Deep Learning

Deep Learning

From Big Data to Artificial Intelligence with R

Stéphane Tufféry
Associate Professor,
University of Rennes 1,
France

This edition first published 2023
© 2023 John Wiley & Sons Ltd

Registered Offices
John Wiley & Sons Ltd, The Atrium, Southern Gate, Chichester, West Sussex, PO19 8SQ, UK

Editorial Office
9600 Garsington Road, Oxford, OX4 2DQ, UK

For details of our global editorial offices, customer services, and more information about Wiley products visit us at www.wiley.com.

Wiley also publishes its books in a variety of electronic formats and by print-on-demand. Some content that appears in standard print versions of this book may not be available in other formats.

Library of Congress Cataloging-in-Publication data applied for

Hardback: ISBN: 9781119845010

Cover Design: Wiley
Cover Images: Courtesy of Stéphane Tufféry; Maxger/Shutterstock
Printed and bound by CPI Group (UK) Ltd, Croydon, CR0 4YY

C9781119845010_271022

To my parents

Contents

Acknowledgements *xiii*
Introduction *xv*

1   **From Big Data to Deep Learning**   *1*
1.1   Introduction   *1*
1.2   Examples of the Use of Big Data and Deep Learning   *6*
1.3   Big Data and Deep Learning for Companies and Organizations   *9*
1.3.1   Big Data in Finance   *10*
1.3.1.1   Google Trends   *10*
1.3.1.2   Google Trends and Stock Prices   *11*
1.3.1.3   The quantmod Package for Financial Analysis   *11*
1.3.1.4   Google Trends in R   *13*
1.3.1.5   Matching Data from quantmod and Google Trends   *14*
1.3.2   Big Data and Deep Learning in Insurance   *18*
1.3.3   Big Data and Deep Learning in Industry   *18*
1.3.4   Big Data and Deep Learning in Scientific Research and Education   *20*
1.3.4.1   Big Data in Physics and Astrophysics   *20*
1.3.4.2   Big Data in Climatology and Earth Sciences   *21*
1.3.4.3   Big Data in Education   *21*
1.4   Big Data and Deep Learning for Individuals   *21*
1.4.1   Big Data and Deep Learning in Healthcare   *21*
1.4.1.1   Connected Health and Telemedicine   *21*
1.4.1.2   Geolocation and Health   *22*
1.4.1.3   The Google Flu Trends   *23*
1.4.1.4   Research in Health and Medicine   *26*
1.4.2   Big Data and Deep Learning for Drivers   *28*
1.4.3   Big Data and Deep Learning for Citizens   *29*
1.4.4   Big Data and Deep Learning in the Police   *30*
1.5   Risks in Data Processing   *32*
1.5.1   Insufficient Quantity of Training Data   *32*
1.5.2   Poor Data Quality   *32*
1.5.3   Non-Representative Samples   *33*
1.5.4   Missing Values in the Data   *33*

1.5.5	Spurious Correlations	*34*
1.5.6	Overfitting	*35*
1.5.7	Lack of Explainability of Models	*35*
1.6	Protection of Personal Data	*36*
1.6.1	The Need for Data Protection	*36*
1.6.2	Data Anonymization	*38*
1.6.3	The General Data Protection Regulation	*41*
1.7	Open Data	*43*
	Notes	*44*

2	**Processing of Large Volumes of Data**	*49*
2.1	Issues	*49*
2.2	The Search for a Parsimonious Model	*50*
2.3	Algorithmic Complexity	*51*
2.4	Parallel Computing	*51*
2.5	Distributed Computing	*52*
2.5.1	MapReduce	*53*
2.5.2	Hadoop	*54*
2.5.3	Computing Tools for Distributed Computing	*55*
2.5.4	Column-Oriented Databases	*56*
2.5.5	Distributed Architecture and "Analytics"	*57*
2.5.6	Spark	*58*
2.6	Computer Resources	*60*
2.6.1	Minimum Resources	*60*
2.6.2	Graphics Processing Units (GPU) and Tensor Processing Units (TPU)	*61*
2.6.3	Solutions in the Cloud	*62*
2.7	R and Python Software	*62*
2.8	Quantum Computing	*67*
	Notes	*68*

3	**Reminders of Machine Learning**	*71*
3.1	General	*71*
3.2	The Optimization Algorithms	*74*
3.3	Complexity Reduction and Penalized Regression	*85*
3.4	Ensemble Methods	*89*
3.4.1	Bagging	*89*
3.4.2	Random Forests	*89*
3.4.3	Extra-Trees	*91*
3.4.4	Boosting	*92*
3.4.5	Gradient Boosting Methods	*97*
3.4.6	Synthesis of the Ensemble Methods	*100*
3.5	Support Vector Machines	*100*
3.6	Recommendation Systems	*105*
	Notes	*108*

4   **Natural Language Processing**   *111*
4.1   From Lexical Statistics to Natural Language Processing   *111*
4.2   Uses of Text Mining and Natural Language Processing   *113*
4.3   The Operations of Textual Analysis   *114*
4.3.1   Textual Data Collection   *115*
4.3.2   Identification of the Language   *115*
4.3.3   Tokenization   *116*
4.3.4   Part-of-Speech Tagging   *117*
4.3.5   Named Entity Recognition   *119*
4.3.6   Coreference Resolution   *124*
4.3.7   Lemmatization   *124*
4.3.8   Stemming   *129*
4.3.9   Simplifications   *129*
4.3.10   Removal of Stop Words   *130*
4.4   Vector Representation and Word Embedding   *132*
4.4.1   Vector Representation   *132*
4.4.2   Analysis on the Document-Term Matrix   *133*
4.4.3   TF-IDF Weighting   *142*
4.4.4   Latent Semantic Analysis   *144*
4.4.5   Latent Dirichlet Allocation   *152*
4.4.6   Word Frequency Analysis   *160*
4.4.7   Word2Vec Embedding   *162*
4.4.8   GloVe Embedding   *174*
4.4.9   FastText Embedding   *176*
4.5   Sentiment Analysis   *180*
           Notes   *184*

5   **Social Network Analysis**   *187*
5.1   Social Networks   *187*
5.2   Characteristics of Graphs   *188*
5.3   Characterization of Social Networks   *189*
5.4   Measures of Influence in a Graph   *190*
5.5   Graphs with R   *191*
5.6   Community Detection   *200*
5.6.1   The Modularity of a Graph   *201*
5.6.2   Community Detection by Divisive Hierarchical Clustering   *202*
5.6.3   Community Detection by Agglomerative Hierarchical Clustering   *203*
5.6.4   Other Methods   *204*
5.6.5   Community Detection with R   *205*
5.7   Research and Analysis on Social Networks   *208*
5.8   The Business Model of Social Networks   *209*
5.9   Digital Advertising   *211*
5.10   Social Network Analysis with R   *212*
5.10.1   Collecting Tweets   *213*
5.10.2   Formatting the Corpus   *215*

5.10.3   Stemming and Lemmatization   *216*
5.10.4   Example   *217*
5.10.5   Clustering of Terms and Documents   *225*
5.10.6   Opinion Scoring   *230*
5.10.7   Graph of Terms with Their Connotation   *231*
          Notes   *234*

6   Handwriting Recognition   *237*
6.1   Data   *237*
6.2   Issues   *238*
6.3   Data Processing   *238*
6.4   Linear and Quadratic Discriminant Analysis   *243*
6.5   Multinomial Logistic Regression   *245*
6.6   Random Forests   *246*
6.7   Extra-Trees   *247*
6.8   Gradient Boosting   *249*
6.9   Support Vector Machines   *253*
6.10   Single Hidden Layer Perceptron   *258*
6.11   H2O Neural Network   *262*
6.12   Synthesis of "Classical" Methods   *267*
          Notes   *268*

7   Deep Learning   *269*
7.1   The Principles of Deep Learning   *269*
7.2   Overview of Deep Neural Networks   *272*
7.3   Recall on Neural Networks and Their Training   *274*
7.4   Difficulties of Gradient Backpropagation   *284*
7.5   The Structure of a Convolutional Neural Network   *286*
7.6   The Convolution Mechanism   *288*
7.7   The Convolution Parameters   *290*
7.8   Batch Normalization   *292*
7.9   Pooling   *293*
7.10   Dilated Convolution   *295*
7.11   Dropout and DropConnect   *295*
7.12   The Architecture of a Convolutional Neural Network   *297*
7.13   Principles of Deep Network Learning for Computer Vision   *299*
7.14   Adaptive Learning Algorithms   *301*
7.15   Progress in Image Recognition   *304*
7.16   Recurrent Neural Networks   *312*
7.17   Capsule Networks   *317*
7.18   Autoencoders   *318*
7.19   Generative Models   *322*
7.19.1   Generative Adversarial Networks   *323*
7.19.2   Variational Autoencoders   *324*

7.20   Other Applications of Deep Learning   *326*
7.20.1   Object Detection   *326*
7.20.2   Autonomous Vehicles   *333*
7.20.3   Analysis of Brain Activity   *334*
7.20.4   Analysis of the Style of a Pictorial Work   *336*
7.20.5   Go and Chess Games   *338*
7.20.6   Other Games   *340*
            Notes   *341*

8   Deep Learning for Computer Vision   347
8.1   Deep Learning Libraries   *347*
8.2   MXNet   *349*
8.2.1   General Information about MXNet   *349*
8.2.2   Creating a Convolutional Network with MXNet   *350*
8.2.3   Model Management with MXNet   *361*
8.2.4   CIFAR-10 Image Recognition with MXNet   *362*
8.3   Keras and TensorFlow   *367*
8.3.1   General Information about Keras   *370*
8.3.2   Application of Keras to the MNIST Database   *371*
8.3.3   Application of Pre-Trained Models   *375*
8.3.4   Explain the Prediction of a Computer Vision Model   *379*
8.3.5   Application of Keras to CIFAR-10 Images   *382*
8.3.6   Classifying Cats and Dogs   *393*
8.4   Configuring a Machine's GPU for Deep Learning   *408*
8.4.1   Checking the Compatibility of the Graphics Card   *408*
8.4.2   NVIDIA Driver Installation   *409*
8.4.3   Installation of Microsoft Visual Studio   *409*
8.4.4   NVIDIA CUDA Toolkit Installation   *409*
8.4.5   Installation of cuDNN   *410*
8.5   Computing in the Cloud   *411*
8.6   PyTorch   *417*
8.6.1   The Python `PyTorch` Package   *417*
8.6.2   The R `torch` Package   *424*
            Notes   *428*

9   Deep Learning for Natural Language Processing   431
9.1   Neural Network Methods for Text Analysis   *431*
9.2   Text Generation Using a Recurrent Neural Network LSTM   *432*
9.3   Text Classification Using a LSTM or GRU Recurrent Neural Network   *438*
9.4   Text Classification Using a H2O Model   *450*
9.5   Application of Convolutional Neural Networks   *454*
9.6   Spam Detection Using a Recurrent Neural Network LSTM   *458*
9.7   Transformer Models, BERT, and Its Successors   *459*
            Notes   *477*

10   **Artificial Intelligence**   *479*

10.1   The Beginnings of Artificial Intelligence   *479*

10.2   Human Intelligence and Artificial Intelligence   *484*

10.3   The Different Forms of Artificial Intelligence   *486*

10.4   Ethical and Societal Issues of Artificial Intelligence   *491*

10.5   Fears and Hopes of Artificial Intelligence   *495*

10.6   Some Dates of Artificial Intelligence   *498*

Notes   *501*

Conclusion   *505*

Note   *506*

Annotated Bibliography   *507*

On Big Data and High Dimensional Statistics   *507*

On Deep Learning   *509*

On Artificial Intelligence   *511*

On the Use of R and Python in Data Science and on Big Data   *512*

Index   *515*

Acknowledgements

I warmly thank Franck Berthuit and Ricco Rakotomalala for their careful reading and helpful comments. I am also pleased to thank all the people I met at the University of Rennes 1, at the Ensai (École Nationale de la Statistique et de l'Analyse de l'Information) and at the Institute of Actuaries of Paris, where I taught the courses on data science, big data, and deep learning from which this book was derived.

Introduction

This book is dedicated to deep learning, which is a recent branch of a slightly older discipline: machine learning.[1] Deep learning is particularly well suited to the analysis of complex data, such as images and natural language. For this reason, it is at the heart of many of the artificial intelligence applications that we will describe in this book. Although deep learning today relies almost exclusively on neural networks, we will first look at other machine learning methods, partly because of the concepts they share with neural networks and which it is important to understand in their generality, and partly to compare their results with those of deep learning methods. We will then be able to fully measure the effectiveness of deep learning methods in computer vision and automatic natural language processing problems. This is what the present book will do, recalling the theoretical foundations of these methods while showing how to implement them in concrete situations, with examples treated with the open source deep learning libraries of Python and mainly R, as indicated below. As we will see, the prodigious development of deep learning and artificial intelligence has been made possible by new theoretical concepts, by more powerful computing tools, but also by the possibility of using immense masses of various data, images, videos, audios, texts, traces on the Internet, signals from connected objects ... these big data will be very present in this book.

The Structure of the Book

Chapter 1 is an overview of deep learning and big data with their principles and applications in the main sectors of finance, insurance, industry, transport, medicine, and scientific research. A few pages are devoted to the main difficulties that can be encountered in processing data in machine learning and deep learning, particularly when it comes to big data. We must not neglect the IT risks inherent in the collection and storage, sometimes in a cloud, of large amounts of personal data. The news about certain social networks regularly reminds us of this. At the opposite end of the spectrum from their commercial vision of big data are open data, which closes the chapter.

Chapter 2 deals with concepts that data scientists must know when dealing with large volumes of data: parsimony in modeling, algorithmic complexity, parallel computing and its generalization, which is distributed computing. We devote a few pages to the MapReduce algorithm at the basis of distributed computing, its implementation in the Hadoop system, and to the database management systems, known as NoSQL and column-oriented, particularly adapted to big data. We will see that "analytical" applications such as machine learning have particular computing requirements that require specific solutions: Spark is one of them. We then review the hardware and software resources to be implemented, whether they are on the user's machine or in a cloud. We talk about the processors that enable deep learning computations to be accelerated, as well as the two most used open source software in statistics, machine learning, and deep learning: R and Python. A synoptic table compares the main machine learning methods implemented in R, Python (scikit-learn library) and Spark (MLlib). We also found it interesting to mention quantum computing, for which specific versions of algorithms are starting to be designed, notably in linear algebra, machine learning, optimization, and cryptography. The prospects of quantum computing are still distant but very promising, with the possibility of a considerable reduction in computing time.

Chapter 3 recalls some essential principles of machine learning and data science: the bias-variance dilemma in modeling, complexity reduction methods, optimization algorithms, such as gradient descent, Newton or Levenberg-Marquardt, ensemble (or aggregation) methods by random forests, Extra-Trees or boosting, and useful methods for big data, such as incremental algorithms and recommendation systems used by social networks and online commerce. Apart from these reminders, it is assumed that the reader is familiar with machine learning methods but, if required, a bibliography is given at the end of the book and notes are provided in each chapter for specific references.

Chapter 4 presents natural language processing methods. The principles of textual analysis are introduced, including segmentation into units or tokenization, part-of-speech tagging, named entity recognition, lemmatization, and other simplification operations that aim to reduce the volume of data and the complexity of the problem as much as possible while retaining the maximum amount of information, which is a constant concern in statistics and machine learning. We then describe the operations of vector representation of words, which go from the classical document-term matrix to the methods of word embedding, which started with Word2Vec, GloVe, and fastText, and the list of these is continuously growing. We speak of embedding because each word is associated with a point in a vector space of fairly small dimensions, of the order of a few hundred, i.e. much less than different terms, with the remarkable property that two semantically close words correspond to close points in the vector space, and that arithmetic operations in this vector space can lead to identities such as "King" – "Man" + "Woman" = "Queen". These vector embeddings preserve not only the proximity of words but also their relations. They are therefore an efficient way to transform documents for analysis, for example, to classify them into categories: spam or non-spam, type of message, subject of the complaint, etc. We also discuss topic modeling, which uses methods such as latent Dirichlet allocation to detect all the topics present in a corpus of documents. We present another current method of natural language processing, sentiment analysis, which seeks to detect the sentiments expressed in a text, either in a binary form of positive or negative sentiments, or in a more elaborate form of joy, fear, anger, etc. Neural methods applied to natural language processing are discussed in Chapter 9, after the one devoted to the principles of deep learning.

Chapter 5 shows how to analyze social networks, starting from the notions of graph theory and taking the example of Twitter. We are particularly interested in the so-called centrality and influence measures, as they are very important in social networks and web search engines. We are also interested in the detection of communities, which are the dense sub-graphs that can constitute a partition of the studied graph. The search for communities in a graph is an active field of research, in various domains (biology, sociology, marketing), because the vertices of a same community tend to have in common interesting properties. Some considerations are turned to the economic model of social networks and to digital advertising and what is called programmatic advertising.

Chapter 6 deals with the classical problem of recognizing handwritten digits on bank checks and postal codes on envelopes, among others. On a well-known dataset (MNIST), it compares the different machine learning methods previously discussed in the book: in particular penalized regression, random forests, gradient boosting, and support vector machines.

Chapter 7 is a long and important chapter on deep learning. It explains the principles of deep learning and the architecture of deep neural networks, especially convolutional and recurrent networks, which are those most widely used for computer vision and natural language processing today. The many features designed to optimize their performance are presented, such as pooling, normalization, dropout, and adaptive learning, with indications on how best to use them. We review the fundamental learning mechanism of neural networks, backpropagation, the difficulties encountered in its application to multilayer networks with the vanishing gradient phenomenon that led for a while to the "winter of artificial intelligence," and the solutions found in the last ten years by new ideas and increased computing power. Particular networks are described: autoencoders for data compression, and generative neural networks that are increasingly being developed to have artificial intelligence produce texts, images or music. Illustrations show the interest of deep learning for subjects ranging from object detection to strategy games.

Chapter 8 presents the application to computer vision of the methods seen in Chapter 7, using MXNet, Keras-TensorFlow, and PyTorch libraries. In particular, they are applied to three classical datasets: (1) the MNIST database already discussed in Chapter 6, which allows the performances of classical and deep learning methods to be compared; (2) the CIFAR-10 image database; and (3) a database of cat and dog pictures. We apply transfer learning. We sketch the question of the explicability of machine learning algorithms by applying the LIME method to images to find out on which parts of the image the model relies for its predictions. We show how to configure a computer with a Windows operating system to use its graphics processing unit (GPU) for deep learning computations, which are much faster on these graphics processors than on classical processors (CPUs). This configuration is not very simple and it is necessary to follow the different steps indicated. The chapter concludes with examples of cloud computing, using the Google Colab platform with a Jupyter notebook running Python code.

Chapter 9 returns to natural language processing, applying to it the deep learning methods described in Chapter 7: generative models and recurrent neural networks. An example application is given of the creation of poems by a neural network which has been provided with an example for its training (Shakespeare's *Sonnets*) but no other information on the English language, no dictionary, and no grammar rules. We also show how to apply LSTM and GRU recurrent networks to document classification, and we compare them to classical machine learning methods. We then show how recent "transformer" models have led to a refinement of the word embedding methods seen in Chapter 4, with the BERT algorithm and its successors able to take into account the context of a polysemous word to compute its embedding. But these transformer models are much more than word embedding methods and they are today the state of the art for all natural language processing tasks, document classification, translation, question-answering, text generation, automatic summarization, etc. We give an insight into their performance by applying the BERT model to the same example of document classification as the previous LSTM model.

Finally, Chapter 10 describes artificial intelligence with its concepts, its relationship with human intelligence, its links with symbolic methods, machine learning and deep learning, its applications and, of course, the hopes and debates it raises.

The book concludes with an annotated bibliography and an index.

In the examples in this book, R has been used more often than Python. Even if Python's successes are growing in data science, R remains the reference software in this field, the richest in statistics, and it has progressively caught up in the field of deep learning. Indeed, the main methods and first of all the convolutional and recurrent neural networks, initially interfaced with Python (the calculations themselves are often implemented in C++ and CUDA) are also increasingly being interfaced with R. It should be noted, however, that the use of TensorFlow and Keras, even with R, requires the prior installation of Python, at least in a minimal distribution such as Miniconda. As for the PyTorch library, until 2020, it had not been ported to R and required writing Python code for its use, which we do at the end of Chapter 8. Since then, the project "torch for R" supported by RStudio has implemented the PyTorch library in R, directly from C++ code without going through the Python interface.[2]

Another reason for choosing R is that many books have already been published on Python, while few describe the use of R in deep learning. Of course, these issues are the subject of articles and discussions in forums, but the interesting elements are disseminated and not necessarily complete and coherent between them. We have therefore favored an approach that is perhaps more circumscribed, but, we hope, coherent and likely to allow the reader to solve the problems of data science and deep learning. Since this is the objective of this book, and not a systematic comparison of software libraries, we have chosen not to increase the volume of the book by presenting all the code both in R and Python versions. For the same reason, we have not presented examples of the use of all deep learning libraries, but only three of the main ones: Keras-TensorFlow, MXNet, and PyTorch.

Many running times are shown, to illustrate the differences in computational performance between different methods or ways of programming, or sometimes between different software. Most of the deep neural network training examples were implemented on a laptop computer with a quad-core Intel i5-8300H processor running at 2.3 GHz, with 8 GB of RAM, a 64-bit Windows 10 operating system, and an NVIDIA GeForce GTX 1050 graphics card. The execution times are sometimes compared with and without the use of this GPU. They would of course be very different if they were measured on other machines, and it is better to look at the differences in computing time between two approaches than at their absolute value.

The duration and some results of the computations can also sometimes depend on the version of R, and those presented in this book were mostly obtained with versions 3.6.x to 4.1.x of R. The reader should not be surprised by differences that one can obtain with other more or less recent versions. This is especially true of the big data and deep learning packages, which are frequently evolving like the methods they implement.

The methods presented in this book go far beyond the field of statistics to cover statistical learning and machine learning, of which deep learning is a particular branch.

In short, we can say that if statistics seeks to predict phenomena, it seeks above all to explain them and therefore to provide a description in the form of models. A model is a representation of reality that assumes that the data follow certain probability distributions. The statistician carries out tests to check this assumption and to ensure that this model is well founded. If it is proven that the observed data do follow the assumed probability distribution, or at least do not deviate too much from it, all that remains is to estimate the parameter(s) of this distribution and to verify, once again by means of statistical tests, the significance of this estimate (in common language: its reliability).

In machine learning, we are primarily interested in the predictive power of the methods and the generalization capacity of the models obtained. We do not ask them to provide a formalized description of reality and the notion of hypothesis testing takes a back seat.[3] This is all the more true since we are interested in phenomena that are sometimes too complex to be described by simple probability distributions, and these phenomena are described by much more complex mechanisms, deep learning mechanisms that are not without analogy with the functioning of the brain and can partly explain their important place in artificial intelligence.

Notes

1 We include here in the same term statistics, statistical learning, and machine learning, for the sake of brevity and because the boundaries are shifting, despite our attempt to draw them at the end of this Introduction.
2 https://www.rstudio.com/blog/torch/.
3 According to Brian Ripley's quip (*useR! 2004*, Vienna): "Machine learning is statistics minus any checking of models and assumptions."

1

From Big Data to Deep Learning

The first chapter of the book begins with a presentation of big data, which is both a growing field of study and application (with algorithms and tools) and its raw material (data sets). The term data is in the plural (of datum) as it should be in English, and we can talk about the plurality of data sources, but we can also think of the discipline in the singular, with a set of concepts and methods, a mixture of machine learning[1] and computer technology. In the first sense of the term, big data can be understood as large collections of data, too large for traditional data-processing systems, but this translation only emphasizes the voluminous aspect of these data, whereas their variety is often also essential, as the following pages will show. Of the machine learning methods, we will focus on deep learning methods, which are the best for dealing with big data such as text, voice, image, and video. We will then go on to examine some key points in the processing of data, especially big data, and we will conclude with questions of personal data protection and some elements on open data.

1.1 Introduction

Big Data covers all the issues associated with the collection and exploitation of very large sets of data, of very varied natures and formats (texts, photographs, clicks, signals from sensors, connected objects, etc.), and in very rapid, even continuous evolution. They are invading many fields of activity: health, industry, transport, finance, banking and insurance, retail, public policy, security, scientific research, etc.

The economic stakes are high: McKinsey[2] estimates that big data could save healthcare policies in the United States $300 billion per year and generate $600 billion in consumption by using consumer location data.

We will see that the impacts of big data are very important for both people and business, and that the technological challenges are formidable.

Before going into detail about big data, let's take a quick historical look at the developments that led to them. For a several decades, the rise of computing power has accompanied the explosion of data production. This rise has developed over several eras:

- before 1950, the beginnings of statistics with a few hundred individuals and a few variables, collected in a laboratory according to a strict protocol of experimental design for a scientific study;

- in the 1960s–1980s, data analysis with a few tens of thousands of individuals and a few dozen variables, rigorously collected for a specific survey;
- in the 1990s and 2000s, data mining with several million individuals and several hundred variables, collected in the information system of companies for decision-making;
- from the 2010s, big data with several hundred million individuals and several thousand variables, of all types, collected in companies, systems, the Internet, for decision-making and new services.

From the end of the nineteenth century until the 1950s was the era of classical statistics. It precedes the invention of computers, so the means of calculation are manual and very limited, and it is characterized by:

- small volumes studied;
- the strong hypotheses on the statistical distributions followed (triad: linearity, normality, homoscedasticity);
- models derived from theory and confronted with data;
- the probabilistic and statistical nature of the methods;
- laboratory use.

The predominance of the hypothetico-deductive method and the importance of tests and inferential statistics can be noted. Data are collected and analyzed within a strict, often scientific, framework in order to verify a theory, which can be refuted by the result of a test. The foundations of mathematical statistics, but also important predictive methods, such as linear discriminant analysis and logistic regression, date from this period.

In the 1960s and 1980s, the emergence of computers revolutionized the discipline, allowing for much more complex and rapid calculations than before, on thousands of analyzed individuals and dozens of variables, with the construction of "Individuals x Variables" tables. This was a time of great theoretical creativity, during which many fundamental methods were invented that are still widely used today. This is the golden age of data analysis and especially of factorial analysis, and visual representation begins to take on great importance.

The 1990s saw the advent of the concept of *data mining*, which is not only characterized by an explosion of computing resources and the quantity of data to be processed, but also by a profound change in the role of quantitative analysis. Even if it uses the tools of statistics, data mining differs from statistics in many qualitative and quantitative aspects:

- millions or tens of millions of individuals, and hundreds or thousands of variables are analyzed:
- many variables are non-numerical, sometimes textual;
- weak assumptions are made about the statistical distributions followed;
- data are collected prior to the study, and often for other purposes;
- the populations studied are constantly changing;
- outliers (out of the norm, at least in terms of the distributions studied) are present;
- the data are imperfect, with data entry errors, coding errors, missing values;
- fast calculations are needed, sometimes in real time;
- we are not always looking for the mathematical optimum, but sometimes for the model that is easiest to understand for non-statisticians;

- the models are derived from the data and sometimes attempts are made to derive theoretical elements from them;
- some methods are starting to come from information theory or *machine learning;*
- used in companies, and not only in labs and universities.

Two major changes have occurred. On the one hand, the data analyzed often were not collected for the needs of the study and were collected for management needs, with all that this implies in terms of redundancy, imprecision, and even errors. Data mining involves a long and important work of "cleaning" the data prior to modeling. On the other hand, the aim is not essentially scientific, or even sometimes explanatory, but rather to assist in decision-making. It is not a question of formulating theoretical hypotheses and then verifying them with the help of observations, but of finding models that fit the observed data as well as possible, and can, in some very specific cases, suggest theoretical clues.

For example, in the commercial field, we do not try to elaborate a theory of customer behavior and its hidden motives, and we simply try to characterize the profiles of those customers most likely to buy a given product, and possibly know when and at what price.

A new era began in the 2010s when big data appeared, with hundreds of millions of individuals and thousands of variables, of all types, sometimes very noisy, collected in companies, objects, the Internet, to provide decision support, and also, more than with data mining, new services. The concept of big data was born out of the explosion in the production of all kinds of data: traces left on the Web (sites visited, videos seen, clicks, keywords searched for, etc.), opinions expressed in social networks (about a person, a company, a brand, a product, a service, a movie, a restaurant), posts in social media and content shared on websites (blogs, photographs, videos, music tracks, etc.), geolocation by GPS or IP address, information gathered by industrial, road and climate sensors, RFID chips, NFC devices and connected objects (smartphones, connected watches and wristbands, intelligent personal assistants,[3] cameras, electricity meters, household appliances, scales, clothes, medical devices, cars, glasses with augmented reality ...) that form what is called the *Internet of Things* (IoT).

These big data are characterized by what Doug Laney has called[4] the "three Vs": volume, velocity and variety.[5]

The volume of data involved has given Big Data its name, with an order of magnitude that can reach the petabyte (10^{15} bytes). The increase in data volume comes from the increase in:

- the number of individuals observed (more numerous or at a finer level);
- the frequency of observation and data recording (from monthly to daily or hourly);
- the number of observed features.

This increase also comes from the observation of new data, especially from connected objects, geolocation, and the Web.

Thus, in one minute on the Internet:[6]

- 120 new accounts are created on LinkedIn;
- 571 websites are created;
- 600 Wikipedia pages are created or updated;
- 1,500 blogs are posted
- 46,740 photographs are posted on Instagram;

- 154,200 calls are made on Skype;
- 752,000 dollars are spent online;
- $258,750 in sales are made by Amazon;
- 342,000 smartphone applications are downloaded;
- 456,000 tweets are sent;
- 900,000 people log on to Facebook;
- 4.1 million videos are viewed on YouTube;
- 3.6 million searches are made on Google;
- 16 million SMS are sent;
- 156 million emails are sent (including over 100 million spam emails).

This aspect of volume is perhaps the most visible and spectacular feature of big data, but it is not entirely new, since the retail, banking, and telecom industries have long been handling huge volumes of data, with annual numbers of transactions routinely exceeding one billion. However, if the number of objects or individuals processed (the rows of the databases) was very large, the number of their observed characteristics (the columns of the databases) was not so large, and this is rather where the novelty of big data lies, and their theoretical and practical difficulties. The main theoretical difficulty is the so-called "curse of dimensionality," to which we return in Section 1.5.1. From a practical point of view, it is sometimes said that big data begin when we can no longer load data into memory and, more generally, when we can no longer process it by "conventional" means (in a rather vague sense, which can, for example, refer to non-distributed computer architectures). What sounds like a joke is at the same time pragmatic, and refers to the technical and software tools that can manipulate data that cannot reside in memory.

The variety of big data is due to the fact that these data are of very diverse natures and forms: numerical, graphs, web logs, texts in various forms (documents, emails, SMS, etc.), sounds, images, videos, functional data … This variety makes it difficult to use the usual databases and requires a variety of methods: graph analysis, deep neural networks, text mining, web mining … Heterogeneous data can be crossed: for example, sales data matched with social network data, or pollution sensor data matched with weather data and traffic sensors.

The velocity of big data comes from the fact that these data are updated rapidly, sometimes in real time and in a continuous flow, or at least at high frequency, and must often be processed just as quickly. By data streams, we mean the continuous flow of data from industrial, meteorological, and astronomical sensors. An autonomous vehicle must be able to continuously and immediately process an enormous quantity of data, estimated at 30 terabytes per day. On merchant sites, the customer's decision on the Web is made quickly because it only takes one click to change site, so it is necessary to instantly make them the best commercial offer. Another example: credit card fraud must of course be detected in real time. In some cases, the limitation of the calculation time can induce an error to be estimated and controlled.

Note that in some cases, it is not only the application of the statistical model but its update that is done in real time or at least very frequently. Velocity thus has three components:

- data velocity;
- the speed of the treatments to be implemented;
- the speed of updating the models.

The concept of data science has recently developed to address the theoretical and technical challenges raised by big data. The modeling methods applied to big data are far from being new but they have seen strong motivation and important work related to big data. We can mention in particular some advanced techniques of sampling, optimization, machine learning, deep learning, penalized estimators of the Lasso or Danzig type, incremental learning, spatial statistics, the use of graphs, and of course the analysis and generation of natural language, both written and spoken.

Sampling issues are important, as they can help to reduce the volume of data to make it more easily manipulated, and to infer general conclusions from partial observations. But the representativeness of samples is difficult to establish, with multiple data sources, which do not cover the same populations and have a significant number of missing values. This raises problems of sampling techniques and sample adjustment. For example, it is necessary to assign appropriate weights to the observed units in order to obtain a representative sample of the population studied. There is also the issue of matching individual data from different sources and using auxiliary information. These methods are already used by the national statistical institutes (such as French INSEE), which uses numerous data sources (surveys, population census, and administrative files), as well as by media audience measurement institutes.

Incremental learning refers to methods that allow us to build a model, not on the basis of a complete sample, but on the basis of data that arrive in smaller chunks and from which we must update the model without having to take into account past observations. These methods make it possible to analyze data arriving in streams or which are too large to be processed at once. They are found in certain decision trees, the Very Fast Decision Trees, which rely on a theoretical limit, the Hoeffding bound, to determine a sufficient number of observations to obtain a split of each node of a tree close enough to the split that would have been obtained with all the observations. By this sampling, these trees can treat data so massive that the calculations would be too long or even impossible. Another widely used incremental algorithm is Alan Miller's "Memory Bounded Algorithm" AS 274 which is used for linear regression and is implemented in the `biglm` package of R. Incremental algorithms also exist in deep learning.

Machine learning methods, such as model aggregation (ensemble methods), support vector machines, and neural networks discussed in this book, are used for their high predictive power, in situations where model readability is not required and their "black box" characteristic is not an insurmountable obstacle, especially since some methods of explainability (Section 1.5.7) of their predictions are beginning to develop.

Deep learning is used for problems as complex as image, video, text and speech recognition, it uses sophisticated machine learning techniques such as convolutional neural networks, and it relies on massively parallel computer architectures, especially for computations with graphics processors, which we discuss later. Along with big data, deep learning is the main topic of this book because it is at the heart of modern data science. Most big data could not be analyzed without deep learning.

Whether the images are from social networks or medical imaging, advanced algorithms are needed to process them, not just to retouch or enhance them, but to recognize faces, places, or tumor cells. Unfortunately, deep learning can also create fake images or videos, manufacturing *deepfakes*. "Multimodal artificial intelligence" methods, combining image, voice and text recognition, are being implemented to try to flush out these deepfakes. Deep learning is also becoming indispensable for processing data as numerous and complex as those produced by genetic analysis, astronomy, or particle physics. Deep learning has also made it possible to achieve unequaled performance in text and voice processing, whether it is answering human questions in writing or orally, or helping users in their searches on the Web: today, huge transformer neural networks (Section 9.7) analyze the requests of Internet users to find the most relevant information.

1.2 Examples of the Use of Big Data and Deep Learning

Examples of the use of big data and deep learning abound in a wide variety of sectors. This section gives a quick overview before we come back to discuss several of them.

In the field of transport, it is about the improvement of road traffic by geolocation, the search for free parking spaces, the billing of parking in paying areas thanks to the reading and the optical recognition of characters on the license plates, the dynamic fixing of the price of airline tickets.

This last application is part of dynamic pricing, also called yield management or revenue management. It concerns activities with fixed available capacities, high fixed costs, perishable products (to be sold before a certain date) and that can be sold in advance at differentiated prices. Dynamic pricing determines in real time the appropriate quantities to put on sale, at the appropriate price, at the appropriate time, in order to maximize the profit generated by the sale. It is about maximizing margin without reducing demand. It was born in the 1980s in the airline industry with American Airlines, but has since spread to many other areas of transport, hotels, advertising space, tourism, entertainment. For example, it is applied by Uber to regulate the number of drivers behind the wheel at a given time: lowering fares when supply exceeds demand should encourage Uber drivers not to drive at that time. Dynamic pricing is also used in fashion, where it is more difficult to implement for new products with less predictable sales.

To take the example of air transport, here is what Stéphane Ormand, head of the "revenue management" department at Air France-KLM Group, says about dynamic pricing in an interview in *La Croix* on June 27, 2016:

> Nearly a year in advance, they [pricers] virtually carve up an aircraft for each flight into a multitude of fares, taking into account a multitude of factors – everything from the economic crisis in Brazil to falling exchange rates in Venezuela or Nigeria, or the Euro soccer tournament in France … Analysts must keep a constant watch on the competition, local or global events that can disrupt demand for a given flight and adapt the sales strategy.

A single economy class cabin can be divided into fifteen or so fares, with fare differentials of 1 to 10, and the number of seats between these fares can be adjusted according to demand.

In a sense, dynamic pricing is a return to the age-old practice of prices that were not fixed and posted, but were the result of negotiation. Here, we cannot speak of negotiation because the price is set without the buyer's knowledge, but it is the overall behavior of all buyers that influences the price. Dynamic pricing must be legally regulated so as not to discriminate against certain customers on the basis of their individual profile or the place where they live.

In marketing, geolocation allows you to send a promotion or a coupon on your smartphone when you pass near a business. This geolocation (or *geofencing*) uses the GPS of smartphones, Wi-Fi hotspots, beacons.

Another marketing application of big data is the analysis of preferences, recommendations, possibly linked to sales data, to target consumers more efficiently (Section 3.6).

A classic in the retail industry is the analysis of receipts and its cross-referencing with loyalty program data. Consider that these analyses are done in real time, and that it is at the moment of checkout that the customer is warned, based on the contents of their shopping cart, that they may have forgotten to buy an item. There is a lot of talk about Internet big data, but 90% of sales in the world are still made in physical stores, and Wal-Mart remains the leading retail group in the world, even if Amazon comes in third place in Deloitte's Top 250 in 2020.[7] It was in sixth place in 2016 and in 186th place in 2000. Moreover, it should be noted that Amazon is starting to open physical stores and to make agreements with mass retail chains. Under the terms of an agreement between Google and Carrefour, since 2020, Google's voice assistant can be used to order purchases at Carrefour, through a smartphone or a connected speaker. Such an agreement was made in August 2017 in the United States between Google and Wal-Mart. With big data, physical stores can try to exploit their advantages over online businesses.

Combining the two types of businesses, Amazon Go is a physical store that relies on sensors to know which items have been picked up by customers (and not put back on the shelf). Payment is made automatically when leaving the store, if one has an Amazon account and a smartphone with the Amazon Go app. Like online visits and purchases, those made in this store can be tracked by Amazon, which can use them to derive relevant recommendations.

Perhaps less mediatized than the previous applications of big data, the scientific applications are important and varied in fields that are big users of massive data, such as meteorology, seismology, oceanography, ecology, genomics, epidemiology, medical imaging, astronomy, and nuclear physics.

For example, the Large Synoptic Survey Telescope (LSST) records 30 terabytes of images each day, with real-time alerts for changes in the position or brightness of celestial objects. The Large Hadron Collider (LHC) used to discover the Higgs boson records 60 terabytes of data every day, at each of its 100 million collisions per second. The Discovery supercomputer at the NASA Center for Climate Simulation (NCCS) stores 32 petabytes of climate data and climate model simulations.

In literature, the millions of digitized texts cover the entire history of literature and can be analyzed for comparative literature or to study the diffusion of cultural movements in a society, according to the historical or social context. They are also available and downloadable on sites such as Gutenberg[8] for texts in the public domain. In archeology, computer vision can be applied to the identification of patterns on ancient objects, their comparison with other known objects, their dating, and the study of their technical and stylistic evolution.[9] These applications of deep learning are part of the disciplines called *digital humanities*.

Artificial intelligence comes to the aid of paleography, that is, the study of ancient writings, to distinguish minute differences in the style of two texts. Thus, in April 2021, scientists from the University of Groningen in the Netherlands published an article in *PLOS One* revealing that two scribes, and not just one, had probably written one of the Dead Sea Scrolls, the Great Isaiah Scroll.

In journalism, data journalism relies on the analysis of digital data to verify, produce, and distribute information. These data are increasingly numerous, notably thanks to Open Data (Section 1.7) and social networks (Section 5.1). This is different from infographics, which only aims to represent data. It can also rely on natural language processing tools, machine translation, and automatic text generation to comment on data. Among the applications of data journalism, we can mention the identification of individuals or events in photographs, the detection of fake photographs or videos, the detection of fake news and fact-checking, the exploration and analysis of archives and large databases, the automatic monitoring of social media to detect emerging topics, the "breaking news" to be announced before the others, the analysis of political speeches, or the detection of propaganda, of influences. We can also mention the recommendation systems (Section 3.6) that suggest to readers new articles likely to interest them, based on those they have already read.

In the field of human resources, job boards rely on machine learning methods, and companies use résumé analysis enriched by searching CV libraries, detecting links made by the candidate on social networks, events in which he or she participates, his or her career path, etc. This sourcing allows start-ups to detect candidates who best match the position offered and the company's culture more quickly than headhunters, and at a lower cost. Interview reports with employees can also be analyzed to automatically detect positive or negative tones, situations of discomfort, the expression of difficulties. More recently, AI has been used to automate telephone or video-conference interviews with candidates, but with results that are sometimes unreliable in evaluating the aptitudes of candidates for a position. Recruitment is a field where particular attention is paid to the absence of bias and discrimination.

Applications of big data to education are the development of applied technologies to education (EdTech) and the analysis of social networks to learn about the popularity of lessons and student satisfaction, and to adapt teaching to the progress of each student.

In computer science, big data tools are used to monitor machines and networks, and to detect failures or security incidents. The Swiss company DeepCode uses artificial intelligence trained on open source lines of code to help programmers, detecting bugs in their lines of code and suggesting fixes based on other programmers' fixes. It does this for JavaScript, TypeScript, Java, C/C++, and Python. In 2021, the French startup SourceAI uses GPT-3 (Section 9.7) to translate natural language queries (in English, French, German, or Spanish) into computer code in over 40 programming languages. Some envision the end of the programmer's job in a few decades, as programming can be done entirely by artificial intelligence.

In June 2021, Google engineers announced that they had successfully used reinforcement learning (Section 7.1) to design the layout of their next TPU chips (Section 2.6.2), i.e., to organize the arrangement of the billions of transistors that make them up, so as to minimize the surface area, the length of the wires, and the power consumption, and to maximize the performance.[10] Six hours of calculations produce a result at least as good as several months of work by specialized engineers.

In their hunt for fraud, tax authorities are increasingly relying on information found on the Web and social networks, which can reveal a taxpayer's lifestyle, address, commercial and financial transactions, more effectively than reading the celebrity pages of magazines.

Security, along with video surveillance and intelligence, is also increasingly using big data and artificial intelligence tools, with the possible drifts mentioned in Section 1.4.3. Some intelligence agencies admit to using artificial intelligence to prevent cyberattacks, to fight against disinformation by detecting deepfakes, to combat security threats and crime, while relying on ethical principles. But security can also be endangered by big data, whether it is the myriad of connected objects that can fall under the control of malicious people (to direct them in server attacks, for example), or even connected autonomous vehicles (Section 1.4.2) that could also be remotely controlled and used in terrorist attacks. Since 2016, the Mirai malware has been regularly used to infect connected objects such as video surveillance cameras to form networks, botnets, capable of massive attacks on servers, in the form of message streams saturating those servers (known as a *denial of service attack*). The advent of 5G and the growth in the number of connected objects have led to fears that the frequency of these attacks will increase. Video surveillance facial recognition is also of interest to banks, which are beginning to see it as a way to identify dangerous individuals and enhance the security of their employees. Facial recognition algorithms were first defeated by the wearing of health masks during the Covid-19 crisis, before being refined to work under these new conditions, and they can also be used to detect the presence of people without masks.

Big data are present even in sports, in soccer, basketball, baseball or tennis, in the collection and analysis of data on the position, the movements of the ball and the players, their heart rate, the history of the matches played, these big data being used to develop new game tactics, to predict the results of competitions, to improve performance, to study the trajectories on the field, to measure the impact of fatigue, to limit the risks of injury, or to adapt training. They were used by the German national team during the 2014 World Cup, and we can also mention the use of data from the Hawk-Eye system on the trajectory of balls and players in sports such as cricket, tennis, badminton or volleyball. A lot of data has also been collected for a long time in motorsports. The collection and communication of physiological data from sportsmen and women to their coaches and team managers, and even to sports journalists, raise obvious confidentiality problems.

1.3   Big Data and Deep Learning for Companies and Organizations

The contribution of big data to business is fourfold:

- increase in audience and market share, loyalty, with, for example, the increase in sales induced by recommendations;
- decision support, with the example of forecasting stock market and macroeconomic trends using the analysis of web searches and social media posts;
- improving operational processes, for example, by forecasting the company's needs and the price of raw materials (according to various meteorological and economic criteria) over time, allowing the company to purchase the right quantities at the right time, or

forecasting store traffic according to weather conditions and external events, or even predictive maintenance;

- the creation of new innovative products and services, in which the customer himself benefits from a decision-making system, whether for downloading films or music (recommendation systems) or for driving, as we will see in Section 1.4.2.

With big data, we are witnessing a shift from analytics to decision-making. Data are no longer used only to help the company make decisions, but are used to offer new products and services to the customer, as personalized as possible, and to set prices with precision thanks to yield management.

The second industrial revolution with the invention of the assembly line by Henry Ford in 1913 led to mass production and a standardization of the offer, thus to mass consumption, mass media, and mass culture. In the opposite direction, big data allow companies to adapt their offer more specifically to each customer and allow a tailor-made production. Moreover, it is no longer just a matter of performing complex analyses on large volumes of data, but of creating new functions at the heart of real-time operational applications. However, there is a caveat to this optimistic observation: recommendation systems tend to lock people into profiles determined by algorithms and only offer them products, contracts, and information that are supposed to correspond to their profile. This is what is called algorithmic containment (Section 10.5).

1.3.1 Big Data in Finance

Big data can be used in the financial industry to analyze stock market risk, financial risk and fraud risk.

On the subject of stock market risk, a study published in *Scientific Reports*[11] in 2013 shows a correlation between certain keywords entered on Google and the evolution of stock market prices: before a fall in stock market indices, investors are concerned and search the Web for information helping them decide whether to hold or sell their shares. We will come back to this example later.

In the analysis of financial risk, social media posts and press articles can provide information on the sentiment of economic operators. For example, what people say about a company, its image among its partners, financial analysts or the general public, its difficulties, its reputation, its image in terms of quality, innovation, social and environmental respect, all these elements can provide information on its financial health and be integrated into the analysis. The management of certain funds relies on this type of analysis, also provided by economic information specialists such as Ellisphere (formerly Coface Services).

For credit card fraud risk detection, geolocation data of smartphone holders can be compared with payment terminal information to ensure consistency.

1.3.1.1 Google Trends

Google Trends[12] allows us to see how often a term has been searched on Google, with a visualization by region of the associated searches and certain headlines in the news. The frequencies associated with several terms can be overlaid as in Figure 1.1. The data can be downloaded in CSV (comma-separated values) format. Google Trends is used in various fields such as health (Section 1.4.1) and financial markets.

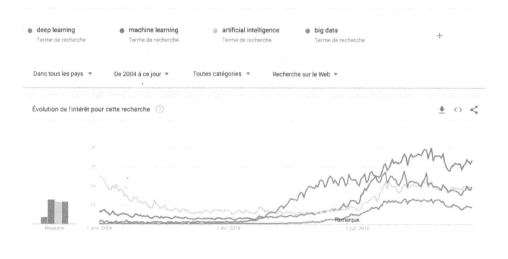

Figure 1.1 Google Trends.

1.3.1.2 Google Trends and Stock Prices

The use of Web searches for forecasting stock market prices is based on the principle that decision-making is preceded by a search for information, which is increasingly done on the Web.

Here is how the study published in *Scientific Reports* (2013) was conducted. From January 2004 to February 2011, 98 terms were analyzed on Google Trends: debt, stocks, portfolio, inflation, Dow Jones, etc.,. and for each term, the proportion $n(t)$ of the total searches of week t was recorded. During the same period, the closing prices $p(t)$ of the Dow Jones Industrial Average (DJIA, often shortened to Dow Jones, the oldest index of the New York stock exchanges) were taken at the beginning of each week t.

The hypothesis tested is that $p(t + 1)$ is correlated with $n(t)$, specifically with:

$$\Delta n(t, \Delta t) = n(t) - \text{average of } n(t) \text{ between } t - 1 \text{ and } t - \Delta t,$$

with Δt varying between 1 and 6 weeks in the study.

The test was translated into a "Google Trends strategy" consisting of:

- sell the DJIA at the price $p(t + 1)$ on the 1st day of week $t + 1$ if $\Delta n(t, \Delta t) > 0$, then buy the DJIA at the price $p(t + 2)$ at the end of the 1st day of week $t + 2$;
- buy the DJIA at price $p(t + 1)$ on the 1st day of week $t + 1$ if $\Delta n(t, \Delta t) < 0$, then sell the DJIA at price $p(t + 2)$ at the end of the 1st day of week $t + 2$.

The highest gain, 326% between 2004 and 2011, was obtained with the term "debt" and $\Delta t = 3$, while a "Dow Jones strategy" of replacing $\Delta n(t, \Delta t)$ with $\Delta p(t, \Delta t)$ ('buy at the sound of the gun and sell at the sound of the bugle') yields a gain of only 33% over the same period.

1.3.1.3 The quantmod Package for Financial Analysis

Stock market and currency prices and other financial information can be found in sources such as Yahoo Finance. Quantitative data are represented by symbols, such as ^FCHI for

Figure 1.2 Stock market price.

the French CAC 40. The R quantmod package allows one to access, analyze, and represent these financial data. Here is how we can retrieve the CAC 40 prices between 2007 and 2018, and display them (Figure 1.2).

```
> library(quantmod)
> getSymbols("^FCHI", src="yahoo")
> head(FCHI)
           FCHI.Open FCHI.High FCHI.Low FCHI.Close FCHI.Volume FCHI.Adjusted
2007-01-02   5575.76   5621.65  5575.63    5617.71    85910000       5617.71
2007-01-03   5621.00   5623.67  5596.82    5610.92   118580700       5610.92
2007-01-04   5573.73   5585.54  5547.17    5574.56   130465700       5574.56
2007-01-05   5552.64   5566.24  5517.35    5517.35   126420500       5517.35
2007-01-08   5532.57   5555.67  5509.06    5518.59   115053800       5518.59
2007-01-09   5549.01   5563.48  5532.62    5533.03   151688200       5533.03

> plot(FCHI[,c("FCHI.Adjusted")], type="l")
```

For the rest of our analysis, we transform the quantmod data into a data frame, and remove any rows with missing data. This is the case here for May 1, 2014. We put the date, which is the name of the rows, in a specific variable, and we extract the month.

```
> cac40_value <- as.data.frame(FCHI)
> cac40_value <- cac40_value[which(!is.na(cac40_value$FCHI.Volume)),]
> cac40_value <- cbind("date" = rownames(cac40_value), cac40_value)
> rownames(cac40_value) <- NULL
> cac40_value$mois <- substr(cac40_value$date,1,7)
> head(cac40_value)
        date FCHI.Open FCHI.High FCHI.Low FCHI.Close FCHI.Volume FCHI.Adjusted    mois
1 2007-01-02   5575.76   5621.65  5575.63    5617.71    85910000       5617.71 2007-01
2 2007-01-03   5621.00   5623.67  5596.82    5610.92   118580700       5610.92 2007-01
3 2007-01-04   5573.73   5585.54  5547.17    5574.56   130465700       5574.56 2007-01
```

```
4  2007-01-05   5552.64   5566.24  5517.35    5517.35   126420500      5517.35 2007-01
5  2007-01-08   5532.57   5555.67  5509.06    5518.59   115053800      5518.59 2007-01
6  2007-01-09   5549.01   5563.48  5532.62    5533.03   151688200      5533.03 2007-01
```

We then calculate the monthly average of the adjusted closing price, and transform the month-year into a 01-month-year date of the usual POSIXct class. This data frame can be merged with Google Trends data.

```
> cac40_monthly <- aggregate(cac40_value[,"FCHI.Adjusted"],
    list(date=cac40_value$mois), mean)
> cac40_monthly$date <- as.POSIXct(paste(cac40_monthly$date,
    "01", sep="-"), format='%Y-%m-%d', tz= "UTC")
> colnames(cac40_monthly) <- c("date", "value")
> head(cac40_monthly)
        date      value
1 2007-01-01 5586.986
2 2007-02-01 5684.217
3 2007-03-01 5495.406
4 2007-04-01 5831.803
5 2007-05-01 6053.903
6 2007-06-01 6014.926
```

1.3.1.4 Google Trends in R

The gtrendsR package allows access to the Google Trends statistics, i.e. the frequency of queries normalized on a scale from 0 to 100,[13] by entering one or several search keywords, and possibly a region and dates. With the first versions of the package on CRAN, up to version 1.3.5, you had to have a Gmail address and log in with your address and password. Around mid-2017, the Google Trends API[14] changed and the gtrendsR package was updated accordingly. It no longer requires authentication, but it has the disadvantage of only providing monthly, not weekly, series if you go back more than five years. A Python package exists, pytrends, with the same parameters as the R package.

You can specify a geographical area and a resolution:

- with a resolution of "1h," "4h", "1d," "7d," Google Trends returns data for the last one hour, four hours, one day, and seven days;
- a resolution not shown is weekly for any period between three months and five years, and daily for any period between one and three months.

A parameter (gprop) of the gtrends() function can specify the Google product on which the search should be performed: Web (default), news, images, YouTube... Here, we are interested in web searches, and we extract the search statistics in France between January 1, 2007 and December 31, 2015.

```
> library(gtrendsR)
> cac40_trend <- gtrends("CAC 40", geo="FR", time="2007-01-01
    2015-12-31")
> head(cac40_trend$interest_over_time)
```

```
          date hits keyword geo gprop category
1 2007-01-01   10  CAC 40  FR  web          0
2 2007-02-01   10  CAC 40  FR  web          0
3 2007-03-01   12  CAC 40  FR  web          0
4 2007-04-01   11  CAC 40  FR  web          0
5 2007-05-01   10  CAC 40  FR  web          0
6 2007-06-01    9  CAC 40  FR  web          0
> plot(cac40_trend)
```

The `plot()` function displays the evolution of the search frequencies of an expression on Google over time (Figure 1.3).

1.3.1.5 Matching Data from `quantmod` and Google Trends

We now merge the adjusted closing prices and the queries frequencies on Google Trends in order to obtain a double set of monthly values.

```
> cac <- merge(cac40_monthly, cac40_trend$interest_over_time[,1:2])
> head(cac)
        date    value hits
1 2007-01-01 5586.986   10
2 2007-02-01 5684.217   10
3 2007-03-01 5495.406   13
4 2007-04-01 5831.803   10
5 2007-05-01 6053.903   10
6 2007-06-01 6014.926    9
```

As explained above, there is a negative correlation between the frequency of queries on Google Trends and the CAC 40 prices, slightly stronger for the correlation of ranks.

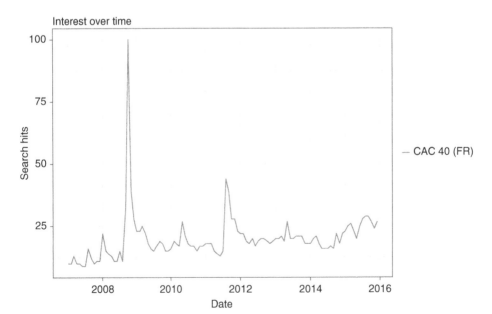

Figure 1.3 Google search queries.

```
> cor(cac$value, cac$hits)
[1] -0.3378188
> cor(cac$value, cac$hits, method="spearman")
[1] -0.3956836
```

By transforming the previous data frame into a multiple time series using the `ts()` function, we can search for the lag of the Google search series that maximizes its linear cross-correlation with the CAC 40 price series. We indicate that the series starts in January 2007 and that it is monthly. The graphs of the two time series can be plotted on the same time axis (Figure 1.4) or the two time series can be overlaid on the same graph (Figure 1.5) by first standardizing (centering and scaling) the data with the `scale()` function in order to put the two series on the same scale.

```
> cac.ts <- ts(data = cac, start = c(2007,1), frequency = 12)
> cac.ts
                date     value hits
Jan 2007 1167606000 5586.986   10
Feb 2007 1170284400 5684.217   10
Mar 2007 1172703600 5495.406   13
Apr 2007 1175378400 5831.803   10
May 2007 1177970400 6053.903   10
Jun 2007 1180648800 6014.926    9
...

> plot(cac.ts[,-1])
> plot(scale(cac.ts[,-1]), plot.type = "single", lty = 1:2)
```

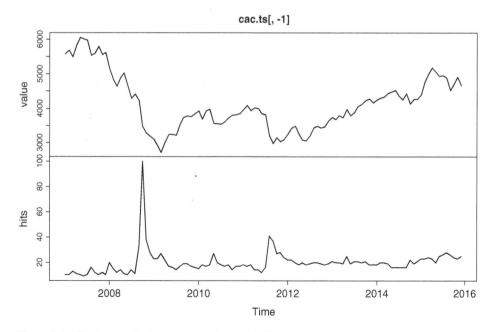

Figure 1.4 Stock market prices and search queries time series.

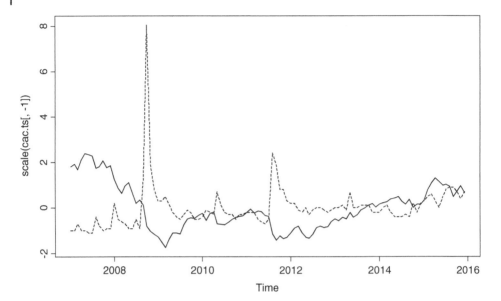

Figure 1.5 Stock market prices and search queries overlay.

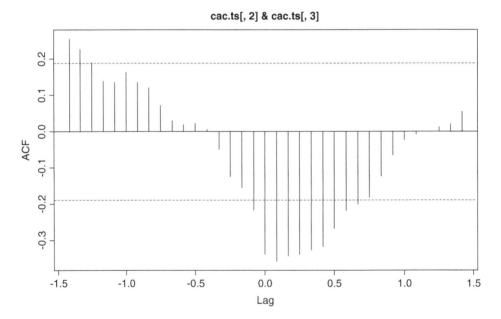

Figure 1.6 Correlogram.

We plot the correlogram (Figure 1.6) and we see that the linear correlation is maximal (in absolute value) when the trend series precedes the CAC 40 price series by one month. This correlation is then −0.357.

```
> cross <- ccf(cac.ts[,2],cac.ts[,3], type = c("correlation"),
    plot = TRUE)
> cross$lag[which.max(abs(cross$acf))]*12
[1] 1
> cross$acf[which.max(abs(cross$acf))]
[1] -0.3569695
```

We can also calculate the Spearman correlogram of correlations and see that the correlation is maximal (in absolute value) when the trend series precedes by one month that of the CAC 40 prices.

```
> cross <- ccf(rank(cac.ts[,2]),rank(cac.ts[,3]),
    type = c("correlation"), plot = TRUE)
> cross$acf[which.max(abs(cross$acf))]
 [1] -0.3963044
```

This rank correlation equal to -0.396 is not surprisingly stronger than the linear correlation.

The following calculation shows that the correlation is less strong in 2012, 2013, and 2015. In fact, we even see that the direction of the correlation reverses slightly in 2012 and cancels in 2013. These differences in correlation across years can be seen in Figure 1.5.

```
> library(lubridate)
> cac$an <- year(cac$date)
> sapply(2007:2015, function(x) {cor(cac[which(cac$an==x),]
    $value, cac[which(cac$an==x),]$hits, method="spearman")})
[1] -0.8297550 -0.6208354 -0.6926184 -0.5920817 -0.6678821
    0.1043598  0.0000000 -0.6250023 -0.3697275
```

The same calculation can also be done using annual windows in the time series.

```
> sapply(2007:2015, function(x) {scac <- window(cac.ts,
    start=c(x,1), end=c(x,12)) ; cor(scac[,2],scac[,3],
    method="spearman")})
[1] -0.8297550 -0.6208354 -0.6926184 -0.5920817 -0.6678821
    0.1043598  0.0000000 -0.6250023 -0.3697275
```

Finally, we can check that the CAC 40 prices are correlated to other Google searches, but the gtrends() function only allows at most five terms simultaneously to be queried.

```
> cac40_trend_all <- gtrends(c("crise", "dette", "chômage",
    "inflation", "croissance"), geo="FR", time="2007-01-01
    2015-12-31")
> CAC <- merge(cac40_monthly,
    cac40_trend_all$interest_over_time[,1:3])
> sapply(c("crise","dette","chômage","inflation","croissance"),
    function(x) {cor(CAC[which(CAC$keyword==x),]$value,
    CAC[which(CAC$keyword==x),]$hits, method="spearman")})
      crise       dette     chômage    inflation   croissance
-0.50732425 -0.19880401  0.20049101 -0.08707338  0.19189605
```

The negative correlation with "crisis" is expected, but the positive correlation with "unemployment" is more surprising.

1.3.2 Big Data and Deep Learning in Insurance

Big data are present in both branches of insurance: property and casualty (P&C) insurance, and health insurance.

In P&C insurance, auto insurance, with the possibility of geolocating insured drivers, is very interested in the contribution of big data.

Some insurers have developed a smartphone application that analyzes the driving style of drivers in order to offer them appropriate rates. This application analyzes the number of kilometers driven, the time, the type of road, and takes measurements (acceleration, braking, speed in curves, and speed in relation to traffic) allowing the calculation of a monthly score influencing the pricing. GPS data can also be used. You have to be careful about a radical change in behavior, which could lead to the suspicion of fraud.

Some apps allow you to analyze your driving in order to adjust your insurance premium and offers automatic assistance calls in case of an accident.

Sensors on the car could even signal the risk of breakdown, telling the driver what to do and where to find the nearest breakdown mechanic. These solutions are in the interest of the insurer and the insured (and society): reduction of the risk of breakdown and accident.

Another application of deep learning algorithms for computer vision is the analysis of photos of crashed vehicles to estimate their damage and repair costs. This automatic analysis is not always efficient enough but it is very fast and can help experts in their work.

In health insurance, "pay as you live" contracts are developing in the same way, the aim of which is to suggest lifestyles deemed better for the insured and the insurer. In order to know if you have a really healthy lifestyle, the insurer could be tempted to look at your activities as they appear on social networks, at least as soon as the progress of artificial intelligence will make it possible to use these data in a sufficiently fast and reliable way.

1.3.3 Big Data and Deep Learning in Industry

The numerous sensors (temperature, pressure, vibration, wear) placed on the components of a machine, an elevator, an engineering structure (bridge, tunnel, building) or a transport vehicle permit data to be retrieved in real time and remotely, which, once analyzed and modeled, can provide a probability of failure, of breakage of a part, and allow an arbitration between:

- unnecessarily heavy and frequent maintenance operations, leading to unnecessary expenses and unavailability of the productive apparatus;
- insufficient maintenance operations, leading to costly and even dangerous failures.

The interest in these predictive maintenance devices is the fact that the measured stresses are the real ones and not the ones foreseen in the design. Predictive maintenance allows us to intervene earlier, at the first signs of weakness, and therefore at a lower cost and for less time than if we wait for the actual degradation of the device. Some estimate that predictive maintenance and the industrial internet of things could save several hundred billion euros per year worldwide.

In addition to productive devices, examples of applications are of course aeronautics (the sensors on an airplane generate 1 gigabyte of data during a Paris-New York flight), automotive, bridge monitoring, with their tension, corrosion, temperature and wind speed sensors, and smart meters.

Smart meters allow real-time prediction of consumption of electric energy, but also of malfunctions, and faster and more economical billing. These smart meters can measure and transmit in near real time (at short intervals throughout the day) the energy consumption of a building.

The uses of smart meters are many: to monitor networks in real time, to balance supply and demand, to regulate consumption, to read consumption remotely and to produce accurate bills, to identify breakdowns and defaults, and to refine forecasting models. It is a component of smart grids (intelligent electrical networks).

The data transmitted continuously (readings every ten minutes) are big data in their scope, and they will provide fairly accurate information on the lifestyle of the building's occupants, especially since it is planned that various connected objects will communicate their data to the smart meter: the boiler, thermostat, heat pump, radiators, etc. It will be possible to identify devices in operation from their load curve.

Examples of big data use abound in the power generation and distribution industry:

- sensors in the plants;
- measures on the networks (regulation, optimization);
- results of simulations (production planning);
- connected devices' load curves ;
- letters from customers ;
- Web site log files ;
- social networks, forums ;
- telephone records.

Voluminous data, coming from various sources and often in a continuous flow (electrical consumption, sensors), thus big data, intervene in the following:

- smart grids: smart meters, electric vehicles;
- smart home: energy management, Internet of Things, connected speakers;
- smart cities: traffic management, lighting, energy management.

Smart meters also exist to measure water or natural gas consumption, and they can detect abnormal consumption and especially leaks.

Other contributions of big data are the optimization of the supply chain and the improvement of the design of future aircraft.

Deep learning is used in computer vision, useful in particular to learn how to distinguish a defective part from a compliant part. This is a binary classification problem on images, as we will see in Section 8.3, except that here it is not a question of distinguishing animals or objects, but defective parts or not. The learning of a deep neural network is done on a sample of images of already classified parts. These models are used in real time during the welding of parts monitored by a camera. The camera is connected to an algorithm that triggers an alert if a bad weld is detected. The stakes are high when we know that a defective part can cause a breakdown or an accident, and cost the manufacturer a lot of money, and that at the same time there are not enough human inspectors to ensure this level of surveillance. This system is used in particular by automotive and agricultural equipment manufacturers. Other manufacturing processes can benefit from the same type of algorithm.

1.3.4 Big Data and Deep Learning in Scientific Research and Education

The applications of big data in science are not the most publicized but are not the least important.

1.3.4.1 Big Data in Physics and Astrophysics

Particle physics and astrophysics are interested in objects that are so numerous that the contribution of big data is decisive. The DEUS (Dark Energy Universe Simulation) project seeks to model the evolution of the entire observable universe, from the Big Bang to the present day. It applies the standard cosmological model to simulate the behavior of 550 billion particles, in order to gain a better understanding of the nature of dark energy and its influence on the structure of the universe, as well as the origin of the distribution between dark matter and galaxies. The calculations were performed on the CURIE supercomputer of the GENCI consortium (Grand Équipement National de Calcul Intensif), which includes the French government (49%), the CEA (20%), the CNRS (20%), universities (10%) and INRIA (1%). Housed at the CEA, CURIE has 92,000 processors and a capacity of 2 petaflops: it is one of the five most powerful computers in the world. The calculations generate 150 petabytes of data but only 1 petabyte of data needs to be stored. The first simulations were carried out in April 2012 and won the Big Data prize from the American magazine *HPCwire* in 2013.[15] The *Large Hadron Collider* (LHC) is also a huge source of data: 60 terabytes per day.

Modern telescopes provide a gigantic quantity of images and therefore of data: for example, the *Very Large Telescope* (VLT), in fact is composed of four optical telescopes in the Atacama desert in the north of Chile, which each collect 15 terabytes per night. We can also mention the future Vera C. Rubin Observatory (or LSST: *Large Synoptic Survey Telescope*) built in Chile, which will record 30 terabytes of data per night, with a camera of 3.2 billion pixels, the largest existing digital camera. From 2023, it will provide the precise position of more than 10 billion galaxies and new information on dark matter and dark energy, but to do this will require computing power adapted to big data.

As for Euclid, the space mission of the European Space Agency (ESA), whose objective is to understand the origin of the acceleration of the expansion of the universe and the nature of its source: dark energy, Euclid will be based on a telescope to be launched in 2022 and will be able to observe ten billion astronomical sources in visible light and in the infrared, going back 10 billion years to the period when dark energy played a significant role in the acceleration of the expansion of the universe. This telescope will produce in ten years about 10 petabytes of images that will be analyzed in nine computing centers working for more than one hundred European laboratories, and will provide a wealth of data to astronomers for decades to come.

1.3.4.2 Big Data in Climatology and Earth Sciences

The study of the climate, the forecasting of its evolution and in the shorter term the weather forecasts naturally involve huge amounts of data. Examples include the Discovery supercomputer at the NASA Center for Climate Simulation (NCCS), which stores 32 petabytes of climate data and climate model simulations. In 2017, the UN launched the *Data for Climate Action* challenge to encourage researchers to use big data to find solutions for climate change mitigation and adaptation.[16]

In addition, work is being done to estimate the probability of an earthquake occurring at a given location.

1.3.4.3 Big Data in Education

Data analysis is increasingly being used to monitor students, particularly in distance learning which has recently become widespread. Faced with the difficulties of this type of teaching, where the teacher does not see the student, data analysis is used to adapt teaching to the student's progress and to identify the risks of dropping out and send alerts to the teaching team. The objective is to increase the success rate by individualizing the teaching.[17] This analysis can be based on the time spent, the way of following the program, of watching videos, of searching on the Web ... and even on the analysis of clicks and data entry. It is important to beware of crossing the line between these analyses and those of student behavior or automatic evaluation, which is tempting to reduce costs but carries the risk of incorrect evaluations.

These methods can be applied in particular to MOOCs ("massive online open courses"), which aim to bring together as many learners as possible online. OpenClassrooms[18] was created in 1999 (under the name "Le site du Zéro") and offers free online courses accessible to all, on computer science, science, and business. France Université Numérique[19] (FUN) is a MOOC that was launched in October 2013 and has offered about 100 courses since January 2014. One of the best-known MOOCs, Coursera,[20] offers several hundred courses.

1.4 Big Data and Deep Learning for Individuals

Following the previous section, which looked at big data applications from the perspective of companies and organizations, this section takes the perspective of individuals, in whose lives big data are becoming increasingly important.

1.4.1 Big Data and Deep Learning in Healthcare

Just as medicine has long made extensive use of statistics, known as biostatistics, so it was one of the first users of deep learning, particularly in medical imaging, and of big data generated by medical devices and measuring instruments, the processing of which is of course of capital interest for public health. The use of big data is part of the *4 P's of medicine*: personalized, preventive, predictive, and participative.

1.4.1.1 Connected Health and Telemedicine

Big data are first encountered in remote medical monitoring, for example, for the detection of heart attack risks, or Diatelic for the remote monitoring of dialysis patients. DeepMind has developed the Streams application, which analyzes the medical data of patients suffering from kidney disease, in real time, in order to alert their doctors of a risk of acute renal failure.

Remote monitoring tools, or even simple applications for smartphones, can analyze the data transmitted by sensors (heart rate, blood pressure, oxygen saturation, blood sugar, temperature, etc.). They can reduce the costs of patient care while improving their quality of life, especially for diabetics. In 2018, the first connected watch with an electrocardiogram sensor appeared. Artificial intelligence is increasingly present, through numerous start-ups, to analyze medical images, electrocardiograms or genetic data, optimize radiotherapy treatments, or reduce the duration of MRI examinations.

A distinction must be made between connected health, or eHealth, and telemedicine. Connected health is reserved for minor ailments and the monitoring of patients by themselves, using algorithms. It can also simply help to adopt a healthier lifestyle or increase the autonomy of the elderly. Telemedicine is aimed at serious illnesses, focuses on clinical aspects and uses much greater resources, with secure networks permanently connected to medical teams. The same device can be used for both connected health and telemedicine, for example, a blood pressure monitor can be connected to a doctor to monitor a high risk of high blood pressure (following certain medical treatments) or be connected to a simple algorithm if the risk of blood pressure is limited. A connected scale can be used to track a baby's weight after a difficult birth or to track the weight of a person on a diet. We can guess that the commercial stakes are not far from connected health. Neither are the economic and ethical stakes: should we stop reimbursing a patient whose remote monitoring has shown that he or she is not respecting his or her medical treatment and is not taking his or her medication? We know that the rate of non-adherence reaches 50% in certain pathologies. The fear of penalties could also slow down the acceptance of connected health, as well as the fear of not respecting medical confidentiality.

Other questions also arise about connected health: its usefulness, its effectiveness and of course its reliability. The latter is crucial when a connected object is an insulin pump that will automatically inject a diabetic patient (artificial pancreas) when required.

1.4.1.2   Geolocation and Health

In Kenya, the geolocation of cell phone users (15 million users and 12,000 antennas) can analyze the movements of the population and discover that some movements had little impact on the spread of malaria (near Nairobi) or, on the contrary, had a lot (near Lake Victoria).

With geolocation data from more than 150,000 cell phones, in 2014, the Swedish NGO Flowminder analyzed the movements of populations in West Africa and tried to predict the location of Ebola fever outbreaks, which allowed for better location of treatment centers.[21] The difficulty with these analyses is that cell phone equipment is uneven across countries, and also that people's behavior changes during the epidemic, which complicates their modeling.

After the Haiti earthquake in 2010, geolocation helped facilitate aid distribution by analyzing crowd movements based on cell phone data.[22] During the subsequent cholera outbreak, phone data were used to identify areas at risk.

During the 2015 earthquakes in Nepal, Flowminder again distinguished itself by using cell phone data to locate population movements, as a large proportion of Nepalese were equipped with them.

In March 2020, data from European mobile operators were used to track the spread of the Covid-19 epidemic and conduct spatial epidemiology analyses.

1.4.1.3 The Google Flu Trends

By analyzing the keywords entered on its search engine, Google was able to establish a correlation between certain requests and the appearance of an epidemic of influenza (Figure 1.7). This correlation was corroborated by health monitoring organizations and was published in the journal *Nature*.[23]

This example illustrates the V of big data velocity (Section 1.1), with daily data updates and not weekly updates as in traditional health monitoring: yet, the sooner an epidemic is detected, the better it is fought.

Google began this project in 2008, following other work on searches or clicks on certain sites. Google analyzed billions of queries on its search engine in the United States between September 2003 and March 2007, and extracted the 50 million most frequent queries (keyword or combination of keywords, for example "indications of flu" or "cold/flu remedy"). Note that keywords with no apparent connection to influenza were not excluded *a priori*.

These queries were aggregated on a weekly basis, and normalized across regions of the United States by dividing the *RC* number of queries containing a certain keyword combination by the total *RT* number of queries in the region.

Specifically, nine regions were considered: those of the Centers for Disease Control and Prevention (CDC), which provide epidemiological data, including the weekly percentage of physician visits with influenza-like illness *(ILI)*: temperature greater than 100°F (37.8°C) with a cough or sore throat.

For each region of the United States, and for each of the 128 weeks considered, the percentage *P* of influenza-like visits, the *RC/RT* ratio, and a linear regression of their logit was sought:

$$logit(P) = \beta_0 + \beta_1.logit\left(^{RC}/_{RT}\right) + \varepsilon.$$

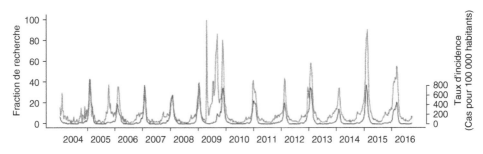

Figure 1.7 Google Flu Trends. Source: Sentinel Network; http://www.sentiweb.fr/france/fr/?page=google.

For each of the 50 million queries:

- nine linear regressions were each fitted on 128 points (i.e. 450 million regressions, distributed over several hundred machines);
- the correlation coefficients of the predicted and observed values of P were calculated for each of the nine regions;
- the average correlation of the nine linear regressions was calculated.

The queries with the highest average correlation were kept as they best corresponded to the evolution of influenza symptoms (simultaneously in all nine regions, to reinforce the significance of the result), and then they were combined together in new linear models. The same combinations were then tested in all nine regions. The combination of the 45 best queries gave the best overall result. In particular, when a combination of 81 queries was reached (the last being "Oscar nominations"), the correlation of the overall model dropped (Figure 1.8).

In these top 45 queries, 91% are directly related to the flu. In the next 55 queries, only 55% are directly related to the flu. For example, there is "high school basketball" which is in season in winter.

A linear model was finally fitted on these 45 best queries, over all nine regions, i.e. $1152 = 128 \times 9$ observations. It was validated on 42 weeks more recent than the training data sample (March 2007 to May 2008) and on all nine regions, showing a correlation coefficient $= 0.97$ (average between regions). This model can be applied continuously (including outside the periods monitored by the CDC) and provides predictions for the next day, whereas the CDC data are available in one to two weeks. This time saving is precious to take preventive measures: alerting populations, vaccination, detection of a new strain. But traditional networks are complementary, providing more accurate data and also data such as age and address that are absent from web queries.

As can be seen on its website,[24] Google Flu Trends has been distributed in 29 countries. It was also followed in 2011 by a Google Dengue Trends.

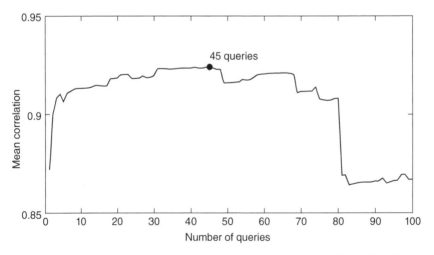

Figure 1.8 Number of queries in Google Flu Trends. Source: *Nature*, 457 (2009), 1012–1014.

Thus, the Google Flu Trends (GFT) model forecasts were initially 97% correlated with CDC forecasts. The quality of these forecasts declined from 2013 onwards, with an overestimation (sometimes double) of influenza cases.[25] Several causes have been identified:

- internal to Google: the Google engine has evolved since 2008, in particular with the auto-completion of additional search terms, i.e. semi-automatic entry based on the previous searches of Internet users, which artificially increases the prevalence of certain terms (searches no longer depend solely on the state of health of the Internet user, but also on the operation of the search engine);
- external to Google: the number of searches can also increase if the news talks more about the disease (as in the case of H1N1) or a drug related to the disease, or even when a media outlet, such as *The New York Times* in 2008, publishes an article on the GFT giving an example of a query analyzed by Google, a query immediately entered by many Internet users (this is the reason given by Google for not publishing the list of GFT queries).

Other causes are not new: Google users are not a representative sample of the whole population, symptoms may be poorly described, and moreover some words with the same search pattern as the flu have no relation to the disease.

Google revised its model in 2009 (after the H1N1 flu epidemic), in 2013 (after the H3N2 flu epidemic) and in 2014, trying to take into account the impact of media coverage of the flu on Google searches. It also refined its regression model by substituting an elastic net regression[26] (Section 3.3). But Google eventually closed its Google Flu Trends website to the public in August 2015, though the data remained available to researchers.

Despite the use of elastic net, there was a probable overfitting of the GFT model, especially on winter epidemics, resulting in poor generalization to other periods, as the GFT model detects cold and winter and not only influenza.

Google's work has been criticized for its forecasting errors and lack of information provided to the scientific community,[27] but the GFT can be useful in countries without a health surveillance network as efficient as the Centers for Disease Control and Prevention in the United States, and in conjunction with health surveillance data.

It was shown[28] that the Google Flu Trends model improved the use of only historical CDC data in an ARIMA model, decreasing the mean absolute error (MAE) by 16% with a 32-week learning window. Other work[29] showed that GFT data could be used in an auto-regressive model incorporating a hidden Markov chain, which is more robust, more accurate, and incorporates seasonality: the ARGO (AutoRegression with GOogle search data) model.

The use of health surveillance data is important to ensure the reliability of local-level predictions, which are both the least accurate in the GFT model and the most important for prevention, vaccine delivery, and distribution actions.

Other projects include Flu Near You (US) and GrippeNet.fr (France). Some projects are based on analysis of Twitter (MappyHealth, Crowdbreaks, Sickweather), Yahoo! and Wikipedia, but the signal-to-noise ratio is low, and the young age of users makes the sample unrepresentative.

Another example is provided by the Covid-19 outbreak in 2020. Recall that it appeared at the end of November 2019 in the Chinese region of Wuhan and that the Chinese authorities recognized the existence of this new pneumopathy at the end of December 2019. The World Health Organization (WHO) announced on January 9, 2020 that this epidemic was due to a new RNA virus, SARS-CoV-2, of the coronavirus family like SARS-CoV (responsible for the SARS epidemic in 2003) and MERS-CoV (responsible for the MERS epidemic in 2012). This new virus is the causative agent of this new respiratory infectious disease called Covid-19 (for **C**orona**VI**rus **D**isease). The human-to-human transmissibility and the number of actual cases in Wuhan were guessed in mid-January 2020, notably from studies by Imperial College London based on cases reported far from Wuhan, in Thailand and Japan. The late announcement of the WHO and its initial underestimation of the pandemic were surprising, and have since been attributed to the influence of China and its desire to exonerate its responsibility in the dissemination of the virus.

The Canadian company BlueDot had detected the epidemic and its spread in Asia a few days before the WHO alert, based on an algorithm that takes into account not only data from Google searches for symptoms, but also from online forums, news feeds in 65 languages, health bulletins and official statements, as well as air travel. The algorithm's analyses are verified by epidemiologists who validate the information before sending it to health authorities, airlines, and public hospitals in several countries.

1.4.1.4 Research in Health and Medicine

The collection of patient data makes it possible to detect epidemics or to evaluate the side effects of a treatment. It is possible to match medical data with environmental data to study, for example, the effect of exposure to pesticides or endocrine disruptors. Genomic data can also be matched with clinical, medical imaging or socio-economic data to explain the onset of a disease or the response to a treatment.

In addition to these public projects, there are private projects such as Google's *Baseline* project, which wants to map human health by collecting medical data from volunteers equipped with connected sensors.

In population genomics, we seek to identify the regions of the genome affected by selection processes, from domestication to the recent improvement of breeds used in production, and understanding artificial selection can help to improve natural selection. Genome-wide association studies (GWAS) are the analysis of genetic variants in individuals, and the study of their correlations with phenotypic traits such as diseases (rheumatoid arthritis, Crohn's disease, breast cancer, Alzheimer's disease). These studies require massive data, which can involve hundreds of thousands of individuals and millions of variables: the nucleotide polymorphisms (SNPs: single-nucleotide polymorphisms) which are the genetic variants studied. These SNPs represent about 90% of human genetic variants and correspond to the substitution of one nucleotide for another at a specific location in the genome. For example, at a specific position in the genome, the C (cytosine) nucleotide may appear in most individuals, but in a minority of individuals, the position is occupied by a T (thymine) nucleotide. This means that there is a SNP at this position in the genome. On average, a SNP is encountered every 100 to 1000 nucleotides and there are about 5 million SNPs in a human genome (i.e., compared to a reference genome), distributed irregularly across the chromosomes. Fortunately, not all of these genetic variants are associated with pathologies, but some are associated with pathologies and responses of the body to treatments, hence the interest of genome-wide association studies. One difficulty with these studies is that genome-wide databases are scarce and lack representativeness for certain populations.

Neuroimaging benefits greatly from deep learning techniques. Brain imaging, for example, by MRI, allows us to map the areas activated during the performance of certain tasks and thus associated with certain mental processes. It is also possible to link the observed shape of the brain to certain characteristics, such as age, and to learn to distinguish by imaging the normal aging of a brain from a neurodegenerative disease. For a long time, brain imaging was limited to small datasets because of acquisition and processing costs, and the conclusions were unreliable and sometimes contradictory, due to the importance of experimental variations. It can now handle larger datasets, thanks to image compression methods and the use of distributed computing, and can rely on computer vision algorithms using deep neural networks. These algorithms can detect hidden patterns indicative of a pathology such as Alzheimer's disease, allowing an earlier diagnosis than the appearance of clinical signs and thus likely to increase the chances of successful therapies.

Deep learning, with methods based, for example, on generative models (Section 7.19), is beginning to be used to design new molecules for therapeutic purposes. In December 2018, DeepMind announced some very interesting results on protein folding, a challenging and important question in understanding the mechanisms of life and certain diseases. Deep neural network models were trained to predict the 3D shape of proteins based on their constituent amino acids. Proteins are chains of amino acids and folding can occur between each amino acid in the chain, leading to an extremely large number (about 20^{300} for 300 amino acids in a protein) of different combinations and structures. With the same amino acids, two proteins can have different shapes and therefore different functions. So the three-dimensional shape of a protein is very important, and a wrong folding of a protein can prevent it from fulfilling its function properly and be the cause of diseases such as diabetes or Alzheimer's. In order to understand this protein folding mechanism, and the diseases caused by its defects, that researchers are organizing competitions to predict the shape of proteins. The challenge is to predict the structures of recently discovered, but not yet made public, proteins based on their amino acid sequence. The team that comes closest to reality wins. DeepMind's AlphaFold algorithm won a competition (CASP13) by finding the most accurate prediction for 24 of the 43 proposed structures,[30] while the runner-up managed to do so for only 14 structures. It had been trained on thousands of known proteins, taking into account the distance between the amino acids and the angles formed by the folds, to find the shape that requires the least energy, which is the one taken by the protein. It was also able to predict in March 2020 the 3D structure of several proteins associated with the SARS-CoV-2 coronavirus, and an improved version trained on 170,000 proteins, AlphaFold 2, won the CASP14 competition in November 2020. The results of this competition are measured by a global distance test (GDT) between the predicted structure and the actual shape of a protein observed in laboratory. This distance is normalized on a scale of 0 to 100 and AlphaFold 2 obtained a GDT score above 90 for two-thirds of the proteins. Its GDT score for the most difficult protein to predict was even 25 points higher than the next team, while in 2018 the lead was only 6 points. Now, a distance as small as that reflected by a GDT score above 90 falls within the measurement uncertainty interval and means that AlphaFold 2 predictions are as good as the imaging data. AlphaFold 2 has been described in a paper published in *Nature*,[31] along with an open source software and a database of the structures of hundreds of thousands of proteins from several species.

It is envisaged to use this type of algorithm to create proteins fulfilling a particular function, useful for certain health or environmental problems, and start-ups are being created in this field. A new Alphabet company called Isomorphic Labs has thus been launched in November 2021 to apply these methods to the discovery process of new drugs.[32]

BERT models have also been applied to this question of the 3D structure of proteins,[33] their attention mechanisms connecting amino acids that are distant in sequence but close in 3D structure.

We will see in Section 7.20.3 that very promising projects of brain-machine interfaces allow a paralyzed person to pilot an exoskeleton by thought, as a kind of artificial spinal cord, or a mute person to express himself or herself using a vocal device decoding their brain signals.

Of course, its successes cannot hide for the moment the limits of artificial intelligence in the medical field, as we will see in Section 10.2.

1.4.2 Big Data and Deep Learning for Drivers

Big data and deep learning are present in automotive driving assistance, using:

- intelligent guidance system (integrating vehicle location, traffic status and history, presence of hazards, weather conditions and driver's time constraints);
- economic driving assistance (by integrating the consumption of the vehicle in its various phases of operation: stop, acceleration, cruising, braking);
- driving assistance systems based on information communicated by other vehicles, such as the presence of a broken-down vehicle, a hill or a descent allowing to anticipate an increase or a decrease of the engine speed (this is under study in some road transport companies);
- detection of driver fatigue by analyzing the driver's behavior.

Big data can be used for tracking systems in case of theft, similar to cell phones.

Big data also enables personalized maintenance based on information collected by multiple sensors: brake wear, engine speed, fluid pressure, etc. Analyzing these data and comparing them with data collected on other vehicles helps determine the optimal time to perform a service. These data are sent to a cloud to feed statistical models and send alerts to the driver if an anomaly is detected.

Agreements were announced in 2018 between automakers and GAFAMs: a Google/Renault-Nissan-Mitsubishi agreement for the use of Google Assistant artificial intelligence, and a Microsoft/Volkswagen agreement for the Volkswagen Automotive Cloud to use the Microsoft Azure platform.

These applications shift from individual to collective interests. The collection of information provided in real time by drivers' smartphones also provides information to the community about road traffic conditions, smoothing the traffic and even avoiding accidents. This information can also send alerts on road conditions, saving detection costs. Weather sensors on in-vehicle smartphones can provide more detailed information than the national weather service.

The biggest innovation expected in the next decades in the transport sector is the advent of the autonomous vehicles: train, bus, truck, car and maybe even planes. The self-driving car should free up time, reduce traffic jams, reduce the number of parking spaces needed, facilitate vehicle sharing, and of course reduce the number of accidents (the majority of which are due to human error).[34] More generally, the financial and human cost of transport will decrease. However, some people will suffer: taxi drivers and truck drivers, perhaps garage owners.

The self-driving vehicle uses sensors and cameras to reconstruct the road situation in 3D and the position of other vehicles, and artificial intelligence algorithms to analyze these data in real time and act accordingly on the vehicle's controls to accelerate, slow down, brake, turn, depending on the road configuration, traffic conditions, external disturbances and of course obstacles. It must ensure both the safety and comfort of passengers.

Several levels of autonomy have been defined and must be reached over time by the vehicles.[35]

- At level 0, the vehicle is not automated at all, and the driver has total control of the main functions of the vehicle (engine, gas pedal, steering, brakes) at all times.
- In Level 1, the vehicle has some driver assistance features, such as Anti-lock Braking System (ABS) or Electronic Stability Program (ESP) that assist the driver but still leave the vehicle under the driver's control.
- At Level 2, partial automation of the vehicle's main functions allows the driver to be replaced in some situations, such as parking the vehicle, but leaves the driver fully responsible for driving in all other situations.
- Level 3 is limited autonomous driving, where in certain situations, for example, on the highway, the driver can hand over full control of the vehicle to the automated system, which will then be responsible for the main functions and will be able to accelerate, brake, and change lanes. The driver must nevertheless remain attentive and be ready to recover control of the vehicle at any time.
- Level 4 is autonomous driving throughout a journey, where the driver does not need to watch the road or hold the steering wheel, but only on appropriate routes (good enough road) and provided that the weather conditions are suitable (no fog or snow, for example).
- At Level 5, driving is fully autonomous in all circumstances and the driver can even leave the driver's seat or even be absent.

Developing these autonomous vehicles employs an enormous number of possible driving scenes, including vehicle malfunctions, and requires massive simulations of millions of kilometers, on any type of road, in any type of weather conditions and in any type of circumstance, including the failure of a computer or sensor. A particular difficulty for artificial intelligence is predicting human behavior: while a driver will guess that a pedestrian running after a bus is likely to cross the road suddenly, this will be much more difficult for an artificial intelligence.

1.4.3 Big Data and Deep Learning for Citizens

Local authorities can analyze social networks, discussion forums, blogs, and the online press to help them build dashboards and opinion barometers to help them define public policies. The analysis of these documents allows a city to detect the expectations and concerns of its inhabitants, in order to better target its investments, its renovation works, its new services, or its communication.

We must not hide the risk of drifting toward surveillance of citizens' opinions and personal networks, or of manipulation as shown by the cases that have involved Facebook since 2016, particularly around the American presidential elections.

Particularly worrying is the example of China, where a mass surveillance system is being set up using video surveillance cameras and facial recognition algorithms to track everyone in the country. The regime's goal is to cover all of China's public places with 450 million cameras by 2020, allowing it to find any person in a city within minutes (as tested by a BBC journalist who was found in seven minutes in the city of Guiyang from a photograph). Even more worrying, it is planned that this system will be coupled with a "social credit system" evaluating the behavior of each citizen in order to grant or withdraw rights. This algorithm is kept secret, but it is known that it is based on financial data, purchasing habits, and social contacts, among other things. This evaluation could lead to denying a person access to certain means of transport, hotels, purchase of an apartment, etc. Blacklists are disseminated on the Web and people calling them are informed by a message that their correspondent is on the blacklist. In 2019, China tested the extension of this social credit system to foreign companies, with a system that constantly monitors compliance with three hundred standards and downgrades the rating of a company that does not comply with them, which could make this system a political weapon.

The abuses of facial recognition are not limited to states, with applications allowing anyone to find on the Web all the photographs of themselves or of any person from whom they have obtained a photograph, even without their knowledge, even providing for alerts to be sent as soon as a new photograph is detected.

Social networks can also be scrutinized to anticipate election results, but polls remained more effective in predicting the results of the first round of the French presidential election in 2017. We know the importance of big data in the 2012 American presidential elections. Both in the campaign of the candidates to target potential voters by the right means (email, phone call, home visit) and focus on voters supposedly more undecided, adapt the communication of a candidate in real time based on messages on Twitter. And both in the prediction of results by statistician Nate Silver in his blog FiveThirtyEight.com, correct prediction in each of the 50 states (his predictions were correct in 49 of the 50 states in 2008, and in 31 of the 33 states where Senate elections were held in 2012). His model is known to rely heavily on polling but has not been disclosed. Social networks can also be used to estimate election results before the close of polling stations.

In everyday life, deep learning algorithms are used in many applications: voice recognition and synthesis to communicate with a chatbot, automatic reading of checks, early detection of fires from a network of ground cameras, infrastructure monitoring, etc.

1.4.4 Big Data and Deep Learning in the Police

The use of big data and machine learning in predictive policing has developed a lot in the United States, where there is a logic of "proactive policing" whose objective is to prevent crimes and not only to react and arrest the perpetrators. This policy is not quite the same in Europe, and in particular in France, where the arrest of a person can only be carried out in the event of the "beginning of execution" and where the simple control of a person can only be done on the basis of objective elements. The prediction provided by a software is not always considered to be such an element (whereas the nose of a dog will be for drug detection), but France and Europe are nevertheless beginning to take an interest in such software.

In France, the PredVol software was tested in 2016–2017 to predict vehicle crime. It provided a cartographic representation of the tested department and pointed out the risk areas according to a weekly forecast, from a five-year history. It specified the offence: car theft, motorcycle or bicycle theft or theft from a vehicle. Its evaluation showed that it tended to predict that risky areas would remain risky. As it did not provide any really new information, it was abandoned. The national police force then acquired another software system, Paved, which predicts a higher risk of vehicle theft or burglary in a given area, perhaps a little more accurately than PredVol. It is not based on personal data but on the history of delinquency in that area.

PredPol (now Geolitica)[36] is software developed by researchers at the University of California Los Angeles (UCLA) by analyzing 13 million crimes, and operated since 2011 by the Los Angeles Police Department and other US police departments. This provides them with a daily updated mapping of 200 x 200 meter areas where there is a high probability of a crime or offense occurring, which allows them to define patrol zones. The details of PredPol's algorithm are not published, but it is known that it is based on a seismology model by French researcher David Marsan that predicts aftershocks from an earthquake. PredPol explains future events by past events: people break in more often where they have already broken in. Like the previous software mentioned, PredPol makes predictions about areas and not about people. This police prediction system has been quite successful and has spread to other cities. Compared to the classic pins planted on a map, it has an undeniable practicality with its predictions sent to police officers' smartphones.

It has since been criticized[37] in two opposite directions: the duster effect and the streetlight effect. The duster effect means that the predictions of the algorithm may be accurate but that they do not reduce crime, which would only shift to a new location. The streetlight effect implies that the algorithm's predictions may not even be accurate, but they give the appearance of being accurate because police forces concentrate according to the predictions and thus record crime more often in predicted areas than in others. The crimes might not be more where the algorithm says they are, but they would simply be recorded better. In any case, these are the places where crime is usually concentrated, which could be predicted to be at risk without the help of software.

It should be considered that the purpose of this software is actually less to predict crime itself than to optimize police patrols according to risk, like its competitor Hunchlab from the American company Azavea. Nevertheless, it continues to be regularly accused of perpetuating economic and racial bias.[38]

We can also mention the Key Crime system in Italy and Precobs (Pre Crime Observation System, but this is also a nod to the *precogs* of *Minority Report*) in Germany.

Unlike PredPol and its emulators, the American company Palantir's model (named after the "vision stones" in *The Lord of the Rings*) relies on the personal data of previously convicted individuals, including of course their backgrounds, and establishes a network between them like those studied in Chapter 5, making it possible to highlight central individuals and increase their risk score. This solution interested the French Direction Générale de la Sécurité Intérieure (DGSI), before being extended to other activities and other French and European clients, despite the reluctance fueled by Palantir's relationship with American intelligence and fears of data leakage to an American agency.

1.5 Risks in Data Processing

The challenges of big data and deep learning lie not only in the computing power to store and process data, but also in its security and quality. There are several pitfalls to avoid:

- too little training data;
- poor data quality;
- missing values;
- non-representative samples;
- spurious correlations;
- overfitting;
- lack of explainability of models.

1.5.1 Insufficient Quantity of Training Data

An essential difficulty of Big Data comes from what is called the "curse of dimensionality". This curse comes from the fact that the individuals studied are points in a space whose number of dimensions is equal to the number of characteristics observed: each of these characteristics is a coordinate of the individual. With big data, the individuals are therefore represented in high-dimensional spaces, and of course the individuals must be sufficiently close, the space must be sufficiently dense, so that the learning of rules and models can be carried out on a representative basis. However, it is very difficult to fill a high dimensional space. For example, in the subspace $[0,1]^d$, 10^d points are needed to be separated by a distance equal to 0.1. Thus, in dimension 1, ten points in the interval $[0,1]$ make it possible to cover a phenomenon with a step equal to 0.1, but it takes one hundred points to obtain the same coverage in $[0,1]^2$ and it takes ten billion in $[0,1]^{10}$, which is much greater than the number of individuals commonly present in a dataset. This explains why the predictive power of a model increases with the number of explanatory variables used up to a certain point before decreasing (the Hughes effect).

Now, if we consider images, we realize that a training sample can only contain a tiny proportion of all possible pixel configurations: even with extremely simple images of 28 × 28 pixels, each taking only 2 values (white/black), the number of configurations, the dimension of the solution space, is $2^{28\times28}$, i.e. 10^{236}, a huge number!

1.5.2 Poor Data Quality

Data quality is always critical, and even more so with big data because:

- many data come from external and heterogeneous sources;
- their rapid evolution makes it more difficult to control them;
- they may be used in automatic algorithms;
- some data, typically those collected on the Web and social networks, contain a large amount of noise, missing values or even errors.

Let's recall the main quality requirements when processing data:

- the definition of the data must be known and adequate;
- the data must not be erroneous;
- non-missing values must be present in the attributes that require them;
- the matching of data between different data sources must not reveal any inconsistencies;
- the data values must be up to date;
- data should not be unduly duplicated;
- the history, processing and location of the data in question must be easily traceable.

It is also important to avoid errors that could occur when reconciling data sources between which no universal keys exist.

1.5.3 Non-Representative Samples

A basic rule of modeling is to train the model on a representative sample of the population to which the model will be applied. A lack of representativeness is the most common cause of systematic errors in model prediction, commonly referred to as "algorithmic bias."

Representative sampling is not necessarily simple random sampling, and it is not uncommon to stratify a sample to ensure that each type of individual, even the rarest ones, are adequately represented. This is a common practice in public opinion polling, where one wishes to control for gender and age representation in order to improve the accuracy of the results for the entire population. But there are rules for determining the optimal size of strata, and in all cases, one should not exclude from the sample a stratum on which one will then want to make predictions or obtain results.

It is also known that a linear regression model is only valid for the range of observed values. We know that medical results cannot be extrapolated from one type of patient to another. We know that an image recognition algorithm will sometimes fail miserably to recognize an image absent from its training sample, as recalled below (Section 1.5.6).

1.5.4 Missing Values in the Data

A particular cause of unrepresentativeness of a sample is the presence of missing values for some variables, or even missing individuals altogether, which is the case of non-respondents in surveys or credit applicants who have been denied credit. In this case, since these individuals did not obtain credit, we cannot assume that they would have repaid it or not, and therefore they do not have a good or bad payer label and are necessarily absent from the training dataset of a scoring model. Non-response is then total, whereas it is only partial when some of the responses were provided or some of the variables were observed. If the values or responses are not missing at random, as is often the case, they render the sample unrepresentative and lead to the existence of a bias in the results.

This is what we try to remedy with imputation methods, i.e. the replacement of missing values. There are deterministic imputation methods, in which the imputed value is always the same for each individual, and random methods, in which the imputed value varies with each application of the method. Among the deterministic methods, we find the imputation of Y by its mean or median over the respondents, or imputing Y by a regression $Y = f(X_i)$ on other variables X_i without missing values.

These methods are useful for obtaining values for each individual, but sometimes one is not specifically interested in individual predictions but rather in results over the whole population, whether it is to calculate correlation coefficients, regression coefficients or other statistical parameters. The objective of imputation is not to obtain the best possible predictions of the missing values, but to replace them with plausible values in order to make the best use of the available information to make inferences about the parameters of the population. However, deterministic methods obviously do not respect the distributions of the imputed variables or their relationships with the other variables. In particular, they underestimate the variance of the imputed variables. This is why we often turn to random imputation methods.

The first method consists of adding a random residue to the previous regression, which is then written $Y = f(X_i) + \varepsilon$. This residual can be drawn from a parametric distribution fixed *a priori*, or drawn randomly from the prediction errors of the deterministic imputation method observed on the respondents. Another method is the "hot deck" imputation[39] in which the missing value of an observation is replaced by the non-missing value of another observation drawn at random from the same sample. A third method is Donald B. Rubin's multiple imputation.[40] In a single imputation, each missing value is replaced by an assumed value. In multiple imputation, each missing value is imputed by several (often of the order of five) values. This results in several completed datasets without missing values, which allows the desired statistical analyses to be performed on each of these datasets, and then the results obtained are combined into a set of estimated parameters with their variance. This allows us to add the variance between the datasets to the variance within each dataset.

The advantage of these random imputation methods is that they preserve the distributions of the imputed variables, but this comes at the cost of additional variance, due to the random selection of residuals or individuals. One can try to limit this variance by a good implementation of these methods, but other approaches have been proposed to limit the imputation variance, such as the balanced imputation of Chauvet *et al.*[41] This has several advantages: it is as simple as simple imputation, it can be applied to qualitative or quantitative variables, and it preserves the distribution of the imputed variables

In computer vision, each image is defined by a set of pixels and missing parts of the image correspond to pixels with missing values. We can use the previous imputation methods but a more natural solution is to represent an image as a graph, where each pixel is a vertex, and two neighboring pixels are connected by an edge. When pixels are missing in an image, the corresponding graph has fewer vertices but this does not change the way it is processed. In particular, we can apply to it the methods of Spatial Graph Convolutional Networks (SGCN) and perform on these graphs the classical convolution operations on images. Compared to simple graph networks that only take into account the neighborhood of the pixels, spatial graph networks take into account their spatial coordinates, which is more precise information. This approach has achieved good results.[42]

1.5.5 Spurious Correlations

It is known that a strong correlation between margarine consumption and the divorce rate in Maine, or between crude oil imports from Norway and driver deaths in collision with railway train, does not reflect any causality. These are two of many examples presented on a well-known website.[43] It would never occur to anyone to use such spurious correlations in a model, even if their R^2 is greater than 0.95. And yet, there is a great risk that tools designed, and even praised, to look for any correlation in big data, detect such absurd correlations and implement them in an "AutoML" approach, i.e. automatic machine learning.

This risk can only be avoided by careful analysis of the data and knowledge of the business behind it. This knowledge is necessary because not all spurious correlations, which do not correspond to any causality, present themselves in such a burlesque light. For example, in the field of risk prediction, certain apparent risk factors are not due to an inherent risk but to the company's management rules in the face of this risk, rules that are valid at a given moment but not immanently. A model built on these rules will appear reasonable and will provide correct predictions at first, but will quickly show its limits and a decrease in its predictive power.

In an attempt to discern true causality among correlations, epidemiologist Bradford Hill set out nine criteria for causality,[44] including temporality, correlation strength, plausibility, and reproducibility. Temporality (cause precedes effect) is obvious, and the intensity of the correlation can be measured by the data scientist, but plausibility requires business expertise and therefore exchanges between data scientists and business experts.

Beware, however: not all unexpected correlations are spurious.

1.5.6 Overfitting

We speak of overfitting of a model when too much complexity leads it to follow all the fluctuations of the training sample, to learn the noise in addition to the signal, to detect false links with the risk of applying them wrongly to other samples.

When we talk about a model being too complex, it is normally in comparison with the size of its training sample, and a larger sample can allow the training of a more complex model, in the larger number of cases the model allows a larger number of parameters to be fitted. However, the quantitative size of the training sample is not enough, and its representativeness is also important: its cases must represent the largest possible number of cases. This seems obvious but is not always easy to obtain. For example, in computer vision, a deep neural network will be able to learn to identify fish, but as these fish will have been represented in the vast majority of cases on a seabed, the network will have learned to recognize a fish on a seabed and may not be able to recognize it in an unusual context. Examples are quite frequent of animals or objects not recognized when they are not in their usual environment. Examples include husky dogs mistaken for wolves when photographed in the snow.[45] A famous paper shows how a photograph of a panda can be imperceptibly modified to be mistaken for a photograph of a gibbon by the GoogLeNet neural network.[46] This kind of "attack" that could mislead deep learning models is taken seriously and studied, as it could lead to accidents if it involves autonomous vehicles which are made to take one road sign for another.

1.5.7 Lack of Explainability of Models

By moving from classical regression models to deep neural network models or ensemble models aggregating large numbers of decision trees, we have moved from "white boxes" to "black boxes". The direct apprehension that one has of the coefficients of a regression gives the impression that one understands the model well, and it is true that they allow one to justify one's predictions perfectly. But we refer to the previous discussion on correlations that are not necessarily causalities, to warn against the illusion of believing that the mathematical justification of predicted values provides a real explanation of the model. "Predicting is not explaining," to quote the title of a famous book by the mathematician René Thom.[47] And most methods of "model explainability" consist solely of determining the influence (intensity and meaning) of the variables in the predictions of the model. However, the importance of the variables measured in this way does not mean the existence of causality, and the change in one variable may imply changes in other variables: one cannot often measure the influence of a variable "all other things being equal"/ (*ceteris paribus*). We have thus obtained a form of explanation of the model, in the sense that we can justify our predictions with arguments that are understandable to a human being, but this justification may not be satisfactory if it does not indicate the underlying causes at play. It will answer the question "how was such a high score calculated for this individual?" rather than "why is this score so high for this individual?". This is why, alongside purely predictive models, causal models are being developed, such as Bayesian networks.

Recognizing their limitations, model explainability methods can nonetheless be useful, particularly in a regulatory setting, for responding to auditors and ensuring that no criterion has a disproportionate weight in a prediction or is likely to cause bias. The simplest methods estimate the global weight of a variable in a model (for example, by measuring the decrease of the predictive power of the model after randomly swapping the values of the variable), but more recent methods, such as LIME[48] and Shapley's[49] method, can be applied in machine learning and even deep learning models to estimate the contribution of each characteristic in the prediction made for a specific individual (Section 8.3.4). They are implemented in R (`shapr`, `fastshap`, `lime`, `iml`) and Python (`shap`, `lime`, `skater`) packages and more general tools such as *Google AI Explanations* available on Google Cloud Platform, and *AI Fairness 360* from IBM available in R and Python.

1.6 Protection of Personal Data

All that is technically possible is not legally and even less ethically possible, and the overuse of personal data would be counterproductive for any company that engaged in it. Negligence is not acceptable either: data security is crucial when large amounts of personal data are stored. This is both for financial reasons (these data are valuable) and for the protection of personal data, and therefore for reasons of trust. The data must be safe from theft, loss or damage, and protection against hacking and cyberattacks must be reinforced.

1.6.1 The Need for Data Protection

Legislation on personal data protection will probably have to evolve to take into account the existence of the immense amounts of personal data available on the Internet, of which the holder is probably not even aware. The massive use of data collected by social networks has, however, been the subject of awareness on the occasion of several recent cases, including the scandal revealed in March 2018 of the processing of personal information of more than 85 million people, collected through Facebook by Cambridge Analytica. This company was able to collect a lot of data from Facebook users thanks to a personality questionnaire available on Facebook, which was to be used by Cambridge researchers to study the psychological profile of a person thanks to their activity on Facebook. One of the researchers sold these data, which belonged not only to the people who had installed the application but also to their friends on Facebook, to Cambridge Analytica, which allowed political figures to use it to influence the vote for Donald Trump during the 2016 US presidential election, by sending elements that could orient their vote to the voters' Facebook feed. Since then, it has also been discovered that Facebook allowed advertisers to target their marketing messages by using the phone number provided by Facebook users to secure their account, and also by using contacts from the user's phone address book (which the social network has access to after the user has authorized it to scan their contacts for "friends").

In addition, numerous cases of data theft have highlighted security breaches:

- the theft of 100 million LinkedIn user email addresses and passwords revealed in May 2016;
- the theft of 68 million Dropbox user email addresses and passwords revealed in August 2016;
- the hacking of at least 500 million Yahoo! accounts in 2014, revealed only in September 2016;
- the theft of at least 143 million consumers' personal data from Equifax databases revealed in September 2017;
- the theft of 57 million Uber customers' personal data in October 2016, revealed only in November 2017;
- the hacking of at least 50 million Facebook accounts in September 2018;
- the theft of personal data (login, password, and in some cases name, phone number, place of residence, birthday) of 533 million Facebook accounts of users from 106 countries, theft carried out in 2019 but revealed only in April 2021 by its posting on a hackers' forum;
- the theft of card and bank account data, and other personal information of 100 million U.S. customers of Capital One Bank in March 2019, during the migration of its IT system to the cloud, by a former AWS employee.

The users concerned were not always notified by the company, or beyond the legal deadlines.

Particular attention should be paid to objects connected to the Internet, video surveillance cameras, routers, thermostats ... whose knowledge of the IP address can allow the takeover by an unwanted third party and be used in denial of service attacks, which consist in saturating the target's servers by concentrating toward it a huge flow of requests from the hacked objects (which then constitute a *botnet*). An even more direct and serious danger could come from taking control of a connected autonomous vehicle (Section 1.4.2), as it was already partially the case in 2016 when Chinese researchers from the Keen Security Lab took remote control of some functions of a Tesla Model S car, including the dashboard lock and the braking! Terrorists could even take control of an entire fleet of vehicles and turn them into deadly weapons. We are beginning to advocate the presence of a button on these vehicles that would allow them to be disconnected from the Internet.

The strengthening of legislation on the protection of personal data (Section 1.6.3) and its adaptation to the Internet era will have to accompany and provide a framework for the development of a digital economy based on the exploitation of enormous quantities of data provided by Internet users, social networks, and even all citizens, most often without their knowledge, because of their activity, their expression, their purchases, their movements, but also quite simply because of their lives in a world of increasingly connected sensors and devices. The acceptance of the digital economy model will require better control of its protagonists.

Thus, geolocation by smartphones can track individuals, and know their habits, the places they frequent to the nearest address. This geolocation is based on the recovery of the addresses of the relay antennas to which the smartphones are connected. The development of connected sensors also generates large amounts of individual data, especially in the field of health, where data are sensitive. The use of the cloud raises the issue of data transfer to countries that do not have legislation protecting personal data, and under conditions that do not always ensure total data security.

Cryptography is essential for encrypting data to ensure that it cannot be misused if it falls into the possession of the wrong people. Some data are only stored and exchanged in encrypted form. For example, payment data transmitted over the Internet is encrypted. It is even possible to perform certain operations on encrypted data without having to decrypt it. Unfortunately, cryptographic methods can also be used by hackers who manage to encrypt all the data on a computer, or even an entire company network, and demand a ransom in exchange for the decryption key: this is known as ransomware.

1.6.2 Data Anonymization

Not to mention criminal cases, anonymization may be desired in order to study sensitive data, such as medical data, without making it possible to identify the individuals concerned. In other fields, such as commercial, banking, there is a "right to be forgotten" provided for by the legislation so that the data of a former customer is no longer accessible by name a certain time after the customer's departure. Nevertheless, the company possessing these data may wish to be able to use it for statistical studies that do not contain names, or to meet regulatory obligations for risk analysis in the case of a bank.

Anonymization methods do exist, but they do not always offer total protection. On the one hand, each Internet user, even if not identified, can be associated with a very precise profile of behavior or even personality. On the other hand, it has been demonstrated[50] that the combination of certain information, known as quasi-identifiers, often corresponds to a unique person, who can then be identified if we have a database in which this person appears with an identifier and their quasi-identifiers. It is enough to match the two databases containing these quasi-identifiers, one containing the identifier, the other not, to be able to identify the individual in the second database. The quasi-identifiers can be the sex, the date of birth and the postal code together.

A famous example of de-anonymization of a database is that of Netflix, which in October 2006 launched its prize for the best recommendation model (see Section 3.6) by providing a database of 100 million ratings of movies seen by 480,000 users whose name had been replaced by an anonymous identifier. A few weeks later, two researchers from the

University of Texas, Narayanan and Shmatikov, announced that a de-anonymization algorithm allowed them to find a user in the Netflix database:[51]

- in 84% of the cases by knowing 6 ratings of the user,
- in 99% of the cases by knowing 6 ratings with their date within 14 days,
- in 68% of the cases by knowing 2 ratings with their date to within 3 days.

They applied their result to the public IMDb (Internet Movie Database) and the ratings it contains, assuming that the ratings of the same user of Netflix and IMDb are highly correlated. They showed that their de-anonymization is effective even if the intersection of the two databases is small.

The problem with this breach in anonymity is that a Netflix user does not want their ratings to become public, revealing their personality traits.

The same misfortune happened the same year to AOL, which had given access to 20 million web searches of 650,000 users, some of whose identities were found by two journalists of *The New York Times*.

The basic anonymization known as pseudonymization is therefore often not sufficient. This method consists of replacing an individual's identifier with a pseudonym or a random key (which must, however, allow for file matching).

More sophisticated methods of anonymization do exist,[52] such as data noise (e.g. by adding Gaussian noise to continuous variables) and especially k-anonymization[53] which consists of a kind of "blurring" of the data. In this method, we start by determining the quasi-identifiers, whose combination of values can be unique, and by making the values of the quasi-identifiers of each individual equal to those of at least $(k\text{-}1)$ other individuals: we replace these values by intervals of values by grouping adjacent quasi-identifiers. For example, we group the individuals by age groups and we replace the age of each individual by its age group. The value of k must be well chosen: small enough not to degrade the precision of the analyses that will be performed on the data, but large enough not to reveal too precisely the values of the sensitive data.

The k-anonymization may present a technical difficulty for the replacement of some data, for which a good "blurring", whether it is about the constitution of bins for a quantitative variable or the grouping of categories for a categorical variable, may require a non-trivial and somewhat long human or machine processing.

But the main limitation of this method arises when a sensitive data item varies little in each grouping of quasi-identifiers. In this case, it would be enough to know the value of this sensitive data item for an individual that we have managed to identify, to have a fairly accurate idea of the value of this data item for the $(k\text{-}1)$ other individuals of their group. If we want to avoid this, we can increase the level of aggregation of the individuals and constitute larger groups.

Another possibility is to group individuals according to another quasi-identifier, for example, the postal code, which will better mix the values of the sensitive data to be protected. However, this mixing can be detrimental to the analyses: it will not be possible to verify the existence of a link between age and a phenomenon if we only know the occurrence of the phenomenon for heterogeneous age groupings.

In both cases, the objective is that of the l-diversity method: to add a constraint so that not only each group of quasi-identifiers contains at least k individuals, but that the sensitive variable takes at least l distinct values.

A third method is *t*-proximity since *l*-diversity does not remove all useful information, it is further disguised by constructing the groups of quasi-identifiers so that the distribution of values of the sensitive variable is approximately the same in each group of quasi-identifier. The disadvantage of *t*-proximity is that it limits the possible analyses since it reduces the possibility of discovering useful correlations between the quasi-identifiers and the sensitive variable.

A fourth method is differential privacy.[54] It is appreciated by specialists because it provides theoretical bounds on the risk of identifying an individual. However, it is difficult to implement, and it creates fictitious data that are not always plausible (but which can be for geolocation data).

A fifth method consists of generating a dataset that recreates all or part of the variables in the dataset but preserves their distributions and relationships. This makes it possible to fit a model whose parameters are very close to those that would have been calculated on the initial data. At the same time, since the data are synthetic, they can no longer be linked to a person, which completely preserves anonymity. This method can be implemented using the R package `synthpop`.

Here's how it's done: the set of variables is divided into two subsets:

- those which are not synthesized (possibly empty set);
- those that are synthesized.

The non-synthesized variables are not modified (be careful not to leave any quasi-identifier in them, unless you delete them).

For synthesized variables:

- the first variable is sampled with replacement from the initial dataset;
- the second variable is sampled conditionally to the first variable according to a method:
  - non-parametric: we build a CART decision tree on this variable whose predictor is the first variable;
  - parametric: a model is built on this variable whose type determines the model (linear regression for a continuous variable, logistic regression for a binary variable, multinomial or ordinal logistic regression);
  - sampling with replacement from the initial dataset (risk of not respecting the links between variables);
  - from a user-defined model (e.g. a neural network).
- the *pth* variable is sampled in the same way conditionally to the *p-1* previous variables.

Obviously the synthesis models (conditional distributions) are calculated on the observed data and not on the synthesized data.

Note that in all methods, it is better to start by removing the extreme values that are easier to identify and more difficult to anonymize.

Another avenue for privacy is *federated learning*. It was born in 2016 from a Google paper[55] proposing to replace the learning of deep learning models on large centralized databases with collaborative learning among users relying on a decentralized architecture.

In federated learning, a global model trained on all individuals is replaced by the aggregation of several local models each trained on a subset of individuals. The model training is first initialized (randomly or by transfer learning) on a server, then deployed on each client terminal (e.g. smartphones) where the training continues based on the client data only, then the model updates are encrypted and sent to the server, which then aggregates all the updates into an optimized global model that is deployed on each client terminal. It is assumed that reverse engineering does not allow the central actor to guess the data of a local terminal from its updates.

The interest is in preserving the privacy of users, whose data do not leave their device. This is interesting for models trained on the Internet of Things, on medical data that will not leave the processing center, or on data from a consortium of companies that would like to work together without sharing their data. Moreover, the cost of data transfers is reduced.

A variant is where the variables, not the individuals, are divided into subsets. In all cases, the idea is that no one sees the whole data set.

The limitation of federated learning is the quality of the data. On the one hand, the theoretical distributions presupposed for the modeling are less frequently met locally than globally. On the other hand, by not gathering all the variables on all the individuals, we do not permit cross-tabulations which often allow us to detect inconsistencies and data quality problems. Finally, by only sending back to the central server the results of the local models and not the data that were used to train them, the quality of the backtesting *of* the models is severely limited: we can possibly follow their performance but we can no longer link this performance to the data of the model and note that a performance drop is linked to such or such data that should be corrected or replaced.

There is a Python library for federated learning: `PySyft`.

1.6.3 The General Data Protection Regulation

Harmonizing and strengthening the various existing European regulations, the General Data Protection Regulation (GDPR) which came into force on May 25, 2018, establishes new rules for the protection of personal data of European citizens, including:

- the right to erasure ("right to be forgotten"), i.e. the possibility for an individual to obtain the erasure of all personal data concerning him or her;
- the right of every individual not to be subject to a decision based exclusively on automated processing that produces legal effects concerning him or her or significantly affects him or her in a similar way;
- a new right to data portability: the individual must be able to recover, in a structured and commonly used computer format, his or her data communicated to an operator in order to keep them or transmit them to another operator;
- a duty to fully inform the person whose data are being collected in order to obtain their explicit and informed consent;
- taking into account the protection of personal data (*privacy by design*), from the very first stages of the design of the product or service that will process these data, in a way that is inherent to the company's/organization's information system (for example, by using pseudonymization and encryption);
- the application by default of the highest level of personal data protection (e.g. only necessary data should be processed, short retention period and limited and controlled accessibility) without any intervention from the user (whose default profile should preserve the confidentiality of his privacy) (*privacy by default*);

- the replacement of *a priori* declarations of processing by the obligation (*accountability*) for any data controller to be able to demonstrate compliance with data protection rules at any time, and therefore to have an internal control system;
- the appointment of a data protection officer in companies and organizations carrying out large-scale personal processing;
- the obligation for companies and organizations to notify as soon as possible to the national protection authority the cases of serious personal data breaches, and this authority may require the company to notify individually each person concerned;
- in the event of non-compliance with the GDPR, financial penalties of up to 4% of the company's annual worldwide turnover or €20 million, whichever is higher.

The GDPR applies to all companies processing personal data of EU citizens, even if they are established outside the EU or if their processing is carried out outside the EU.

The challenge of this regulation is to protect data without preventing its legitimate use, which requires, among other things, the ability to match data. If medical data cannot be matched with patients' socio-demographic and geographic data, it is obvious that their analysis loses some of its acuity.

The aim is to make those responsible for processing personal data accountable, in order to restore the confidence of those who entrust their data and, for those who use them, confidence in the quality and lawfulness of the collection of these data.

On April 21, 2021, the European Commission published its proposals for the regulation of artificial intelligence.[56] It wishes to both promote the development of artificial intelligence while addressing the risks it poses to the security and fundamental rights of Europeans. It classifies artificial intelligence systems into four categories according to their potential risk, which is judged:

- unacceptable, if AI aims to do the following:
  - manipulate human behavior to deprive users of their free will;
  - allow for social scoring by states;
- high, for AI use in:
  - biometric identification of persons;
  - critical infrastructures that could endanger the life and health of citizens;
  - education or vocational training;
  - product safety components (e.g. in robot-assisted surgery);
  - employment, workforce management and access to self-employment (e.g., résumé screening);
  - essential private and public services (e.g., credit risk assessment);
  - law enforcement;
  - the management of migration, asylum and border controls;
  - administration of justice and democratic processes;
- limited, if AI contributes:
  - for example, to conversational agents such as chatbots;
- minimal, if AI enters a majority of applications, including:
  - anti-spam filters;
  - video games.

The latter category is not regulated. To the limited risk category, specific transparency obligations apply: when talking to a conversational agent, a user must know that he or she is interacting with a machine in order to make an informed decision about whether to proceed.

High-risk artificial intelligence systems will have to meet strict conditions in order to be put on the market, including:

- adequate risk assessment and mitigation systems (risk management system);
- high quality of the data fed into the system;
- registration of activities in a public European database to guarantee the traceability of results;
- detailed documentation providing all the necessary information on the system and its purpose to enable the authorities to assess its compliance;
- clear and adequate information for the user;
- appropriate human control;
- a high level of robustness, security, and accuracy.

These rules still need to be adopted by the Member States and the European Parliament, but we can already see that the algorithms are in America and the standards are in Europe. This can lead to embarrassing situations, such as when regulatory authorities have difficulty understanding that in epidemiology a medical cohort must last a long time, and when in the midst of the Covid-19 pandemic they slow down the creation of a new cohort intended to study the locations of contamination. Moreover, the Cloud Act adopted in 2018 in the United States allows the American administration to seize all data relating to the electronic communications of a company or an individual, stored on the servers of an American company or operating in the United States, whether these servers are located in the United States or in another country, and without that individual being informed. This concerns, among others, all clients of GAFAM and the Cloud Act obviously conflicts with the GDPR since the data of a European citizen can be seized by the American authorities.

A new legal approach to data protection began to emerge from 2018: the patrimonialization of data that, belonging to the individual, could only be sold on a data market with the owner's consent (which is already the consequence of the legislation) and possibly with to be paid for, justified by the benefits derived from it by their users, starting with GAFAM.

1.7 Open Data

Open data are free public data, numerous and reputed to be reliable. However, they require a lot of work to widely share data collected for a specific use. They are mainly used in the fields of transport, health, libraries. They satisfy the growing demand of transparency of citizens and their wish to participate in public life.

Open data are the basis of a new business model, which has seen the creation of start-ups to exploit and value data better than the large companies or organizations that originate the data, and to provide services to individuals or other companies. For example, there are many smartphone applications on the topic of transport, using geolocation and data on infrastructure and schedules.

Crowdsourcing is the use of contributions from a large number of people to perform a task. Contributors may bring varying degrees of expertise, machine time from individual computers, or low-skilled but numerous volunteer labor. The motivations are diverse: personal development, distraction, play, self-promotion or altruism.

The general public can participate in the advancement of certain research, including:

- Wikipedia projects;
- papyrus transcription (https://www.ancientlives.org/#/);
- the Old Weather project (https://www.oldweather.org/) to capture nineteenth-century ship's logs containing interesting Arctic weather information;
- the Galaxy Zoo project (https://www.zooniverse.org/projects/zookeeper/galaxy-zoo/) to classify more than one million galaxies;
- more generally, the Zooniverse portal (www.zooniverse.org) and its dozens of collaborative projects in medicine, biology, climatology, science, history, literature, art.

We can also say that Google Flu Trends (Section 1.4.1.3) is a passive form of crowdsourcing. The same is true for certain authentication systems on the Internet (CAPTCHA) that ask the user to recognize a car, a bridge, an animal in a series of photographs that are presented. This system is used not only to confirm that the user is a human being and not a robot, but also to make the user label images, which will then be used to train computer vision algorithms.

Crowdsourcing is most often voluntary and in several of the examples cited, it is qualified. Another form of activity, described as digital labor, is (poorly) paid and unskilled. It is the one performed by people who connect to platforms (the best known being Amazon Mechanical Turk), sometimes as a main activity but most often in addition to another salaried activity, to perform repetitive tasks that are necessary to train supervised algorithms: identifying and classifying images and videos, writing reviews, searching for information in documents, translating texts, transcribing recordings of intelligent voice assistants, etc. They are millions of "Turkers" (contraction of worker and Turk) and digital workers on other microwork platforms, who supplement their income in conditions that may seem undignified (low pay, lack of employment contract, lack of welfare benefit) but which are flexible and useful to them. It is not without humor that Amazon has given its platform a name that refers to the "Mechanical Turk," a so-called automaton from the end of the eighteenth century that could play chess and beat many human players. In reality, a real human player was hiding inside the cabinet and it can be seen as a metaphor for human intelligence, which is still indispensable in tasks that artificial intelligence alone cannot always perform well enough, whether it is analyzing images or words.

Notes

1 We include here in the same term statistics, statistical learning, and machine learning, for the sake of brevity and because the boundaries are shifting, despite our attempt to draw them in the Introduction.

2 McKinsey, Big Data, the Next Frontier for Innovation, Competition and Productivity, 2011. www.mckinsey.com/business-functions/mckinsey.

3 The best-known being Google Home, Amazon Echo, and Apple HomePod, allowing voice control of devices in a home. Amazon claims in early 2019 to have connected its Alexa smart voice assistant to more than 100 million devices worldwide, from its Echo connected speaker, of course, to home appliances and soon Volkswagen cars.

4 Laney, D., 3D Data Management: Controlling Data Volume, Velocity and Variety. META Group Research Note. 6 (70) (2001).

5 Two more "V's" have since been added: veracity and value, but veracity has always been at the heart of statisticians' concerns, and the importance of value was already affirmed in data mining.

6 See, for example, https://www.domo.com/learn/data-never-sleeps-5, http://www.visualcapitalist.com/happens-internet-minute-2017/ and also http://www.internetlivestats.com.

7 https://www2.deloitte.com/content/dam/Deloitte/at/Documents/consumer-business/at-global-powers-retailing-2020.pdf.

8 http://www.gutenberg.org.

9 Pawlowicz, L.M. and Downum, C.E., Applications of Deep Learning to Decorated Ceramic Typology and Classification: A Case Study Using Tusayan White Ware from Northeast Arizona, *Journal of Archaeological Science*, 130 (2021), 105375.

10 Mirhoseini, A., Goldie, A., Yazgan, M. *et al.* (2021). A Graph Placement Methodology for Fast Chip Design. *Nature*, 594 (2021), 207–212.

11 Preis, T., Moat, H.S, and Stanley, H.E., Quantifying Trading Behavior in Financial Markets Using Google Trends, *Scientific Reports* 3 (2013), 1684, http://www.nature.com/srep/2013/130425/srep01684/full/srep01684.html.

12 https://trends.google.com/.

13 https://support.google.com/trends#topic=6248052.

14 An API (Application Programming Interface) is a programming interface that allows software to provide services to other software. We will discuss several of them in this book.

15 http://www2.cnrs.fr/en/2013.htm.

16 https://www.unglobalpulse.org/data-for-climate-action.

17 http://www.scientificamerican.com/article.cfm?id=how-big-data-taking-teachers-out-lecturing-business&page=2

18 https://openclassrooms.com/.

19 https://www.fun-mooc.fr/.

20 https://www.coursera.org/.

21 http://www.flowminder.org/publications/containing-the-ebola-outbreak-the-potential-and-challenge-of-mobile-data.

22 http://www.plosmedicine.org/article/info%3Adoi%2F10.1371%2Fjournal.pmed.1001083

23 Ginsberg, J., Mohebbi, M.H., Patel, R.S., Brammer, L., Smolinski, M.S. and Brilliant, L., Detecting Influenza Epidemics Using Search Engine Query Data, *Nature* 457 (2009), 1012–1014, http://www.nature.com/nature/journal/v457/n7232/full/nature07634.html. See also http://www.google.org/flutrends/intl/en_us/about/how.html and http://websenti.u707.jussieu.fr/sentiweb/?page=google.

24 https://www.google.org/flutrends/.

25 *Nature*, 494 (2013), 155–156, 14 February 2013 (http://www.nature.com/news/when-google-got-flu-wrong-1.12413).

26 https://static.googleusercontent.com/media/research.google.com/en//pubs/archive/41763.pdf.

27 Justified by Google, which argues that the disclosure of the search terms used in its model immediately leads to an artificial increase in the input of these terms.

28 Preis, T. and Moat, H.S., Adaptive Nowcasting of Influenza Outbreaks Using Google Searches. *Royal Society Open Science*, 1 (2014), 140095, http://rsos.royalsocietypublishing.org/content/1/2/140095.

29 Yanga, S., Santillanab, M., and Koua, S., Accurate Estimation of Influenza Epidemics Using Google Search Data Via ARGO, *PNAS*, 112(47) (2015), 4473–4478.

30 Senior, A.W. *et al.*, Improved Protein Structure Prediction Using Potentials from Deep Learning, *Nature*, 577 (2020), 706–710.

31 Jumper, J. *et al.*, Highly Accurate Protein Structure Prediction with AlphaFold, *Nature*, 596 (7873) (2021), 583–589.

32 https://www.isomorphiclabs.com/.

33 Vig, J., Madani, A., Varshney, L.R., Xiong, C., Socher, R., and Rajani, N.F., BERTology Meets Biology: Interpreting Attention in Protein Language Models, arXiv:2006.15222. (2020).

34 In this regard, we should not forget the first fatal accident in May 2016 when a Tesla car hit a truck that it had not seen turning. Tesla said at the time that this was the first fatal accident in more than 200 million miles already driven by its vehicles. In March 2018, another accident involved an autonomous vehicle and a pedestrian who was hit by the vehicle and killed by the collision.

35 SAE International (J3016) Automation Levels.

36 https://geolitica.com/.

37 https://cortecs.org/wp-content/uploads/2014/10/rapport_stage_Ismael_Benslimane.pdf.

38 https://themarkup.org/show-your-work/2021/12/02/how-we-determined-crime-prediction-software-disproportionately-targeted-low-income-black-and-latino-neighborhoods.

39 Andridge, R. and Little, R., A Review of Hot Deck Imputation for Survey Nonresponse, *International Statistical Review*, 78 (2010), 40–64.

40 Rubin, D.B., Multiple Imputations in Sample Surveys: A Phenomenological Bayesian Approach to Nonresponse, in *Proceedings of the Survey Research Methods Section* (American Statistical Association, 1978), pp. 20–34.

41 Chauvet, G., Deville, J.C., and Haziza, D., On Balanced Random Imputation In Surveys, *Biometrika*, 98 (2011), 459–471.

42 Danel, T. *et al.*, Processing of Incomplete Images by (Graph) Convolutional Neural Networks (2020). arXiv:2010.13914v1

43 http://www.tylervigen.com/spurious-correlations.

44 Hill, A. B., The Environment and Disease: Association or Causation?, *Proceedings of the Royal Society of Medicine* 58 (5) (1965), 295–300.

45 Ribeiro, M. T., Singh, S., and Guestrin, C., "Why Should I Trust You?": Explaining the Predictions of Any Classifier (2016). arXiv:1602.04938.

46 Goodfellow, I.J., Shlens, J., and Szegedy, C. Explaining and Harnessing Adversarial Examples (2014). arXiv:1412.6572.

47 Thom, R., *Prédire n'est pas expliquer* (Éditions ESHEL, 1991).

48 Ribeiro, *et al.*, op. cit.

49 Štrumbelj., E. and Kononenko, I., Explaining prediction Models and Individual Predictions with Feature Contributions. *Knowledge and Information Systems* 41(3) (2014), 647–665.

50 Allard, T., Nguyen, B., and Pucheral, P. L'art de préserver l'anonymat, *Pour la science*, 98 (2018), 98–103.

51 Narayanan, A., and Shmatikov, V., How to Break the Anonymity of the Netflix Prize Dataset (2007). arXiv:cs/0610105.

52 Nguyen, B., Techniques d'anonymisation. *Statistique et Société*, Société française de statistique, 2(4) (2014), 53–60.

53 Samarati, P., and Sweeney, L. Generalizing Data to Provide Anonymity When Disclosing Information (Abstract), in *PODS '98: Proceedings of the Seventeenth ACM SIGACT-SIGMOD-SIGART Symposium on Principles of Database Systems* (1998).

54 Dwork, C., Differential Privacy. Paper presented at International Colloquium on Automata, Languages and Programming (ICALP) (2006).

55 McMahan, H.B., Moore, E., Ramage, D., and Aguera y Arcas, B. Federated Learning of Deep Networks Using Model Averaging (2016). arXiv:1602.05629v1.

56 https://ec.europa.eu/commission/presscorner/detail/en/IP_21_1682.

2

Processing of Large Volumes of Data

The processing of large volumes of data raises theoretical, algorithmic, and computational issues that we address in this chapter. Some of the principles stated here should be kept in mind because they are not linked to any particular software or programming language, and are of very general use. Parallel computing is discussed, which can, under certain conditions, accelerate calculations, then the chapter turns to distributed computing which aims at treating massive data by distributing them on several machines. Cloud computing is explored, which allows the greatest number of people to access machine learning and deep learning resources, and a great deal of computing power. Some processors are particularly adapted to deep learning and will be presented. The open source tools R and Python are described: they are both software and languages, and they are currently the most used in data science. Finally, at the end of the chapter, the promises of quantum computing are mentioned.

2.1 Issues

If a dataset is too large to be analyzed in a reasonable amount of time, there are four factors that can be used:

- the size of the dataset:
  - the number of observations, thanks to sampling;
  - the number of variables, by selection or compression methods.
- the complexity of the algorithm, understood as a function of the number of elements (observations and variables) to be processed, giving the order of magnitude of the number of steps to be performed for this processing;
- the quality of the IT implementation;
- the hardware or software computing power, both of which can be intertwined, especially when a software is able to take advantage of a parallel architecture of the machine, or of the arithmetic capabilities of the machine's processor.

The first question is the number n of observations. If n is large, this may pose a practical problem of computation time, and if n is small, this may pose a statistical problem of reliability of the results. The more observations we have, the easier the inferences and the modeling are, especially since many statistical estimators have good asymptotic

Deep Learning: From Big Data to Artificial Intelligence with R, First Edition. Stéphane Tufféry.
© 2023 John Wiley & Sons Ltd. Published 2023 by John Wiley & Sons Ltd.
Companion website: www.wiley.com/go/Tuffery/DeepLearning

properties, starting with the maximum likelihood estimator. It is generally when the number of observations is small that non-trivial statistical problems arise: it is sometimes necessary to use so-called exact tests.

Then there is the question of the number of variables. In principle, a large number of variables does not pose any statistical problems except when it exceeds the number of individuals, in which case, specific methods, such as PLS regression or Lasso must be used.

A problem that is more computational than theoretical arises when both the number of variables is very large and the number of individuals is very large: the complexity of the problem must then be reduced so that it becomes scalable, which can be done in the following ways:

- by dimension reduction, by projecting the space of variables onto a lower dimensional subspace by a change of variables minimizing the loss of information, as in factor analysis which operates a kind of information compression;
- by variable selection, looking for a "parsimonious" model.

2.2 The Search for a Parsimonious Model

A parsimonious model is a model that uses only a part of the available data: the explanatory variables deemed most relevant to the desired objective are selected. This principle of parsimony is similar to the one formulated by William of Ockham (1319) who stated "multiples should not be used without necessity." We speak of Ockham's razor because it allows us to eliminate, to "shave off," what is useless. It is fundamental and universal in statistical learning, where one seeks the best possible explanation by the simplest possible model.

We generally look for variables that minimize the empirical risk penalized by a measure of model complexity (Section 3.3). This penalty is a function that can be seen as a distribution over all the models. The simplest penalties are based on the number of variables selected (the Akaike and Schwartz criteria). The minimization of this penalized risk is a combinatorial problem of too great a complexity when the number of variables exceeds several tens, except for convex penalties since a local minimum is then global.

When we are interested in L^δ-norm penalties, so called because the penalty is the L^δ-norm of the coefficients of the variables, these penalties are convex if and only if $\delta \geq 1$. The Akaike and Schwartz criteria are L^0 penalties, since the sum of the 0 powers of the coefficients is equal to the number of variables multiplied by 1. The penalties in L^δ-norm are differentiable if and only if $\delta > 1$.

The most famous convex penalty is the Lasso (L^1 norm), but since it is not differentiable, we cannot use gradient descent (Section 3.2), which we replace with subgradient descent.

We are interested in the conditions under which non-convex penalties could allow a minimization of the penalized empirical risk without an exhaustive search. This is achieved by first searching for a minimum for a Lasso type penalty, and then in the neighborhood of this solution, we seek the solution of the problem for the non-convex penalty. These non-convex penalties can have interesting properties. Thus, the penalty known as Smoothly Clipped Absolute Deviation (SCAD) penalty[1] is close to the Lasso penalty for small coefficients but approaches a constant penalty for large coefficients. It addresses the problem of bias of large coefficients in the Lasso penalty.[2]

2.3 Algorithmic Complexity

Let's start with the algorithmic complexity as a function of the number n of observations.

Some algorithms, such as linear regression or linear discriminant analysis, have a linear complexity with respect to the number n, but this complexity is generally not linear: the computation time is not proportional to n, but to $n.\log(n)$, n^2, n^3, etc. Thus, k-nearest neighbors and decision trees have a complexity in $n.\log(n)$ or n^2 depending on the case. Support vector machines have a complexity in n^3. The agglomerative hierarchical clustering often has a complexity in n^2, but we can use mixed clustering by preceding the agglomerative hierarchical clustering with a fast clustering, by k-means. As for sorting algorithms, their complexity is often in n^2 or $n.\log(n)$.

Let's turn to the algorithmic complexity as a function of the number p of variables. As a function of the number of variables, the complexity of the algorithms is generally linear in clustering (agglomerative hierarchical clustering, k-means) and non-linear in factor analysis and classification: this is the case of logistic regression, linear discriminant analysis and linear regression which have a complexity in $n.p^2 + p^3$, as well as principal component analysis, with a complexity $O(n.p^2)$ of the computation of the covariance matrix, and a complexity $O(p^3)$ of the eigenvalue decomposition. Multiple correspondence analysis has a complexity of the order of $(l.m)^{3/2}$, where l and m are the numbers of rows and columns. Decision trees and neural networks have a complexity $O(p)$.

The complexity of fitting a model also depends on the mode of variable selection: global, step-by-step, or input without selection. If we want to explore all the possible models with 0 to p variables, the complexity of the problem becomes exponential because there are 2^p of them. Furnival and Wilson have somewhat optimized this exhaustive search by their *leaps and bounds*[3] algorithm.

The complexity of exact tests is not usually expressed by a simple formula, but it is often great and may require the use of Monte Carlo simulations or asymptotic tests.

The Apriori algorithm[4] for association rule detection has an exponential complexity with respect to the number of items.

2.4 Parallel Computing

In the 2000s, processor manufacturers began to stop the race for power, as they reached the physical limits in terms of component size and dissipation of the heat produced. This partly explains the expectations of quantum computing (Section 2.8), but also the decision to build processors with multiple cores, even in personal computers. This allows parallel computing.

Parallel computing consists of breaking down processing into different tasks that are performed on several cores or several processors of a machine. A processor can have several cores, as is now often the case with personal computers, and a machine can have several processors, as is the case with traditional servers. They are called CPUs: central processing units. But in parallel computing, the machine is unique and the memory is usually shared, unlike in distributed computing, which is the subject of Section 2.5.

Unlike other programming techniques, parallelization does not reduce the total computation time but spreads it over several machine resources and therefore reduces the time between the beginning and the end of the computations.

Parallelization assumes that there are:

- several CPUs, either a multi-core processor (a personal computer) or several processors on one machine (a server);
- an adapted software (for example, R or Python: see Section 2.7);
- a treatment that is appropriate for this, with numerous tasks that can be performed independently of each other.

On this last point, it should be noted that computations are better parallelized than reads/writes. Also, optimization algorithms or adaptive algorithms such as boosting do not naturally parallelize. On the other hand, cross-validation, bootstrapping, random forests, and deep learning algorithms parallelize well.

K-means parallelize moderately well: the objects to be clustered are distributed in the different nodes (the initial centers being replicated in each node), the assignment to the centers and the recalculation of these centers are done in each node, but a global calculation of the center of each cluster must be done at the end of each iteration, hence the need for communication between the nodes.

Parallelization can benefit from a change of computational method. Thus, for the solution of a system of linear equations, the Jacobi method converges less quickly than the Gauss-Seidel method but parallelizes better.

Not all processes are faster after parallelization. If a part P of the treatments can be parallelized, and if N is the number of CPUs, then the gain of parallelization is:

$$\frac{1}{[(1 - P) + (P/N)]}$$

according to Amdahl's law.[5] For example, if $P = 90\%$, we will not be able to divide the computing time by more than 10.

On the other hand, parallelization is more efficient on a sufficient volume of data, because the parallelization mechanism itself consumes time. For this reason, it is important to avoid parallelizing tasks on too many threads.

2.5 Distributed Computing

In distributed computing, unlike the parallel computing of Section 2.4, the processing is broken down into tasks that are carried out on several machines, without shared memory. Between these machines, data must be exchanged through a network of sufficient size not to slow down the calculations too much. In return for a lower speed and a higher complexity, the distributed architecture can process volumes of data that would be too large for a single machine. This is why it is often used for big data and this is its main interest. We talk about a "cluster" of servers, and the processing as well as the data are distributed in the nodes of the cluster spread over several machines.

However, distributed architecture should not be confused with the grid architecture used for grid computing: in the latter, despite the objective of sharing resources, the machines hosting these resources are autonomous (not controlled by a common unit), weakly connected, often numerous, remote, and heterogeneous, with operating systems and file management systems that may be different. On the contrary, in distributed computing, the machines of a cluster are homogeneous and not autonomous. Grid computing generalizes distributed computing which generalizes parallel computing.

Distributed architecture is one of the technological breakthroughs initiated by Google and Yahoo, followed by Facebook, Twitter, Netflix, and Amazon, to crawl the web and respond to Internet users' requests. These uses require large data collection, storage, and analysis capacities, with changing data and power requirements, which have necessitated the implementation of new computer, hardware and software architectures in recent years. Often open source, they address three needs:

- the need to distribute storage and computation to match needs and capacities at a reasonable cost, which the distributed architecture and the MapReduce algorithm address;
- the need to manage data that are more flexible and less structured than the usual data, to which schema-less databases respond;
- the need to access significant computing power on demand, which cloud computing addresses.

The first two needs are addressed in this section, and cloud computing is discussed a little later in Section 2.6.3.

2.5.1 MapReduce

MapReduce is a programming algorithm developed by Google researchers[6] to perform operations on a cluster of servers. It consists of dividing and distributing data over several nodes where tasks are performed (the "Map" operation) and then aggregating the results (the "Reduce" operation).

Data are represented by pairs (key, value):

- the Map step reads the data and returns a result in the form of a pair (key, value) per input record;
- an intermediate step "shuffle" sorts the pairs by keys and sends to the same next step the pairs that have the same key;
- the Reduce step aggregates the values that have the same key.

It can be noted like this:

$$\text{map}(k1, v1) \rightarrow \text{list}(k2, v2)$$
$$\text{reduce}(k2, \text{list}(v2)) \rightarrow \text{list}(k3, v3)$$

In particular, in the case of word count:

- in the Map phase:
  - k1 is the name of the file, v1 is the text content in the file;
  - k2 is each word, v2 is "1" for each word;
- In the Reduce phase, the "1's" for each word are added together and the list of words with their count is returned.

An example of word counting in MapReduce is shown in Figure 2.1.

This example of counting words in a text is typical of MapReduce. The *k-means* algorithm provides another illustration of the MapReduce principle. The Map step reads the data and

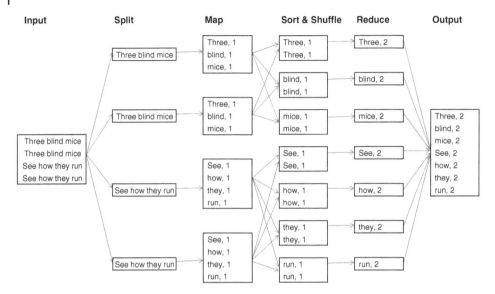

Figure 2.1 MapReduce.

calculates the distance separating each observation from each of the initial centers. The result of this step is provided as a (key, value) pair for each observation (value), with the corresponding key being the center to which the observation is closest. The Reduce step aggregates the values that have the same key by computing the cluster barycenters, i.e. the averages of the values of the variables of the observations belonging to the same cluster because they are associated with the same key.

The MapReduce algorithm doesn't always offer optimal performance, but it does have some interesting features such as its "scalability" (especially since the number of nodes is adaptable) and fault tolerance (a node can replace another node that fails) which allows large volumes to be stored on ordinary hardware that is less expensive than high reliability hardware. Scalability means the ability to support an order of magnitude change in data, with data being ten or a hundred times larger. Fault tolerance is MapReduce's big advantage over the Message Passing Interface (MPI) architecture, which is also used for distributed computing.

MapReduce can be programmed in Java, Python, R (with `RHadoop` and `SparkR`) and other languages.

2.5.2 Hadoop

The implementation of the MapReduce algorithm in the open source world and the Apache Foundation gave birth to the Hadoop project. Following work published in 2003 by Google on the Google File System,[7] Doug Cutting and Mike Cafarella developed a new distributed file system that they named after a toy of Cutting's son: a yellow elephant named Hadoop, which also stands for *High-Availability Distributed Object-Oriented Platform.*

Hadoop is a Java implementation of MapReduce. It is based on the HDFS (Hadoop Distributed File System) but also relies on other tools: Pig, Hive, HBase... Hadoop has become a reference for distributed computing and is widely used in Internet environments: Yahoo, Facebook, Twitter, eBay...

The structure of Hadoop consists of a "master," the NameNode, and "slaves," the DataNodes. The master receives requests and controls access to the databases of the "client" computer, and distributes the data to the DataNodes, which store and retrieve it. The data are stored in the DataNodes in the form of blocks that are often 64 megabytes in size, and are replicated, usually three times, in several DataNodes, on several machines. This redundancy ensures tolerance of failures, which are somewhat more likely when the mass of data requires it to be distributed over a larger number of servers. Each block of data is processed by a DataNode, but this responsibility can be transferred to another DataNode if the first one has stopped working. To signal that it is working, it must send a message every three seconds to the NameNode. If the latter stops working, it is of course much more annoying, and this is why there is a secondary NameNode as a backup. The NameNode selects the DataNodes to which it distributes data in order to optimize access times, i.e. by choosing those with the highest bandwidth.

Hadoop can be used as follows:

- by download from the Apache Foundation website (www.apache.org);
- by installing a "distribution" (such as Ubuntu or Debian for Linux): MapR, Cloudera-Hortonworks (which merged in 2018), or PureData System for Hadoop;
- directly ready to use from Cloud Computing providers: Microsoft Azure, Amazon Web Services, Google Cloud Platform.

2.5.3   Computing Tools for Distributed Computing

Just as relational database management systems (RDBMS) are adapted to structured data, distributed file systems are adapted to unstructured and expanding data. But Hadoop is not the only tool, other tools have been developed to handle big data, such as NoSQL (Not Only SQL), which extends the SQL (Structured Query Language) to the specific problems of big data and unstructured data.

The SQL language was designed for traditional DBMS (Database Management Systems), adapted to structured relational databases and to operations (joins...) and constraints (e.g., concurrent data updates) that increase the complexity of processing and their execution time.

However, in the giant databases of websites with very large audiences such as Google, Amazon, Facebook, and eBay, the data are not very structured, what matters is fast access to the data, in read mode without updating, and the expensive features of relational DBMS are useless, whereas the load balancing on a relational database requires optimization which can be difficult. On the other hand, it is necessary to be able to distribute the data over a large number of servers in order to allow multiple simultaneous accesses. In addition, it is necessary to be able to continuously add new data, which is not easily possible with relational databases whose schema is difficult to modify. This is why NoSQL databases were created for big data.

Hadoop and NoSQL have in common that they both are:

- open source
- scalable

- fault-tolerant
- adapted to unstructured data.

Among the big data computing tools, we can also mention the Pig programming language, which makes it possible to write MapReduce instructions at a level comparable to the SQL language, thus higher than Java.

Originally developed by Yahoo in 2006, Hive is a data warehouse infrastructure for Hadoop. The HiveQL language is based on SQL, but its statements are transformed (compiled) into MapReduce statements. The PyHive interface allows you to run Hive queries in Python.

Oracle Big Data SQL allows you to generate a single SQL query that can be executed in both an Oracle database and a Hadoop and NoSQL environment, allowing you to use both the SQL skills of DBAs and the advanced security features of the Oracle database.

The notion of a *data lake* has recently emerged to meet the storage and analysis needs of the big data. A data lake is a vast reservoir of raw data of heterogeneous structures, fed by external data sources and on which various analyses and explorations can be performed. Unlike traditional data warehouses, data lakes offer integrated data storage without a predefined schema. In the absence of a data schema, an effective metadata system is essential to make the data searchable and prevent the lake from becoming an unworkable "data swamp." Many data lakes are based on Hadoop technology, but not all.

2.5.4 Column-Oriented Databases

A change has occurred in some NoSQL DBMS, which are *column-oriented* instead of *row-oriented*. In a traditional, row-oriented DBMS, Table 2.1 is stored as:

> 1, Smith, Joe, 50; 2, Jones, Peter, 60; 3, Williams, Mary, 40; …

whereas in a column-oriented DBMS, it is stored as;

> 1,2, 3; Smith, Jones, Williams; Joe, Peter, Mary; 50,60,40; …

This second form makes it easier to insert a new column, facilitates data compression when the data in a column are similar, but is not suitable for quick access to specific rows.

An example of a column-oriented NoSQL DBMS is Cassandra, a project of the Apache Foundation written in Java. As a column-oriented database, Cassandra is more suitable for sequential data processing than for direct access to individual rows.

Cassandra is a fully distributed system: each node in a cluster has the same role, and there is no master, which makes configuration simpler, supports higher loads, and promotes fault

Table 2.1 Data table.

	Last name	First name	Age
1	Smith	Joe	50
2	Jones	Peter	60
3	Williams	Mary	40

tolerance. Cassandra is simple to implement and suitable for multi-server deployment. A SQL-like CQL language has been developed for Cassandra. But Cassandra does not allow joins or aggregations, and requires another tool, such as Spark (Section 2.5.6).

HBase is another column-oriented database from the Apache Foundation, a sub-project of Hadoop and therefore fully compatible with HDFS. It can handle very large volumes of data. It can be used with the Apache Phoenix database engine, which allows you to execute SQL queries on HBase by converting them into HBase statements. Phoenix is more specifically dedicated to HBase than Hive and is much faster. In addition, it also provides a JDBC driver.

MongoDB is a popular NoSQL DBMS because of its flexibility and variety of applications, written in C++, and can manipulate objects in a format derived from JSON.

CouchDB is another database from the Apache Foundation, which is not relational but manages the different versions of stored documents. This, along with its simplicity of use, makes it interesting.

2.5.5 Distributed Architecture and "Analytics"

Distributed architecture emerged to store huge volumes of data, not for "analytics." This is visible in the algorithmic complexity of MapReduce: not everything can easily be implemented, and the classic example of counting words in a text is not very simple. With this architecture, some processing can take longer than with traditional architectures. Moreover, Hadoop does the following:

- performs long tasks rather than quick tasks that can be restarted;
- is fault-tolerant but replicates data;
- works with distributed storage rather than in centralized memory;
- is used more in mass treatments than in interactive treatments.

It was therefore necessary to design adapted algorithms and tools because distributed computing tools had rudimentary user interfaces, and little or no statistical and machine learning algorithms. This motivated the development of Spark, an open source Apache framework designed for data manipulation and machine learning. However, it is not clear that a distributed computing architecture is as suitable for intensive machine learning calculations as a centralized architecture with a memory that can hold a large amount of data. We will come back to this in Section 2.5.6.

This has not prevented the appearance in recent years of numerous packages of the open software R and Python, adapted not only to parallel computing, but also to distributed computing and MapReduce (Hadoop, Spark): they benefit from the capabilities of MapReduce and the simplicity of R and Python (see Section 2.7), and from statistical methods being implemented, including the machine learning library MLlib of Spark integrated into the packages `sparklyr` and `SparkR` of R and the `PySpark` library. Python also supports parallel or distributed computing with the Dask library. Commercial packages and software have also been developed by editors around R, such as Microsoft Machine Learning Server and Oracle R Enterprise, and around Python such as Micro Focus VerticaPy.

In addition, we can mention Mahout,[8] which is a free Java library of statistical learning algorithms (implemented on Hadoop for the old algorithms). However, it still needs to be completed and made more reliable, and is no longer very popular with data scientists.

Commercial software publishers are also mobilized by big data issues, with Oracle Advanced Analytics, for example, and SAS Viya, which can perform calculations in shared or distributed memories.

Finally, there are data visualization or dashboarding software and many start-ups are active in this field. We can mention Apache Superset which can create beautiful graphs and dashboards from very large databases. Other well-known software systems are Tableau, Power BI, and QlikView.

2.5.6 Spark

Spark is an open source environment of algorithms for distributed computing for data processing, statistics, and machine learning. It was created in 2009 by Matei Zaharia in the Algorithms, Machines and People Lab (AMPLab) at UC Berkeley, became an Apache Foundation project in 2013, and is now maintained and developed by the Berkeley alumni company Databricks. Spark version 3.2.2 was released on July 17, 2022.

Spark provides an answer to a major drawback of Hadoop: in an iterative algorithm, each iteration communicates with the next by writing the results and then reading them into an HDFS file, which results in slow execution. Spark keeps data in memory between the iterations of MapReduce steps, which permits much faster processing than Hadoop.

Unstructured data are stored in Resilient Distributed Datasets (RDDs), which have a parallel, fault-tolerant data structure, while columned data are stored in Spark DataFrame class objects, which have a more optimal structure when a schema, i.e., a structure, is defined on the data.

Spark accesses all Hadoop data formats (HDFS, HBase, Hive, Cassandra) and other formats (Parquet, JSON, CSV). It is written in Java and its native language is Scala, but it can also be used with Python and R. It can be run alone, on a personal computer, a server, a Hadoop cluster, Mesos or in the cloud (EC2). It is included in Hadoop distributions like the one from Cloudera-Hortonworks.

Spark has tools for data management (Spark SQL), graph analysis (GraphX), data streams (Spark Streaming) and, since Spark 1.5, machine learning (MLlib).[9] Tables can be created with Spark SQL which has an SQL or HiveQL syntax. The structure of Spark DataFrame is gradually replacing that of RDD in MLlib. The machine learning algorithms in MLlib are quite numerous and listed in Table 2.3 (see Section 2.7). This list can be further enriched by the Sparkling Water project[10] which combines Spark and H2O:[11] H2O can convert Spark RDDs into H2O data frames and vice versa, and one can use H2O algorithms in Spark. It should be noted that the MLlib library does not contain deep learning algorithms, which does not prevent the use of Spark to format data that will be presented to TensorFlow[12] or Keras.[13]

But deep learning on distributed data reduces the training data sample for each node and may decrease the quality of learning, so this solution should not be considered if the volume of data does not dictate it. In general, Spark is better suited for data manipulation than for machine learning analysis. This is because the distribution of data across nodes in the Spark cluster is not a problem for data transformation, which can generally easily be parallelized, but machine learning algorithms often require loading data into memory, which is more problematic on a Spark cluster, since the data must be loaded into memory on each node in the cluster. Each node does not necessarily have as much memory as a powerful machine with centralized memory.

MLlib is to Spark what Mahout is to Hadoop. However, some of its functions are optimized for massive data thanks to simplifications made at the expense of their theoretical qualities. Thus, the implementation of random forests was made with choices intended to optimize machine resources but not always predictive performance, with the default limitation of the maximum number of bins in the discretization of continuous variables performed for the search of an optimal split (`max.bins` parameter), and the maximum depth of the trees by default is equal to 5,[14] which is not much when we are looking for the maximum decorrelation of the trees (see Section 3.4.2). By comparison, this maximum tree depth has been set to 20 by H2O, which permits starting from one million individuals to arrive at about one individual per node, which is expected for random forests applied in classification. Let us add that for the user of R or scikit-learn, the outputs of MLlib seem frustrating and offer little help to the interpretation of the results.

Many forums mention the power of Spark but the tests they show of its use in machine learning are rare beyond the eternal Titanic (2201 observations) and Fisher's iris (150 observations), interesting datasets but not very conducive to highlighting the qualities of massive data management. An exception is a chapter by Besse et al.[15] that compares in detail R, Python, and MLlib in three typical machine learning applications: (1) handwritten digit recognition; (2) a recommendation system; and (3) logistic regression on textual data. Its conclusion is that "current implementations of classical learning methods (logistic regression, random forests) in MLlib or SparkML do not compete or compete poorly with a usual use of these methods (R, Python scikit-learn) in an integrated architecture in the sense of non-distributed."

The chapter also notes (on p. 12) the frequent difficulties and even crashes related to Spark's memory management. Spark's ability to handle large data does not come with the ability to store complex models, and makes its use sometimes problematic for machine learning. In addition, Spark does not process instructions as it encounters them in the code, but rather processes them all together when it needs them, i.e. when a new instruction calls on it, whether to display the number of rows, to display the first rows resulting from processing, or to perform a machine learning calculation. Until then, Spark only registers the fact that it will have to execute the processing (but a *checkpoint* instruction can force this execution). The advantage and the reason for this particular operation, different from R or Python, are that it allows Spark to optimize the distribution of the treatments. The disadvantage is that it can cause Spark to execute a large amount of processing, which can exceed the memory capacity. This is where the *checkpoint* instruction can be useful. We can also try to increase the number of partitions in which the RDDs and DataFrame are distributed, using the `repartition()` function.

Thus, it seems that a distributed architecture on physically separate nodes is better suited to data management and preparation tasks, which do not require simultaneous manipulation of all the data, than to complex modeling tasks, in which computational requirements prevail over input/output requirements.

A conference paper[16] compares computation times for factoring very large matrices (several terabytes) with Spark and MPI (implemented in C), and notes in conclusion that Spark's task management creates bottlenecks and that "the time spent in these bottlenecks is several orders of magnitude greater than the time spent in actual computation... which limits the scalability achievable by Spark for highly iterative algorithms." The synchronous execution mode causes the slowest tasks to slow down the entire set of tasks. The MPI (Message Passing Interface) architecture is compared to Spark, is much faster here, and is also a distributed memory architecture, usable with C, C++, Fortran, and more recently Perl, Java, Python and R (Rmpi package) languages. The paper suggests that Spark could benefit from MPI integration.

Finally, another journal article[17] also compares the computation times of Spark and an MPI/OpenMP architecture. The OpenMP architecture differs from MPI in that it is parallelized but not distributed: all memory is shared and each task has access to all data. The hybrid MPI/OpenMP architecture can exploit a clustered configuration, such as MPI and a multi-core configuration, such as OpenMP. Two methods are used for comparison: *k*-nearest neighbors and SVMs. The article concludes that the MPI/OpenMP architecture outperforms Spark in terms of speed, with computations ten times faster, conceding to Spark some data management advantages (MPI programming is difficult) and its fault tolerance. The authors also suggest integrating the MPI/OpenMP architecture into Spark to increase its performance, possibly at the cost of a concession to Spark's fault tolerance, which has a negative impact on its performance.

2.6 Computer Resources

Another factor we can include to facilitate the processing of large volumes of data and deep learning is the hardware configuration of the machines used for the calculations.

2.6.1 Minimum Resources

Of course, it is necessary to provide sufficient power, especially in terms of RAM (installed on the motherboard), and have at least 4 gigabytes of memory.

Then you need to be equipped with a 64-bit operating system rather than a 32-bit one. Indeed, the usable RAM is limited to 2 or 3 gigabytes on a 32-bit machine, several terabytes on a 64-bit machine (depending on the operating system)... far from the theoretical limits of 4 gigabytes in 32 bits (1 gigabyte = 2^{30} bytes) and 16 exabytes in 64 bits.

A multi-core machine is obviously required to implement parallelization.

Traditional mechanical hard disks (HDD: Hard Disk Drive) are increasingly being replaced by solid state drives (SDD: Solid State Drive), with read/write speeds increasing from a few dozen megabytes per second to several hundred megabytes per second.

The use of the graphics processing unit (GPU) allows for a very significant reduction in computation time in deep learning (see Section 2.6.2). Besides AMD and Intel cards, NVIDIA cards are still the most used and "entry-level" models (GeForce GTX 1050 or 1060) already have interesting performances, as we will see later in the book. The implementation of a GPU processor in a Windows environment is described in Section 8.4. Some deep neural network libraries can use multiple GPUs simultaneously.[18]

One can ask the question of which operating system to use: Windows or Unix (or Linux)? Unix would be more powerful, more economical with the resources of the machine, and some (rare) R packages do not exist for Windows.

2.6.2 Graphics Processing Units (GPU) and Tensor Processing Units (TPU)

A few years ago, it was discovered that graphics processing units (GPUs), initially created to perform complex calculations of image animation in video games, could also be very useful for scientific computing. A first application to traditional neural networks showed that the calculation time could be divided by 20 on a GPU,[19] and this application was quickly extended to convolutional neural networks.[20] Indeed, if graphics processors are generally slower processors than CPUs, the structure of these GPUs is highly parallel. Thus, as early as 2015, some GPUs had nearly 6000 cores. This high level of parallelism is adapted to intensive computing and especially to mathematical computing, but less so to computing on massive data. Indeed, the GPUs' memory is significantly smaller than the memory of CPUs and, for massive data, this forces the user either to distribute them on several GPUs, or to store the data in the memory of the CPU and perform exchanges between CPU and GPU, but these exchanges are slowed down by the bandwidth of the bus connecting them.

Programming on these GPUs was difficult until the appearance in 2007 of the CUDA (Compute Unified Device Architecture) language, which is a kind of C language developed by NVIDIA.[21] Since then, GPU computing has been increasingly used for scientific computing and for deep learning which makes great use of matrix computing.

For example, the neural network deep learning libraries, TensorFlow, Keras, MXNet, and PyTorch (see Section 7.2), routinely incorporate the ability to run their computations indifferently on CPU or GPU, without even having to change the instruction code. Section 8.4 describes the configuration of a Windows machine equipped with an NVIDIA graphics card for deep learning on GPU.

For scientific computing and, in particular, matrix computing, some packages of R and Python can use GPUs, as well as Julia, Matlab, and others.

For Python, we can mention the `PyCUDA`, `PyOpenCL` and `pyculib` libraries.

The R package `gputools` was one of the first to exploit GPUs. It was based on the CUDA parallel processing API of NVIDIA graphics processors and required a CUDA-compatible GPU card. It was available on Linux, but not Windows, and has since been removed from CRAN. Another package, `gmatrix`, was created to perform linear algebra calculations in CUDA, but it also has been removed from CRAN.

More recently, the R package `gpuR` was usable on all GPUs because it was based on the OpenCL free language compatible with all GPUs, unlike NVIDIA's CUDA. It was available on the CRAN but was also removed.

In 2015, Google began using Tensor Processing Units (TPUs), which are even faster than CPUs and GPUs in machine learning and deep learning tasks, in which these new processors are specialized (and not for graphical calculations). TPUs have since been made available to Google Cloud Platform and Google Colab users (see Section 8.5).

2.6.3 Solutions in the Cloud

Finally, for a prompt need for computing power, whether in terms of storage space, CPU, GPU or software, one can consider renting servers in the cloud, the best-known offers being Elastic Compute Cloud (EC2) from Amazon Web Service (AWS), Microsoft Azure, and Google Cloud Platform. Facebook's absence from this market can be explained by the significant investment required, not only from a technical point of view, but also from a commercial point of view, to build a competitive offer in the cloud. This commercial effort was difficult for Microsoft, which had suffered the bursting of the dot-com bubble in 2000, but this turn, initiated since 2014 by Satya Nadella, from PC software to cloud computing, has largely contributed to Microsoft's recent growth and placed it second in the cloud, behind AWS.

The user can create virtual machines as private virtual servers, with several categories of virtual machines depending on their amount of memory, storage space and cores, and the user pays according to the category of the virtual machine and its usage time. Physically, these virtual machines are hosted on thousands of physical servers around the world. Their total storage capacity is kept secret.

Obviously, these cloud computing solutions are interesting for occasional power needs but expensive for continuous use. Moreover, data can be dispersed in the cloud and the available power can vary according to the moment, contrary to resources specifically reserved for one use. For this reason, and also for reasons of IT security, which can be particularly important in some cases, other solutions than the pure cloud, still called "public cloud," have been developed. There are also "private clouds," which are architectures similar to those of public clouds but deployed in the information system of companies, and "hybrid clouds."

Cloud solution providers typically offer three tiers of services: (1) infrastructure as a service (IaaS); (2) platform as a service (PaaS); and (3) software as a service (SaaS). IaaS provides machines and storage space. PaaS also provides operating systems, databases, and development environments. SaaS provides ready-to-use applications and data.

The solutions for computing in a cloud allow one to choose the number and type of processors and the amount of memory used.[22] Pricing depends on these choices as well as the time of use. There are free solutions for individuals, students, and researchers, and pricing is adapted to academic institutions. We will come back in Section 8.5 to the free cloud computing solutions with examples of its implementation.

2.7 R and Python Software

R and Python are both software and scripting languages, interpreted, running on Unix, Windows, macOS, and under open license. If R is the reference software in statistics and machine learning, Python, which comes from the world of computer development, has been enriched with machine learning libraries that are now widespread in the scientific world, and it has even become the reference for deep learning, with its implementations of PyTorch, TensorFlow, Keras, and MXNet. These libraries are also available in R packages, but for TensorFlow and Keras, the R packages are based on Python for which they are an interface.

There are several reasons why R is successful as a statistical and machine learning software:

1) R is free, open source, and available on various platforms (Unix, Windows, macOS), which makes it accessible to everyone and allows wide distribution of analysis and experience.

2) R is functionally very rich, with more than 18,300 packages available in August 2022 on the CRAN[23] website[24] (more than 2000 on Bioconductor[25] and thousands on GitHub), covering a wide range of methods for data processing, statistics, machine learning, deep learning, data visualization.

3) The centralization in an open repository (CRAN) of such a large number of tested[26] and documented packages, with a secure download, is a strong point of R compared to Python.

4) The packages are often developed to accompany research work, and are therefore at the cutting edge of the state of the art.

5) The R language is close to mathematical language, elegant, concise, readable, and allows for more efficient development and maintenance of programs. It is easier to learn and write than some computer languages such as C++, which speeds up the writing of programs and limits the risk of errors.

6) The R language makes it possible to write complex functions capable of executing operations that are not yet provided for in the many existing packages.

7) With a variety of graphical interfaces and integrated development environments, the best known and most recognized of which is RStudio, R is accessible to all types of users, whether they are programmers or not.

8) One can almost always find the answer to a question on R quickly, thanks to the many active forums, mailing lists, publications, and conferences.

9) R makes it easy to produce beautiful and elaborate graphics and to create web applications with the `shiny` package.

10) R allows the user to adjust quite fine computer parameters (parallelization, memory management, GPU) without requiring advanced computer knowledge.

11) R is compatible with fast languages such as C and C++, which means that it is possible to execute code written in these languages with R.

12) R is evolving fast, especially in big data issues, with the creation of packages to handle massive data, parallel computing and amounts of very varied data.

The Python language resembles the R language in some ways, and in particular its dynamic typing of variables, but it is perhaps simpler than the R language and more "unequivocal" than R, which often offers several ways of programming the same thing, some of which may be less efficient in terms of calculation time. There is a peculiarity of the Python language that leaves mixed feelings among programmers: indentation is part of the syntax,[27] since it is not symbols such as brackets that delimit blocks of instructions (e.g. to be executed under a certain condition), it is indentation, in the form of four spaces. This can lead to errors if these spaces are not present, and if they have been replaced by a tab with the same visual appearance, for example.

One difficulty is that the installation of Python in its basic distribution[28] is not easy, especially for some packages: you have to find the packages on websites, download the right version, type "pip" commands (which is a package management utility), etc. It is therefore often preferred to the Anaconda distribution proposed by the company Continuum Analytics[29] and easier to install. But the Anaconda distribution is only free for solo practitioners, students, and researchers.[30] The Anaconda repository contains more than 250 Python packages in addition to the 150 packages automatically installed with Anaconda, and these packages cover a large part of its users' needs. Additional packages are available in the Anaconda cloud.[31] Anaconda also provides access to integrated development environments such as Spyder (which is similar to RStudio) and Jupyter. We will see in Section 8.6.1 an example of Python code entered and executed in a Jupyter notebook.

Python is used more by programmers and developers, especially web developers, while R is used more by statisticians and actuaries. This is due to a difference in approach: Python favors simplicity, productivity, and automation, while R favors finesse, interpretability, and graphical representation of results. For example, there is no pruning of decision trees in Python.

The reference implementation of Python is the CPython interpreter written in C, which produces and executes bytecode. PyPy is a newer and faster interpreter, but not all Python libraries (like NumPy) are compatible with PyPy. Numba is a just-in-time compiler, which speeds up Python processing without changing the code.

Of course, in terms of computational speed, R and Python are very far from C# and C++, the latter being up to 100 times faster than Python. The advantages of Python are its simplicity of programming and the variety of its libraries, those of C++ and C# being their performance and the greater rigor of their syntax. On a scale of difficulty of computer languages from 1 to 10, some people[32] place Smalltalk at level 1, Python at level 3, most languages at level 5, Java at level 6, C# at level 7, Scala at level 8, and C++ at level 10. This explains the popularity of Python in computer developments that need to be fast, because the gain in development speed can be much greater than the loss in performance, which is not very noticeable if the processing is simple (for the same reason, Java is also often preferred to C++ and this is what led Microsoft to create C#, which is the "Microsoft's Java").

Python has partly made up for the gap it had at the beginning compared to R in terms of statistics and machine learning, with the arrival of scikit-learn, which is an open source library of machine learning algorithms, based on Python's scientific libraries NumPy and SciPy. It has the advantage of grouping all the machine learning functions in a single package, whereas these functions are scattered in many R packages (except for the `caret` and `mlr` packages, which group many methods). But the scikit-learn library still has some limitations. For example, it only handles numerical data (preferably without missing values), and not factors[33] which must be replaced by the dummy indicators of their levels (an encoder is provided for this purpose)[34] but at the cost of dissociating the different levels of a factor. It works in memory. The output of scikit-learn is far from being as detailed as those of R functions. The list of its machine learning algorithms is given in Table 2.3 while Table 2.2 compares some of the R and Python packages. Other comparisons can be found on the Web.[35]

In Table 2.3 the statistical and machine learning functions existing in the classical R packages are compared (we usually mention only one package, even if several exist), in

Table 2.2 Comparison of Python and R packages.

Tasks	Python packages	R packages
IDE	Spyder, Rodeo, PyCharm, Jupyter Notebook (ex IPython)	RStudio, RCode, Jupyter Notebook
Data handling[a]	Pandas, dask	data.table, dplyr, tidyr
Statistics	statsmodels, linearmodels	MASS, stats, glmnet, nlme, robust, robustreg, tseries, survival
Machine Learning	scikit-learn, XGBoost, lightgbm, h2o	caret, mlr, e1071, rpart, randomForest, ranger, xgboost, lightgbm, h2o
Data visualization	Matplotlib, Seaborn, plotly, Bokeh, Pygal	ggplot2, lattice, ggvis, rgl, plotly, shiny
SQL queries	pandasql	sqldf
Date management	datetime	lubridate
Web Scraping	Beautifulsoup, Scrapy	Rvest, RSelenium
Big Data	PySpark	sparklyr, SparkR
Deep Learning	TensorFlow, PyTorch, Keras, Caffe, MXNet, transformers	tensorflow, keras, torch, mxnet
Natural language processing	NLTK, spaCy, gensim, TextBlob	tm, koRpus, quanteda, cleanNLP, spacyr, RTextTools, R.TeMiS
Explicability	shap, lime, skater	shapr, fastshap, lime, iml

a) See a comparison here: http://datascience-enthusiast.com/R/pandas_datatable.html.

R ffbase, bigmemory, gputools, h2o, RevoScaleR packages, as well as in Python scikit-learn and Spark MLlib libraries.

We regularly read that Python is faster than R, but detailed and argued comparisons tend to show comparable computation times for both software, or even lower for R (especially with the data.table package)[36] except in the task of creating new variables, which is accomplished faster by the Python[37] pandas library. A more recent comparison[38] incorporated other tools than pandas and data.table, with the R package dplyr, Spark, Julia, datatable, which is a Python package inspired by data.table, and the Python package dask, which parallelizes the calculations. The results show that no tool stands out from the others in all cases, but that data.table is almost always in the top two and that Spark starts to do well on the largest volumes.

Note that the R package rPython can execute Python in R, as well as the package reticulate[39] which permits a Python session inside an R session, to access Python objects, to import Python models, etc. Conversely, the Python package rpy2 can execute R in Python.

Table 2.3 Comparison of machine learning functions.

Method	R base	ffbase	bigmemory	gputools	H2O	RevoScaleR	scikit-learn	MLlib
k-means	kmeans		bigkmeans		h2o.kmeans	rxKmeans	x	x
Agglomerative hierarchical clustering	cluster			gpuHClust			x	
Linear regression	lm	bigglm.ffdf	biglm	gpuLm	h2o.glm	rxLinMod	x	x
Logistic regression	glm	bigglm.ffdf	bigglm	gpuGlm	h2o.glm	rxLogit	x	x
GLM	glm	bigglm.ffdf	bigglm	gpuGlm	h2o.glm	rxGlm	x	x
Penalized regression	glmnet				h2o.glm		x	x
Cox survival model	survival				h2o.coxph			
PLS regression	pls						x	
Decision trees	rpart					rxDTree	x	x
Random forests	randomForest				h2o. randomforest	rxDecisionForest	x	x
Extra-Trees	extraTrees						x	
Gradient boosting	gbm, xgboost				h2o.gbm, h2o.xgboost		x	x
SVM with linear kernel	e1071						x	x
SVM with non-linear kernel	e1071						x	
Naive Bayesian classifier	e1071				h2o.naiveBayes		x	x
PCA	stats				h2o.prcomp		x	x
Artificial neural networks	nnet, mxnet				h2o. deeplearning		x	x
Graph analysis	igraph						x	x
Latent Dirichlet allocation	topicmodels, lda						x	x
Word2Vec word embedding	rword2vec				h2o.word2vec		x	x
Collaborative filtering	recommenderlab						x	x

2.8   Quantum Computing

A much more distant but very promising prospect for high performance computing and deep learning is quantum computing. It was initiated by the works of the mathematician Yuri Manin and those of the physicist Paul Benioff, and in particular his paper[40] describing a quantum model of the Turing machine. The physicist Richard Feynman quickly saw the great potential of quantum computing.[41] A first application came from Shor's quantum algorithm,[42] which permits one to decompose a number into a product of prime factors in a polynomial time, that is to say exponentially faster than classical algorithms.

While information is encoded in binary bits (0 or 1) in a classical computer, it is encoded in qubits (*quantum bits*) in a quantum computer, where a qubit can be in either a $|0>$ or $|1>$ state, but also in any $\lambda|0> + \mu|1>$ superposition of these two states. A classical computer with n bits at any time can be in *one* state among 2^n, while a quantum computer with n qubits can be in any superposition of the 2^n elementary states. Qubits can thus encode an enormous amount more information than bits. Another quantum property of matter, entanglement, permits one to massively parallelize the calculations by entangling the different qubits of the computer, since the knowledge of the state of a qubit permits one to know the state of any other qubit.

However, the fabrication of quantum computers faces three considerable difficulties: (1) how to create a sufficient number of qubits (currently a few tens); (2) how to combine them in entangled states; and (3) how to maintain the coherence of these states long enough to perform the calculations.

But on October 23, 2019, Google researchers published an article in *Nature* announcing the first act of "quantum supremacy," with a 54-qubit processor (named Sycamore) that managed to perform in 200 seconds a calculation that a supercomputer would have taken 10,000 years to perform.[43] This claim of duration was quickly disputed by IBM, which announced in turn on November 15, 2021 that it had made a processor with 127 qubits. Eagle is the first processor to have exceeded the threshold of 100 qubits, but it is estimated that it will take at least 1000 qubits for a processor to be able to perform really realistic and useful calculations. This is what IBM expects to achieve in 2023 with its future Condor processor with 1121 qubits.

In 2022, quantum computers are only capable of factoring very small numbers using Shor's algorithm, but if they reached a sufficient number of qubits held long enough in decoherence-free and noise-free entangled states, Shor's algorithm would make it possible to break all public-key cryptographic systems, with far-reaching consequences for the entire world.

Alongside large companies such as Google, IBM, and Atos, start-ups are being created and are following various approaches: superconductors, photons, trapped ions, cold atoms, etc. We can mention IonQ, Rigetti Computing, Pasqal, Quandela, Alice & Bob, Xanadu, etc. An ecosystem is being created with the establishment of platforms for writing quantum algorithms and "quantum computing as a service," just as there is an IaaS and a PaaS (see Section 2.6.3). For example, IBM has been offering resources for quantum computing on the cloud since 2016 (IBM Quantum Lab)[44] and has been developing the Qiskit Python library[45] since 2017, which allows quantum programs to be written and run, either on a quantum computer in the IBM Quantum Lab or on a quantum simulator on a classical computer. Other solutions exist, such as Amazon Braket[46] and Google Quantum Computing Service[47] based on its Sycamore processor and its Python Cirq library.[48]

One of the fundamental results of quantum computing is Grover's algorithm,[49] which permits one to find with a high probability in a time $O(\sqrt{N})$ an element satisfying some criteria among N elements. It can thus be a question of finding an x such that $f(x) = y$ given in a set of N pairs (x, y), i.e. to invert a function not explicitly known. Grover's algorithm improves on classical algorithms that find such a solution in a time $O(N)$: it clearly takes at least $N/2$ steps to find the solution. Using an application of Grover's theorem may offer the possibility of breaking a cryptographic key of length 128 bits in 2^{64} iterations instead of 2^{128}. A general application of this theorem is in optimization, the search for the minimum of a function. It can be an error function and Grover's algorithm finds natural applications in machine learning,[50] and even in deep learning.

There is a quantum version, qBLAS, of the BLAS (Basic Linear Algebra Subprograms)[51] algorithms useful for linear algebra, least squares, principal component analysis, gradient descent, etc. Various methods, from SVM to Boltzmann machines, can benefit from it.[52]

Of course, quantum computing still poses considerable challenges from a hardware and software point of view. On the applications of quantum algorithms, one can consult the very documented and rich in references web page of the American laboratory NIST (National Institute of Standards and Technology): Quantum Algorithm Zoo.[53]

Notes

1 Fan, J. and Li, R. Variable Selection Via Nonconcave Penalized Likelihood and Its Oracle Properties. *Journal of the American Statistical Association*, 96 (2005), 1348–1360.

2 Bühlmann, P. and van de Geer, S. *Statistics for High-Dimensional Data* (Berlin: Springer, 2011). See Section 2.5.1.

3 Furnival G.M. and Wilson, R.W. Regression by Leaps and Bounds. *Technometrics*, 16 (1974), 499–511.

4 Agrawal, R., Imielienski, T., and Swami, A.N. Mining Association Rules between Sets of Items in Large Databases. In: *Proceedings of the 1993 ACM SIGMOD International Conference on Management of Data* (New York: ACM Press, 1993), pp. 207–216.

5 Amdahl, G. Validity of the Single Processor Approach to Achieving Large-Scale Computing Capabilities. *AFIPS Conference Proceedings*, 30 (1967), 483–485.

6 Dean, J. and Ghemawat, S. MapReduce: Simplified Data Processing on Large Clusters. Paper presented at OSDI'04: Sixth Symposium on Operating System Design and Implementation, San Francisco (2004), pp. 137–150.

7 Ghemawat, S., Gobioff, H., and Leung, S-T. The Google File System. In: *Proceedings of the 19th ACM Symposium on Operating Systems Principles* (Bolton Landing: ACM, 2003), pp. 20–43.

8 https://mahout.apache.org/.

9 http://spark.apache.org/docs/latest/ml-guide.html.

10 https://www.h2o.ai/sparkling-water/.

11 H2O is an open source library of machine learning algorithms that are run on a Java virtual machine, optimized for a 64-bit operating system. It was created by the Californian company H2O.ai. The algorithms are generalized linear model, random forests, boosting, XGBoost gradient boosting, principal component analysis, *k*-means, perceptron neural network, stacking and Word2Vec embedding. H2O can be implemented on a single machine, server, Hadoop or Spark distributed data cluster. H2O has interfaces for R, Python, Scala, Java, and CoffeeScript. There is an R package h2o which relies on a REST API to execute instructions written in R in an H2O cluster.

12 https://cloud.google.com/blog/big-data/2017/11/using-apache-spark-with-tensorflow-on-google-cloud-platform.

13 http://maxpumperla.com/elephas/.

14 https://spark.rstudio.com/reference/ml_random_forest/.

15 Besse, P., Guillouet, B., and Loubes, J.-M. (2017). Apprentissage sur Données Massives; trois cas d'usage avec R, Python et Spark. In : M. Maumy-Bertrand, G. Saporta, and C. Thomas-Agnan, *Apprentissage Statistique et Données Massives* (Journées d'Études en Statistique, Éditions Technip, 2018).

16 Gittens, A. *et al*. Matrix Factorizations at Scale: A Comparison of Scientific Data Analytics in Spark and C+MPI Using Three Case Studies. Paper presented at 2016 IEEE International Conference on Big Data (2016), arXiv:1607.01335.

17 Reyes-Ortiz, J.L., Oneto, L., and Anguita, D. Big Data Analytics in the Cloud: Spark on Hadoop vs MPI/OpenMP on Beowulf. *Procedia Computer Science*, 53 (2015), 121–130.

18 https://www.tensorflow.org/tutorials/images/deep_cnn.

19 Oh, K.-S. and Jung, K. GPU Implementation of Neural Networks. *Pattern Recognition*, 37(6) (2004), 1311–1314.

20 Chellapilla, K., Puri, S., and Simard, P. High Performance Convolutional Neural Networks for Document Processing. Paper presented at Tenth International Workshop on Frontiers in Handwriting Recognition (2006).

21 See the CUDA installation: https://developer.nvidia.com/cuda-downloads.

22 See a comparison: https://towardsdatascience.com/maximize-your-gpu-dollars-a9133f4e546a.

23 Comprehensive R Archive Network.

24 https://cran.r-project.org/.

25 https://www.bioconductor.org/.

26 https://cran.r-project.org/web/packages/policies.html#Submission.

27 This concept was invented in 1966 by Peter J. Landin, under the name of *off-side rule*.

28 https://www.python.org/downloads/.

29 https://www.anaconda.com/.

30 https://www.anaconda.com/pricing.

31 https://docs.anaconda.com/anaconda/.

32 https://www.quora.com/On-a-scale-of-1-10-how-hard-is-it-to-learn-Python-programming-from-scratch.

33 Which are, however, managed by the `Pandas` library.

34 http://scikit-learn.org/stable/modules/preprocessing.html#encoding-categorical-features.

35 See https://www.dataquest.io/blog/python-vs-r/ and https://github.com/matloff/R-vs.-Python-for-Data-Science.

36 See, for example, https://github.com/Rdatatable/data.table/wiki/Benchmarks-%3A-Grouping.

37 https://www.statw,orx.com/de/blog/pandas-vs-data-table-a-study-of-data-frames-part-2/.

38 https://h2oai.github.io/db-benchmark/.

39 https://rstudio.github.io/reticulate/.

40 Benioff P. The Computer as a Physical System: A Microscopic Quantum Mechanical Hamiltonian Model of Computers as Represented by Turing Machines. *Journal of Statistical Physics*, 22 (1980), 563.

41 Feynman, R. Simulating Physics with Computers. *International Journal of Theoretical Physics.* 21 (6/7) (1982), 467–488.

42 Shor, P.W. Algorithms for Quantum Computation: Discrete Logarithms and Factoring. In: *Proceedings of 35th Annual Symposium on Foundations of Computer Science* (IEEE Computer Society Press, 1994), pp. 124–134.

43 Arute, F. *et al.* Quantum Supremacy Using a Programmable Superconducting Processor. *Nature*, 574 (2019), 505–510.

44 https://quantum-computing.ibm.com/lab.

45 https://qiskit.org/.

46 https://aws.amazon.com/fr/braket/.

47 https://quantumai.google/quantum-computing-service.

48 https://quantumai.google/cirq.

49 Lov, K.G. A Fast Quantum Mechanical Algorithm for Database Search. In: *Proceedings, 28th Annual ACM Symposium on the Theory of Computing* (1996). arXiv:quant-ph/9605043.

50 Wittek, P. *Quantum Machine Learning: What Quantum Computing Means to Data Mining* (New York: Academic Press, 2014).

51 Linear algebra libraries developed since the 1970s for different computers, first in Fortran and then in C. We went from the simplest level BLAS-1 in 1979 (operations on scalars) to BLAS-3 in 1987 (vector operations).

52 Biamonte, J., Wittek, P., Pancotti, N., Rebentrost, P., Wiebe, N., and Lloyd, S. Quantum Machine Learning (2018). arXiv:1611.09347, https://arxiv.org/abs/1611.09347.

53 https://quantumalgorithmzoo.org/.

3

Reminders of Machine Learning

This chapter is a synthesis of the most used machine learning methods in data science, starting with optimization algorithms, continuing with penalized regression and complexity reduction methods, ensemble methods, and then support vector machines. A specific section is dedicated to recommendation systems. Typical deep learning methods will be discussed in Chapter 7. For more details, we refer to our other books published by Technip, to the classic work by Hastie, Tibshirani and Friedman,[1] the book by James, Witten, Hastie and Tibshirani,[2] or, for historical aspects, to the article by Gilbert Saporta.[3]

3.1 General

Machine learning can be defined as a set of methods that allow an algorithmic system to evolve through a process of learning from the data, in order to perform tasks (often predictions) sometimes more efficiently than by classical algorithms. This learning is done by computing an error function and and making the system parameters change in order to minimize the error, by gradient-based methods or other optimization algorithms (Section 3.2).

When systems are organized in more or less complex hierarchical structures, representing different levels of reality, from the particular to the general, from the local to the global, we speak of deep machine learning or deep learning. These methods are used in artificial intelligence in complex tasks such as image or text recognition, and are described later in this book.

The main modeling methods applied to big data are based on advanced sampling techniques, optimization, machine learning, deep learning, Lasso-type estimators, functional data, incremental learning, and of course on the natural language processing methods (Chapters 4 and 9). We can add the detection of association rules, used in the retail industry for the analysis of cash register receipts (market basket analysis), which are big data with numbers of receipts of several hundred million and numbers of products of several tens or hundreds of thousands.

Sampling issues are important, as they can help to reduce the volume of data to make them more easily processed, and to infer general conclusions from partial observations. But sample representativeness can be tricky to establish, when multiple data sources do not cover the same populations and have a significant number of missing values.

Deep Learning: From Big Data to Artificial Intelligence with R, First Edition. Stéphane Tufféry.
© 2023 John Wiley & Sons Ltd. Published 2023 by John Wiley & Sons Ltd.
Companion website: www.wiley.com/go/Tuffery/DeepLearning

There is the issue of matching individual data from different sources that sometimes have no data in common except for a subsample. This poses problems of sampling, merging, and sample adjustment.

Adjustment consists of assigning weights to the observed units in order to obtain a representative sample of the population studied by restoring the distribution of a few well-chosen variables. It is done at the time of calculating the estimator, unlike stratification or balanced sampling, which is done beforehand, when the sample is drawn.

One might think that big data would provide samples that are as representative as they are massive, but this is not the case. To see this, we need only take the example of population movements studied from GPS location data provided by cell phone operators: the elderly or disadvantaged are visibly under-equipped and therefore under-represented. This type of situation is known as coverage error, where the sampling frame, from which the samples are drawn, differs from the target population to be studied. One can try to match such a sampling frame with other databases to compensate for this under-representation, but this type of matching poses difficulties that are not trivial.

The study of *high-dimensional matrices* arises naturally, where matrices whose rows are customers and columns are downloaded, purchased, or recommended products. It can also be matrices representing relationships between individuals, in the context of marketing, sociology, biostatistics or between financial institutions (daily returns) in the context of studying systemic risk. These matrices are often sparse and have particular estimators, with penalties of the Lasso or Group Lasso type.

We can search these large matrices for sub-matrices (clusters) corresponding to relevant subsets of products and individuals interested in these products. This is also the idea of biclustering (or co-clustering) which operates the simultaneous clustering of rows and columns. It can be about finding groups of documents characterized by certain groups of words, or associating groups of phenotypes to groups of genes.

High dimensional regression poses the classical problem of variable selection (see Section 2.2). One also encounters, for example in biostatistics (DNA sequencing) or in chemometrics (statistics applied to chemical data), situations where the number of variables is higher, or even much higher, than the number of individuals, and where the classical regression methods do not apply and give way to methods such as Lasso, elastic net, or PLS regression. The number of variables studied can vary between 10^4 and 10^8, while the number of observations is a few hundred. This situation is symbolized by writing $p \gg n$, and one can of course also have $n \gg 0$ for big data.

Functional data are data that are not punctual but continuous, such as curves or images. These data have multiplied with the technological progress that allows the collection and storage of increasingly fine observations, continuously capturing information on a studied object (meteorological, environmental, medical, food ...). These data are large, and also pose problems of high correlation between two close observations of the same continuous phenomenon.

The interest of functional data is that, instead of discriminating individuals on the basis of a few characteristics in finite number observed in a few selected moments, we have no preconceived ideas about the time and duration of the differences between two evolution curves, which leads us to consider them in their entirety instead of discretizing them.

In predictive models on functional data, the explanatory and to be explained variables can be of finite or infinite dimension or both.

Machine learning methods (ensemble methods, support vector machines, neural networks) are used for their high predictive power, in situations where model readability is not necessary and where their "black box" aspect is not a drawback.

We can take the example of an online bookstore, which wants to recommend titles to its customers. In this recommendation problem (see Section 3.6), the variables (titles already purchased) are excessively numerous and create sparse matrices that are difficult to model. A common approach is to decompose the customer base into a very large number of segments, possibly thousands, which are continuously recalculated by statistical techniques that allow us to place each customer in a small cluster of customers with similar tastes. Then, the customer is offered the titles often acquired by other customers in their cluster, which the customer has not yet acquired. These calculations are constantly redone, without any search for robust and comprehensible clusters and models.

Incremental algorithms make it possible to develop and update a model using new data as it arrives, without having to reprocess old data. This is called data stream analysis, or on-line learning, as opposed to batch or offline learning. This is useful for data streams and data that are too massive to be processed in a single block in their entirety.

Some decision trees are incremental: notably the Very Fast Decision Trees[4] which sample the input data to process them in reasonable times even when they are massive. They are based on the Hoeffding bound which gives the number of observations that allow a split in the tree to be made with a sufficient level of confidence, i.e. with a result close enough to the split that would have been obtained with all the observations. In this type of tree, the first observations are used to split the root of the tree, the following observations are used to split the nodes immediately below the root, etc. These trees have since been generalized (CVFDT, VFDTc, OVFDT) and implemented on Hadoop.[5]

Random forests (see Section 3.4.2) also have their incremental version with the On-line Random Forests of Saffari *et al.*[6] Each new observation is used k_i times in each tree i, where k_i is drawn according to the Poisson distribution to simulate a bootstrap sample. A sample of candidate explanatory variables is drawn but the Extra-Trees method (see Section 3.4.3) is preferably used for splitting. This saves a useful amount of time due to the larger number of operations performed.

In incremental algorithms, the training data are all supposed to come from the same distribution or, on the contrary, to undergo an evolution of their distribution (concept drift) over time, an evolution that could reduce the predictive power of the models but that the principle of incremental algorithms, with the incorporation of recent training data, can help take into account. This is notably the case of the CVFDT and VFDTc trees.

Ensemble methods, also called *aggregation methods*, as well as *stacking*, consist of combining predictive methods. In stacking, different methods are combined; in ensemble methods, the same method is applied a large number of times.

When aggregating predictive models, sometimes simply by averaging their predictions, it is better to aggregate simpler models, which are individually less efficient, to obtain a better final model! This is because the more advanced individual models are more similar to each other, and the gain from aggregating them is much smaller (see Section 3.4). This touches on the need for power to process big data, as these methods can be very time-consuming if the data are massive and the number of aggregated models is large.

Alongside the classical methods, more modern methods are used (ensemble methods, for example) but also recent improvements of classical methods (penalized methods, for example). It is like the so-called classical music, which did not stop in the nineteenth century, and which is constantly enriched by new works, some of them more innovative and original than works of so-called modern music.

The difficulties to be taken into account in big data modeling are linked, on the one hand, to the quantity of data and the expected processing speed, but, on the other hand, to data quality problems. We are therefore looking for algorithms that are resistant to noise and bias:

- the diversity of data sources and their more or less easy access lead to sampling biases that can be very important;
- data may be missing or mislabeled;
- noise can be very important, especially for data coming from the Web and social networks.

Data preparation is therefore even more important than in a traditional context, but it is not always easy, due to lack of time and lack of information on the source of the data.

3.2 The Optimization Algorithms

The use of optimization algorithms is constant in modeling where they are applied primarily to find the parameters of models that minimize their prediction errors. We recall the principle of the most widespread algorithms.

The *Newton* (or Newton-Raphson) *algorithm* is the standard method for finding the minimum of a derivable function (for example, an error function) that is approximated by a quadratic function using its Taylor expansion of order 2, thus of order 1 for the derivative. One can then write:

$$f'(\widehat{\beta}) \approx f'(\beta_k) + (\widehat{\beta} - \beta_k) + f''(\beta_k).$$

Now, if $f(\widehat{\beta})$ is minimum, then $f'(\widehat{\beta}) = 0$ which leads to:

$$\widehat{\beta} \approx \beta_k - f'(\beta_k)/f''(\beta_k).$$

Hence, the iterative algorithm:

$$\beta_{k+1} = \beta_k - \frac{f'(\beta_k)}{f''(\beta_k)}.$$

In dimension > 1, the gradient $\nabla f(\beta) = \frac{\partial}{\partial \beta_i} f(\beta)$ generalizes $f'(\beta)$ and the Hessian matrix $H(f)(\beta) = \frac{\partial 2}{\partial \beta_i \beta_j} f(\beta)$ generalizes $f''(\beta)$. One can write:

$$\beta_{k+1} = \beta_k - H(f)(\beta_k)^{-1} \nabla f(\beta_k).$$

This algorithm has three limitations.

First, it is designed to find points where the gradient ∇f is 0 (the "critical points") which may correspond to a minimum (the Hessian matrix is positive definite at that point), a maximum (the Hessian matrix is negative definite at that point) but also a saddle point (see below) of f. In the neighborhood of a saddle point, Newton's algorithm can converge to this point instead of converging to a point where the error is minimal. At a saddle point, the Hessian matrix is neither positive nor negative definite. We recall that a matrix A is positive definite if $(Ax, x) > 0$ for all x, or equivalently if all its eigenvalues are positive. It is positive semidefinite if $(Ax, x) \geq 0$ for all x, where equivalently if all its eigenvalues are positive or zero.

Then, if f is convex quadratic, Newton's algorithm converges in a single iteration, but otherwise it must perform several iterations, each time performing a second-order approximation of the function. If it starts close enough to the solution, it will converge with a quadratic speed, but if it starts far from the solution or at an inappropriate point, this algorithm may converge slowly or not at all. The convergence of Newton's algorithm is fast but local. The opposite is a global convergence, guaranteed from any initial point.

Finally, it requires inverting the Hessian matrix (matrix of partial second derivatives), which, unless one has an exact formula of the first and second derivatives, is costly in high dimension, with a complexity in $O(np^2 + p^3)$ for the computation and the inversion of the matrix, and may moreover present a risk of instability.

This complexity makes Newton's method less appropriate than others in high dimension, as well as the presence of saddle points, which are all the more numerous as the dimension is high (see below).

Recall that a function is convex (respectively strictly convex) if and only if its Hessian matrix is positive semidefinite (respectively positive definite) at any point. Conversely, a function is concave (respectively strictly concave) if and only if its Hessian matrix is negative semidefinite (respectively negative definite) at any point. In this case, a local extremum is also a global extremum.

Quasi-Newton methods approximate the entire Hessian matrix (or rather its inverse) by a matrix M of the same size, computed from the previous gradients, which avoids having to compute the Hessian matrix. The counterpart of this approximation is that the convergence requires a larger number of iterations than the Newton method. The necessary storage of this matrix M in memory can be a difficulty in high dimension.

The most common algorithm is that of Broyden, Fletcher, Goldfarb and Shanno (BFGS, 1970) implemented in the `optim()` R function and the `minimize()` Python SciPy function.

The BFGS algorithm is based on the whole set of gradients and the L-BFGS (Limited-memory BFGS) variant is based only on the m most recent gradients, often with m often less than 20, which requires much less memory than the BFGS algorithm. This is appreciable when the number of variables is very large, and can even improve the convergence by forgetting the first gradients far from the solution. We see an analogy with the ADADELTA and RMSprop algorithms (see Section 7.14).

As for the BFGS-B and L-BFGS-B algorithms, they are variants with bounds on the variables of the function to minimize.

The *Gauss-Newton algorithm* is used for a least squares search of a nonlinear function, i.e. the minimization of the sum of its squared errors. It approximates a part of the Hessian matrix: it is a modification of Newton's algorithm, which is easier to implement because it does not compute the second derivatives, but which does not always converge well, in case of strong nonlinearity or in case of starting far from the solution.

The *gradient descent algorithm* dates back to Cauchy (1847) and consists of finding the minimum of a differentiable real function by moving in the data space in the opposite direction to the gradient of the function, so as to make this function decrease. Gradient descent uses only the first derivatives and replaces the inverse of the Hessian matrix by a constant or time-dependent step (called learning rate in machine learning) ε_k:

$$\beta_{k+1} = \beta_k - \varepsilon_k \nabla f(\beta_k).$$

This is called a fixed step gradient descent if ε_k is constant and variable step otherwise. We will see in Section 7.14 several variable step size gradient descent algorithms. A special case is the optimal step gradient descent, whose step size minimizes the function in the direction of the gradient, i.e. minimizes the function: $x \to \beta_k - x \nabla f(\beta_k)$. This optimal step size can be difficult to determine in the general case and one does not always try to do so, except in some special cases, such as that of a quadratic functional where one can explicitly calculate the optimal step size from the matrix A. This case is the one where the function whose minimum is sought is of the form:

$$\frac{1}{2}(Ax, x) - (b, x) = \frac{1}{2}\sum_{i,j=1}^{n} a_{ij}x_i x_j - \sum_{i=1}^{n} b_i x_i,$$

where A is a symmetric matrix (n x n).

We speak of an *elliptic* quadratic function if moreover the matrix A is positive definite, i.e. if $(Ax, x) > 0$ for all x, or equivalently if all its eigenvalues are positive. An elliptic quadratic function is strictly convex.

This case is often studied, as it both approximates real cases and yields many theoretical results. One of these results is that the optimal step gradient descent always converges. Another result is that the fixed rate gradient descent converges if and only if $\varepsilon < 2/\lambda_{max}$, where λ_{max} is the largest eigenvalue of the matrix A.

Since the quadratic function $\frac{1}{2}(Ax, x) - (b, x)$ has derivative $Ax - b$, the search for its minimum was motivated by the resolution of the linear equation system $Ax = b$, which is a method sometimes more efficient than its direct resolution, in particular when the matrix A is sparse because in this case the calculation of Ax is fast.

We can take the example of the quadratic function in dimension 2:

$$Q_a(x, y) = x^2 + y^2 + axy, a \in \mathbb{R}.$$

For $-2 < a < 2$, $Q_a(x, y)$ has a unique minimum $= 0$ which it reaches at $(x, y) = (0, 0)$. This case is illustrated in Figure 3.1.

For $a = 2$, $Q_a(x, y) = 0$ on the line with equation $x - y = 0$.

For $a = -2$, $Q_a(x, y) = 0$ on the line with equation $x + y = 0$.

If $a < -2$ or $a > 2$, $Q_a(x, y)$ has a single stationary point, the saddle point $(0,0)$. This case is illustrated in Figure 3.2.

The matrix $\begin{pmatrix} 2 & a \\ a & 2 \end{pmatrix}$ associated with this quadratic form has eigenvalues 3 and 1 for $a = 1$, eigenvalues 4 and 0 for $a = 2$, and eigenvalues 5/2 and 3/2 for $a = 0.5$.

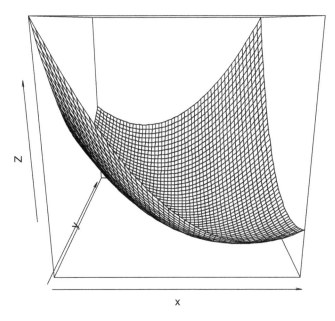

Figure 3.1 $x^2 + y^2 + xy$.

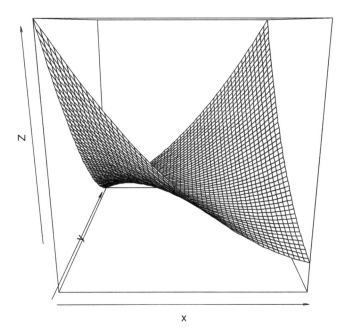

Figure 3.2 $x^2 + y^2 + 3xy$.

From the previous result, the fixed-step gradient descent converges if and only if its step size is $< 2/3$ for $a = 1$. Figure 3.3 verifies the absence of convergence with a fixed step size $> 2/3$.

Figure 3.4 shows that the gradient descent converges with a fixed step size $< 2/3$, but with significant oscillations. We can decrease the value of the step size to reduce these oscillations, but we then see, as in Figure 3.5, that the convergence is much slower. The determination of a fixed step is thus delicate and can lead to a very slow convergence, a very irregular convergence, or an absence of convergence. This shows the interest in calculating an optimal step size when it is feasible. In some cases, one can compute the best possible fixed step, which for a function $\frac{1}{2}(Ax, x) - (b, x)$ equals $2/(\lambda_{min} + \lambda_{max})$, which is 0.5 in the previous case $x^2 + y^2 + xy$.

Figure 3.6 thus shows that the optimal step gradient descent (in dashed line) is faster than the previous fixed step descent. Below we present another descent method, the conjugate gradient, which converges in fewer iterations than the classical gradient, as seen in the solid line on Figure 3.6, with just the same first step, the one corresponding to the black line. The dilemma with these methods is that they converge in fewer iterations than the fixed step gradient, but computing an optimal direction adds complexity to each iteration. Therefore, they are not always more efficient. There is no single answer to this dilemma and the choice of the best method depends on the problem encountered.

Beyond a few tens of thousands of observations, the *stochastic gradient* variant is often used, i.e. the calculation of the gradient on a random sample (hence the term *stochastic*), or even the *online gradient* which is recalculated on each observation and not on all observations (see Section 7.3). The computation of the gradient alone is faster but the

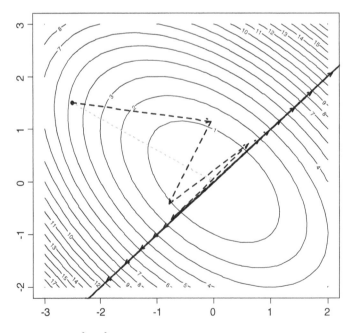

Figure 3.3 $x^2 + y^2 + xy$ – Fixed step = 0.7.

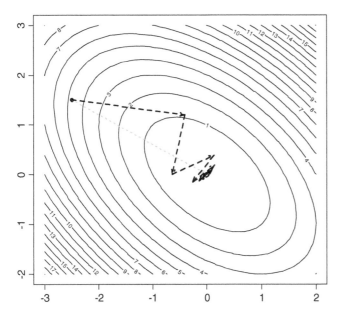

Figure 3.4 $x^2 + y^2 + xy$ – Fixed step = 0.6.

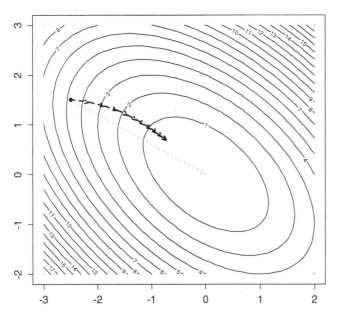

Figure 3.5 $x^2 + y^2 + xy$ – Fixed step = 0.1

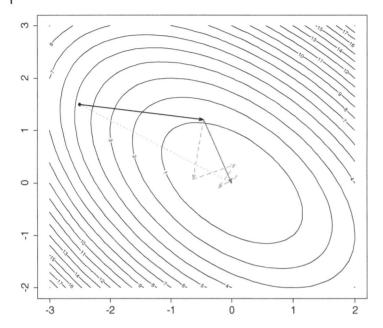

Figure 3.6 $x^2 + y^2 + xy$ – Optimal step descent (in dashed line) and conjugate gradient (in solid line).

algorithm requires a larger number of iterations to converge, since each iteration decreases the error less, or even increases it when an atypical observation is encountered. Solutions have been considered to reconcile a fast computation and a fast convergence, such as the *averaged stochastic gradient*[7] which uses its memory of the previous values of the gradient.

The gradient descent algorithm has several advantages. It is efficient on large volumes of data. It has a global convergence: it is possible to start far enough from the solution, especially if the space to be covered is convex. In the latter case, a local minimum is a global minimum, which is well suited to the gradient, which is a local information. Finally, for multi-layer neural networks, we can easily compute the first derivatives of compound functions according to the formula $(g \circ f)' = (g' \circ f)f'$, as we shall see in Section 7.3.

But this algorithm has limits. The gradient descent using only the first derivatives converges less quickly than Newton's algorithm and the algorithms approximating the Hessian matrix. Indeed, the gradient gives the direction to move toward to find the minimum, but does not use the information brought by the second derivatives to optimize the step of the descent. Furthermore, the gradient descent can be problematic in case of bad conditioning of the Hessian matrix.

On the one hand, this Hessian matrix can have eigenvalues of opposite signs: we then have a "saddle point" (Figure 3.7). This point is a maximum of the function in certain directions (eigenvectors with negative eigenvalues) and a minimum in other directions (eigenvectors with positive eigenvalues). This is the example of the function $f(x, y) = x^2 - y^2$ whose eigenvalues of H(f) are 2 and −2 at point (0,0). We have seen that in the presence of a saddle point, Newton's algorithm can be attracted to this point instead of converging to a minimum of the error, which is a limitation of this algorithm. This drawback becomes major when the dimension increases because these saddle points are then more

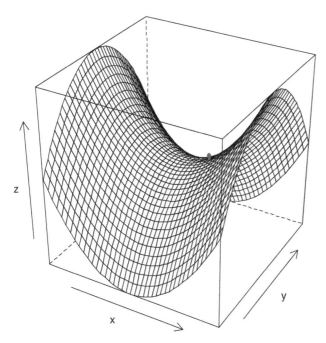

z

y

x

Figure 3.7 Saddle point.

numerous since it becomes very unlikely that all the eigenvalues are of the same sign. On the other hand, the gradient descent can generally escape a saddle point, but in a time that can be exponentially long. The convergence of the gradient descent is then slowed down.

On the other hand, the Hessian matrix can have eigenvalues of equal signs but very different values. In this case the matrix is said to be ill-conditioned. An ill-conditioned Hessian matrix has stronger second derivatives in certain directions, where the curvature of the surface is greater, as in a canyon that has steep slopes (eigenvalue $\gg 0$) in one direction and a smooth slope (eigenvalue > 0) in the perpendicular direction that descends to the minimum. The gradient will descend in the direction of the steeper slope, but too fast, because the gradient predicts a descent without seeing that the slope then quickly begins to rise again. Based on the gradient, we overshoot the minimum of the function (the bottom of the canyon), and we start again too quickly on the other slope. We go down in the direction where the gradient is the steepest but where we go down for less time. We have to decrease the step of the gradient but we then go down too slowly in the direction of the lowest slope. The result is that the descent of the gradient will zigzag from one slope to the other of the first direction instead of going directly down in the second direction. This phenomenon is most pronounced when the conditioning $\lambda_{max}/\lambda_{min}$ is high (Figure 3.8) but it is already apparent with lower conditioning, as in the $x^2 + y^2 + xy$ example where the conditioning is equal to 3/1 and Figure 3.4 already shows zigzags.

Faced with this problem, we have three solutions.

The first is to improve the conditioning of the matrix, i.e., to decrease the ratio $\lambda_{max}/\lambda_{min}$ of the matrix, which is achieved by a product $P^{-1}A$ with an appropriate matrix P (e.g., the

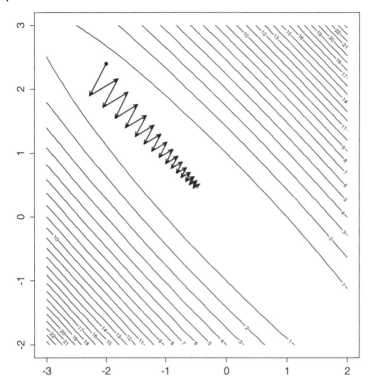

Figure 3.8 Gradient descent with an ill-conditioned Hessian matrix $x^2 + y^2 + 1.9xy$ has eigenvalues 39/10 and 1/10.

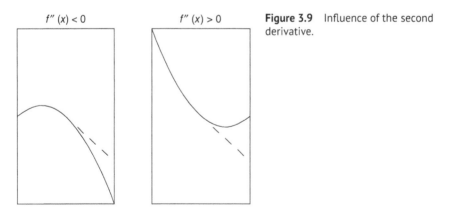

Figure 3.9 Influence of the second derivative.

diagonal of A). This preconditioning has the geometric translation of making the contour lines less elliptical and more circular.

The second solution is to take into account the second derivatives and not only the first, which is Newton's method. Figure 3.9 shows the interest of taking into account the second derivative: when it is negative (on the left), it takes into account the fact that f decreases faster than the gradient indicates, and when it is positive (on the right), it takes into account the fact that f decreases less quickly than the gradient indicates.

The third solution consists in replacing the directions opposite to the gradients by "conjugate" directions, which are the main axes of a quadratic function $f(x) = \frac{1}{2}x^T A x - x^T b$ approximating the function to be minimized. The solution is no longer sought in the opposite direction of the gradient but in the vector space generated by all the previous gradients.

The *conjugate gradient*[8] is an "intermediate" algorithm between the gradient descent (slower convergence) and Newton's algorithm (heavier calculation with the Hessian matrix to be inverted).

The first vector p_0 is the opposite of the gradient and we iteratively search for the conjugate vectors p_k vectors:

- orthogonal (that's what "conjugate" means)[9] two by two for the scalar product $\langle p_k, p_{k+1} \rangle = p_k^T A p_{k+1}$;
- we calculate the residual $r_k = b - A x_k \ (= -\nabla f(x_k))$;
- from the residual, we compute a surrogate α_k to the step;
- p_k is calculated from p_{k-1} and the residual r_k;
- we calculate $x_{k+1} = x_k + \alpha_k p_k$.

Using the information from the previous step, this algorithm converges faster than gradient descent. More precisely, when the function to be minimized is an elliptic quadratic function of p variables, we are assured of a convergence in at most p steps (except for rounding errors). The number of steps is generally larger for a non-quadratic function but smaller than with gradient descent. In Figure 3.6, the convergence is obtained in two steps by the conjugate gradient (in solid line) and more than five steps by the optimal step gradient descent. We check that the first step is done in the same direction for both methods.

This convergence is even faster with a well-conditioned matrix A (see above). A well-conditioned matrix increases the speed of convergence of the optimal step gradient descent, but increases much more the speed of convergence of the conjugate gradient, in a proportion which can be very large. This is because the number of iterations required is proportional to $\lambda_{\max}/\lambda_{\min}$ for the optimal step gradient descent and $\sqrt{\lambda_{\max}/\lambda_{\min}}$ for the conjugate gradient. This quadratic convergence of the conjugate gradient is optimal for first-order methods without second derivatives calculation, but it is equaled by some descent methods using a moment (see Section 7.3).

Finally, this algorithm is particularly efficient when the matrix A is sparse, with few matrix operations at each iteration, and this makes it a popular method in this case, especially since this advantage is added to the speed of convergence. On the other hand, when the matrix A is full, the number of operations to perform is of the order of $2n^3$, and this algorithm is then not the fastest.

With these methods, which need to compute derivatives of functions of several variables, the calculations can be difficult for complicated functions. The *coordinate relaxation method*, or *coordinate descent*, can be interesting in this case: it consists in searching for the minimum of the function in a single direction at each iteration. We thus have a simpler optimization problem since it consists in finding the minimum of a function of only one real variable, the other variables being fixed. This minimum can be found by gradient descent for a differentiable function, but the gradient is then easier to calculate than in the general case. Other methods even can find the minimum of a non-derivable function.

The most natural method is the cyclic coordinate descent, in which we look for the minimum in the direction of the first coordinate axis, then the second axis, then the third, etc. A generalization of coordinate descent is the block coordinate descent and this consists in searching for the minimum in a subspace of dimension > 1 of the space of all variables: the optimization is not done variable by variable, but by blocks of variables.

It can be shown that, like the optimal step gradient descent, the coordinate descent always converges for an elliptic quadratic function. But this convergence is not guaranteed for all functions. For some non-derivative functions such as:

$$Q(x, y) = x^2 + y^2 - 2(x + y) + 2|x - y|,$$

the descent can remain stuck in (0,0) while the minimum is in (1,1). Indeed, the function increases in both x and y directions.

On the other hand, the convergence of the coordinate descent can be very slow when the value of one variable influences the optimal value of another variable. This is the case for the following function:

$$Q(x, y) = \alpha(x - y)^2 + x^2 + y^2, \alpha > 0.$$

Indeed, the second term pushes toward solutions close to (0,0), but the first term pushes the two variables to have close values, and convergence will be slower the larger α is. By comparison, the minimum of this function is found in one iteration by Newton's method and two iterations by the conjugate gradient method.

Thus, coordinate descent is most efficient with functions whose variables play independent roles, in optimization problems whose parameters do not depend on each other. If this condition is met, coordinate descent can be an interesting method with big data and functions whose gradient would be expensive to compute.

The *Levenberg-Marquardt algorithm* is used for a least squares search of a nonlinear function. It interpolates the Gauss-Newton algorithm and the gradient descent algorithm with a damping factor λ_k adjusted at each iteration:

$$\beta_{k+1} = \beta_k - (H(f)(\beta_k) + \lambda_k I)^{-1} \nabla f(\beta_k).$$

This factor decreases in the regions where the function is almost linear and increases elsewhere, so that the algorithm is close to the Gauss-Newton algorithm if λ_k is small and to the gradient descent if λ_k is large.

Compared to Newton's algorithm and its local convergence, Levenberg-Marquardt algorithm brings a global convergence and can find a solution even by starting far away. It also converges in fewer iterations, but since each one requires longer computations, its convergence is generally slower.

Another way to go from local Newton's convergence to global convergence is the *damped Newton's method*, in which one introduces a regularization term $\gamma_k \in [0, 1]$, closer to 1 when far from the solution and closer to 0 when approaching the solution:

$$\beta_{k+1} = \beta_k - \gamma_k H(f)(\beta_k)^{-1} \nabla f(\beta_k).$$

There are also direct optimization methods without calculating derivatives.

The *simplex algorithm*[10] is based on the following principle. In p dimensions, we construct a simplex with $p + 1$ vertices, we search for its vertex where the function is maximal and we replace it by its symmetric x_s with respect to the center of gravity of the p remaining vertices, we stretch the simplex in the direction of x_s if $f(x_s) < \min\{f(x_i)\}$, and so on. This algorithm is fast and robust, but it may converge to a solution far from a minimum. In this case, a practiced solution is to restart from the last obtained solution. It is implemented in the `optim()` R function and the `minimize()` Python SciPy function.

The *iteratively reweighted least squares* (IRLS) *method* is one of the most widely used methods for computing the maximum likelihood estimator in the generalized linear model. With the canonical link function (e.g. logit for logistic regression and logarithm for Poisson regression), this method converges to the maximum likelihood estimator, like Newton's method but more quickly since it does not require the computation of the Hessian matrix. It is known as the Fisher scoring method.

This method is iterative: at each iteration one starts from the β_k coefficients of the previous step (those of the linear regression, for example, for the first iteration), one calculates the predictions $\pi_{\beta_k}(x_i) (= 1/ + \exp(-\beta_k x_i)$ for the logit) from which a weighting variable $W(x_i)$ and a new explanatory variable $V(x_i)$ can be derived, the ordinary linear model $V \sim X$ is fitted to the W-weighted observations, keeping the same explanatory variables X, new coefficients β_{k+1} are obtained, and the next iteration is performed. The coefficients converge to the maximum likelihood estimate. This is indeed an iterated weighted least squares method.

We can also mention the *alternating least squares method*, which can be quite fast but at the cost of poor convergence, and *simulated annealing*.

Genetic algorithms[11] are interesting and can find solutions in complex spaces, but they are very slow.

3.3 Complexity Reduction and Penalized Regression

Before talking about machine learning methods, it is good to recall a few theoretical elements, and to recall what the *bias-variance dilemma* so important in modeling consists of, and how it requires mastering the complexity of models.

If a model f links X and Y so that $Y = f(X) + \varepsilon$, with $E(\varepsilon) = 0$ and $V(\varepsilon) = \sigma^2$, and if $\widehat{f}$ estimates f, common loss functions L are:

- for y continuous, the function $L(y,\widehat{f}(x)) = (y - \widehat{f}(x))^2$,
- for $y = -1/+1$, the function $L(y,\widehat{f}(x)) = \frac{1}{2}|y - \widehat{f}(x)|$.

The risk is by definition the expectation of the loss function over all possible values of the data (x, y). As the theoretical joint probability distribution of x and y is generally unknown, one can only estimate the risk. The most common estimate is the empirical risk

$$\frac{1}{n} \sum_{i=1}^{n} (y_i - \widehat{f}(x_i))^2 \text{ or } \frac{1}{n} \sum_{i=1}^{n} \frac{1}{2}|y_i - \widehat{f}(x_i)|$$

where n is the population size. In the second formula, we find the error rate for $y = -1/+1$. The empirical risk is so called because it is based on the empirical distribution, which associates the probability $1/n$ with each observation, and which is the natural probability distribution in the absence of any information other than that given by the observations.

In the quadratic case, the risk is decomposed into three terms:

$$\mathbb{E}[Y - \widehat{f}(X)]^2 = \mathbb{E}[Y - f(X)]^2 + \mathbb{E}[Y - \mathbb{E}[\widehat{f}(X)]]^2 + \mathbb{E}[[\mathbb{E}[\widehat{f}(X)] - \widehat{f}(X)]^2].$$

These three terms are:

- the Bayesian risk independent of the model (irreducible error);
- the square of the difference between the expectation of the prediction $\widehat{f}(X)$ and the mean value of Y (square of the model bias);
- the variance of the prediction (model variance).

The more complex a model is, the more its bias decreases but the more its variance increases, and it can increase more than the bias decreases, so that the error of the model can increase while its complexity increases. It is therefore necessary to find the right compromise between bias and variance of the model, between fitting to the training data (bias) and generalization capacity (variance). To ensure a good generalization of the model, it is the sum of "bias^2 + variance" that must be minimized.

In the simplest cases, the complexity of a model is equal to $p + 1$, where p is the number of its parameters. However, it is not always possible to reduce the number of parameters of the model, especially when its future users want to see a certain number of criteria appear simultaneously (even if they are strongly correlated). This will be the case, for example, in medicine, with physiological measurements, analysis results, or in banking, with qualitative criteria on companies.

Fortunately, complexity can be reduced in some models without reducing the number of parameters, in particular by introducing bounds $\|\beta\| \leq C$ in the search for the coefficients of a regression model. We then have the inequality:

$$\text{complexity} \leq \min [\text{integer part } (R^2 C^2), p] + 1,$$

the observations being contained in a sphere of radius R. This is called *penalized* or *regularized regression*. In the case of support vector machines, the complexity can be reduced by increasing the margin of the SVM. Finally, in ensemble methods, it is the aggregation of the models that can reduce their variance and possibly their bias. We will see how these methods operate, but we start by recalling the definition of penalized regression,[12] which is very important in big data modeling.

In the regression with penalty L^δ ($\delta \geq 0$), instead of simply minimizing the deviance (-2.log-likelihood), we minimize the sum of the deviance and a penalty:

$$-2. \log\text{-likelihood} + \lambda \sum_{j=1}^{p} |\beta_j|^\delta, \text{with } \lambda \geq 0,$$

This is equivalent to minimizing:

$$-2. \log\text{-likelihood with constraint } \sum_{j=1}^{p} |\beta_j|^\delta \leq C, \text{with } C \geq 0.$$

This is also true in the framework of the generalized linear model, and in the framework of linear regression by replacing the deviance by the sum of residual squares.

The larger the penalty λ (or the smaller the bound C), and the smaller the coefficients β_j will have to be so that the term $\lambda \sum_{j=1}^{p} |\beta_j|^{\delta}$ does not increase too much. The improvement in regression fit that causes the deviance or sum of residual squares to decrease usually goes hand in hand with increasing the coefficients, but if the coefficients become large, the term $\lambda \sum_{j=1}^{p} |\beta_j|^{\delta}$ will increase more than the deviance will decrease and we will move away from the desired minimum. The increase in the penalty λ thus leads to a limitation of the size of the coefficients of the model and a limitation of its fit, which is the price to pay for a better generalization to other samples.

There are two situations in the penalized regression: (1) when $\delta \leq 1$, the increase in the penalty λ leads to the progressive cancelation of the coefficients (Figure 3.10), and thus operates a selection of the explanatory variables. We have the AIC (Akaike) and BIC (Schwartz) criteria if $\delta = 0$, and the Lasso regression if $\delta = 1$; (2) when $\delta > 1$, increasing the penalty λ leads to a shrinking of the coefficients but not to their cancelation (Figure 3.11). The ridge regression ($\delta = 2$) is the most common. It reduces the coefficients in all directions, and even more so in directions with low variance. In other words, the coefficient of the ridge regression on the first principal component of the data decreases less than the coefficient of the ridge regression on the second principal component, etc.

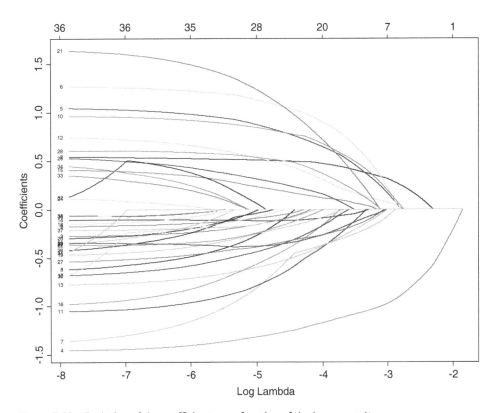

Figure 3.10 Evolution of the coefficients as a function of the Lasso penalty.

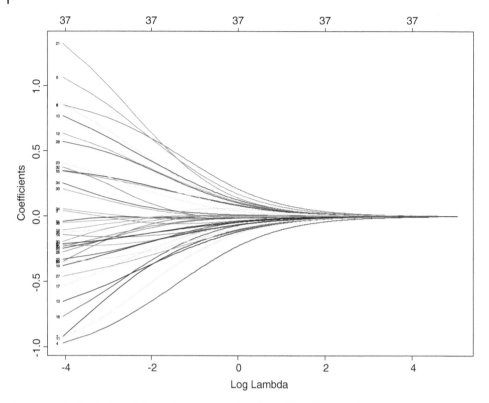

Figure 3.11 Evolution of the coefficients as a function of the ridge penalty.

In some cases, we want to both shrink the coefficients (like the ridge regression) and cancel some of them (like the Lasso regression), while eventually having more non-zero coefficients than individuals. This is what the "elastic net" allows, in which the penalty is of the form:

$$\lambda \left[(1 - \alpha) \sum_j \beta_j^2 + \alpha \sum_j |\beta_j| \right],$$

with varying between 0 (ridge model) and 1 (Lasso model).

The complexity can also be reduced by PLS (Partial Least Squares) regression. It is shown that with a single PLS component, the signs of the coefficients are equal to the signs of the correlations between the explanatory variables and the variable to be explained.[13]

It has been found that PLS regression reduces the coefficients in directions with low variance, but can cause too large an increase in directions with high variance, so the prediction error of PLS is often somewhat larger.[14]

Python scikit-learn library and many R packages implement these methods: `glmnet`, `penalized`, `grplasso`, `grpreg`, `relaxo`, `lasso2`, `lars`, `glmpath`, `elasticnet`, `pls`, `plsRglm`...

3.4   Ensemble Methods

The reduction of the variance of a model by ensemble methods (or model aggregation) is based on the observation that the mean of B i.i.d. (independent identically distributed) random variables of variance σ^2 has a variance σ^2/B (and an expectation equal to the expectation of each variable), and that the variance of the mean is $\rho\sigma^2 + \frac{1-\rho}{B}\sigma^2$ when the variables are identically distributed but dependent, with a positive correlation ρ.

This formula can be applied to the prediction function defined by each model in the aggregation, and we see that if these functions are highly correlated, the aggregation will reduce the variance of predictions little, even if B is large.

3.4.1   Bagging

By averaging models (e.g. decision trees) on B bootstrap samples of the training dataset, we obtain a model whose bias has not decreased but whose variance has decreased the more the correlation between the models is low. This is the principle of bagging: **B**ootstrap **AGG**regat**ING**.[15]

The B models can be aggregated:

- by a vote or an average of probabilities $P(Y = 1|X)$ when you know how to calculate this average (classification);
- by an average of the estimates $E(Y|X)$ (regression).

The voting procedure applied to low quality trees can lead to a worse result during aggregation. To show this, suppose that $Y = 1$ for all x and that each model predicts 1 with probability 0.4 and 0 with probability 0.6. The classification error of each model will be 0.6 but aggregation by voting will result in a model whose error is 1.

In bagging, the base model is the same for each iteration. It is most often a decision tree but sometimes a neural network.

The correlation between models is decreased both by the bootstrap mechanism, but also by the increase in complexity: bagging is best applied to classifiers with low bias and high variance. This is why it is most often used with decision trees, whose pruning strategy is then simple: we prune the trees as little as possible so that they are as deep as possible, with the highest variance and the lowest correlation. The apparent paradox of bagging is that it seeks what is most often avoided: models with high variance, which could be described as not very robust. Moreover, bagging is inefficient on a strong classifier, whose different models will be too correlated to reduce the variance.

Bagging is implemented in two R packages: `ipred` and `randomForest`.

3.4.2   Random Forests

It has been observed that bagging is inefficient when the models are too correlated and we therefore want to decorrelate them. The idea of random forests[16] is to introduce a second randomization: it is not only the individuals that are randomly drawn, as in bagging, but also the explanatory variables, by drawing, at each splitting of a tree, a subset of candidate variables of size q (constant during the training) among the set of p explanatory variables.

As the correlation of the models decreases (it can go down to $\rho = 0.05$ or even less when aggregating trees with q close to 1), the variance of the aggregated model decreases, according to the previous formula $\rho\sigma^2 + \frac{1-\rho}{B}\sigma^2$.

At each splitting of the tree, not all the explanatory variables are tested and likely to provide the splitting criterion of the node, but only a subset of q explanatory variables, which avoids seeing the same most discriminant variables appear too often. Each elementary tree performs less well, but the aggregation leads to a better performing aggregate model: the increase in bias is more than compensated by the decrease in variance.

Random forests are implemented in several R packages: `randomForest` and `ranger` based on the CART tree, `party` based on the CTree tree, as well as in H2O, Spark, and Python.

Decreasing the number q of candidate variables increases the bias but decreases the correlation between the models and the variance of the final model, and q thus adjusts the trade-off between bias and variance.

For classification, Breiman suggests a subset of $q = \lceil\sqrt{p}\rceil$ variables ([x] denoting the integer part of x), $[\log(p) + 1]$ variables or a single variable. However, this number q should not be too small if a high proportion of variables is not very discriminant.

Random forests start to be very efficient when the probability of selecting a discriminant explanatory variable is greater than 0.5. This probability is given by the hypergeometric distribution. If, for example, 6 discriminant variables are mixed with 30 non-discriminant variables, the probability of drawing at least one discriminant variable among 6 is:

```
> sum(dhyper(1:6, 6, 30, 6))
[1] 0.6951548
```

Random forests are easy to implement because the number q of explanatory variables is the only parameter to be set. The number of iterations is less sensitive to adjust, and it is in our interest to choose a high number of iterations, especially since several implementations of random forests are fast, especially the one of `ranger`, even on large numbers. The number of models to aggregate should in principle increase with the number of predictors.

An interesting advantage of random forests is that they are resistant to overfitting (unlike neural networks and boosting) even when the number of aggregated models is large. This makes the choice of the number of trees in the forest less sensitive.

There are similarities between random forests and penalized ridge regression.

First, narrowing the coefficients in the ridge regression by introducing a penalty λ is equivalent to selecting $q < p$ explanatory variables randomly from the p explanatory variables. Increasing λ or decreasing q:

- increases the bias, since the solution is sought in a subspace fixed by the constraint;
- reduces the variance, so as to compensate for the increase in bias.

Another analogy is that all explanatory variables can appear in the model:

- by shrinking their coefficients in the ridge regression;
- or by random selection in random forests.

In both cases, the task of selecting the variables is simplified.

The final commonality between these two methods is their high predictive power.

Random forests and penalized ridge regression also have several differences. The penalty λ allows a continuous adjustment of the bias-variance, while the number q is discrete. It permits one to adjust the coefficients with the help of the ridge plot, so that all the coefficients have a coherent sign, or even some coefficients are higher than a threshold fixed by the domain experts.

The penalized regression is deterministic. Penalized regression calculations are inherently faster, even though random forest calculations can be parallelized.

But the main difference, which is also the main disadvantage of random forests, is the lack of readability of a random forest model, which by aggregation destroys the tree structure.

3.4.3 Extra-Trees

Extra-Trees, or Extremely randomized Trees,[17] are an extension of random forests, with which they have several similarities:

- At each split, q candidate explanatory variables are selected by a random draw, among the p available explanatory variables;
- the best split is selected among the q possible ones, based on the Gini index for the classification and the variance for the regression.

The difference between Extra-Trees and random forests is that the determination of each split of a node is not supervised but totally random in Extra-Trees. For a continuous explanatory variable, the splitting threshold can be drawn according to the uniform distribution between the minimum and maximum values of the explanatory variable, and not determined in such a way as to minimize an impurity function (Gini index for the CART tree).

The bias is increased but the variance is decreased, in a proportion that can make the bias-variance trade-off favorable to decreasing the error. The bias can eventually be decreased by building each tree on the whole population, without bootstrapping.

In addition to the reduction in variance, the obvious advantage of Extra-Trees over random forests is the speed of their training.

An extreme case of Extra-Trees is the one where $q = 1$: as only one explanatory variable is randomly selected at each split, the construction of the tree is then totally random and independent of the variable to be explained Y. Obviously, the prediction is not random and the variable to be explained is taken into account at one stage of the process: when each terminal node (and therefore each individual) is assigned to a class of Y (classification) or a value of Y (regression), which is done according to the usual assignment rules. In this case, the bias is maximal, but the decrease in variance can be interesting.

In practice, the tests of Geurts *et al.* show that:

- In classification problems, the square root of p is generally a good compromise between bias and variance, which minimizes the error;
- in regression problems, the bias seems to increase with the decrease of the number of selected explanatory variables, more rapidly than in classification, and they obtain good results with $q = p$.

Extra-Trees are implemented in Python and in the `extraTrees` package of R. We show an example implementation in Section 6.7.

3.4.4 Boosting

Boosting is an ensemble method that consists of successively applying the same classification or regression algorithm to versions of the initial training sample modified at each step to account for the classification or prediction errors of the previous step,[18] and then combining the models thus constructed to obtain a better performing final model. Very typically, the modifications that occur at each step are an overweighting of the misclassified or misfit observations from the previous step. We force the learning process to focus on the cases that are the most difficult to predict or fit, while trying to limit the risk of overfitting during the final aggregation by weighting the models by their quality.

Boosting differs from other ensemble methods because it is an adaptive and generally deterministic algorithm. Another difference is that boosting not only reduces the variance of the models but can also reduce their bias. Its principle is attractive and its performance is sometimes very high, with a very low prediction error, but it is frequently subject to overfitting. There are many variants, the Discrete AdaBoost, the Real AdaBoost, the Gentle AdaBoost, the LogitBoost, the Arcing (Adaptive Resampling and Combining), whose performances are nevertheless not always very different on real data.

Boosting is implemented in the Python scikit-learn library and in several R packages, including `ada`, `gbm`, `xgboost`, and `mboost`, not to mention H2O, Spark, and Python.

The boosting mechanism can be illustrated by an example given in a book by the inventors of boosting[19] and in a lecture by one of them.[20] Figure 3.12, where the misclassified observations are surrounded by a circle, shows that a sufficiently large number of iterations can allow the adjustment on irregular data.

The discussion in this section will be simplified by considering that the binary variable to be explained has values of ±1 and that the prediction of the classification function f is the sign of f. Thus, well-classified individuals are those for whom the product $y.f$ is positive. We also speak of the $y.f$ margin by thinking of support vector machines.

One of the earliest and most widely used versions of boosting is the Discrete AdaBoost algorithm[21] which is shown below:

1) Initialize the weights of the N observations of the training data sample: $p_i = 1/N, i = 1, 2, ..., N$.
2) Repeat for $m = 1$ to M (the number of iterations):
   - fit the model $f_m(x) \in \{-1, +1\}$ on the training sample weighted by the weights p_i;
   - calculate the weighted error rate ε_m of $f_m(x)$ (with the rate taking into account the weight p_i of each misclassified observation) and calculate $\alpha_m = log(1 - \varepsilon_m/\varepsilon_m)$;

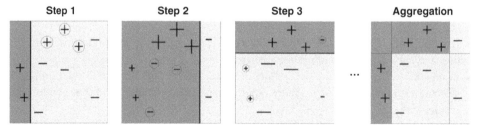

Figure 3.12 Adaptive boosting mechanism. *Source*: Schapire, R.E. and Freund, Y. *Boosting: Foundations and Algorithms* (Cambridge, MA: MIT Press, 2012).

- we can multiply α_m by a learning rate $\lambda < 1$ to decrease the intensity of the adaptive mechanism;
- if $\varepsilon_m < 0.5$, multiply the weight p_i of each misclassified (resp. well-classified) observation by $exp(\alpha_m)$ (resp. $exp(-\alpha_m)$) (otherwise: stop the algorithm or reset the weights); this is equivalent to multiplying in all cases the weight by $exp(-\alpha_m y_i f_m(x_i))$ since an observation (x_i, y_i) is well classified when $y_i f_m(x_i) > 0$;
- normalize the weights p_i so that their sum is 1.

3) The boosted model is the sign of the sum $\sum_m \alpha_m f_m(x)$ (or the average value of $\alpha_m f_m(x)$).

We observe that the misclassified observations all have their weights multiplied by the same value, contrary to another version of boosting called arc-x4,[22] and that this multiplier $exp(\alpha_m)$ is all the smaller as the error rate is greater (Figure 3.13). This prevents a model that is poorly fitted during an iteration from having an inappropriate importance in the evolution of the weights, and limits the risks of overfitting. For each coefficient α_m to be positive, the error rate ε_m must be strictly less than 0.5, and if this is no longer the case, we can reset the weights $p_i = 1/N$.

When the base classifier does not return a binary value but a continuous value, typically a probability, the Discrete AdaBoost algorithm can be replaced by the Real AdaBoost algorithm. The aggregation thus takes into account for each base model a more precise information than the predicted class.

Here is the algorithm in the case of the exponential loss function:

1) Initialize the weights of the N observations:

$$p_i = 1/N, i = 1, 2, \ldots, N.$$

2) Repeat for $m = 1$ to M (the number of iterations):
- calculate the probability $p_m(x) = P(Y = 1|x)$ on the training sample weighted by the weights p_i;
- if $p_m(x) = 0$ or 1, reset the weights $p_i = 1/N$.

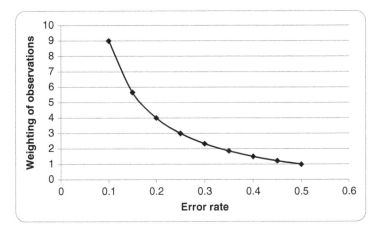

Figure 3.13 Weighting of observations according to the error rate.

- otherwise:
  - calculate $f_m(x) = \frac{1}{2} \log \left(\frac{p_m(x)}{1 - p_m(x)} \right)$;
  - (or the bounded function $f_m(x) = p_m(x) - (1 - p_m(x)) \in [-1, 1]$ in the Gentle AdaBoost);
  - multiply the weight p_i of each observation (x_i, y_i) by the exponential loss function $exp(-\lambda. y_i f_m(x_i))$ for $i = 1, 2, ..., N$, where $\lambda \leq 1$ is as above a learning rate;
  - normalize the weights p_i so that their sum is 1.
3) The boosted classifier is the sign of the sum $\sum_m f_m(x)$.

This algorithm gives a weight > 1 to misclassified observations and a weight < 1 to well-classified observations. Its disadvantage is that the half-logit by which the weights are multiplied can be very large for well-separated observations ($p_m(x)$ close to 0 or 1), thus causing instability of the weights. When this happens, we can turn to other types of boosting, for example, the Gentle AdaBoost, which does not have this drawback of the Real AdaBoost even if it has the same exponential loss function.

We can verify that the results obtained with Real AdaBoost rarely differ much from those obtained with Discrete AdaBoost, thus confirming an observation of an article[23] that just points out the inferior performance of Discrete AdaBoost on *stumps*.

Stumps are trees of depth 1, with only two leaves, which therefore have a low variance but a high bias. Their individual discriminant power is of course low, but their boosting leads to a discriminant power often superior to that of a good model such as logistic regression. Random forests are also efficient on stumps.

The reason why boosting is subject to overfitting is the adaptive mechanism that leads to overweighting misclassified individuals in some cases because they are atypical. To minimize overfitting, the ada and gbm packages propose to automatically determine an optimal number of iterations that minimizes the error rate (ada) or the loss function (gbm). This number is determined on the training sample, on a test sample (ada), or by cross-validation (gbm). It is generally recommended to limit the aggregation to this number or another determined value, for example, by measuring the area under the ROC curve on a test sample. Like some neural networks, boosting is subject to overfitting and the test error can increase after a certain number of iterations, and we gain by performing the well-known early stopping of neural networks.

```
> pred.boost <- predict(boost, test, type='prob', n.iter=1800)[,2]
```

Other solutions consist in using another loss function or to decrease the learning rate λ (also called penalty or regularization or shrinkage parameter).

This importance of the choice of the loss function comes from the fact that Friedman *et al.*[24] have shown that the Discrete AdaBoost algorithm is equivalent to a step-by-step minimization of the expectation of the exponential loss function $exp(-y.F_m)$, where y is the variable to be explained and F_m is a classification function which is obtained by adding at each iteration a basis function (a decision tree, for example) to the function F_{m-1} and which converges to the searched classification function $f = F_M$. Now, this exponential loss function is a continuous convex approximation of the most natural ranking loss function: the misclassification function $1_{(sign(f) \neq Y)}$. Convexifying a loss function is a common operation in machine learning, as it is easier to find the minimum of a convex function.

Another loss function used is the logistic loss (or binomial deviance)

$$\log(1 + \exp(-2y.f)).$$

This is another approximation of the function $1_{(sign(f) \neq Y)}$ which penalizes misclassifications more than it improves good classifications. But the exponential function penalizes misclassification exponentially, not linearly, giving much greater importance to misclassified individuals. For this reason, the exponential function may be less appropriate than the logistic function in the presence of many atypical individuals. We call the variant of boosting that relies on the logistic loss function LogitBoost.

Other examples of convex loss functions can be used for binary ± 1 classification problems, such as the quadratic loss $(y - f)^2$ and the vector support $(1 - yf)_+$ (positive part). These are other convex approximations of the function $1_{(sign(f) \neq Y)}$. The choice of an appropriate loss function allows one to adapt to a variety of situations.

In regression, in the presence of extreme values, the quadratic loss function may be less appropriate than the absolute value or the Huber function:

$$L_\delta(y,f) = \begin{cases} \frac{1}{2}(y-f)^2 \ si \ |y-f| \leq \delta \\ \delta\,(|y-f| - \delta/2) \ si \ |y-f| > \delta \end{cases}.$$

Another variant is the gradient boosting functional, or Friedman[25,26] gradient boosting, which relies on the gradient descent method to find the minimum of the expectation of the loss function. The opposite of the gradient indicates the direction in which the largest decay in the expectation of the loss function occurs and which must be added to F_{m-1} to obtain F_m. In this method, a decision tree is fitted on the opposite of the gradient. See Section 3.4.5 for more details.

We have seen above that it is possible to penalize the addition of each new model to the aggregation and to adjust the descent of the error surface using a parameter called the learning rate or shrinkage. This parameter is 1 in the original AdaBoost equivalent algorithm, but it can be chosen to be smaller (e.g. 0.1 or even less) for a slower gradient descent and a finer search for an optimal solution with less risk of overfitting. A decrease in the learning rate slows down the convergence and forces an increase in the number of iterations, thus the computation time. But the most common way to try to limit overfitting is to decrease the learning rate λ. We see from Figure 3.14 to Figure 3.16 that a low rate $\lambda = 0.01$ is required so that the training error, represented by the lower curve, does not quickly fall to 0 but instead gradually decreases.

Boosting has been studied in many works and is prized for its effectiveness. However, it does have several limitations:

- its sensitivity to noise due to the adaptive mechanism that emphasizes observations that are difficult to classify or fit, a sensitivity that can be reduced by choosing an adapted loss function (absolute value or Huber function rather than quadratic function for regression);
- its inefficiency on a stable base classifier (linear discriminant analysis, logistic regression on fixed variables), because in this case it will often be the same observations that will be misclassified, and their weight will increase strongly, as well as the error rate;
- its computation time, which is longer than that of random forests that can easily be parallelized;

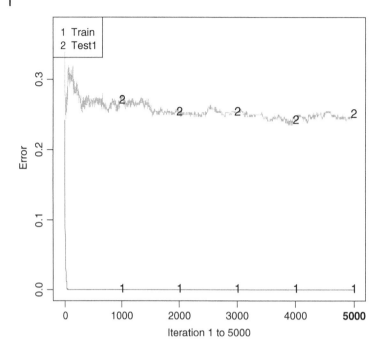

Figure 3.14   Effect of learning rate on boosting convergence ($\lambda = 1$).

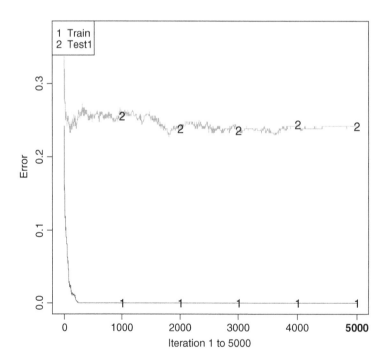

Figure 3.15   Effect of learning rate on boosting convergence ($\lambda = 0.1$).

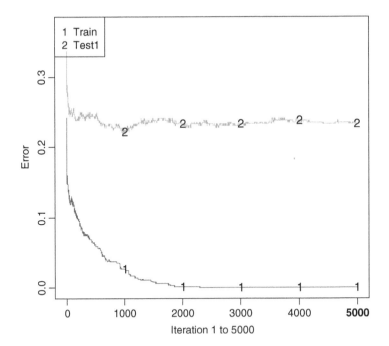

Figure 3.16 Effect of learning rate on boosting convergence ($\lambda = 0.01$).

- its convergence to an optimal performance is generally slower, particularly sensitive when the boundary between the classes to be predicted is poorly delimited and AdaBoost loses time to reweight the classification errors of the observations that are close to the boundary;
- the complexity and sensitivity of its settings (loss function, number of iterations, learning rate).

Nevertheless, boosting often has a very high predictive power, especially in its gradient boosting versions presented in Section 3.4.5.

3.4.5 Gradient Boosting Methods

The gradient boosting presented here is a variant of boosting that gives very good results and is very popular, especially in its XGBoost implementation. We introduce it by going back to the definition of boosting in mathematical terms.

We can reformulate the definition of boosting seen in Section 3.4.4 more precisely by saying that it is an iterative algorithm in which the estimator $\hat{f}$ is obtained at each step m by minimizing an expression:

$$\hat{f}_m = \arg\min_f \frac{1}{n} \sum_{i=1}^{n} L(y_i, \hat{F}_{m-1}(x_i) + f(x_i)),$$

with L a loss function, $\hat{F}_{m-1} = \sum_{k=1}^{m-1} \alpha_k \hat{f}_k$ and f in a given family of functions.

This family is frequently that of decision trees: $f(x) = \sum_{j=1}^{J} \beta_j 1_{R_j}(x)$, R_j being the region of the jth leaf of the tree and β_j its value in this leaf.

At the end of the training, we obtain the estimator $\widehat{f} = \widehat{F}_M = \sum_{m=1}^{M} \alpha_m \widehat{f}_m$.

We often replace the model $\widehat{F}_m = \widehat{F}_{m-1} + \alpha_m \widehat{f}_m$ by $\widehat{F}_{m-1} + \nu\alpha_m \widehat{f}_m$ where ν between 0 and 1 is a constant learning rate. A low value may require an increase in the number M of iterations but it has the advantage of reducing the risk of overfitting. We often use a value $\nu < 0.3$ or even $\nu < 0.1$ in regression.

But looking for $\widehat{f}_m$ and α_m such that $\widehat{F}_m = \widehat{F}_{m-1} + \alpha_m \widehat{f}_m$ fits as well as possible to Y (α_m is used to weight the model $\widehat{f}_m$) is equivalent to fitting $\alpha_m \widehat{f}_m$ on the residuals $y_i - \widehat{F}_{m-1}(x_i)$.

The idea of gradient boosting is that the gradient of the quadratic loss function is the opposite of the previously defined residual:

$$L(y, F(x)) = \frac{1}{2}(y - F(x))^2 \implies -\left(\frac{\partial L(y, F(x))}{\partial F(x)}\right) = y - F(x).$$

This suggests the following iterative algorithm:

- $\widehat{F}_0 = \arg\min_\alpha \frac{1}{n}\sum_{i=1}^{n} L(y_i, \alpha)$ is a constant function.

Then, for $m = 1$ to M:

- we calculate the opposite of the gradients $r_{i,m} = -\left(\frac{\partial L(y_i, F(x_i))}{\partial F(x_i)}\right)_{F=\widehat{F}_{m-1}}$ for $i = 1 \ldots n$,
- we find $\widehat{f}_m$ by adjusting it to $(x_i, r_{i,m})_{i=1\ldots n}$,
- we are looking for the multiplier $\alpha_m = \arg\min_\alpha \frac{1}{n}\sum_{i=1}^{n} L(y_i, \widehat{F}_{m-1}(x_i) + \alpha\widehat{f}_m(x_i))$,
- we update the model $\widehat{F}_m = \widehat{F}_{m-1} + \alpha_m \widehat{f}_m$.

The final model is $\widehat{F}_M$.

We recognize the formula of the gradient descent:

$$\widehat{F}_m = \widehat{F}_{m-1} - \alpha_m \frac{1}{n}\sum_{i=1}^{n} \frac{\partial L(y_i, \widehat{F}_{m-1}(x_i))}{\partial \widehat{F}_{m-1}(x_i)}.$$

This formulation of boosting in the form of a gradient descent is more general than the residual fitting formulation. It corresponds to the case where L is the quadratic loss, but the loss functions can be varied.

With some loss functions, the gradient is less sensitive to outliers than the residuals related to the quadratic function. This is of course the case with the absolute value and the Huber function. Indeed, the gradient of the quadratic loss is $y - F(x)$, while the gradient of the absolute value is the sign of $y - F(x)$, and the gradient of the Huber function is $y - F(x)$ (if $|y - F(x)| \leq \delta$) or $\delta.sign(y - F(x))$ (if $|y - F(x)| > \delta$).

In Friedman's TreeBoost algorithm, we look for the model in the form:

$$\widehat{F}_m = \widehat{F}_{m-1} + \alpha_m \widehat{f}_m,$$

where $\widehat{f}_m(x) = \sum_{j=1}^{J_m} \beta_{j,m} 1_{R_{j,m}}(x))$ is a decision tree.

From there, we can simplify $\alpha_m \beta_{j,m}$ and rewrite the model:

$$\widehat{F}_m = \widehat{F}_{m-1} + \sum_{j=1}^{J_m} \alpha_{j,m} 1_{R_{j,m}}(x),$$

with $\alpha_{j,m} = \arg\min_\alpha \sum_{x_i \in R_{j,m}} L(y_i, \widehat{F}_{m-1}(x_i) + \alpha)$.

Empirically, the number of terminal J of terminal nodes in trees is often chosen between 4 and 8.

A penalty can be introduced: $\sum_{m=1}^{M} \left(\gamma J_m + \frac{1}{2}\lambda\|\alpha_{j,m}\|_2^2 + \mu\|\alpha_{j,m}\|_1 \right)$ to reduce the risk of overfitting.

Among the gradient boosting algorithms, the XGBoost[27] (eXtreme Gradient Boosting) algorithm has several particularities that contribute to its performance:

1) We compute the second derivatives, i.e. the Hessian matrix $H(L) = \left(\frac{\partial^2 L(y_i, F(x_i))}{\partial F(x_i)\partial F(x_j)} \right)$ and not only the gradient ($\nabla L = \frac{\partial L(y_i, F(x_i))}{\partial F(x_i)}$) for the update of the model (*Newton boosting*).
2) We replace the gradient descent $\hat{F}_m = \hat{F}_{m-1} - \alpha_m \nabla L$ by Newton's method $\hat{F}_m = \hat{F}_{m-1} - H(L)^{-1}\nabla L$ method, which takes better advantage of the information provided by the data.
3) It is no longer on ∇L but on $H(L)^{-1}\nabla L$ that the decision trees are adjusted.
4) We can penalize the base models as indicated above.
5) We can apply the random forest mechanism which consists in sampling the explanatory variables at each tree or each split of each decision tree.

The XGBoost algorithm has shown in many cases (including Kaggle competitions) an excellent predictive power combined with a certain speed of calculation. It relies on its good optimization method, on its penalization of the complexity of the base models and on an efficient parallelization of the calculations. It is implemented in R, Python, H2O and Spark (see Section 6.8).

Another algorithm based on gradient boosting is well known, especially for its handling of categorical variables: the CatBoost algorithm.[28,29] It implements gradient boosting for classification and regression, with an optimized handling of categorical variables.

CatBoost is based on a variant of gradient boosting, *ordered boosting*, analogous to classical boosting where at each iteration m we adjust $\alpha_m \hat{f}_m$ on the residuals $y_i - \hat{F}_{m-1}(x_i)$, except that CatBoost computes each residual from a model $\hat{F}_{m-1}^{i-1}$ different for each individual, because it is trained on the previous individuals x_i. So we compute the residual $y_i - \hat{F}_{m-1}^{i-1}(x_i)$. The goal of ordered boosting is to reduce overfitting: the residual of an individual is calculated with a model trained without this individual, thus without the bias of a residual calculated from a model trained with this individual. If there is not a natural order (for example, temporal) of the individuals, a random permutation is introduced at each iteration.

The number of calculations is very large since n models are fitted at each iteration, but optimizations can reduce the number of models.

One way to decrease the computation time and perhaps reduce the risk of overfitting is to use oblivious trees, characterized by the fact that it is the same variable that intervenes in each split of a given level of depth of the tree (but not necessarily the same one in two different levels).

Categorical variables are coded by a variant of *target encoding*: instead of replacing each category with the mean value of the response variable in the category, the risk of overfitting is reduced by coding each x_i by calculating the mean value in the category for the individuals before x_i i.e. for the $x_j, 1 \leq j < i$. In the calculation of this average, we can add 1 to the denominator (number of individuals in the category) and a prior p to the numerator (sum of the values of Y for the individuals in the category), this prior often being the mean value of Y in the whole population.

Finally, Microsoft's LightGBM algorithm[30] is a well-documented, very fast and memory-efficient implementation of gradient boosting.[31] It relies on the Gradient-based One-Side Sampling (GOSS) method not to examine all individuals in order to find the best split of each tree node, by subsampling those that contribute the least to the gradient.

Another technique (EFB: Exclusive Feature Bundling) is used to reduce the number of explanatory variables by grouping those that are "exclusive" in the sense that they rarely take non-zero values simultaneously.

Its pruning mechanism can produce complex trees, so there is a risk of overfitting, which is reduced by numerous possible settings, including an early stopping feature. LightGBM easily provides a very good prediction, sometimes better than XGBoost, and it is so fast that one can test several settings in a reasonable time. It is available in Python and R (package `lightgbm`) and one can consult the following documentations:

1) https://lightgbm.readthedocs.io/en/latest/Python-Intro.html
2) https://lightgbm.readthedocs.io/en/latest/R/index.html

It can run on classical, parallel or distributed architecture, on CPU or GPU.

3.4.6 Synthesis of the Ensemble Methods

The comparison of the ensemble methods is presented in Table 3.1.

3.5 Support Vector Machines

Support vector machines are a kind of generalization of linear discriminant analysis, in which the linear separation of classes, when it is not possible in the initial space, is achieved by embedding into a space of higher, possibly infinite, dimension. The linear separation obtained in this enlarged space is equivalent to a non-linear separation in the initial space, but it has a simpler form (see Figure 3.18). Another difference with linear discriminant analysis is the way the linear separation is determined: in SVMs, one looks for the separation that maximizes the margin between classes, i.e., the width of the corridor between the observations of the two classes. In the example in Figure 3.17, we prefer the B1 boundary to the B2 boundary. This maximization of the margin reduces the complexity of the resulting model and ensures a better generalization. This is understandable: in a sample other than the training sample, the points will not all fall on the right side of the margin and may therefore sometimes be misclassified; however, this risk is all the smaller the wider the margin. As in the penalized regression (see Section 3.3), we add a constraint to find a more robust solution.

Searching for the optimal separation amounts to searching for a hyperplane of equation $a * x + b = 0$ ($a * x$ is the scalar product of a and x) satisfying simultaneously two conditions:

- it separates well the classes to be discriminated A and B (good fit of the model), in the sense that the function defined by $f(x) = a * x + b$ is > 0 if and only if $x \in A$, and $f(x) \leq 0$ if and only if $x \in B$;
- it is as far as possible from all observations (robustness of the model), knowing that the distance of an observation x to the hyperplane is $|a * x + b|/\|a\|$.

Table 3.1 Comparison of bagging, random forests, extra-trees, and boosting.

Bagging	Random forests Extra-Trees	Boosting
Features		
Bagging is a random mechanism	Like bagging	Boosting is an adaptive and generally (except for arcing, XGBoost and LightGBM) deterministic mechanism
At each iteration, training is done on a different bootstrap sample	Like bagging	Generally (except arcing, XGBoost and LightGBM), at each iteration, training is done on the complete initial sample
At each iteration, training is done on all the predictors	At each iteration, training is done on a random subset of predictors	At each iteration, training is done on all the predictors
At each iteration, the model produced must perform well on all observations	At each iteration, the model produced must also perform well on all the observations, but less so than the bagging, since not all the predictors are used	At each iteration, the model produced must perform well on some observations; a model that performs well on some atypicals will perform less well on the other observations
In the final aggregation, all models have the same weight	Like bagging	In the final aggregation, the models are generally weighted according to their error rate
Advantages and disadvantages		
Variance reduction technique by model aggregation	Like bagging, but with a greater reduction in variance (even more for Extra-Trees)	Can decrease the variance and bias of the base model But the variance can increase with a stable base model
Loss of readability of the base decision tree model	Loss of readability of the base decision tree model	Loss of readability of the base decision tree model
Quite effective on stumps	Quite effective on stumps	Very effective on stumps
Possibility of parallelizing the algorithm	Like bagging	Sequential algorithm more difficult to parallelize
No overfitting: superior to boosting in the presence of noise	Like bagging	Risk of overfitting if the number of iterations is large or the data are noisy
Bagging is the simplest but is less discriminant than random forests and boosting	Random forests are always better than bagging and sometimes better than boosting. Depending on the case, Extra-Trees are more or less predictive than random forests (but always faster)	Boosting is often more efficient than bagging or even random forests, at least on not too noisy data

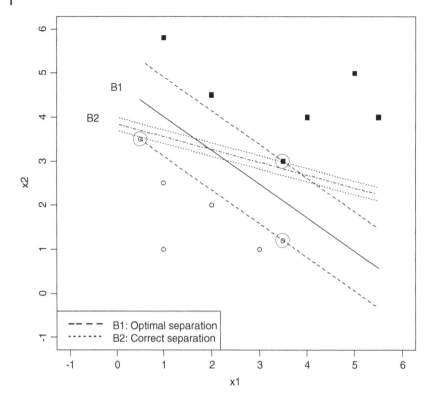

Figure 3.17 Correct separation (B2) and optimal separation (B1).

The margin, which is by definition the width of the corridor, is $2/\|a\|$ and must be maximized.

Given the points (x_i, y_i), with $y_i = 1$ if x_i is in A and $y_i = -1$ if x_i is in B, finding the optimal hyperplane $a * x + b = 0$ is equivalent to finding a pair (a, b) simultaneously satisfying the two conditions:

- for all i, $y_i(a * x_i + b) \geq 1$ (good separation);
- ½ $\|a\|^2$ is minimum (maximum margin).

This is a constrained optimization problem, whose solution provides an expression:

$$a = \sum_i \alpha_i y_i x_i$$

hence:

$$f(x) = \sum_i \alpha_i y_i(x * x_i) + b, \alpha_i \geq 0,$$

whose sign indicates the class to which the observation x should be assigned.

What is remarkable about this expression, which looks like a usual score function, is that the only non-zero coefficients α_i are those corresponding to points x_i that are exactly on the boundaries of the margin: the support vectors. In the example in Figure 3.17, these points are the ones that are circled. In other words, the optimal hyperplane depends only on the support vectors, the closest points. This is in contrast to linear discriminant analysis in which the distant points also influence the solution. This is generally considered to be favorable to the robustness of SVMs, insofar as the distant points can be outliers or in any case damaging to a good generalization capacity. This capacity is all the greater when the number of support points is small, since the model is then simpler, and we will be interested in the proportion of support points later.

In practice, when the two populations to be discriminated are not perfectly separated but overlap, some individuals fall inside the margin or are misclassified, i.e. fall on the wrong side outside the margin. To quantify the misclassification error, for each previous individual we measure the distance separating it from the margin boundary on the side of its class. We then normalize this distance by dividing it by the half-margin and obtain a term ξ_i, called the slack variable. An individual is inside the margin if $\xi_i \in]0, 1]$ and an "error" in the model is an individual for which $\xi_i > 1$. The sum of all ξ_i represents the set of classification errors. To the constraint of maximizing the margin is then simultaneously added a constraint of minimizing the sum of errors, and the hyperplane separating the classes must satisfy both conditions:

- for all i, $y_i(a * x_i + b) \geq 1 - \xi_i$;
- $\frac{1}{2} \|a\|^2 + C \sum_i \xi_i$ is minimum.

If $\xi_i > 0$, the condition $y_i(a * x_i + b) \geq 1 - \xi_i$ is a relaxation from the initial condition $y_i(a * x_i + b) \geq 1$. This occurs, not only for misclassified observations ($\xi_i > 1$), but also for those within the margin ($\xi_i \in]0, 1]$).

In the second condition, a cost parameter $C > 0$ is used to penalize errors and control the fit of the model. The larger C is, the greater the sensitivity to errors: the fit will also be greater. Because of the penalty for errors and individuals within the margin, a larger cost will decrease the width of the margin and the generalization ability of the model; but it will be more accurate on the training sample, with fewer classification errors. It is therefore necessary to choose C carefully to guarantee a good compromise between adjustment and robustness. This choice of C can be made by cross-validation or testing on another sample, as we will see later.

The solution of the previous problem admits the same form as in the separable case, with a separating hyperplane of equation $f(x) = 0$, where $f(x)$ is expressed as a function of score:

$$f(x) = \sum_i \alpha_i y_i(x * x_i) + b,$$

with the particularity that the coefficients α_i are all in $[0, C]$. The only non-zero α_i coefficients are those of the support points:

- the points x_i that are exactly on the boundaries of the margin, as in the separable case;
- points x_i misclassified or in the margin (points with variable slack > 0), in which case $\alpha_i = C$.

Even when the populations to be discriminated are relatively well separated, the separation may not be linear. One then seeks, by means of a non-linear transformation Φ, to pass from the original space into a space of greater dimension (possibly infinite) but endowed with a scalar product (the Hilbert space) and where a linear separation exists. The transformation example of Φ in Figure 3.18 shows how the change of space from a dimension 2 to a

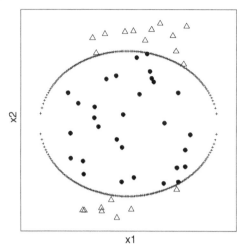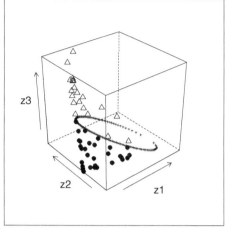

Figure 3.18 Example of transformation in an SVM: $\Phi(\vec{x}) = \left(x_1^2, \sqrt{2}x_1x_2, x_2^2 \right)$.

dimension 3 takes into account the non-linearity. The boundary ellipse is replaced by a hyperplane.

We have seen that the equation $f(x)$ of the separating hyperplane is expressed in terms of scalar products $x * x'$. After transformation by Φ, it is expressed in terms of scalar products $\Phi(x) * \Phi(x')$:

$$f(x) = \sum_i \alpha_i y_i \Phi(x) * \Phi(x_i)) + b.$$

The quantity $k(x, x') = \Phi(x) * \Phi(x')$ is called the *kernel*. In the algorithm, it is the kernel k and not Φ that is chosen, and if we do it correctly, we can compute $k(x, x')$ without showing Φ. The beauty of SVMs is to be able to express $f(\Phi(x))$ as a function of x without explicitly using Φ. The calculations are then done in the input space, and become much simpler and faster. For this reason, we speak of a *kernel machine*. Here are some examples of kernels:

- linear $k(x, x') = x * x'$; the simplest, used on large volumes of data, especially sparse tables as encountered in text mining;
- polynomial $k(x, x') = (x * x' + c)^d$, where d is the degree of the polynomial; this kernel is intuitive, used in image processing;
- $k(x, x') = e^{-\frac{\|x-x'\|^2}{2\sigma^2}}$; one of the most commonly used with the radial basis function kernel;
- radial basis function (RBF) $k(x, x') = e^{-\gamma \|x-x'\|^2}$, $\gamma \geq 0$;
- radial Laplacian $k(x, x') = e^{-\gamma \|x-x'\|}$, $\gamma \geq 0$; also of general interest;
- sigmoidal $k(x, x') = tanh(\gamma(x * x') + \theta)$, where γ is the gain and θ the threshold; and where we recognize the transfer function often used for the multilayer perceptron.

If we take the example of the polynomial kernel of degree 2 and the function

$$x = (x_1, x_2) \rightarrow \Phi(x) = \left(x_1^2, \sqrt{2}x_1x_2, x_2^2 \right),$$

we see that the scalar product $\Phi(x) * \Phi(x') = (x_1x_1' + x_2x_2')^2 = (x.x')^2$ is expressed in the feature space without showing Φ.

Depending on the choice of kernel, the computation time will be more or less important, but this choice also permits one to model various problems. This may explain the success of SVMs in domains, such as image, sound or natural language recognition, where the data have a particular shape to which a well-chosen kernel can be expected to adapt. One can note in the expression of the scalar product $\Phi(x) * \Phi(x')$ that the dimension of the feature space can increase rapidly, for example, with the degree in the case of a polynomial kernel, and that, contrary to a decision tree, for example, an SVM will not select any variable and will instead keep all the components of $\Phi(x) * \Phi(x')$. If the number of variables in the input space is important, it will be much more important in the feature space. This will be even more annoying if some of the variables are irrelevant and only bring noise, because the SVM will struggle to find a subspace of the feature space in which the separation is well done. In particular, if the class boundary is quadratic, a polynomial kernel of degree 2 will be appropriate, but a kernel of higher degree will have its classification error significantly increased.[32]

The SVMs initially dedicated to classification have been extended to regression. The basic principle is similar to that of SVM classification: minimize a penalized loss function, the penalty being the inverse of the square of the margin, and the loss function that can be in regression the "ε-insensitive" function, defined by:

$$\|y - f(x)\|_\varepsilon = \max(0, \|y - f(x)\| - \varepsilon).$$

The analogy with classification comes from the fact that it is equivalent to minimize

$$\left(\frac{1}{margin}\right)^2 + \frac{C}{2} \sum_i \xi_i$$

or to minimize

$$\left(\frac{1}{C}\right)\left(\frac{1}{margin}\right)^2 + \sum_i (1 - y_i f(x_i))_+,$$

where $(.)_+ = \max(0, .)$ is the "positive part" function. We have $(1 - y_i f(x_i))_+ = 0$ for the (x_i, y_i) such that $y_i f(x_i) > 1$, i.e. the points that are well ranked and outside the margin. The other points are the only ones involved in the classification and they are the support vectors. In regression, the only points that intervene are those that go out of the "tube" of width ε around the solution y; for the others we have $\|y - f(x)\|_\varepsilon = 0$. This regression method, called ε-regression, is the most common one for SVMs. It requires the setting of another parameter than the cost: the parameter ε sometimes set by default to 0.1. We have seen by the way that SVM and SVR are penalized methods, like the ridge and Lasso regressions.

3.6 Recommendation Systems

Recommendation (or recommender) systems cover several aspects, including the recommendation of friends, products (or contents) and routes.[33] In general, a recommender system is used when one wants to propose to agents (customers, visitors, drivers, patients) options (products, advertisements, job offers, itineraries, medical treatments) among sets of possible options, and when, in view of the result (purchase of the product, click or not on the advertisement, travel time, effect of the treatment), one wants to modify the subsequent proposals of options to improve the satisfaction of the agents. There is a difficulty of principle and a practical difficulty. The practical difficulty is the very large number of agents and options, which makes the computations very complex, even though they must often be performed quickly. The difficulty in principle is that we do not know what the result would have been if other options had been proposed. However, the agent concerned may have reacted to other options and other agents may have reacted to the same option, and it is then a question of seeing whether these other agents are close to the first, given the options already chosen. This idea is implemented in the collaborative filtering described below.

The recommendation of friends is practiced by social networks to recommend "friends" (contacts) to a person. We look for the vertices of the graph of this network (Section 5.3) having the most common friends with this person, assuming that the friends of my friends can probably be my friends.

The route recommendation consists in geolocating a visitor, following their route, proposing information related to their position and suggesting a visit according to the route already taken and the things to see.

Item recommendation has grown significantly with online commerce and consists of suggesting appropriate items and products to customers to maximize their likelihood of purchasing them.

One form of this recommendation consists in analyzing the navigation of an Internet user, their clicks until the "transformation," which can be a purchase, an appointment or simply a click on a banner on a website.

The most common form of item recommendation is collaborative filtering, which gets its name because the prediction for one person is made through the "collaboration" of other people: the preferences of the set of people are analyzed, either through observation (online purchases, downloads made, viewing time, opinions on social networks) or because they have been asked to rate items or provide a list of preferences, and the prediction of a person P's liking for an item A is made by examining the liking for that item of the set of people who are similar to person P. Those who have agreed so far should agree next.

In collaborative filtering, the data are presented in the form of a matrix of individuals x items, where the element of the ith row and the jth column indicates the presence/absence of purchase of the jth item by the ith individual, or the score attributed to this item by this individual. We obtain a matrix which is in practice very large but also very sparse, which causes computational problems. These problems can be accentuated when we want to take into account contextual elements, such as the day of the week, gender, or age. We then go from a matrix "individuals x items" to a higher-order tensor, for example, "individuals x items x days," which is even sparser.

The similarity of individuals can be measured in various ways, and in particular by the correlation coefficient of their rows in the "individuals x items" matrix: for two individuals, we calculate this correlation coefficient on the set of items rated by both of them. Once we have measured this similarity and constituted groups of individuals who are similar but have not bought exactly the same items, we aggregate their scores in order to identify individuals with a high score for an item they have not yet bought and that we will therefore propose to them.

Without even mentioning the possibilities of manipulation, or the case of atypical individuals, the three main difficulties of collaborative filtering are the "cold start," the volume of data and its sparsity. The cold start is due to the principle of the method, and to the fact that we cannot properly evaluate a new individual until they have rated a sufficient number of articles, nor a new article until they have received a sufficient number of ratings. The difficulty related to the volume of data is the need for a large computing power when analyzing millions of individuals and hundreds of thousands of articles. Finally, the sparseness of data comes from the fact that even the most active individuals rate only a very small proportion of articles, and even the most popular articles are rated by only a very small proportion of individuals. In such an empty space, as in interstellar space, nothing is close, and one recognizes in this situation the curse of dimensionality described in Section 1.5.1.

An efficient solution used to decrease the size and sparseness of the "individuals x articles" matrix is also used for the "terms x documents" matrix of the textual analysis, and this solution is described in more detail in Section 4.4.4. This is the latent semantic analysis, which consists in finding a low rank approximation of the "individuals x articles" matrix. We decrease the number of rows by replacing several rows with a linear combination if they correspond to similar items, and we move the rows and columns of the matrix to form high-density rectangles, meaning that individuals in the rows of a rectangle will frequently have the same opinions or ratings on items in the columns of the rectangle.

Another approach is content-based filtering, in which one does not predict the behavior of an individual by analyzing the behavior of other individuals, but by analyzing the characteristics of the items purchased by that individual to build a model that can be applied to other individuals and items.

Content-based filtering does not suffer from the difficulties faced by collaborative filtering, but in practice, there is benefit in combining the two, as in the Netflix example. The Netflix prize is one of the best-known examples of collaborative filtering algorithm research.[34] In 2006, Netflix offered a prize[35] of one million dollars to the team able to improve its recommendation system by 10%, i.e. to lower its mean square error by 10%. The task was to process 5 billion ratings (from 1 to 5 stars), of which 100 million were for training the model and 1.5 million for the public ranking. The prize was won in September 2009 by BellKor's Pragmatic Chaos team with a 10.06% decrease in error, but with a very complex result (104 models) and it was difficult to implement. Simpler models found in 2007 are still used: the Korbell team won an "intermediate" prize of $50,000 with an 8.43% decrease in error. The Netflix prize was then discontinued due to privacy concerns and a threat of class action, as Netflix users could be identified (see Section 1.6). The notoriety of this challenge comes from the fact that it was the first challenge of this type and importance (before Kaggle competitions), and from the fact that it triggered a lot of work on recommender systems.

Another well-known movie recommendation system is MovieLens, a non-commercial system created in 1997 and based on the work of the University of Minnesota's *GroupLens Research* laboratory. It is accessible to users of its website,[36] and makes available to the community different datasets, from the *MovieLens 25M Dataset* (25 million ratings applied to 62,000 movies by 162,000 users) to the *MovieLens 100K Dataset*, available online,[37] on Kaggle and in R packages like `recommenderlab`.

Notes

1 Hastie, T., Tibshirani, R., and Friedman, J. *The Elements of Statistical Learning: Data Mining, Inference and Prediction* (Heidelberg: Springer, 2009).

2 James, G., Witten, D., Hastie, T., and Tibshirani, R. *An Introduction to Statistical Learning, with Applications in R* (Heidelberg: Springer, 2021).

3 Saporta, G. Une brève histoire de l'apprentissage. In: M. Maumy-Bertrand, G. Saporta, and C. Thomas-Agnan (eds) *Apprentissage Statistique et Données Massives*, Journées d'Études en Statistique (Paris: Éditions Technip, 2018).

4 Domingos, P. and Hulten, G. Mining high-speed data streams. In: *Proceedings of KDD 2000* (New York: ACM Press, 2000), pp. 71–80.

5 Desai, S., Roy, S., Patel, B., Purandare, S., and Kucheria, M. Very Fast Decision Tree (VFDT) algorithm on Hadoop. Paper presented at 2016 International Conference on Computing Communication Control and automation (ICCUBEA) (2016), pp. 1–7.

6 Saffari, A., Leistner, C., Santner, J., Godec, M., and Bischof, H. On-line Random Forests. Paper presented at 3rd IEEE ICCV Workshop on On-line Computer Vision (2009).

7 Schmidt, M., Le Roux, N., and Bach, F. Minimizing Finite Sums with the Stochastic Average *Gradient* (2013). arXiv:1309.2388.

8 Ciarlet, P.G. *Introduction to Numerical Linear Algebra and Optimisation* (Cambridge: Cambridge University Press, 1989).

9 Hence the expression "conjugate gradient" since these vectors are conjugate to the gradient.

10 Nelder, J. A. and Mead, R. A Simplex Method for Function Minimization. *Computer Journal*, 7 (4) (1965), 308–313.

11 Holland, J.H. *Adaptation in Natural and Artificial Systems* (Ann Arbor, MI: University of Michigan Press, 1975).

12 See a more complete presentation in Tufféry, S. *Modélisation prédictive et Apprentissage statistique avec R* (Paris: Éditions Technip, 2017).

13 Saporta, G. *Probabilités, analyse des données et statistique* (Paris: Éditions Technip, 2011), 3rd edition, Section 17.5.3.

14 Frank, I. and Friedman, J. A Statistical View of Some Chemometrics Regression Tools (with Discussion). *Technometrics*, 35(2) (1993), 109–148.

15 Breiman, L. Bagging Predictors. *Machine Learning*, 26(2) (1996), 123–140.

16 Breiman, L. Random Forests. *Machine Learning*, 45 (2001), 5–32.

17 Geurts, P., Ernst, D., and Wehenkel, L. Extremely Randomized Trees. *Machine Learning*, 63(1) (2006), 3–42.

18 Freund, Y. and Schapire, R.E. A Decision-Theoretic Generalization of Online Learning and an Application to Boosting. *Journal of Computer and System Sciences*, 55(1) (1997), 119–139.

19 Schapire, R.E. and Freund, Y. *Boosting: Foundations and Algorithms* (Cambridge, MA: MIT Press, 2012).

20 http://videolectures.net/mlss05us_schapire_b/.

21 Freund and Schapire (1997), op. cit.

22 In Breiman's x-4 arcing, at each iteration, the weighting of each observation does not depend on the overall weighted error rate, but is equal (up to normalization) to $1 + m(i)^4$, where $m(i)$ is the number of classification errors of that ith observation in all previous iterations. Furthermore, there is no final weighting of the models.

23 Friedman, J., Hastie, T., and Tibshirani, R. Additive Logistic Regression: A Statistical View of Boosting (with discussion). *Annals of Statistics*, 28 (2000), 337–407.

24 Ibid.

25 Friedman, J.H. Greedy Function Approximation: A Gradient Boosting Machine. *Annals of Statistics* (2001), 1189–1232.

26 Friedman, J. Stochastic Gradient Boosting. *Computational Statistics & Data Analysis,* 38 (2002), 367–378.

27 Chen, T. and Guestrin, C. XGBoost: A Scalable Tree Boosting System. In: *KDD '16: Proceedings of the 22nd ACM SIGKDD International Conference on Knowledge Discovery and Data Mining*, (2016), pp. 785–794, arXiv:1603.02754.

28 Dorogush, A.V., Ershov, V., and Gulin, A. CatBoost: Gradient Boosting with Categorical Features Support (2018). arXiv:1810.11363v1.

29 Prokhorenkova, L., Gusev, G., Vorobev, A., Dorogush, A.V., and Gulin, A. CatBoost: Unbiased Boosting with Categorical Features (2019). arXiv:1706.09516v5.

30 Ke, G. *et al.* LightGBM: A Highly Efficient Gradient Boosting Decision Tree, *Advances in Neural Information Processing Systems*, 30 (NIPS 2017): 3149–3157. http://papers.nips.cc/paper/6907-lightgbm-a-highly-efficient-gradient-boosting-decision.

31 https://lightgbm.readthedocs.io/en/latest/.

32 Hastie, T., Tibshirani, R., and Friedman, J.H. *The Elements of Statistical Learning* (Heidelberg: Springer Verlag, 2009), 2nd edition, Section 12.3.4.

33 One can read E. Viennet *et al.* Systèmes de recommandation sociaux. In: M. Maumy-Bertrand, G. Saporta, and C. Thomas-Agnan (eds.). *Apprentissage Statistique et Données Massives*, Journées d'Études en Statistique (Paris: Éditions Technip, 2018) This overview proposes a unifying framework for the different methods presented, based on the bipartite graph of users and items, under the name of "social filtering." See also: F. Fogelman-Soulié *et al.*, Recommender Systems and Attributed Networks. In: E. Diday, R. Guan, G. Saporta, and H. Wang (eds.). *Advances in Data Science* (Hoboken, NJ: Wiley, 2020).

34 Bennett, J. and Lanning, S. The Netflix Prize. In: *Proceedings of KDD Cup and Workshop* (2007), 35.

35 http://www.netflixprize.com/

36 https://movielens.org/.

37 https://grouplens.org/datasets/movielens/.

4

Natural Language Processing

Natural language processing is the application of linguistics, statistical analysis, machine learning, and deep learning to create algorithms capable of analysing and interpreting text or spoken words in natural human language, in order to solve particular problems or perform specific tasks, or eventually to provide results or answers in natural language. It began in the early twentieth century with the work on lexical statistics of Jean-Baptiste Estoup and George Kingsley Zipf, which was followed by researchers, such as Benoît Mandelbrot, George Udny Yule, Pierre Guiraud, Charles Muller, Gustav Herdan, Maurice Tournier, Pierre Lafon, Etienne Brunet, André Salem, and Ludovic Lebart. Text data analysis developed a lot in the 1960s and 1970s and then gave birth to text mining, at the time when data mining commenced. In recent years, text mining has become a branch of Natural Language Processing (NLP). The latter goes beyond the framework of text mining because it is interested in writing but also in speech. Speech, of course, poses specific and complex problems. Natural Language Processing is a vast discipline, which also includes the inverse operations of the previous ones: Natural Language Generation and Text-to-Speech. In this chapter, we will focus on the analysis of textual data, illustrated by examples treated with the software R, which will be used to manipulate texts and strings, to transform them by word embedding methods and to analyse them by supervised and unsupervised statistical and machine learning methods. We will also discuss methods of topic modeling and sentiment analysis.

4.1   From Lexical Statistics to Natural Language Processing

The first analyses of word frequencies can be found in the work of the psychologist Benjamin Bourdon,[1] but these analyses really developed with the work of Estoup[2] and Zipf.[3] The study of the frequency of an occurrence of a word in a text gave rise to Zipf's very interesting law, which links the frequency of a word to its rank in the frequency table. The example of James Joyce's *Ulysses* is famous: the 10th word appears 2653 times, the 100th word 265 times, the 1000th word 266 times and the 10000th word twice. This reflects the fact that the product of rank r and frequency f is approximately constant:

$$r \times f = \text{constant}.$$

This law is not valid in all contexts with the same precision, and it has been generalized by replacing r by r^a (a being an exponent depending on the language and the type of

Deep Learning: From Big Data to Artificial Intelligence with R, First Edition. Stéphane Tufféry.
© 2023 John Wiley & Sons Ltd. Published 2023 by John Wiley & Sons Ltd.
Companion website: www.wiley.com/go/Tuffery/DeepLearning

speaker), but it is universal, because it applies to all types of texts in all languages, and it even applies to other "rank-size" problems: the rank of cities in a country related to their size, the rank of companies related to their turnover, the rank of individuals related to their incomes, etc.

Lexical statistics (synonyms: "linguistic statistics," "quantitative linguistics," "lexicometrics") developed with the description and characterization of vocabulary in texts and corpora, and experienced a great expansion in the 1960s and 1970s when it came closer to the multidimensional analysis developed by the school of Jean-Paul Benzécri, helped by the emergence of computer tools, to allow a true analysis of textual data. At that time, two main sources of study emerged: on the one hand, corpora made up of a few rather long documents; on the other, corpora made up of short and numerous documents, possibly accompanied by complementary variables for each document.

Among the former, we find political speeches (those of presidents are a great classic of textual analysis, on both sides of the Atlantic), and we also find literary works (more often novels than poems), which stylometry studies in order to identify an author, to characterize his vocabulary and style, or to date a work, or to follow the semantic and stylistic evolution of a corpus through space and time. These studies are part of the *digital humanities*.

In the second type of corpus, we find the answers to open-ended questions in opinion surveys, and also, more recently, emails, messages, and other tweets. Their complementary variables can be metadata on the texts themselves (structure, date) or socio-demographic variables on their speakers.

Text mining, or textual data mining, is interested in this second type of corpus. It appeared in the 1980s to automatically process textual data in natural language in ever-increasing quantities. The perspective here is that of a synthetic and non-literary view of the text, of the discovery of hidden information and topics (themes) or of automatic decision-making. Text mining differs from stylometry in that it is not interested in the text for its own sake, but rather in the useful information it can extract from it. It relies particularly on the graphical form extracted from raw texts, on the one hand, because it seems unbiased and not linked to any presuppositions about the texts, and, on the other, because this extraction can be automated quite well. This extraction is accompanied by a simplification of the lexicon by various operations that we will see later.

If text mining has its roots and some of its methods in lexical statistics, it owes its development, on the one hand, to the enormous volume of textual data created and disseminated in our society (laws, decrees, regulations, contracts, emails, tweets, SMS), and, on the other, to the widespread computerized capture and storage of these data (which are moreover increasingly directly produced in electronic format), and finally to the development of exceptionally powerful tools in statistics, multidimensional data analysis, machine learning, and lately in deep learning and artificial intelligence.

The notion of *natural language processing* tends to subsume all textual data analysis, whereas it obviously originates from the aim to automate linguistic tasks using a computer tool, which obeys more utilitarian than scientific considerations, and therefore does not cover all aspects of textual data analysis. It must be said that the development of the Internet, social media, and connected objects (voice assistants) has created a huge mass of multilingual language data, which for one reason or another (intelligence, politics, marketing) we wish to analyse as quickly as possible. This has led to the expansion of natural language processing, especially since its scope includes not only written but also oral data, and can be combined with images.

Natural language processing can be based on symbolic or statistical methods. The former require a lot of work, because they involve lexical and morphosyntactic analysis, named entity recognition (Section 4.3.5) and coreference resolution (Section 4.3.6), in order to recognize the constituents of the text (sentences, words), their nature and their relations. It also requires knowledge of domain-specific vocabulary.

Statistical methods are based on quantitative analyses which have developed a lot in the last few years, due to the availability of ever larger and more varied text data sets. With the contribution of machine learning, word embedding methods (Section 4.4) and deep neural networks (Chapter 9), today statistical methods can achieve high performance, in tasks as diverse as classification, annotation, and translation of documents, faster and with a higher level of automation than rule-based symbolic methods.

4.2 Uses of Text Mining and Natural Language Processing

The main sources of textual data are emails, job applications, business or medical interview reports, news agency dispatches, documentation and expert reports, the Internet and online databases, historical archives, and more recently speech transcripts from videos or telephone conversations, social networks, blogs, micro-blogs, and SMS.

There are two types of methods in textual data analysis. *Descriptive methods* allow the identification of the topics (themes) addressed in a set of documents, without knowing these topics in advance. *Predictive methods* look for rules that allow a document to be automatically assigned to a category of documents, among several predefined categories, as we do, for example, to detect spam or automatically direct an email or a résumé to the appropriate department.

Specifically, descriptive methods are used to discover hidden information, detecting emerging trends in social media, analysing medical test reports, searching for case-related legislation or case law, detecting plagiarism, or searching for fraud in claims.

Predictive methods are used for decision-making, illustrated by the automatic routing of mail and calls to technical or commercial support, email filtering, information filtering, and news filtering.

One of the most advanced uses of natural language processing is machine translation (and computer-assisted translation), which, after a difficult start, has made significant progress in recent years, thanks in particular to recurrent neural networks (Section 7.16) and transformer models (Section 9.7). It is now possible to instantly translate speech from one language into another. Another very common application of NLP is spelling and grammar correction, as well as autocorrection or autocompletion of text in word processing applications and Internet search engines. We can also mention conversational agents, or chatbots, which allow dialogues between humans and machines and which are increasingly used in commercial or technical customer support. They are becoming so fluid that machines are beginning to pass the Turing test (Section 10.1). We are touching here on speech recognition and its reverse operation, speech synthesis, of which we can see demonstrations on the DeepMind website,[4] whose convolutional network WaveNet can speak with a perfect human voice. Some banks are starting to offer voicebots that allow a customer to consult his accounts or make a transfer, operations that he triggers by voice using an assistant like Google Home. Among others, Lyrebird (a bird capable of imitating many sounds), a start-up founded by three PhD students at the University of Montréal, has developed a text-to-speech solution capable of imitating a person's voice with a given emotion. Less than a minute of audio recording of a person is enough to generate an imitation of their voice of such quality that it could fool those who hear it. This obviously raises serious questions about the risks of manipulation, fraud and fake news. This can also have an effect on the job of voice actor in the cinema.

Deep learning is beginning to be successfully applied to source discrimination in speech recognition in the presence of multiple sound sources. Cochlear implants have benefited from recent advances allowing them to amplify only useful sounds and not background noise.

Text and image data can be matched, when images or pictures are placed in the middle of text, and text and image identification can be improved by performing them simultaneously. Deep neural networks can also recognize images and describe them through automatic text generation (Section 7.16).

4.3 The Operations of Textual Analysis

This section describes the various lexical analyses that are often performed to categorize documents or to detect the topics contained in a set of documents. We will call this set of documents a corpus, without giving this term the rigorous definition of Sinclair[5] for whom a corpus "is a collection of language data that are selected and organized according to explicit linguistic criteria to serve as a sample of language." For us, a corpus will not aim at being representative of a sample, which should perfectly represent a language, a type of work or a field of specialization. A corpus will be a collection of texts obtained more pragmatically than scientifically, simply because they are available and we want to exploit them, with an operational rather than a knowledge purpose.

These analyses go through a series of operations: tokenization, part-of-speech tagging, named entity recognition, coreference resolution, and lemmatization or stemming. These operations are required to make text data accessible to an algorithm. They consist in cutting out units in the textual chain, the lexical entities which are the sequences of non-separating characters, then grouping them together by identifying compound words, locutions, equivalent terms, in order to represent the corpus in the form of a matrix crossing the documents (in rows) and the terms or lexical entities (in columns). We will see in Section 4.4 that such a representation can apply classical statistical and factorial analyses, or more recent machine learning methods (Bayesian classifier, gradient boosting, support vector machines, etc.) to this matrix. This matrix representation is sometimes replaced by a more elaborate vector representation, such as Word2Vec embedding, taking into account the semantic relations between words.

This method of content analysis is implemented in many commercial and especially free software. We can quote the commercial software SPAD.T (Système Portable pour l'Analyse des Données Textuelles = Portable System for Text Data Analysis) and the academic software Dtm-Vic of Ludovic Lebart,[6] a specialist who also was involved in the origin of SPAD.T. These analyses are also available in many Python and R packages,[7] and, in particular, the `tm` package by Ingo Feinerer, which is the "historical" package for creating, manipulating, and analysing text corpora. This package has been integrated, with some others (like `ca` for correspondence analysis) in the `R.TeMiS` (R Text Mining Solution) package by Milan Bouchet-Valat and Gilles Bastin,[8] which benefits from the graphical environment of *R Commander* and forms a complete text mining suite. We will also show `quanteda` and `cleanNLP` packages in action. For Python, the `NLTK` (Natural Language ToolKit) library is the best known and is very complete, including for the number of languages processed. The `spaCy` library is increasingly being used because it is fast and is regularly enriched to the point today of allowing the use of transformer models, such as BERT (Section 9.7). The `gensim` library has functions for word embedding, topic modeling (latent semantic analysis, latent Dirichlet allocation), and deep learning. The `Polyglot` and `Pattern` Python libraries can also be mentioned.

4.3.1 Textual Data Collection

Extracting textual data requires the ability to deal with various data formats, and is not trivial in some cases, such as web data analysis, where text has to be extracted in the middle of other components of a web page (HTML markup, JavaScript scripts). The extraction of the content of a web site is done using *web scraping* techniques.

It is important to know how to use the information contained in this metadata, such as hyperlinks that can help to structure the documents between them, to link them and to represent them in graphs. Words in titles can be overweighted in some analyses compared to other words, and hashtags are useful for social network analysis. Before deleting special characters, it is necessary to check that they do not refine the analysis, such as emoticons (smileys) for opinion detection or sentiment analysis.

Blogs and micro-blogs such as Twitter have become an important source of data, but they can also come from more traditional TXT, CSV, or XML files.

In all cases, it is often necessary to perform an initial formatting of the text by eliminating certain special characters, line breaks or useless spaces, punctuation marks, and possibly by lower-casing all capitalized characters. Several R packages store the textual data in an internal "corpus" structure to which they then apply a whole set of transformations and operations, such as those described in the following sections.

4.3.2 Identification of the Language

The Web, among other things, requires multilingualism to be managed, sometimes within the same document. Some software systems, such as R and its package `koRpus`, are able to automatically detect the language of a text. The `textcat` package is very efficient in this task: based on the work of Cavnar and Trenkle,[9] it calculates the frequency of n-grams of characters in the analysed text, which it compares to a database of 74 languages. A character n-gram is a sequence of *n* contiguous characters in a word. For example, the 2-grams (bigrams) of "word" are "_w," "wo," "or," "rd" and "d_."

```
> library(textcat)
> textcat(c("This is an English sentence.", "Das ist ein
    deutscher Satz.", "Esta es una frase en español.", "C'est
    une phrase en français.", "E' una frase in italiano."))
[1] "english" "german" "spanish" "french" "italian"
```

Another package, `franc`, has the additional advantage of allowing one to limit the search to certain languages or to exclude certain languages from the search, either on the basis of a list of languages or on the basis of a minimum number of speakers.

```
> sapply(c("This is an English sentence.", "Das ist ein
   deutscher Satz.", "Esta es una frase en español.", "C'est
   une phrase en français.", "E' una frase in italiano."), franc)
 This is an English sentence.    Das ist ein deutscher Satz.
                     "eng"                            "deu"
Esta es una frase en español. C'est une phrase en français.
                     "spa"                            "fra"
    E' una frase in italiano.
                     "ita"
```

4.3.3 Tokenization

Tokenization, or segmentation into primary lexical entities, consists in dividing the text into smaller units: paragraphs, sentences or terms most often, but also characters, or units separated by particular signs. This segmentation is not trivial, because it requires in particular to have identified the compound words to separate the terms, and to have located the limits of sentences. These can be separated by punctuation marks such as the dot, but a dot can also follow an abbreviation or an acronym, or be a decimal separator in Anglo-Saxon notation, and therefore is not to be taken into account for tokenization. It is also necessary to manage the contracted forms of the English language ("I'm"). As for compound words, they can be separated by a space, by a hyphen or pasted. We can see that it is better to have identified the language before proceeding with this segmentation, and also to possibly use a lexicon containing specialized terms. We are not talking about languages like Chinese or Japanese in which words are not separated by space character, which makes tokenization particularly difficult. Several R packages have tokenization functions, such as `tokenizers`, `tm` and `quanteda`, and for Python we can mention the NLTK library.

The previous "tokens" (characters, words) are 1-grams, which can be generalized into n-grams, i.e. sequences of n consecutive tokens. The character n-grams mentioned in Section 4.3.2 are tools for the user of a smartphone or a search engine whose auto-completion suggests the end of a word input. Word n-grams allow a much more subtle analysis of texts than just words, taking into account negations ("doesn't like," "isn't happy") and more generally the context surrounding the words.

The tools of tokenization are often enriched with functions of extractions of the n-grams. It is possible to keep all signs (letters, numbers, punctuation marks) or to exclude some of them.

Here is an example of segmentation obtained with the `quanteda` package (Section 4.4.2) and its `tokens()` function.

```
> text <- "To be or not to be, that is the question."
```

We will start with the tokenization in words, keeping all signs.

```
> tokens(text)
tokens from 1 document.
text1 :
 [1] "To"        "be"        "or"       "not"      "to"        "be"
 [7] ","         "that"      "is"       "the"      "question" "."
```

And now the search for word digrams, eliminating punctuation marks:

```
> tokens_ngrams(tokens(text, remove_punct = TRUE), n = 2)
Tokens consisting of 1 document.
text1 :
 [1] "To_be"         "be_or"        "or_not"        "not_to"
 [5] "to_be"         "be_that"      "that_is"       "is_the"
 [9] "the_question"
```

Skip-grams are a more subtle way of taking into account the context surrounding words. The n-grams are formed by association of n adjacent tokens: they are 0-skip-n-grams. They generalize into k-skip-n-grams which are formed by association of n tokens each separated by k tokens. Thus, in a 1-skip-gram we take only one word out of two. Skip-grams can detect associations of words that are neighbors without being strictly adjacent. The `tokens_ngrams()` function of the `quanteda` package can generate simultaneously 0-skip-grams, 1-skip-grams, etc.

```
> tokens_ngrams(tokens(text, remove_punct = TRUE), n = 2,
    skip = 0:1, concatenator = " ")
Tokens consisting of 1 document.
text1 :
 [1] "To be"    "To or"    "be or"    "be not"   "or not"   "or to"
     "not to"
 [8] "not be"   "to be"    "to that"  "be that"  "be is"
[ ... and 5 more ]
```

The question also arises of dividing the corpus into documents, which are to the corpus what observations are to the sample. If it is not naturally divided into documents, such as emails, tweets, or answers to a questionnaire, the corpus can simply be divided into paragraphs, each paragraph becoming a document.

4.3.4 Part-of-Speech Tagging

Part-of-speech tagging (POS tagging is the identification of the grammatical nature of words in a text: nouns, verbs, adjectives, articles, pronouns, adverbs, etc. It can look for additional information such as gender and number for a noun or adjective, or mode and tense for a verb, distinguish proper nouns from common nouns, so that several dozen grammatical categories can be commonly distinguished. The number of categories is even greater for highly inflected languages such as ancient Greek or Latin, but the number of inflections in a language tends to decrease over time. In agglutinative languages, such as Turkish, suffixes that agglutinate with each other make part-of-speech tagging very difficult.

The general difficulty of part-of-speech tagging is that the same word can have several homographs of different natures, but one can try to remedy this by performing a grammatical analysis of the nearby context, relying on the fact that there are more or less frequent grammatical constructions.

First, simple rules can be applied. For example, in English or French, if a word that is not at the beginning of a sentence is capitalized, it is probably a proper noun. In English, if a word ends in "ment," it is a common noun.

Grammatical tagging is also often done by taking into account the probability of occurrence of a form: in French, "permissions" is more likely to be a noun than the imperfect subjunctive of the verb "permettre," especially in a recent text. In English, "dog" is more likely to be a noun than a verb. This probability is calculated on the basis of a reference corpus already tagged or a tagged training corpus more directly related to the analysis performed. For the English language, the first reference was in 1967 the Brown corpus, or the Brown University Standard Corpus of Present-Day American English, with its 500 texts of various genres, each listed with 2000 words, for a total of one million words, all tagged for many years. More recently, the British National Corpus has 100 million words in written (90% of the corpus) or spoken (10%) British English.

A more elaborate method consists in taking into account the probability of occurrence of a sequence of two or three tags. This probability can be calculated on a corpus or determined by machine learning, but we can also use grammatical rules indicating that certain grammatical constructions are obligatory or, on the contrary, forbidden. In the latter case, the probability of the sequence will be zero.

Examples of grammatical rules include:

- the indefinite article is not used before an adverb if there is no adjective after the adverb:
  - the house gets its water from a well (adv. or n.) → noun,
- a word between an article and a common noun is an adjective,
- the indefinite article is not used before a verb:
  - I need a tire (v. or n.) for my car → noun,
- no noun after a pronoun:
  - we rose (v. or n.) early → verb.

Between the sequences of probability 0 or 1 provided by grammatical rules, the analysis can assign intermediate probabilities to sequences: for example, the word following an article has a probability 0.4 of being a noun, a probability 0.3 of being an adjective, etc.

An even more accurate method is to calculate the probability that a given sequence of words corresponds to a sequence of grammatical tags.

One difficulty with these approaches is that they require tagged corpora, which are not always available for certain types of texts. Moreover, some tags or sequences of tags may exist but are rare and absent from the corpus, which could lead to the false belief that their probability is zero.

Another difficulty, concerning the rules of grammatical form sequences, is that they are based on the analysis of close words, which must themselves be analysed, which thus requires a cascade analysis. Here is an example of pronoun recognition in French: "je le sens → verbe" where the ambiguity of "le" (pronoun or article) is removed by the pronoun "je."

An additional difficulty arises when a text contains words belonging to several languages, which are sometimes just labelled as "foreign word."

We see that part-of-speech tagging often requires a delicate disambiguation. Nevertheless, the best taggers achieve an accuracy of 97%, a value that seems difficult to exceed today. Some labellers choose not to resolve all ambiguities and to indicate if a word is a noun or a verb, a noun or an adjective, etc.

The oldest (1994) and one of the best-known part-of-speech taggers is Helmut Schmid's "TreeTagger,"[10] which performs part-of-speech tagging in more than fifteen languages (English, German, French, Italian, Spanish, Russian, etc.) and is used in Dtm-Vic and the `koRpus` package of R. TreeTagger can be used on its own, but it does not have a built-in graphical interface other than the one developed by Ciarán Ó Duibhín for Windows.[11] We have to provide it with texts in UTF-8 format. We give an example of how it works in Section 4.3.7 on lemmatization.

Another example is the Stanford Tagger[12] (2003), trained on the Penn Treebank corpus.[13] This corpus was compiled between 1989 and 1996 and consists of 7 million words in American English from *Wall Street Journal* articles, computer manuals, transcripts of telephone conversations, and other sources. This corpus was grammatically tagged into 36 POS tags and 12 tags for punctuation and currency symbols, initially automatically before being verified by human annotators. The Penn Treebank is often used because of its high reliability.

4.3.5 Named Entity Recognition

A named entity is an expression referring to a specific and unique entity: person, organization, place, date. Document analysis should recognize that expressions such as "June 6, 1944," "His Holiness," and "the Wars of the Roses" are groups of words referring to a date, a person, and an event. In the following, we will use the term "term" to refer to both such a sequence of graphic forms or a graphic form of length 1 (a "word").

The recognition of named entities is a complex operation, which must be based both on a grammatical analysis and on the use of a dictionary, or even a specialized lexicon of the field studied, because a good analysis must be based on the knowledge of idiomatic expressions. It is useful for extracting information from documentary corpora, which aims at automatically feeding structured databases with natural language data. It can also be used to detect personal data in texts in order to anonymize them: first names can thus be replaced by other first names.

The `cleanNLP` and `spacyr` R packages have named entity recognition features. We will illustrate this with the first lines of *Pride and Prejudice* (1813) by Jane Austen.

It is a truth universally acknowledged, that a single man in possession of a good fortune, must be in want of a wife.

However little known the feelings or views of such a man may be on his first entering a neighbourhood, this truth is so well fixed in the minds of the surrounding families, that he is considered the rightful property of some one or other of their daughters.

"My dear Mr. Bennet," said his lady to him one day, "have you heard that Netherfield Park is let at last?"

Mr. Bennet replied that he had not.

"But it is," returned she; "for Mrs. Long has just been here, and she told me all about it."

Mr. Bennet made no answer.

"Do you not want to know who has taken it?" cried his wife impatiently.

"You want to tell me, and I have no objection to hearing it."

The `cleanNLP` package is all the more complete because it is based on several NLP backends. The richest is the CoreNLP library from Stanford.[14] However, it is not the fastest, and it requires a Java environment (and the `rJava` package) and the prior installation of the NLP library files, including large *jar* files. This installation can be done in the following ways:

- by download;[15]
- or by running in R the command `cnlp_download_corenlp()` (or the command `cnlp_download_corenlp(lang="xx")` to use a language xx other than English).

In both cases, a compressed file is downloaded. It must then be unzipped in the R directory of the `cleanNLP` package (for example, "C:\Users\tuffery\Documents\R\win-library\4.0\cleanNLP\extdata" which the `cnlp_download_corenlp()` command does automatically.

If you want to manipulate another language than English, you have to download a Java file such as "stanford-english-corenlp-2016-10-31-models.jar," either at https://stanfordnlp.github.io/CoreNLP/download.html to have the latest version, or at https://stanfordnlp.github.io/CoreNLP/history.html to choose an older version (if you are not using the most recent version of R).

To specify the use of the CoreNLP library, call the `cnlp_init_corenlp()` function.

Another available backend is the `spaCy` package of Python, which must be installed before its first use. In the `cleanNLP` package, this installation can be done using the function `cnlp_download_spacy(model_name = "en")`. To use it, we then call each time the `cnlp_init_spacy()` function.

The Python package `spaCy` can also be installed and used via the R package `spacyr`, which creates a specific conda environment named `spacy_condaenv`. The English language model `en_core_web_sm` is installed. This installation of the `spacyr` package does not allow the use of the `spaCy` backend with `cleanNLP`. If we rely on an existing installation of Python, we have to indicate its location:

```
> spacy_install(conda =
    "C:/Users/<name>/Miniconda3/Library/bin")
```

In this case, the path to the spaCy environment will be:

```
> spacy_install(conda = "D:/anaconda3/envs/spacy_condaenv")
```

The spaCy package has a good function for named entity recognition and a good lemmatizer, also in French, which can be used after downloading the corresponding language model:

```
> spacy_download_langmodel(model="fr_core_news_sm",
    conda="D:/anaconda3/Library/bin")
```

Each time we use the `spacyr` package, we have to execute the `spacy_initialize()` function which detects and initializes the Python `spaCy` library. We may need to specify the path to the conda environment of `spaCy` if there are several installations of Python on the machine. If we use a language model other than the English one installed by default

Table 4.1 Comparison of parsing features.

	POS lemmatization	Named entity recognition	Extraction of dependencies	Coreference resolution	Sentiment analysis	fastText embedding
CoreNLP	x	x	x	x	x	
spaCy	x	x	x			x
Udpipe	x		x			

with spaCy, we have to specify it after downloading it. Here is how we would specify both the conda environment and the use of the French language model:

```
> spacy_initialize(model = "fr_core_news_sm",
    condaenv="D:/anaconda3/envs/spacy_condaenv")
```

Not all the features of the Python package are included in R, such as its convolutional neural network document classifier.

By specifying `cnlp_init_udpipe()` we use the R package udpipe (to be installed beforehand), whose installation is faster and simpler than the two previous backends, since Udpipe has no external dependencies and does not require installing anything other than a 16-megabyte dictionary.

To complete the process, a final backend is integrated by default in the `cleanNLP` package, which relies on the `tokenizers` package but only allows tokenization and not the more elaborate operations of the other backends.

All these backends do not have the same functionality (Table 4.1) and only coreNLP offers analysis in languages other than English. The language is therefore the first parameter of the `cnlp_init_corenlp()` function.

```
> library(cleanNLP)
> cnlp_init_corenlp("en", anno_level = 2,
    lib_location = NULL, mem = "4g", verbose = FALSE)
Loading required namespace: rJava
> txt <- c(" It is a truth universally acknowledged,
    that a single man in possession of a good fortune, must
    be in want of a wife.
...
+ 'You want to tell me, and I have no objection to hearing
    it.'")
```

The `cnlp_init_corenlp()` function also indicates the location of the directory containing the backend on the machine (NULL if it is the one for the default R installation), the memory used, and the level of these analyses (anno). When this last parameter is 0, only tokenization, part-of-speech tagging, and lemmatization are performed, when it is 1, dependencies are searched and sentiment analysis is performed, for anno = 2 named entities are searched, and for anno = 3 coreferences (Section 4.3.6) are searched. The computation time is obviously greater when the analyses are numerous and it can become considerable on a vast corpus. In all cases, we must start by "annotating" the text.

```
> annotation <- cnlp_annotate(txt)
```

Once this is done, we can obtain a lot of information about the text, provided in several data frames, one for each of the analyses mentioned in Table 4.1. These data frames identify sentences by their *sid* identifier ("s" for "sentence") and words by their *tid* identifier ("t" for "token").

The first data frame contains the words of the text, with their grammatical nature and their lemmatized form.

```
> cnlp_get_token(annotation)
       id sid tid          word        lemma upos  pos cid
2    doc1   1   1            It           it PRON  PRP   1
3    doc1   1   2            is           be VERB  VBZ   4
4    doc1   1   3             a            a  DET   DT   7
5    doc1   1   4         truth        truth NOUN   NN   9
6    doc1   1   5   universally  universally  ADV   RB  15
7    doc1   1   6  acknowledged  acknowledge VERB  VBD  27
8    doc1   1   7             ,            ,    .    ,  39
9    doc1   1   8          that         that  ADP   IN  41
10   doc1   1   9             a            a  DET   DT  46
11   doc1   1  10        single       single  ADJ   JJ  48
12   doc1   1  11           man          man NOUN   NN  55
13   doc1   1  12            in           in  ADP   IN  59
14   doc1   1  13    possession   possession NOUN   NN  62
15   doc1   1  14            of           of  ADP   IN  73
16   doc1   1  15             a            a  DET   DT  76
17   doc1   1  16          good         good  ADJ   JJ  78
18   doc1   1  17       fortune      fortune NOUN   NN  83
19   doc1   1  18             ,            ,    .    ,  90
20   doc1   1  19          must         must VERB   MD  92
21   doc1   1  20            be           be VERB   VB  97
22   doc1   1  21            in           in  ADP   IN 100
23   doc1   1  22          want         want VERB   VB 103
24   doc1   1  23            of           of  ADP   IN 108
25   doc1   1  24             a            a  DET   DT 111
26   doc1   1  25          wife         wife NOUN   NN 113
...
```

Another data frame contains the named entities. We identify people, places, durations, sometimes events or dates...

```
> cnlp_get_entity(annotation)
      id sid tid tid_end entity_type           entity entity_normalized
1 doc1   1  16      16      ORDINAL            first               1.0
2 doc1   1  44      44       NUMBER              one               1.0
3 doc1   2   4       4       PERSON           Bennet
4 doc1   2  11      12     DURATION          one day               P1D
5 doc1   2  18      19     LOCATION Netherfield Park
6 doc1   3   2       2       PERSON           Bennet
7 doc1   4  10      10       PERSON             Long
8 doc1   5   2       2       PERSON           Bennet
```

Another data frame describes the dependencies, i.e. the syntactic relations between the words. We see that between words 3 ("a") and 4 ("truth") there is a determiner relation, that between words 2 ("is") and 4 ("truth") there is a copula verb relation ("attributive"), that between words 5 ("universally") and 6 ("acknowledged") there is a modifier adverb relation, and that between words 10 ("single") and 11 ("man") there is an adjectival relation (*amod*: adjectival modifier).

```
> cnlp_get_dependency(annotation))
      id sid tid tid_target  relation relation_full
1    doc1   1   0           4      root          root
2    doc1   1   4           1     nsubj         nsubj
3    doc1   1   4           2       cop           cop
4    doc1   1   4           3       det           det
5    doc1   1   6           5    advmod        advmod
6    doc1   1   4           6       acl           acl
7    doc1   1   4           7     punct         punct
8    doc1   1  22           8      mark          mark
9    doc1   1  11           9       det           det
10   doc1   1  11          10      amod          amod
```

A data frame contains the coreferences described in Section 4.3.6.

One operation is only possible with the spaCy backend: the fastText vector embedding (Section 4.4.9) which consists of representing each word by its coordinates in a vector space, this representation having the very useful property of making words be neighbors in the vector space when they have a close meaning or are used in the same contexts. But a simpler embedding is possible with the other backends: the transformation of the text into a document-term matrix with different weights such as TF-IDF (Section 4.4.3). It is sufficient to use the `cnlp_get_tfidf()` function.

Finally, the `cnlp_get_sentence()` function specific to the coreNLP backend assigns a sentiment score to each sentence, which detects the tonality of the sentence and is equal to 0 (very negative), 1 (negative), 2 (neutral), 3 (positive) or 4 (very positive). We will see in Section 4.5 a more precise approach.

```
> cnlp_get_sentence(annotation)
     id sid sentiment
1 doc1   1         3
2 doc1   2         2
3 doc1   3         2
4 doc1   4         2
5 doc1   5         1
6 doc1   6         2
7 doc1   7         2
8 doc1   8         2
9 doc1   9         1
```

With coreNLP, it is possible to perform the same analysis on a French, German, Spanish, or Chinese text, provided that the Java file corresponding to the desired language has been downloaded from the Stanford NLP library[16] (only the English file is installed by default with the `cleanNLP` package).

4.3.6 Coreference Resolution

In a text, anaphora pose problems of ambiguity that must be resolved. We take "anaphora" here in its grammatical sense of coreference: the repetition of a word by another word that refers to it, most often a pronoun ("he," "she," "him," "this one."..). These anaphors are all the more frequent in texts as a common rule of stylistics advises using them to avoid repetitions. More generally, coreferences are multiple references to the same entity. They are treated by coreference resolution, which aims at identifying the entity to which the anaphora refers, but requires a fairly good grammatical quality of the text studied and its prior tagging.

The package `cleanNLP` already seen can find the coreferences. Here are those of the Jane Austen novel already discussed:

```
> (coreference <- cnlp_get_coreference(annotation))
      id rid mid     mention mention_type  number   gender    animacy sid tid  tid_ tid_
                                                                               end  head
1   doc1  49  41          it  PRONOMINAL SINGULAR NEUTRAL INANIMATE   7  11    11   11
2   doc1  49  49          it  PRONOMINAL SINGULAR NEUTRAL INANIMATE   9  15    15   15
3   doc1  34  35          it  PRONOMINAL SINGULAR NEUTRAL INANIMATE   5   3     3    3
4   doc1  34  34          it  PRONOMINAL SINGULAR NEUTRAL INANIMATE   5  25    25   25
5   doc1  43   5      a wife     NOMINAL SINGULAR  FEMALE   ANIMATE   1  24    25   25
6   doc1  43  43    his wife     NOMINAL SINGULAR  FEMALE   ANIMATE   8   2     3    3
7   doc1  44  10  such a man     NOMINAL SINGULAR    MALE   ANIMATE   2   9    11   11
8   doc1  44  11         his  PRONOMINAL SINGULAR    MALE   ANIMATE   2  15    15   15
9   doc1  44  16          he  PRONOMINAL SINGULAR    MALE   ANIMATE   2  36    36   36
10  doc1  44  27     My dear      PROPER SINGULAR    MALE   ANIMATE   3   2     5    5
                  Mr. Bennet
11  doc1  44  21         his  PRONOMINAL SINGULAR    MALE   ANIMATE   3   9     9    9
12  doc1  44  23         him  PRONOMINAL SINGULAR    MALE   ANIMATE   3  12    12   12
13  doc1  44  25         you  PRONOMINAL  UNKNOWN UNKNOWN   ANIMATE   3  18    18   18
14  doc1  44  28  Mr. Bennet      PROPER SINGULAR    MALE   ANIMATE   4   1     2    2
15  doc1  44  29          he  PRONOMINAL SINGULAR    MALE   ANIMATE   4   5     5    5
16  doc1  44  37  Mr. Bennet      PROPER SINGULAR    MALE   ANIMATE   6   1     2    2
17  doc1  44  40         you  PRONOMINAL  UNKNOWN UNKNOWN   ANIMATE   7   3     3    3
18  doc1  44  42         his  PRONOMINAL SINGULAR    MALE   ANIMATE   8   2     2    2
19  doc1  44  44         You  PRONOMINAL  UNKNOWN UNKNOWN   ANIMATE   9   2     2    2
20  doc1  46  26          My  PRONOMINAL SINGULAR UNKNOWN   ANIMATE   3   2     2    2
21  doc1  46  32          me  PRONOMINAL SINGULAR UNKNOWN   ANIMATE   5  22    22   22
22  doc1  46  45          me  PRONOMINAL SINGULAR UNKNOWN   ANIMATE   9   6     6    6
23  doc1  46  46           I  PRONOMINAL SINGULAR UNKNOWN   ANIMATE   9   9     9    9
24  doc1  31  36         she  PRONOMINAL SINGULAR  FEMALE   ANIMATE   5   8     8    8
25  doc1  31  31         she  PRONOMINAL SINGULAR  FEMALE   ANIMATE   5  20    20   20
```

The `rid` column contains a single reference and if it appears in several coreferences, this `rid` reference is carried over several rows whose `mid` column contains the coreference. It seems to be considered here that "a wife" and "his wife" refer to the same person (whose gender and animacy have been identified in passing), who would be mentioned in the first sentence (words 24 and 25) and the eighth sentence (words 2 and 3). This is not correct because "his wife" refers to Mrs Bennet. Second, "such a man" and "his" are rightly equated with the same person, but they are also incorrectly considered to be coreferences of Mr Bennet. On the other hand, all the following coreferences to Mr Bennet, nouns and pronouns, are correct.

4.3.7 Lemmatization

Part-of-speech tagging also allows lemmatization. While the previous steps were aimed at improving the comprehension of the text studied, lemmatization is a way to simplify the text. It consists of reducing the terms to their canonical form (lemma): nouns reduced to the singular, adjectives reduced to the masculine singular and verb inflections reduced to the infinitive.

The lemma, or dictionary form, or citation form, is the form in which words are presented in a general dictionary, which contains only the canonical forms and not the inflected forms. French, Spanish, Russian, and German have numerous inflected forms (conjugations or declensions). German also has the particularity of creating compound words by agglomeration of several nouns, and the question may arise of splitting these units into elementary fragments.

Stemming (Section 4.3.8) is quite commonly used with English, but lemmatization is more suitable for German or Latin languages like French, which have a high rate of inflection. It is more complex and time-consuming than stemming, but more accurate and relevant.

The difficulty of lemmatization is that the same graphic form can correspond to several canonical forms, for example, an adjective and a present participle, or a verb and an auxiliary, or a verb and a noun. Thus, the terms in French: suis (suivre, être), été (être, été), avoué (avoué, avouer), sens (sens, sentir). Or in English: flown (fly, flown), dove (dive, dove), given (give, given), left (left, leave). One method of treatment is the aforementioned part-of-speech tagging, and another consists of sorting out the possibilities by means of a probabilistic calculation.

Not all software can perform lemmatization, but we can mention SPAD.T and the aforementioned TreeTagger, which perform lemmatization in the same languages as POS tagging. Some software offer semi-automatic lemmatization, which only suggests lemmas. Here is an example of an analysis of the incipit of Marcel Proust's *À la recherche du temps perdu*, using the `treetag()` function of the `koRpus` package, which uses TreeTagger for POS tagging and lemmatization. Other R packages know how to lemmatize, such as `spacyr`, `udpipe` and `cleanNLP`.

```
> library(koRpus)
> library(koRpus.lang.fr)
> tagged.text <- treetag("Longtemps, je me suis couché de bonne heure.", for-
mat="obj", treetagger="manual", lang="fr", add.desc = TRUE, TT.options=list
    (path="C:/TreeTagger/", preset="fr"))
> tagged.text@TT.res
```

	token	tag	lemma	lttr	wclass	desc	stop	stem
1	Longtemps	ADV	longtemps	9	adverb	adverb	NA	NA
2	,	PUN	,	1	punctuation	punctuation	NA	NA
3	je	PRO:PER	je	2	pronoun	personal pronoun	NA	NA
4	me	PRO:PER	me	2	pronoun	personal pronoun	NA	NA
5	suis	VER:pres	suivre|être	4	verb	verb present	NA	NA
6	couché	VER:pper	coucher	7	verb	verb past participle	NA	NA
7	de	PRP	de	2	preposition	preposition	NA	NA
8	bonne	ADJ	bon	5	adjective	adjective	NA	NA
9	heure	NOM	heure	5	noun	noun	NA	NA
10	.	SENT	.	1	fullstop	Sentence ending punctuation	NA	NA

The `TT.res` component contains the results, which go up to the tense of the verbs. The lemmatized text can be recovered.

```
> paste(taggedText(tagged.text)$lemma, collapse=" ")
[1] "longtemps , je me suivre|être coucher de bon heure ."
```

The koRpus package can perform analyses in English, German, Spanish, French, Italian, Dutch, Portuguese, and Russian, each of these languages having its own associated package, called koRpus.lang.xx, where xx indicates the language. The following command shows which packages are available and which are already installed. If we wanted to install a new package, the one corresponding to Russian, we would have to run the command install.koRpus.lang("ru").

```
> available.koRpus.lang()
The following language support packages are currently avail-
able:

  koRpus.lang.en [installed]
  koRpus.lang.de [installed]
  koRpus.lang.es [installed]
  koRpus.lang.fr [installed]
  koRpus.lang.it [installed]
  koRpus.lang.nl
  koRpus.lang.pt
  koRpus.lang.ru


To install all missing packages, run:

  install.koRpus.lang(c("nl", "pt", "ru"))
```

The koRpus package also contains functions for calculating lexical diversity (lex.div) and readability (readability). These readability indices are more popular in English-speaking countries than in French-speaking countries, where a finer stylistic analysis is preferred to simple quantitative and pragmatic criteria. Readability indexes have been particularly developed in the United States to help write texts that are easy and quick to read, whether they are official, administrative, or advertising texts. This is why these indices are often calibrated on the English language, even if some, such as the Flesch index, have a French version.

Here are some of the diversity and readability criteria calculated on the whole of Proust's *La Recherche* (see Section 4.4.4).

We start with the automated readability index (ARI), based on a count of the number of characters, words and sentences, and equal to:

$$ARI = 4{,}71 \left(\frac{\#characters}{\#words} \right) + 0{,}5 \left(\frac{\#words}{\#sentences} \right) - 21{,}43$$

The higher the level of education required to read it, the higher the rate; at 13.45 in the example of Proust, it approaches university level.

```
> ARI(tagged.text)

Automated Readability Index (ARI)
  Parameters: default
       Grade: 13.45

Text language: fr
```

A variant is the Coleman-Liau index. Another common readability index is the Flesch-Kincaid index, which replaces the number of characters with the number of syllables. The Simple Measure of Gobbledygook (SMOG index) is a little different, since it counts the number of words of at least three syllables in a given number of sentences and takes the square root. Gunning's FOG index also looks at the number of words with at least three syllables and their proportion in the total words. When the index is high, the reader is likely to get lost in the fog.

Indices based on a syllable count and not on a character count are naturally much longer to compute, since they require a prior breakdown of the text into syllables (performed by the `hyphen()` function).

```
> coleman.liau(tagged.text)

Coleman-Liau
  Parameters: default
        ECP: 51% (estimted cloze percentage)
      Grade: 9.19
      Grade: 9.19 (short formula)

Text language: fr
> SMOG(tagged.text)
Hyphenation (language: fr)

Simple Measure of Gobbledygook (SMOG)
  Parameters: default
      Grade: 11.66
        Age: 16.66

Text language: fr
> FOG(tagged.text)
Hyphenation (language: fr)

Gunning Frequency of Gobbledygook (FOG)
  Parameters: default
      Grade: 14.15

Text language: fr
> flesch.kincaid(tagged.text)
Hyphenation (language: fr)

Flesch-Kincaid Grade Level
  Parameters: default
      Grade: 11.4
        Age: 16.4

Text language: fr
```

As for lexical diversity indices, they relate the number of different words (types) to the total number of words (tokens) themselves. For example, the Guiraud index divides the number of different words by the square root of the total number of words. More simple, but perhaps a little less refined because it is more sensitive to the length of the text, is the TTR index which relates the number of different words to the total number of words. The Herdan index relates the logarithm of the number of different words to the logarithm of the total number of words. On the contrary, the MTLD (Measure of Textual Lexical Diversity) index of McCarthy is more elaborate: it computes the TTR index for increasing sample sizes of the text, and since this index tends to decrease when the length of the sample increases (this is its drawback), a quantity called the number of factors is increased by 1 for each decrease of the TTR below a certain threshold. At the end of the text, the MLTD index is obtained by dividing the total number of words by the number of factors.

```
> TTR(tagged.text)
Language: "fr"


Total number of tokens: 1300161
Total number of types:   40633
Total number of lemmas: 29235


Type-Token Ratio
   TTR: 0.03

> R.ld(tagged.text)
Language: "fr"


Total number of tokens: 1300161
Total number of types:   40633
Total number of lemmas: 29235


Guiraud's R
   R: 35.64

> MTLD(tagged.text)
Language: "fr"


Total number of tokens: 1300161
Total number of types:   40633
Total number of lemmas: 29235


Measure of Textual Lexical Diversity
              MTLD: 112.75
   Number of factors: 11531.06
         Factor size: 0.72
     SD tokens/factor: 38.09 (all factors)
                       38.09 (complete factors only)
```

By any standard, Proust's prose is very rich!

Modeling work has been done[17] to predict the difficulty of a text, for example, on the Common European Framework of Reference for Languages (CEFR) scale, ranging from A1 (beginner) to C2 (experienced). These machine learning models rely on explanatory variables such as the previous indices to predict the level of the text among the six possible ones.

4.3.8 Stemming

One of the simplest ways to reduce the complexity of a text's vocabulary is stemming. It is the passage to the root, or radical, i.e. the removal of the prefix and the suffix. The disadvantage of this process is that the root is not always a real word and the result lacks readability and relevance. It can be followed by a "stem completion" step, which consists in replacing each root by its most frequent original form (or the first one, or at random) in a specified dictionary or in the original text.

```
> library(tm)
> stemDocument("fraises", language = "french")
[1] "frais"
> stemDocument("cherche", language = "fr")
[1] "cherch"
> stemDocument("cherchent", language = "fr")
[1] "cherchent"
```

The best-known stemming algorithm is that of Martin Porter,[18] which he implemented in his program Snowball. This algorithm is used in the R packages `SnowballC` and `tm`.

The first advantage of stemming is that it is simpler than lemmatization since it does not require part-of-speech tagging. Another advantage of stemming is that it is not very sensitive to spelling mistakes. It can be useful in document classification operations, for which it is more the general topic than the grammatical and stylistic variants that is important. But if one wants to proceed to a syntactic analysis or a part-of-speech tagging, stemming should obviously not be performed before these steps.

4.3.9 Simplifications

The previous steps have allowed a better understanding of the documents. Next, we need to simplify them, obviously without changing the meaning, so that we can more easily identify the main topics. The aim is to reduce the number of different terms while losing as little information as possible.

A first frequent simplification, and sometimes even necessary, is the deletion of rare words, whose frequency of appearance in the corpus is lower than a given threshold. The rarest words are the hapax, which appear only once.

A second simplification takes place by grouping the variants of terms present in the documents. We count the graphic variants (gray = grey), possibly the syntactic variants, the synonyms (US = USA = United States = Uncle Sam), the parasynonyms (words with similar meanings: discontent, anger, dissatisfaction), and the development of acronyms (€ = EUR = euro, EU = European Union). Expressions and metaphors should be identified, for example, by replacing "the Chancellor of the Exchequer" by "the British Ministry of Finance." Like the lexicon of compound words, a dictionary of synonyms can be used.

The analogies are then grouped together using a thesaurus, which is a dictionary that presents the terms by grouping them into topics and structuring them in a hierarchical manner. In this way, it is possible to go from the most precise concepts to the most general ones. To do this, we can rely on lexical databases, the most famous of which is WordNet,[19] hosted at Princeton University and freely available, with analysis tools. It can be used in R thanks to the `wordnet` package and after installing the Windows program WordNet-2.1 or the Unix/Linux program WordNet-3.0 (most recent versions) downloaded from the Princeton University site.[20] The approximately 200,000 words (nouns, verbs, adjectives, and adverbs) in WordNet are grouped into about 117,000 "synsets" (synonym sets) which are groups of synonymous words. If it has more than one meaning, a word can be present in more than one group. Synsets are linked by semantic relations. In particular, from a synset a hierarchy of increasingly general and abstract concepts can be developed: car → vehicle → transport … These hyperonyms form an ontology, i.e. a system of categories able to classify the elements of a universe. This passage from topics to concepts is made difficult by the presence of homonyms and we mention in Section 4.4.4 the topic models intended to detect the topics of a corpus of documents.

Here is an example of a search on WordNet with the `wordnet` package:

```
> setDict("C:/Program Files (x86)/WordNet/2.1/dict")
> filter <- getTermFilter("ExactMatchFilter", "power", TRUE)
> terms <- getIndexTerms("NOUN", 5, filter)
> synsets <- getSynsets(terms[[1]])
> sapply(synsets, getWord)
[[1]]
[1] "power"         "powerfulness"

[[2]]
[1] "power"

[[3]]
[1] "ability" "power"

[[4]]
[1] "world power" "major power" "great power" "power" "superpower"

[[5]]
[1] "office" "power"

[[6]]
[1] "power" "force"

[[7]]
[1] "might" "mightiness" "power"

[[8]]
[1] "exponent" "power" "index"

[[9]]
[1] "baron"   "big businessman"  "business leader"  "king"         "magnate"   "mogul"
[7] "power"   "top executive"    "tycoon"
```

4.3.10 Removal of Stop Words

A frequent and easy simplification of the corpus is to remove stop words. These are terms, such as prepositions, articles, pronouns, and conjunctions ("grammatical words"), which, as opposed to "lexical words" (nouns, adjectives, verbs), provide little information because their distribution is uniform in most texts. As they are quite numerous, about 20–30% of the words in a standard text, it is interesting to remove them, which is done with the help of an "anti-dictionary," which can be enriched according to the context.

Here are the English stop words from the R tm package:

```
> stopwords("en")
  [1] "i"            "me"          "my"          "myself"
  [5] "we"           "our"         "ours"        "ourselves"
  [9] "you"          "your"        "yours"       "yourself"
 [13] "yourselves"   "he"          "him"         "his"
 [17] "himself"      "she"         "her"         "hers"
 [21] "herself"      "it"          "its"         "itself"
 [25] "they"         "them"        "their"       "theirs"
 [29] "themselves"   "what"        "which"       "who"
 [33] "whom"         "this"        "that"        "these"
 [37] "those"        "am"          "is"          "are"
 [41] "was"          "were"        "be"          "been"
 [45] "being"        "have"        "has"         "had"
 [49] "having"       "do"          "does"        "did"
 [53] "doing"        "would"       "should"      "could"
 [57] "ought"        "i'm"         "you're"      "he's"
 [61] "she's"        "it's"        "we're"       "they're"
 [65] "i've"         "you've"      "we've"       "they've"
 [69] "i'd"          "you'd"       "he'd"        "she'd"
 [73] "we'd"         "they'd"      "i'll"        "you'll"
 [77] "he'll"        "she'll"      "we'll"       "they'll"
 [81] "isn't"        "aren't"      "wasn't"      "weren't"
 [85] "hasn't"       "haven't"     "hadn't"      "doesn't"
 [89] "don't"        "didn't"      "won't"       "wouldn't"
 [93] "shan't"       "shouldn't"   "can't"       "cannot"
 [97] "couldn't"     "mustn't"     "let's"       "that's"
[101] "who's"        "what's"      "here's"      "there's"
[105] "when's"       "where's"     "why's"       "how's"
[109] "a"            "an"          "the"         "and"
[113] "but"          "if"          "or"          "because"
[117] "as"           "until"       "while"       "of"
[121] "at"           "by"          "for"         "with"
[125] "about"        "against"     "between"     "into"
[129] "through"      "during"      "before"      "after"
[133] "above"        "below"       "to"          "from"
[137] "up"           "down"        "in"          "out"
[141] "on"           "off"         "over"        "under"
[145] "again"        "further"     "then"        "once"
[149] "here"         "there"       "when"        "where"
[153] "why"          "how"         "all"         "any"
[157] "both"         "each"        "few"         "more"
[161] "most"         "other"       "some"        "such"
[165] "no"           "nor"         "not"         "only"
[169] "own"          "same"        "so"          "than"
[173] "too"          "very"
```

This step should not be performed too early in the analysis, and not before the recognition of named entities, tokenization, part-of-speech tagging, and lemmatization, because the presence of stop words is necessary for the proper performance of these operations.

We also sometimes simplify the corpus by deleting the shortest words, including those that are not stop words.

4.4 Vector Representation and Word Embedding

4.4.1 Vector Representation

The analysis of textual data is most often done on vector representations of the data, which are stored in matrices containing the documents in rows and the terms in columns (or the reverse). Each coefficient c_{ij} of such a matrix is the number of occurrences (possibly weighted or in binary form "presence/absence") of term j in document i. The number of columns is generally very large because the number of different terms increases very quickly with the size of the corpus. But most of the cells of the matrix are equal to 0 because each document contains only a small part of the terms of the corpus, especially if the documents are short (tweets, emails, dispatches): these matrices are sparse. In order to reduce the number of columns and to have fewer sparse document-term matrices, the number of terms is reduced by the deletion of stop words, rare words, and the stemming and lemmatization operations described above.

This document-term matrix format allows the application of a large number of exploratory data analysis methods, ranging from distance calculations between documents or between terms to clustering, and including factor analysis. Note that the line vector associated with a short text is sparse, so its Euclidean norm is small; the Euclidean distance is therefore often calculated by normalizing the vectors, or it is replaced by the cosine distance.

Such analyses can also be enriched with metadata about the documents (date and purpose of the document, type of document, department to which the document is addressed, etc.) or their authors (socio-demographic characteristics, relations with the organization, etc.), and this metadata can be matched with the textual data.

This matrix approach is central in software such as SPAD.T and Dtm-Vic, which are often used to analyse short texts or responses to opinion polls with open and closed questions. Each answer to an open question corresponds to a row of a matrix called "whole lexical table," whose columns are the terms of the lexicon (possibly reduced by lemmatization, deletion of stop words, etc.).

If we also have information on the respondents or authors of the texts, which are in the form of categorical variables, we can construct an "aggregate lexical table" that contains:

- one line per word of an answer to an open question;
- one column per category of each categorical variable (age group, socio-professional category) or per possible answer to a closed question;
- in each cell c_{ij} the number of texts/questionnaires whose author/respondent is in the jth given category and has used the ith word.

These tables can be used for factorial analysis or clustering. Thus, a correspondence analysis on the whole lexical table can identify co-occurring words. A multiple correspondence analysis on the aggregated lexical table makes it possible to reconcile the words and the descriptive variables of the respondents or the authors, and to answer the question "who says what?."

Clustering, either hierarchical or by *k*-means, allows us to divide a corpus into groups of documents, and to search for the terms that are most characteristic of each group.

4.4.2 Analysis on the Document-Term Matrix

To show an example of the creation of the document-term matrix of a corpus and the first analyses that can be performed, we use the `quanteda` package[21] of R. It is a very complete package, which can perform a certain number of the operations seen previously: creation of a corpus, tokenization, stemming, extraction of n-grams, cleaning. Moreover, it is fast because it is parallelized, and it relies on the `stringi` package for the manipulation of the text (and its libraries in C++), the `data.table` package and the `Matrix` package for the processing of the sparse matrices. It also relies on the `readtext` package for reading text files or data from the Web, Facebook, or Twitter. It is accompanied by other packages for correspondence analysis of the document-term matrix, document classification, word cloud display. A package dedicated to sentiment analysis is in preparation.

We are going to look at a list of 13,845 job offers extracted from the American site Craigslist[22] and available on the H2O.ai website (Section 2.5.6) which uses it in its documentation.[23] As we will try to classify the offers by categories, we define this variable as a factor. The text of the ads is converted to ASCII format which will be readable by all machine learning functions used later, and in particular by the classification function of LightGBM which was sensitive to this encoding in the version we tested.

```
> craigslist <- read.csv("https://raw.githubusercontent.com/h2oai/sparkling-water/
    rel-1.6/examples/smalldata/craigslistJobTitles.csv")
> names(craigslist) <- c("category", "text")
> craigslist$text <- iconv(craigslist$text, from = 'UTF-8', to = 'ASCII')
> craigslist$category <- as.factor(craigslist$category)
> head(craigslist)
    category                                                    text
1 education                                  After School Supervisor
2 education *****TUTORS NEEDED - FOR ALL SUBJECTS, ALL AGES*****
3 education                                 Bay Area Family Recruiter
4 education      Adult Day Programs/Community Access/Job Coaches
5 education                    General Counselor - Non Tenure track
6 education            Part-Time Summer Math Teachers/Tutors
```

We then create the document-term matrix using the `dfm()` function. Until version 3 of `quanteda`, this matrix was created from a corpus, a list of documents that `quanteda` created and manipulated.

```
> library(quanteda)
> craigs <- corpus(craigslist)
> summary(craigs, showmeta = TRUE)
Corpus consisting of 13845 documents, showing 100 documents:

    Text Types Tokens Sentences  category
   text1     3      3         1 education
   text2     9     19         1 education
   text3     4      4         1 education
    ...
```

From now on, we need to start by tokenizing the documents, which is possible with the quanteda tokens() function, using its built-in tokenizer or an external tokenizer. The result is a list where each element corresponds to an input document and is a vector of tokens. We can also remove words, symbols, punctuation … and pass the characters in lower case.

```
> toks <- tokens(craigslist$text, remove_punct = TRUE,
    remove_symbols = TRUE) %>%
+       tokens_tolower() %>%
+       tokens_remove(pattern = stopwords("en"))
```

The option remove_numbers = TRUE would remove words that are numbers. Here is an example of using an external tokenizer, the one from spaCy.

```
> toks <- tokens(spacy_tokenize(craigslist$text),
    remove_punct = TRUE, remove_symbols = TRUE) %>% …
```

With this done, the document-term matrix can be created using the dfm() function, and it should be noted that dfm() creates it as a sparse matrix to reduce the memory its storage takes up. We can then search for the most frequent terms in the job offers:

```
> dtm <- dfm(toks)
> topfeatures(dtm,20)
       assistant         service          needed          hiring        customer
            1473             937             899             846             825
         manager          office            time            make         teacher
             818             731             707             706             527
              hr  administrative            week       part-time             now
             503             499             467             433             413
            full          wanted            part     coordinator       accountant
             408             404             377             376             354
```

Here is an excerpt from the resulting matrix:

```
> dtm[1:10, 1:10]
Document-feature matrix of: 10 documents, 10 features (81% sparse).
10 x 10 sparse Matrix of class "dfm"
       features
docs    school supervisor tutors needed subjects ages bay area family recruiter
   text1      1          1      0      0        0    0   0    0      0         0
   text2      0          0      1      1        1    1   0    0      0         0
   text3      0          0      0      0        0    0   1    1      1         1
   text4      0          0      0      0        0    0   0    0      0         0
   text5      0          0      0      0        0    0   0    0      0         0
   text6      0          0      1      0        0    0   0    0      0         0
[ reached max_ndoc ... 4 more documents ]
```

We can look for the most related terms to specified terms, by considering the cosine distance (as here), the correlation, the Jaccard distance (the cardinal of the intersection over that of the union). For this, a quanteda companion package is required.

```
> library(quanteda.textstats)
> sim <- textstat_simil(dtm, dtm[,"consultant"], method = "cosine", margin =
    "features")
> lapply(as.list(sim), head, 6)
$consultant
   leasing  architect    solution     sharing apartments    -banking-
 0.3920462  0.2409658   0.2199707   0.1796053  0.1796053    0.1796053
```

It is also possible to count the most frequent words, possibly by category. We can see how many times a word appears and in how many documents, here in how many offers:

```
> head(textstat_frequency(dtm, groups=craigslist$category))
      feature frequency rank docfreq      group
1  accountant       344    1     344 accounting
2  accounting       253    2     251 accounting
3     manager       192    3     192 accounting
4      senior       153    4     153 accounting
5   bookkeeper       153    4     153 accounting
6    accounts       131    6     129 accounting
```

Basic statistics can be calculated on the number of signs present in the documents, including URLs and emojis:

```
> summary(textstat_summary(dtm))
   document          chars            sents           tokens           types           puncts
 Length:13845    Mode:logical    Mode:logical    Min.   : 0.000   Min.   : 0.000   Min.   :0
 Class :character NA's:13845      NA's:13845      1st Qu.: 3.000   1st Qu.: 3.000   1st Qu.:0
 Mode  :character                                Median : 4.000   Median : 4.000   Median :0
                                                 Mean   : 4.621   Mean   : 4.582   Mean   :0
                                                 3rd Qu.: 6.000   3rd Qu.: 6.000   3rd Qu.:0
                                                 Max.   :13.000   Max.   :12.000   Max.   :0
    numbers          symbols           urls                tags              emojis
 Min.   :0.0000   Min.   :0       Min.   :0.0000000   Min.   :0.000000   Min.   :0
 1st Qu.:0.0000   1st Qu.:0       1st Qu.:0.0000000   1st Qu.:0.000000   1st Qu.:0
 Median :0.0000   Median :0       Median :0.0000000   Median :0.000000   Median :0
 Mean   :0.1338   Mean   :0       Mean   :0.0005056   Mean   :0.001734   Mean   :0
 3rd Qu.:0.0000   3rd Qu.:0       3rd Qu.:0.0000000   3rd Qu.:0.000000   3rd Qu.:0
 Max.   :4.0000   Max.   :0       Max.   :1.0000000   Max.   :1.000000   Max.   :0
```

It can also be interesting to search for word associations:

```
> library(quanteda.textstats)
> head(textstat_collocations(toks, size=3, min_count=10))
              collocation count count_nested length    lambda        z
1       flexible car needed    17            0      3 10.833428 4.395079
2      cleaners start week     35            0      3  8.916335 4.103301
3       needs drivers make     68            0      3  9.850946 4.003554
4   hiring part-time tutors    44            0      3  7.979223 3.921877
5       cleaner wanted make    27            0      3  7.441901 3.589317
6         wanted make 1000    27            0      3  7.202669 3.469253
```

For most analyses, the large number of columns in the document-term matrix is a drawback, and we use the `dfm_trim()` function to simplify it, here by keeping only terms appearing at least 200 times and in at least 20 documents. We see that the sparsity goes from 99.9% to 97%, with 51 terms instead of the initial 5408.

```
> dtm
Document-feature matrix of: 13,845 documents, 5,408 features
    (99.92% sparse) and 0 docvars.
> dtmsp <- dfm_trim(dtm, min_termfreq = 200, min_docfreq = 20)
> dtmsp
Document-feature matrix of: 13,845 documents, 51 features
    (97.04% sparse) and 0 docvars.
```

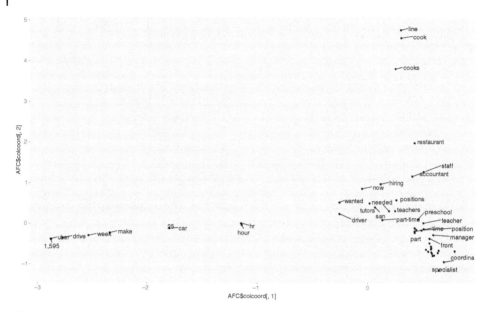

Figure 4.1 CA on document-term table.

We can then proceed to a correspondence analysis, using the `textmodel_ca()` function which is incorporated in the `quanteda.textmodels` package. It is adapted to sparse matrices, and we specify that this is the case with the option `sparse = TRUE`. This option is essential here.

```
> library(quanteda.textmodels)
> AFC <- textmodel_ca(dtmsp, nd = 2, sparse = TRUE)
> library(ca)
> plot.ca(AFC, what=c("none","all"))
```

The correspondence analysis function of the `quanteda` package creates a `ca` object, which can be displayed using the `plot()` function of the `ca` package. The code presented here displays all the columns, i.e. the terms, but not the rows, i.e. the text numbers, which are so numerous that they would obscure the graph. Nevertheless, the graph produced by the `plot()` function is not very readable and we prefer a graph produced by the `geom_text_repel()` function of the `ggrepel` package which improves the readability of the graph by pushing back the labels (an arrow indicating their real location) to avoid their overlapping (Figure 4.1). We notice the logical proximity of some terms.

```
> library(ggplot2)
> library(ggrepel)
> ggplot(as.data.frame(AFC$colcoord), aes(x=AFC$colcoord[,1],
    y=AFC$colcoord[,2])) + geom_point() + geom_text_repel
    (aes(label=rownames(AFC$colcoord)), hjust=1, vjust=1,
    size=5, segment.size = 0)
```

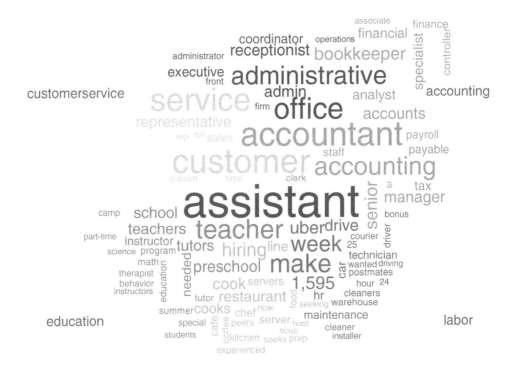

Figure 4.2 Word cloud.

We then create a document-term matrix aggregating the documents according to a criterion, in this case the job offer category, so that the new matrix has only one row per group:

```
> dtm.gp <- dfm_group(dtm, groups=craigslist$category)
> dtm.gp
Document-feature matrix of: 6 documents, 5,408 features
    (71.591% sparse).
```

This allows us to display a *comparison cloud*, which is a word cloud comparing term frequencies across multiple document categories (Figure 4.2). The visualization of word clouds requires the package `quanteda.textplots`.

```
> library(quanteda.textplots)
> textplot_wordcloud(dtm.gp, min_count = 30,
      random_order = FALSE, comparison = TRUE, max_words=100,
      color=gray.colors(3))
```

Let us now see how easy it is to match a job offer to its category. Using the `textmodel_nb()` function of the `quanteda.textmodels` package, we perform the training of the naive Bayesian classifier on a training set composed of half of the jobs, the remaining ones being for model testing. They are formed from the sparse matrix with 5408 terms.

Let us recall the principle of this predictive method. We are interested in the probability that an offer belongs to a category G_i knowing that it contains certain words $X_1, \ldots, X_p$. Bayes' theorem allows us to write this probability as:

$$P\left(G_i/X_1 \ldots X_p\right) = \frac{P(G_i)P(X_1 \ldots X_p/G_i)}{\sum_j P(G_j)P(X_1 \ldots X_p/G_j)}.$$

Assuming "naively" the independence of the presence of words in each category (one word is not more likely if another is present), we can then write:

$$P\left(G_i/X_1 \ldots X_p\right) = \frac{P(G_i)\prod_{k=1}^{P}P(X_k/G_i)}{\sum_j P(G_j)\prod_{k=1}^{P}P(X_k/G_j)}.$$

The probability sought is thus obtained from the frequency of each word of the offer in each of the categories of offers, the frequency of which is calculated during the training of the model. The calculation also involves the probabilities $P(G_i)$ called *priors*. These *priors* can be based on the frequency of documents (prior = "docfreq"), be the same probabilities for each category (prior = "uniform"), or be based on the frequency of words in each category (prior = "termfreq"). We choose the latter prior for our test. It will be different from the first prior as not all documents will have the same number of words:

```
> y <- craigslist$category
> set.seed(235)
> s <- sample(1:nrow(craigslist), nrow(craigslist)*0.5)
> (classif <- textmodel_nb(dtm[s,], y[s], prior = "termfreq",
    distribution = "multinomial"))

Call:
textmodel_nb.dfm(x = dtm[s, ], y = y[s], prior = "termfreq",
    distribution = "multinomial")

Distribution: multinomial ; priors: 0.1292012 0.1646752
    0.1701757 0.17939 0.1804 0.176158 ; smoothing value: 1 ;
    6922 training documents; fitted features.
```

The confusion matrix and correct classification rate on the test set are as follows:

```
> table(y[-s], predict(classif, dtm[-s,]))
```

	accounting	administrative	customerservice	education	foodbeverage	labor
accounting	611	109	35	5	5	7
administrative	48	1003	134	21	9	27
customerservice	26	145	768	34	60	145
education	12	50	19	1120	10	24
foodbeverage	9	57	78	5	980	140
labor	5	35	95	35	47	1010

```
> sum(y[-s] == predict(classif, dtm[-s,])) / length(y[-s])
[1] 0.7932977
```

The correct classification rate approaches 80% in validation, which is correct for a classification of documents in six categories, some of which are obviously not very separated. We can verify that this rate would be only slightly lower if we replaced the word frequency-based prior with the uniform prior or with the document frequency-based prior.

The `quanteda.textmodels` package also relies on the `LiblineaR` package to provide modeling by support vector machine with linear kernel.

```
> (classif <- textmodel_svm(dtm[s,], y[s]))

Call:
textmodel_svm.dfm(x = dtm[s, ], y = y[s])

6,922 training documents; 23,676 fitted features.
Method: L2-regularized L2-loss support vector classification
dual (L2R_L2LOSS_SVC_DUAL)
```

Here is the confusion matrix and the correct classification rate on the test sample:

```
> table(y[-s], predict(classif, dtm[-s,]))

                 accounting administrative customerservice education foodbeverage
                 labor
accounting              667            59              23         3           10         10
administrative           60           940             152        25           20         45
customerservice          26           132             791        26           62        141
education                 9            38              31      1122           10         25
foodbeverage              4            44              69         3         1006        143
labor                     0            34              81         9           71       1032
Warning message:
1463 features in newdata not used in prediction.
> sum(y[-s] == predict(classif, dtm[-s,])) / length(y[-s])
[1] 0.8028311
```

The correct classification rate exceeds 80% in validation, which is even better than the naive Bayesian classifier.

Another function in the `quanteda.textmodels` package relies on the `glmnet` package to perform penalized multinomial regression (Section 3.3). However, the rarest terms must be removed beforehand so that they are not absent from the test sample while present in the training sample, which would cause a `glmnet` error. A message warns that this function automatically searches for the best value of the regularization parameter lambda, which is determined by cross-validation.

```
> dtmsp <- dfm_trim(dtm, min_termfreq = 10)
> (classif <- textmodel_lr(dtmsp[s,], y[s]))
Call:
textmodel_lr.dfm(x = dtmsp[s, ], y = y[s])
6,922 training documents; 902 fitted features.
Method: multinomial logistic regression
Warning messages:
1: from glmnet Fortran code (error code -95); Convergence for
   95th lambda value not reached after maxit=10000 iterations;
   solutions for larger lambdas returned
```

...

This is the confusion matrix and the correct classification rate on the test sample, which is at the same level as the naive Bayesian classifier.

```
> table(y[-s], predict(classif, dtmsp[-s,]))

           accounting administrative customerservice education foodbeverage
           labor
accounting         652            55              36         4            8
                    17
administrative       55           960             142        24           16
                    45
customerservice      27           105             781        22           56
                   187
education             5            41              30      1110           15
                    34
foodbeverage          5            36              86         6          980
                   156
labor                 3            23              99        14           48
                  1040
> sum(y[-s] == predict(classif, dtmsp[-s,])) / length(y[-s])
[1] 0.7977755
```

We now test classification methods absent from the `quanteda.textmodels` package. The random forest model (Section 3.4.2) of the `ranger` package leads to a good classification rate of 75.7% in test, lower than the previous "classical" models. We build a data frame from the document-term matrix and the category of each document, removing the first variable which is the document number, which is useless for the classification:

```
> train <- data.frame(dtm[s,], category=craigslist$category[s])
> train$doc_id <- NULL
> valid <- data.frame(dtm[-s,], category=craigslist$category[-s])
> valid$doc_id <- NULL
> rg <- ranger(category ~ ., data=train, importance = "impurity", num.trees=500,
    mtry=50, replace=T, write.forest=T, seed=235)
> pred.rg <- predict(rg, dat = valid[,-ncol(valid)])
> table(valid[,ncol(valid)], pred.rg$predictions)

           accounting administrative customerservice education foodbeverage
           labor
accounting         608            82              41         9            4
                    28
administrative       47           982             115        15           14
                    69
customerservice      18           136             662        17           80
                   265
education            18            70              20      1046           24
                    57
foodbeverage         12            74              73         4          902
                   204
labor                10            35              61        13           66
                  1042
> sum(pred.rg$predictions == valid[,ncol(valid)]) / nrow(valid)
[1] 0.7571862
```

The boosting model (Section 3.4.4) of the gbm package leads to a good classification rate of 76.5% in test.

```
> boost <- gbm(category ~ ., data=train, n.trees = 500,
    distribution='multinomial', shrinkage = 0.2,
    n.minobsinnode = 5, verbose=T)
> pred.boost <- predict(boost, valid[,-ncol(valid)],
n.trees=100, type="response")
> dim(pred.boost)
[1] 6923    6    1
```

The predict() function returns six probabilities, one for each of the categories to be predicted, so we need to write a small function that will return the category with the highest probability among the six:

```
> f <- function(i) {
+ names(which.max(pred.boost[i,,1]))
+ }
> pred.gbm <- Vectorize(f)(1:nrow(valid))
> sum(pred.gbm == valid[,ncol(valid)]) / nrow(valid)
[1] 0.7651307
> table(valid[,ncol(valid)], pred.gbm)
                pred.gbm
                 accounting administrative customerservice education foodbeverage
                 labor
  accounting            629             54              41         5           10           33
  administrative         55            944             132        14           19           78
  customerservice        25            113             688        17           78          257
  education              10             59              28      1047           23           68
  foodbeverage            5             45              82         6          941          190
  labor                   3             29              81         9           57         1048
```

A better classification is achieved using the XGBoost algorithm (Section 3.4.5). In less than a minute, we obtain a model that correctly ranks 80.6% of the job offers. Here, the iterations are stopped early, before the expected 1000 iterations. This early stopping feature, also used in neural networks, allows us to stop the training process when the error has reached a low point that is not reached again in the next ten iterations. The first step is to transform the previous data frames into sparse matrices, then into matrices in the XGBoost Xgb format. In these matrices, the variable to be explained is indicated and coded in numerical form between 0 and the number of classes – 1.

```
> library(xgboost)
> library(Matrix)
> # transformation of data frames into sparse matrices
> train.mx <- sparse.model.matrix(category ~ ., train)
> valid.mx <- sparse.model.matrix(category ~ ., valid)
> # transformation of sparse matrices into Xgb matrices
> # note that the variable to be explained must be in [0,1] (binary:logistic) or in
    [0,num_class-1]
> dtrain    <- xgb.DMatrix(train.mx, label=as.numeric(train$category)-1)
> dvalid    <- xgb.DMatrix(valid.mx, label=as.numeric(valid$category)-1)
> set.seed(235)
> system.time(train.gdbt <- xgb.train(params=list(objective="multi:softmax",
    num_class=6, eval_metric="mlogloss", eta=0.15, max_depth=6, colsample_bytree=0.5),
    data=dtrain, nrounds=1000, early_stopping_rounds = 10, watchlist=list(eval=dvalid)))
[1]      eval-mlogloss:1.663432
Will train until eval_mlogloss hasn't improved in 10 rounds.
[2]      eval-mlogloss:1.579211
[3]      eval-mlogloss:1.515369
...
[587]    eval-mlogloss:0.573533
[588]    eval-mlogloss:0.573481
Stopping. Best iteration:
[578]    eval-mlogloss:0.573320
utilisateur      système        écoulé
      72.31        21.18          49.70
> pred.gbm <- predict(train.gdbt, newdata=dvalid)
> sum(pred.gbm == as.numeric(valid$category)-1) / nrow(valid)
[1] 0.8057201
> table(pred.gbm, as.numeric(valid$category)-1)
                                    .
pred.gbm     0     1     2     3     4     5
       0   648    49    23     6     6     2
       1    55   980   112    44    40    23
       2    37   134   797    26    81    89
       3     3    20    21  1107     3    10
       4     9    22    51    22   988    45
       5    20    37   174    30   151  1058
```

Finally, we implement the gradient boosting of the LightGBM algorithm.

We have to start by transforming the previous sparse matrices, not into Xgb matrices as for XGBoost, but into LGB datasets:

```
> library(lightgbm)
> dtrain <- lgb.Dataset(data=train.mx, label=as.numeric
    (train$category)-1)
> dvalid <- lgb.Dataset.create.valid(dtrain, valid.mx,
    label=as.numeric(valid$category)-1)
```

LightGBM is very fast and the training of the model is done in a few seconds. Its parameters are quite similar to those of XGBoost, with the addition here of a Lasso penalty.

```
> lgb.grid = list(seed = 123, objective = "multiclass",
    num_class = 6, metric = "multi_error", boosting_type =
    "gbdt", max_depth = 6, num_leaves = 32, learning_rate = 0.3,
    feature_fraction = 0.75, bagging_fraction = 1,
    num_threads = 1, lambda_l1=0.01, verbosity=1)
> system.time(lgb.model <- lgb.train(params = lgb.grid,
    data = dtrain, nrounds = 1000, valids = list(test = dvalid),
    early_stopping_rounds = 10))
```

But the rate of correct classification in test is lower than that of XGBoost, which remains here the best model for the classification of job offers.

```
> pred.lgb <- predict(lgb.model, valid.mx, reshape=TRUE)
> pred.lgb <- max.col(pred.lgb) - 1
> sum(pred.lgb == as.numeric(valid$category)-1) / nrow(valid)
[1] 0.7618085
```

The above examples provide only a small glimpse into the possibilities of textual data analyses. As a first step, these analyses could perhaps be refined by lemmatizing and restricting the factor analyses and classification models to lemmatized nouns and verbs, to extract more information from the corpus without increasing the size of the processed matrices. We will continue our investigations in another direction, replacing the simple document-term matrix by more elaborate vector representations.

4.4.3 TF-IDF Weighting

We often apply weighting rules to the document-term matrices, for example, by overweighting the terms appearing in a small number of documents, but occurring frequently in these (few) documents. Indeed, a term appearing in the majority of the documents of the corpus contributes less to the differentiation of the documents than a term appearing in a small number of documents. On the other hand, if this term appears multiple times in this document, it characterizes this document all the better. These two criteria are combined in the so-called TF-IDF weighting, which is the product of two terms:

- the term frequency *tf*, equal to the ratio $n_{ij}/length(j)$, where n_{ij} is the number of occurrences of term *i* in document *j*, divided by the number of terms in document *j* to measure the frequency of the term in the document;
- the term *idf* ("inverse document frequency"), equal to the logarithm $log(n/n_i)$, where *n* is the total number of documents and $n_i \geq 1$ the number of documents in the corpus containing the term *i*.

The product $tf_{ij}.idf_i$ thus gives the weight of term *i* in document *j*, which is 0 if the term is absent from the document. A term present in all the documents has a zero term *idf*, thus a zero weight. Stop words can thus be naturally neutralized, at least if the documents are long enough. Conversely, a rare term has a high weight, and the logarithm is used precisely to avoid an excessive overweighting of the rarest terms. In any case, the rarest terms of the corpus, and at least the hapax ($n_i = 1$), are often eliminated before the weighting is calculated. It is also important to take care that if the corpus is split into too long documents, most of the terms would be present in all the documents and would therefore have a zero weighting. The TF-IDF weighting can be used to select the terms of a corpus, as those which have a TF-IDF weighting higher than a certain threshold for at least one document. Sometimes this TF-IDF weighting is only used for term selection, while the classical document-term matrix continues to be used for analysis.

With the `quanteda` package, the TF-IDF weighting of a document-term `dtm` matrix is calculated as follows:

```
> tfidfDtm <- dfm_tfidf(dtm)
```

Let's take the example of the Prologue of the Gospel of Saint John.

```
> txt <- c("In the beginning was the Word, and the Word was
    with God, and the Word was God.", "The same was in the
    beginning with God.")
```

We start by computing the document-term matrix.

```
> dtm <- dfm(tokens(txt))
> as.matrix(dtm)
        features
docs    in the beginning was word , and with god . same
  text1  1   4         1   3    3 2   2    1   2 1    0
  text2  1   2         1   1    0 0   0    1   1 1    1
```

The `dfm_tfidf()` function of the `quanteda` package is used to compute the TF-IDF weighting, with options `scheme_tf` for the TF frequency and `scheme_df` for the IDF inverse. The base of the logarithm is 10 by default but can be replaced by another base, for example, *exp*(1) or 2 as in the `weightTfIdf` weighting of the `tm` package. By default, the TF term is not the frequency as defined above, but the number n_{ij} of occurrences, and we specify the option `scheme_tf = "prop"` to get the frequency. Other possibilities are $log(1 + n_{ij})$, the ratio $n_{ij}/\max_k n_{kj}$ over all terms *k*, and others. For the IDF term, its definition above is indeed the default `scheme_df = "inverse"`.

```
> dtm <- dfm_tfidf(dfm(tokens(txt)), scheme_tf = "prop", scheme_df = "inverse")
> as.matrix(dtm)
       features
docs    in the beginning was    word       ,    and with god .    same
  text1  0   0         0   0 0.0451545 0.030103 0.030103   0   0 0 0.00000000
  text2  0   0         0   0 0.0000000 0.000000 0.000000   0   0 0 0.03344778
```

In this example, the words "in", "the", "beginning", "was", "with", "God" are in both documents, so IDF = 0 and therefore TF.IDF = 0. An option avoids this cancelation of the IDF term by introducing a term $k \geq 0$ in the denominator of the logarithm: $log(n/(k + n_i))$ instead of $log(n/n_i)$.

For the word "word" (punctuation marks are counted with the words):

- in document 1: we have TF = 3/20 and IDF = $log_{10}(2/1)$, hence TF.IDF = 0.0451545;
- in document 2: we have TF = 0, hence TF.IDF = 0.

For the word "same":

- in document 1: we have TF = 0, hence TF.IDF = 0;
- in document 2: we have TF = 1/9 and IDF = $log_{10}(2/1)$, hence TF.IDF = 0.03344778.

With the options `scheme_tf = "count"` and `scheme_df = "inverse"` by default, we get the following result.

```
> dtm <- dfm_tfidf(dfm(tokens(txt)))
> as.matrix(dtm)
       features
docs    in the beginning was    word      ,    and with god .    same
  text1  0   0         0   0 0.90309 0.60206 0.60206   0   0 0 0.00000
  text2  0   0         0   0 0.00000 0.00000 0.00000   0   0 0 0.30103
```

For the word "word", in document 1, we have TF = 3 and IDF = $log_{10}(2)$, hence TF.IDF = 0.90309, and in document 2, we have TF = 0, hence TF.IDF = 0. For the word "and", in document 1, we have TF = 2 and IDF = $log_{10}(2)$, hence TF.IDF = 0.60206, and in document 2, we have TF = 0. And for the word "same", in document 1, we have TF = 0, and in document 2, we have TF = 1 and IDF = $log_{10}(2)$, hence TF.IDF = 0.30103.

4.4.4 Latent Semantic Analysis

With the document-term matrix representation and the commonly used distances, two terms are close if they are common to many documents, and two documents are close if they have many terms in common. The limitation of this approach is that it does not handle synonymous or analogous terms, appearing in similar contexts. If two synonyms, for example, "automobile" and "car," are used, the first in some documents, and the second in other documents, and if no document mixes the two terms, these two synonyms will not be matched, unless of course their documents have other terms in common. Conversely, if the same term has two meanings, or if two homonyms (homographs) are present in the documents, some documents will be unduly matched, while their other terms are very different. Finally, the idf overweighting of a rare term, whose use is more stylistic than thematic, can lead to inappropriate matches between documents.

Solutions to these limitations have been sought, the first of which is Latent Semantic Analysis (LSA),[24] which seeks to detect "latent concepts" in documents. A latent concept corresponds to the presence of co-occurrences and correlations, not two by two, but multiple, between several terms. If we are only interested in the two-by-two correlations, the use of the word "chair" in an administrative and furniture sense can lead to very distinct documents being brought together, but if we take into account the multiple correlations that can link the terms "chair," "executive board," "steering committee"… on the one hand, and "chair," "armchair," "table," "dining room" … on the other, and if we compare all the documents between them, and not only two by two, then two documents which have in common speaking about chairs and which would tend to be close, can be, on the contrary, distant by the other terms which they contain, rather administrative for the first document and rather furniture for the second, at least if the two topics "administrative" and "furniture" are sufficiently represented in the corpus to have been identified.

Conversely, if two documents speak, one about cars and the other about automobiles, and if they have no terms in common, they could be very far apart. However, if the topic "transport" has been identified with its associated terms, the two documents could be brought together, if the first one also speaks of truck, road, tolls … and if the second one speaks of engine, bodywork, garages …

At the end of the latent semantic analysis, each term is associated with one or more topics that it contributes to characterize, and each document is associated with one or more topics that it contains. We can thus see that a document is 50% related to topic A, 20% to topic B and 30% to topic C. This is also known as latent semantic indexing (LSI) in the context of information retrieval.

Mathematically, the latent semantic analysis consists in finding an approximation of the document-term (or term-document) matrix M by a matrix of rank k smaller than the rank of M,i.e. whose row or column vectors generate a vector space of smaller dimension. This is done by a Singular Value Decomposition (SVD) of the document-term matrix, whose k largest eigenvalues correspond to the k identified latent concepts.

The singular value decomposition of rectangular matrices generalizes the diagonalization of square matrices. It writes any matrix M of dimension $d \times n$ and rank $r (\leq \min(d, n))$ as a product of three matrices:

$$M = D\Delta^t T,$$

in which:

- D = unit matrix (and even here orthogonal since M is real) $d \times d$;
- Δ = matrix whose diagonal terms (the others are zero) contain the singular values of M (these singular values are the square roots of the eigenvalues of matrices $M^t M$ and $^t MM$);
- T = unit matrix (here orthogonal) $n \times n$.

Recall that the orthogonality of matrices D and T means that $^t DD = I_d$ and $^t TT = I_n$.

To avoid unnecessarily expensive computations, the "compact SVD" only performs the computations for the vectors corresponding to the non-zero singular values, thus for the following smaller matrices:

- D = matrix $d \times r$;
- Δ = diagonal matrix $r \times r$ containing the only non-zero singular values;
- T = matrix $n \times r$.

For all $k \leq$ r the previous decomposition can be written:

- $D = (D_k \; D_{r-k})$ with D_k matrix d x k and D_{n-k} matrix d x $(r - k)$;
- $\Delta = \begin{pmatrix} \Delta_k & 0 \\ 0 & \Delta_{r-k} \end{pmatrix}$ with Δ_k diagonal matrix k x k of k largest singular values;
- $T = (T_k \; T_{r-k})$ with T_k matrix n x k and T_{d-k} matrix n x $(r - k)$.

We can then define the rank approximation k of the matrix M as the matrix

$$M_k = D_k \Delta_k^t T_k.$$

According to the Eckart-Young-Mirsky theorem, M_k is the best approximation of rank k of the matrix M (in the sense of the Frobenius norm). If $k' > k$, the matrix $M_{k'}$ is a better approximation of M than M_k but the k first columns of M_k and $M_{k'}$ are the same, because M_k is obtained by canceling the singular values $> k$.

Here is a small example of singular value decomposition. The svd() function of the base package of R computes the singular value decomposition of a matrix and returns its components in a list:

```
> (m <- matrix(c(1,2,0,2,1,3),2,3, byrow = TRUE))
     [,1] [,2] [,3]
[1,]   1    2    0
[2,]   2    1    3
> (svd <- svd(m))
$d
[1] 3.939644 1.865262
$u
             [,1]        [,2]
[1,] -0.3553806 -0.9347217
[2,] -0.9347217  0.3553806
$v
             [,1]        [,2]
[1,] -0.5647271 -0.1200692
[2,] -0.4176729 -0.8117159
[3,] -0.7117813  0.5715774
```

We find the initial matrix by the product $u.Diag(d).^t v$:

```
> svd$u %*% diag(svd$d) %*% t(svd$v)
     [,1] [,2]         [,3]
[1,]   1    2 1.110223e-16
[2,]   2    1 3.000000e+00
```

We obtain the rank 1 approximation by keeping only the first diagonal term of the matrix d.

```
> diag(c(svd$d[1],0))
         [,1] [,2]
[1,] 3.939644    0
[2,] 0.000000    0
> (a <- svd$u %*% diag(c(svd$d[1],0)) %*% t(svd$v))
          [,1]      [,2]      [,3]
[1,] 0.7906592 0.5847726 0.9965458
[2,] 2.0795912 1.5380685 2.6211140
```

We check that the matrix *a* is of rank 1:

```
> a[2,]/a[1,]
[1]  2.630199 2.630199 2.630199
```

In latent semantic analysis, we set *k* to the desired rank, and we obtain the approximation M_k of *M* in order to reduce the dimension by removing the noise, the insignificant terms. We have:

- D_k = matrix *d x k* of the distribution of *d* documents by topic;
- T_k = matrix *n x k* of the distribution of *n* terms by topic.

From the above, when we go to $k' > k$, new topics are taken into account but the first ones do not change.

We find the matrices *D* and *T* of the latent Dirichlet allocation (Section 4.4.5), but their coefficients here are not probabilities.

Latent semantic analysis can be performed with R using the `lsa()` function in the `lsa` package, but the `textmodel_lsa()` function in the `quanteda.textmodels` package gives the same results much faster.

We will show its application to the corpus *À la recherche du temps perdu* by Marcel Proust in which we will try to discern topics.

The `proustr` package contains the complete text of the seven volumes of this novel, with their 1.2 million words (not counting punctuation marks). We display the year of publication of each volume.

```
> library(proustr)
> proust <- as.data.frame(proust_books())
> library(quanteda)
> length(unlist(tokens(proust[[1]])))
[1] 1382049
> length(unlist(tokens(proust[[1]], remove_punct = TRUE)))
[1] 1204975
> table(proust$book, proust$year)
```

	1913	1919	1921	1922	1923	1925	1927
À l'ombre des jeunes filles en fleurs	0	792	0	0	0	0	0
Albertine disparue	0	0	0	0	0	259	0
Du côté de chez Swann	1004	0	0	0	0	0	0
La Prisonnière	0	0	0	0	365	0	0
Le Côté de Guermantes	0	0	1610	0	0	0	0
Le Temps retrouvé	0	0	0	0	0	0	89
Sodome et Gomorrhe	0	0	0	412	0	0	0

To detect topics more easily, we rely on lemmatization which reduces, as we saw in Section 4.3.7, each word to its canonical form (singular for a noun, infinitive for a verb). It proceeds by first identifying the grammatical type of the word, and we use it here to keep only nouns and adjectives, which are more meaningful for identifying topics (the addition of verbs does not help to distinguish topics).

We perform the lemmatization using the `spacyr` package (Section 4.3.5). First, we have to execute the `spacy_initialize()` function which initializes the Python library spaCy and in which we specify the use of the French language model. We then apply its `spacy_parse()` function to the Proust novel. It identifies the grammatical type `pos` of each word and its `lemma` form.

```
> library(spacyr)
> spacy_initialize(model = "fr_core_news_sm", condaenv="D:/anaconda3/envs/
    spacy_condaenv")
> parsed <- spacy_parse(proust$text, entity = FALSE)
> head(parsed,10)
   doc_id sentence_id token_id    token     lemma   pos
1   text1           1        1 Longtemps longtemps   ADV
2   text1           1        2         ,         , PUNCT
3   text1           1        3        je        je  PRON
4   text1           1        4        me        me  PRON
5   text1           1        5      suis      être   AUX
6   text1           1        6    couché   coucher  VERB
7   text1           1        7        de        de   ADP
8   text1           1        8     bonne       bon   ADJ
9   text1           1        9     heure     heure  NOUN
10  text1           1       10         .         . PUNCT
```

With the `str_pad()` function, we add "0's" to the text numbers so that text0001 is followed by text0002, instead of text1 being followed by text10, and the paragraphs remain in order.

```
> library(stringr)
> parsed$doc_id <- paste("text",str_pad(substr(parsed$doc_id,
    5,8), 4, pad = "0"), sep="")
```

Only nouns and adjectives are preserved, as we have indicated.:

```
> parsed <- parsed [parsed$pos %in% c("NOUN", "ADJ"), c(1,5:6)]
```

We then group the lemmas by `doc_id` value, i.e., by paragraph of the novel. We go from a data frame with one row per lemma to a data frame with one row per paragraph, on which the sequence of lemmas of the paragraph has been combined in a single column.

```
> parsed <- aggregate(lemma ~ doc_id, data = parsed,
    FUN = cbind)
```

We then create a document-term matrix by removing punctuation and stop words. We do this as in Section 4.4.2, starting by tokenizing the documents using the `quanteda` `tokens()` function.

```
> toks <- tokens(parsed$lemma, remove_punct = TRUE) %>% tokens_tolower()
    %>% tokens_remove(stopwords("french"))
> dtm <- dfm(toks)
> dtm
Document-feature matrix of: 4,590 documents, 18,256 features (99.72% sparse)
    and 0 docvars.
      features
docs    bon heure peine bougie éteint oeil temps demi-heure pensée sommeil
  text1   1     2     1      1      1    3     2          1      2       1
  text2   0     0     0      0      0    0     0          0      0       0
  text3   0     0     0      0      0    1     1          0      0       2
  text4   0     0     1      0      0    1     0          0      0       1
  text5   0     2     1      0      0    0     2          0      0       2
  text6   0     1     0      0      0    0     1          0      3       0
[ reached max_ndoc ... 4,584 more documents, reached max_nfeat ... 18,246
    more features ]
```

The svd() function provides the SVD decomposition, while the fast.svd() function of the corpcor package calculates the rank of the matrix to be decomposed and provides its compact SVD decomposition.

```
> svd <- svd(dtm, nrow(dtm), ncol(dtm))
> str(svd)
List of 3
 $ d: num [1:4590] 343.7 151.6 105.6 86.4 79.5 ...
 $ u: num [1:4590, 1:4590] -0.00619 -0.00339 -0.00365 -0.00435 -0.008 ...
 $ v: num [1:18256, 1:18256] -0.07444 -0.087567 -0.040735 -0.000573 -0.002296 ...

> library(corpcor)
> svd <- fast.svd(as.matrix(dtm))
> str(svd)
List of 3
 $ d: num [1:4450] 343.7 151.6 105.6 86.4 79.5 ...
 $ u: num [1:4590, 1:4450] -0.00619 -0.00339 -0.00365 -0.00435 -0.008 ...
 $ v: num [1:18256, 1:4450] -0.07444 -0.087567 -0.040735 -0.000573 -0.002296 ...
```

The dimension of the matrices of the compact SVD decomposition shows that the rank of the dtm matrix is equal to 4450, which can be verified by the rankMatrix() function.

```
> library(Matrix)
> rankMatrix(dtm)
[1] 4450
```

We can now apply the textmodel_lsa() function to the dtm matrix. We choose a rank $k = 4$ to detect four topics.

```
> library(quanteda.textmodels)
> lsa <- textmodel_lsa(dtm, nd=4)
```

We thus obtain the matrices of the singular value decomposition, in the three components sk (diagonal matrix $k \times k$), docs (matrix $d \times k$) and features (matrix $n \times k$). The sk component contains the singular values.

```
> head(lsa$sk)
[1] 343.69748 151.55526 105.58045  86.42939
```

The doc component is the document matrix, which gives the distribution of topics by documents. The rows correspond to the documents and the columns to the topics.

```
> dim(lsa$docs)
[1] 4590    4
> head(lsa$docs)
               [,1]          [,2]           [,3]          [,4]
text1 -0.006188504 -0.006993114 -0.0006273152 -0.015453178
text2 -0.003394630 -0.005197517 -0.0010327879 -0.012838936
text3 -0.003652339 -0.004684278 -0.0001029639 -0.007284384
text4 -0.004352975 -0.006538686  0.0016028111  0.017625602
text5 -0.008004603 -0.008483685 -0.0022833970 -0.006456630
text6 -0.009515893 -0.011958244 -0.0014088870 -0.019654664
```

The `features` component is the term matrix, which gives the distribution of topics by terms. The rows correspond to the terms and the columns to the topics.

```
> dim(lsa$features)
[1] 18256     4
> head(lsa$features)
                  [,1]            [,2]            [,3]            [,4]
bon    -0.0744396074  0.0167486302 -0.0298049157 -0.0176964529
heure  -0.0875673670 -0.0583135973  0.0080038566 -0.1638602034
peine  -0.0407352180 -0.0255249517 -0.0015329882 -0.0005291873
bougie -0.0005734231 -0.0011529806  0.0001981098 -0.0017873016
éteint -0.0022959741  0.0005492143  0.0011716490 -0.0047997850
oeil   -0.0723262136 -0.0306430384 -0.0077233687 -0.0412766997
```

The `matrix_low_rank` component contains the low rank approximation, equal to the product `lsa$docs %*% diag(lsa$sk) %*% t(lsa$features)`.

```
> identical(lsa$matrix_low_rank, lsa$docs %*% diag(lsa$sk) %*%
    t(lsa$features))
[1] TRUE
```

We can verify that the approximation by a matrix of rank k is all the better as k is larger, for example, by comparing the first five rows and columns of the document-term matrix to its rank 5, 500, and 2000 approximations.

```
> dtm[1:5,1:5]
Document-feature matrix of: 5 documents, 5 features (68.00%
    sparse) and 0 docvars.
         features
docs     bon heure peine bougie éteint
  text1   1    2     1     1      1
  text2   0    0     0     0      0
  text3   0    0     0     0      0
  text4   0    0     1     0      0
  text5   0    2     1     0      0
```

Here is the approximation of rank $k = 5$.

```
> lsa <- textmodel_lsa(dtm, nd=5)

> lsa$matrix_low_rank[1:5,1:5]

            bon       heure      peine       bougie       éteint
text1 0.17656516  0.46405900 0.11303656  0.0046169245  0.009545295
text2 0.09759462  0.32882310 0.06823904  0.0035188291  0.007334304
text3 0.10139770  0.25252453 0.06842100  0.0025009772  0.004621854
text4 0.04444035 -0.05536809 0.08776472 -0.0003376456 -0.002298689
text5 0.24081152  0.39634339 0.13982808  0.0032341362  0.003756161
```

Here is the approximation of rank $k = 500$.

```
> lsa <- textmodel_lsa(dtm, nd=500)
> lsa$matrix_low_rank[1:5,1:5]
            bon       heure       peine      bougie        éteint
text1  0.960734685 1.95369358 0.92545662 0.19417725   0.130625994
text2 -0.006281429 0.01559383 0.03444897 0.03715665  -0.015522169
text3 -0.024108106 0.02511236 0.01495448 0.01207025  -0.001331632
text4 -0.011669259 0.08165571 0.89017469 0.02530461  -0.021295917
text5  0.025767264 1.99637922 0.89064899 0.01403057   0.011502556
```

And here is the approximation of rank $k = 2000$.

```
> lsa <- textmodel_lsa(dtm, nd=2000)
             bon         heure         peine        bougie         éteint
text1  0.9997826693  2.003307e+00 0.9991555976  0.926404522   0.9274621108
text2  0.0039173562  9.819338e-05 0.0007255252 -0.007228610   0.0056216724
text3  0.0003477475 -4.408717e-03 0.0059821337 -0.004763289  -0.0187019354
text4  0.0012279073 -4.192828e-04 0.9858057613 -0.020318168  -0.0293600081
text5 -0.0031378700  2.004074e+00 0.9965088555  0.003884611   0.0001082076
```

The following function is used to determine the first terms of each topic:

```
> toptopics <- function(x){
+ top <- order(lsa$features[,x],decreasing=T)
+ row.names(lsa$features)[head(top,20)]
+ }
> sapply(1:4,toptopics)
           [,1]              [,2]          [,3]          [,4]
 [1,] "enfoncez"        "m."          "mme"         "femme"
 [2,] "securæ"          "mme"         "duchesse"    "homme"
 [3,] "sunt"            "baron"       "princesse"   "autre"
 [4,] "nostræ"          "gens"        "femme"       "amour"
 [5,] "vitæsumu"        "monsieur"    "salon"       "jeune"
 [6,] "enim"            "duchesse"    "amie"        "vie"
 [7,] "sodomitæign"     "princesse"   "albertine"   "duchesse"
 [8,] "tantum"          "duc"         "dame"        "désir"
 [9,] "saint-hilair"    "nom"         "mlle"        "maîtresse"
[10,] "peu"             "mari"        "guermante"   "être"
[11,] "pardi"           "salon"       "nom"         "tel"
[12,] "intimidé"        "charlu"      "petit"       "personne"
[13,] "remonte"         "morel"       "grand"       "œuvre"
[14,] "incendien'"      "air"         "visite"      "fille"
[15,] "caneva"          "marquis"     "mondain"     "vice"
[16,] "antiphonaire"    "ajouta"      "mère"        "monde"
[17,] "quadrivium"      "roi"         "temps"       "plaisir"
[18,] "trivium"         "vieux"       "parme"       "goût"
[19,] "historié"        "homme"       "année"       "sentiment"
[20,] "atlantique"      "ah"          "mari"        "relation"
```

It can be seen that the four topics obtained by latent semantic analysis are not very well characterized, significantly less well than the four obtained by latent Dirichlet allocation

(Section 4.4.5). With latent semantic analysis, the number of topics must be higher, often between 100 and 300, to obtain a good approximation of M. We will therefore see that the latent Dirichlet allocation provides an easier interpretation of the topics.

Finally, here is the frequency of the first topic of each document:

```
> table(max.col(textmodel_lsa(dtm, nd=4)$docs))
```

```
   1    2    3    4
  27 1047 2343 1173
```

4.4.5 Latent Dirichlet Allocation

Latent Dirichlet Allocation (LDA)[25] is another method for identifying the topics of which documents are composed and distinguishing the sets of terms that characterize these topics. It assumes that:

- each document is a mixture of topics among a set of K topics, and that this mixture follows a Dirichlet distribution[26] of order K;
- each topic is a mixture of terms, and that this mixture follows another Dirichlet distribution, depending on the topic.

This means that in each document, each of the K topics appears with a certain probability, the sum of these K probabilities being 1. And in each topic, each term has a certain probability of belonging to the field of this topic, the sum of the probabilities on all the terms being 1 for each topic.

We have to determine these probabilities. To do this, we start by drawing a set of topics for each document according to a Dirichlet distribution, before drawing a set of terms for each topic: we thus generate a set of terms for each document. The modeling consists of finding the distributions of topics and terms which generated the documents of the corpus with the highest possible probability, i.e. to maximize the likelihood of the terms of the documents. The latent Dirichlet allocation is a generative model.

Let's specify the determination of the model. The Dirichlet distribution of order K and parameters $(\alpha_1, \alpha_2, \dots \alpha_K)$ has for probability density the function:

$$f(x| \alpha) = \frac{\Gamma\left(\sum_{i=1}^{K} \alpha_i\right)}{\prod_{i=1}^{K} \Gamma(\alpha_i)} \prod_{i=1}^{K} x_i^{\alpha_i - 1} = \frac{1}{\beta(\alpha)} \prod_{i=1}^{K} x_i^{\alpha_i - 1}$$

where $\alpha_i > 0$, $\Gamma(t)$ is the Gamma function (generalization of the factorial function), $\sum_{i=1}^{K} x_i = 1$ and $x_i \geq 0$ for all $i \in [1, K]$.

In this density function, the normalization constant is the inverse of the beta function $\beta(\alpha)$. Given the α_i, we can derive x_i which are the parameters of a multinomial distribution. In the LDA, these α_i are determined for the whole corpus, and for each document of this corpus are drawn x_i which are the probabilities of each topic in the document. The sum $\alpha = \sum \alpha_i$ is a concentration parameter which controls the homogeneity of the x_i. The larger α is, the closer the probabilities of the topics are, and the smaller α is, the more each document focuses on a small number of topics. This will happen the more the number of topics is high, and α is therefore generally inversely proportional to the number K of topics. A common initialization value is $\alpha = 50/K$.

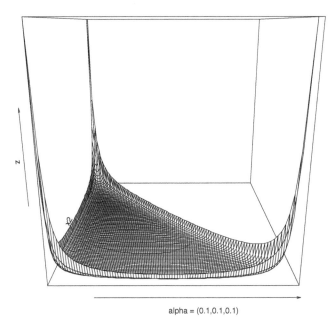

alpha = (0.1,0.1,0.1)

Figure 4.3 Density of a Dirichlet distribution of order 3 and parameters (0.1, 0.1, 0.1).

This concentration on a few topics for a small value of α comes from the density function of the Dirichlet distribution, as shown in Figure 4.3 representing this density for a Dirichlet distribution of order 3 and parameters (0.1, 0.1, 0.1). Each corner corresponds to a topic and we can see that the documents are concentrated in the corners.

Figure 4.4 shows the distribution of topics in the documents for parameters (10, 10, 10) of the Dirichlet distribution. It can be seen that a majority of the documents have a significant mix of topics.

Here is the R code for these figures:

```
library(gtools)
x1 <- seq(0.01,1, by=0.01)
x2 <- seq(0.01,1, by=0.01)
Concentration parameter
alpha <- c(0.1,0.1,0.1)
alpha <- c(10,10,10)
z <- matrix(0, nrow=length(x1), ncol=length(x2))
f <- function(x,y)
{
 if(x+y < 1) {a <- c(x, y, 1-x-y); diric <- ddirichlet(a,alpha)}
 else {diric <- NA}
 return(diric)
}
z <- outer(x1,x2,Vectorize(f))
persp(x1,x2,z, xlab="alpha = (10,10,10)")
```

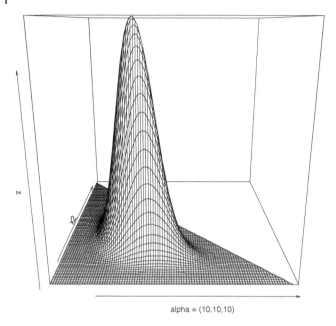

alpha = (10,10,10)

Figure 4.4 Density of a Dirichlet distribution of order 3 and parameters (10, 10, 10).

Once the probabilities x_i of the topics of a document are drawn according to the Dirichlet distribution $Dir(K, \alpha)$ of the corpus, we can draw, for each word of the document:

- a topic i according to the multinomial distribution given by the probabilities x_i;
- a term according to the multinomial distribution given by the probabilities $\beta_{i,j}$ of each term j in the topic i.

So we want to estimate the parameters $\alpha = (\alpha_i)$ and $\beta = (\beta_{ij})$ which is classically done by looking for those that maximize the log-likelihood of the words m_d observed in the set of D documents:

$$l(\alpha, \beta) = \sum_{d=1}^{D} \log(P(m_d|\alpha, \beta)).$$

We want to maximize the probability of the observed words given the parameters α and β. This probability has a complex formula:

$$P(m_d|\alpha, \beta) = \int \left\{ \sum_{t_i} [\prod_{j=1}^{N} P(m_j|t_i, \beta) P(t_i|x)] \right\} P(x|\alpha) dx =$$

$$= \int \left\{ \sum_{t_i} [\prod_{j=1}^{N} \beta_{ij} P(t_i|x)] \right\} P(x|\alpha) dx.$$

The $x = (x_i) \geq 0$ are the parameters of the multinomial distribution drawn according to the Dirichlet distribution of parameter α. They are the probabilities of the topics t_i in the document.

The preceding log-likelihood is therefore in practice too difficult to calculate directly, but we can use an expectation-maximization algorithm in two steps: step E calculates the expectation of the log-likelihood conditionally on the parameters $\alpha^{(t)}$ and $\beta^{(t)}$ parameters, and the M step searches for the $\alpha^{(t+1)}$ and $\beta^{(t+1)}$ that maximize this expectation. This EM algorithm[27] computes the log-likelihood of data (here, the words of the documents) which depend on unobserved latent variables (here, the topics). It is often that the value of the parameter α obtained by maximization of the log-likelihood is significantly smaller than the initial value = $50/K$. This means that each document contains a small number of topics.

The latent Dirichlet allocation assumes that the topics are uncorrelated, and there is a generalization that admits the correlation of the topics: the Correlated Topics Model (CTM) of Blei and Lafferty.[28]

The two approaches, latent semantic analysis and latent Dirichlet allocation, can be compared in the analysis of a corpus, as it does not seem obvious that one is systematically superior to the other. They are quite different, since the first is based on linear algebra and the second on generative probabilistic models.

These two unsupervised methods belong to what is called "topic modeling," an important field in natural language processing. Between them, we can also mention Probabilistic Latent Semantic Analysis (PLSA). These are bag *of* words methods in which the position of words in a document is not taken into account, but only their frequency. In a sense, they are less grammatically sophisticated than the analyses of Section 4.3 such as part-of-speech tagging, dependency parsing, or coreference resolution, but they allow simpler and faster analyses, without parameterization and without a language-specific dictionary.

They match terms, but also, symmetrically, documents, and constitute an approach to document classification. They are useful to understand a corpus and to synthesize its content,[29] without having to rely on a dictionary of synonyms, and they can also be used to group news articles by subject, or for collaborative filtering (Section 3.6) in the recommendation of articles or movies.

Latent Dirichlet allocation can be done with R using the `topicmodels` package by Bettina Grün and Kurt Hornik and the `lda` package by Jonathan Chang. We will test the first package, which has the advantage of being well documented[30] and integrated with the `text mining` and `quanteda` packages. It implements the CTM model and the variational expectation-maximization algorithm (in C), as well as Gibbs sampling (in C++). The latter requires less memory and should therefore be preferred for large corpora, but the original method described by the authors of LDA is the variational expectation-maximization algorithm. The `lda` package relies exclusively on Gibbs sampling, programmed in C.

We will take the example of Marcel Proust *À la recherche du temps perdu* to try to discern topics using the latent Dirichlet allocation, after having done so using the latent semantic analysis (Section 4.4.4).

Recall that we have created the document-term matrix `dtm` of this corpus by removing punctuation, as well as the stop words of the `proustr` package. The `LDA()` function of the `topicmodels` package implement the latent Dirichlet allocation but it cannot be performed on a document-term matrix where some documents have no more terms after the previous transformations. One can directly delete the empty rows or equivalently use the `convert()` function of the `quanteda` package to convert the matrix into "topicmodels."

```
> dtm <- dtm[rowSums(as.matrix(dtm)) > 0,]
> dtm <- convert(dtm, to = "topicmodels")
```

This matrix has 18,256 columns. This may not seem like a lot, but it should be remembered that we have only kept the canonical forms of nouns and adjectives, which greatly reduces the number of terms. We can verify that after deleting the documents without terms, there are 4586 rows left in the matrix.

We then run the latent Dirichlet allocation by specifying the number of four topics. Without specifying the method used, it is the variational expectation-maximization (VEM) algorithm that is applied, but here with Gibbs sampling, the topics clearly emerge:

```
> library(topicmodels)
> lda <- LDA(dtm, k = 4, control = list(seed = 235),
    method = "Gibbs")
```

Since each topic is a mixture of terms, we are interested in the first k terms of each topic, i.e. the terms that have the highest probability of belonging to the topic, given by the function `terms(lda,k)`. In other words, the ith column below ($1 \leq i \leq 4$) contains the term m_{i1} that has the highest probability β_{i1} in the i^e topic, followed by the term m_{i2} that has the second highest probability β_{i2} in the i^e thematic, followed by the 3rd term, etc.

```
> terms(lda,20)
        Topic 1     Topic 2      Topic 3       Topic 4
 [1,]  "petit"     "autre"      "mme"         "femme"
 [2,]  "air"       "vie"        "m."          "tout"
 [3,]  "jour"      "nouveau"    "homme"       "jour"
 [4,]  "heure"     "tout"       "tout"        "autre"
 [5,]  "oeil"      "chose"      "gens"        "plaisir"
 [6,]  "chambre"   "tel"        "monde"       "amour"
 [7,]  "côté"      "grand"      "grand"       "fille"
 [8,]  "tout"      "fois"       "nom"         "chose"
 [9,]  "regard"    "temps"      "duchesse"    "albertine"
[10,]  "grand"     "idée"       "ami"         "jeune"
[11,]  "moment"    "souvenir"   "monsieur"    "moment"
[12,]  "maison"    "sorte"      "princesse"   "fois"
[13,]  "tête"      "seul"       "femme"       "désir"
[14,]  "soir"      "année"      "personne"    "mère"
[15,]  "fleur"     "premier"    "bon"         "temps"
[16,]  "pied"      "œuvre"      "père"        "seul"
[17,]  "instant"   "esprit"     "air"         "amie"
[18,]  "porte"     "différent"  "duc"         "mort"
[19,]  "rue"       "réalité"    "petit"       "vie"
[20,]  "voiture"   "moment"     "dame"        "premier"
```

These probabilities $\beta_{i1}, \beta_{i2}, \beta_{i3} \ldots$ are contained in the `terms` component of the `posterior` object. Here are the probabilities of the first ten terms of the corpus:

```
> t(posterior(lda)$terms[,1:10])
                    1            2            3            4
bon        1.392319e-06 1.310915e-06 7.995678e-03 3.777547e-03
heure      1.090325e-02 1.061841e-04 1.411530e-05 5.633229e-03
peine      1.392319e-06 3.619436e-03 1.283209e-06 3.699686e-03
bougie     1.963170e-04 1.310915e-06 1.283209e-06 1.297680e-06
éteint     1.684706e-04 4.063836e-05 1.283209e-06 4.022808e-05
oeil       9.817244e-03 1.848390e-04 2.322609e-04 3.790523e-03
temps      3.816348e-03 8.771332e-03 3.977949e-05 8.591939e-03
demi-heure 2.798562e-04 1.310915e-06 1.411530e-05 1.297680e-06
pensée     2.102402e-04 3.317926e-03 1.283209e-06 2.129493e-03
sommeil    2.980956e-03 1.310915e-06 1.283209e-06 1.297680e-06
```

Moreover, since each document (i.e. here each paragraph of the novel) is a mixture of topics, we are interested in the first k topics of each document, i.e. the topics which have the highest probability of being those of the document. This is what the `topics(lda,k)` function provides, which allows us to highlight the distribution of the main topic of each paragraph of *La Recherche*.

```
> table(topics(lda,1))

   1    2    3    4
1131  776 1679 1000
```

The first topic is about places (room, house, way), moments (day, evening, moment), nature (air, flower, head, foot) and the glance (eye, glance) that allows us to embrace them. The second topic is that of time (life, time, year, times) and the inner world (memory, idea, work) at the center of Proust's work. The third topic is social (duchess, princess, sir, Mrs, people, great, high society, name) and it is the most frequent one in our corpus, as André Gide had noticed when he refused Proust's first manuscript at Gallimard by declaring: "Too many duchesses and countesses, it is not for us." The fourth topic is marked by feelings and sensations (love, pleasure, desire, alone).

The Hellinger distance calculates the distance between the topics. This distance between 0 and 1 is defined for two discrete probability distributions according to the formula:

$$d_H(P,Q) = \frac{1}{\sqrt{2}}\sqrt{\sum_{i=1}^{N}(\sqrt{p_i} - \sqrt{q_i})^2}.$$

We can naturally apply it to the probabilities of $(\beta_{i.}, \beta_{j.})$ of two topics i and j on all the terms of the corpus.

```
> distHellinger(posterior(lda)$terms)
          [,1]      [,2]      [,3]      [,4]
[1,] 0.0000000 0.8330715 0.8334798 0.8151258
[2,] 0.8330715 0.0000000 0.8251332 0.7812285
[3,] 0.8334798 0.8251332 0.0000000 0.8178204
[4,] 0.8151258 0.7812285 0.8178204 0.0000000
```

The topics all seem to be more or less equidistant.

We can see the interest of this type of analysis, which will certainly not teach the connoisseur of Proust anything, but which can be applied in a few seconds to a vast corpus of any language in order to extract the main topics without any prior knowledge of either the corpus or even the language. Note that these are the dominant topics per document of the corpus, and not topics discovered without constraint. The division of the corpus into documents thus influences the result of the analysis, but the division into paragraphs of the novel is appropriate here: the paragraphs are long enough to make it possible to discern the topics, and short enough to be numerous enough to observe the variety of the topics of the corpus. The division of the corpus into documents always has some important effect on the analyses, and is not always trivial when the corpus is not divided in such an obvious way as in a corpus of emails, tweets, or poems from a collection.

We can compare the VEM, Gibbs, and CTM models on the basis of the diversity of membership probabilities, considering that a model that distinguishes well between topics will assign to each document a maximum probability for one topic and a minimum probability for the others, which translates into a minimum entropy $-\sum_i p_i \log(p_i)$ (ideally, zero). To calculate it, we rely on the fact that the `topics` component of the `posterior` object of the model contains the probability x_i for each document to contain one topic or another (just as the `terms` component of the `posterior` object contains the probability β_{ij} for each term j to belong to a topic i).

For example, here are the probabilities of the first six documents (paragraphs) in the Gibbs model, the second in the list of models calculated on four topics, between the VEM model and the CTM model:

```
> models <- list(VEM = LDA(dtm, k = 4, control =,
    list(seed = 235) method = "VEM"), Gibbs = LDA(dtm, k = 4,,
    control = list(seed = 235), method = "Gibbs"), CTM =,
    CTM(dtm, k = 4, control = list(seed = 235)))
> head(posterior(models[[2]])$topics)
              1         2         3         4
text1 0.3372093 0.2984496 0.1046512 0.2596899
text2 0.3511905 0.1726190 0.1726190 0.3035714
text3 0.3064516 0.3387097 0.1989247 0.1559140
text4 0.2752809 0.3314607 0.1741573 0.2191011
text5 0.3814815 0.3074074 0.1444444 0.1666667
text6 0.4506579 0.2861842 0.1151316 0.1480263
```

We therefore calculate the entropy of each document and then the average entropy over all the documents. Here, the variational model proves to be the most differentiating since its entropy is lower:

```
> sapply(models, function(x) mean(apply(posterior(x)$topics, 1,
    function(z) - sum(z * log(z)))))
      VEM       Gibbs       CTM
0.5333555 1.3482228 0.8396295
```

This is related to the lower value of the concentration parameter α of the variational model.

```
> sapply(models[1:2], slot, "alpha")
      VEM        Gibbs
 0.1154307 12.5000000
```

Note that we know the sum $\alpha = \sum_{i=1}^{K} \alpha_i$ but not each parameter α_i.
We could also have set the value of the concentration parameter ourselves.

```
> lda <- LDA(dtm, k = 4, control = list(alpha = 1, seed = 235),
    method = "Gibbs")
> table(topics(lda,1))

   1    2    3    4
 839 1291 1463  993
```

The `logLik()` function gives us the log-likelihood of each model, which can help in choosing a method or a number of topics.

```
> (models.logLik <- as.matrix(lapply(models, logLik)))
        [,1]
VEM    -2248736
Gibbs  -2081197
CTM    -2253416
```

An indicator derived from the log-likelihood is the perplexity, which also allows us to choose the method and the number of topics, by looking for the minimal perplexity. The `perplexity()` function also computes it on a sample that may be different from the training sample, or by cross-validation, which of course adds to the relevance of this criterion. The distribution of the topics is then not recalculated on the new sample and it is the one of the training that is used. The `perplexity()` function requires the `as.simple_triplet_matrix()` function from the `slam` package.

```
> library(slam)
> (models.perplexity <- as.matrix(lapply(models, function(x)
    perplexity(x, newdata=as.simple_triplet_matrix(dtm)))))
        [,1]
VEM    1990.893
Gibbs  2124.012
CTM    2034.035
```

Other metrics are available in the `ldatuning` package to help choose the number of topics.

```
> library(ldatuning)
> tunes <- FindTopicsNumber(dtm, topics = c(2:40),
    metrics = c("Griffiths2004", "CaoJuan2009", "Arun2010"),
    method = "Gibbs", control = list(seed = 235), mc.cores = 4L,
    verbose = TRUE)
```

```
fit models... done.
calculate metrics:
  Griffiths2004... done.
  CaoJuan2009... done.
  Arun2010... done.
> tunes
    topics Griffiths2004 CaoJuan2009  Arun2010
1      40       -1905376  0.05988517  864.2633
2      39       -1910485  0.06204172  865.8945
3      38       -1908473  0.05936829  872.5899
4      37       -1909443  0.06933416  887.6637
5      36       -1902578  0.06176701  883.9991
6      35       -1905214  0.06154614  889.9165
7      34       -1901061  0.06454038  896.9888
8      33       -1907589  0.07032816  911.0024
9      32       -1910721  0.07204820  916.0142
10     31       -1901064  0.06709663  922.7393
...
> FindTopicsNumber_plot(tunes)
```

Here, with the Gibbs method, the optimal number of topics appears high regardless of the observed metric (Figure 4.5).

The number of topics chosen is often dictated by practical considerations rather than by the minimization of a statistical criterion.

In a generalization of the latent Dirichlet allocation, the hierarchical Dirichlet process (HDP),[31] the number of topics does not have to be fixed *a priori* because it is supposed to be a random variable following a Dirichlet distribution and can be determined from the data. But it depends on a parameter *eta* whose different values can lead to different numbers of topics and different topics.

If we compute models for several numbers of topics, we should not compare entropies computed on different numbers of topics K, or else we should relate them to the maximum entropy $-\log(1/K)$ as in the following example.

```
> models <- lapply(seq(2, 6, by = 1), function(d){LDA(dtm, k=d,
    control = list(seed = 235), method = "Gibbs")})
> sapply(models, function(x) mean(apply(posterior(x)$topics, 1,
    function(z) - sum(z * log(z)))))
[1] 0.6756678 1.0682549 1.3482228 1.5633796 1.7385443
> sapply(models, function(x) {mean(apply(posterior(x)$topics, 1,
    function(z) - sum(z * log(z))))/-log(1/x@k)})
[1] 0.9747826 0.9723676 0.9725372 0.9713823 0.9703001
```

4.4.6 Word Frequency Analysis

If we move away from topic modeling to simpler methods, the `textstat_keyness()` function of the `quanteda.textstats` package allows us to compare the frequency of

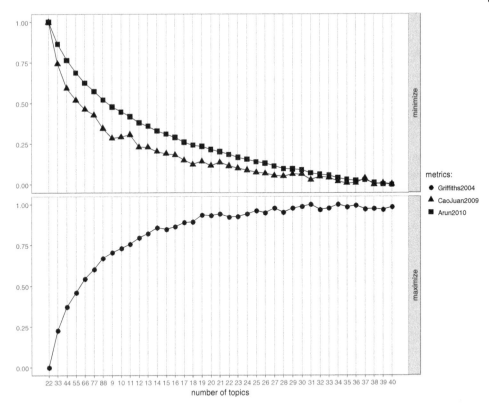

Figure 4.5 Finding the optimal number of topics.

occurrence of terms in two corpora or two sub-corpora, and to measure the significance of the difference in occurrence of each term.

```
> library(proustr)
> proust <- as.data.frame(proust_books())
```

We create a document-term matrix as before, but by aggregating the documents according to a criterion, here the "volume" which corresponds to a part of each book, so that the new matrix has only one row per volume:

```
> library(quanteda)
> toks <- tokens(proust$text, remove_punct = TRUE) %>% tokens_
    tolower() %>% tokens_remove(stopwords("french"))
> dtm <- dfm(toks)
> dtm <- dfm_subset(dtm, proust$book %in% c("Du côté de
    chez Swann"))
> dtm.gp <- dfm_group(dtm, groups=proust$volume[which
    (proust$book %in% c("Du côté de chez Swann"))])
```

The `textstat_keyness()` function then computes a statistic associated with the frequency table of each term, crossed with a "target" variable which is one of the categories of the previous `group` variable, i.e. here one of the parts of the novel. This statistic is the χ^2 statistic in the absence of any other specification, but can also be the Fisher exact statistic or the likelihood ratio.

```
> library(quanteda.textstats)
> keyness <- textstat_keyness(dtm.gp, target = "Deuxième par-
tie - Un amour de Swan")
> head(keyness)
      feature      chi2 p n_target n_reference
1    verdurin 306.3393 0      258           0
2      odette 303.5933 0      261           2
3       qu'il 269.7319 0      731         296
4       swann 218.4023 0      511         183
5    d'odette 150.9892 0      130           1
6 forcheville 116.1621 0       98           0
```

Thanks to a function of the `quanteda.textplots` package, this statistic is then represented in Figure 4.6, which shows here that, within Proust's *Du côté de chez Swann,* in the second part, *Un amour de Swann,* there is much more frequent mention of the Verdurins, Odette, and Swann, while the other two parts, *Combray* and *Noms de pays: le nom,* are dominated by the presence of the narrator's parents and especially also of the cook Françoise.

```
> library(quanteda.textplots)
> textplot_keyness(keyness, labelsize = 5, show_legend = F)
```

Another useful function of the `quanteda` package is the `kwic()` function, which can find all the contexts in which a word appears. Note that the word "grand-mère" appears only three times with this spelling in *La Recherche,* against 676 times with the spelling "grand'mère."

```
> toks <- tokens(proust$text)
> kwic(toks, "grand-mère")
Keyword-in-context with 3 matches.
[text2094, 174]          pensais à ce que ma | grand-mère |
     faisait seule, je me
[text2668, 485]          , il fallut que ma | grand-mère |
     s'habillât. Ayant refusé obstinément
[text3292, 909] En souvenir de madame votre | grand-mère | ,
     j'avais fait relier pour

> dim(kwic(toks, "grand'mère"))[1]
[1] 676
```

4.4.7 Word2Vec Embedding

In the ordinary vector representation, two words are close if they occur in the same documents. It has already been said that if some documents talk about cars and never

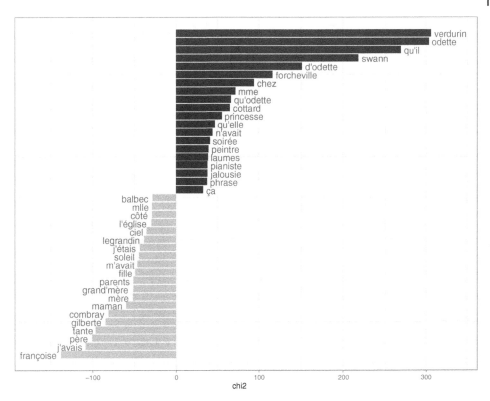

Figure 4.6 Frequency of words in *Un amour de Swann* (in blue) and in *Combray* and *Noms de pays: the name* (in grey).

about automobiles, and other documents do the opposite, the two sets of documents will never be reconciled, unless they have other terms in common. But this last condition makes the matching of terms dependent on a corpus that may be small and limited. On the other hand, the other terms that allow the reconciliation of the first terms may be found in distant parts of the documents, without any close relation with the first terms. This is the interest of the Word2Vec vector representation which (1) relies on models developed on corpora which can be very large, and (2) only takes into account the neighborhood of each term. On these two points, Word2Vec differs from topic modeling methods such as latent semantic analysis and latent Dirichlet allocation.

Word2Vec offers a more sophisticated vector representation than the usual bag of words representation because two texts will not be close in this vector space simply because they share a certain number of co-occurring words (with the problem that one text can talk about cars and another about automobiles and seem distant), but especially because they share words with close meanings and relations in a large corpus which was used to learn the Word2Vec model used. This learning allows us to identify certain words that play similar roles in many sentences, and whose vectors will be close in the word embedding space, from a sufficiently rich corpus. The learning is done with a hidden layer neural network whose number of units is the dimension of the vector space in which the words are embedded.

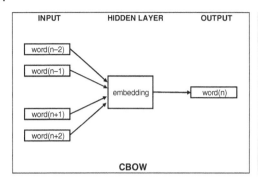 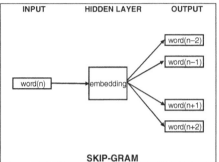

Figure 4.7 Word2Vec embedding models.

This dimension, usually between 100 and 1000, is much smaller than the number of words. The Word2Vec vector representation is therefore much more compact than the bag of words representation whose dimension is the number of words. However, this number of words, the size of the vocabulary of the corpus, is generally very large, even if we have taken care to reduce it by the lemmatization operations seen previously, deleting stop words, etc.

The two types of Word2Vec models are *skip-gram* and CBOW (Continuous Bag-Of-Words). In the skip-gram model, the network scans the text with a sliding window that passes over the words, and it uses each word to predict the surrounding words in its window. In the CBOW model, the network predicts each word from those surrounding it in its window (Figure 4.7). Training is done on pairs (context, target word) in which the network must distinguish pairs where the target word is the one in the middle of the context window, from pairs where the same context window is associated with a randomly chosen target word. A refinement of the CBOW model is the *context2vec* model[32] obtained by substituting the simple CBOW network with a bidirectional LSTM network (Section 7.16).

This method is called "self-supervised learning" and is not based on data labeling, for example, "spam" or "non-spam" for e-mails, or the category for a job offer, but on information coming from the data itself, in this case texts: a part of a text is used to predict another part of this text. The interest of self-supervised training is that it does not require human intervention for labeling the data and can therefore easily exploit very large datasets such as those found on the Web, in this case corpora of texts, huge enough to train complex models.

This process has some analogy with that of autoencoders (Section 7.18), with the projection of a high-dimensional space (here, the words) onto a much smaller dimensional space (their vector representations). The training is done on a base containing thousands of sentences with central words and surrounding words. The values that arrive on the hidden units of the network are the vector representations of the "contextual" words, which are adjusted to allow the network to maximize the quality of its word prediction. The skip-gram model is slightly slower than the CBOW model but is said to be more efficient with rare words, since it does not average the distribution of words over a context window.

We can see that the essential difference between the bag of words representation and the Word2Vec representation is that the latter takes into account the context of words. The Word2Vec representations of two words will be close as vectors if these two words present both a semantic similarity and a syntactic similarity. The Word2Vec representation can therefore detect synonymies and analogies, i.e. words appearing in similar contexts. An example of an analogical relation is that a grandfather is to a grandmother what a father is to a mother, that a king is to a queen what a man is to a woman, or that Rome is to Italy what Paris is to France.

In a Word2Vec vector representation of the words:

- the vector "King" – "Man" + "Woman" is close to the vector "Queen" ;
- the vector "Paris" – "France" + "Italy" is close to the vector "Rome."

Remarkably, the Word2Vec representation automatically detects relations such as the ones above (country – capital) without specifying that we were looking for this relation. From this point of view, the Word2Vec representation improves the topic model approach as well as the n-gram approach (the trigram analysis, for example, being a way to take into account the context of the words). It therefore makes high performance possible in document classification. Word2Vec is a so-called "word embedding" method.

We go from the representation of a word to that of a (rather short) text by calculating the center of gravity of the Word2Vec vectors representing the words of this text (after possible cleaning of the text and, for example, deletion of stop words). Each text, for example, an email or a tweet, is represented by a vector of fixed length and the proximity in this vector space of the Word2Vec representations of two texts indicates close meanings and contexts of these texts, beyond simple word coincidences. This shows the interest of this representation for automatic classification. It is also efficient in disambiguation and automatic translation. It is similar to the idea of factorial analysis, which is to perform analyses on data summarized by a few factors; here, we have texts summarized by a few vectors. Word embedding methods are useful for both supervised and unsupervised natural language processing tasks.

Depending on the needs, and of course on the languages, the Word2Vec models can be trained on various corpora, which should be as complete as possible and appropriate to the domain studied. But if the analysed corpora are very large, their vector representation is less so: the number of vector coordinates is equal to the number of distinct words in the corpus, multiplied by the few hundred dimensions. Wikipedia is one of the sources often used, especially since it exists in many languages.

Word2Vec was invented by researchers at Google,[33] which makes resources freely available to the research and user community.[34] Word2Vec is usable in Python thanks to the `gensim` library (which also implements LSA and LDA), and in R thanks to the packages `rword2vec`, `wordVectors` and `h2o`. Pre-trained Word2Vec models are available in several languages, notably in French on Jean-Philippe Fauconnier's website[35] and in English with a model of vectors in dimension 300 learned on 100 billion words from Google News.[36] There are also training datasets, such as the first billion characters of Wikipedia[37] and another dataset of one billion words.[38]

The Doc2Vec algorithm has been proposed[39] to vectorize documents instead of vectorizing words like Word2Vec does. It is notably used in sentiment analysis.[40]

It is very simple to use these models, for example, using the R package `rword2vec`, by loading one of the pre-trained models mentioned above. After installing `rword2vec` (from GitHub), we load the binary file of the pre-trained model.

```
> library(devtools)
> install_github("mukul13/rword2vec")
> library(rword2vec)
> vector <- "D:/Data/NLP/GoogleNews-vectors-negative300.bin"
```

We can then search for the closest terms to a set of prescribed terms, as described above:

```
> (ana <- word_analogy(file_name = vector,
    search_words = "man woman king", num = 5))


Word: man   Position in vocabulary: 251


Word: woman   Position in vocabulary: 641


Word: king   Position in vocabulary: 6147
              word             dist
1            queen 0.711819648742676
2          monarch 0.618967652320862
3         princess 0.590243101119995
4     crown_prince 0.549946367740631
5           prince 0.537733243537903
```

We find the analogy relationship of "queen" with "woman," "king" and "man." We can also test the ability of Word2Vec to identify a relationship from country to capital:

```
> (ana <- word_analogy(file_name = vector,
    search_words = "paris france london", num = 5))


Word: paris   Position in vocabulary: 198365


Word: france   Position in vocabulary: 225534


Word: london   Position in vocabulary: 139693
              word             dist
1           england 0.583685517311096
2            europe 0.552957236766815
3        birmingham 0.518000662326813
4          european 0.512530326843262
5         newcastle 0.510719418525696
```

We can also search, with the distance() function, the closest words to a given word, here the word "king":

```
> (dist <- distance(file_name = "text8.bin",
    search_word = "king", num = 5))
Entered word or sentence: king

Word: king   Position in vocabulary: 187
        word             dist
1     prince 0.744405388832092
2    emperor 0.674374461174011
3      kings  0.65012001991272
4     throne 0.646447896957397
5       duke 0.642947494983673
```

In some languages, a problem may arise with accents, which can be solved by converting to UTF-8 encoding.

```
> dist$word <- iconv(dist$word, from="UTF-8", to="latin1")
```

The `rword2vec` package can load a pre-trained model, in the form of a binary vector file, but the `rword2vec` package also can train a model on a corpus, using the `word2vec()` function. Here is how to train a model stored in a file named `vec.bin`, from the text8 corpus:

```
> model <- word2vec(train_file = "D:/Data/NLP/text8", out-
put_file = "vec.bin", binary=1)
```

The text8 corpus is well known.[41] It is made up of 100 million characters from the English Wikipedia, with all words separated by a space and without line breaks between articles. It is derived from the larger enwik9 corpus: the first billion characters of Wikipedia.[42] More information about these corpora can be found on Matt Mahoney's website.[43]

Thanks to another function of the `rword2vec` package, the binary file resulting from the training can be converted into a text file where each line corresponds to a word and contains its Word2Vec vector coordinates:

```
> bin_to_txt("vec.bin", "vector.txt")
> w2v <- as.data.frame(read.table("vector.txt", skip=1))
> w2v[1:10,]
```

For the detection of compound words, the `word2phrase()` function can combine pairs of adjacent words into a single vector: los_angeles, san_francisco, golden_gate …

```
> word2phrase(train_file = "text8", output_file = "vec.txt")
> model <- word2vec(train_file = "vec.txt",
    output_file = "vec2.bin", binary=1)
```

Similarly, we can use the `wordVectors` package to apply a pre-trained model:

```
> install_github("bmschmidt/wordVectors")
> library(wordVectors)
> library(magrittr)
> vector <- "D:/Data/NLP/text8.bin"
> model <- read.vectors(vector)
Filename ends with .bin, so reading in binary format
Reading a word2vec binary file of 71291 rows and 100 columns
> model %>% closest_to(~"king" - "man" + "woman")
        word similarity to "king" - "man" + "woman"
1       king                              0.8263808
2      queen                              0.6865205
3    empress                              0.6466833
4     prince                              0.6203607
5    emperor                              0.6202348
```

We can train a model on a corpus:

```
> model <- train_word2vec("D:/Data/NLP/craigswords.csv",
"craigs2.bin", vectors=100, threads=4, window=5, iter=10,
    cbow=0, min_count=5, negative_samples=0)
```

We now show an example of a very simple implementation of Word2Vec using the h2o package, on the classical example of spam detection, using a Kaggle dataset,[44] consisting of 5564 English SMS messages, whose variable v1 is the label "ham/spam" [45] and whose variable v2 contains the SMS raw text.

We create Word2Vec vectors using the skip-gram model of the `h2o.word2vec()` function by retaining only words appearing in at least five SMS messages, with a sliding window of five words around each word, a vector representation of dimension 100, and 10 epochs for training the neural network. Unlike the previous examples, we train a model on the SMS corpus, and do not use a pre-trained model. Words are distinguished by the function `h2o.tokenize(x, "\\\\W+" )` which considers any character other than a letter or a number as a word separator, and separates two lines of the data frame x, so here two SMS messages, by a "NA."

The Word2Vec vectors created for each word are then aggregated by an average at the level of each SMS message by the `h2o.transform()` function.

```
> textes <- h2o.importFile(path="C:/Users/.../data_spam.csv",
    header = TRUE)
> words <- h2o.tokenize(textes$v2, "\\\\W+")
> w2v.model <- h2o.word2vec(words, min_word_freq = 5,
    vec_size = 100, window_size = 5, epochs = 10)
> plot.vecs <- h2o.transform(w2v.model, words,
    aggregate = "average")
```

We want to develop a classification model to distinguish spam from non-spam. We use gradient boosting (Section 3.4.4) applied to the Word2Vec vectors of each SMS message. It is implemented in the `h2o.gbm()` function. We start by creating training (80%) and test (20%) datasets from the vector representation of each SMS message, preceded by the label "ham/spam":

```
> data <- h2o.cbind(textes["v1"], plot.vecs)
> data.split <- h2o.splitFrame(data, ratios = 0.8, seed = 235)
> gbm.model <- h2o.gbm(x = names(plot.vecs), y = "v1",
    training_frame = data.split[[1]], validation_frame =
    data.split[[2]], seed = 235)
> h2o.confusionMatrix(gbm.model, data.split[[2]])$Error[3]
[1] 0.01727273
> h2o.confusionMatrix(gbm.model, data.split[[2]])
Confusion Matrix (vertical: actual; across: predicted)
      for max f1 @ threshold = 0.805640932478627:
        ham spam    Error       Rate
ham     966    1 0.001034    =1/967
spam     18  115 0.135338    =18/133
Totals  984  116 0.017273    =19/1100
```

Applying the gradient boosting model to the test set shows that, without any preprocessing of the data, such as removing stop words or short words, our model identifies SMS messages that are spam with a test error rate of only 1.7%. The calculation of the confusion matrix further shows that we have very few false positives, as 1 SMS message out of 967 is mistaken for spam, and conversely 18 SMS messages out of 133 spams are not identified as spams.

A random forest model performs almost as well, with a test error rate of 1.8%, but it has only two false positives:

```
> rf.model <- h2o.randomForest(x = names(plot.vecs), y = "v1",
    training_frame = data.split[[1]], validation_frame =
    data.split[[2]], ntrees = 100, max_depth = 20, mtries = 10,
    seed=235)
> h2o.confusionMatrix(rf.model, data.split[[2]])
Confusion Matrix (vertical: actual; across: predicted)   for max
    f1 @ threshold = 0.57:
        ham spam    Error       Rate
ham     965    2 0.002068     =2/967
spam     18  115 0.135338    =18/133
Totals  983  117 0.018182   =20/1100
```

A perceptron with two hidden layers of ten units each, a hyperbolic tangent activation function and a weight decay ridge gives in 20 epochs an error rate of 1.9% in test.

```
> dl.model <- h2o.deeplearning(x = names(plot.vecs), y = "v1",
    training_frame = data.split[[1]], validation_frame =
    data.split[[2]], hidden = c(10,10), epochs = 20,
    activation = "Tanh", l1 = 1e-6, seed=235)
> h2o.confusionMatrix(dl.model, data.split[[2]])
Confusion Matrix (vertical: actual; across: predicted)   for max
    f1 @ threshold = 0.724988334866501:
        ham spam    Error       Rate
ham     961    6 0.006205     =6/967
spam     15  118 0.112782    =15/133
Totals  976  124 0.019091   =21/1100
```

On this dataset, we verified that a preprocessing with the removal of stop words, short words or words containing a number, a passage of all the characters in lower case, did not improve, on the contrary, the rate of good classification.

Another example is the prediction of the type of a job posting on Craigslist based on the title of the posting. This dataset has already been used in Section 4.4.2.

```
> jobs.path = "https://raw.githubusercontent.com/h2oai/
    sparkling-water/rel-1.6/examples/smalldata/craigslist
    JobTitles.csv"
> jobs <- h2o.importFile(job.titles.path, destination_frame =
    "jobtitles", col.names = c("category", "jobtitle"),
    col.types = c("Enum", "String"), header = TRUE)
```

Here are the categories to predict. The classification task is a bit more difficult with six categories to predict instead of two previously:

```
> h2o.table(jobs$category)
          category Count
1       accounting  1593
2   administrative  2500
3  customerservice  2319
4        education  2438
5      foodbeverage  2495
6            labor  2500
```

We proceed as before, starting with a gradient boosting model on the Word2Vec coordinates of the offers, without any prior data pre-processing:

```
> words <- h2o.tokenize(jobs$jobtitle, "\\\\W+")
> w2v.model <- h2o.word2vec(words, min_word_freq = 5, vec_size = 100, window_size = 5,
    epochs = 10)
> jobs.vecs <- h2o.transform(w2v.model, words, aggregate = "average")
> data <- h2o.cbind(jobs$category, jobs.vecs)
> data <- data[!is.na(data$C1),]
> data.split <- h2o.splitFrame(data, ratios = 0.8, seed = 235)
> gbm.model <- h2o.gbm(x = names(jobs.vecs), y = "category", training_frame =
    data.split[[1]], validation_frame = data.split[[2]], distribution="multinomial",
    ntrees = 300, learn_rate = 0.1, max_depth = 6, seed = 235)
> h2o.confusionMatrix(gbm.model, data.split[[2]])$Error[7]
[1] 0.2151248
> h2o.confusionMatrix(gbm.model, data.split[[2]])
Confusion Matrix: Row labels: Actual class; Column labels: Predicted class
                accounting administrative customerservice education foodbever-
age labor  Error       Rate
```

	accounting	administrative	customerservice	education	foodbeverage	labor	Error	Rate		
accounting	238	56	18	4	2	4	0.2609	=	84 / 322
administrative	10	381	57	11	11	11	0.2079	=	100 / 481
customerservice	6	52	313	7	44	38	0.3196	=	147 / 460
education	3	18	12	432	4	11	0.1000	=	48 / 480
foodbeverage	2	15	35	2	401	38	0.1866	=	92 / 493
labor	6	9	43	6	51	373	0.2357	=	115 / 488
Totals	265	531	478	462	513	475	0.2151	=	586 / 2724

Without pre-processing the data and without extensive research into optimizing the parameters of the gradient boosting model, we have a test error rate of 21.5%. The "education" category is the best predicted, with only 10% error.

A random forest of 200 trees and 10 variables tested at each split yields a slightly higher error rate at 21.8%:

```
> rf.model <- h2o.randomForest(x = names(jobs.vecs), y = "category", training_frame =
    data.split[[1]], validation_frame = data.split[[2]], ntrees = 200, max_depth = 30,
    mtries = 10, seed=235)
> h2o.confusionMatrix(rf.model, data.split[[2]])$Error[7]
[1] 0.2184288
> h2o.confusionMatrix(rf.model, data.split[[2]])
Confusion Matrix: Row labels: Actual class; Column labels: Predicted class
                accounting administrative customerservice education foodbever-
age labor  Error       Rate
```

	accounting	administrative	customerservice	education	foodbeverage	labor	Error	Rate		
accounting	235	53	19	8	2	5	0.2702	=	87 / 322
administrative	14	377	52	10	14	14	0.2162	=	104 / 481
customerservice	6	56	301	13	45	39	0.3457	=	159 / 460
education	4	18	6	441	4	7	0.0813	=	39 / 480
foodbeverage	1	14	30	5	404	39	0.1805	=	89 / 493
labor	5	11	35	9	57	371	0.2398	=	117 / 488
Totals	265	529	443	486	526	475	0.2184	=	595 / 2724

We now perform a pre-processing of the data before retraining the Word2Vec model and the gradient boosting model on the Word2Vec vectors.

The `words <- h2o.tokenize(jobs$jobtitle, "\\\\\W+" )` statement for separating words is replaced by the following ones, in which we pass all words in lower case, and remove words less than two characters long or containing a number, as well as stop words (those in the `tm` package):

```
> library(tm) # for the list of stopwords
> tokenize <- function(sentences) {
+ tokenized <- h2o.tokenize(sentences, "\\\\\W+")
+ tokenized.lower <- h2o.tolower(tokenized)
+ tokenized.lengths <- h2o.nchar(tokenized.lower)
+ tokenized.filtered <- tokenized.lower[is.na(tokenized.lengths)
    || tokenized.lengths >= 2,]
+ tokenized.words <- tokenized.filtered[h2o.grep("[0-9]", tok-
enized.filtered, invert = TRUE, output.logical = TRUE),]
+ tokenized.words[(! tokenized.words %in% stopwords("en")),]
+ }
> words <- tokenize(jobs$jobtitle)
```

We then compute the Word2Vec vectors and the previous gradient boosting model, whose parameters we keep:

```
> h2o.confusionMatrix(gbm.model, data.split[[2]])$Error[7]
[1] 0.1852531
> h2o.confusionMatrix(gbm.model, data.split[[2]])
Confusion Matrix: Row labels: Actual class; Column labels: Predicted class
                accounting administrative customerservice education foodbever-
age labor  Error      Rate
accounting        263        35        12        5        3        2 0.1781    =    57 / 320
administrative     16       396        49       10        6        5 0.1784    =    86 / 482
customerservice     6        54       327        7       28       35 0.2845    =   130 / 457
education           3        19        12      438        1        8 0.0894    =    43 / 481
foodbeverage        2        15        25        1      409       43 0.1737    =    86 / 495
labor               2        10        49        7       35      388 0.2098    =   103 / 491
Totals            292       529       474      468      482      481 0.1853    =   505 / 2726
```

The result of this data preprocessing is sensible, with a test error rate decreasing to 18.53%. We obtain an error rate of 18.45% with a random forest of 200 trees and 20 variables tested at each split. These rates are very slightly lower than the one obtained with a random forest on the document-term matrix in Section 4.4.2. The gain provided by the Word2Vec splitting is limited here because its model was trained on a corpus limited to the documents to be classified.

We will visually check the quality of the word embedding and the ability of the skip-gram algorithm to match semantically close terms. We use again the `h2o.transform()` function but without aggregation, in order to obtain a vector per word and not per document. As the result is a data frame with 100 columns, each containing a vector coordinate of the words, we reconcile this data frame with the one, `words`, containing each word, in a column `C1` which we rename because `C1` is also the coordinate of the first vector.

```
> mots.vecs <- h2o.transform(w2v.model, words,
    aggregate = "none")
> words$mot <- words$C1
> words$C1   <- NULL
> mots.vecs <- h2o.cbind(words, mots.vecs)
> mots.vecs <- mots.vecs[!is.na(mots.vecs$C1),]
> nrow(mots.vecs)
[1] 58602
```

We have 58,602 words but with all their repetitions. We copy this H2O data frame into an R data frame and remove the duplicates. We have only 1417 distinct words.

```
> motsvectsdf  <- as.data.frame(mots.vecs)
> motsvectsdf <- unique(motsvectsdf)
> nrow(motsvectsdf)
[1] 1417
```

Since we cannot display so many words legibly, we select the most frequent words, limiting ourselves to the 50 most frequent.

```
> freq    <- as.data.frame(words$mot)
> freq    <- table(freq$mot)
> freq    <- sort(freq, decreasing=TRUE)
> select <- names(head(freq, 50))
> select
 [1] "assistant"      "time"           "service"
 [4] "needed"         "hiring"         "manager"
 [7] "customer"       "part"           "office"
[10] "make"           "hr"             "full"
[13] "teacher"        "week"           "administrative"
[16] "now"            "wanted"         "coordinator"
[19] "san"            "specialist"     "accountant"
[22] "sales"          "car"            "admin"
[25] "associate"      "uber"           "position"
[28] "representative" "school"         "hour"
[31] "accounting"     "positions"      "drive"
[34] "receptionist"   "cook"           "preschool"
[37] "bonus"          "earn"           "driver"
[40] "restaurant"     "staff"          "tutors"
[43] "teachers"       "front"          "support"
[46] "line"           "executive"      "cooks"
[49] "company"        "entry"
> mots.vect <- motsvectsdf[motsvectsdf$mot %in% select,
    c("mot","C1","C2")]
```

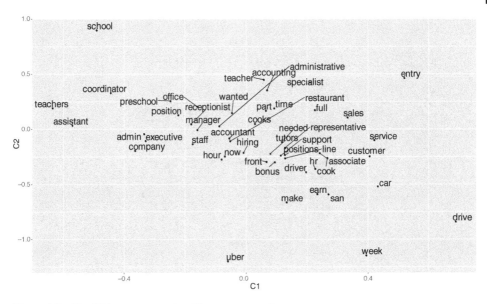

Figure 4.8 Word2Vec representation (first two vectors).

We can then display the words in a plane consisting of the first two Word2Vec vectors (Figure 4.8). We use the `geom_text_repel()` function of the `ggrepel` package which improves the readability of the graph by pushing the labels back (an arrow indicating their true location) to avoid overlapping.

```
> library(ggplot2)
> library(ggrepel)
> ggplot(mots.vect, aes(x=C1, y=C2)) + geom_point() + geom_
    text_repel(aes(label=mot), hjust=1, vjust=1, size=5,
    segment.size = 0)
```

The result may seem a bit disappointing because the neighboring words are not necessarily those whose meaning is close. This is due to the fact that the Word2Vec vectors are not ordered by decreasing information contribution, contrary to the axes of a factorial analysis, and that the first two Word2Vec vectors only provide a part of the information among 98 other vectors. It will therefore be more convincing to perform a principal component analysis on these 100 vectors and to display the words on the factorial plane of the first two axes (Figure 4.9).

```
> pca        <- prcomp(motsvectsdf[,-1])
> pcamots <-   cbind(motsvectsdf$mot, pca$x[,1:2])
> colnames(pcamots)[1] <- "mot"
> motsvectspca <- as.data.frame(pcamots)
> motsvectspca$PC1 <- as.numeric(as.character(motsvectspca$PC1))
> motsvectspca$PC2 <- as.numeric(as.character(motsvectspca$PC2))
> mots.vect <- motsvectspca[motsvectspca$mot %in% select, ]
> ggplot(as.data.frame(mots.vect), aes(x=PC1, y=PC2)) +
    geom_point() + geom_text_repel(aes(label=mot), hjust=1,
    vjust=1, size=5, segment.size = 0)
```

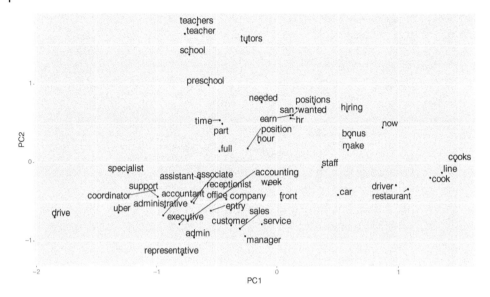

Figure 4.9 Word2Vec representation (first two factorial axes).

After performing this principal component analysis using the `prcomp()` function in the `stats` package, we create a data frame containing each word and its coordinates on the first two factorial axes, but we have to transform them by `as.numeric(as .character(wordsvectspca$PC1))` because the coordinates produced by the `prcomp()` function are factors and not numeric variables.

Homogeneous groups of words can then be clearly distinguished. One of these groups contains the words "restaurant," "line," "cook," and "cooks," which are of course associated with the "foodbeverage" category. Another group contains the words "tutors," "teachers," "teacher," "preschool," and "school," which are associated with the "education" category. It is understandable that a machine learning model manages to separate these categories quite well, and particularly the education job offers, whose words appear the most isolated from the others.

4.4.8 GloVe Embedding

Following Word2Vec, other word representation methods have been studied. One of them is the GloVe representation,[46] which is implemented in the R package `text2vec`.[47]

This representation involves the creation of a co-occurrence matrix whose coefficients M_{ij} are the number of times word i appears in the context of word j, i.e. in a window of a certain size around word j, the weight of the words decreasing when one moves away from the center of the window. We normalize this matrix by the logarithm to avoid having orders of magnitude too different in the frequencies. We then look for a low rank approximation of this matrix, thus a vector space of lower dimension in which we are interested in the embedding of each word. In this embedding, the vector v_i corresponding to each word i must be such that the scalar product $<v_i, v_j>$ of two vectors is equal to the logarithm of M_{ij}. These computations can be time-consuming if performed on a large corpus and it is possible to download pre-trained models, for example, from the Wikipedia corpus.[48]

Let's illustrate this with an example[49] of nine sentences containing the following words, after removing stop words and words that appear only once.

```
texts = [['human', 'interface', 'computer'],
  ['survey', 'user', 'computer', 'system', 'response', 'time'],
  ['eps', 'user', 'interface', 'system'],
  ['system', 'human', 'system', 'eps'],
  ['user', 'response', 'time'],
  ['trees'],
  ['graph', 'trees'],
  ['graph', 'minors', 'trees'],
  ['graph', 'minors', 'survey']]
```

The co-occurrence matrix with a window width of 5 is as follows.

```
[[0 1 1 1 1 1 1 1 0 0 0 0]
 [1 0 1 0 0 2 0 0 1 0 0 0]
 [1 1 0 0 0 1 0 1 1 0 0 0]
 [1 0 0 0 1 1 2 2 0 0 0 0]
 [1 0 0 1 0 1 1 1 0 0 1 1]
 [1 2 1 1 1 2 1 2 3 0 0 0]
 [1 0 0 2 1 1 0 2 0 0 0 0]
 [1 0 1 2 1 2 2 0 1 0 0 0]
 [0 1 1 0 0 3 0 1 0 0 0 0]
 [0 0 0 0 0 0 0 0 0 0 2 1]
 [0 0 0 0 1 0 0 0 0 2 0 2]
 [0 0 0 0 1 0 0 0 0 1 2 0]]
```

The rows and columns correspond in this order to the following words: *computer, human, interface, response, survey, system, time, user, eps, trees, graph,* and *minors*. For example, the last row has a "1" in the 5th column because *minors* is in a window around *survey* (9th text), a "1" in the 10th column because *minors* is in a window around *trees* (8th text) and a "2" in the 11th column because it is in two windows around *graph*.

After weighting the words according to their distance from the center of the window, the matrix becomes the following:

```
[[ 0.    0.5   1.    0.5   0.5   1.    0.33  1.    0.    0.    0.    0.   ]
 [ 0.    0.    1.    0.    0.    2.    0.    0.    0.5   0.    0.    0.   ]
 [ 0.    0.    0.    0.    0.    1.    0.    1.    0.5   0.    0.    0.   ]
 [ 0.    0.    0.    0.    0.25  1.    2.    1.33  0.    0.    0.    0.   ]
 [ 0.    0.    0.    0.    0.    0.33  0.2   1.    0.    0.    0.5   1.   ]
 [ 0.    0.    0.    0.    0.    0.    0.5   1.    1.67  0.    0.    0.   ]
 [ 0.    0.    0.    0.    0.    0.    0.    0.75  0.    0.    0.    0.   ]
 [ 0.    0.    0.    0.    0.    0.    0.    0.    1.    0.    0.    0.   ]
 [ 0.    0.    0.    0.    0.    0.    0.    0.    0.    0.    0.    0.   ]
 [ 0.    0.    0.    0.    0.    0.    0.    0.    0.    0.    1.5   1.   ]
 [ 0.    0.    0.    0.    0.    0.    0.    0.    0.    0.    0.    2.   ]
 [ 0.    0.    0.    0.    0.    0.    0.    0.    0.    0.    0.    0.   ]]
```

We can see that the GloVe representation is both a local method (with a window), like Word2Vec, and a global method of matrix factorization, like the latent analysis methods. It combines the advantages of both types of methods, by exploiting the context of each word better than factorization methods, and by exploiting the statistical properties of the corpus better than local methods.[50] In a local method, we are interested in the context of a word without having a global view of its frequency in the corpus.

The performance of the GloVe representation is not always much better than that of Word2Vec, but GloVe can parallelize itself and therefore process large corpora faster. On the other hand, GloVe requires more memory.

4.4.9   FastText Embedding

The Word2Vec representation has been generalized by Facebook's fastText representation,[51] in which not only words are embedded in a vector space, but all character n-grams formed from these words. In this representation, the vector corresponding to a word is the sum of the vectors corresponding to its n-grams of characters. For example, if we set the minimum and maximum length of the n-grams to 3 and 6, the vector of the word "apple" is the sum of the vectors of the n-grams "<ap," "app," "appl," "apple," "apple>," "ppl," "pple," "pple>," "ple," "ple>" and "le>."

Working with n-grams offers two major advantages over the word embeddings of Word2Vec and GloVe. On the one hand, it is possible to find the vector corresponding to a word that does not exist, for example, when it has been written with a spelling mistake. Indeed, the vector will be computed from the vectors of the n-grams, which exist for the most part. This vector will be close to the word written without spelling mistakes.

On the other hand, the fastText embedding provides a better embedding of rare words. These are present in few contexts and lack neighboring words for a reliable computation of their vector representation. On the other hand, their n-grams are much more frequent and shared with the n-grams of many other words.

The obvious counterpart of these advantages is that the number of n-grams is much larger than the number of words and that the training of the model is much more time-consuming (but perhaps less time-consuming than with the LSTM networks of Section 9.2). In order to control the time and memory required for computation, it is therefore important to pay attention to the proper parameterization of the training, including the minimum and maximum length of the n-grams, as well as the minimum frequency of words considered in the learning, which may need to be raised to limit complexity.

One can also avoid a long training curve by using pre-trained models. Facebook provides on its website[52] fastText models in dimension 300, trained on Wikipedia in nearly 300 languages.

The fastText embedding is implemented in the `fastTextR`[53] package on CRAN and in a Python library. It can be used for text classification or for word representation, depending on the value of the `method` parameter of the R `fasttext()` function: `supervised`, `cbow` or `skipgram`.

To illustrate the classification with `fastTextR`, we return to the example of predicting the type of job offer from the title of the offer (Section 4.4.2). We start by replacing the job category in the first column with the "__label__category" value that is the expected form of fastText. Then we pre-process all the words of the titles in lower case, removing punctuation, stop words, and words less than two characters long or containing a number:

```
> jobs.path = "https://raw.githubusercontent.com/h2oai/
    sparkling-water/rel-1.6/examples/smalldata/craigslistJob
Titles.csv"
> jobs <- h2o.importFile(jobs.path, destination_frame = "jobs",
    col.names = c("category", "jobtitle"), col.types =
    c("Enum", "String"), header = TRUE)
> jobs <- as.data.frame(jobs)
> jobs$category <- paste0("__label__", jobs$category)
> jobs$jobtitle <- gsub("[^[:print:]]", "", jobs$jobtitle)
    # deletion of non-printable characters
> jobs$jobtitle <- gsub("\\<\\w{1}\\>", "", jobs$jobtitle)
    # deletion of words of 1 character
> jobs$jobtitle <- tolower(jobs$jobtitle) # change to lower
    case
> jobs$jobtitle <- gsub("[[:punct:]]", " ", jobs$jobtitle)
    # replace punctuation with a space
> jobs$jobtitle <- gsub("\\<[a-z]*[0-9]+[a-z]*\\>", "",
    jobs$jobtitle) # deletion of words containing a number
> stopw <- paste0("\\b(", paste0(stopwords("en"),
    collapse="|"), ")\\b")
> jobs$jobtitle <- gsub(stopw, "", jobs$jobtitle)
    # deletion of stop words
> jobs$jobtitle <- gsub("[[:space:]]{2,}", " ", jobs$jobtitle)
    # deletion of multiple spaces
```

We save the pre-processed data in a CSV file. Then we read it with the `readLines()` function which creates a vector of strings with one element per line of the file read. We perform fastText's own "normalization" and build a training dataset and a test dataset.

```
> write.table(jobs[-1,], file="D:/Data/NLP/craigsjobs.csv",
    row.names = F, col.names = F)
> jobs <- readLines("D:/Data/NLP/craigsjobs.csv")
> jobs <- ft_normalize(jobs)
> set.seed(123)
> s <- sample(length(jobs), length(jobs)*0.8, replace=F)
> writeLines(jobs[s], con = "D:/Data/NLP/craigslist.train")
> writeLines(jobs[-s], con = "D:/Data/NLP/craigslist.test")
```

To classify the job categories, we then construct a 20-dimensional fastText model from the n-grams between n = 2 and n = 5, with a 5-word sliding window, retaining only words appearing in at least 5 titles, with a learning rate equal to 0.1 and 10 epochs for training the model on four cores of the machine.

```
> cntrl <- ft_control(word_vec_size = 20, window_size = 5,
     learn_update = 100, learning_rate = 0.1, min_count = 5,
     min_ngram = 2, max_ngram = 5, epoch = 10, nthreads = 4)
> system.time(model <- ft_train("D:/Data/NLP/craigslist.train",
     method="supervised", control = cntrl))
utilisateur      système        écoulé
      1.33         0.08          0.45
> model
fastText "supervised" model:
    117,547 tokens, 1,230 words, 6 labels
```

Then we apply the model to the test set:

```
> test.pred <- ft_predict(model, newdata=jobs[-s], k = 1, prob = TRUE)
> (confusion_matrix <- table(gsub("__label__", "", substr(jobs[-s],1,21)),
    gsub("__label__", "", test.pred$label)))
```

	accounting	administrative	customerservice	education	foodbeverage	labor
" accountin	252	37	16	8	2	1
" administr	33	367	50	2	12	10
" customers	12	59	322	13	31	54
" education	5	16	9	438	4	4
" foodbever	2	6	34	1	411	42
" labor " "	2	8	40	8	33	425

```
> 1-sum(diag(confusion_matrix)) / sum(confusion_matrix)
[1] 0.2000722
```

The error rate obtained is not lower than the one previously obtained with the Word2Vec function of the h2o package and does not attribute an advantage to the use of n-grams in this example which does not contain any rare word or spelling mistake.

We turn to the use of the fastTextR package for word representation, which can be performed using the skip-gram or CBOW method. As mentioned in Section 4.4.7, the CBOW method is faster but less accurate. We will not represent here the result it gives but it would clearly appear less satisfactory than the skip-gram method.

To obtain the representation in Figure 4.10, we first build a 20-dimensional fastText model with a parallelized learning of ten epochs:

```
> cntrl <- ft_control(learning_rate = 0.1, word_vec_size = 20,
     epoch = 10, nthreads = 4)
> model <- ft_train("D:/Data/NLP/craigslist.train",
     "skipgram", cntrl)
```

We then retrieve the vectors associated with the studied words. The function get_words() gives the list of these words and the function get_word_vectors(x,y) exports the coordinates of the vectors of the x model associated with the y words. These coordinates are in a matrix of 1233 rows (as many as different words) and 20 columns:

```
> vectors <- ft_word_vectors(model, ft_words(model))
> dim(vectors)
[1] 1230    20
```

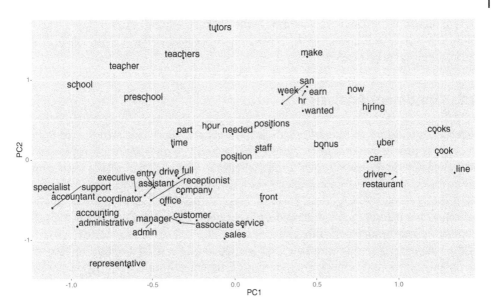

Figure 4.10 FastText representation (first two factorial axes).

We then transform this matrix into a data frame to which we add the word variable from the row names:

```
> motsvectsdf <- as.data.frame(vectors)
> motsvectsdf$mot <- row.names(motsvectsdf)
```

As above, we compute a principal component analysis to represent the words in the first factorial plane. We use the prcomp() function, remembering that the last variable of the data frame contains the words and that we must therefore exclude it from the principal component analysis to keep only the coordinates of the vectors:

```
> pca       <- prcomp(motsvectsdf[,-ncol(motsvectsdf)])
> pcamots <- cbind(motsvectsdf$mot, pca$x[,1:2])
> colnames(pcamots)[1] <- "mot"
> motsvectspca <- as.data.frame(pcamots)
```

We created a data frame containing each word and its coordinates on the first two factorial axes, which we transformed by the statement as.numeric(as.character(words vectspca$PC1)) since the coordinates produced by the prcomp() function are factors and not numeric variables:

```
> motsvectspca$PC1 <- as.numeric(as.character(motsvectspca$PC1))
> motsvectspca$PC2 <- as.numeric(as.character(motsvectspca$PC2))
```

We represent only the most frequent words, and for this purpose we use the select word vector created earlier with the 50 most frequent words:

```
> mots.vect <- motsvectspca[motsvectspca$mot %in% select, ]
> ggplot(as.data.frame(mots.vect), aes(x=PC1, y=PC2)) +
      geom_point() + geom_text_repel(aes(label=mot), hjust=1,
      vjust=1, size=5, segment.size = 0)
```

As in Figure 4.9, in Figure 4.10 we can clearly see the grouping of words by job type. The ability of word embedding to perform these groupings explains why it is possible to classify the job offers quite precisely.

4.5 Sentiment Analysis

A recent application of natural language processing is sentiment analysis (or opinion mining). It aims at automatically detecting and quantifying the sentiments expressed in a document and more generally in a corpus, which can be made up of posts, tweets, emails, movie reviews, or survey responses. Sentiments can be the two polarities (positive/negative) or the basic emotions of joy, fear, anger, sadness, surprise, and disgust. These emotions, as well as the neutral emotion, have been identified by the American psychologist Paul Ekman[54] as being innate and universal.

The simplest approaches are based on particular lexicons, associating to each word its polarity, or its basic emotion(s). These lexicons range from a binary scale (the word is/is not positive) to a 16-notch scale (`syuzhet` package). There are many of them in English, especially for polarities, and probably fewer in French, and *a fortiori* in less spoken languages, but we can mention the French FEEL lexicon,[55] which contains 14,000 words, obtained by automatic translation of the *English Emotional Lexicon NRC-Canada* and validated by a professional translator.

Each word is thus assigned a score, and the score of the document is the sum or average of the scores of its words. We can very simply define the polarity of a document by subtracting the number of negative words from the number of positive words. This approach is limited, since, on the one hand, many words have a meaning that depends on the context, and, on the other, the meaning of a word can be modified by a grammatical construction, and in particular inverted by a negation.

More elaborate approaches exist, based on machine learning methods or topic modeling methods, such as latent semantic analysis and latent Dirichlet allocation, as seen previously. They can build a model capable of predicting a sentiment after being trained on a corpus of documents whose sentiments are known. They can also look at word n-grams, at least digrams, to detect negations, or perform more subtle grammatical analysis, for example, to identify speakers.

Sentiment analysis is widely used with Twitter data (Section 5.10.6) or other social networks to detect opinions about political events or figures, trends before an election, community reactions to a speech or decision, interest in the launch of a new product, the brand image of a company, etc. This analysis can be performed at regular intervals and the evolution of an opinion score can be followed over time.

Several R packages implement sentiment analysis, the following[56] all on CRAN:

- the `meanr` package is very fast (written in C) but it is limited to the basic approach of counting positive and negative words according to a dictionary;
- the `syuzhet` package is based on four dictionaries (including Bing and nrc)[57] and on the sentiment analysis tool of the Stanford NLP group (for the use of which the `coreNLP` package must be installed);
- the `SentimentAnalysis` package uses dictionaries (some specific to finance) and can create them;

- the RSentiment package has its own dictionary and can create one;
- the sentimentr package is based on nine dictionaries of the lexicon package and draws its strength from the consideration of negations (" I do not like it"), amplifications (" I really like it"), attenuations (" I hardly like it") and oppositions (" I like it but it's not worth it").

Full syntactic analyses are very difficult, but simpler and more "local" analyses that consist of dealing with negations and of identifying different markers such as those of intensity (little, much, very) are already very useful in sentiment analysis. Other local analyses consist of identifying markers of spatial relation (at, near, far) and of temporal relation (once, formerly, soon) as in the recognition of named entities (Section 4.3.5).

The sentimentr package takes variations into account with the help of a *shifters* file and rules. The shifters file contains a list of words, each associated with a code. This code is 1 for a negation, 2 for an amplification, 3 for an attenuation and 4 for an opposition. Then, when analyzing a document, the polarity of each word is inflected in the presence of one of these modifiers in a window of four words before and two words after the analyzed word. An odd number of negations turns amplification into attenuation. Here are the first ten modifiers:

```
> head(as.data.frame(lexicon::hash_valence_shifters),10)
              x y
1     absolutely 2
2          acute 2
3        acutely 2
4          ain't 1
5           aint 1
6         almost 3
7       although 4
8         aren't 1
9          arent 1
10        barely 3
```

And here is an example of how to take these variations into account:

```
> txt <- c("I like it",
+ "I do not like it",
+ "I don't like it",
+ "I really like it",
+ "I dislike it",
+ "I really dislike it")
> (sentim <- sentiment(txt))
   element_id sentence_id word_count   sentiment
1:          1           1          3   0.2886751
2:          2           1          5  -0.2236068
3:          3           1          5   0.2236068
4:          4           1          4   0.4500000
5:          5           1          3  -0.5773503
6:          6           1          4  -0.9000000
```

1: -.023

It is a truth universally acknowledged, that a single man in possession of a good fortune, must be in want of a wife. However litle known he feelings or views of such a man may be on his first entering a neighbourhood, this truth is so well fixed in the minds of the surrounding families, that he is considered the rightful property of some one or other of their daughters. 'My dear Mr. Bennet,' said his lady to him one day 'have yoy heard that Netherfield Park is le at last?' Mr. Bennet replied that he had not. 'But it is,' returned she; 'for Mrs. Long has just been here, and she told me all about it.' Mr. Bennet made no answer. 'Do you not want to know who has taken it?' **cried his wife impatiently.** *'You want to tell me, and I have no objection to hearing it.'*

Figure 4.11 Sentiment analysis.

Let's take the incipit of Jane Austen's *Pride and Prejudice* and apply the `sentimentr` package to it.[58]

```
> library(sentimentr)
> txt <- c(" It is a truth universally acknowledged [...] and
    I have no objection to hearing it.'")
```

We obtain the score of each sentence, then aggregated by text passage, i.e. by element of the string vector. Here, we have only one.

```
> sentiment(txt)
   element_id sentence_id word_count   sentiment
1:          1           1         23   0.46915743
2:          1           2         47   0.04375950
3:          1           3         28   0.09449112
4:          1           4         24   0.00000000
5:          1           5         14  -0.48107024
6:          1           6         13   0.06933752
> (sentim <- sentiment_by(txt))
   element_id word_count         sd ave_sentiment
1:          1        149  0.3035809    0.03354882
```

With a version of `sentimentr` at least equal to 2.8.0, the `highlight()` function colors text passages according to their sentiment score (positive = *green*; negative = **pink**), saves them in HTML format and opens them in a web browser (Figure 4.11).

```
> highlight(sentim)
Saved in C:\Users\.../polarity.html
Opening C:\Users\.../polarity.html ...
```

The `sentimentr` package also allows you to identify the most positive and negative sentences in a document.

We start with 5000 reviews on Trip Advisor and we use the `extract_sentiment_terms()` function which allows to extract the positive and negative words of each sentence:

```
> data(hotel_reviews)
> txt <- hotel_reviews$text
> sentim <- sentiment(txt)
> pol_words <- extract_sentiment_terms(txt)
> head(pol_words,5)
   element_id sentence_id negative              positive
1:          1           1                          perfect
2:          1           2
3:          1           3                       exceptional
4:          1           4              friendly,helpful
5:          1           5             enjoyed,beautiful
```

We will match these words with the sentences that contain them to extract the most positive and the most negative sentence.

```
> head(pol_words$sentence,5)
[1] "This hotel is in THE perfect location."
[2] "It's within walking distance to many sites and just a tram
    ride away from everything else."
[3] "The staff in this hotel is exceptional..."
[4] "very friendly and helpful."
[5] "We enjoyed the beautiful rooftop terrace with views of the
    Marmara Sea."
```

Here is the most positive sentence:

```
> pol_words$sentence[which.max(sentim$sentiment)]
[1] "Very relaxing.5) Food - very good quality."
```

Here is the most negative sentence:

```
> pol_words$sentence[which.min(sentim$sentiment)]
[1] "Too much stodgy and fried stuff-and not prepared partic-
ualry well.."
```

We then extract the polarity of the words and sort them by decreasing polarity:

```
> terms <- attributes(pol_words)$counts
> terms <- terms[order(terms$polarity, decreasing=T), ]
```

The five most positive words are found to be as follows:

```
> head(terms,5)
          words polarity   n
1:    excellent        1 939
2:      enjoyed        1 440
3:          top        1 373
4:      pleasant        1 319
5:      quality        1 231
```

The five most negative words are found to be as follows:

```
> tail(terms,5)
       words polarity   n
1:    i wish        -2  34
2:     overly       -2  33
3:   too good       -2   4
4: too often        -2   3
5:     unduly       -2   1
```

The `sentimentr` package handles English but it can be used to specify a dictionary in another language or to modify an existing dictionary. A dictionary is a simple data frame or data table with two columns: the first one containing the words and the second one containing their polarity. You can also modify the predefined shifters file in English.

Notes

1 Bourdon, B. *The Expression of Emotions and Tendencies in Language* (Paris: Félix Alcan, 1892).

2 Estoup, J.B. *Gammes Sténographiques,* 4th edn (Paris: Imprimerie Moderne, 1916).

3 Zipf, G.K. The Psychobiology of Language (Boston: Houghton-Mifflin, 1935). The definitive formulation can be found in: *Human Behavior and the Principle of Least-Effort* (Reading, MA: Addison-Wesley, 1949).

4 https://www.deepmind.com/blog/wavenet-a-generative-model-for-raw-audio.

5 Sinclair, J. (1996). *Preliminary Recommendations on Corpus Typology.* EAGLES Document EAG-TCWG-CTYP/P.

6 http://www.dtmvic.com/

7 See the "CRAN Taskview Natural Language Processing," at https://cran.r-project.org/web/views/NaturalLanguageProcessing.html.

8 Bouchet-Valat, M. and Bastin, G. RcmdrPlugin.temis, a Graphical Integrated Text Mining Solution in R, *The R Journal,* 5(1), (2013), 188–196.

9 Cavnar, W.B. and Trenkle, J.M. n-Gram-Based Text Categorization, in *Proceedings of SDAIR-94, 3rd Annual Symposium on Document Analysis and Information Retrieval,* (1994), pp. 161–175.

10 http://www.cis.uni-muenchen.de/~schmid/tools/TreeTagger/

11 http://www.smo.uhi.ac.uk/~oduibhin/oideasra/interfaces/winttinterface.htm

12 https://nlp.stanford.edu/software/tagger.shtml.

13 Marcus, M.P. et al. Building a Large Annotated Corpus of English: the Penn Treebank, *Computational Linguistics,* 19(2) (1993), 313–320; and Marcus, M.P. et al. The Penn Treebank: Annotating Predicate Argument Structure, *ARPA Human Language Technology Workshop* (1994).

14 Also accessible through the `coreNLP` package.

15 https://stanfordnlp.github.io/CoreNLP/download.html.

16 https://stanfordnlp.github.io/CoreNLP/history.html.

17 See, for example, François, T. Modèles statistiques pour l'estimation automatique de la difficulté de textes de *FLE*. RECITAL 2009 (Senlis. 2009).

18 Porter, M.F. *An Algorithm for Suffix Stripping*, Program, 14(3) (1980), 130–137.

19 http://wordnet.princeton.edu/.

20 https://wordnet.princeton.edu/download/current-version.

21 Benoit, K., Watanabe, K., Wang, H., Nulty, P., Obeng, A., Müller, S., and Matsuo, A. quanteda: An R Package for the Quantitative Analysis of Textual Data, *Journal of Open Source Software*, 3(30) (2018), 774.

22 www.craigslist.org

23 https://raw.githubusercontent.com/h2oai/sparkling-water/rel-1.6/examples/smalldata/craigslistJobTitles.csv.

24 Deerwester, S., Dumais, S.T., Furnas, G W., Landauer, T.K., and Harshman, R. Indexing by Latent Semantic Analysis, *Journal of the American Society for Information Science*, 41(6) (1990), 391-407.

25 Blei, D., Ng, A., and Jordan, M. Latent Dirichlet Allocation. *Journal of Machine Learning Research*, 3 (2003), 993–1022.

26 Multinomial generalization of the beta distribution.

27 Dempster, A.P., Laird, N.M., and Rubin, D.B. Maximum Likelihood from Incomplete Data via the EM Algorithm, *Journal of the Royal Statistical Society*, Series B, 39(1) (1977), 1–38.

28 Blei, D.M. and Lafferty J.D. A Correlated Topic Model of Science, *The Annals of Applied Statistics*, 1(1) (2007), 7–35.

29 The site http://www.princeton.edu/~achaney/tmve/wiki100k/browse/topic-presence.html provides an application to the Wikipedia corpus.

30 Grün, B. and Hornik, K. topicmodels: An R Package for Fitting Topic Models. *Journal of Statistical Software*, 40(13) (2011).

31 Teh Y.W., Jordan M.I., Beal M.J., and Blei D.M. Hierarchical Dirichlet Processes, *Journal of the American Statistical Association*, 101(476) (2006), 1566–1581.

32 Melamud, O., Goldberger, J., and Dagan, I. context2vec: Learning Generic Context Embedding with Bidirectional LSTM, in *Proceedings of the 20th SIGNLL Conference on Computational Natural Language Learning (CoNLL)*, (2016), pp. 51–61.

33 Mikolov, T., Chen, K., Corrado, G., and Dean, J. *Efficient Estimation of Word Representations in Vector Space* (2013). arXiv:1301.3781.

34 https://code.google.com/archive/p/word2vec/.

35 http://fauconnier.github.io/#data.

36 https://drive.google.com/file/d/0B7XkCwpI5KDYNlNUTTlSS21pQmM/edit.

37 http://mattmahoney.net/dc/textdata.html and http://mattmahoney.net/dc/enwik9.zip.

38 http://www.statmt.org/lm-benchmark/1-billion-word-language-modeling-benchmark-r13output.tar.gz.

39 Quoc, V. Le, and Mikolov, T. *Distributed Representations of Sentences and Documents* (2014). arXiv:1405.4053.

40 See https://www.r-bloggers.com/twitter-sentiment-analysis-with-machine-learning-in-r-using-doc2vec-approach/ and https://medium.com/scaleabout/a-gentle-introduction-to-doc2vec-db3e8c0cce5e.

41 Downloadable here: http://mattmahoney.net/dc/text8.zip.

42 Downloadable here: http://mattmahoney.net/dc/enwik9.zip.

43 http://mattmahoney.net/dc/textdata.html.

44 https://www.kaggle.com/uciml/sms-spam-collection-dataset.

45 The term "ham" for non-spam email or SMS message is understandable if you know that the word "spam" is an acronym for "Shoulder of Pork and hAM," which is quoted in a Monty Python sketch parodying a radio commercial for a poor-quality canned ham, SPAM, during which the name of the product is repeated multiple times.

46 Pennington, J., Socher, R., and Manning, C.D. GloVe: Global Vectors for Word Representation, in *Proceedings of the 2014 Conference on Empirical Methods in Natural Language Processing (EMNLP)* (2014), 1532–1543.

47 https://cran.r-project.org/web/packages/text2vec/vignettes/glove.html.

48 https://nlp.stanford.edu/projects/glove/.

49 https://radimrehurek.com/gensim/tut1.html.

50 https://nlp.stanford.edu/pubs/glove.pdf.

51 https://fasttext.cc/.

52 https://github.com/facebookresearch/fastText/blob/master/pretrained-vectors.md?utm_campaign=buffer&utm_content=buffer0df9b&utm_medium=social&utm_source=linkedin.com.

53 https://cran.r-project.org/web/packages/fastTextR/README.html.

54 Ekman, P. An Argument for Basic Emotions, *Cognition and Emotion*, 6(3) (1992), 169–200.

55 http://advanse.lirmm.fr/feel.php.

56 See Naldi, M. *A Review of Sentiment Computation Methods with R Packages* (2019). arXiv:1901.08319.

57 The NRC dictionary has word lists by polarity (+/-), eight categories of feelings (anger, sadness ...) and in several languages (translated from English by Google Translate).

58 https://github.com/trinker/sentimentr.

5

Social Network Analysis

Social networks are at the heart of big data, with their huge quantities of data of all kinds, text, images, video, and audio. They are of interest to both the private sector, with their growing use in marketing campaigns and recommendation systems, and the public sector, which sees them as a means of surveying public opinion. They are also of particular interest to the academic world, especially since these data are partly freely available, as we shall see, and provide rich material for researchers. Researchers often apply methods and tools from graph theory,[1] analyze them, and identify their most interesting characteristics, their most influential members, the diffusion of information, their communities … What has led to the important development of these methods is also that they apply to networks as varied as those found in biology, computer science, telecommunications, or transport. They are the subject of numerous theoretical works and various computer implementations.

5.1 Social Networks

A network is a set of entities connected by links. A social network is a set of human entities (individuals, groups, or organizations) linked by social ties, i.e. family, friends or professionals. It can be represented as a graph where the actors are the vertices and the links are the edges. We can study a graph, its number of vertices, edges, its density, its diameter and its central elements, i.e. those which have the most links.

The following figures give an idea of the difficulty of analysis on social networks, whose data are truly massive, even before being varied.

There are 4.66 billion internet users worldwide in January 2021, with 4.2 billion registered on a social media.[2] Facebook has 2.74 billion monthly active users and over 150 billion connections between friends. YouTube has 2.29 billion active users, and more than 1 billion hours of video are viewed each day. Twitter has 353 million active users, 500 million tweets are sent each day, and an account has an average of 208 followers (the maximum being over 100 million followers). As for Instagram, it has 1.22 billion active users.

Beyond these figures, social networks are evolving rapidly, and we understand the need to have powerful algorithms to analyze them.

Deep Learning: From Big Data to Artificial Intelligence with R, First Edition. Stéphane Tufféry.
© 2023 John Wiley & Sons Ltd. Published 2023 by John Wiley & Sons Ltd.
Companion website: www.wiley.com/go/Tuffery/DeepLearning

5.2 Characteristics of Graphs

Graphs are mathematical objects that were studied as early as 1736 by Leonhard Euler who introduced the concepts to solve the famous problem of the seven bridges of Königsberg: go around the city and return to its starting point by taking each bridge once and only once. Graphs are used to represent social networks in particular and all networks in general. They are sets of vertices (or nodes) linked together by edges (or links). They are described by the following:

- A path is a sequence of edges and vertices connecting two vertices. The length of the path is its number of edges. A cycle is a path whose two ends are the same vertex. Two vertices are said to be adjacent if they are connected by a path of length 1.
- The distance between two vertices is the minimal length of the paths connecting them. It is sometimes expressed in *hop distance*: two adjacent vertices are one-hop neighbors.
- A graph is said to be "small-world" if it has a small average distance between two vertices; more precisely, an average distance less than or equal to the logarithm of the number of vertices.
- The eccentricity of a vertex is its maximum distance from all other vertices, i.e. the distance from the farthest vertex. The radius of the graph is the minimum eccentricity of the vertices, i.e. the smallest distance a vertex can be from all the others. The diameter of a graph is the maximum eccentricity of its vertices, i.e. the maximum distance between two vertices of the graph.
- A graph can be directed or undirected. If it is directed, we distinguish an edge between vertices A and B from an edge between B and A. A directed edge is called an arc or arrow.
- Edges can be weighted (also called "valued"), for example, by the number of messages between A and B. The weight of a path is then the sum of the weights of the edges that compose it. Vertices can also be weighted. A weighted graph is a graph whose edges or vertices are weighted.
- Data can be associated to the vertices and we speak then of a graph with attributes, or an attributed graph. It can be the age and the city of an individual.

We assume from here on that the graph is simple, i.e. without multiple edges (several edges connecting two vertices) nor edges from a vertex to itself (called a "loop," which is a cycle of length 1). We will only talk about unipartite graphs, where all vertices have the same type. An example of a bipartite graph is one where the vertices can be products or customers.

The neighborhood of a vertex is the set of vertices that are adjacent to it, i.e. directly connected.

The degree of a vertex is the number d of its neighbors. The sum of the degrees of the vertices of a graph is equal to twice its number of edges. The distribution of the degree of the vertices varies according to the graphs. A "scale-free" graph is a graph where this distribution follows a power distribution: the number of vertices with a given degree d is proportional to d^{-k}, where k is a constant ≥ 1 (between 2 and 3 for many networks). This reflects the fact that many vertices have a low degree and some vertices have a high degree, in other words, that many are not very connected and some are very connected. We find here a power distribution, associated with the notion of "sparsity," as in Zipf's law (Section 4.1). Scale-free graphs are naturally created when new vertices are connected to existing vertices with a probability proportional to the degree of these vertices. This is called preferential attachment, encountered in particular on the Web: the most cited pages tend to be more and more cited.

The maximum number of edges of a graph, reached when any pair of vertices is directly connected, is:

- $n(n - 1)$ for a directed graph with n vertices,
- $n(n - 1)/2$ for an undirected graph.

The density of a graph is the quotient of the number of edges over the maximum number of edges. A graph with density 1, i.e. all vertices are connected, is called a "clique" or *complete graph*. A *dense graph* is a graph whose density is close to 1, and a *sparse graph* is a graph that conversely has a density close to 0.

A graph is connected if any pair of vertices is connected by a path. In other words, no vertex is isolated. A connected graph does not necessarily have a high density, because the path between two vertices can be more or less long. An unconnected graph has an infinite diameter. Some graphs have a giant connected component: the largest connected component of the Facebook graph contains 99.91% of non-isolated individuals.

The mathematical publication graph contains about 401,000 vertices (authors), including 84,000 isolated vertices (authors without co-authors), and a giant connected component that contains 268,000 vertices, or 84% of the non-isolated vertices.[3]

In fact, this situation is quite frequent. When the average degree of a graph is small, it has many connected components, but when this degree increases, there comes a moment when a connected component is formed which quickly becomes very large until it connects most of the vertices: it is then a giant connected component.

5.3 Characterization of Social Networks

Social networks are graphs with particular properties:

- they are very large and can have millions of vertices, and hundreds of millions or even billions of links;
- vertices have attributes (name, age, city, language, possession of a product, etc.) and links can also have attributes (number of communications between two vertices);
- (homophily property) vertices with close attributes are more often connected (this is especially true of language);
- they are "scale-free" graphs (but Facebook does not exactly follow a power distribution for the degree of its vertices);
- they are "small-world" graphs;
- they have a high *clustering coefficient* (transitivity): this is the probability that two randomly chosen neighbors of a vertex are themselves connected;
- they are generally decomposed into "communities," which are subgraphs whose vertices are strongly connected to each other and weakly connected to the vertices of other communities.

Let's give examples of "small-world" graphs.

Stanley Milgram conducted an experiment in 1967 to test a hypothesis formulated by the author Frigyes Karinthy in 1929, according to which, if two people are connected when they know each other, the distance between two individuals on Earth is always less than or equal to 6: in other words, they are separated by no more than 5 intermediaries. Milgram sent 60 letters to individuals, asking them to forward them to acquaintances in order to reach a specified recipient. The recipient was not always reached, but when it was, five or fewer intermediaries were sufficient.

Other experiments gave average numbers of intermediates varying between 4.4 and 5.7, depending on the group of individuals.

The graph formed by Facebook has an average distance between users of 4.57, with 92% of user pairs having a distance of 5 or less.[4] This average distance is lower (about 4), if we limit ourselves to one country. It decreases over the years (5.28 in 2008, 4.74 in 2011, 4.57 in 2016), and 84% of connections remain within one country.

To say that the average number of intermediaries is 4 means that if we consider two people A and B, in general a friend of a friend of A is a friend of a friend of B.

A 2007 study by Jure Leskovec and Eric Horvitz on 240 million users of an instant messenger (Microsoft Messenger) with 30 billion conversations showed an average distance of 6.6. Another study[5] found that this average distance is 3.43 for Twitter.

Many graphs are "small world": road, telecommunication, genetic, social. But if we add a temporal dimension, networks are generally no longer "small world": all vertices are not contemporary and a family tree is not small world.

5.4 Measures of Influence in a Graph

In many applications of social networks, it is important to identify the most influential individuals. In a graph, the importance of a vertex can be expressed in several ways, the main ones being the degree centrality, the closeness centrality, the betweenness centrality, and prestige. The latter is computed by the PageRank algorithm described later.

In a graph with n vertices, a vertex of degree d has at most $n - 1$ neighbors, and its *degree centrality* is d or, in normalized form, the ratio $d/(n - 1)$. A graph is *complete* when all its vertices have a normalized degree centrality equal to 1. A complete undirected graph with n vertices has $n(n - 1)/2$ edges.

The *closeness centrality* is the inverse of the distance of the vertex from all the others: a high closeness centrality is the sign of a vertex that is close to the others. As this centrality decreases with the number n of vertices of the graph, it is often normalized by multiplying it by $n - 1$.

The *betweenness centrality* is what characterizes the vertices that bring the others closer, because many (shorter) geodesic paths pass through these vertices: these vertices have a greater influence on the network. The betweenness of a vertex is the number of geodesics passing by this vertex, and the betweenness of an edge is the number of geodesics passing by this edge. In fact, for each pair (S, T) of distinct vertices of V, we compute the proportion of geodesics connecting S and T that pass through V, and the betweenness centrality of V is the sum of these proportions for all pairs (S, T).

The degree prestige of a vertex of a directed graph, or its popularity, is the quotient $d_{in}/(n - 1)$, where d_{in} is the number of incoming edges, i.e. the number of edges directed to the vertex. This is the degree centrality limited to incoming edges. This notion is very much used on the Web, which is a particular graph, whose vertices are the HTML pages, and the edges the hyperlinks between the pages. In search engines, we are interested in "authority" pages, i.e. those that are the best sources of information on a topic.

The structure of a classic database makes it possible to extract information, but on the Web the search by keywords does not limit the number of answers to a request. That is why Sergey Brin and Larry Page invented in 1998 an algorithm that ranks Web pages containing keywords according to their popularity, therefore according to the number of links pointing to them, that is to say, according to their degree of prestige in the previous sense. We are interested in authority pages, which have many incoming links, not to be confused with the hubs pages, which have many outgoing links. This algorithm is used by Google, which indexes several billion pages per day.

Brin and Page's algorithm[6] (called PageRank with a pun on the name of the co-founder of Google) perfects the notion of the degree of prestige of a page, by taking into account the degree of prestige of the pages pointing to it. A link from page A to page B increases the PageRank of B, but:

- the higher the PageRank of page A, the higher the PageRank of page B;
- the increase in PageRank of page B is all the more important as page A has few outgoing links.

The PageRank algorithm is recognized as the reference system for academic publications, in which the value of a publication is determined by the number of citations to that publication.

Let $A_1, A_2, ..., A_n$ be the pages pointing to a page B, $PR(A_k)$ the PageRank of A_k, $N(A_k)$ the number of outgoing links present on the page A_k, and d a factor between 0 and 1, often fixed at 0.85. Then the PageRank of B is:

$$PR(B) = (1 - d) + \{d.[PR(A_1)/N(A_1) + ... + PR(A_n)/N(A_n)]\}$$

In particular, if no page points to B, then $PR(B) = 1 - d$. This value $1 - d$ is the probability of arriving randomly on a web page, without having followed a link. The quantity $PR(A_k)$ is the contribution of the page A_k to all the other pages to which it points.

We see that PageRank depends on links and not on clicks. This has sometimes led to the temptation to multiply the links between the pages of a site to improve its rank, or to register it on many directories. Google has reacted against this "spamdexing" by trying to detect these artificial links, and also by integrating qualitative criteria in the analysis of pages, including a criterion of trust that benefits government sites.

For a commercial site, the PageRank is of essential importance, because we know that a site that does not appear on the first page of the search engine has much less chance of being consulted by a user. Obviously, in practice, it is still necessary to choose the keywords of a site, because it is the first search criteria.

5.5 Graphs with R

Several packages like `statnet`, `tnet`, `RBGL`, `sna` and `network` can deal with graphs in R, the `bipartite` package can manipulate bipartite graphs, but the most interesting is perhaps `igraph`, which is based on C/C++ (also interfaced with Python) and is faster.[7]

It can handle millions of vertices and edges, but cannot handle so many vertices and edges for measurements of eccentricity, centrality, and display with most layouts. A "layout" is an algorithm that regulates the arrangement of vertices in the display of a graph, and igraph implements a number of such algorithms: positioning on a sphere, according to a two- or three-dimensional grid, the Fruchterman-Reingold algorithm which is one of the most popular, the Sugiyama algorithm, the Kamada-Kawai algorithm, multidimensional positioning (MDS), Davidson-Harel simulated annealing, GEM algorithms, and for large graphs, DrL (Distributed Recursive (Graph) Layout), LGL (Large Graph Layout), and Michael Schmuhl's graphopt algorithm. You can also choose a random layout or rely on the layout_nicely() function which automatically chooses the most appropriate one from several algorithms.

With the igraph package, we can define a graph directly or create it from a file of edges and vertices, or even simply from a file of edges from which we deduce the vertices (assuming that there are no isolated vertices).

Here is how we define a graph. The first one is undirected, unlike the second one, in which we have an arc from Bob to Cecil, from Daniel to Cecil, and from Eugene to Gordon and Helen.

```
> library(igraph)
> graphe <- graph.formula( Alice-Bob-Cecil-Alice, Daniel-Cecil-
  Eugene, Cecil-Gordon )
> graphe <- graph.formula( Alice +-+ Bob --+ Cecil +-- Daniel,
  Eugene --+ Gordon:Helen )
```

Vertices and edges can carry attributes, which are modifiable, such as their size or color.

```
> V(graphe)$size <- 20
> V(graphe)$color <- "red"
```

We can produce a fixed or interactive representation of a graph using the plot() and tkplot() functions. We can also specify a layout.

```
> plot(graphe)
> plot(graphe, vertex.label=V(graphe)$name, vertex.size=1,
  vertex.label.cex=2, edge.arrow.size=1,
  layout=layout.fruchterman.reingold)
> tkplot(graphe)
```

The creation of a graph from a file of edges and vertices is done as follows, the specification of vertices being optional (vertices = NULL) as said above.

```
> graphe <- graph_from_data_frame(liens, vertices=acteurs, directed=TRUE)
> graphe <- graph_from_data_frame(liens, vertices=NULL, directed=TRUE)
```

Other commands are useful.

```
> V(graph) # list of vertices
> E(graph) # list of edges
> V(graph)$name # names of vertices
> length(V(graph)) # number of vertices
> length(E(graph)) # number of edges
```

Functions exist to analyze connected components:

```
> is.connected(graph) # is the graph connected?
> no.clusters(graph) # number of connected components
> clusters(graph) # size of the components and membership of
   the vertices
> table(clusters(graph)$csize) # size distribution of the
   connected components
```

Functions also exist to analyze the degree of the vertices:

```
> table(degree(graph)) # degree distribution of the vertices
> table(degree(graph, mode="in")) # degree of incoming vertices
> table(degree(graph, mode="out")) # degree of outgoing vertices
> plot(degree.distribution(graph), log="xy") # degree representation
```

The characteristics of a graph and the influence measures can also be calculated:

```
> graph.density(graph) # density of the graph
> transitivity(graph) # clustering coefficient
> table(betweenness(graph)) # betweenness
> plot(closeness(graph)) # closeness centrality
> summary(eccentricity(graph)) # eccentricity of vertices
```

Let's look at the graph whose vertices are R packages and whose edges connect the packages according to their dependency links. In this graph, the existence of a "p → q" edge means that package q depends on package p ("Depends" link) or that package q requires the presence of package p to function ("Imports" link), or that package q relies on C or C++ code from package p, which it must import by include ("LinkingTo" link). In recent versions of R, the import link replaces the dependency link and they can be confused here.[8]

The tools::package_dependencies() function indicates all the dependencies of a package, and it is used in two functions of the miniCRAN package. The first one, the pkgDep(p) function, lists all the packages on which package p depends; in addition to these packages, the suggests = TRUE option gives a list of other packages that can complement p without being essential to its operation; and the enhances = TRUE option gives a list of packages that are enhanced by p. The function pkgDep(p) performs a recursive search for dependencies by looking for dependencies of dependencies, etc. The miniCRAN package itself depends on the following packages:

```
> pkgDep("miniCRAN", suggests = FALSE, enhances = FALSE)
 [1] "miniCRAN"    "httr"       "igraph"      "assertthat" "curl"
 [6] "jsonlite"    "mime"       "openssl"     "R6"         "magrittr"
[11] "Matrix"      "pkgconfig"  "lattice"     "askpass"    "sys"
```

A second function, makeDepGraph(), creates the graph of these dependencies and we can see that it relies in particular on the igraph package for this. Figure 5.1 represents the dependencies between the following packages, the color of the edges indicating the type of dependency. We have chosen them for their interest and popularity.

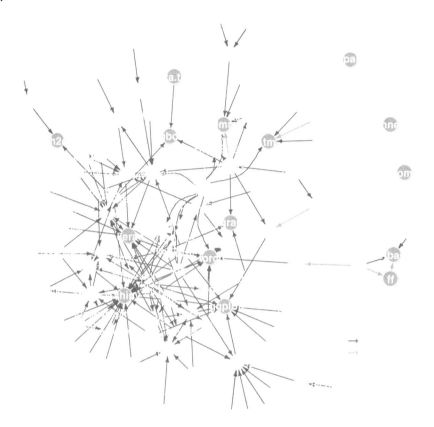

Figure 5.1 Displaying a graph of R packages.

```
> packages <- c("igraph", "ggplot2", "data.table", "glmnet",
    "shiny", "nnet", "randomForest", "rpart", "xgboost",
    "torch", "keras", "ff", "ffbase", "h2o", "tm")
> graphe <- makeDepGraph(packages, suggests = FALSE,
    enhances = FALSE)
> plot(graphe, cex=1.25, legendPosition = c(1, -1))
```

   As of November 27, 2021, the dependencies of these fifteen packages form a graph with 99 vertices and 195 edges. These edges correspond to 12 "LinkingTo" dependencies, 6 "Depends" dependencies and 177 "Imports" dependencies.

```
> length(V(graphe)) # number of vertices
[1] 99
> length(E(graphe)) # number of edges
[1] 195
> table(E(graphe)$type)

  Depends    Imports LinkingTo
        6        177        12
```

When we look at the degree distribution of the vertices, we see that three vertices have no incoming or outgoing dependency links: they correspond to the packages `rpart`, `randomForest` and `nnet` clearly visible in Figure 5.1. We can also see that 52 packages have no incoming dependency, i.e. they do not depend on any other package, and that 13 packages have no outgoing dependency, because no package depends on them.

```
> table(degree(graphe)) # degree distribution of the vertices

 0  1  2  3  4  6  7  8  9 10 11 12 16 20
 3 31 18 15  3  7  4  5  5  2  1  2  1  2
> table(degree(graphe, mode="in")) # degree of incoming vertices

 0  1  2  3  4  5  6  7  8 10 11 20
52 13 10  6  1  3  2  4  3  3  1  1
> table(degree(graphe, mode="out")) # degree of outgoing vertices

 0  1  2  3  4  5  6  7  9 16 20
13 56 13  4  3  2  1  4  1  1  1
```

One package (`shiny`) is dependent on 20 packages, and one package (`rlang`) has 20 outgoing edges, which means that 20 packages depend on `rlang`.

```
> which(degree(graphe, mode="in")==max(degree(graphe,
    mode="in"))) # vertices having the most incoming edges
shiny
    5
> which(degree(graphe, mode="out")==max(degree(graphe,
    mode="out"))) # vertices having the most outgoing edges
rlang
   31
```

We then check if this graph is "scale-free" (Section 5.2), i.e. if the number of vertices with a given degree d is proportional to $d^{-\alpha}$, where α is a constant greater than 1. To do so, we use the function `fit_power_law()` of the `igraph` package. The Kolmogorov-Smirnov statistic is higher, the better the fit is to a power distribution and a p-value higher than 5% shows that we cannot reject the hypothesis that the distribution follows a power distribution. This is the case here for values $d \geq 8$, this threshold `xmin` being determined by the function:

```
> fit <- fit_power_law(degree(graphe))
> fit
$continuous
[1] FALSE

$alpha
[1] 4.126685

$xmin
[1] 8
```

```
$logLik
[1] -39.72802

$KS.stat
[1] 0.06258275

$KS.p
[1] 0.9999998
```

We then see that the graph has four connected components, three components reduced to a single package (with no dependency relationships) and one component containing the remaining 96 packages:

```
> is.connected(graphe)
[1] FALSE
> no.clusters(graphe)
[1] 4
> table(clusters(graphe)$csize)

 1 96
 3  1
```

We then see that the graph is not very dense, and that the probability that two randomly chosen neighbors of a vertex are themselves connected is equal to 0.186, which is a rather low clustering coefficient:

```
> graph.density(graphe)
[1] 0.02009895
> transitivity(graphe)
[1] 0.1856187
```

We can check that the diameter of a graph is not the same depending on whether all paths are taken into account (option `directed=F`) or only the paths in which all edges are directed (option `directed=T`). In the latter case, the distances and the diameter are naturally smaller.

```
> diameter(graphe, directed=F)
[1] 10
> diameter(graphe, directed=T)
[1] 3
```

We wonder if the graph of packages is "small-world," i.e. if the average distance between vertices is less than the logarithm of the number of vertices. This is indeed the case:

```
> mean_distance(graphe)
[1] 1.495298
> log(length(V(graphe)))
[1] 4.59512
```

We are then interested in the PageRank of the vertices of the graph. The calculation of the PageRank is part of the functionalities of the `igraph` package. The `page_rank (<graph name>)` object is a list whose vector element contains the PageRank of each vertex:

```
> page_rank(graphe)$vector
      igraph        ggplot2    data.table       glmnet         shiny
 0.007837758   0.077243416   0.004558256  0.029668587   0.073117355
        nnet   randomForest         rpart      xgboost         torch
 0.004558256   0.004558256   0.004558256  0.009867267   0.026392237
       keras             ff        ffbase          h2o            tm
 0.069021658   0.005849761   0.014696576  0.012371865   0.020540639
...
```

Here are some figures on PageRank and the list of packages whose PageRank exceeds the ninth decile, i.e. the 10% of packages that have the most dependencies. We find not surprisingly packages such as `ggplot2` or `shiny`:

```
> summary(page_rank(graphe)$vector)
    Min.   1st Qu.    Median      Mean   3rd Qu.      Max.
0.004558  0.004558  0.004558  0.010101  0.008594  0.077243
> quantile(page_rank(graphe)$vector,0.9)
       90%
0.02106646
> names(which(page_rank(graphe)$vector >
    quantile(page_rank(graphe)$vector,0.9)))
 [1] "ggplot2"    "glmnet"     "shiny"      "torch"      "keras"
 [6] "tfruns"     "scales"     "tibble"     "bslib"      "tensorflow"
> which(page_rank(graphe)$vector==max(page_rank(graphe) $vector))
ggplot2
      2
```

Here is how we can color in red and increase the size of the 10% of vertices with the highest PageRank, color the edges according to the type of link between the packages (red for the "Imports" link, yellow for the "Depends" link, and black for the "LinkingTo" link), then display the graph (Figure 5.2).

```
> V(graphe)$size <- 2
> V(graphe)$size [which(page_rank(graphe)$vector >
    quantile(page_rank(graphe)$vector,0.9))] <- 10
> V(graphe)$color <- "white"
> V(graphe)$color [which(page_rank(graphe)$vector >
    quantile (page_rank(graphe)$vector,0.9))] <- "red"
> col <- rep("blue", length(E(graphe)$type))
> col[E(graphe)$type=="Imports"] <- "red"
> col[E(graphe)$type=="Depends"] <- "yellow"
> col[E(graphe)$type=="LinkingTo"] <- "black"
> plot.igraph(graphe, layout=layout.fruchterman.reingold)
```

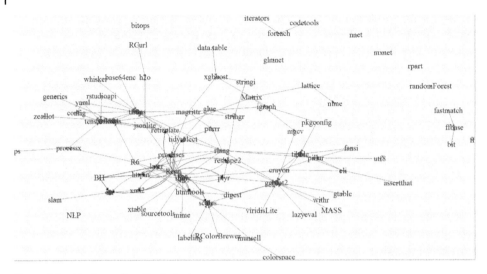

Figure 5.2 Maximum PageRank display.

We now take a look at the graph of all CRAN packages as of November 27, 2021. It is a graph of 18616 vertices and 76337 edges. These edges correspond to 4618 "LinkingTo" dependencies, 8854 "Depends" dependencies and 62865 "Imports" dependencies:

```
> packages <- row.names(available.packages())
> graphe <- makeDepGraph(packages, suggests = FALSE, enhances = FALSE)

> length(V(graphe)) # number of vertices
[1] 18616
> length(E(graphe)) # number of edges
[1] 76337
> table(E(graphe)$type)

  Depends    Imports LinkingTo
     8854      62865      4618
```

The Rcpp package is the one on which the largest number of CRAN packages depend: 4757 packages. The one with the most dependencies is the Seurat package used in genomics.

```
> max(degree(graphe, mode="in"))
[1] 44
> which(degree(graphe, mode="in")==max(degree(graphe, mode="in")))
Seurat
 15129
> max(degree(graphe, mode="out"))
[1] 4757
> which(degree(graphe, mode="out")==max(degree(graphe, mode="out")))
 Rcpp
13161
```

We then want to check if this graph is "scale-free": the p-value associated with the Kolmogorov-Smirnov statistic is much higher than 5%, so we don't reject the hypothesis that the distribution follows a power distribution:

```
> fit <- fit_power_law(degree(graphe))
> fit
$continuous
[1] FALSE

$alpha
[1] 1.966562

$xmin
[1] 35

$logLik
[1] -1795.103

$KS.stat
[1] 0.033408

$KS.p
[1] 0.8674178
```

The graph is not connected, but 86% of the packages are in the same connected component:

```
> table(clusters(graphe)$csize)

    1     2     3 16044
 2490    35     4     1
```

The CRAN package graph is "small-world," with an average distance between vertices well below the logarithm of the number of vertices:

```
> mean_distance(graphe)
[1] 2.841359
> log(length(V(graphe)))
[1] 9.831777
```

The paws package (Interface to Amazon Web Services) has the highest PageRank:

```
> which(page_rank(graphe)$vector==max(page_rank(graphe)$vector))
 paws
11391
```

A completely different graph is one whose vertices are countries and whose edges connect countries sharing a land border (see Section 5.6.5). These data can be found on Wikipedia.[9] We have a graph with 164 vertices and 641 edges.

```
> liens <- read.csv("Borders.csv")
> liens <- na.omit(liens)
> graphe <- graph.data.frame(liens, vertices=NULL, directed=TRUE)
> summary(graphe)
IGRAPH 4cea600 DN-- 164 641 --
+ attr: name (v/c)
```

In reality, we must consider the graph as undirected, which reduces the number of edges:

```
> graphe <- as.undirected(graphe)
> vcount(graphe)
[1] 164
> ecount(graphe)
[1] 329
```

We look at the distribution of the degree of the vertices. Twenty countries have only one neighbor and, on the other hand, one country borders sixteen countries: Russia.

```
> table(degree(graphe))

 1  2  3  4  5  6  7  8  9 10 11 14 16
20 30 29 25 23 15 11  5  2  1  1  1  1
> which.max(degree(graphe))
Russia
   121
```

5.6 Community Detection

Recall that the communities of a graph are a partition of this graph into denser subgraphs, whose vertices are strongly connected to each other and are weakly connected to the vertices of other communities.

We can also define communities based on the notion of clique and quasi-clique. A clique is a graph in which all vertices are connected (Section 5.2) and a quasi-clique is a group of vertices that are highly connected. A community is a subgraph that is both a quasi-clique and a quasi-connected component (not very connected to vertices outside the community).

Note that a graph can contain groups of differentiated vertices that are not communities. For example, there is no community in a star network: a vertex (leader, controller, etc.) is connected to many vertices, but these vertices are not connected to each other. There is a more general notion that includes the notion of community, which is that of cluster. But the most used notion is that of community and the search for the communities of a graph is an important activity in the study of a graph. Many methods have been proposed,[10] of which the following mentions only the main ones. These methods apply to various situations, are based on very different principles, and their complexity is very variable, going from linear complexity to polynomial or exponential complexity with respect to the number of vertices or edges. It is obvious that these last methods will be forbidden on very large graphs. Few methods can handle graphs of at least one million vertices, but we quote one of them.

For graphs whose vertices have attributes, the search for communities can be combined with the vertices clustering: vertices are grouped on the basis of the similarity of their attributes and their connections. For example, we will try to maximize simultaneously the interclass inertia of the attributes and the modularity of the graph.

5.6.1 The Modularity of a Graph

A notion commonly used in this research is that of modularity. The *modularity* of a graph divided into communities is a measure of the quality of this division, a measure that is all the higher as the vertices of the same community (respectively of different communities) are more often (respectively rarely) connected by edges.

The standard measure is the Newman-Girvan modularity[11] of a graph Γ:

$Q(\Gamma)$ = (proportion of intra-community edges of Γ)

– (proportion of intra-community edges in a random graph with the same

number of vertices and the same distribution of their degrees as Γ).

In other words, for the given division into communities, we compare the proportion of edges that are inside the communities:

- for the given graph Γ,
- for a graph whose edges would be randomly arranged between vertices, without consideration of the community structure, but respecting the degrees of the vertices of Γ.

Such a graph is obtained by cutting each edge in two, and by randomly reconnecting each half-edge, called a "stub" to another half-edge. A graph with m edges has $2m$ stubs. If P is the matrix where each element P_{ij} is the probability that there is an edge between vertices i and j, then we have $P_{ij} = d°(i)d°(j)/(2m)$ since there are $d°(i)d°(j)$ stubs connecting i to j. If the graph is weighted, the number m of edges is replaced in the definition of P_{ij} by the sum of their weights.

Furthermore, let A be the adjacency matrix of Γ, defined by:

A_{ij} = 1 if the vertices i and j are connected by an edge,[12] A_{ij} = 0 otherwise.

This matrix is symmetric for an undirected graph. In a weighted graph, the value 1 is replaced by the weight of the edge.

The previous condition is expressed by the equality $\sum_j P_{ij} = \sum_j A_{ij}$ = degree of vertex i.

The matrix $A - P$ is called the modularity matrix. We find the modularity defined previously in the following sum on the set of communities:

$$Q(\Gamma) = \frac{1}{2m} \sum_{i,j} (A_{ij} - P_{ij}) 1_{[community(i)=community(j)]}.$$

Only contributions from intra-community summits are taken into account.

The modularity is by definition comprised in the interval $[-1, +1]$, it is 0 for a random division into communities, and its authors consider that a community structure is significant when the modularity exceeds 0.3.

Maximizing modularity is a way to detect communities. In particular, the modularity must obviously be positive, which means that the number of intra-community edges exceeds the number of intra-community edges that would be obtained at random. Maximizing Q on the set of vertex partitions is an NP-hard problem.

In particular, if a graph has k connected components not linked by an edge, and if its communities are exactly its connected components, then its modularity is $1 - 1/k$ and tends to 1 if k is large.

Conversely, we see that in a graph where each vertex is a community and is not a connected component, the modularity is negative since $A_{ij} = 0$ for any vertex i.

The modularity measure Q is sensitive to the size of the graph, since P_{ij} decreases when m increases. Indeed, in a large graph, one cannot reasonably assume that a vertex is connected to any distant vertex. This results in the following:

- Q tends to 1 when the number of vertices tends to infinity, even in the absence of community structures;
- Q can be positive non-zero for a random graph; in other words, communities eventually appear in large random graphs;
- Q does not allow comparison of two graphs of different sizes;
- the optimization of Q can lead to joining two communities connected by few edges.

Several workarounds have been proposed, such as normalizing the modularity or multiplying P_{ij} by a factor $\gamma > 0$ that can be set to adjust the size of the communities.

But it has also been found that the number of partitions with modularity just below the maximum modularity can be very large, and that it happens that several methods based on modularity maximization discover very different community structures, while having high modularities close to each other.

Nevertheless, modularity remains a very useful notion for community research.

5.6.2 Community Detection by Divisive Hierarchical Clustering

As for the clustering methods of "individuals x variables" tables, there are hierarchical methods of community detection. The classical one is the Girvan-Newman method,[13] based on the betweenness centrality, which is a divisive (top-down) hierarchical clustering method that proceeds by removing edges one by one, starting with those with a higher degree of betweenness. This idea is based on the observation that edges connecting different communities are more often contained in geodesics because there are few paths from one community to another. Modularity provides a criterion for determining the right level in the hierarchy for building communities. The complexity of this method is in $O(m^2.n)$, where n is the number of vertices and m the number of edges, and moreover the degree of betweenness must be recalculated after each edge deletion, which makes this method very slow and hardly applicable to a graph with thousands of edges. It is only applicable to undirected graphs.

The method of Radicchi *et al.*[14] is of the same type, with a complexity only in $O(m^2)$. The method of Fortunato *et al.*[15] is also of the same type (betweenness centrality), but its complexity in $O(m^3.n)$ is high.

The leading eigenvector method[16] is a binary divisive hierarchical clustering based on the diagonalization of the modularity matrix. We look for its maximum eigenvalue, the associated eigenvector, and the sign of each vertex in this eigenvector: the vertices with a positive sign form a community and the vertices with a negative sign form another one, this assignment maximizing the modularity. We then repeat the procedure for each community, as long as the modularity increases. The complexity of this method is in $O(n^3)$. It applies only to undirected graphs.

5.6.3 Community Detection by Agglomerative Hierarchical Clustering

Newman's greedy algorithm,[17] perfected by Clauset, Newman and Moore,[18] is an agglomerative hierarchical clustering starting from the vertices (one community = one vertex) and merging them in order to maximize the modularity function. It applies only to undirected graphs without multiple edges. It is quite fast since its complexity is $O((m+n).n)$, or even $O(n^2)$ for a sparse graph. In the best case, and for sparse graphs, this complexity can be lowered to $O(n.\log^2(n))$. This algorithm has the disadvantage of having a tendency to produce communities of very unequal sizes, by quickly constituting communities of large sizes which are grouped together.

Wakita and Tsurumi's method[19] remedies this by favoring groupings of communities of comparable sizes along with those that increase modularity. For this purpose, the modularity function is multiplied by a "consolidation ratio." Moreover, this method scales well and can handle several million vertices. It is only applicable to undirected graphs. It is not implemented in the `igraph` package but it is in the `modMax` package, which is, however, slow and may lack memory to handle large graphs. Applied to the previous graph of packages, Wakita and Tsurumi's method isolates each package without dependency in a community reduced to itself, but groups the other packages in several quite differentiated communities, one containing rather graphical packages, another one machine learning and deep learning packages, another one around the `ff` package for big data, etc.

The Louvain method[20] is also based on the notion of modularity, and applies only to undirected graphs. It proceeds in several steps:

- Each vertex is considered a separate community.
- The modularity of this partition is computed and it is recalculated after moving a first vertex into the community of each one of its neighbors; when the increase of the modularity is maximal, and if it is positive, the vertex is placed in the corresponding community. If no gain is possible, the vertex remains in its community.
- This is done for each of the vertices, until no local move can increase the modularity.
- Then a new graph is constructed, whose vertices are the communities detected in the previous step. The weight of the edge connecting two of these "super-vertices" is equal to the sum of the weights of the edges connecting the vertices of the two corresponding communities. The edges between the vertices of the same community constitute cycles in the new graph, weighted in the same way.
- We then start the algorithm again from the first step.
- We stop when the modularity no longer increases.

This algorithm converges quickly since the number of communities decreases at each step. Its speed is a great advantage of this method, which has an estimated complexity in $O(m)$. This is what allowed it to be used on more than one hundred million vertices. Another interesting factor of the Louvain method is that it produces a hierarchy of communities, nested within each other, each maximizing modularity locally, which means that it is not possible to reach a higher modularity simply by moving neighbors. On the other hand, the Louvain method tends to produce communities that are sensitive to the order in which the vertices are processed, and perhaps of unequal sizes. For example, applied to the previous graph of packages, Louvain's algorithm isolates each package without dependencies into a community reduced to itself, and groups almost all other packages into a single community, which is not very interesting.

5.6.4 Other Methods

The methods in this section do not rely on the notion of modularity.

The Walktrap algorithm[21] performs a number of random walks, based on the fact that a random walk tends to keep vertices in the same community, since they are weakly connected to vertices in other communities. It can define a distance that can be used in an ascending hierarchical clustering method. Its complexity is in $O(n^2.\log(n))$ or at worst $O(m.n^2)$, where n and m are always the number of vertices and the number of edges of the graph. This algorithm is slower than Newman's greedy algorithm but faster than the Girvan-Newman method based on the degree of betweenness.

The Markov Cluster Algorithm (MCA) of van Dongen[22] starts from the adjacency matrix A_{ij} and computes the transition probabilities $s_{ij} = A_{ij}/d°(i)$ between all vertices. In this matrix, s_{ij} is the probability of a random walk from vertex i to vertex j, and the sum of the coefficients of each column is 1 for a given row (a given vertex i). Then we raise the matrix (s_{ij}) to the power p (an integer often equal to 2) to have the probability m_{ij} of a random walk from i to j in p steps (expansion phase). Then we raise each m_{ij} to the power $\alpha \in \mathbb{R}$, which has the effect of increasing the weight of the large m_{ij}, thus of the pairs of vertices which have a high probability of belonging to the same community (inflation phase). The coefficients of the same row are divided by their sum so that the sum of the coefficients of a row is 1. We return to the expansion phase, and after a few iterations, the matrix converges to a matrix containing only 0's and 1's, which is the adjacency matrix of a graph whose connected components are the communities of the initial graph.

In its basic version, this method has a complexity in $O(n^3)$, quite high because of the matrix product in the expansion phase. This is often remedied by retaining only the k largest coefficients per column after each iteration, before returning to the expansion phase. Thus the complexity is only $O(n.k^2)$, which is all the more advantageous as k can be chosen to be quite small in practice (unless it has to be increased to increase the number of communities).

This method is easy to implement and popular. It can be applied to directed or undirected graphs. Its drawback is that the obtained communities depend on the inflation parameter α. Information and resources can be found on the author's website.[23] It is not implemented in the `igraph` package but it is implemented in the `MCL` package, but without the possibility of keeping only the k largest coefficients, which is inconvenient to handle large graphs.

There are other methods, such as by Harel and Koren, Zhou and Lipowsky, but their complexity in $O(n^3)$ is also great.

We can also mention the Infomap method (on undirected graphs), the spin glass method (on connected graphs), and the simulated annealing method which can give good results but with prohibitive computation times.

5.6.5 Community Detection with R

The `igraph` package implements several methods to detect communities in a graph. Here are several of the methods available, with their code, from those just seen.

```
> cm <- fastgreedy.community(simplify(as.undirected(graphe)))
> cm <- edge.betweenness.community(as.undirected(graphe))
> cm <- cluster_walktrap(graphe)
> cm <- cluster_louvain(as.undirected(graphe))
> cm <- cluster_leading_eigen(as.undirected(graphe))
> cm <- cluster_spinglass(g, spins=2)
> cm <- cluster_spinglass(g, vertex=1)
> cm <- cluster_infomap(as.undirected(graphe))
```

If the graph is not connected, we will apply the spin glass `cluster_spinglass` method to the graph reduced to its first connected component:

```
> vertices <- which(clusters(graphe)$membership==1)
> graphe <- induced.subgraph(graphe,vertices)
```

We can obtain the number and size of communities, and a vector containing the community number of each vertex:

```
> length(cm) # number of communities
> sizes(cm) # size of communities
> membership(cm)
```

By applying several of these methods to the CRAN package graph, we can see that they detect about the same (high) number of communities, but with very different computation times and unequal modularity:

```
> system.time(cm <- cluster_infomap(as.undirected(graphe)))
utilisateur     système      écoulé
     27.12         0.18       27.54
> cm
IGRAPH clustering infomap, groups: 2962, mod: 0.28

> system.time(cm <- walktrap.community(graphe))
utilisateur     système      écoulé
     12.87         0.28       13.49
> cm
IGRAPH clustering walktrap, groups: 2758, mod: 0.42

> system.time(cm <- fastgreedy.community(simplify(as.undirected(graphe))))
utilisateur     système      écoulé
      3.57         0.00        3.60
> cm
IGRAPH clustering fast greedy, groups: 2169, mod: 0.47

> system.time(cm <- cluster_leading_eigen(as.undirected(graphe)))
utilisateur     système      écoulé
      0.88         0.01        0.98
> cm
IGRAPH clustering leading eigenvector, groups: 2129, mod: 0.21
```

```
> system.time(cm <- cluster_louvain(as.undirected(graphe)))
utilisateur     système      écoulé
       0.26         0.00        0.27
> cm
IGRAPH clustering multi level, groups: 2146, mod: 0.49
```

On the graph of countries and their land borders, the Louvain method still gives the highest modularity:

```
> system.time(cm <- cluster_louvain(as.undirected(graphe)))
utilisateur     système      écoulé
          0           0           0
> cm
IGRAPH clustering multi level, groups: 12, mod: 0.75
+ groups:
  $'1'
  [1] "Albania"                "Bosnia_and_Herzegovina"
  [3] "Bulgaria"               "Croatia"
  [5] "Greece"                 "Kosovo"
  [7] "Montenegro"             "North_Macedonia"
  [9] "Serbia"


  $'2'
  [1] "Dominican_Republic" "Haiti"


  + ... omitted several groups/vertices
```

One can prefer the country communities detected by the greedy algorithm, which are slightly less numerous and are obtained with nearly the same computation time:

```
> system.time(cm <- fastgreedy.community(simplify(graphe)))
utilisateur     système      écoulé
       0.00         0.00        0.02
> cm
IGRAPH clustering fast greedy, groups: 11, mod: 0.75
+ groups:
  $'1'
   [1] "Abkhazia"        "Armenia"          "Azerbaijan"
   [4] "Belarus"         "Czech_Republic"   "Estonia"
   [7] "Finland"         "Georgia"          "North_Korea"
  [10] "South_Korea"     "Latvia"           "Lithuania"
  [13] "Moldova"         "Mongolia"         "Norway"
  [16] "Poland"          "Romania"          "Russia"
  [19] "Slovakia"        "South_Ossetia"    "Sweden"
  [22] "Ukraine"


  + ... omitted several groups/vertices
```

We can color the communities in order to represent them on a static or interactive graph (Figure 5.3). We use here the standard "rainbow" palette of R and the Fruchterman-Reingold layout, which is probably the most appropriate here.

```
> colbar <- rainbow(length(cm))
> col <- colbar[membership(cm)]
# static graph
> layout1 <- layout.fruchterman.reingold
> plot(graphe, vertex.color=col, vertex.size=8,
    vertex.label.cex=1, margin=-0.2, layout=layout1)
# interactive graph
> tkplot(graphe, vertex.color=col)
```

We can see that the countries of North and Central America are in the same community. It may seem surprising to find the countries of South America in the same community as the countries of Western Europe; this comes from France which, with Guyana, has a border with Brazil and another with Suriname. The other European countries are in a

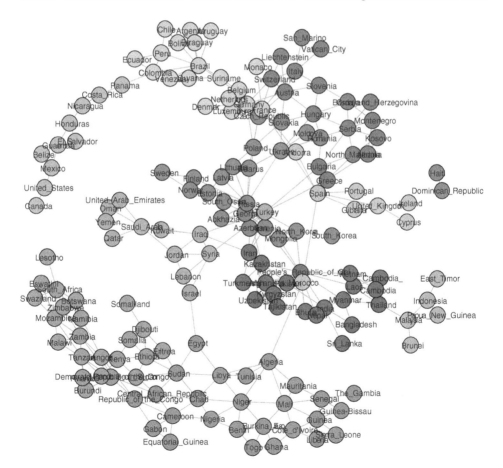

Figure 5.3 Detecting communities in the country graph.

community. The countries of the Middle East form a community. The African countries are divided into two communities, one of which contains the countries of southern and eastern Africa and part of central Africa. Australia and New Zealand are absent; more generally, islands are generally absent because they do not have land borders. Cyprus is an exception because of its border with the United Kingdom, which has two military bases there. Haiti and the Dominican Republic together form an island and therefore a community in the graph. Finally, Asia forms one community, except for the countries around Indonesia which form another community. The communities in the graph of countries are thus well in line with the geography.

5.7 Research and Analysis on Social Networks

The study of social networks and more generally of graphs is a very active research field. This research is interested in many other types of networks: bibliographic networks of publications linked by citations, networks of links between genes (X regulates Y), between proteins, networks of neurons in the brain, telecommunication networks, road networks, networks of buyers and products (two buyers are linked if they bought the same product, and two products are linked if they were bought by the same person), etc. They give rise to generic methods: the search for important proteins in a biological network is of the same nature as the search for important actors in a social network.

Key research topics include:

- link mining, in particular to improve the effectiveness of viral marketing or to help detect fraud;
- identification of the important actors in a graph;
- community detection;
- recommendation systems (Section 3.6), to present to a user what is likely to interest him or her: music, movies, images, news, web pages, contacts;
- roles of individuals based on their relationships;
- joint analysis of links and attributes in a graph;
- analysis of the diffusion of information, influence;
- evolution of graphs and communities;
- comparison of graphs;
- optimization of the paths in social networks (routing algorithms);
- graph compression;
- visualization of large graphs.

Community detection is useful in fields such as viral marketing, economics, sociology, biology, or biochemistry. We search for communities because the vertices of the same community tend to have interesting properties in common. This search is similar to clustering in exploratory data analysis, but the detection of communities is based on the structure of the graph and (except for some hybrid methods) not on the attributes of the vertices.

Networks can be analyzed in other ways: the detection of abnormal links, or, on the contrary, hidden links, for example, by evaluating the score of a link between two vertices. This score can be used to predict the evolution of the graph and can be used in a recommendation system. We can also try to predict the evolution of the size of the communities.

Another application is used for fraud detection: a graph is constructed in which two merchants are linked if the same credit card has been used at both, and we are interested in links that are abnormal due to the geographical distance or the very different type of merchants.

Social networks are also a useful complement to public statistics. For example, analysis of Twitter messages in the Netherlands showed a correlation between sentiments expressed and the public index of household confidence. Bloomberg journalists also incorporate Twitter data. This social media is in high demand during elections, where it competes with polls to measure popularity and voting intentions for a particular candidate. In general, Twitter has taken over from the traditional media in the traditional analyses in the social sciences and humanities of discourse, opinion, etc. It is attractive because of the free and immediate availability of its information, which can be analyzed by many tools, including R (Section 5.10.1).

These examples illustrate the possible contribution of private big data analysis to official statistics, with equivalent indicators but calculated much more quickly and probably at a lower cost. However, if analyses of data collected on the Web complement traditional analyses, they cannot totally replace them, especially because of the permanent evolution of the algorithms of Google, Facebook, Twitter, which can impact the stability and reliability of the analyses that rely on them, as the example of Google Flu Trends shows (Section 1.4.1). Moreover, the users of these networks are not representative of the whole population, and there is a lack of baseline data to adjust these samples.

5.8 The Business Model of Social Networks

The business model of social networks is the provision of free services in exchange for personal data. For example, in a few years, Facebook has evolved from a tool for storing and distributing personal data to a complete system for exploiting these data, allowing third-party companies to access the user information to which they give them access, and even to interact to produce information that may or may not be displayed in a user's information, with some advertisements highlighting your friends' likes. Facebook allows advertisers to serve targeted ads on the network based on your public information, which is basic information (name, gender, photo, networks) and information you share in public mode. Unfortunately, Facebook also allows political parties to send disguised 'ads' for their candidates.

Some credit scoring methods rely on an applicant's business contacts (via LinkedIn) to assess their ability to repay, whether the stated job seems accurate, and how long it would take them to find a job based on their network contacts. Others ask for access to the applicant's Facebook account or other social networks, to identify a possible contact with someone who has already defaulted, or conversely with someone who lives in an affluent neighborhood or is well paid.

Google analyzes the content of emails in Gmail to determine profiles of Internet users that it sells to advertisers to target their ads in real time. Google can connect to your Google+ account and extend its analysis to your contacts and their posts. When a user searches for a term on Google, the *Google AdWords* program displays ads containing that term in the commercial links column to the right of the search results. The display is based on the geographical area chosen by the advertiser and the price he agrees to pay for each click on his ad. He can also set a limit on his daily budget. Possible frauds must be detected, because this daily budget could be used up by a malicious program that would generate many artificial clicks on the ads.

Depending on the services used by its users, Google accesses a huge amount of personal information: emails, contacts, calendar, positions, documents, web browsing history, web searches, applications installed on smartphones, videos seen on YouTube. They can reveal information as sensitive as opinions and health status!

Since 2014, thanks to geolocation, Google has even allowed its advertisers to know whether a person who clicked on a banner ad then visited the corresponding store. And Google has a deal with Mastercard, revealed in 2018, that allows it to know if a click on an ad was followed by a sale in the store. This information is then reported to advertisers in aggregate, that is, not detailed at the buyer level, but globally, indicating the amount and proportion of the advertiser's sales that come from Internet users who have clicked on a Google online ad.

GAFA (Google, Apple, Facebook, Amazon) or GAFAM (adding Microsoft) have developed financial services (payment, insurance, credit) that allow them to:

- collect customer data;
- facilitate purchases (Apple Pay, Amazon Pay);
- consider competing with banks and insurance companies.

Their prospects are to offer financial advice and insurance contracts that will be personalized because they will be based on the detailed knowledge of customer data. They are joined by the Chinese BATX (Baidu, Alibaba, Tencent, Xiaomi).

The challenge for them is to move from setting up efficient technical infrastructures to a global relationship of trust and advice with the customer. They are still far from this, at least Apple, which in 2016 derived 63% of its revenue from the iPhone, Google (Alphabet), which derived 88% of its revenue from advertising, and Facebook (Meta), which derived 97% of its revenue from advertising!

The risk for the traditional players is to lose their role as distributors and become only producers. And the risk for policyholders is to lose the benefit of risk pooling, with the shift to "pay as you drive" or "pay as you live," and to pricing based on an increasingly precise and personalized estimate of the risk.

Faced with this growing hold of an oligopoly, alternative solutions are emerging. Some alternative search engines, unlike Google, Bing,and Yahoo, offer an anonymous search to Internet users, without memorizing their IP address. Since the National Security Agency scandal caused by Edward Snowden, who revealed the NSA's mass surveillance programs, these alternative search engines are growing rapidly: Qwant, Ecosia, DuckDuckGo, Mojeek, StartPage, and others.

Alternative social networks have also appeared, which offer similar services to networks like Facebook, while guaranteeing their users a better control of their data via a decentralized, free, and non-profit system. These networks do not rely on advertising revenues, but on the involvement and donations of their user community. For example, Diaspora,[24] launched in 2010 in the United States by four students, has about 660,000 users. Another example is Movim,[25] created by Timothée Jaussoin, a French computer science student.

For mapping, the collaborative project OpenStreetMap is the open source equivalent of Google Maps.

The marketing use of social networks is of course not reserved to the Web giants, as they give access to some of their data. The analysis of social networks, forums, and search engines makes it possible to discover the interests and preferences of Internet users, and therefore their possible behavior when faced with a product or service proposal. This is particularly useful for companies that do B2B2C, for example, in the food industry, and have contact with distributors but not with their end customers, about whom they have little direct information.

Social network analysis is not only useful for sales, and it can help in the design of new products, through the analysis of positive or negative perception of certain product features (Section 4.5), possibly even through statistical analysis of social media. In 2018, ready-to-wear companies began to draw inspiration from the shapes and colors visible on social networks for the creation of their models.

Another example, in the insurance or credit sector, the research of the profiles of Internet users going on the websites of sales of cars, makes it possible to try to detect in its own customers those which have this profile and would be likely to subscribe soon to an insurance or credit contract.

Of course, if the deluge of data entering the GAFA data centers is worrying, we should not forget that specialized players in many sectors have more data in their sector than the GAFA. For example, it is true that Google can know that we have been to the hospital and what symptoms we have searched for on the Internet, but the example of Google Flu Trends (Section 1.4.1) shows that this is not enough to match the knowledge that the Health Service has about our health. However, it must be recognized that if GAFA has less data in each domain than specialized players, they have the strength of being able to merge data from all these domains, whereas each specialized player will only see a part of it, with a lot of precision, certainly, but without seeing the big picture. And let's not forget the attempts by GAFA to enter other domains than their own, such as Facebook with its Diem (Libra) crypto-currency project finally abandoned in January 2022.

5.9 Digital Advertising

Even if it's not about social networks, what we call programmatic advertising has taken off so much that we have to say a few words about it. This is a marketing campaign management method that relies on big data algorithms to analyze user behavior and buy advertising space in a personalized way for each user. Unlike the traditional marketing approach, which consists of selecting one or more media (television, radio, billboards, press, Internet, etc.) according to the target, the budget and the objectives of the campaign, programmatic advertising is based on targeting Internet users and buying space, impression by impression. Today, it represents the majority of digital marketing investments.

Automated virtual platforms (ad exchange) bring together buyers (advertisers or their agencies) and sellers (publishers or their agencies) of Internet advertising in a real-time bidding system.

When an Internet user arrives at a Web page on which a banner ad is displayed, which is called an impression, the page sends a request (ad call) to the ad exchange platform. This request contains information such as the banner ID, the IP address of the user and a possible identifier, the page from which the user came (referrer), the user's browsing history (thanks to cookies), the browser (Firefox, Edge, Chrome…) and the operating system (user agent). The ad exchange platform sends a bid request to all potential buyers, who respond with a bid. The ad exchange awards the banner to the highest bidder and its ad is instantly displayed on the seller's website (which can filter the advertisers). This process takes a few tens of milliseconds, the time it takes for the web page to load.

Algorithms allow advertisers to determine whether to target the user, the product and the amount of the bid to offer, and the precise content to display according to the characteristics of the user, or the budget for a campaign. They rely on the profile of the user and their browsing history transmitted by the ad exchange, and on analyses that show that the banners have more or less effect on this type of user when they are placed on certain websites.

These techniques owe their success to the fact that advertisers seek to place their advertising in an optimal way for conversion (purchase, download). They call on retargeting specialists who are paid per click. This is the case of a company like Criteo that analyzes more than 230 terabytes of data per day. They know how to spot the sequences of visited websites that best lead to the desired conversion, and they bid when they spot that an Internet user is executing this sequence. Initially, banner ads were statically integrated into Web pages, but they were then dynamically programmed by ad servers to adapt to the Internet user.

5.10 Social Network Analysis with R

Huge amounts of information or at least opinions are constantly circulating on Twitter, which makes it a privileged observatory of political, social, and societal life. For this reason, the analysis of tweets has become a great classic of text mining. It could even constitute a specific branch of it, *tweet mining*, because of the structural particularities of tweets. As for Facebook, its 2.74 billion users make it a privileged means of communication for both individuals and companies.

Software libraries can analyze social networks, such as Twitter or Facebook. They exploit APIs that allow programmatic access to these social networks in order to read, structure, and store them in a way that is suitable for further analysis. As far as R is concerned, we can mention:

- for Twitter, the packages `twitteR` and `rtweet` (see Section 5.10.1) and `streamR` (for capturing streaming tweets);
- for Facebook, the `Rfacebook` package;
- for Instagram, the `instaR` package;
- for YouTube, the `tuber` package;
- for LinkedIn, the `Rlinkedin` package;
- for web scraping, the `RCurl` and `rvest` packages.

As an illustration of web scraping, here is how to extract the population of each country on Wikipedia:

```
> library(rvest)
> url <- "https://en.wikipedia.org/wiki/List_of_countries_and_
  dependencies_by_population"
> pop <- read_html(url) %>% html_table(fill=TRUE) %>% .[[1]]
```

For the example of Twitter that will occupy us in the rest of this section, we can consult the excellent website of Ricco Rakotomalala.[26]

5.10.1 Collecting Tweets

Jeff Gentry's `twitterR` package and Michael W. Kearney's more recent `rtweet` package can collect and analyze tweets. They are simply installed from CRAN or GitHub. Before using them for the first time, one must first connect to the Twitter interface (https://dev .twitter.com/) with an account and create an application with the appropriate access rights settings. You need to retrieve four codes that allow you to connect to the Twitter API and authenticate yourself:

```
> consumer_key <- "YOUR CONSUMER KEY"
> consumer_secret <- "YOUR CONSUMER SECRET"
> access_token <- "YOUR ACCESS TOKEN"
> access_secret <- "YOUR ACCESS SECRET"
```

Then you can install the `twitteR` package and connect to Twitter like this, with a message confirming the authentication:

```
> install.packages('twitteR')
> library(twitteR)
> setup_twitter_oauth(consumer_key, consumer_secret,
    access_token, access_secret)
[1] "Using direct authentication"
```

You can also install the `rtweet` package and connect like this to Twitter, indicating the name of the Twitter application that has been created in the development interface.

```
> devtools::install_github("mkearney/rtweet")
> library(rtweet)
> app <- "nom_application"
> twitter_token <- create_token(app, consumer_key,
    consumer_secret, access_token, access_secret)
```

Here are some basic commands of the `twitteR` package:

```
> getUser("xxx")$followersCount # number of followers
> getUser("xxx")$friendsCount # number of followees
> userTimeline("xxx", n=100) # thread of a user
> trend <- availableTrendLocations() # trends
> getTrends(trend[which(trend$country=="France"),]$woeid)
    # trends on France
```

You can extract the tweets posted on a topic between two dates. You can specify a character string or a hashtag. You can specify the maximum number of tweets to be extracted, but often fewer are retrieved, either because there are not as many tweets that meet the conditions, or because of the availability of the Twitter infrastructure, or because the tweets are too old: indeed, the Twitter API limits the availability of tweets to about ten days. If you want to access older tweets, there are some free solutions[27] but most of them are not free:

```
# extraction of tweets with the package twitteR
> tweets <- searchTwitter("#AI", lang='en', n=100000,
    since= '2021-12-01', until='2021-12-31')


# extraction of tweets with the package rtweet
> tweets <- search_tweets("#AI", lang='en', n = 100000,
    include_rts = FALSE, retryonratelimit = TRUE)
```

We can note an interesting option of the search_tweets() function, retryonratelimit = TRUE, which asks the package to re-interrogate the Twitter API every 15 minutes if the number of extracted tweets has reached the approximate limit of 18000. Indeed, the Twitter API forbids retrieval of more tweets in this time frame.

The tweets extracted with the package twitteR are in a list that can be converted into a data frame by one of the following three equivalent commands. The third one is slightly faster and uses the rbindlist() function of the data.table package. The tweets extracted with the rtweet package are in a *tibble*, a particular type of data frame:

```
> df <- twListToDF(tweets)
> df <- do.call("rbind", lapply(tweets, as.data.frame))
> library(data.table)
> df <- rbindlist(lapply(tweets, as.data.frame))
```

In the form of a data frame, tweets are easier to manipulate and they are also much smaller, both in memory (this can be checked with the object.size() function) and on disk if saved in RData format. Several pieces of information are accessible, in addition to the df$text of the tweet:

```
> table(as.Date(df$created)) # date of tweets
> table(df$screenName) # authors of the tweets
> length(unique(df$screenName)) # number of authors
> table(df$longitude), table(df$latitude) # location
> table(df$isRetweet) # messages that are re-tweets (T/F)
> length(which(!df$isRetweet)) # number of original tweets
> table(df$retweeted) # retweeted messages (T/F)
> table(df$retweetCount) # number of re-tweets of the
    original tweet
```

A command allows you to remove non-printable characters, i.e. special characters that may hinder the analysis of the text extracted from each tweet:

```
> texte <- unlist(lapply(df$text, function(x) gsub("[^[:print:]]", "", x)))
```

5.10.2   Formatting the Corpus

Formatting the corpus of tweets can be done with the help of the `tm` package (Section 4.3) by a series of operations intended to progressively simplify the corpus in order to reduce the number of terms and to allow statistical operations of analysis and modeling, as we have seen in Chapter 4.

Compared to the documents usually processed by these methods, tweets have two particularities. The first is that they are very short, which forces their authors to use ellipses, abbreviations, and to abuse the syntax. This complicates the task of analysis and makes the preliminary work of preparing the corpus even more crucial. On the other hand, the analysis can be facilitated by the second particularity of tweets: they often contain special characters indicating metadata, such as authors (@ symbol) and subjects (hashtag # symbol). Thus, a hashtag in front of a keyword or a group of words in a tweet can be used to classify it in a category.

We start by creating the corpus, i.e. the structured set of documents:

```
> myCorpus <- Corpus(VectorSource(texte))
```

To limit the number of graphic variants that are not significantly different, all characters are lower-case:

```
> myCorpus <- tm_map(myCorpus, content_transformer(tolower))
```

We remove the words beginning with @, which in tweets are the names of users. A retweet starts with RT followed by @<user> to indicate the re-tweeted user:

```
> myCorpus <- tm_map(myCorpus, function(x)
    gsub("@[[:alnum:]]*", "", x))
```

Then we remove the URLs (addresses) of the web pages, which are not terms to analyze:

```
> myCorpus <- tm_map(myCorpus, function(x)
    gsub("http[[:alnum:]]*", "", x))
```

Punctuation marks are removed. An option of the `removePunctuation()` function keeps hyphens in compound words, but other separators, such as apostrophes, are also removed which has the effect of pasting words that should not be pasted. We therefore propose a more complete function based on the `gsub()` function:

```
> myCorpus <- tm_map(myCorpus, function(x) removePunctuation
    (x, preserve_intra_word_dashes = TRUE))
> myCorpus <- tm_map(myCorpus, function(x) gsub("[[:punct:]]*
    *(\\w+[&'-]\\w+)|[[:punct:]]+ *| {2,}", " \\1", x))
```

Numbers can be removed if they are deemed irrelevant:

```
> myCorpus <- tm_map(myCorpus, removeNumbers)
```

We then simplify the corpus by deleting the stop words (Section 4.3.10), whose lists are provided by the `stopwords()` function of the `tm` package and can be optionally enriched with additional words, such as "rt" here to remove the retweet symbol:

```
> myStopwords <- c(stopwords('english'), "rt", "via", "amp")
> myCorpus <- tm_map(myCorpus, removeWords, myStopwords)
```

Simpler but not useless is the removal of unnecessary spaces:

```
> myCorpus <- tm_map(myCorpus, stripWhitespace)
```

The `gsub()` function can be used to correct mistakes or make other desired changes:

```
> myCorpus <- tm_map(myCorpus, gsub, pattern=
    "artificialintelligence", replacement="ArtificialIntelligence")
```

We can create a data frame containing the text with its previous modifications, as well as some metadata:

```
> texte.corpus <- data.frame(text=unlist(lapply(myCorpus,
    as.character)), date=as.Date(df$created), lon=df$longitude,
    lat=df$latitude, stringsAsFactors=F)
```

5.10.3 Stemming and Lemmatization

The aim of the previous transformations is to reduce the number of different terms while losing as little information as possible. The aim is to reduce the sparsity in order to simplify the subsequent analyses. A slightly more elaborate transformation than the previous ones is the change to the radical of each word, i.e. the removal of the prefix and suffix of the words, which is called stemming (Section 4.3.8).

It can be performed as follows on our corpus. We must first load the `SnowballC` package, which implements Martin Porter's stemming algorithm:

```
> library(SnowballC)
> corpus.stem <- tm_map(myCorpus, stemDocument, language = "fr")
```

We saw in Section 4.3.8 that the disadvantage of stemming is that the root is not always a real word and that the result lacks readability and relevance. We have also seen that it is possible to partially avoid this by performing a "stem completion," which is the replacement of each radical by its most frequent original form (or the first one, or at random) in a specified dictionary, which can be, as here, the corpus itself:

```
> dictCorpus <- myCorpus
> corpus.stem <- tm_map(corpus.stem, stemCompletion,
    dictionary=dictCorpus)
```

In Section 4.3.7 we presented a more sophisticated and text-friendly operation than stemming: lemmatization. Its disadvantage is its complexity, and the fact that the tools to perform it are rarer, especially in open source and in languages other than English (but the koRpus package was mentioned).

5.10.4 Example

We will extract the tweets talking about artificial intelligence and more precisely the hashtag #AI. Limiting ourselves to tweets in English, this still represents more than one million tweets extracted between October 27 and November 27, 2021. In reality, they were obtained by running the `searchTwitter()` function several times, on several dates, because of the limit indicated above on the number of days that the Twitter API allows to go back:

```
> tweets.ia <- searchTwitter("#AI", lang='en', n=1500000,
    since='2021-10-27', until='2021-11-27')
> df <- twListToDF(tweets.ia)
> dim(df)
[1] 1054494      16
> table(as.Date(df$created))
```

```
2021-10-27 2021-10-28 2021-10-29 2021-10-30 2021-10-31
     29259      26343      28239      24924      19979
2021-11-01 2021-11-02 2021-11-03 2021-11-04 2021-11-05
     34842      36851      34429      33449      31778
2021-11-06 2021-11-07 2021-11-08 2021-11-09 2021-11-10
     31442      29098      32493      33071      35685
2021-11-11 2021-11-12 2021-11-13 2021-11-14 2021-11-15
     37438      38674      31363      30747      33139
2021-11-16 2021-11-17 2021-11-18 2021-11-19 2021-11-20
     33028      36564      35563      35324      31504
2021-11-21 2021-11-22 2021-11-23 2021-11-24 2021-11-25
     33124      50946      38383      53695      28093
2021-11-26 2021-11-27
     23858      21169
```

Here are the first six tweets:

```
> head(df$text)
[1] "RT @KirkDBorne: Download Free eBook (47-page PDF) —
    The #Mathematics needed in preparation for an introductory
    class in #MachineLearning :…"
[2] "RT @KirkDBorne: [FREE download 185-page PDF]
    \nComprehensive Guide to #MachineLearning for
    #DataScientists → https://t.co/rEvJ7hNalv\n————\n#…"
[3] "RT @TheIncLab1: ♪ This #AI song generator lets you
    pick your topic, genre and mood! https://t.co/lxa1SzG6Tu"
[4] "RT @LEAD_Coalition: #ArtificialIntelligence reveals
    current drugs that may help combat #Alzheimers disease
    https://t.co/fpCBDUgLwP\n\n#AI #de…"
[5] "RT @enricomolinari: Citi names crypto team chief, looks to
    hire 100 more in digital asset effort
    \n\nhttps://t.co/YsGx5JntyE @bankingdive #fi…"
[6] "RT @Ronald_vanLoon: For the 1st Time Scientists Used Tiny
    #Robots to Cure Infections\nby @wef\n\n#HealthTech
    #HealthCare #IoT #ML #AI #FutureO…"
```

We see that retweets are more frequent than original tweets:

```
> table(df$isRetweet)


 FALSE    TRUE
220702 833792
```

Some tweets are retweeted a huge number of times:

```
> summary(df$retweetCount)
   Min. 1st Qu.  Median    Mean 3rd Qu.    Max.
    0.0     3.0    14.0   127.2    43.0  9775.0
```

The most retweeted one was a tweet from Nima Roohi (CEO and Cofounder of BloomingHealth) about reinforcement learning:

```
> df[df$retweetCount==max(df$retweetCount), c('created',
   'screenName','text','retweetCount')]
                     created       screenName
1006908 2021-10-29 08:04:13 AbdlbassetKABOU
text
1006908 RT @NimaRoohiS: Reinforcement Learning
   #MachineLearning #AI\n https://t.co/bzvfgUzIxv
        retweetCount
1006908         9775
```

If a tweet has been retweeted multiple times in our observation window, the retweets will appear multiple times with exactly the same text. We don't necessarily want to give too much influence to these multiple-replicated messages and decide to remove the duplicates:

```
> dim(df)
[1] 1054494       16
> df <- df[!duplicated(df$text),]
> dim(df)
[1] 318234        16
```

The number of tweets was divided by more than three. Retweets may remain if the original tweet was not in the retrieval.

The main authors of these tweets are the following:

```
> d <- as.data.frame(table(df$screenName))
> d <- d[order(d$Freq, decreasing=T), ]
> names(d) <- c("User","Tweets")
> head(d)
                   User Tweets
16193    education_24x7  11590
55499           zeditip   8236
4994   Artificialbrain    6748
24690   InversoSignals    2969
26614     JobPreference    2931
2292          AINewsFeed    2740
```

Some authors only retweet and disappear from the list if we exclude retweets from our count:

```
> d <- as.data.frame(table(df$screenName[which(!df$isRetweet)]))
> d <- d[order(d$Freq, decreasing=T), ]
> names(d) <- c("User","Tweets")
> head(d)
                  User Tweets
38387          zeditip   8219
17254 InversoSignals   2969
18530  JobPreference   2931
1576        AINewsFeed   2740
7968        cppsecrets   1888
4263         BalanceOt   1863
```

The main source of these tweets is the Twitter web interface, ahead of iPhones and Android smartphones. We also note the presence of other Twitter interfaces than those of Twitter itself, such as Buffer and IFTTT, which offer solutions that may be of interest to companies that want to follow several Twitter accounts or several other social media simultaneously:

```
> d <- as.data.frame(table(df$statusSource))
> d <- d[order(d$Freq, decreasing=T), ]
> names(d) <- c("Source", "Tweets")
> head(d)
Source Tweets
995      <a href="https://mobile.twitter.com" rel="nofollow">Twitter Web App</a> 81947
165             <a href="http://twitter.com/download/android" rel="nofollow">Twitter for
Android</a> 29371
166             <a href="http://twitter.com/download/iphone" rel="nofollow">Twitter for
iPhone</a> 21563
954                        <a href="https://ifttt.com" rel="nofollow">IFTTT</a>  11958
686     <a href="https://help.twitter.com/en/using-twitter/how-to-tweet#source-labels"
rel="nofollow">education-bot</a>  11590
446                        <a href="https://buffer.com" rel="nofollow">Buffer</a>  11246
```

Having seen above that hashtags play a particular role in tweets by highlighting certain topics, we are naturally interested in the hashtags contained in the tweets and we extract them to identify the most frequent. We therefore retrieve all the words preceded by a # sign, using the is_hashtag vector with values +1 for the #s and –1 for the others:

```
> words <- unlist(strsplit(df$text," "))
> is_hashtag <- regexpr("^#[[:alnum:]_]*", words)
> list_hashtags <- regmatches(words, is_hashtag)
```

We have recovered no fewer than 712,870 hashtags, of which 34,457 are different, and we will sort them by decreasing frequency before displaying the first ones:

```
> length(liste_hashtags)
[1] 712870
> length(unique(liste_hashtags))
[1] 34457
```

```
> hashtags <- sort(table(list_hashtags), decreasing=TRUE)
> head(hashtags, 10)
liste_hashtags
```

#AI		#ai	
115984		20350	
#MachineLearning		#DataScience	
18572		13846	
#BigData		#IoT	
12649		12395	
#ArtificialIntelligence		#Python	
10430		8971	
#ML		#Analytics	
8716		8292	

The most frequent hashtag by far is, of course, #AI, since this is our criterion for extracting tweets. We can represent the hashtags in a word cloud, which will highlight the most frequent hashtags, by displaying them in larger characters and placing them in the center of the graph (Figure 5.4). We took care to exclude the most frequent hashtag #AI from the word cloud to prevent them from taking up all the space. The second and third most frequent hashtags are then #ai and #MachineLearning and are therefore the most frequent hashtags displayed in the word cloud. Their central position comes from the option `random.order = FALSE`, which makes frequent words to be displayed first, in the center of the graph. We had to limit the number of words and impose a minimum frequency. We have chosen to have 20% of the words arranged vertically (`rot.per` instruction).

```
> library(wordcloud)
> wordcloud(names(hashtags)[-1], hashtags[-1], min.freq=500,
    random.order = FALSE, rot.per=.2, max.words=500)
```

The word cloud highlights some of the concepts naturally associated with artificial intelligence (machine learning, data science, big data, innovation), some of its tools (Python, PyTorch, cloud), and some of its most frequent applications (Internet of Things, analytics, healthcare, chatbot, robotics).

We then format the tweets, transforming the corpus as we saw in Section 5.10.2, but without stemming. All characters are lower case to avoid differentiating between cases of the same term. We replace #s with spaces so that we can identify terms and abbreviations. We remove the URLs and the words beginning with @.

Once this is done, we can delete the stop words to which we have added terms such as "rt" designating retweets. We remove punctuation marks except in compound words. We also delete the short words (1 or 2 letters) because not all of them are stop words already deleted. Before deleting the short words, we replaced the abbreviation "ai" with "artificial intelligence." This must be done before deleting the short words because this abbreviation is a short word that would be deleted. We delete words containing only numbers. Then we can replace some words or correct mistakes.

Figure 5.4   Hashtag word cloud.

```
> text <- unlist(lapply(df$text, function(x) gsub("[^[:print:]]", "", x))
> myCorpus <- Corpus(VectorSource(text))
> # change to lower case
> myCorpus <- tm_map(myCorpus, content_transformer(tolower))
> # removal of hashtags
> myCorpus <- tm_map(myCorpus, function(x) gsub("#", " ", x))
> # deletion of words beginning with @ (before deleting punctuation)
> myCorpus <- tm_map(myCorpus, function(x) gsub("@[[:alnum:]]*", "", x))
> # deletion of URLs (before removing punctuation)
> myCorpus <- tm_map(myCorpus, function(x) gsub("http[[:graph:]]*", "", x))
> # definition of stop words, adding personal words
> myStopwords <- c(stopwords('english'), "amp", "rt", "via", "will")
> myCorpus <- tm_map(myCorpus, removeWords, myStopwords)
> # removal of punctuation (except in compound words)
> myCorpus <- tm_map(myCorpus, function(x) gsub("[[:punct:]]*
+    *(\\w+[&'-]\\w+)|[[:punct:]]+ *| {2,}", " \\1", x))
```

```
> # replacement of abbreviations
> myCorpus <- tm_map(myCorpus, function(x) gsub("\\<ai\\>",
  "artificial intelligence", x))
> # deletion of short words
> myCorpus <- tm_map(myCorpus, function(x) gsub("\\<\\w{1,2}\\>", "", x))
> # deletion of words containing only numbers
> myCorpus <- tm_map(myCorpus, function(x) gsub("\\b[0-9]+\\b", "", x))
> # error correction
> myCorpus <- tm_map(myCorpus, gsub, pattern="artificialintelligence",
  replacement="artificial intelligence")
> myCorpus <- tm_map(myCorpus, gsub, pattern="machinelearning",
  replacement="machine learning")
> myCorpus <- tm_map(myCorpus, gsub, pattern="deeplearning",
  replacement="deep learning")
> myCorpus <- tm_map(myCorpus, gsub, pattern="datascience",
  replacement="data science")
```

An important transformation is then lemmatization (Section 4.3.7) which allows us to reduce each word to its canonical form. We perform the lemmatization using the `spacyr` package (Section 4.3.5). First, we have to execute the `spacy_initialize()` function to initialize the spaCy library. Then we apply its `spacy_parse()` function to the `unlist(myCorpus)` vector containing the texts of the tweets. It identifies the grammatical type (`pos`) of each word and its lemmatized form (`lemma`):

```
> library(spacyr)
> spacy_initialize(condaenv="D:/anaconda3/envs/spacy_condaenv")
> #spacy_initialize()
> parsed <- spacy_parse(unlist(myCorpus), entity = TRUE)
> head(parsed,10)
     doc_id sentence_id token_id      token       lemma    pos entity
1  content1           1        1                           SPACE
2  content1           1        2   download    download   VERB
3  content1           1        3       free        free    ADJ
4  content1           1        4      ebook       ebook   NOUN
5  content1           1        5      -page       -page   NOUN
6  content1           1        6        pdf         pdf   NOUN
7  content1           1        7 mathematics mathematics  PROPN
8  content1           1        8     needed        need   VERB
9  content1           1        9 preparation preparation  NOUN
10 content1           1       10 introductory introductory  ADJ
```

Only nouns and adjectives will be kept, all the other words not being informative enough for the continuation of our analyses. Some tweets disappear. The spaces separating the tweets are also kept (`pos = SPACE`) and are used in the instruction `unlist(strsplit(parsed, " "))` to split the character vector into tweets. The canonical form "datum" is returned to the plural "data" which is its usual form.

```
> dim(parsed)
[1] 3679923        7
> parsed <- parsed[parsed$pos %in% c("NOUN", "ADJ", "SPACE"),5:6]
> parsed <- paste(parsed$lemma, collapse =" ")
> parsed <- gsub("datum", "data", parsed)
> parsed <- gsub("machinelearning", "machine learning", parsed)
> parsed <- gsub("deeplearning", "deep learning", parsed)
> parsed <- gsub("artificialintelligence", "artificial intelligence", parsed)
```

```
> parsed <- gsub("datascience", "data science", parsed)
> parsed <- unlist(strsplit(parsed, "  "))
> parsed <- parsed[parsed!=""]
> length(parsed)
[1] 224623
```

Here is the result of this lemmatization:

```
> head(parsed,10)
 [1] "free ebook -page pdf preparation introductory class
     machine"
 [2] " free download -page pdf comprehensive guide machine
     learning datascientist"
 [3] " artificial intelligence song generator topic genre mood"
 [4] " coalition artificial intelligence current drug
     combat artificial intelligence"
 [5] " citi name team chief digital asset effort"
 [6] " vanloon 1st time scientist tiny robot artificial
     intelligence futureo"
 [7] " artificial intelligence modern world artificial
     intelligence selfdrivingcar connectedcar"
 [8] " meta interesting upload human artificial intelligence
     artificial intelligence"
 [9] " aisoma arrogance underestimation human artificial
     intelligence great danger society"
[10] " meta interesting upload human artificial intelligence
     artificial intelligence artificial intelligence work
     startup enterprise artificial intelligence tech learn"
```

Many analyses are based on a document-term matrix constructed from the corpus. As we saw in Section 4.4, this matrix form is perfectly adapted to factorial analysis, clustering methods, etc. We see that we have here 57,834 terms and a very sparse matrix: 99.98% of zero coefficients.

```
> library(quanteda)
> dtm <- dfm(tokens(parsed))
> dtm
Document-feature matrix of: 224,623 documents, 57,834
   features (99.98% sparse) and 0 docvars.
...
```

We can check Zipf's law (Section 4.1) and represent it in Figure 5.5. The beginning of the curve is distorted by the previous deletion of some frequent words, short words, stop words, which results in a frequency for some words lower than that which should correspond to their rank. In addition, the specific search for the hashtag AI led to an extremely high frequency of the term "artificial intelligence" compared to the other terms.

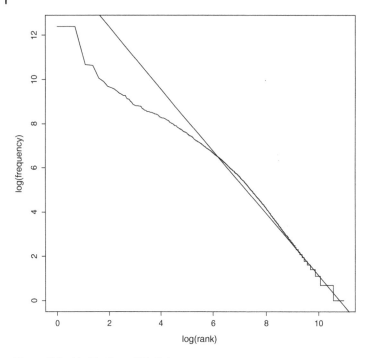

Figure 5.5 Verification of Zipf's law.

```
> Zipf_plot(dtm)
(Intercept)              x
  15.232285      -1.409951
```

The ten most frequent terms in the corpus are the following:

```
> topfeatures(dtm,10)
  artificial  intelligence          data      machine      science
      242743        242171         42608        41261        23462
         new       bigdata    technology      analytic     business
       19997         15982         15067         14229        13197
```

In the word cloud (Figure 5.6), we notice the preponderance of certain terms related to artificial intelligence. To create it, we rely on the textplot_wordcloud() function seen in Section 4.4.2.

```
> library(quanteda.textplots)
> textplot_wordcloud(dtm, min_count = 2000,
    random_order = FALSE, comparison = FALSE, max_words=100,
    max_size = 3, color=gray.colors(1))
```

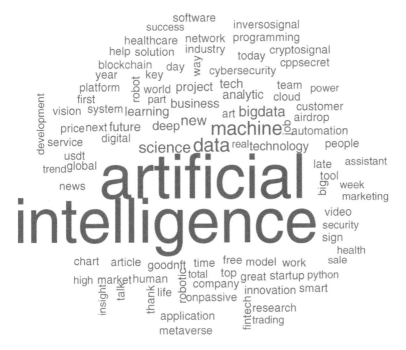

Figure 5.6 Word cloud.

5.10.5 Clustering of Terms and Documents

The word cloud is aesthetically pleasing but of limited statistical interest, because it matches terms according to their frequency but not according to their proximity in the corpus. It does not therefore allow the detection of topics. For that, it is necessary to cluster the terms.

By this clustering, we want to bring closer the neighboring terms in the corpus, by considering terms as being closer, the more they co-occur in a greater number of documents. The constructed matrix structure permits one to apply the usual methods of factorial analysis and clustering, here, for example, an agglomerative hierarchical clustering.

To do this, we start with the document-term matrix. As we are only interested in the most frequent terms, we use the `dfm_trim()` function of the `quanteda` package to build the document-term matrix by keeping only the terms appearing at least 5000 times in 500 documents. We then calculate the distance between the terms in the matrix, using the `textstat_dist()` function, which is more optimized than the usual `dist()` function because it processes the sparse matrix created by the `dfm_trim()` function. However, the result is a `quanteda` object, which must be transformed into a distance matrix for `hclust()` using the `as.dist()` function. Then we perform an agglomerative hierarchical clustering with Ward's distance,[28] and we display its dendrogram (Figure 5.7).

```
> dtmsp <- dfm_trim(dtm, min_termfreq = 5000, min_docfreq = 500)
> library(quanteda.textstats)
> distMatrix <- textstat_dist(dtmsp, margin="features")
> h <- hclust(as.dist(distMatrix), method="ward.D2")
> plot(h)
```

Cluster Dendrogram

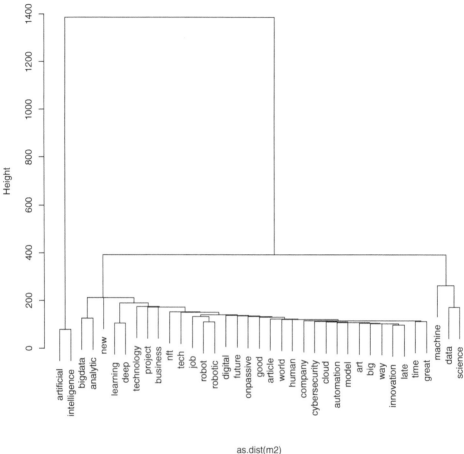

Figure 5.7 Clustering of terms.

In this dendrogram, the terms "artificial" and "intelligence" are of course very close, and there are coherent groups of terms, such as one that refers to data science, deep learning, analytic and big data, robot and robotic, etc.

We can perform the usual analyses and in particular look for the number of clusters optimizing a certain criterion. A classical criterion is the maximization of the between-cluster inertia, i.e. the R^2. However, this R^2 is maximum when each cluster is reduced to one element, and each grouping of two clusters leads to a decrease in the R^2. In order not to end up with a trivial clustering, the criterion must be refined: the decrease of the R^2 is calculated by going from $k + 1$ clusters to k clusters, which is called the semi-partial R^2 ($SPR^2(k)$), and the objective then becomes to find the number of clusters which maximizes the ratio $SPR^2(k)/SPR^2(k + 1)$. In other words, we stop at $k + 1$

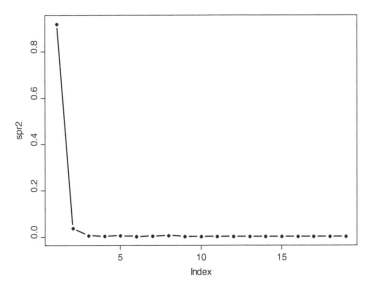

Figure 5.8 Graph of the semi-partial R².

clusters when the passage to k clusters decreases the value of the R^2 too much. Figure 5.8 shows that $SPR^2(1)/SPR^2(2)$ is maximum and that the choice of two clusters optimizes the semi-partial R^2.

The calculation of the semi-partial R^2 can be done as follows. First, we calculate the sum of total squares (totalss). For each value k of the number of clusters between 1 and 20, we compute the within-cluster sum of squares (wss), the between-cluster sum of squares (bss), the ratio bss/totalss (ev: explained variance) which is the R^2, and the Calinski-Harabasz index (between-cluster variance/within-cluster variance):

$$\frac{bss/k-1}{wss/n-k}.$$

We then compute the spr2 differences which give the evolution of the R^2, then the ratios spr2[k]/spr2[k+1]. Since the optimal number of clusters is $k+1$ when spr2[k]/spr2[k+1] is maximal, we deduce here that the optimal number of clusters is 2, according to the semi-partial R^2 criteria. This can be seen in Figure 5.8 produced by the plot(spr2) command, where the cluster composed of the terms "artificial" and "intelligence" is clearly distinguished from clusters composed of the other terms.

```
# total inertia
> totss <- function(dmatrix) {
+ globalmean <- apply(dmatrix, 2, mean)
+ sum(apply(dmatrix, 1, function(x) {(sum((x-globalmean)^2,
    na.rm = T))}))
+ }
> (totalss <- totss(scale(m2)))
[1] 2970
```

```
> wss.total <- function(dmatrix, groups) {
+ wsstot <- 0
+ l <- length(unique(groups))
+ for(i in 1:l) wsstot <- wsstot + totss(subset(dmatrix,
  groups==i))
+ wsstot
+ }
> kmax <- 20
# within-cluster inertia
> wss <- numeric(kmax)
> for(k in 1:kmax) {
+ labels <- cutree(h, k=k)
+ wss[k] <- wss.total(scale(m2), labels)
+ }
> # between-cluster inertia
bss <- totalss - wss
> # calculation of the R² and the Calinski-Harabasz index for
  each possible number of clusters
> n <- dim(scale(m2))[1]
> (inertia <- cbind(k=1:kmax, wss, bss, ev=bss/totalss,
  ch=(bss/0:(kmax-1))/(wss/(n-(1:kmax)))))
        k        wss        bss         ev         ch
 [1,]   1 1332.00000     0.000 0.0000000        NaN
 [2,]   2  104.09261 1227.907 0.9218524  412.8704
 [3,]   3   55.73700 1276.263 0.9581554  389.2651
 ...
[20,]  20   10.56199 1321.438 0.9920706  111.9428
> spr2
 [1] 0.9218523971 0.0363030069 0.0046557177 0.0033364302
 [5] 0.0045232810 0.0020301007 0.0021531304 0.0050187475
 [9] 0.0020056666 0.0020575811 0.0013110324 0.0011740251
[13] 0.0008669468 0.0009106079 0.0008714360 0.0007997252
[17] 0.0007209021 0.0007787509 0.0007010918
> plot(spr2, type="b", pch=16)
> sapply(1:19, function(n) (spr2[n]/spr2[n+1]))
 [1] 25.3932794   7.7975103   1.3954189   0.7376129   2.2281067
 [6]  0.9428601   0.4290175   2.5022841   0.9747691   1.5694358
[11]  1.1166988   1.3542067   0.9520527   1.0449510   1.0896692
[16]  1.1093396   0.9257159   1.1107688         NA
> 1+which.max(sapply(1:19, function(n) (spr2[n]/spr2[n+1])))
[1] 2
```

In the same way as the terms, we can classify the documents. To do this, we transpose the term-document matrix to have the documents in rows and the terms in columns. Several clustering methods are commonly used: *k*-means, *k*-medoids, etc.

Some methods can determine an optimal number of clusters according to a certain criterion, such as *k*-means with the `clusterSim` and `fpc` packages which rely on a criterion such as the Calinski-Harabasz index or the Rousseeuw Silhouette index, which is closer to +1 when there is a small distance between elements of the same cluster and a larger average distance between them and the elements of another cluster. We compute these indices on a sample of terms to avoid a too long computation:

```
> dtmsp <- dfm_trim(dtm, min_termfreq = 500, min_docfreq = 50)
> m2 <- textstat_dist(dtmsp, margin="features")
> dim(m2)
[1] 647 647
> m3 <- t(m2)
> library(fpc)
Warning message:
le package 'fpc' a été compilé avec la version R 3.6.3
> clustering.ch <- kmeansruns(m3, krange=2:8, criterion="ch")
> clustering.ch$crit
[1]    0.000 2476.620 3179.606 4351.608 5610.011
[6] 7222.365 7369.401 8970.928
> (k <- clustering.ch$bestk)
[1] 8
```

The Calinski-Harabasz criterion identifies eight clusters, which are searched by the *k*-means algorithm, run with the option `nstart=10`, i.e. run ten times with different random draws from the initial centers to keep the best of the ten runs: the one that minimizes the within-cluster inertia:

```
> set.seed(123)
> kmeansResult <- kmeans(m3, k, nstart=10)
```

These clusters are characterized by the following terms:

```
> for (i in 1:k) {
+   cat(paste("cluster ", i, " : ", sep=""))
+   s <- sort(kmeansResult$centers[i,], decreasing=T)
+   cat(names(s)[1:5], "\n")
+ }
cluster 1 : artificial intelligence data machine science
cluster 2 : artificial intelligence data machine science
cluster 3 : artificial intelligence new project technology
cluster 4 : artificial intelligence data machine science
cluster 5 : artificial intelligence data machine science
cluster 6 : com mytradingpet gem perfect century
cluster 7 : artificial intelligence data machine nft
cluster 8 : artificial intelligence data machine science
```

The clusters of documents are of unequal size, indicating that a few documents deal with very specific topics (in cluster 6), and that many documents have many terms in common:

```
> kmeansResult$size
[1]   85   16    2 161   53    2    7 321
```

5.10.6 Opinion Scoring

We will now compute an opinion score for each (non-lemmatized) tweet, using the sentimentr package described in Section 4.5. We have seen that it relies on dictionaries to detect the polarity (positive or negative) of each document, but that it is also able to inflect this polarity in the presence of negations, amplifications, attenuations, and oppositions.

The sentiment_by() function returns the opinion score of each tweet:

```
> library(sentimentr)
> corpus.txt <- data.frame(text=head(unlist(myCorpus),
    length(text)), date=as.Date(df$created), stringsAsFactors=F)
> txt <- get_sentences(corpus.txt$text)
> opinion <- sentiment_by(txt)
> head(opinion)
   element_id word_count sd ave_sentiment
1:          1         12 NA     0.3752777
2:          2          9 NA     0.8833333
3:          3          9 NA     0.1666667
4:          4         13 NA    -0.1109400
5:          5         10 NA     0.3478505
6:          6         15 NA     0.3872983
```

Knowing the opinion score and the date of each tweet, we can then compute the daily mean and median score to track the evolution of the opinion score of the topic of interest over time (Figure 5.9). We therefore aggregate the score values by the day the tweet was sent, and retrieve the fourth and third components of the summary() function, which are the mean and median of a numerical vector:

```
> evol.score <- aggregate(opinion$ave_sentiment,
    by=list(corpus.txt $date), summary)
> plot(evol.score$Group.1, evol.score$x[,4],
    type="l", xlab="Date", ylab="", ylim=c(floor(range(evol.
    score$x[,4])[1]), ceiling(range(evol.score$x[,4])[2])),
    col="red", lab=c(10,10,0), cex.axis=0.1)
> axis(2, cex.axis=1.5)
> lines(evol.score$Group.1, evol.score$x[,3], type="l",
    xlab="Date", ylab="", lty=3, col="blue")
> mtext("Mean score", 2, line=2, col="red", cex=2)
> mtext("Median score", 4, line=0.5, col="blue",
    cex=2)
> axis.Date(side=1, cex.axis=1.2, at=seq(range(evol.
    score$Group.1)[1], range(evol.score$Group.1)[2], "days"))
```

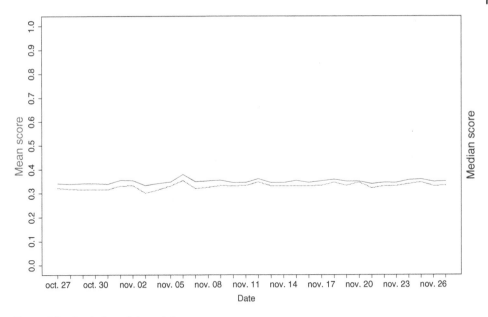

Figure 5.9 Evolution of the opinion score.

We can also search for the most positive or negative tweets:

```
> sentim <- sentiment(txt)
> pol_words <- extract_sentiment_terms(txt)
> head(pol_words)
   element_id sentence_id           negative                                          positive
1:          1           1                                                            free,learning
2:          2           1                                       free,comprehensive,guide,learning
3:          3           1                                                             intelligence
4:          4           1 combat,disease coalition,intelligence,intelligence
5:          5           1                                                              hire,asset
6:          6           1                                                          cure,intelligence
> pol_words$sentence[sentim[which.max(sentim$sentiment)]$element_id]
[1] "top easy deep learning frameworks beginners top10 deep learning deep
    learning"
> pol_words$sentence[sentim[which.min(sentim$sentiment)]$element_id]
[1] "drug addiction risk algorithm grim toll chronic pain sufferers artificial
    intelligence"
```

Here we see some stability in the score and the predominance of positive feelings about artificial intelligence. We do not see any tweets containing the fears sometimes expressed about artificial intelligence (Section 10.5).

5.10.7 Graph of Terms with Their Connotation

We can conduct other analyses by creating an undirected graph whose vertices are the terms, and whose edges connect two terms if they are co-occurring in a document. To do this, we start with the document-term matrix, which we transpose into a term-document matrix after having removed the least frequent terms, in order to have fewer than 100 terms and a readable graph:

```
> dtm <- dfm(tokens(corpus.txt$text, remove_punct = TRUE))
> dtm <- dfm_trim(dtm, min_termfreq = 3500, min_docfreq = 300)
> dtm <- t(as.matrix(dtm))
> dim(dtm)
[1]     82 318234
```

We switch to a Boolean matrix that we transform into an adjacency matrix: the element m_{ij} is the number of documents containing the terms i and j. From the adjacency matrix, the adjacency graph is created, by definition, the one in which two terms are connected if they are co-occurring in a document. Loops and multiple edges are removed by the simplify() function.

```
> dtm[dtm>=1] <- 1
> termMatrix <- dtm %*% t(dtm)
> library(igraph)
> g <- graph.adjacency(termMatrix, weighted=T, mode="undirected")
> g <- simplify(g)
```

Graphically, we choose to match the most frequent terms to larger vertices, by searching the frequency of each term in a data frame associating its frequency to each term, i.e. to the name of the corresponding vertex:

```
> freq <- sort(rowSums(dtm), decreasing=TRUE)
> d <- data.frame(word=names(freq), freq=freq)
> V(g)$size <- log(d[match(V(g)$name, d$word),2])*5
> V(g)$color <- "white"
> V(g)$label.cex <- 2
```

We can display a fixed or interactive graph (Figure 5.10) using the plot() or tkplot() function and the Fruchterman-Reingold layout:

```
> plot(g, vertex.label=V(g)$name, vertex.size=V(g)$size,
    vertex.label.cex=1, edge.arrow.size=0.5,
    layout=layout.fruchterman.reingold)
> library(tcltk)
> tkplot(g)
```

Detecting communities in the term graph can be done using several of the methods seen in Section 5.6, including Newman's greedy algorithm, the Girvan-Newman's divisive method, the Walktrap algorithm, and the Louvain algorithm.

```
> cm <- fastgreedy.community(g)
> cm <- edge.betweenness.community(g)
> cm <- walktrap.community(g)
> cm <- cluster_louvain(g)
```

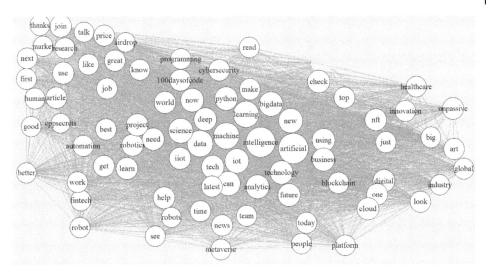

Figure 5.10 Term adjacency graph.

Once this detection is done, we can calculate the number and size of the communities:

```
> length(cm) # number of communities
> sizes(cm) # community sizes
```

Communities can be colored with colors or grayscale (better rendered here by the `Greys` palette of the `RColorBrewer` package than by the standard `grey` palette). The `membership` vector contains the community identifier of each vertex:

```
> colbar <- rainbow(length(cm))
> col <- colbar[membership(cm)]

> library(RColorBrewer)
> colbar <- brewer.pal(length(cm), "Greys")
> col <- colbar[membership(cm)]
```

The display of an interactive graph is done like this:

```
> tkplot(g, vertex.color=col)
```

Four communities are detected with the greedy algorithm and with the Louvain algorithm (Figure 5.11), whose sizes are as follows:

```
> sizes(cm)
Community sizes
 1   2   3   4
13  61   4   4
```

The most important community of terms concerns everything that relates to artificial intelligence in general. Another community is about machine learning, deep learning, and big data. A third community is about robotics and jobs, and, finally, the last community is about a platform for data engineers.

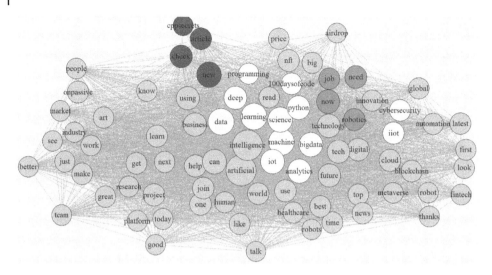

Figure 5.11 Communities with the Louvain algorithm.

The representation of the terms of the tweets in a graph with the detection of its communities is a good way to identify the main topics of the tweets.

Notes

1 It is interesting to read: Emmanuel Viennet. Analyse des réseaux sociaux. In Myriam Maumy-Bertrand, Gilbert Saporta, and Christine Thomas-Agnan, *Apprentissage Statistique et Données Massives*, Journées d'Études en Statistique (Paris : Éditions Technip, 2018).

2 *Digital in 2021 Global Overview* by We Are Social and Hootsuite; see https://wearesocial .com/digital-2021.

3 See http://wwwp.oakland.edu/enp/trivia/.

4 See Ugander *et al.*, The Anatomy of the Facebook Social Graph (2011), arXiv:1111.4503v1. Backstrom *et al.*, Four Degrees of Separation (2012), arXiv:1111.4570v3. Edunov *et al.*, Three and a Half Degrees of Separation, Facebook Research (2016), https://research .facebook.com/blog/three-and-a-half-degrees-of-separation/.

5 Bakhshandeh *et al.* Degrees of Separation in Social Networks, in *Proceedings, The Fourth International Symposium on Combinatorial Search* (SoCS-2011). (2011).

6 Page, L., Brin, S., Motwani, R., and Winograd, T. The Pagerank Citation Ranking: Bringing Order to the Web, Technical report, Stanford Digital Library Technologies Project (1998).

7 In addition to R, another software is popular for manipulating graphs: Gephi, an open source software for network analysis and visualization, written in Java, but more adapted to visualization than to computation on large graphs.

8 https://r-pkgs.org/dependencies.html.

9 https://en.wikipedia.org/wiki/List_of_countries_and_territories_by_land_borders.

10 For a full discussion of the state of the art, see Santo Fortunato, Community Detection in Graphs, *Physics Reports* 486 (2010), 75–174, arXiv:0906.0612.

11 Girvan, M. and Newman, M.E.J. Finding and Evaluating Community Structure in Networks. *Physical Review E*, 69(2) (2004),:026113, arXiv:cond-mat/0308217.

12 Or $A_{ij} = weight(edge(i,j))$ if the graph is weighted.

13 Girvan, M. and Newman, M.E.J. Community Structure in Social and Biological Networks, *Proceedings of the National Academy of Sciences of the U.S.A.*, 99 (2002), 7821–7826.

14 Radicchi, F. Castellano, C., Cecconi, F., Loreto, V., and Parisi, D. Defining and Identifying Communities in Networks, *Proceedings of the National Academy of Sciences of the U.S.A.*, 101(9): (2004). 2658–2663.

15 Fortunato, S., Latora, V., and Marchiori, M. Method to Find Community Structures Based on Information Centrality. *Physical Review E*, 70(5) (2004), 056104.

16 Newman, M.E.J. Finding Community Structure Using the Eigenvectors of Matrices, *Physical Review E*, 74 (2006). 036104.

17 Newman, M.E.J. Fast Algorithm for Detecting Community Structure in Networks. *Physical Review E*, 69(6) (2004), 066133, arXiv:cond-mat/0309508.

18 Clauset, A., Newman, M.E.J., and Moore, C. Finding Community Structure in Very Large Networks. *Physical Review E*, 70 (2004), 066111.

19 Wakita, K. and Tsurumi, T. Finding Community Structure in Mega-scale Social Networks (2007), arXiv:cs/0702048.

20 Blondel, V D., Guillaume, J-L., Lambiotte, R., and Lefebvre, E. Fast Unfolding of Communities in Large Networks, *Journal of Statistical Mechanics*, P10008, (2008). 1–12, arXiv:0803.0476.

21 Pons, P. and Latapy, M. Computing Communities in Large Networks Using Random Walks, *Computer and Information Sciences – Iscis 2005, Proceedings 3733*, (2005), 284–293, arXiv:physics/0512106.

22 van Dongen, S. Graph Clustering by Flow Simulation. PhD thesis, University of Utrecht, (2000).

23 https://www.micans.org/mcl/.

24 https://diasporafoundation.org/.

25 https://movim.eu/.

26 http://eric.univ-lyon2.fr/~ricco/tanagra/fichiers/fr_Tanagra_tweets_analysis.pdf.

27 https://github.com/Jefferson-Henrique/GetOldTweets-python.

28 The "ward.D2" method used in the `hclust()` function is the "true" Ward method, in which the numerator of the Ward distance $d(A, B) = \frac{d(a,b)^2}{\frac{1}{n_A} + \frac{1}{n_B}}$ distance is squared, which is not the case in the "ward.D" method.

6

Handwriting Recognition

In this chapter we implement the machine learning methods described in Chapter 3, from penalized multinomial logistic regression to Extra-Trees, as well as some others, such as linear and quadratic discriminant analysis. We apply them to the MNIST dataset and compare their performance in handwritten digit recognition. The best performing methods are not seen in this chapter, because they are related to deep learning and will be discussed in Chapter 8, which shows the advantages they bring in this type of complex problem.

6.1 Data

The applications of character recognition are numerous: postal address interpretation, bank check processing, use of touch screens, car license plate recognition, etc. Some of the character recognition problems involve handwritten characters and others involve printed or typewritten characters. Among the handwritten characters, some are recognized off-line (this is the case treated in this chapter) and others are recognized on-line, i.e. at the time they are drawn, with a device that captures the movements of a pen or stylus on a sensitive surface. On-line recognition is difficult, because it is affected by the speed and precision of the stroke, the inclination of the pen, changes in direction. Generally speaking, the recognition of printed characters is part of what is called optical character recognition (OCR), and it is easier than the recognition of handwritten characters where some difficulties can arise due to the segmentation of words into characters for cursive handwriting. This is why often machine learning is used. Many handwritten character recognition methods have been tested and published.[1]

The best-known database is that of handwritten digits collected by the National Institute of Standards and Technology in the USA. The complete database is available on the NIST site[2] and is composed of 814,255 images written by 3699 people (employees and students) – but it is not free. A database of 70,000 images extracted from the previous one by the MNIST (Modified National Institute of Standards and Technology) is composed of digits written by about 250 people, free, often used by researchers. It is accompanied by explanations, bibliographic references and the mention of error rates obtained on this dataset using a number of modeling methods.[3]

The MNIST images are also pre-processed, with centered, deslanted, and normalized size digits (Figure 6.1).

Deep Learning: From Big Data to Artificial Intelligence with R, First Edition. Stéphane Tufféry.
© 2023 John Wiley & Sons Ltd. Published 2023 by John Wiley & Sons Ltd.
Companion website: www.wiley.com/go/Tuffery/DeepLearning

Figure 6.1 Images from the MNIST database.

6.2 Issues

Handwritten character recognition is a classification problem: it is about associating each image with a number from 0 to 9, or with a character in other examples. The methods most often cited in the literature are neural networks, k-nearest neighbors, support vector machines, and decision tree boosting.

Without data pre-processing, the published error rates on MNIST are:[4]

- about 12% by linear discriminant analysis;
- greater than 10% for a classical neural network (perceptron) with a hidden layer;
- 7.7% for boosted stumps;
- 5% for the k-nearest neighbors;
- 4.7% for a perceptron with two hidden layers.

Ad hoc data pre-processing can provide a significant gain by taking advantage of features present at several points in a person's handwriting. Other methods construct tangential distances[5] invariant by rotation, translation and homothety, or distances used in supervised methods, such as k-nearest neighbors.

But for several years, the best good classification rates have been obtained with deep neural networks, convolutional or capsule networks (Section 7.15). Unlike other methods, these deep networks use the fact that the variables are pixels constituting an image, in which they can recognize a handwritten digit even if it is not always in the same place in the image, depending on how it was written.

6.3 Data Processing

On the reference website,[6] the MNIST images are saved in IDX format by Yann LeCun and Corinna Cortes who indicate that it is enough to use a simple program to read it,[7] but we can find them in CSV format on Kaggle[8] and other websites.[9] On the latter website we get the images in a `train.csv` file and a `test.csv` file. They are 28 x 28 pixels in size.

The train.csv file has 60,000 rows and 785 columns: the label variable which is the digit between 0 and 9, and the pixel0 to pixel783 variables which are the 784 = 28 x 28 pixels of the number image. The test.csv file has 10,000 rows and the same number of columns. The pixel values are grey levels between 0 and 255.

It should be noted that all the error rates quoted, whether in the literature or in our tests, have an optimistic bias because they are measured on this sample of 10,000 images, which is the same sample used for the optimization of the model parameters and for the measurement of the error rate. To be rigorous, we would have to measure this error rate on a sample that was not used to optimize or choose the models, but this is not done in the references we cite.

We read the files with the read.csv() function. Each line corresponds to an image and to display it we use the image() function after loading the line into a matrix. The following code displays the first thirty digits of the base (Figure 6.2). Note that the columns of the matrix are processed from the last to the first, because of the operation of the image() function, for which the row number corresponds to the x axis and the column number corresponds to the y axis, but with the first column being the horizontal line $y = 0$. As the image is filled starting from the top, y[,ncol(y):1] must be written.

```
> old <- par(no.readonly = TRUE)
> par(mfrow = c(5,6), mar = c(2,2,2,2))
> for(i in 1:30) {
+    y = as.matrix(train[i, 2:785])
+    dim(y) = c(28, 28)
+    image(y[,ncol(y):1], axes = FALSE, col = gray(0:255/255))
+ }
> par(old)
```

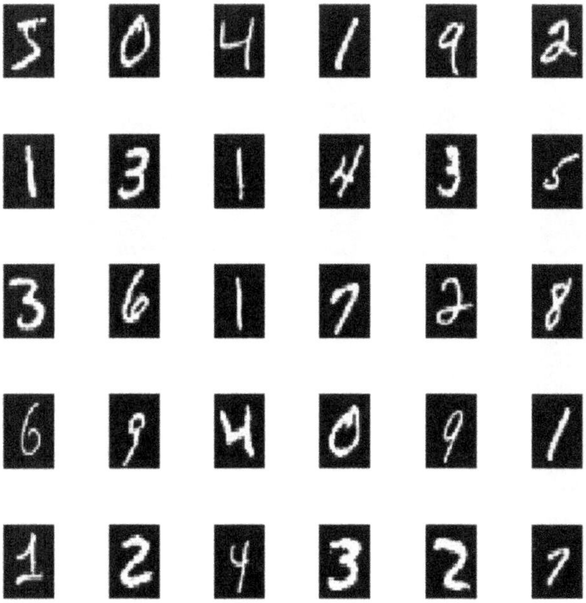

Figure 6.2 Reading the MNIST database.

It is always a good idea to begin analyses by examining the data. Here, we can calculate the "average digits" obtained by superimposing the pixels of all the images corresponding to the same digit.

```
> avg.digits <- matrix(NA,10,785)
> avg.digit = function() {
+ for (i in (0:9)) {
+ avg.digits[i+1,1] <- i
+ avg.digits[i+1,2:785] <-
    t(as.matrix(colMeans(train[which(train$label==i),2:785])))
+ }
+ return(avg.digits)
+ }
> avg.digits <- avg.digit()
```

The representation of these average digits is done as before and gives Figure 6.3.

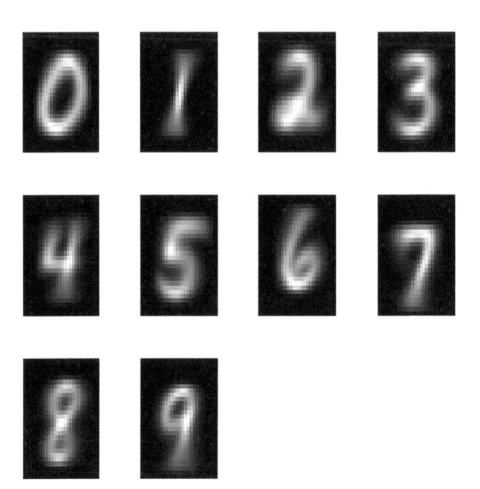

Figure 6.3 Average digits from the MNIST database.

```
> par(old)
> old <- par(no.readonly = TRUE)
> par(mfrow = c(3,4), mar = c(2,2,2,2))
> for(i in 1:10) {
+    y = avg.digits[i, 2:785]
+    dim(y) = c(28, 28)
+    image(y[,ncol(y):1], axes = FALSE, col = gray(0:255/255))
+ }
> par(old)
```

We can then test a first method of identifying the digits, by creating a `score(i)` function returning for the ith image the average digit it is closest to, i.e. the average digit j whose pixel vector `digits.moy[j,2:785]` is the most correlated to the pixel vector of the image. The average digits have been determined on the training dataset and with the `Vectorize()` function we apply the `score` function to each of the `nrow(test)` images of the test dataset.

```
> score = function(i) {
+ dist.digit <- sapply(1:10, function(j)
   cor(as.numeric(test[i,-1]), avg.digits[j,2:785], method =
   "spearman"))
+ return(which.max(dist.digit)-1)
+ }
> pred.avd.digit <- Vectorize(score)(1:nrow(test))
```

Maximizing the Spearman rank correlation to the ten average digits yields a prediction with an error rate of 17.53%.

```
> pred.cm <- pred.avd.digit
> sum(pred.cm != test[,1]) / nrow(test)
[1] 0.1753
> table(test[,1], pred.cm)
      pred.cm
         0    1    2    3    4    5    6    7    8    9
  0    906    4    0    5    2   15   22    1   22    3
  1      0 1118    2    3    0    2    5    0    5    0
  2     21   75  778   26   10    0   56   14   47    5
  3      5   27   26  841    1   13    9   13   40   35
  4      0    9    3    0  746    0   33    0   24  167
  5     19   50    2  119   31  548   25    8   54   36
  6     19   33    5    0   13   20  861    0    7    0
  7      1   32   16    2   11    0    2  853   24   87
  8      6   55    5   67   15   22   12   12  726   54
  9      6   12    2   10   49   12    1   16   31  870
```

One could verify that maximizing the Pearson correlation gives a prediction with an error rate of 17.92%.

Another classical way to reduce the dimension is the principal component analysis. This is not about reducing the number of images by focusing on the average images, but about reducing the number of variables, by replacing the many pixels by their first principal components.

We start by reducing the explanatory variables to have pixels between 0 and 1.

```
> X <- train[,-1]
> Y <- train[,1]
> Xreduced <- X/255
```

We then perform a principal component analysis on the covariance matrix of the previous data, using the `prcomp()` function of the `stats` package. This package contains another principal component analysis function, `princomp()`, and they differ in several ways. First of all, `prcomp()` normalizes the data with $n-1$ in the denominator, and `princomp()` puts the number n in the denominator, but more importantly `prcomp()` uses the Singular Value Decomposition (section 4.4.4), which is considered more stable than the eigenvalue decomposition used by `princomp()`.

```
> Xcov <- cov(Xreduced)
> pcaX <- prcomp(Xcov)
```

We then calculate the eigenvalues and the cumulative sums of the variances. We see that the first ten components already represent 87% of the inertia.

```
> ev <- pcaX$sdev^2
> head(cumsum(ev/sum(ev)), 10)
 [1] 0.2525604 0.4179995 0.5426700 0.6375159 0.7090430
     0.7684616 0.8022281 0.8295837 0.8524195 0.8706786
```

The principal component analysis performs a very strong compression of the images since:

- the first 26 components represent 97% of the inertia;
- the first 32 components represent 98% of the inertia;
- the first 44 components represent 99% of the inertia;
- the first 58 components represent 99.5% of the inertia;
- the first 82 components represent 99.8% of the inertia;
- the first 106 components represent 99.9% of the inertia.

In the following, we will test several values of the number of axes. We create the training matrix as input to the model by multiplying the matrix `as.matrix(Xreduced)` containing the 60,000 images in rows and the 784 pixels in columns, by the matrix `pcaX$rotation[,1:nbaxes]` containing the 784 pixels in rows and the selected axes in columns.

```
> nbaxes <- 44
> Xfinal <- as.matrix(Xreduced) %*% pcaX$rotation[,1:nbaxes]
```

In the same way, we create the test matrix from the principal component analysis.

```
> testreduced <- test[,-1]/255
> testreduced <- as.matrix(testreduced) %*%
    pcaX$rotation[,1:nbaxes]
```

6.4   Linear and Quadratic Discriminant Analysis

Linear discriminant analysis, with the lda() function of the MASS package gives an error rate of 12.70% in about one minute of calculation. It is necessary to eliminate the constant variables beforehand, as otherwise an error message will appear.

```
> lda <- lda(label ~ ., data=train)
> pred.lda <- predict(lda, test)$class
> sum(pred.lda != test[,1]) / nrow(test)
[1] 0.127
> table(test[,1],pred.lda)
   pred.lda
      0    1    2    3    4    5    6    7    8    9
0   940    0    1    4    2   13    9    1    9    1
1     0 1096    4    3    2    2    3    0   25    0
2    15   32  816   34   21    5   37    9   57    6
3     5    5   25  883    4   25    3   16   29   15
4     0   12    6    0  888    4    7    2   10   53
5     8    8    4   44   12  735   15   10   38   18
6    12    8   11    0   25   29  857    0   16    0
7     2   30   15    9   22    2    0  864    4   80
8     7   27    8   27   20   53   10    6  790   26
9     9    7    1   13   63    6    0   37   12  861
```

This method is very fast but completely unsuitable for this type of problem.

We can also test the quadratic discriminant analysis implemented in the qda() function of the same package. With this function, we must not only eliminate the constant variables but also eliminate any collinearity between the explanatory variables. A simple way to do this is to use the jitter() function to add some noise to each of the explanatory variables, i.e. each column of the data frame train. We can then compute the quadratic discriminant analysis model and its predictions on the test basis.

```
> train.J <- train
> train.J[,-1] <- apply(train.J[,-1], 2, jitter)
> system.time(qda <- qda(label ~ ., train.J))
utilisateur     système      écoulé
      58.17        2.80       62.16
> pred.qda <- predict(qda, test)$class
> sum(pred.qda != test[,1]) / nrow(test)
[1] 0.2063
```

The error rate of the quadratic discriminant analysis model obtained, 20.63%, is much higher than that of the linear discriminant analysis, which can be explained by the complexity of the model to be fitted, with many more coefficients to determine. In passing, we check that we can apply the lda() function of linear discriminant analysis to the variables noised by jitter() and we find an error rate of 12.66% very close to the previous one, which shows that this noise makes it possible to fit the model without disturbing it.

Given this greater complexity of quadratic discriminant analysis, it seems all the more important to reduce the number of variables in the model, as allowed by principal component analysis. As mentioned above, we create the `Xfinal` and `testreduced` matrices by selecting the first 32 principal components, and we create the `trainreduced` data frame from `Y` and `Xfinal`. We are forced to create this data frame because creating a model directly from the vectors without going through a data frame poses a problem in the `predict()` function, which expects a `newdata` of the same length as the training sample (60000 rows). So we cannot directly write `qda(Y ~ Xfinal)`. We also need `testreduced` to be a data frame to apply the MASS `predict()` function to it.

```
> trainreduced <- data.frame(Y, Xfinal)
> system.time(adq <- qda(Y ~ ., data=trainreduced))
utilisateur     système      écoulé
       0.50        0.11        0.61
> pred.qda <- predict(adq, newdata=data.frame(testreduced))$class
```

We then calculate the test error rate and the confusion matrix, and find that the error rate became much lower. Tests with 26 or 44 components slightly increased the error rate. As for the linear discriminant analysis, it does not benefit from principal component analysis, and its error rate remains above 12%.

```
> sum(pred.qda != test[,1]) / nrow(test)
[1] 0.0371
> table(test[,1], pred.qda)
   pred.qda
        0    1    2    3    4    5    6    7    8    9
0     967    0    1    0    0    6    2    1    3    0
1       0 1101   12    4    0    1    1    0   15    1
2       3    0 1008    3    2    0    3    2   11    0
3       1    0    7  971    0   10    0    5   12    4
4       1    0    4    0  964    0    3    2    2    6
5       3    0    0   17    0  864    2    0    5    1
6       7    1    0    0    2   14  927    0    7    0
7       0    4   29    4    4    4    0  951    8   24
8       5    0    9   16    0    3    2    3  928    8
9       4    3    9    7   10    3    0    6   19  948
```

If the `jitter()` function can be used to overcome collinearity, the most natural solution is principal component analysis, which provides orthogonal components. We also notice here that principal component analysis has a strong power of "compression" on the images, which allows it to control the complexity of the quadratic discriminant analysis model by limiting the number of explanatory variables in the model input. The quadratic discriminant analysis then has an excellent ratio of accuracy to computation time, with 3.71% of errors committed for a training lasting less than one second (after the principal component analysis).

6.5 Multinomial Logistic Regression

Another natural solution to collinearity is to keep all the variables, i.e. all the pixels of the images, but to process them with a penalized method, for example, ridge or Lasso (Section 3.3). As this solution is obviously more expensive than the previous one in terms of computation time, we use for its implementation the h2o package of R because of its speed. The function h2o.glm() implements multinomial logistic regression, which can be applied to a classification problem with more than two classes.

We obtain an error rate of 7.15% with Lasso regression, penalty = 0.0001 and the quasi-Newton optimization algorithm (limited to a maximum of 500 iterations to limit computation time) which leads more quickly to an interesting solution than the iterated reweighted least squares algorithm. A ridge regression gives an error rate of 7.52% with the same penalty, and weaker or stronger penalties give here higher error rates with the Lasso or ridge regression:

```
> system.time(glmh2o <- h2o.glm(y = 1, x = 2:785,
    training_frame = train, family = "multinomial",
    solver="L_BFGS", alpha=1, lambda = 0.0001, max_iterations =
    500, validation_frame = test))
utilisateur      système      écoulé
       0.54         0.20      256.76
> prediction <- h2o.predict(glmh2o, newdata=test)
> pred.label <- max.col(prediction[,-1]) - 1
```

For the calculation of the prediction, it is necessary not to take into account the first column which contains the label. We obtain the error rate and the confusion matrix as follows:

```
> sum(pred.label != as.vector(test$label)) / nrow(test)
[1] 0.0715
> table(as.vector(test$label), pred.label)
   pred.label
      0    1    2    3    4    5    6    7    8    9
0   957    0    2    2    0    7    6    5    1    0
1     0 1111    4    2    0    1    4    2   11    0
2     7    7  931   15    9    3   13    9   34    4
3     3    2   18  924    0   25    2    8   22    6
4     1    1    4    3  921    0   10    4    7   31
5     8    4    3   33    8  779   14    8   31    4
6     9    3    7    2    7   12  914    2    2    0
7     0   10   23    5    3    1    0  954    2   30
8     7    7    4   22    9   24    9   10  871   11
9    10    9    1   10   24    5    0   22    5  923
```

This error rate is much lower than that of linear discriminant analysis, but it is still very high, especially compared to the methods that will now be examined.

6.6 Random Forests

Ensemble methods should presumably be more appropriate for a complex problem such as handwriting recognition, and we start with random forests (Section 3.4.2). To implement them, we preferred the `ranger` package by Wright and Ziegler (2016), which is less well known than the `randomForest` package by Liaw and Wiener (2002) that interfaces with R the Fortran program by Breiman and Cutler. This choice is motivated by the fact that the `ranger` package is much faster than the `randomForest` package and also the `party` package. It is also faster than the `h2o.randomforest()` function of the `h2o` package. It comes from a software written in C++ that has carefully optimized the memory usage.[10] It is called *ranger* for "RANdom forest GEneRator" and can be used independently of R. It implements random forests of classification, regression and survival trees, as well as Extra-Trees (Section 3.4.3).

We used the `ranger()` function without specifying the minimum population size of the nodes of the decision trees, keeping the default value equal to 1 in classification, and we varied the number of trees, and the number of explanatory variables randomly selected at each tree split.

We obtained the results in Table 6.1, with error rates and computation times, which shows a minimum error rate of 2.70% obtained for 1000 trees and 30 selected variables. The computation takes almost 8 minutes, but it would take about ten times longer with the `randomForest` package.

We observe a rise in the error rate when the number of trees in the forest exceeds 1000. Here is the random forest obtained with 1000 trees and 30 explanatory variables at each split, leading to the lowest error rate of 2.70%.

```
> library(ranger)
> train[,1] <- as.factor(train[,1])
> rg <- ranger(label ~ ., data=train, importance = "none",
    num.trees=1000, mtry=30, replace=T, write.forest=T, seed=235)
> pred.rg <- predict(rg, dat = test[,-1])
```

Table 6.1 Random forests with the `ranger` package.

# variables (mtry) # trees (num.trees)	10	20	30	40	50
100	3.25 % 26 s.	3.20 % 40 s.	3.07 % 55 s.	3.05 % 73 s.	2.96 % 83 s.
300	3.16 % 69 s.	3.03 % 104 s.	2.85 % 165 s.	2.88 % 195 s.	2.83 % 223 s.
500	3.17 % 104 s.	2.90 % 169 s.	2.80 % 229 s.	2.85 % 305 s.	2.82 % 367 s.
1000	3.17 % 198 s.	2.80 % 326 s.	**2.70 %** 474 s.	2.82 % 603 s.	2.72 % 770 s.
2000	3.18 % 396 s.	2.82 % 666 s.	2.78 % 930 s.	2.80 % 1285 s.	2.75 % 1522 s.

```
> table(test[,1], pred.rg$predictions)
```

	0	1	2	3	4	5	6	7	8	9
0	971	0	1	0	0	2	1	1	4	0
1	0	1123	3	3	0	2	2	0	1	1
2	6	0	1001	4	3	0	4	8	6	0
3	0	0	8	979	0	5	0	9	6	3
4	1	0	1	0	960	0	5	0	2	13
5	3	0	0	9	3	863	6	1	4	3
6	7	3	0	0	3	3	939	0	3	0
7	1	2	17	0	0	0	0	996	2	10
8	4	0	6	7	3	5	3	3	932	11
9	5	5	2	9	9	2	1	4	6	966

```
> sum(pred.rg$predictions != test[,1]) / nrow(test)
[1] 0.027
```

There are more confusions between 7/2 and 4/9.

6.7 Extra-Trees

Extremely randomized Trees, or Extra-Trees (Section 3.4.3), are a variant of random forests. They are implemented in the packages extraTrees and ranger.

Table 6.2 shows the test error rates obtained with a minimum of 1 individual per node during training. We note that the error rate increases after 50 selected variables. It is not certain that a larger number of trees would further decrease the error rate, which we note is significantly lower than that of a random forest. We have not parallelized the calculations (numThreads = 1).

The Extra-Trees package offers a possibility not foreseen in the original Extra-Trees algorithm: for each explanatory variable, test several random splits and not only one, which allows testing of several solutions even with mtry = 1. This constitutes a "trade-off" between Extra-Trees *stricto sensu* and random forests. Table 6.3 shows the error rates obtained with three random splits tested.

Compared to the single split test, testing multiple random splits can decrease the error rate, especially when only a small number of explanatory variables are selected. A lower

Table 6.2 Models obtained with the extraTrees package (numRandomCuts = 1).

# variables (mtry) # trees (ntree)	10	20	30	40	50
100	2.84 %	2.62 %	2.57 %	2.57 %	2.64 %
	37 s.	73 s.	103 s.	123 s.	151 s.
300	2.72 %	2.49 %	2.49 %	2.38 %	2.42 %
	113 s.	194 s.	283 s.	395 s.	499 s.
1000	2.66 %	2.40 %	2.49 %	2.41 %	**2.32 %**
	369 s.	689 s.	977 s.	1400 s.	1794 s.

Table 6.3 Models obtained with the `extraTrees` package (numRandomCuts = 3).

# variables (mtry) # trees (ntree)	10	20	30	40	50
300	2.59 % 162 s.	2.43 % 291 s.	2.36 % 427 s.	2.39 % 599 s.	2.39 % 698 s.
1000	2.50 % 724 s.	2.37 % 1962 s.	2.35 % 2386 s.	2.38 % 2624 s.	**2.29 %** 2785 s.

error rate of 2.29% is achieved with 1000 trees, 50 explanatory variables and 3 random splits tested.

Before loading the `extraTrees` package, it is necessary to specify the memory allocated to R (heap size), the default value of 1 gigabyte being insufficient for the recognition of the MNIST digits. We allocate here 3 gigabytes. It is sometimes also necessary to specify the Java directory of the machine.

```
> options ( java.parameters = "-Xmx3g" )
> Sys.setenv (JAVA_HOME='C:/Program Files/Java/jdk1.8.0_181')

> library (extraTrees)
Le chargement a nécessité le package : rJava
> set.seed (235)
> et <- extraTrees (train[,-1], cible, ntree=1000, mtry=50,
    numRandomCuts=3, nodesize=1, numThreads=1)
> pred.et <- predict (et, test[,-1], probability=F)
```

We calculate the error rate and the confusion matrix on the test sample:

```
> sum (pred.et != test[,1]) / nrow (test)
[1]  0.0229
> table (test[,1], pred.et)
   pred.et
        0    1    2    3    4    5    6    7    8    9
0     973    0    0    0    0    2    1    1    2    1
1       0 1124    3    3    0    2    1    1    1    0
2       6    0 1003    3    2    0    3   10    5    0
3       1    0    7  984    0    4    0    8    5    1
4       1    0    0    0  960    0    5    1    3   12
5       2    1    0    7    1  870    5    1    3    2
6       6    3    0    0    3    3  941    0    2    0
7       1    2   16    0    1    0    0 1003    1    4
8       3    0    4    4    2    5    1    3  943    9
9       5    5    2    6   10    1    1    4    5  970
```

As above, there are more confusions between the 7/2 and 4/9.

We note the interest of certain ensemble methods, particularly Extra-Trees. Their random splitting principle makes them faster than random forests, and they are also more discriminant here.

6.8 Gradient Boosting

Among the implementations of gradient boosting (Section 3.4.5), the most popular is currently XGBoost[11] (eXtreme Gradient Boosting), which is an open source gradient boosting library designed for parallel computing (and even distributed with Spark), with interfaces for C++, R, Python, Julia and Java, in Linux, macOS and Windows environments. XGBoost is initially a project of the DMLC group: Distributed (Deep) Machine Learning Common.

XGBoost performs the boosting of decision trees (`booster=gbtree`) or linear models (`booster=gblinear`), for regression, ranking and classification. It sets the learning rate, the maximum depth of the trees, the minimum size of nodes, and the L^1 and L^2 penalty of the linear models. It can save and reload a model to continue training. It can parallelize its calculations on several cores and work on CPU (`predictor="cpu_predictor"`) or GPU (`predictor="gpu_predictor"`).

XGBoost is one of the most used machine learning algorithms in Kaggle competitions. It is available in R (package `xgboost`), Python, Julia, Java, and C++. The R package is available on CRAN (stable version) and on GitHub and can be installed as follows:

```
> library(devtools)
> install_github('dmlc/xgboost', subdir='R-package')
> library(xgboost)
```

To use it, you must first transform the data frames into sparse matrices (or ordinary matrices with the function `model.matrix()`):

```
> library(Matrix)
> train.mx <- sparse.model.matrix(label~., train)
> test.mx  <- sparse.model.matrix(label~., test)
```

Then we have to transform the sparse matrices into Xgb matrices:

```
> dtrain   <- xgb.DMatrix(train.mx, label=train$label)
> dtest    <- xgb.DMatrix(test.mx, label=test$label)
```

As seen above, the `xgboost` package sets a number of parameters to optimize the model.[12]

The learning rate eta is in the interval]0, 1[and limits overfitting when decreased. The default value 0.3 is quite suitable here but we can hope to decrease the error with a smaller value of eta.

The maximum depth of the trees, which is 6 by default, can be modified and it is appropriate here to lower it to 5.

As in random forests, in tree boosting, one can select only a random sample of explanatory variables at each split (`colsample_bylevel` parameter), or at each tree (`colsample_bytree` parameter). The default value of 1 for the `colsample_bytree` parameter can be lowered to 0.5 or 0.25.

One can try to limit overfitting by selecting only a random sample of the observations for learning. Here, lowering the default value of 1 for this subsample parameter does not seem to decrease the error, on the contrary.

If we decrease one of the previous parameters, in particular eta, we must consider increasing the number of iterations.

Here is an example implementation of the xgboost package in which we use the softmax function for multiclass classification and cross-entropy as a loss function. We set the number of iterations to 1000, and look for values of eta (between 0.05 and 0.25) and colsample_bytree (between 0.2 and 0.5) that minimize the error, as these ranges of values were found to be relevant enough for our data. We therefore perform with the outer() function a double loop on the learning rate and the proportion of selected variables, calculating each time the error rate that we return in an array. We specify a seed to ensure the reproducibility of the results, and we use the four cores of the machine:

```
> i <- seq(0.05,0.25,by=0.05)
> j <- seq(0.2,0.5,by=0.05)
> f <- function(i,j)
+ {
+ set.seed(123)
+ train.gdbt <- xgb.train(params=list(booster = "gbtree",
    objective="multi:softmax", num_class=10,
    eval_metric="mlogloss", max_depth=5, subsample=1, eta=i,
    colsample_bytree=j), data=dtrain, nrounds=1000, nthread = 4,
    verbose=0, watchlist=list(eval=dtest))
+ pred.gbm <- predict(train.gdbt, newdata=dtest)
+ return(sum(pred.gbm != test$label) / nrow(test))
+ }
> system.time(k <- outer(i,j,Vectorize(f)))
utilisateur      système       écoulé
  281523.33      1714.71      80122.48
> k
        [,1]    [,2]    [,3]    [,4]    [,5]    [,6]    [,7]
[1,]  0.0212 0.0216 0.0210 0.0216 0.0221 0.0223 0.0216
[2,]  0.0199 0.0210 0.0211 0.0208 0.0211 0.0215 0.0205
[3,]  0.0199 0.0207 0.0199 0.0210 0.0202 0.0204 0.0213
[4,]  0.0210 0.0209 0.0204 0.0213 0.0205 0.0206 0.0218
[5,]  0.0209 0.0207 0.0217 0.0210 0.0203 0.0208 0.0208
```

An error rate of 1.99% is achieved with eta = 0.10 and 20% of selected variables, and with eta = 0.15 and 20 or 30% of selected variables. Other values of the learning rate or a higher sampling rate of the explanatory variables lead to a larger error.

We compute the confusion matrix of the second solution:

```
> set.seed(123)
> system.time(train.gdbt <- xgb.train(params=list(booster =
    "gbtree", objective="multi:softmax", num_class=10,
    eval_metric="mlogloss", max_depth=5, subsample=1, eta=0.15,
    colsample_bytree=0.2), data=dtrain, nrounds=1000,
    nthread = 4, verbose=0))
utilisateur      système      écoulé
    5607.17        43.02     1599.21
> pred.gbm <- predict(train.gdbt, newdata=dtest)
> sum(pred.gbm != test$label) / nrow(test)
[1] 0.0199
> table(test$label, pred.gbm)
   pred.gbm
        0    1    2    3    4    5    6    7    8    9
  0   971    0    1    0    0    1    2    1    3    1
  1     0 1127    2    1    0    1    1    1    2    0
  2     4    0 1008    4    2    0    2    7    5    0
  3     0    0    4  991    0    3    1    6    4    1
  4     1    0    3    0  956    0    4    0    2   16
  5     2    0    1    5    0  871    6    3    3    1
  6     4    2    0    0    1    3  942    0    6    0
  7     2    3   13    0    1    0    0 1001    2    6
  8     5    1    2    1    3    1    2    3  954    2
  9     4    4    2    5    7    0    1    4    2  980
```

The error rate of 1.99% is achieved in over 26 minutes, which is not very fast compared to other methods.

We can test another gradient boosting algorithm presented in Section 3.4.5: LightGBM. To compare the `lightgbm` package to `xgboost`, in terms of accuracy and computation time, we will do so with similar settings: maximum tree depth equal to 5, maximum 1000 iterations with an early stopping after 10 iterations without improvement of the evaluation metric on the validation sample. We did not introduce any L1 or L2 penalty, which did not seem to improve the accuracy here. The only difference with the `xgboost` package is the use of the Extra-Trees option (Section 6.7) available on `lightgbm`.

We need to start by transforming the previous sparse matrices, not into Xgb matrices as for XGBoost, but into LGB dataset:

```
> library(lightgbm)
> dtrain <- lgb.Dataset(data=train.mx, label=train$label)
> dtest  <- lgb.Dataset.create.valid(dtrain, test.mx,
    label=test$label)
```

We then search the best values of the learning rate and the proportion of selected variable:

```
> i <- seq(0.03,0.05,by=0.005)
> j <- seq(0.1,0.4,by=0.05)
> f <- function(i,j)
+ {
+ lgb.grid = list(seed = 123, objective = "multiclass",
    num_class = 10, metric = "multi_logloss", boosting_type =
    "gbdt", max_depth = 5, num_leaves = 256, learning_rate = i,
    feature_fraction = j, bagging_fraction = 1, extra_trees =
    "true", num_threads = 4, verbosity=-1)
+ lgb.model <- lgb.train(params = lgb.grid, data = dtrain,
    nrounds = 1000, eval_freq = 20, valids = list(test = dtest),
    early_stopping_rounds = 10)
+ pred.lgb <- predict(lgb.model, test.mx, reshape=TRUE)
+ pred.lgb <- max.col(pred.lgb) - 1
+ return(sum(pred.lgb != test$label) / nrow(test))
+ }
> system.time(k <- outer(i,j,Vectorize(f)))
utilisateur      système      écoulé
  45133.70      1620.74     15869.05
> k
        [,1]    [,2]    [,3]    [,4]    [,5]    [,6]    [,7]
[1,]  0.0194  0.0184  0.0178  0.0182  0.0181  0.0171  0.0178
[2,]  0.0186  0.0178  0.0174  0.0172  0.0173  0.0170  0.0176
[3,]  0.0184  0.0174  0.0162  0.0176  0.0176  0.0173  0.0177
[4,]  0.0182  0.0174  0.0167  0.0174  0.0184  0.0173  0.0170
[5,]  0.0174  0.0180  0.0173  0.0174  0.0182  0.0176  0.0174
```

An error rate of 1.62% is achieved with a learning rate equal to 0.04 and 20% of the variables selected. We compute the confusion matrix of this solution:

```
> lgb.grid = list(seed = 123, objective = "multiclass",
    num_class = 10, metric = "multi_logloss", boosting_type =
    "gbdt", max_depth = 5, num_leaves = 256, learning_rate =
    0.04, feature_fraction = 0.2, bagging_fraction = 1,
    extra_trees = "true", num_threads = 4, verbosity=-1)
> system.time(lgb.model <- lgb.train(params = lgb.grid,
    data = dtrain, nrounds = 1000, eval_freq = 20, valids =
    list(test = dtest), early_stopping_rounds = 10))
utilisateur      système      écoulé
    773.53        63.61       286.88
> pred.lgb <- predict(lgb.model, test.mx, reshape=TRUE)
> pred.lgb <- max.col(pred.lgb) - 1
> sum(pred.lgb != test$label) / nrow(test)
[1] 0.0162
```

```
> table(test$label, pred.lgb)
   pred.lgb
        0    1    2    3    4    5    6    7    8    9
0     972    1    0    0    0    1    2    1    2    1
1       0 1126    3    1    0    1    2    1    1    0
2       4    0 1012    4    1    0    0    6    5    0
3       0    0    2  996    0    2    0    6    2    2
4       1    0    3    0  964    0    4    0    2    8
5       2    0    1    5    0  874    5    1    3    1
6       4    2    0    0    2    3  942    0    5    0
7       0    1   10    2    1    0    0 1008    2    4
8       2    0    2    2    3    1    0    2  959    3
9       3    4    1    5    6    0    0    3    2  985
```

A comparison of the `lightgbm` and `xgboost` packages shows that `lightgbm` achieves a 1.62% error rate in less than 5 minutes, compared to the 1.99% error rate achieved by `xgboost` in 26 minutes. A completely comparable test would be obtained without the Extra-Trees option of `lightgbm`, in which case the error rate is 2.04%. This option of the LightGBM algorithm clearly shows its interest here.

6.9 Support Vector Machines

We now build an SVM model (Section 3.5) whose variables are the first 58 components of the principal component analysis on the MNIST digits, which we have seen represent 99.5% of the inertia. We will therefore work on the `Xfinal` matrix created earlier (one row per image and one column per principal component) and we use the well-known package `e1071`.

We can verify that the linear kernel $k(x, x') = x * x'$ leads here to a rather high error rate, of the order of 6% with a cost parameter $\delta = 1$ or 10. We will therefore focus on the polynomial kernel and the radial kernel.

The polynomial kernel $k(x, x') = (\gamma x * x' + c)^d$ is known to be well suited for computer vision. We start with a polynomial of degree 2. The `tune.svm()` function of the `e1071` package can find the parameters that minimize the classification error rate: here we vary the constant c, the parameter γ and the cost. The search for the best model can be done by cross-validation, but we have specified here a test sample. Note also that we have to specify that the variable to be explained Y is a factor to indicate that we are looking for a classification model and not a regression model:

```
> library(e1071)
> system.time(svmpol <- tune.svm(Xfinal, factor(Y),
    kernel="polynomial", degree=2, gamma=10^(-3:-1),
    cost=10^(0:2), coef0=seq(0.1,0.3,by=0.1),
    validation.x = testreduced, validation.y = factor(test[,1]),
    tunecontrol = tune.control(sampling = "fix", fix=1)))
```

After a search that can be long if the ranges of values tested for the parameters are large, we display the best model found:

```
> svmpol$best.model
```

```
Call:
best.svm(x = Xfinal, y = factor(Y), degree = 2, gamma =
    10^(-3:-1), coef0 = seq(0.1, 0.3, by = 0.1), cost = 10^(0:2),
    kernel = "polynomial", validation.x = testreduced,
    validation.y = factor(test[, 1]), tunecontrol = tune.control
    (sampling = "fix", fix = 1))


Parameters:
   SVM-Type:  C-classification
 SVM-Kernel:  polynomial
       cost:  10
     degree:  2
      gamma:  0.01
     coef.0:  0.1


Number of Support Vectors:  10426
```

The summary() function displays the error of each SVM model tested.

```
> summary(svmpol)


Parameter tuning of 'svm':

- sampling method: fixed training/validation set

- best parameters:
 degree gamma coef0 cost
      2  0.01   0.1   10


- best performance: 0.0169

- Detailed performance results:
   degree gamma coef0 cost   error dispersion
1       2 0.001   0.1    1  0.0704         NA
2       2 0.010   0.1    1  0.0189         NA
3       2 0.100   0.1    1  0.0198         NA
4       2 0.001   0.2    1  0.0695         NA
5       2 0.010   0.2    1  0.0195         NA
6       2 0.100   0.2    1  0.0198         NA
```

```
7        2 0.001   0.3    1 0.0681              NA
8        2 0.010   0.3    1 0.0206              NA
9        2 0.100   0.3    1 0.0199              NA
10       2 0.001   0.1   10 0.0425              NA
11       2 0.010   0.1   10 0.0169              NA
12       2 0.100   0.1   10 0.0208              NA
13       2 0.001   0.2   10 0.0434              NA
14       2 0.010   0.2   10 0.0174              NA
15       2 0.100   0.2   10 0.0199              NA
16       2 0.001   0.3   10 0.0439              NA
17       2 0.010   0.3   10 0.0174              NA
18       2 0.100   0.3   10 0.0203              NA
19       2 0.001   0.1  100 0.0216              NA
20       2 0.010   0.1  100 0.0205              NA
21       2 0.100   0.1  100 0.0208              NA
22       2 0.001   0.2  100 0.0231              NA
23       2 0.010   0.2  100 0.0201              NA
24       2 0.100   0.2  100 0.0199              NA
25       2 0.001   0.3  100 0.0242              NA
26       2 0.010   0.3  100 0.0198              NA
27       2 0.100   0.3  100 0.0203              NA
```

The SVM model that has the lowest error rate on the test sample has constant $c = 0.1$, parameter $\gamma = 0.01$, and cost $\delta = 10$. Here is the application of the optimal parameterization found by tune.svm():

```
> system.time(svmpol <- svm(Xfinal, factor(Y),
   kernel="polynomial", degree=2, coef0=0.1, gamma=0.01,
   cost=10, probability=TRUE))
utilisateur      système       écoulé
     748.94         4.46       758.69
> print(svmpol)
Call:
svm.default(x = Xfinal, y = Y, kernel = "polynomial",
   degree = 2, gamma = 0.01, coef0 = 0.1, cost = 10,
   probability = TRUE)
Parameters:
   SVM-Type:  C-classification
 SVM-Kernel:  polynomial
       cost:  10
     degree:  2
      gamma:  0.01
     coef.0:  0.1
Number of Support Vectors:  10426
```

We apply the SVM model to the test sample to get the error rate and the confusion matrix:

```
> pred.svm <- predict(svmpol, newdata=testreduced,
    decision.values=T)
> sum(pred.svm != test[,1]) / nrow(test)
[1] 0.0171
> table(test[,1], pred.svm)
    pred.svm
        0    1    2    3    4    5    6    7    8    9
  0   971    1    1    0    0    1    2    0    2    2
  1     0 1129    1    0    0    1    1    2    1    0
  2     4    1 1009    1    1    0    2    8    6    0
  3     0    0    2  995    0    4    0    2    6    1
  4     0    0    2    0  967    0    4    1    0    8
  5     3    0    0    7    0  870    3    1    7    1
  6     3    2    3    0    2    4  939    1    4    0
  7     0    2    9    0    1    1    0 1008    0    7
  8     2    0    2    3    2    1    1    3  958    2
  9     2    2    2    0    5    9    2    0    4  983
```

In less than 13 minutes, we obtained a model with an error rate in test equal to 1.71%, which is already a very good performance.

Similarly, we test a model with a polynomial kernel of degree 3: $k(x, x') = (\gamma x * x' + c)^3$. The following parameters give a good result:

```
> system.time(svmpol <- svm(Xfinal, factor(Y),
    kernel="polynomial", degree=3, coef0=0.2, gamma=0.01,
    cost=10, probability=TRUE))
utilisateur      système      écoulé
   1130.97         7.94      1153.19
> print(svmpol)

Call:
svm.default(x = Xfinal, y = factor(Y), kernel = "polynomial",
    degree = 3, gamma = 0.01, coef0 = 0.2, cost = 10,
    probability = TRUE)


Parameters:
   SVM-Type:  C-classification
 SVM-Kernel:  polynomial
       cost:  10
     degree:  3
      gamma:  0.01
    coef.0:  0.2


Number of Support Vectors:  13357
```

This is verified by applying the SVM model to the test sample:

```
> pred.svm <- predict(svmpol, newdata=testreduced,
    decision.values=T)
> sum(pred.svm != test[,1]) / nrow(test)
[1] 0.0155
> table(test[,1], pred.svm)
    pred.svm
       0    1    2    3    4    5    6    7    8    9
  0  973    1    0    0    0    1    3    0    1    1
  1    0 1128    2    1    0    1    1    0    1    1
  2    5    1 1011    1    1    0    1    7    5    0
  3    0    0    3  994    1    5    0    1    6    0
  4    0    0    2    0  971    0    1    0    0    8
  5    3    0    0    6    0  878    4    0    1    0
  6    3    2    0    0    2    4  945    0    2    0
  7    0    2    9    1    2    1    0 1005    1    7
  8    3    0    2    2    3    1    0    2  959    2
  9    2    3    0    4    8    4    0    4    3  981
```

In 19 minutes, we obtained a model with a test error rate equal to 1.55%, improving the performance of the degree 2 polynomial kernel, and matching that of the 200-hidden-unit neural network of section 6.10 but in five times less computation time.

We finally test the radial kernel $k(x, x') = e^{-\gamma \|x - x'\|^2}$ with the same values of γ and cost:

```
> system.time(svmrad <- svm(Xfinal, factor(Y),
    kernel="radial", probability=TRUE, gamma=0.01, cost=10))
utilisateur      système      écoulé
    1239.24         4.57     1248.07
> print(svmrad)

Call:
svm.default(x = Xfinal, y = Y, kernel = "radial", gamma = 0.01,
    cost = 10, probability = TRUE)


Parameters:
   SVM-Type:  C-classification
 SVM-Kernel:  radial
       cost:  10
      gamma:  0.01


Number of Support Vectors:  12201
```

We apply the found SVM model to the test sample:

```
> pred.svm <- predict(svmrad, newdata=testreduced, decision.values=T)
> sum(pred.svm != test[,1]) / nrow(test)
[1] 0.0164
```

```
> table(test[,1], pred.svm)
   pred.svm
        0    1    2    3    4    5    6    7    8    9
  0   971    0    1    0    0    2    3    1    2    0
  1     0 1127    3    1    1    1    1    1    0    0
  2     4    2 1004    2    1    0    2    7    8    2
  3     0    0    3  992    0    3    0    4    6    2
  4     0    0    4    0  961    0    3    0    3   11
  5     2    0    0    7    0  872    6    1    4    0
  6     5    2    0    0    3    4  941    0    3    0
  7     0    5   10    1    1    1    0 1000    2    8
  8     3    0    1    4    3    3    2    3  953    2
  9     4    4    1    4    8    4    0    6    1  977
```

In 21 minutes, we obtained a model with a test error rate equal to 1.64%, a little higher than that of the previous polynomial kernel of degree 3 which remains the best obtained here with an SVM.

6.10 Single Hidden Layer Perceptron

The deep neural networks will be tested in Chapter 8. Before that, we test the perceptron, which is the oldest neural network, since it dates back to 1957 in the initial form applied by Frank Rosenblatt, and to the 1980s in its current form with its hidden layers whose learning is done by gradient backpropagation. It is probably still the most widespread type of neural network.

A multilayer perceptron consists of at least three levels or layers: (1) the input layer receiving the data; (2) the output layer returning the expected result; and (3) an intermediate, so-called "hidden" layer (Section 7.3). Each layer consists of neurons or units, which receive signals (data) from the units of the previous layer, combine them in a scalar product with weights (which are the parameters of the network and are determined by learning) and return a new signal to the next layer, possibly transformed by an activation function which can be a sigmoid function to introduce nonlinearity, or its softmax generalization which estimates probabilities in multi-class classification. A perceptron without hidden layer performs a linear or logistic regression depending on whether its activation function is linear or sigmoid. The units of a network are thus connected to each other, and data are transmitted from one layer to another by these connections as signals are transmitted from one natural neuron to another by their synapses.

In this section we will use Brian Ripley's nnet package, which is the classic R package for neural networks, and is in fact one of the 15 "recommended" R packages, along with cluster, lattice, MASS, Matrix, rpart, etc. These packages are installed in any distribution of R, but you have to load them to use them, unlike the "base" packages.

The nnet package is very simple and implements only the single hidden layer perceptron, whose number of units is the size parameter. Its learning is based on the BFGS (quasi-Newton) algorithm of the optim() function of R, and it has only few options and in particular no early stopping function. With ten classes to predict, the activation function is softmax but it is useless to specify it because it is the choice of the nnet() function with a variable to be explained that is a factor.

We start our tests with a single unit network in the hidden layer, which is of course derisory compared to the complexity of the problem with its 784 pixels to recognize. And in fact, the result is very bad, since the network predicts only one value: "1." The error rate is 88.65% on the test sample.

```
> library(nnet)
> system.time(rn <- nnet(factor(label) ~ ., data=train,
    size=1, maxit=100))
# weights:  805
initial  value 144340.726695
iter  10 value 138155.098012
final  value 138069.550362
converged
utilisateur      système       écoulé
     135.05          0.67       136.37
> pred.rn <- predict(rn, newdata=test[,-1], type="class")
> table(pred.rn)
pred.rn
    1
10000
> # test error rate
> sum(pred.rn != test[,1]) / nrow(test)
[1] 0.8865
```

With two hidden units, the network has 1600 weights and we need to specify a sufficient value of the MaxNWts parameter which is the maximum number of weights of the network and is 1000 by default. In general, a neural network with one hidden layer will have here a structure with 784-x-10 units (input, x units in the hidden layer, output), hence 794.x weights, plus the 10+x weights of the "bias" units. It follows that the model is very long to compute unless x is very small.

```
> set.seed(235)
> system.time(rn <- nnet(factor(label) ~ ., data=train, size=2,
    maxit=100, MaxNWts =10000))
# weights:  1600
initial  value 144564.759274
iter  10 value 124450.790275
...
iter 100 value 120646.747753
final  value 120646.747753
stopped after 100 iterations
utilisateur      système       écoulé
     913.65          0.97       920.36
> pred.rn <- predict(rn, newdata=test[,-1], type="class")
> # test error rate
> sum(pred.rn != test[,1]) / nrow(test)
[1] 0.7902
```

After 15 minutes of computation, the network predicted only two classes and its test error rate remains very high, at 79%!

We find that the complexity of the problem far exceeds the capabilities of the network as we envisioned it. To really improve the predictions, we would need so many weights in the network that its computation time would be prohibitive. To simplify the problem, we again turn to principal component analysis.

Before creating the `Xfinal` matrix as above, we first shuffle the images to improve learning. This precaution is classical with neural networks (Section 7.3).

```
> train <- train[sample(nrow(train)),]
```

Moreover, we have to replace the vector of 60000 digits to predict by a matrix of 60000 rows and 10 indicator columns, one per digit, with a value 0 in each column, except for the column corresponding to the considered digit, which will have the value 1. This is what the function `class.ind()` of the nnet package does.

```
> Y <- class.ind(Y)
```

We can then retrain the perceptron, having replaced the original pixels with their first 58 principal components. In this way, we can go from 2 units to 23 hidden units without increasing the number of weights of the network.

```
> set.seed(235)
> system.time(rn <- nnet(Xfinal, Y, size=23, softmax=TRUE,
    maxit=100, MaxNWts =10000))
# weights:  1597
initial  value 162946.169894
iter  10 value 54687.761787
...
iter 100 value 7424.825882
final  value 7424.825882
stopped after 100 iterations
utilisateur      système      écoulé
    197.52         0.12       198.56
> rn
a 58-23-10 network with 1597 weights
options were - softmax modelling
```

We apply the model to the test set to determine its confusion matrix and error rate, equal to 4.82%:

```
> pred.rn <- predict(rn, newdata=testreduced, type="class")
> sum(pred.rn != test[,1]) / nrow(test)
[1] 0.0482
> table(test[,1], pred.rn)
   pred.rn
```

	0	1	2	3	4	5	6	7	8	9
0	958	0	4	3	2	4	5	1	1	2
1	0	1122	3	1	1	1	0	1	6	0
2	6	2	972	11	10	2	3	9	16	1
3	1	3	17	944	1	11	0	9	18	6
4	4	0	1	0	944	1	6	1	3	22
5	7	1	1	15	3	834	14	3	4	10
6	9	2	3	1	10	7	922	0	3	1
7	2	4	20	6	5	1	0	976	1	13
8	7	1	5	15	4	8	10	6	914	4
9	6	2	1	11	25	7	1	11	13	932

We can see that applying the network to the first principal components rather than to the 784 pixels allowed us to simultaneously divide by 16 the error rate and by more than 4 the computation time!

We continue by increasing the number of hidden units, because 23 is a very small number compared to the 784 pixels of the images. We retrain the network with 100 hidden units, a maximum number of 300 iterations, and a weight decay (L^2 norm penalty of the weights, see Section 7.13) equal to 1 to penalize the error. By default, there is no weight decay in nnet and the value 1 was chosen among values between 0.5 and 10 because it gave a good prediction.

We obtain in 40 minutes a neural model with an error rate on the test set as low as 1.82%. If we are patient, we can even decrease this error rate further, keeping the previous values of weight decay and maximum number of iterations:

- error rate = 1.55% with 200 hidden units (97 minutes of calculation);
- error rate = 1.40% with 300 hidden units (199 minutes of calculation).

Here are the details of this last test:

```
> system.time(rn <- nnet(Xfinal, Y, size=300, softmax=TRUE,
   maxit=300, MaxNWts =30000, decay=1))
# weights:  20710
initial  value 406255.722777
iter  10 value 58754.980989
...
iter 300 value 2969.623986
final  value 2969.623986
stopped after 300 iterations
utilisateur      système      écoulé
   11832.99         2.26     11935.49
> rn
a 58-300-10 network with 20710 weights
```

```
options were - softmax modelling  decay=1
> pred.rn <- predict(rn, newdata=testreduced, type="class")
> # test error rate
> sum(pred.rn != test[,1]) / nrow(test)
[1] 0.014
# confusion matrix
> table(test[,1], pred.rn)
   pred.rn
```

	0	1	2	3	4	5	6	7	8	9
0	975	0	1	0	0	1	1	1	1	0
1	0	1127	2	1	0	0	2	1	2	0
2	3	0	1011	2	2	0	2	6	6	0
3	0	0	3	997	0	3	0	2	4	1
4	1	1	2	0	969	0	2	1	0	6
5	2	0	0	8	0	875	3	1	3	0
6	3	2	0	1	3	2	946	0	1	0
7	0	3	6	1	0	0	0	1013	1	4
8	2	1	2	2	0	1	1	1	962	2
9	2	2	0	4	7	6	0	3	0	985

This error rate of 1.40% is the lowest we have obtained, but at the cost of a significant calculation time.

6.11   H2O Neural Network

The multilayer perceptron is implemented in several R packages: besides nnet, we can mention deepnet, neuralnet, monmlp, RSNNS, AMORE, mxnet and h2o. In the h2o package, it is the deeplearning() function that implements the perceptron.

Contrary to what its name suggests, the H2O neural network is not a deep convolutional network or of such an advanced type, but it shares several characteristics of deep networks: several hidden layers, several available activation functions, dropout possible, an adaptive learning rate... and parallelization.

It also has the advantage, over other implementations, of having a *checkpoint* function that allows a model to be saved and then resumed at a later time, as well as a *grid search* function that allows a large set of models differing according to certain parameters, such as the activation function, the number of hidden layers and units, the weight decay, or the learning rate, to be trained at once.

The H2O network has an override_with_best_model option that keeps the best model encountered in training, which is better than a simple early stopping that interrupts training when the error increases (Section 7.13), but may thereby miss a better solution that would have been obtained by continuing training.

In the H2O network, the input data are automatically reduced centered, the initial weights can be controlled, the error function is the quadratic error or entropy, and the activation function can be the hyperbolic tangent, ReLU, or the Maxout function (Section 7.3). Training is performed by the stochastic gradient descent algorithm (Section 7.3). It is possible to add to the error a weight penalty term of the ridge or Lasso type, which is called the "weight decay" in L^1 or L^2 norm (Section 7.13).

Two other interesting features for the improvement of training are, on the one hand, the manual or automatic adjustment of the learning rate and momentum, and on the other, the implementation of the dropout mechanism (Section 7.11) which is usually rather the prerogative of deep neural networks.

The h2o.deeplearning() function offers the possibility of setting the dropout rate of the input layer of the network (input_dropout_ratio parameter, 0 by default, but often tested with the value 0.2), and the dropout rate of the hidden layers (hidden_dropout_ratio parameter, 0.5 by default). A different ratio can be specified for each hidden layer, for example, c(0.3,0.5,0.5) with three hidden layers. In the activation function specification, one must choose one of the three functions "TanhWithDropout," "RectifierWithDropout" or "MaxoutWithDropout" to have the dropout rate of the hidden layers taken into account. In other words, there is no dropout of hidden units with the "Tanh," "Rectifier," and "Maxout" functions.

To further improve the training process, we can apply a bound on the L^2 norm of the weights arriving on each hidden unit. If the L^2 norm exceeds this bound, the weights are renormalized by division. The use of an *a priori* constraint rather than (or in addition to) a penalty permits one to start the learning with a high learning rate, thus having large modifications of the weights, without fearing that they become too large (H2O does not perform batch normalization). This can explore a larger part of the solution space. This is even more useful with an unbounded activation function such as ReLU or Maxout. This bound (parameter max_w2) is the same for each unit. Its default value is deliberately very large: $3.4028235.10^{38}$.

Let's start with a first test of h2o.deeplearning() function, with the hyperbolic tangent as the activation function, a 20% dropout in the input layer, three hidden layers of 50 units each, and ten epochs for training:

```
> dlh2o <- h2o.deeplearning(x = 2:785, y = 1, training_frame = train,
    validation_frame = test, activation = "Tanh",
    input_dropout_ratio = 0.2, hidden = c(50,50,50), epochs = 10)
> print(dlh2o)
IP Address: localhost
Port      : 54321
Parsed Data Key: train.hex
Deep Learning Model Key: DeepLearning_bb5b2cc97ec68f47f12e7be98a424cd2
Training classification error: 0.02090592
Validation classification error: 0.0372
Confusion matrix:
Reported on test.hex
          Predicted
Actual     0    1    2    3    4    5    6    7    8    9   Error
   0      967    0    1    1    0    3    3    2    2    1 0.01327
   1        0 1127    2    2    0    0    1    0    3    0 0.00705
   2        7    0  988    7    6    1    6    6    8    3 0.04264
   3        0    1   10  965    2    3    3    7   13    6 0.04455
   4        1    0    6    2  955    0    3    5    0   10 0.02749
   5        3    0    0   14    2  840   13    2   10    8 0.05830
   6        5    2    2    4    5    5  934    0    1    0 0.02505
   7        2    6   12    7    3    1    0  982    4   11 0.04475
   8        5    3    9    9    5   12    3    4  919    5 0.05647
   9        3    6    2    7   16   11    1   10    2  951 0.05748
Totals   993 1145 1032 1018  994  876  967 1018  962  995 0.03720
```

We obtain an error rate of 3.72% in test.

The same setting with only adding a dropout in the hidden layers, with `hidden_dropout_ratios = c(0.5,0.5,0.5)`, causes a very large increase in the error rate to 19.78%. The "Maxout" activation function also leads to a very high error rate.

On the other hand, choosing the "Rectifier" activation function, without modifying the other parameters, reduces the error to 3.05%. This error doubles if we add a 50% dropout in each of the hidden layers:

```
> dlh2o <- h2o.deeplearning(x = 2:785, y = 1, training_frame = train,
    validation_frame = test, activation = "Rectifier",
    input_dropout_ratio = 0.2, hidden = c(50,50,50), epochs = 10)
> print(dlh2o)
IP Address: localhost
Port       : 54321
Parsed Data Key: train.hex
Deep Learning Model Key: DeepLearning_8a13dc1e44281e7c39305d4946a84755
Training classification error: 0.01344937
Validation classification error: 0.0305
Confusion matrix:
Reported on test.hex
           Predicted
Actual    0    1    2    3    4    5    6    7    8    9   Error
  0     968    0    1    2    1    1    4    1    1    1 0.01224
  1       0 1122    3    0    0    1    4    2    3    0 0.01145
  2       7    2  988    6    5    3    3    7    8    3 0.04264
  3       0    0    3  978    0    4    0    9    1   15 0.03168
  4       0    0    3    0  961    1    6    2    0    9 0.02138
  5       4    0    1   11    1  854   12    1    3    5 0.04260
  6       7    4    0    2    4    4  935    0    2    0 0.02401
  7       1    5   10    0    4    1    0  993    4   10 0.03405
  8       1    0    4    4    9    8    3    8  926   11 0.04928
  9       3    3    1    5   16    3    1    5    2  970 0.03865
  Totals 991 1136 1014 1008 1001  880  968 1028  950 1024 0.03050
```

Other parameters will further reduce the error.

Adding a `max_w2 = 10` bound lowers the error rate from 3.05% to 2.9%, then adding a ridge = 0.001 penalty lowers it to 2.4%.

```
> dlh2o <- h2o.deeplearning(x = 2:785, y = 1, training_frame = train,
    validation_frame = test, activation = "Rectifier", max_w2 = 10,
    l2 = 1e-3, input_dropout_ratio = 0.2, hidden = c(50,50,50),
    epochs = 10)
> print(dlh2o)
IP Address: localhost
Port       : 54321
Parsed Data Key: train.hex
Deep Learning Model Key: DeepLearning_832f5d61c71e86e0420e6f8aa6ff4de1
Training classification error: 0.01349608
Validation classification error: 0.024
Confusion matrix:
Reported on test.hex
```

```
         Predicted
Actual     0    1    2    3    4    5    6    7    8    9   Error
   0     968    0    2    1    1    2    4    1    1    0 0.01224
   1       0 1122    5    1    0    2    3    1    1    0 0.01145
   2       4    0 1013    0    2    0    1    7    5    0 0.01841
   3       0    0    5  981    0    6    2    7    4    5 0.02871
   4       2    1    2    0  963    0    5    1    1    7 0.01935
   5       2    0    0   11    2  861    7    2    5    2 0.03475
   6       5    2    0    1    3    4  939    0    3    1 0.01983
   7       1    5   10    1    4    0    0  995    2   10 0.03210
   8       1    1    3    5    7    4    5    5  937    6 0.03799
   9       3    2    1    7   10    1    0    3    1  981 0.02775
 Totals  986 1133 1041 1008  992  880  966 1022  960 1012 0.02400
```

Then we increase the number of hidden units to 100 units per layer, and the error rate drops to 1.89%, falling to 1.83% with 20 epochs instead of 10. The next improvement is to increase the max_w2 bound to 20: the error rate then drops to 1.77%, then to 1.68% with 300 units per hidden layer, 1.65% with 400 units per layer, and 1.55% with 500 units per layer:

```
> dlh2o <- h2o.deeplearning(x = 2:785, y = 1, training_frame = train,
    validation_frame = test, activation = "Rectifier", max_w2 = 20,
    l2 = 1e-3, input_dropout_ratio = 0.2, hidden = c(500,500,500),
    epochs = 20)
> print(dlh2o)
IP Address: localhost
Port      : 54321
Parsed Data Key: train.hex
Deep Learning Model Key: DeepLearning_88f876b9122030b2cdc242651d784e85
Training classification error: 0.005938242
Validation classification error: 0.0155
Confusion matrix:
Reported on test.hex
         Predicted
Actual     0    1    2    3    4    5    6    7    8    9   Error
   0     972    1    1    0    0    1    3    1    1    0 0.00816
   1       0 1125    1    1    0    3    2    2    1    0 0.00881
   2       1    0 1020    2    2    0    0    5    2    0 0.01163
   3       0    0    2  999    0    2    0    4    3    0 0.01089
   4       0    0    2    0  960    0    3    3    2   12 0.02240
   5       3    0    0    7    0  874    3    1    3    1 0.02018
   6       3    3    0    0    1    2  947    0    2    0 0.01148
   7       0    1    7    1    0    0    0 1012    3    4 0.01556
   8       2    1    2    5    0    3    0    2  954    5 0.02053
   9       1    2    0    5    6    5    0    6    2  982 0.02676
 Totals  982 1133 1035 1020  969  890  958 1036  973 1004 0.01550
```

On the other hand, we can see that the addition of a fourth hidden layer does not improve the recognition of handwritten digits.

We then performed more exhaustive tests, training networks with three hidden layers (of 784 units each), the "Rectifier" activation function and ten epochs. We tested the following variants:

- penalty L^1 = 0, 10-2, 10-3, 10-4 or 10-5;
- penalty L^2 = 0, 10-2, 10-3, 10-4 or 10-5;
- dropout in the input layer = 0 or 20%;
- dropout in hidden layers = 0 or 50%;
- bound on the L^2 norm of the weights = 0, 10 or 20.

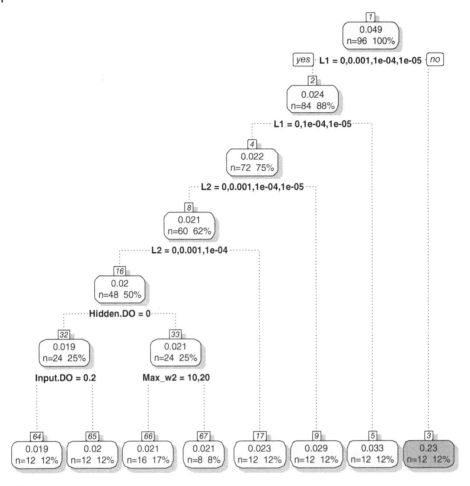

Figure 6.4 Explanation of the error rate.

We measured the error rate on the test set and explained this error rate as a function of the parameters using a decision tree (Figure 6.4). We can then observe the following facts.

A large Lasso penalty (10^{-3} and especially 10^{-2}) greatly increases the error. A high ridge penalty (10^{-3} and 10^{-2}) also increases the error. Dropout in hidden layers slightly increases the error. The dropout in the input decreases the error very slightly due to the large number of variables. The ridge or Lasso penalty has a more noticeable effect on the discriminative power than the dropout in the input or hidden layer.

These findings lead us to the parameterization of a more efficient model than the previous ones.

```
> system.time(dlh2o20 <- h2o.deeplearning(x = 2:785, y = 1, training_frame = train,
    validation_frame = test, activation = "Rectifier", l1 = 1e-5, max_w2 = 5,
    input_dropout_ratio = 0.2, hidden = c(1024,1024,2048), epochs = 100))
utilisateur      système       écoulé
     223.44        49.04     30226.35
```

```
Model Details:
==============
H2OMultinomialModel: deeplearning
Model ID:  DeepLearningModel__8a5781aec9a873e966cc61ef50f342ce
Status of Neuron Layers:
      layer      units      type dropout       l1        l2 mean_rate rate_RMS momentum
1 1.000000   717.000000    Input 20.00 %
2 2.000000  1024.000000 Rectifier  0.00 % 0.000010 0.000000  0.543019 0.410533 0.000000
3 3.000000  1024.000000 Rectifier  0.00 % 0.000010 0.000000  0.446066 0.386899 0.000000
4 4.000000  2048.000000 Rectifier  0.00 % 0.000010 0.000000  0.835448 0.311782 0.000000
5 5.000000    10.000000   Softmax         0.000010 0.000000  0.732272 0.376156 0.000000
   mean_weight weight_RMS mean_bias bias_RMS
1
2     0.000289   0.018487 -0.021783 0.050587
3    -0.003844   0.022540  0.560643 0.311657
4    -0.001678   0.014739  0.007128 0.054715
5    -0.008275   0.049088 -1.318202 0.774780
H2OMultinomialMetrics: deeplearning
** Reported on training data. **
Description: Metrics reported on temporary training frame with 9842 samples


Validation Set Metrics:
=====================
Metrics reported on full validation frame
Extract validation frame with `h2o.getFrame("mnist_test.hex_2")`
MSE: (Extract with `h2o.mse`) 0.00988638
R^2: (Extract with `h2o.r2`) 0.998821
Logloss: (Extract with `h2o.logloss`) 0.05680076
Confusion Matrix: Extract with `h2o.confusionMatrix(<model>,valid=TRUE)`)
=======================================================================
         X0   X1   X2   X3  X4  X5  X6   X7  X8   X9      Error         Rate
0       975    0    0    0   0   1   0    1   1    2 0.005102041     5 / 980
1         1 1129    1    2   0   0   0    0   2    0 0.005286344   6 / 1 135
2         1    1 1022    3   1   0   0    3   1    0 0.009689922  10 / 1 032
3         0    0    2  995   0   2   0    2   4    5 0.014851485  15 / 1 010
4         1    0    1    0 971   0   4    1   0    4 0.011201629    11 / 982
5         2    0    0    2   0 881   3    1   2    1 0.012331839    11 / 892
6         3    3    0    0   3   3 945    0   1    0 0.013569937    13 / 958
7         3    2    5    1   0   0   0 1015   2    0 0.012645914  13 / 1 028
8         0    0    0    3   1   3   0    1 963    3 0.011293634    11 / 974
9         2    3    0    2   5   2   1    2   0  992 0.016848365  17 / 1 009
Totals  988 1138 1031 1008 981 892 953 1026 976 1007 0.011200000 112 / 10 000
```

An error rate of 1.12% is achieved in the test, admittedly after more than eight hours of computation, due to the high number of hidden units and especially the 100 epochs required. The accuracy is expensive, because the best result obtained previously with only 20 epochs and 100 units per hidden layer, was an error rate of 1.77% obtained in about 18 minutes.

6.12 Synthesis of "Classical" Methods

The methods we call "classical" are the "shallow" learning methods, whose results are presented in Table 6.4. We will see in Chapter 8 that for handwritten digit recognition, deep learning methods outperform classical methods, by quickly decreasing the error rate below the 1% threshold. Thus, we obtain with MXNet (Section 8.2.2) a model with an error rate equal to 0.45% on the test set after 50 training epochs. As for Keras (Section 8.3.2), it will allow us to obtain almost the same error rate (0.58%) with the same number of epochs.

Table 6.4 Classical methods applied to the MNIST database.

Method	R package	Error rate (%)	Calculation time[a]
Linear discriminant analysis	MASS	12.70	1 mn
Quadratic discriminant analysis, applied to the first 32 axes of a PCA	MASS	3.71	1 s.
Lasso Multinomial logistic regression	h2o	7.15	4 mn
Random forests (1000 trees and 30 predictors tested at each split)	ranger	2.70	8 mn
Extra-Trees (1000 trees and 3 random splits tested for 50 predictors)	extraTrees	2.29	46 mn
Gradient Boosting XGBoost	xgboost	1.99	26 mn
Gradient Boosting LightGBM	lightgbm	1.62	5 mn
SVM with polynomial kernel of degree 3 applied to the first 58 axes of a PCA	e1071	1.55	19 mn
Single layer perceptron of 300 units, applied to the first 58 axes of a PCA	nnet	1.40	199 mn
Multilayer perceptron with three hidden layers of (1024, 1024, 2048) units, input dropout, rectifier activation and a Lasso penalty $= 10^{-5}$	h2o	1.12	500 mn
Multilayer perceptron with three hidden layers of (100, 100, 100) units, input dropout, rectifier activation and a ridge penalty $= 10^{-3}$	h2o	1.77	18 mn

a) Note: With an Intel Core I3 processor and 8 GB of RAM. The calculation time of the principal component analysis is not counted.

Notes

1 See, for example, Hastie, T., Tibshirani, R., and Friedman, J. *The Elements of Statistical Learning* (New York: Springer, 2009), Section 11.7, pp. 404-409.

2 http://www.nist.gov/srd/nistsd19.cfm.

3 http://yann.lecun.com/exdb/mnist/.

4 Ibid.

5 See, for example, Hastie, Tibshirani and Friedman, op.cit., section 13.3.3.

6 http://yann.lecun.com/exdb/mnist/.

7 See, for example, https://gist.github.com/brendano/39760.

8 https://www.kaggle.com/c/digit-recognizer. Note that the split between training and test is different from LeCun's original, with 42,000 digits in the training dataset and 28,000 digits in the test dataset.

9 http://www.pjreddie.com/projects/mnist-in-csv/.

10 Wright, M.N. and Ziegler, A. Ranger: A Fast Implementation of Random Forests for High Dimensional Data in C++ and R (2015). arXiv:1508.04409.

11 Chen, T. and Guestrin, C. XGBoost: A Scalable Tree Boosting System (2016). arXiv:1603.02754v3.

12 http://xgboost.readthedocs.io/en/latest/parameter.html.

7

Deep Learning

Deep Learning is a branch of machine learning largely based on neural networks that is particularly well suited to learning complex data in order to create advanced supervised or unsupervised models. It is the basis of the best models for computer vision and natural language processing, in particular, for machine translation and text generation, and it can even combine them to automatically generate the description of an image or even an animated scene. Its great capabilities make it popular in a wide range of applications, from medical image analysis to autonomous vehicles. It can also defeat the best human players at go, chess, and is making rapid progress in strategy video games. It has been able to develop thanks to new theoretical ideas but also thanks to the computing power of recent processors, especially those of graphics cards.

7.1   The Principles of Deep Learning

Deep learning seeks to model complex phenomena (voice recognition, computer vision, natural language understanding, etc.) using mechanisms inspired by neuroscience. It is based on the observation that, faced with complexity, the brain works less by simplifying signals through pre-processing than by hierarchical structures of units that each use as input the output of the previous unit.

Deep Learning uses both supervised and unsupervised methods, and particularly neural networks which are coming back into fashion. It currently includes more empirical than theoretical results, even if the work of theorists is of course expected to be the basis of this discipline. We can cite those of Stéphane Mallat.[1]

Improving the performance of deep learning models often requires the construction of more complex networks, made possible by the increase in computing power. This is due to the development of graphics processing units (GPUs) which are much more efficient than central processing units (CPUs) for the learning of developed hierarchical models, thanks to their parallel computing capabilities.

In machine learning, "deep" and "classical" ("shallow") architectures are thus opposed. A classical architecture is a (more or less manual) process of extracting relevant features (dimension reduction, variable selection) followed by a more or less sophisticated classifier. A deep architecture consists of the simultaneous learning of a hierarchy of: (1) several levels for feature extraction (from the simplest to the most complex), and (2) a fairly simple

Deep Learning: From Big Data to Artificial Intelligence with R, First Edition. Stéphane Tufféry.
© 2023 John Wiley & Sons Ltd. Published 2023 by John Wiley & Sons Ltd.
Companion website: www.wiley.com/go/Tuffery/DeepLearning

classifier. Thus, in image recognition, the network learns both to identify relevant patterns in an image and to classify these patterns. Deep learning could be called hierarchical learning, which would perhaps correspond better to its specificity.

This hierarchical organization is inspired by the work of Hubel and Wiesel in 1959 (winners of the Nobel Prize for Physiology or Medicine in 1981), who showed that biological vision is organized hierarchically, with simple cells and complex cells in the visual cortex. The simple cells distinguish local, specific shapes, while the complex cells recognize more global shapes, independently of their precise position (spatial invariance).

This organization corresponds to an operation in which the detection of visual scenes is organized hierarchically, from fine and low-level features (high resolution) to global and more invariant features (low resolution). This hierarchical representation with an increasing level of abstraction is found in several contexts:

- pixel → line → edge → part of an object → object
- character → word → group of words → proposition → sentence → speech
- wave → sound → phoneme→ phone → syllable → word.

A characteristic of the data that can be modeled by deep learning is, in addition to their large quantity (in number of observations and features), the fact that they are low-level data, such as the pixels of an image, and not structured and elaborated data, such as, for example, the socio-demographic data of an individual.

To model these situations, "deep" models have been invented over the last decades. What characterizes them? Yann Le Cun considers that a model is deep when it contains at least two levels of non-linear transformations. Thus, a decision tree is not deep because all decisions are made in the space of input variables: there is no hierarchy. A support vector machine (SVM) is not deep because it has only one possibly non-linear level: its kernel. A classical neural network with a hidden layer, what is called a perceptron, is not deep. We discuss in Section 7.3 the basic notions of neural networks, which will occupy us a lot because they are present in most deep learning methods.

Hornik's theorem[2] shows that one can approximate any continuous function on a bounded closed space of $\mathbb{R}^p$ with a single hidden layer perceptron (three layers with input and output layers) whose activation function is not polynomial. A special case was previously proved for sigmoid activation functions.[3] But it says nothing about the number of units in this hidden layer, its "width," which can be very large, with a risk of over-fitting that deep architectures avoid. After these theorems on "wide networks," other results have been proved on "deep networks" and in particular the fact that one can approximate any Lebesgue integrable function of $\mathbb{R}^p$ in $\mathbb{R}^q$ with a perceptron which has ReLU activation functions, possibly several hidden layers, but each of which has at most $\max(p+1, q)$ units.[4] This bound is optimal and cannot be decreased. But no upper bound is given on the number of hidden layers needed. The conditions of this theorem are more general than those of Hornik's theorem since any continuous function on a bounded closed space is integrable in the sense of Lebesgue but the opposite is not true.

The deep models most used today for image recognition and completion, natural language processing (NLP) and speech processing, are the convolutional neural networks that will be described in this chapter. They are even the basis of programs like AlphaGo that can beat human champions in some games. These are the networks we will discuss most in this chapter, but others will be mentioned, such as the recurrent neural networks that are particularly appropriate for speech recognition, translation, and in general for natural language processing.

Convolutional neural networks were introduced in 1980 by Fukushima,[5] who, with his Neocognitron, was the first to design an arrangement of simple and complex neural layers, like the cells discovered by Hubel and Wiesel. But the Neocognitron lacked a training mechanism based on the reduction of prediction error, and its training was somewhat blind, which nevertheless allowed it to accomplish simple tasks such as number recognition. The learning device came in 1989 with the backpropagation mechanism applied to convolutional networks by LeCun *et al.*[6, 7] These networks were then perfected in 1998 by LeCun, Bottou, Bengio, and Haffner,[8] and they were the first winners in 2012 of the annual ILSVRC ImageNet competition (Section 7.15), with a spectacular performance and a strong lead over the others: the AlexNet network used dropout, data augmentation, and the graphics processing units for fast computations. In 2012, convolutional neural networks reached a classification error rate of handwritten digits in the MNIST dataset (Section 6.1) equal to 0.23% and thus very close to that of a human ($\approx 0.20\%$).

To conclude this introduction, let us mention a third type of learning, next to supervised learning and unsupervised learning: *reinforcement learning*. This is learning by trial and error. It consists in rewarding good answers and good actions, and penalizing bad ones, as we do in training an animal. It is based on a reward function and an algorithm to maximize this function. The goal is to maximize a sum of rewards, corresponding to a sequence of actions, and the objective is therefore both short-term and long-term.

The difference between reinforcement learning and supervised learning is that it does not rely on *a priori* examples of positive or negative actions. Reinforcement learning occurs when we can say *a posteriori* that an action is positive without being able to give *a priori* examples of positive actions. Supervised learning can be implemented when we have a labeled training dataset, such as a set of moves that we know we will win or lose, but reinforcement learning is indispensable in the absence of such a training dataset, for example when the machine must learn a game by playing against itself and not by using a base of games already played.

The scarcity of labeled bases, which most often require human labor for this labeling, explains the interest in reinforcement learning, but it is, on the other hand, much slower because it requires a very large number of iterations. This is not a problem when it comes to learning a game like chess, because the machine can play millions or even billions of games against itself, even in a short time, if we have a lot of computing power: the machine starts by playing less well than a beginner before quickly overtaking the human beginner and eventually overtaking the champions. This is, however, problematic in the physical world, when, for example, it is required to teach movements to a robot whose execution speed is necessarily limited.

Reinforcement learning has been developed very recently and is still limited to specific applications, such as games, but it is bound to develop in other fields: autonomous vehicles, robotics, education, etc.

7.2 Overview of Deep Neural Networks

The main deep learning methods are based on neural networks, whose structure differs, however, from that of classical neural networks, such as the perceptron (Section 7.3), and is adapted to the realization of complex images, videos and written and spoken natural language recognition tasks. Thanks to their local connections, shared weights, and mechanisms, such as pooling and dropout, they can have many hidden layers without over-fitting, which would be impossible for a perceptron.

Among these networks, *convolutional neural networks* excel in image recognition because they reproduce with their deep hierarchical structure the increasing levels of complexity of an image, from the fine and low level features of the image (edges, contours, textures) to the global features (parts of objects, objects) independent of their precise position.

This hierarchical organization has been well known since the work of Hubel and Wiesel on biological vision. It is also found in other domains, such as language recognition, where the complexity grows from the level of words to the level of sentences and speech.

Convolutional neural networks are therefore also successfully applied to the processing of texts written in natural language. Each word or sentence is a matrix that has one row for each possible sign (letter, number, punctuation) and one column for each character of the words: the whole column contains 0 except for the row corresponding to the sign, which contains 1. A character is thus the equivalent of a pixel, and a sentence or a text segment corresponds to an image in its matrix form.[9] We can also make the rows correspond to the words of the vocabulary and the columns to the sentences, and have a non-zero value in the matrix when a word is used in a sentence (Figure 7.1).

The matrix structure of convolutional neural networks can also be applied to sound recognition, each row corresponding to a frequency and each column to a different instant, and a piece of music or a speech is described by the evolution in time of the different intensities of each frequency.

the	young	man	in	anger	in	the	S	bus
↓	↓	↓	↓	↓	↓	↓	↓	↓
1	0	0	0	0	0	1	0	0
0	1	0	0	0	0	0	0	0
0	0	1	0	0	0	0	0	0
0	0	0	1	0	1	0	0	0
0	0	0	0	1	0	0	0	0
0	0	0	0	0	0	0	1	0
0	0	0	0	0	0	0	0	1

Figure 7.1 Matrix representation of a text.

However, convolutional networks are not useful in analyzing data that do not have a spatial or equivalent structure. *A fortiori*, they are not adapted to the analysis of heterogeneous data, as found in many classical problems where quantitative and qualitative data are mixed.

For natural language processing, translation, recognition, and speech synthesis, the most used networks are *recurrent neural networks* (Section 7.16) and *transformer models* (Section 9.7). Recurrent neural networks are neural networks that have recurrent connections in their hidden layers, which can take into account at each moment a certain number of past states. Each unit of a hidden layer has two connections: the usual connection coming from the input layer, and a "recurrent" connection coming from the previous state of the hidden layer.

Recurrent neural networks are thus adapted to situations where the data are sequences, and where what we want to detect depends on the context and on a temporal evolution. However, the memory of recurrent neural networks has often proved to be too short-term, limited to a few dozen iterations. This is due to the backpropagation mechanism, in which the weights of the units receive an update proportional to the gradient of the error (Section 7.3). This gradient decreases exponentially as a function of the number of iterations, which causes recurrent neural networks to quickly "forget the past."

A solution was found in 1997 with the invention of *Long Short-Term Memory*[10] (LSTM) recurrent neural networks by Jürgen Schmidhuber and his student Sepp Hochreiter, who had studied and explained the general problem of vanishing gradient in his thesis.[11] They added a memory unit to the recurrent network to prevent gradient vanishing and to increase the memory depth of the network, thus making it possible to process long sequences of words, but also sequences of images as in a video, and more generally time series. LSTM networks have proven to be very useful and have been breaking all records for speech recognition quality for several years, and are implemented by Google, Apple, and Amazon in their Allo, Siri, and Alexa assistants. Since then, a simpler variant of LSTM networks has been devised: GRU (Gated Recurrent Units) networks,[12] which are sometimes a little less powerful, but faster than LSTMs due to the smaller number of their parameters, and which can have comparable performance in natural language processing.

Another type of model that is highly effective in a wide range of natural language processing tasks appeared in 2017: transformer models (Section 9.7).

Neural networks for deep learning are implemented in a number of software libraries, almost all of which are open source:

- Theano is a library written in Python at the University of Montreal (in MILA: Montreal Institute for Learning Algorithms), which can compile Python into CUDA instructions for GPUs; presumably due to Python being less efficient than C++, and less easy to use, Theano is less prevalent in industry than academia, and the discontinuation of its development was announced by Yoshua Bengio (head of MILA) in late 2017; however, Theano paved the way for TensorFlow.
- TensorFlow is a library implemented in C++ and CUDA (for computations) with a Python scripting language, which is comprehensive, widely used, and therefore well documented, created by Google and, since 2015, used in open source under Apache license, and with Python and R interfaces (`tensorflow` package).

- Keras can rely on the TensorFlow, Theano, or Microsoft Cognitive Toolkit libraries (and PlaidML for GPU computations), which perform computations such as convolutions and for which Keras provides an interface and simpler code; Keras is written in Python and can also be used with the `keras` and `kerasR` packages of R.
- Torch is one of the first deep learning libraries, said to be fast, easy to use, implemented in C and CUDA with a Lua-based scripting language (LuaJIT), and more recently the basis for the Python PyTorch library and the R `torch` package; it is the result of a collaboration of researchers from Facebook, Twitter, and DeepMind, and primarily maintained by Facebook.
- Caffe (Convolutional Architecture for Fast Feature Embedding) is a library written in C++ at UC Berkeley, with Python and MATLAB interfaces, many pre-trained models, rather specialized in computer vision; the Caffe2 version incorporating recurrent networks merged in March 2018 with PyTorch.
- fastai is an interface to PyTorch, as Keras is for TensorFlow, which allows one to quickly implement efficient neural networks; it is an open-source Apache project resulting from the work of the fast.ai group[13] created to "democratize deep learning," in particular, by the MOOC *Practical Deep Learning for Coders*.[14]
- MXNet is a widely used Apache-licensed library, especially on Amazon's cloud, well documented, written in C++, with interfaces for Python, R, MATLAB and Julia; it gets its name from "mix-net" because it combines imperative (implemented in Torch) and symbolic programming (implemented in Caffe, Theano, and TensorFlow, where computations are represented by symbolic graphs that must be "compiled"[15] to be transformed into executable functions).
- `darch` is an R package implementing the ideas of Hinton *et al.* published in 2006[16] (notably on restricted Boltzmann machines).
- Deeplearning4j from Skymind is a parallelized Java library implementing restricted Boltzmann machines, recurrent neural networks, convolutional neural networks, Word2Vec, and GloVe dives.
- MatConvNet for Matlab was developed by the *Visual Geometry Group* of the University of Oxford, also the creator of the convolutional neural networks VGG16 and VGG19, which we will discuss later.
- Hugging Face provides a large number of pre-trained transformer models (Section 9.7).

We can see that some of these libraries come from university laboratories and others from technology companies, with sometimes back and forth between the two worlds.

The implementation of these algorithms in software, such as Python and R, has greatly "democratized" deep learning by making it accessible with a minimum of programming and already quite high performances on ordinary machines.

7.3 Recall on Neural Networks and Their Training

Before studying deep neural networks, we start with some general information about neural networks. They are presented as sets of *units* (or *neurons*) connected to each other, each unit being activated by receiving a bit of data and sending another one. These sets of

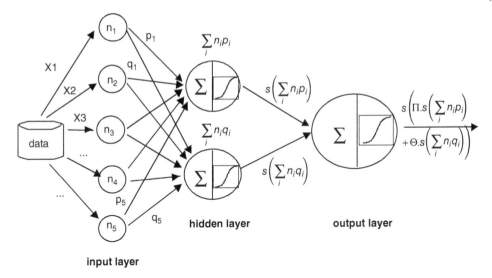

Figure 7.2   Hidden layer perceptron.

units are organized in levels called *layers*, and each layer sends its data to the next layer, like neurons transmitting a signal through their synapses.

Figure 7.2 shows the most common model of a shallow (non-deep) neural network: the perceptron, here a single hidden layer perceptron. In the perceptron, the connection between two units i and j, i.e. the equivalent of a synapse, is made by multiplying the output n_i of unit i by a certain weight p_{ij}. The unit j is activated by the signal $\sum_i p_{ij} n_i$, with the sum taken from all the units i of the previous layer. We can add a "constant" to the model with a particular unit (the "bias") which always transmits the value 1. We can possibly apply an *activation function* $s(\sum_i p_{ij} n_i)$ to this signal. The first level, the input layer, is composed of units that receive the data from the training dataset.

Neural networks can be used for clustering or prediction, and in networks used for prediction (regression or classification), the variable to be explained corresponds to a level called the output layer, with a single unit in the case of regression, and a unit for each category of the variable to be explained when it has at least three categories. If the variable to be explained is binary, the output layer can have one or two units, as explained below.

Between the input layer and the output layer are sometimes connected units belonging to an intermediate level: the *hidden layer*, so called because it corresponds to latent data. A network can have several hidden layers (see Figure 7.2). When a signal x is transmitted from one layer to another, an activation function $s(x)$ is applied to it.

When the signal arrives at a hidden layer, the most used activation functions in classical neural networks are the sigmoid $1/(1 + e^{-x})$ and the hyperbolic tangent $(e^x - e^{-x})/(e^x + e^{-x})$. This can transmit to the layer a normalized data (in [-1, +1] for the hyperbolic tangent, or in [0, +1] for the sigmoid), which we will see later is of interest in the activation of a unit. We also use the absolute value of $tanh(x)$ and the "scaled tanh" $\alpha.tanh(\beta x)$ (with α and $\beta > 0$) as activation functions.

The first neural networks used the threshold function as their activation function, which is 1 if x exceeded a certain threshold, and 0 otherwise. But the units of these networks "saturated" immediately upon receiving a signal exceeding the threshold, instead of reacting gradually. A small change in the input signal caused an abrupt change (infinite gradient) or no change (zero gradient). These networks with a "threshold" activation function were the neuron of McCulloch and Pitts and the single-layer perceptron of Rosenblatt (Section 10.1).

In deep neural networks, the activation function $f(x) = max(x, 0)$, called "Rectifier" or "Rectified Linear Unit" (ReLU), is often used in image recognition, because it allows a much faster training than the sigmoid or the hyperbolic tangent: on the one hand, its computation is faster, and, on the other hand, the absence of unit saturation for large x means that ReLU limits the risks of gradient vanishing (Section 7.4) and the gradient descent converges faster (Figure 7.3). The fact that the second derivative of ReLU is zero makes an optimization algorithm, such as a gradient descent, which uses only the first derivative, all the more advantageous.

But another problem can occur in backpropagation (cf. *infra*), called "dying ReLU": if the distribution of input data to a unit with ReLU makes most of the values negative, the ReLU

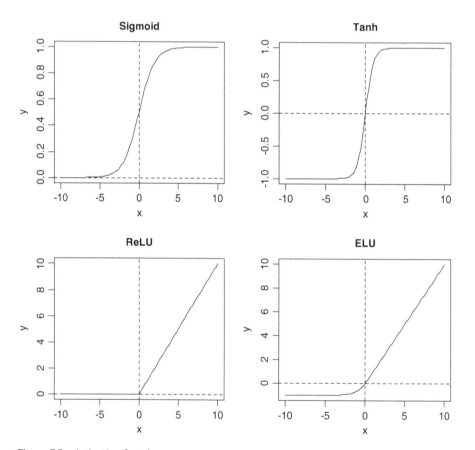

Figure 7.3 Activation functions.

and its gradient will be zero for most of the values: the weights will then not be updated and the unit becomes inactive or "dead." This can happen if the learning rate is too high and can compromise the training of the network if many units are involved. It is sometimes overcome by using the "leaky ReLU," defined by $f(x) = x$ if $x > 0$ and $f(x) = \alpha x$ otherwise (instead of $f(x) = 0$), where α has a small value often equal to 0.01. One can also use batch normalization (Section 7.8), with what is denoted BN-ReLU.

Another variant of ReLU is the ELU (Exponential Linear Unit) function, defined by $f(x) = x$ if $x > 0$ and $f(x) = \alpha(e^x - 1)$ if $x \leq 0$ (see Figure 7.3). It converges to $-\alpha$ when x tends to $-\infty$. The coefficient α often takes values between 0.1 and 0.3. It is fixed and cannot be changed by training. The ELU function has a double advantage: like the leaky ReLU it avoids the dying ReLU phenomenon, and moreover it is everywhere derivable. The fact that it takes negative values can also be useful. But the presence of the exponential increases its computation time.

The ReLU function is relevant on sparse data, i.e. with many 0s. It was published in 2000[17] but only became widespread ten years later,[18] because of its disadvantage compared to classical activation functions of not being derivable in 0.

More recently, another activation function has been proposed:[19] the Maxout $= \max\limits_i p_{ij} n_i$ which consists in taking the maximum of the signals arriving on the unit rather than their sum $\sum_i p_{ij} n_i$. The output is the maximum of the inputs. This function shares with ReLU the property of not saturating for large input values, but moreover it does not cancel out over part of its definition domain, unlike ReLU. There is no "dying Maxout."

The choice of the activation function $s(x)$ is different between the output layer and the layer preceding it. It is usually advised:

- for a regression, thus an output layer taking any numerical values, to take the identity $s(x) = x$ or a linear function $s(x) = ax + b$;
- for a regression with values in [0,1], to take the sigmoid as the activation function (logistic function);
- for the binary classification $Y = 0/1$ with a single output unit, to take as activation function the sigmoid, whose value in [0,1] is an estimator of $P(Y = 1|x)$;
- for multi-class (and possibly also binary) classification, with one unit per class, apply the "softmax" function:

$$s_k(x) = \frac{e^{x_k}}{\sum_{l=1}^{K} e^{x_l}}$$

to the kth component x_k of the output; this ensures that we have a sum $\sum_{k=1}^{K} s_k(x) = 1$ on all the K classes, and each output is an estimator $P(Y = k|x)$.

The training of a neural network consists of determining the weight of each of its connections. If there are n connections in the network, each tuple $(p_1, p_2, \ldots, p_n)$ of weights is used to calculate the output values obtained on the training sample. These output values are compared to the expected values, and an error ε is calculated. The weights to be determined by training are those that minimize the error.

Table 7.1 Choice of activation and error functions.

Problem	Activation of the output	Error function
Regression	Linear	Squared error
Regression in [0,1]	Sigmoid	Squared error
Binary classification	Sigmoid or softmax	Cross-entropy
Multi-class classification	Softmax	Cross-entropy

For regression problems, the error function is usually the expectation of the quadratic loss function $(f(x) - y)^2$ or L^2 loss:

$$L(f, (x,y)) = \|f(x) - y\|^2 = \sum_i (f(x_i) - y_i)^2.$$

The absolute error (L^1) can also be used:

$$L(f, (x,y)) = \sum_i |f(x_i) - y_i|.$$

Quadratic or absolute loss is less suitable for classification problems, and cross-entropy $-\sum_{k=1}^{K} y_k \log(f_k(x))$ is generally used. In the binary case $Y = 0/1$, its expectation the error function is:

$$L(f, (x,y)) = -\sum_i \{y_i \log(f(x_i)) + (1 - y_i) \log(1 - f(x_i))\}.$$

In the multi-class case, it is:

$$L(f, (x,y)) = -\sum_i \sum_{k=1}^{K} y_{ik} \log(f_k(x_i)),$$

y_{ik} being the 0/1 variable to be explained associated with the kth class for the ith observation. By setting $f(x) = P(Y = 1|X = x)$, we recognize in this expression half of the deviance of the generalized linear model.[20] Minimizing the error is therefore the same as finding the maximum likelihood. The maximum likelihood gives the weights sought for these units.

Table 7.1 shows the most common choices of activation and error functions.

The objective of training is to adjust the weights to decrease the error ε. When the weights vary, the set of values $(p_1, p_2, \ldots, p_n, \varepsilon)$ is a surface (or rather a hypersurface) in an $n + 1$ dimensional space, the "error surface," and adjusting the weights in order to minimize the error function can be seen as moving on the error surface to find the minimum point. Unlike linear models in which the error surface is a well-defined and well-known mathematical object (e.g., parabolic shape) whose minimum point can be determined by calculation, neural networks are non-linear models whose error surface has a complex, and often even non-convex, shape, which implies that a local minimum is not necessarily global.

For the search of the minimum error, the optimization algorithms are most often gradient descent or quasi-Newton methods (Section 3.2). The Newton method itself, with its computation of the inverse of the Hessian matrix, can be unstable and this is why quasi-Newton's methods are preferred. On big data, the gradient descent is the most used method because it is more efficient, computing only the first derivatives. Although a quasi-Newton method may converge in fewer iterations than a gradient descent, it may be faster to perform a gradient descent with an increased number of iterations. In the gradient descent, we move on the error surface following the line of greatest slope, in the opposite direction to the gradient since we want to go in the direction of the decrease, not the increase of the error, to arrive at a point as low as possible (Section 3.2).

In the gradient descent algorithm, at each iteration, the mean error and its gradient are computed with respect to the network weights, and the weights are updated. This processing at each iteration can be performed:

- on all observations (batch gradient);
- on a subset called a mini-batch (stochastic gradient);
- on a mini-batch reduced to one observation (online gradient).

The idea of the stochastic gradient is that if the data are massive and redundant, it is not necessary to wait to have processed all the observations to calculate the gradient, a sample already will give a good approximation. This assumes of course that the error function of a set of observations can be decomposed into a sum of errors on each observation, which is in practice always the case of the error functions we use.

The size B of the mini-batches is a parameter of the neural network. If B is small, the gradient is faster to compute and the convergence is generally faster, but more irregular with fluctuations within the mini-batches. These fluctuations can be limited by shuffling the observations, which avoids the case where some mini-batches are too atypical. The risk of a small batch is that it does not reflect the distribution of the input data. Moreover, if the batches are small, the calculations are more numerous and the updates of weights more frequent.

We can choose B to be larger if the error surface is convex or regular enough to allow the convergence directly to a solution, without having to pull out local minima by recalculating the weights on many small mini-batches. Moreover, the size of B can be all the larger as the memory available for the computations is more important, because the vectorization of the computations in memory makes them faster.

A common compromise between speed and stability of convergence leads to mini-batches of size between 32 and 256 observations (for example, images or audio files). Sizes that are powers of 2 are preferred for a better management of memory allocation.

A fairly large number of iterations may be necessary to process all the observations and to pass the whole training sample through the network, which is called an *epoch*. The number of epochs is a parameter of the network; the range of possible epochs is very large, from several tens to several thousands. If, for example, the size of the mini-batches is 32 and the training sample has 3200 cases, 100 iterations are needed for an epoch.

The following general formula gives the weight θ_{t+1} at the $t+1^{\text{st}}$ iteration, according to the weight θ_t at the tth iteration, the error $L(\Theta, (x_i y_i)) = \frac{1}{n} \sum_{i=1}^{n} \frac{1}{2}(y_i - \hat{f}_\theta(x_i))^2$, the considered mini-batches $m_b \subseteq (x_i, y_i)_{i=1...n}$ of size $B [\in 1,n]$, and the learning rate $\varepsilon(t)$:

$$\theta_{t+1} = \theta_t - \varepsilon(t)\frac{1}{B} \sum_{b=0}^{B-1} \frac{\partial L(\theta_t, m_b)}{\partial \theta}.$$

The *learning rate* is a parameter that controls the amount of change in weights during the training process and regulates the speed of descent of the error surface slope. This is the step mentioned in Section 3.2 on the gradient descent. This speed is therefore proportional to the slope of the surface and the learning rate. The higher the learning rate, the faster the training, but the higher the risk of the network converging to a globally non-optimal solution. This rate, between 0 and 1, determines the importance of the modification of the weights during the training process. It is interesting to vary this rate, which will be important at the beginning of the training process to allow a quick exploration of the error surface and a quick approach to the minima of the surface, then it will decrease at the end of the training process to arrive as close as possible to an optimal solution.

A refinement has been made to this method, in order to avoid the zigzags seen in the gradient descent when the gradients are much larger in some directions than in others, i.e. when the Hessian matrix is ill-conditioned (Section 3.2). We add a quantity called *momentum* that speeds up the descent when the gradient keeps the same direction and slows down the descent when the gradient changes direction. Each update of θ_t is done by adding to the negative gradient a "velocity" v that accumulates previous gradients and keeps it in the same direction the higher the moment $\alpha(t) \in [0, 1]$ is.

$$v_t = \alpha(t)v_{t-1} - \varepsilon(t)\frac{1}{B}\sum_{b=0}^{B-1}\frac{\partial L(\theta_t, m_b)}{\partial \theta},$$

$$\theta_{t+1} = \theta_t + v_t.$$

Equivalently, we can write:

$$\theta_{t+1} = \theta_t - \varepsilon(t)\frac{1}{B}\sum_{b=0}^{B-1}\frac{\partial L(\theta_t, m_b)}{\partial \theta} + \alpha(t)(\theta_t - \theta_{t-1}).$$

The inertia $\alpha(t)(\theta_t - \theta_{t-1})$ tends to keep the weight updates in the same direction. This is referred to as the "heavy ball" method. The higher the momentum, the more the update of weights tends to keep the same direction of evolution, as a prevailing factor incorporates the previous weight updates. The momentum helps to achieve convergence by limiting oscillations, such as those seen in Figure 3.4. Convergence can be as fast as that of the conjugate gradient, which also searches for the minimum by exploiting the gradient history (Section 3.2). Just as one strategy is to decrease the learning rate as training proceeds, a similar strategy is to increase the momentum during training, to allow the network to slowly approach a globally optimal solution. A momentum value of 0.9 is common at the end of the training. The notion of momentum introduces the idea of looking at the history of gradients and not just the last computed gradient, an idea developed in the adaptive algorithms described in Section 7.14.

In summary, the learning rate controls the speed of movement and the momentum controls the speed of directional changes on the error surface: at the beginning of training, we go fast and in all directions; at the end, we slow down and turn less.

A variant of the classical moment is the Nesterov momentum,[21] or Nesterov Accelerated Gradient (NAG), in which the gradient is calculated after applying the velocity term.

$$v_t = \alpha(t)v_{t-1} - \varepsilon(t)\frac{1}{B}\sum_{b=0}^{B-1}\frac{\partial L(\theta_t + \alpha(t)v_{t-1}, m_b)}{\partial \theta},$$

$$\theta_{t+1} = \theta_t + v_t.$$

The gradient is calculated not with respect to the current parameter but with respect to its future values: we anticipate the momentum correction in the gradient calculation to avoid the state where the inertia that is brought by the classical momentum prevents it from sufficiently approaching the optimum. In some favorable cases, the rate of convergence of the Nesterov gradient is of the order of $O(1/k^2)$ against $O(1/k)$ for the classical gradient descent. But this is not always the case and the Nesterov gradient may even converge more slowly than the gradient descent.[22]

Up to now, we have acted as if the neural network had only one layer and therefore only one set of weights to fit. But as soon as multi-layer networks appeared, the question arose of training them: how to combine the adjustment of weights on several layers? The solution is the *backpropagation algorithm*. This algorithm dates back to the 1970s and in particular to the thesis of Paul Werbos,[23] and it has been popular since the work of Rumelhart, Hinton, and Williams in 1986 on its application to multi-layer neural networks[24] (after other precursor articles in previous years). The principle of the backpropagation algorithm is to backpropagate (i.e. to propagate from the output to the input) the error of the output layer of the network on each unit of each of the intermediate layers, from the last to the first, by distributing the error on each synaptic weight, which is then updated, in a way that is all the more important as it has contributed more to the error. Several methods could be used to update the synaptic weights and gradient descent is the most commonly used. The standard neural network training algorithm is therefore gradient descent backpropagation. And since it is necessary to backpropagate a gradient (of the error) on all the layers of the network, i.e. to calculate the first derivatives as functions of the weights of the different layers, the basic idea is to use the chain derivation rule of a compound function $(g \circ f)' = (g' \circ f)f$, applying it to the neural network activation functions. The gradient descent with backpropagation was not applicable to the first neural networks whose outputs were binary and became applicable when networks with continuous outputs (for example, sigmoidal) appeared, as we will explain in the next section. We will see that this algorithm encounters difficulties on multi-layer networks, which have been a limitation on its use for several years and have restricted the use of neural networks.

The basic model of a single hidden layer neural network (perceptron) can be coded as follows, x being the input, y being the output, t being the expected output of the network, w_1 the weights between the input and the hidden layer, w_2 the weights between the hidden layer and the output, and h the activation of the hidden layer.[25] We assume that there is a single unit in the hidden layer and omit biases to simplify the notations. Otherwise, we would have to replace, for example, the formula $h = \sigma(x.w_1)$ by the formula $h = \sigma\left(\sum_k x_k . w_{1k}\right)$.

The backpropagation algorithm is encoded in the `backpropagate` function below, which applies gradient descent (Section 3.2) to weights w_1 and w_2. This function is determined by computing the gradient of the squared error $E = \frac{1}{2}(\hat{y} - y)^2$ with respect to the weights w_1 and w_2, knowing that in order to calculate the gradient through several layers we use as seen above the derivation rule of a compound function $(g \circ f)' = (g' \circ f)f'$.

Here f is the sigmoid activation function $\sigma(x) = 1/(1+e^{-x})$.

The output signal seen as a function of the weight $w1$ can be written as $y(w1) = \sigma(h.w_2) = \sigma(\sigma(x.w_1).w_2)$. The derivative of the sigmoid is $\sigma'(x) = e^{-x}/(1+e^{-x})^2 = \sigma(x)(1 - \sigma(x))$ and the derivative of $\sigma(x.w_1)$ as a function of $w1$ is therefore $x.\sigma(x.w_1)(1 - \sigma(x.w_1))$. The particular form of the derivative of the sigmoid function explains that this derivative tends towards 0, and that consequently the learning does not progress any further, when the sigmoid $\sigma(x)$ tends towards +1 or 0, i.e. when x tends towards more or less infinity. We are then on the almost horizontal part of the curve.

If we note $o = h.w_2$, the output of the hidden layer before its activation, we have $y = \sigma(o)$ and the gradient of the error E with respect to the weight w_2 is therefore:

$$\frac{\partial E}{\partial w_2} = \frac{\partial E}{\partial y} \times \frac{\partial y}{\partial o} \times \frac{\partial o}{\partial w_2}$$

$$= (\hat{y} - y)\sigma(o)(1 - \sigma(o))h$$

$$= (\hat{y} - y)y(1 - y)h.$$

The gradient of the error E with respect to the weight w_1 is:

$$\frac{\partial E}{\partial w_1} = \frac{\partial E}{\partial y} \times \frac{\partial y}{\partial o} \times \frac{\partial o}{\partial h} \times \frac{\partial h}{\partial w_1}$$

$$= (\hat{y} - y)\sigma(o)(1 - \sigma(o))w_2\sigma(x.w_1)(1 - \sigma(x.w_1))x$$

$$= (y - \hat{y})y(1 - y)w_2 h(1 - h)x.$$

Here is the R code of the basic model of the single hidden layer perceptron, corresponding to the previous explanations (but reintroducing the biases and several units in the hidden layer, whose number is given by the `size` parameter).

```
sigmoid <- function(x) {1 / (1 + exp(-x))}

feedforward <- function(x, w1, w2) {
  z1 <- cbind(1, x) %*% w1
  h  <- sigmoid(z1)
  z2 <- cbind(1, h) %*% w2
  list(output = sigmoid(z2), h = h)
}

backpropagate <- function(x, y, y_hat, w1, w2, h, learn_rate) {
  dw2 <- t(cbind(1,h)) %*% (y_hat-y) %*% y %*% (1-y)
  dw1 <- t(cbind(1,x)) %*% (h*(1-h) * (y_hat-y) %*% t(w2[-1,]))
  w1 <- w1 - learn_rate * dw1
  w2 <- w2 - learn_rate * dw2
  list(w1 = w1, w2 = w2)
}

perceptron <- function(x, y, size = 5, learn_rate = 1e-2, itera-
tions = 1e4) {
  d <- ncol(x) + 1
  w1 <- matrix(rnorm(d * size), d, size)
  w2 <- as.matrix(rnorm(size + 1))
  for (i in 1:iterations) {
    ff <- feedforward(x, w1, w2)
    bp <- backpropagate(x, y, y_hat = ff$output,
                        w1, w2, h = ff$h,
                        learn_rate = learn_rate)
    w1 <- bp$w1 ; w2 <- bp$w2
  }
  list(output = ff$output, w1 = w1, w2 = w2)
}
```

We can apply this perceptron to a dataset, for example, the spam dataset of the `kernlab` package. The 58th variable of the data frame is the variable to be explained "spam / non-spam." There are 1813 emails that are spam and 2788 that are not. We shuffle the observations by the `sample()` function as advised to do for the training of a neural network, which must avoid having successive observations which are similar.

```
> library(kernlab)
> data(spam)
> x <- data.matrix(spam[sample(nrow(spam)),-58])
> y <- spam$type == "spam"
> mynnet <- perceptron(x, y, size = 10, iterations = 1e3)
> library(pROC)
> auc(y, as.numeric(mynnet$output), quiet=TRUE)
Area under the curve: 0.4329
```

We see that our perceptron does not discriminate spam from non-spam at all. If we look at the output of the `mynnet$output` perceptron, we realize that all its values are extremely small. This is because we need to normalize the input data of a neural network, in order to avoid the phenomenon mentioned above: input data of the sigmoidal activation function that are concentrated in the areas where the gradient is almost zero and the training that no longer progresses. The normalization by the `scale()` function has an immediate effect on the discriminative power of our model.

```
> x <- scale(data.matrix(spam[sample(nrow(spam)),-58]))
> mynnet <- perceptron(x, y, size = 10, iterations = 1e3)
> auc(y, as.numeric(mynnet$output), quiet=TRUE)
Area under the curve: 0.6638
```

Of course, the spam detection model can be improved by increasing the number of units in the hidden layer. The area under the ROC curve reaches 0.963 and we find a score threshold above which 78% of the emails are spam, and below which 95% of the emails are not spam. Other thresholds may be used, depending on whether we want to reduce the number of false positives or false negatives. The complexity of the network increases sharply as does its computation time.

```
> mynnet <- perceptron(x, y, size = 100, iterations = 1e3))
> auc(y, as.numeric(mynnet$output), quiet=TRUE)
Area under the curve: 0.9629
> (tab <- table(y, (mynnet$output > 0.5)))

y        FALSE TRUE
  FALSE   2636  152
  TRUE     392 1421
> sum(diag(tab)/nrow(spam))
[1] 0.8817648
> cbind(prop.table(tab,1), addmargins(tab,2))
            FALSE        TRUE FALSE TRUE  Sum
FALSE 0.9454806 0.05451937  2636  152 2788
TRUE  0.2162162 0.78378378   392 1421 1813
```

This is of course only a "toy example" to understand the mechanism of backpropagation and the need to normalize the data. We get much better performance using the textual data processing methods presented in Chapters 4 and 9.

7.4 Difficulties of Gradient Backpropagation

The training of the different layers of a multilayer neural network does not occur at the same speed, and it is generally slower for the first layers of the network, which are farther from the output layer. This is because, to calculate the gradient across several layers, we use the derivation rule of a compound function $(g \circ f)' = (g' \circ f)f$ and we multiply the gradients.

If the gradients are less than 1, their products decrease with the number of layers, as numbers less than 1 are multiplied an increasing number of times. This produces a phenomenon called the "vanishing gradient" in the backpropagation to the first layers, the consequence of which is a slower and slower training of the first layers of the network. If the gradients are greater than 1, their products increase with the number of layers, resulting in an "exploding gradient." This last situation is uncommon. Indeed, if the activation function σ is the sigmoid, its derivative is at most $\sigma'(0) = 0.25$ (and it is < 1 at all points for the derivative of the hyperbolic tangent, except at 0 where it is 1). Moreover, we generally initialize the weights w_i to values less than 1. The products $w_i\sigma'(h)$ are therefore less than 1, unless the weights increase sufficiently during training.

This tricky problem in training a complex network has long hindered the use of neural networks. Several solutions to vanishing gradient have been devised over the years, and they have been implemented in deep networks:

- a non-random initialization of the weights based on an unsupervised pre-processing, for example, an autoencoder (Section 7.18) according to the ideas of Hinton and Salakhutdinov in 2006;[26]
- reducing the number of parameters (weights and biases) by sharing them as in the convolutional structure (Section 7.5);
- replacing the sigmoid activation function by the ReLU function (Section 7.3), whose gradient is equal to 1 (or 0 for negative input values, which can then pose the problem of "dying ReLU");
- the creation of *residual neural networks*[27] (ResNet), in which the outputs of one layer are added to the outputs of the previous layers to preserve the gradient, which makes it possible to build very deep networks, such as the 152-layer ResNet152 (Section 7.15); thus, as in Figure 7.4, a unit of one layer l can be connected to both a unit of the previous layer, but also to a unit of the layer $l - 2$ or even $l - 3$ by what is called a "skip connection;"
- the use of more powerful computer architectures (GPU graphics processors) to allow the training of a larger number of cases with a larger number of epochs in a reasonable time.

We will return to the second solution by describing convolutional networks in the next section.

The first solution, to determine the initial weights by a auto-encoding mechanism rather than randomly, is a different idea, which was very successful before the advent of convolutional networks and the use of the "brute force" of GPUs, and which is still useful when only a small training dataset is available for modeling.

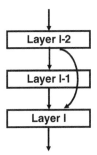

Figure 7.4 Residual networks.

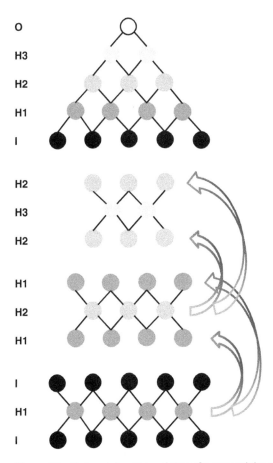

Figure 7.5 Determining the weights of a network by autoencoding.

This can be illustrated in Figure 7.5. We begin by determining the weights of the units in the first hidden layer $H1$ by squeezing them between the repeated input units I in the output, so that the weights of the $H1$ layer are adjusted to allow the I values to be found in the output with as little deviation as possible. Having thus determined the weights of the $H1$ layer, we can then determine the weights of the $H2$ layer units by squeezing them in turn between the $H1$ layer activations that are repeated in input and in output. We proceed in this way. We will see in Section 7.18 that this is the principle of a type of network called an "autoencoder." The weights determined in this way respect the structure of the data: if there are patterns, for example, clusters of individuals, that are clearly identifiable in the input layer *I*, they will remain so in the following layers linked by the weights calculated by the autoencoders, which will facilitate supervised learning.

7.5 The Structure of a Convolutional Neural Network

Convolutional neural networks (CNNs) are the most widespread in deep learning, especially in computer vision. They have several layers, like the perceptron, but with a particularity adapted to the extraction of local features. They exploit the fact that the input variables are not independent but are linked by an underlying spatial structure, contrary to classical neural networks which ignore this spatial structure. It appears on this subject, once again, that machine learning methods, however sophisticated they may be, do not ignore any prior knowledge about the analyzed data, but on the contrary rely on the information that can be known *a priori* about these data, in this case, their spatial organization.

In a perceptron, a unit of a hidden layer is fully connected to all the units of the previous layer, while in a convolutional network, a unit is connected only to a subset of the units of the previous layer, this subset corresponding to a local region (we speak of a "local receiver"). The complexity of a convolutional network is also reduced by the use of shared weights, which reduce the number of parameters, facilitate the backpropagation of the gradient, limit the risk of over-fitting, and facilitate the generalization of the model.

Figure 7.6 illustrates the principle of local connections, and of moving from local to global to exploit the correlation of nearby spatial data: each unit of a layer is connected to three adjacent units of the previous layer, but the unit of layer $l + 1$ is connected to the five units of layer $l - 1$.

Figure 7.7 illustrates the principle of shared weights: all the weights of the same type of line (vertical lines, right oblique lines, left oblique lines) are the same, which allows the detection of specific shapes present in several places in the image, for example, invariants of the writing. Note that even if the unit weights are shared, the biases can be either specific or shared.

We will see in the next section that these local and shared connections occur naturally in the so-called convolutional neural network layers, and that the convolution mechanism has even greater advantages for computer vision than local and shared connections.

A convolutional neural network consists of several levels (Figure 7.8):

- the input layer;
- for feature extraction, one or more levels, each consisting of generally at least three[28] layers:
  - a convolution layer, where the training of the $w_{k,l}$ filters and the biases is done,
  - an activation layer, generally non-linear: *tanh*, |*tanh*|, sigmoid or ReLU = *max*(0,x),
  - a pooling layer ensuring spatial independence;
- for classification, one or more layers each fully connected to the previous one (as in a perceptron);
- the output layer (fully connected to the previous one).

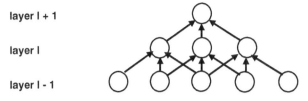

Figure 7.6   Local connections.

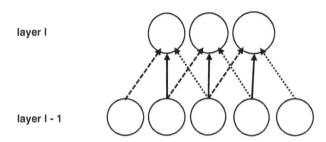

Figure 7.7   Shared weights.

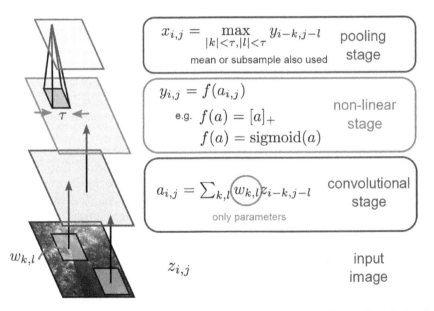

Figure 7.8   Structure of a convolutional network. *Source*: Richard E. Turner, Convolutional neural networks for computer vision, December 2014; http://learning.eng.cam.ac.uk/pub/Public/Turner/Teaching/ml-lecture-3-slides.pdf.

In a convolutional neural network, the first convolution layer extracts simple shapes (vertical, horizontal line, etc.) from the input pixels, the second layer extracts more complex shapes from the basic shapes, and so on: each layer sees larger and larger portions of the image.

It is not uncommon to have four or five levels of convolution, two or three fully connected layers (also called *dense*), at least 100,000 units and a million parameters (weights) in the network, several days of learning computation, which is often at least ten to twenty times faster on GPUs (graphics processors) than on CPUs (section 2.6.2). We will see later (Table 8.2) that the most elaborate networks have several tens of millions of parameters and we will come back in Section 10.4 to the question of the energy consumption of deep neural network training.

Very interesting examples can be found on the Web, such as the images in the CIFAR-10 dataset[29] (Section 7.15) or other data.[30]

A rather rare case is that of a layer with local connections but without shared weights. This configuration can be relevant in some cases, such as images centered on a face: we do not then seek spatial independence, because we know where the eyes and the nose are; in this case, shared weights are not appropriate.

7.6 The Convolution Mechanism

In a convolutional neural network, convolution is performed by applying a sliding window (called a *kernel*, or *filter*) to an input matrix, multiplying the input data and the kernel data term by term,[31] and then adding them. In two dimensions, the (i,j) output value is obtained by applying the kernel to the portion of the input matrix centered on (i,j). In Figure 7.9, the kernel centered on the value "13" yields the value "26."

We recognize in this two-dimensional convolution the formula of a convolution of functions of two variables $(f * g)(i,j) = \sum_{u=-\infty}^{+\infty} \sum_{v=-\infty}^{+\infty} f(u,v)g(i-u,j-v)$.

We recall the simpler and better known formula of convolution of functions of one variable: $(f * g)(i) = \sum_{j=-\infty}^{+\infty} f(j)g(i-j)$.

It is known that the sign $-$ is present in the mathematical formula to ensure commutativity: $f * g = g * f$. As this commutativity is not important for a neural network, for simplicity we replace the negative sign by a positive sign.

1D convolution is used for text processing, 2D for image processing, 3D for video or medical imaging. A fast convolution calculation can be performed by Fourier Transform.

In the convolution of neural networks, the edges of the input matrix must be filled with 0s if we want to convolve to the (i,j) edges of the input matrix: this filling is called padding (or zero-padding). Without this optional padding, the output matrix is smaller. Figure 7.9 shows an example with a kernel of size (3,3) and without padding: the values 11, 24, 7... are not transformed by the convolution.

The interest in convolution lies in the reduction of complexity related to shared weights and local connections, but also in the convolution mechanism itself which is suitable for the detection of any type of visual feature, provided the appropriate convolution filter is used.

Figure 7.10 suggests that each convolution filter detects one type of shape, the combination of which by the different levels of the network results in the detection of increasingly complex shapes. Convolution allows one to move from an elementary object to a more complex object, moving from level to level: from pixels to features, from features to edges, from edges to parts of objects, and from parts of objects to objects.

A hierarchy of several convolution layers can go from the elementary level of pixels to the detection of complex objects. This hierarchy makes the detection particularly efficient. Let's say we want to identify cars in an image. If the algorithm processed only the elementary features, with a high resolution, it would be able to recognize wheels but would not be able to make the link between the presence of four wheels and the fact of being a car. If, on the other hand, the algorithm processed only the global characteristics, with a low

11	24	7	20	3
4	12	25	8	16
17	5	**13**	21	9
10	18	1	14	22
23	6	19	2	15

$\star$

	0	1	0	
	1	-2	1	
	0	1	0	

$=$

		26		

$$26 = 25 + 5 - (2 \times 13) + 21 + 1$$

Figure 7.9 Convolution in a neural network.

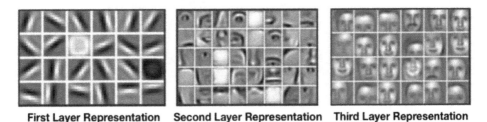

First Layer Representation   **Second Layer Representation**   **Third Layer Representation**

Figure 7.10 Convolution pattern detection. *Source*: Honglak Lee, Roger Grosse, Rajesh Ranganath,nd Andrew Y. Ng. Convolutional Deep Belief Networks for Scalable Unsupervised Learning of Hierarchical Representations, *Proceedings of the 26th International Conference on Machine Learning*, Montreal, Canada, 2009, http://web.eecs.umich.edu/~honglak/icml09-ConvolutionalDeepBeliefNetworks.pdf.

resolution, it would see the four wheels of each car but would not decompose the image into its elements such as the wheels, and would only be able to recognize a car globally and not from its characteristics. The consequence is that it would only be able to recognize cars that looked like those it had already seen, and that it would not be able to abstract the concept of cars from their four wheels (and other elements of course). This would be a disadvantage comparable to the global reading method.

Moreover, this detection is possible without prejudging the precise positioning of objects in the image, thanks to the shared weights of the convolution kernel which will detect the same type of shape, wherever it is in the image. In this way, convolutional neural networks often do not require any pre-processing of the data, except for normalization.

The difficulty of image recognition is broken down into elementary elements: each convolution filter is specialized and simpler (has fewer parameters) than a layer of a classical neural network. It is the juxtaposition of filters at each level, and the stacking of levels, that can go from simple to complex. A classical neural network cannot do this, because even if it has several hidden layers, each of them has the same detection abilities and cannot go from simple to complex: the increase in performance is more quantitative than qualitative.

We talked about filter juxtaposition because each convolution layer is usually composed of several "activation maps," or "feature maps," each corresponding to a different kernel (and bias). Each kernel can detect one type of feature, for example, a vertical line, wherever it is found in the input. Convolution is applied to an input feature map to produce an output feature map, but when we speak of a feature map or an activation map, we mean an output map.

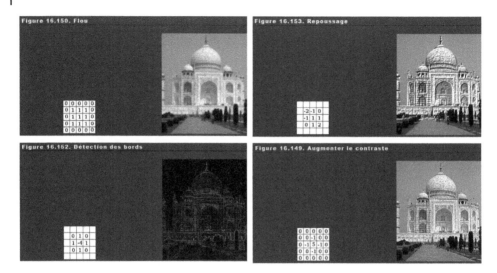

Figure 7.11 Examples of convolution. *Source*: GNU Image Manipulation Program (GIMP); https://docs.gimp.org/2.6/fr/plug-in-convmatrix.html.

To detect color images, we add to the kernel a third dimension called "channel": the three channels are RGB (red, green, blue), and their corresponding kernels usually have different weights.

The Taj Mahal example in Figure 7.11 shows the value of having several maps with different kernels to extract several different features from the processed image. Their results are combined and their parameters are determined by training the neural network. This architecture is parallelizable and can gain particularly from the use of GPUs. A convolutional neural network could have fixed convolution kernels and not be determined by training, but this method would be more like traditional machine learning than deep learning.

In Figure 7.11 four convolution matrices (bottom left of each thumbnail) are applied, the 0s of a matrix corresponding to black pixels and 1s to white pixels.

At the top left, the average of a pixel with its neighbors blurs the image. Bottom left, the difference between a pixel and its neighbors highlights the edges. Top right, we can give relief with a dissymmetrical convolution kernel. Bottom right, the difference between a pixel and its neighbors sharpens the edges.

7.7 The Convolution Parameters

The first parameter, which must always be specified, because it has no natural default value, is the size of the convolution kernel. However, we can say that this size is usually odd, in order to be able to center the kernel on the original unit.

For a small image, about 32 x 32 pixels:

- 7 x 7 can be too large, with too much overlap;
- 5 x 5 is a value often used, at least if we want to limit the number of convolution layers;
- 3 x 3 may be too small, with sometimes too little overlap of sliding windows to capture all the information, unless you have a large enough number of convolution layers, because smaller and more numerous kernels may be preferred.

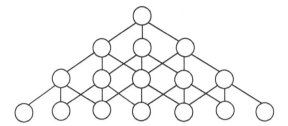

Figure 7.12 Stacking of convolution layers.

An example will help us to understand the reason for this. In a convolution layer with a 7 x 7 convolution kernel, each unit is connected to 7 x 7 units of the previous layer. In a stack of three convolution layers with a stride (see below) equal to 1 and a 3 x 3 convolution kernel, each unit is connected to 3 x 3 units of the previous layer, 5 x 5 of the layer before the previous one, and 7 x 7 units of the first layer (Figure 7.12).

The *receptive field* of a unit is the number of pixels in the image that are connected to that unit. Here, if the first layer is the input layer of the neural network, the receptive field of the unit in the last layer will in both cases be of dimension 7 x 7. More generally, with convolutions of stride 1, the width of the receptive field of a unit in the kth layer is:

$$R_k = 1 + \sum_{i=1}^{k} (N_i - 1).$$

the dimension of the ith layer being N_i x N_i.

So the result seems equivalent, but the 7 x 7 convolution kernel requires 49 parameters, instead of 27 parameters for the stack of 3 layers with 3 x 3 convolution kernels: 9 parameters for the kernel of each layer.

In addition to this gain in the number of parameters, a single kernel computes a linear combination of the input data, while a stack of several kernels separated by nonlinear activation functions introduces nonlinearity in the modeling.

It is therefore better to stack several convolution layers rather than a single layer with a larger convolution kernel: more complex features can be detected with fewer parameters. But more memory is needed to store the results of the intermediate layers during training.

The second parameter of the convolution kernel is the size of the padding. We have seen above that it is the number of rows of 0 added to the edges of the image to complete it. A convolution without padding is called "narrow," or "valid" because the kernel only uses valid input data. Otherwise the padding is called "wide" (or "same" when it is such that the dimension of the output image is the same as the input). It is obvious that the narrow convolution decreases the size of the images since the kernel cannot reach the edge of the input image.

Narrow convolution of an image of size 5 by a kernel of size 3 yields an output image of size 3. Narrow convolution of an image of size 5 by a kernel of size 5 yields an image of size 1. More generally, narrow convolution of an image of size N by a kernel of size n produces an image of size $N - n + 1$. The wide convolution of an image of size N by a kernel of size n and padding p produces an image of size $N - n + 1 + (2p)$.

A padding equal to $(n - 1)/2$ therefore does not reduce the size of the image. However, padding is not always necessary, except with a large kernel or if the information on the edge of the image is important.

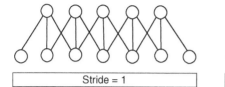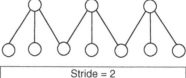

Figure 7.13 Convolution stride.

A third parameter is the "stride" or "skipping factor." This is how many pixels the kernel is moving between two applications to the input image. The most common value is 1, as in the left image of Figure 7.13, whose right image shows a stride equal to 2. A stride equal to 1 is the most common because it does not reduce the image size.

The image produced by a kernel of size n, padding p and stride S has a size equal to $[N - n + (2p)]/S + 1$.

Without padding, with a stride $= 1$ and an $n \times n$ filter, each convolution layer reduces the image size from N to $(N - n + 1)$.

Another important parameter is of course the number of maps per convolution layer. According to rules of thumb, one often retains between 5 and 20 maps in the first layer, between 20 and 100 in the second layer ...

7.8 Batch Normalization

Sometimes a batch normalization layer[32] is introduced between a convolution or fully connected layer and the activation layer that follows it. This normalization layer is useful when the distribution of input data to the convolution or fully connected layer changes during training. This can happen even if we have taken care to normalize the input data of the neural network (we showed in Section 7.3 how necessary it was), since this normalization is only done at the input of the network and not in the hidden layers, and this normalization is only done at the beginning of the training. However, the adjustment of the weights during the training process inevitably leads to a change in the distribution of the data in the layers following each weight. Such a drift of the distribution in the layers of the network during the training process requires a decrease in the learning rate (Section 7.3), which slows down the training process. Indeed, the gradient, by which the learning rate is multiplied, ends up having very different values in the units of the convolution layer. However, if we have a high learning rate, the units which have a higher gradient than the others will see their weights more strongly updated and the value arriving at the input of the activation function will be much larger (or smaller), leading to the saturation of this activation function (with the sigmoid and the hyperbolic tangent) or its explosion or cancelation (with the linear rectifier). It is understandable that it is difficult to apply the same learning rate to units with very different gradients. As the learning does not have the same speed in the different units, this speed has to be set on the slowest ones, which is harmful.

We will see in Section 7.14 that there are adaptive learning algorithms capable of adjusting the learning rate of each unit, in a variable step gradient descent (Section 3.2). However, their efficiency is not high enough in deep neural networks where divergences between units propagate and increase from one layer to another.

The much more efficient solution discovered by Ioffe and Szegedy is *batch normalization*, which consists in applying a normalization of each unit of each layer throughout the training process to ensure that the input of each activation function has values that do not bring it into a saturation, explosion or cancelation zone.

This normalization gets its name from the fact that it is calculated for each batch of observations (Section 7.3). It consists in standardizing (centering and scaling) the observations of each batch by calculating the mean and the variance of each unit in the batch. If we take the example of a network composed of only one unit per layer and whose output of the jth layer is $a_j = s(w_j a_{j-1} + b_j)$, s being the activation function, the w_j being the weights and the b_j being the layer biases, then batch normalization will replace the value

$$a_j = s(w_j a_{j-1} + b_j)$$

by the value

$$a_j = s(BN(w_j a_{j-1} + b_j)).$$

The BN transformation is determined by calculating the mean μ and the variance σ^2 of each $z_j = w_j a_{j-1} + b_j$ on all the observations of the batch. In fact, we do not have exactly

$$BN(z_j) = \frac{z_j - \mu}{\sigma}$$

but

$$BN(z_j) = \gamma_j \frac{z_j - \mu}{\sqrt{\sigma^2 + \varepsilon}} + \beta_j.$$

On the one hand, we add a term ε to avoid possible divisions by 0, and, on the other hand, we follow the standardization with an affine transformation $\gamma x + \beta$ (where the values of γ and β are determined during the training process), because the data have no reason to have a zero mean and a variance equal to 1, and we want to stabilize them during the training process, but not necessarily at respective values 0 and 1.

Batch normalization makes training less dependent on the initialization of the weights and allows a higher learning rate and thus faster training. It limits the risk of gradient vanishing by avoiding the situation where the values arriving on the sigmoid (respectively ReLU) activation layer are concentrated in the saturation (respectively. negative) areas where the gradient cancels.

We will see in Section 8.2.2 an illustration of the effectiveness of this normalization.

7.9 Pooling

Pooling (or *subsampling*) is an operation very frequently performed after convolution to reduce the dimension of the layers of the network, and thus reduce its number of parameters, its training time, and its risk of over-fitting.

The observation window is divided into sub-windows (or *tiles*) whose information is reduced to one element: most often the maximum value of the sub-window (*max pooling*), or sometimes its average, or its L^2 norm (square root of the sum of the squares of the values). Max pooling is illustrated in Figure 7.14. A limit case is when we have a single sub-window, as large as the observation window, which is reduced to a single piece of information.

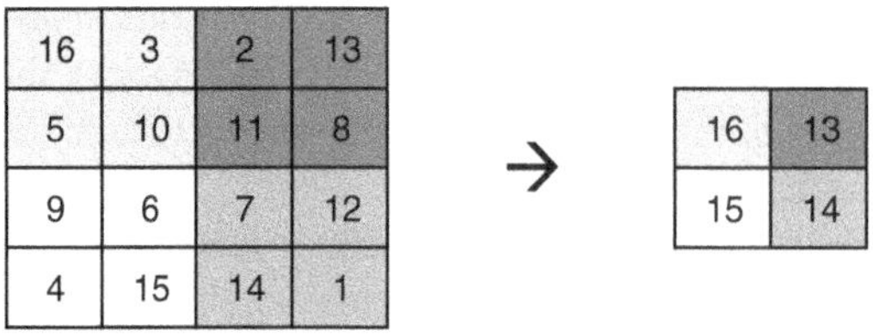

16	3	2	13
5	10	11	8
9	6	7	12
4	15	14	1

→

16	13
15	14

Figure 7.14 Max pooling.

The maximum allows an important global information to be retained, such as the presence of a high value in a region, even if it is not precisely localized, and even if we translate or rotate the image by a few pixels. This is the strategy of the winning neuron: the most active in its region.

The idea of pooling is that it is not the exact position of a feature that matters, but its position relative to other features. Pooling allows an object to be recognized in slightly different positions, even if it has moved a few pixels, because it is the presence of certain features that matters, not their exact position.

The pooling that has just been presented is the one performed at the output of a convolution filter, and it facilitates invariance by translation. Pooling can also be performed at the output of several different filters, and it facilitates rotation invariance: if several filters can recognize a digit, each with a different orientation, the max pooling layer will be activated as soon as one of the filters is activated, i.e. as soon as the digit is read, whatever its orientation.

The successive sub-windows are shifted by a "stride" which is equal to their size when we want to avoid their overlapping. The most common pooling is with 2 x 2 filters and a stride of 2, to divide the size by 4 and reduce the computation time. Larger filters of course reduce the computation time even more but lose a lot (and maybe too much) of information.

Overlapping pooling is sometimes used to reduce over-fitting and to help detect the positions of large features relative to each other. One can thus have pooling with 3 x 3 filters and a stride = 2. The reduction in error obtained by this overlap can be surprising (Section 8.2.2).

A recent refinement of pooling is Fractional Max-Pooling.[33] It assumes that a pooling filter α x α with $1 < \alpha < 2$ allows the number of units and the amount of information to be divided by a factor α^2 strictly less than 4, preventing deeper neural networks from losing any more information. Thus, with $\alpha = \sqrt{2}$, two successive filters do not decrease the amount of information more than a single 2 x 2 filter.

In Fractional Max-Pooling, the pooling regions are of the form $P_{ij} = [a_{i-1}, a_i - 1]$ x $[b_{i-1}, b_i - 1]$, but the a_i and b_i are no longer $a_i = 2i$ (as for 2 x 2 max-pooling) but $a_i = ceiling(\alpha(i + u))$, i.e., the smallest integer greater than or equal to $\alpha(i + u)$, where u is drawn randomly between 0 and 1 and is different for each filter. A variant is with regions $P_{ij} = [a_{i-1}, a_i]$ x $[b_{i-1}, b_i]$ for overlapping pooling.

Here is an example of increments to go from a 25 x 25 window to 18 x 18: 112112121121211212.

Fractional Max-Pooling can cause under-fitting if combined with dropout (Section 7.11) or data augmentation (Section 7.13). Its contribution is therefore not always obvious. It can nevertheless be tested, especially since it is implemented in the Theano, TensorFlow, and Torch libraries.

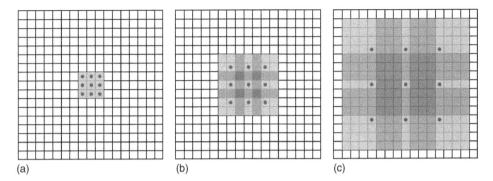

Figure 7.15 Dilated convolution. *Source*: Yu, F. and Koltun, V. Multi-Scale Context Aggregation by Dilated Convolutions (2016). arXiv:1511.07122.

7.10 Dilated Convolution

Fisher Yu and Vladlen Koltun's dilated convolution[34] is another process that enlarges the size of the receptive field of a unit of a layer, i.e., the number of units of the previous layer connected to this unit by a convolution filter.

The 2D convolution with a dilation factor k is defined as follows:

$$(f * g)(i,j) = \sum_{u=-\infty}^{+\infty} \sum_{v=-\infty}^{+\infty} f(u,v)g(i + k.u, j + k.v).$$

With $k = 1$, we find the usual convolution.

With $k = 2$, the first (respectively 2nd...) element of the kernel is multiplied by the 2nd (respectively 4th...) element of the input layer, as in Figure 7.15 by these authors, where image (a) corresponds to the dilation of order 1, image (b) corresponds to the dilation of order $k = 2$, and image (c) corresponds to the dilation of order $k = 4$. We see that with a 3 x 3 filter and a dilation of order 2 (respectively 4), each unit is connected to 7 x 7 (respectively 15 x 15) units of the previous layer, and not 3 x 3.

Figure 7.15 explains why the term "atrous convolution" is also used.

The dilated convolution is useful when the interesting information (images, sounds) can be distant and we want to take them into account without increasing the number of parameters too much. With dilation convolution, a small number of levels each made of small filters, thus a network with a limited number of parameters, allows a larger spatial area to be reached. To extract multi-scale information, convolutions with dilation of increasing orders 2^0, 2^1, 2^2... are an alternative to successive pooling layers, which progressively decrease the resolution. The receptive field of these dilation convolutions grows exponentially with a linearly increasing number of parameters.

7.11 Dropout and DropConnect

The dropout is a mechanism used for the training of neural networks, in which, for each epoch and each training case, each unit has a probability $p > 0$ to see its activation canceled. Its authors recommend a value $p = 0.5$ for each hidden unit. We refer to their paper[35] or to the work of Goodfellow *et al.*[36] for more details.

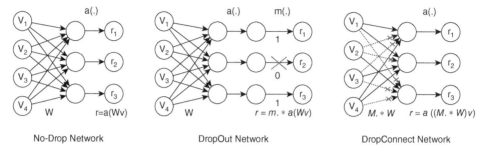

Figure 7.16 Dropout and DropConnect. *Source*: New York University, Center for Data Science; https://cds.nyu.edu/projects/regularization-neural-networks-using-dropconnect/.

In the test phase of the network, there is no dropout, all units are activated and the weights calculated in training are multiplied by p to compensate for the fact that all units are active in the test phase.

It is a mechanism somewhat analogous to that of random forests, an aggregation of neural networks, since with N hidden units, we test up to 2^N different networks. However, there are limits to the analogy.

On the one hand, in the dropout, the subnetworks are not actually created, which very quickly would be impossible because of the computation time and the huge amount of memory that would be needed, given the exponential number of these subnetworks. On the other hand, the different trees of a random forest are independent, while the different subnetworks created by the dropout share the same weights. Indeed, when the weights are updated at each iteration (i.e. at each mini-batch), each unit has the same weight in all the subnetworks where it is present. This simplifies the mechanism.

Dropout aims to avoid over-fitting, by preventing the response of one unit from adapting to the response of other units (co-adaptation) according to a pattern that would be present in the training dataset but would not be generalizable, and that would make the weight of this unit meaningless in itself but only in relation to other weights. We therefore force the units to adapt to general situations. We also avoid a unit acquiring a disproportionate weight at the expense of the other units. This is a device that is considered more effective than weight decay in combating over-fitting. Moreover, it can be used in most neural networks, and not only in deep convolutional and recurrent networks, but also in perceptrons like the H2O software does (Section 6.11).

Dropout can also be applied to the input layer units if the data are noisy. The input dropout is generally lower (of the order of $p = 0.2$) because the information "dropped" in the input is then completely lost.

Figure 7.16 suggests that the dropout before the output layer could cause a case to have no more connections arriving on the output, and thus no longer would participate in training during an epoch. The probability of this happening is very low, and it is even much lower if it happens for all epochs of the network and the case does not participate in network training at all.

For the control of weights and training, it is sometimes replaced by batch normalization (Section 7.8), which can allow, if not eliminate, at least an decrease in the dropout rate.

Despite its universal use, the dropout is less interesting when the training dataset is very large. In this case, its effect is limited, and it must be considered in the light of the fact that the complexity of the network must be increased, and therefore the number of epochs required to train it. However, this disadvantage is slight because the dropout does not significantly increase the computation time for a comparable configuration.

DropConnect[37] is a generalization of dropout. While dropout annihilates the activation of a unit, DropConnect annihilates only a portion of the connections arriving on a unit, as shown in the authors' illustration depicted in Figure 7.16. DropConnect achieved the lowest error rate on MNIST: 0.21%.[38]

7.12   The Architecture of a Convolutional Neural Network

In a convolutional network, convolution layers extract features while fully connected layers perform classification by combining (non-linearly) the extracted features. There are rarely more than two or three fully connected layers.

As for the input layer, it is a square. In the absence of padding, the dimension of the side of this square is often a multiple of 16 so that it can be divided by 2 a fairly large number of times. For example: 32 (CIFAR-10 base), 96 (STL-10 base) or 224 (ImageNet base). If necessary, the images can be completed by 0 on their edges to reach a side multiple of 16.

A possible convolutional network architecture is as follows: we have an image of 32 x 32 pixels a first convolution layer with 5 x 5 filters switches to maps of dimension 28 x 28 → a 2 x 2 pooling layer switches to 14 x 14 maps → a second convolution layer with 5 x 5 filters switches to 10 x 10 maps → a second 2 x 2 pooling layer switches to 5 x 5 maps → they are too small to apply a third convolution layer to them, and are therefore fully connected to a 320-unit layer (Figure 7.17).

We can note the configuration of a neural network:

$$INPUT \rightarrow [[CONV \rightarrow ACTI1]^*N \rightarrow POOL?]^*M \rightarrow [FC \rightarrow ACTI2]^*K \rightarrow FC$$
$$\rightarrow ACTI3 \rightarrow OUTPUT.$$

- *n indicates repetition n times;
- CONV = convolution layer;
- ACTI1 and ACTI2 = ReLU or Tanh or |Tanh| or sigmoid activation;
- ACTI3 = identity, linear, sigmoid or softmax activation;
- POOL? = optional pooling layer;
- FC = layer fully connected to the previous one.

We have $N \geq 0$ (often $N \leq 3$), $M \geq 0$ and $K \geq 0$ (often $K \leq 2$).

The classical perceptron is noted as follows:

$$INPUT \rightarrow [FC \rightarrow ACTI]^*K \rightarrow FC \rightarrow ACTI3 \rightarrow OUTPUT.$$

The classical convolutional network LeNet-5 (Section 7.15) is noted:

$$INPUT \rightarrow [CONV \rightarrow SIGM \rightarrow POOL]^*2 \rightarrow FC \rightarrow TANH \rightarrow FC \rightarrow RBF \rightarrow$$
$$OUTPUT,$$

where SIGM is a sigmoidal activation and RBF is a radial basis function activation.

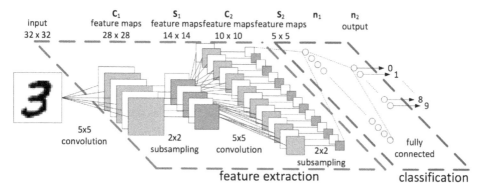

Figure 7.17 Example of a convolutional network. *Source*: https://github.com/tavgreen/cnn-and-dnn.

A fairly common configuration is as follows:

$$\text{INPUT} \rightarrow [\text{CONV} \rightarrow \text{ACTI1} \rightarrow \text{POOL}]^*2 \rightarrow \text{FC} \rightarrow \text{ACTI2} \rightarrow \text{FC} \rightarrow \text{SOFTMAX} \rightarrow \text{OUTPUT},$$

with in particular ACTI1 = ACTI2 = ReLU or Tanh. It is tested in Section 8.2.2. Another effective configuration is:

$$\text{INPUT} \rightarrow [\text{CONV} \rightarrow \text{RELU} \rightarrow \text{CONV} \rightarrow \text{RELU} \rightarrow \text{POOL}]^*3 \rightarrow \text{FC} \rightarrow \text{RELU} \rightarrow \text{FC} \rightarrow \text{SOFTMAX} \rightarrow \text{OUTPUT}.$$

Pooling does not intervene between each convolution layer, so as not to simplify the network too much.

A deeper configuration, with more parameters, may require more computation time for each epoch but fewer epochs to achieve a low error rate.[39] Recall that an epoch in a neural network is a training step during which all the observations of the training set are processed to update the weights of the network. We distinguish an epoch from an iteration, during which not all observations are usually processed (Section 7.3).

Fully connected layers represent both the largest number of parameters (see below) and therefore the longest computation time, but also the smallest contribution to performance.[40] Therefore, some networks, the "Fully Convolutional Networks" (FCN) have only convolution layers and no fully connected layer. However, it is necessary to move from the 2D convolutional maps to the 1D output map. The 2014 ILSVRC winner GoogLeNet (Section 7.15) replaced the fully connected layers with an average pooling layer, which allowed it with 12 times fewer parameters than the 2012 ILSVRC winner to nevertheless achieve a large performance increase (Section 7.15): a top-5 error of 6.67% versus 15.3% for the 2012 ILSVRC winner AlexNet.

In general, convolution layers are always more numerous than fully connected layers, and we have seen that it is better to have more layers with smaller filters. The number of convolution layers is increased when the images are larger, not only to increase the capacity of the network, but also (provided that a narrow convolution is performed, without padding) to decrease the size of the images arriving on the fully connected layers and avoid them having a very large number of units.

Let's take an example to illustrate the increase in the number of parameters of fully connected layers. If we have a convolution layer of 6 maps 26 x 26 obtained by applying

4 x 4 filters to a 29 x 29 map, this layer contains 6 x 26 x 26 = 4056 units, and 6 x (4^2+1) = 102 weights (by adding a bias to the convolution product). Each of the 4056 units has 29^2 possible connections with the previous layer. If the connections were not local and the units of the two layers were fully connected, as in a classical multilayer network, there would be 4056 x (29^2+1) = 3,415,152 weights instead of 102. If the connections were local but the weights of the connections were not shared, these would be different in each receiving unit, so that there would be 4056 x (4^2+1) = 68,952 weights instead of 102.

7.13 Principles of Deep Network Learning for Computer Vision

The principles outlined in this section are applied to deep learning, especially for computer vision. But some of these principles actually apply to all neural networks.

The learning is done by gradient descent (Section 3.2). In its on-line version, the update of the weights takes place after each processed image. Otherwise, this update takes place when a batch of several images has been processed. In a convolutional network, the learning is done by descending the gradient on the set of fully connected layers (classifier) and convolution layers (feature extraction).

To facilitate the descent of the gradient, it is recommended to mix the observations to avoid having successive observations which are similar, because the convergence is slower in the presence of a large number of consecutive observations of the same class to be explained. Moreover, in the descent of the stochastic gradient, it is preferable to avoid having batches that are too atypical, so as not to go in the wrong directions, and this is best achieved by mixing the observations.

It is recommended to normalize the input data to the network, for example, by subtracting the mean image, and even to normalize the input data to each activation layer, by batch normalization (Section 7.8), so that the variances of the inputs to each unit are of the same order of magnitude. This allows the network to be trained at the same speed for all units, and avoids the risk of gradient vanishing by preventing the values arriving on the activation layer from being concentrated in the areas where the gradient cancels.

The weights in each layer are initialized by autoencoding (Section 7.18) or by random draw, according to, for example, the uniform distribution in [-0.05, 0.05] or the centered normal distribution with a standard deviation equal to 0.01. The weights should not be too large to avoid saturation of the units.

The activation function is often the ReLU rectifier, or otherwise the hyperbolic tangent or sigmoid (Section 7.3).

As we will see in the examples in Chapter 8, the images to be processed are often too large (too many pixels) for the capacities of the machines and a reasonable computation time. We therefore often resize these images to a smaller size, a common value being 224 x 224 pixels, by means of functions ("resize") provided by the deep learning libraries. These functions usually proceed by bilinear or bicubic interpolation of neighboring pixels to determine the colors of pixels in a reduced version of an image. The quality of the images is of course reduced but these transformations aim at maximizing the perceptual quality of the reduced images. However, recent work has shown that an optimal quality for human eyes is not necessarily optimal for a convolutional neural network that must recognize objects in images.[41] They suggest that this objective will be better met by an image resizing model whose parameters are trained at the same time as the neural network. The goal of the training will then be to simultaneously optimize the size of the images (as small as possible) and the accuracy of the classification.

As these neural networks are asked to detect very complex and numerous features, such as natural images, sometimes divided into more than 1000 classes, these networks have a high complexity which leads to a risk of over-fitting because the number of training cases is "not so great." Several solutions exist to reduce this risk:

- the use of shared weights of convolutional neural networks, and the use of pooling, to reduce the number of parameters;
- dropout in fully connected layers to avoid co-adaptation of units;
- increasing the sample size by "data augmentation," which consists in generating new images with the same labels by translations, rotations, and zooming of the original images (this augmentation can take place only once or at the beginning of each epoch, but any symmetry or rotation is not always allowed, otherwise a "6" could be mistaken for a "9");
- initiating learning on another larger dataset and transfer learning.

Transfer learning consists in dealing with a problem by starting from a network pre-trained on another problem rather than by starting the training from scratch. This network has been pre-trained with a complex architecture (many layers and weights) on a large dataset using a powerful machine capable of performing a sufficient number of epochs to obtain a very low error. One of the interesting possibilities of deep learning is to use such models that could not have been trained with ordinary resources, taking advantage of some generic aspects of the model. For example, we may need to identify items in a catalog, and use one of the well-known models pre-trained on the ImageNet dataset of fourteen million photographs of objects and animals (Section 7.15) even though our image base to be identified is different from ImageNet. A large model pre-trained on ImageNet may perform better than a small model trained on our specific base. This is because the pre-trained model has learned to recognize features common to all images (vertical and horizontal features, contours ...) or more elaborate features (eyes, ears, mouths). These features have been learned by a pre-trained neural network that is generic enough to be applied to different situations, provided of course that they are not too different. Under this condition, transfer learning allows us to obtain efficient models with less training data and a shorter training time. Many pre-trained models have been trained on the ImageNet dataset, especially since it has been shown in a variety of cases that there is a strong correlation between the accuracy of a pre-trained model on the ImageNet data and the accuracy on a new dataset of a model benefiting from the transfer of the pre-trained model.[42] It has even been verified that this correlation remains high if only the architecture of the pre-trained model is kept, and not its weights.

We show an example of transfer learning in Section 8.3.3. Transfer learning is also applied with very good results in natural language processing (Section 4.4.7).

We can also penalize the network weights as in a ridge or Lasso regression (see Section 3.3), using a device called "weight decay." It consists in adding to the network error a term $\lambda \sum_i p_i^2$ (weight decay in L^2 norm) or $\lambda \sum_i |p_i|$ (weight decay in L^1 norm), p_i being the network weights and λ a penalty similar to that of the ridge and Lasso regressions.

Increasing the decay is an efficient way to reduce over-fitting: it progressively cancels the weights (weight decay in L^1 norm), which simplifies the network and reduces the noise, or decreases them enough (weight decay in L^2 norm) to bring the output of a unit close to 0, thus close to the linearity zone of the activation function. A λ value in the range of 10^{-4} to 10^{-5} is generally used.

More directly than weight decay, we can apply a bound on the L^2 norm of the weights arriving on each hidden unit, which is sometimes implemented with a high initial learning rate.

We have seen (Section 7.3) that it is better to have an adaptive learning rate, decreasing over the course of learning. For example, one can divide this rate every x epochs of the training or use one of the algorithms in Section 7.14. One can also program the training process so that the learning rate decreases every time the error no longer decreases on a test set. For example, at each epoch, we measure this error and after ten epochs without a decrease in the error, we divide the learning rate by 10.

This is accomplished with the help of a *callback function*. A callback function in a neural network is a function that has access to intermediate results of the network during its learning, without having to wait for the end of it, so results can be used to perform some actions: saving the model, changing the learning rate, early stopping of the training, etc. Early stopping is used in neural networks to avoid seeing them converge towards a locally but not globally optimal solution, and it consists of evaluating the error of the network during training and in stopping the training before convergence of the algorithm when the error on a test set no longer decreases.

Some software such as Keras or MXNet (Chapter 8) even allow more complex operations to be programmed, like text generation (Section 9.2). Callback functions can be used in all types of neural networks and not only in computer vision.

7.14 Adaptive Learning Algorithms

As seen with gradient descent in Section 3.2, a constant learning rate is generally not appropriate: we have also seen (Section 7.3) that it is better to learn quickly at the beginning (high rate) and slowly at the end (low rate). Some algorithms progressively decrease the learning rate, linearly or exponentially, or divide it by some factor (often between 2 and 10) every x epochs. But this approach does not take into account the real structure of the data. A more common approach is to reduce the learning rate each time a plateau is reached in the evolution of the error measured on the test dataset. It is possible to program this in deep learning libraries using the so-called callback functions (Section 7.13). However, the reduction factor of the learning rate must be fixed in a somewhat arbitrary way, and moreover a rate common to all the units of the network does not take into account the fact that the updates must be more important for rarer features.

Several adaptive optimization algorithms have been created to best manage the evolution of the learning rate, making it depend on the data and not on a pre-defined scheme. Here are the main ones.

- ADAGRAD[43] operates an automatic update of the learning rate of each weight by dividing it by the square root of the sum of the squares of the gradients of that weight since the start of training. It is suitable for sparse data with larger updates for sparser features, such as in word embedding with rare words. It is also consistent with the idea of starting training with a high learning rate and gradually reducing it (Section 7.3). But taking into account the entire history of gradients (so-called gradient accumulation) since the start of training can cause a premature drop in learning rate. This drop would be even steeper and more damaging if the square root of the sum of the squares of the gradients was not taken. ADAGRAD is therefore rarely optimal in practice and is not widely used.
- RMSprop (Root Mean Square propagation), proposed by Hinton in a Coursera online class,[44, 45] is a refinement of ADAGRAD aimed at preventing the learning rate from dropping too much. In RMSprop, the learning rate of a weight is divided at iteration t by the square root of the sum:

$$r_t = \rho r_{t-1} + (1 - \rho)g_t^2,$$

which weights the square of the last gradient g_t^2 and the sum r_{t-1} of the squares of the previous gradients. Hinton proposes the value $\rho = 0{,}9$ which is sufficient to reduce the weight of the history during training, which is the drawback of ADAGRAD. But we can give another value to the "decay" $\rho \in [0, 1]$ to limit the weight of the history, with the value $\rho = 0{,}5$ coming back to ADAGRAD. Moreover, Hinton recommends an initial value equal to 0.001 of the learning rate. RMSprop is one of the most efficient algorithms.
- ADADELTA[46] is another refinement of ADAGRAD, designed independently of RMSprop. It performs the same moving average computation r_t as RMSprop but then it does not require specification of the learning rate, even initially. This learning rate is replaced by the square root of the moving average of the squares of the deltas, which are each the difference between a weight and its update.
- ADAM (Adaptive Moment Estimation)[47] is another adaptive method for calculating the learning rate for each weight, relying on past gradients (such as momentum) and the squares of past gradients (such as RMSprop), weighting by a factor ρ_1 the sum of the previous gradients and by a factor ρ_2 the sum of the squares of the previous gradients. It is often used with an initial value equal to 0.001 of the learning rate, and values $\rho_1 = 0.9$ and $\rho_2 = 0.999$. This method combines the advantages of using the moment and an adaptive learning rate. It is considered robust and not very sensitive to the choice of parameters ρ_1, ρ_2 and the initial learning rate. It is therefore one of the most used with RMSprop.
- In addition, we can mention AdaMax,[48] a variant of ADAM described in the same article, as well as NADAM,[49] which replaces in ADAM the ordinary moment with the Nesterov momentum (Section 7.3).

We compared three of these algorithms in handwritten digit recognition (MNIST dataset, see Section 6.1) using the MXNet library (Section 8.2). We train a convolutional network whose structure is:

$$20C5 \rightarrow RELU \rightarrow P \rightarrow 60C5 \rightarrow RELU \rightarrow P \rightarrow DO \rightarrow 500FC \rightarrow RELU \rightarrow 10FC$$
$$\rightarrow SOFTMAX$$

The two pooling layers P are overlapping, with a size of 3 and a stride of 2, and the dropout rate DO is 0.5.

With ADAGRAD, batches of 128 images and ten epochs, we obtain in ten minutes a solution ... very bad since the rate of good classification is only 10% on the test sample: the same value was detected for all handwritten digits:

```
> system.time(model <- mx.model.FeedForward.create(symbol=lenet,
    X=train.array, y=train.y, ctx=device.cpu, num.round=10,
    array.batch.size=128,
+ optimizer="adagrad", eval.data=list(data=test.array,
    label=test$label), wd=0.00001, eval.metric = mx.metric.accuracy))
...
[10] Train-accuracy=0.103228278251599
[10] Validation-accuracy=0.10067246835443
utilisateur     système      écoulé
    1729.08     453.18       602.11
```

This result is all the more disappointing since the basic stochastic gradient descent algorithm, which is non-adaptive, leads with a learning rate equal to 0.10 to an error rate of 0.96% on the test sample:

```
> system.time(model <- mx.model.FeedForward.create(symbol=lenet,
    X=train.array, y=train.y, ctx=device.cpu, num.round=10,
    array.batch.size=128,
+ optimizer="sgd", learning.rate=0.1, momentum=0.65,
    eval.data=list(data=test.array, label=test$label), wd=0.00001,
    eval.metric = mx.metric.accuracy))
Auto-select kvstore type = local_update_cpu
Start training with 4 devices
[1] Train-accuracy=0.111778846153846
[1] Validation-accuracy=0.114022943037975
...
[9] Train-accuracy=0.979311034115139
[9] Validation-accuracy=0.989121835443038
[10] Train-accuracy=0.982209488272921
[10] Validation-accuracy=0.990407436708861
utilisateur     système      écoulé
    1782.30     426.08       629.80
```

With ADADELTA and the same parameters, we obtain a very good solution in 11 minutes since the error rate is only 0.76% on the test sample:

```
> system.time(model <- mx.model.FeedForward.create(symbol=lenet,
    X=train.array, y=train.y, ctx=device.cpu, num.round=10,
    array.batch.size=128,
+ optimizer="adadelta", eval.data=list(data=test.array,
    label=test$label), wd=0.00001, eval.metric = mx.metric.accuracy))
...
[10] Train-accuracy=0.986607142857143
[10] Validation-accuracy=0.992385284810127
utilisateur     système      écoulé
    1822.69     510.84       660.10
```

Seeing that ADADELTA achieves great progress, we tested it by increasing the number of epochs to 50. The validation error rate dropped to 0.57%:

```
> system.time(model <- mx.model.FeedForward.create(symbol=lenet,
    X=train.array, y=train.y, ctx=device.cpu, num.round=50,
    array.batch.size=128,
+ optimizer="adadelta", eval.data=list(data=test.array,
    label=test$label), wd=0.00001, eval.metric = mx.metric.accuracy))
[50] Train-accuracy=0.99555237206823
[50] Validation-accuracy=0.994264240506329
utilisateur      système      écoulé
   8998.87      2526.50      3123.07
```

We now test RMSprop, and find that the error rate in validation is even lower: 0.51%:

```
> system.time(model <- mx.model.FeedForward.create(symbol=lenet,
    X=train.array, y=train.y, ctx=device.cpu, num.round=50,
    array.batch.size=128,
+ optimizer="rmsprop", eval.data=list(data=test.array,
    label=test$label), wd=0.001, eval.metric = mx.metric.accuracy))
[50] Train-accuracy=0.996818363539446
[50] Validation-accuracy=0.994857594936709
utilisateur      système      écoulé
   9240.27      2603.10      3288.93
```

We will have other opportunities to implement these adaptive algorithms.

7.15 Progress in Image Recognition

Image recognition is the first application to have benefited from deep learning methods, whose contribution, especially that of neural networks, has achieved spectacular progress in a few years. Moreover, it is the most natural, intuitive, and widespread example of high dimensional data. The following examples show the universal appeal of image recognition, whose uses range from recognizing handwritten postal codes on envelopes to driverless cars, and of course to recognizing people and landscapes in social media. The methods have progressed to the point where the best algorithms are now reaching the same level of recognition quality as the human brain.

Let's recall what makes the strength of deep neural networks in image recognition: the ability to recognize characteristic features of a shape or an object without assuming their exact position in space. It can recognize that two animals belong to the same breed even when their pictures are taken from completely different angles, and that two animals belong to different breeds even in pictures taken in exactly the same way. Yet, in the second case, the two photos could appear closer if they were analyzed pixel by pixel without taking into account their spatial relationships, which is what the usual machine learning methods do. If we want to apply these usual methods on image recognition problems, we have to try to perform a complex pre-processing of the data, which deep methods avoid, and with more success.

Historically, image recognition started with handwritten digits, and the MNIST dataset (Section 6.1) has been used to develop and compare generations of image recognition methods, including convolutional neural networks. It is the preferred benchmark for many deep learning researchers and the literature on this subject is abundant.[50] Figure 7.18, taken from a seminal article by Yann LeCun *et al.*[51] summarizes the state of performance achieved in 1998.

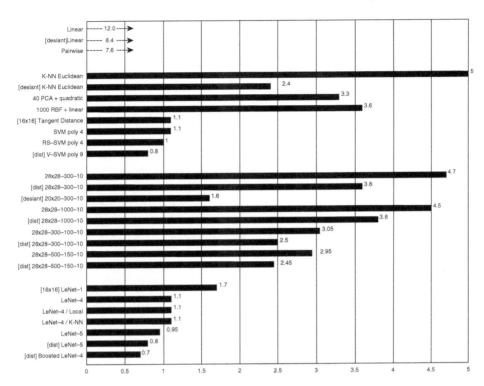

Figure 7.18 MNIST in 1998. *Source*: LeCun, Y., Bottou, L., Bengio, Y., & Haffner, P. Gradient-based learning applied to document recognition, *Proceedings of the IEEE, 86*(11) (1998), 2278–2323.

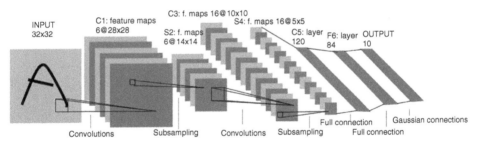

Figure 7.19 LeNet-5 network. *Source*: : LeCun, Y., Bottou, L., Bengio, Y., & Haffner, P. Gradient-based learning applied to document recognition, *Proceedings of the IEEE, 86*(11) (1998), 2278–2323.

One of the lowest error rates in 1998 was provided by the LeNet-5 convolutional neural network. It was very complex for its time, but today it is common to have layers of more than 40 maps, whereas LeNet-5 had only 6 maps in its first layer (Figure 7.19). LeNet-5 came into industrial use in the late 1990s with its implementation in bank check reading systems, which were then able to process half of the checks with less than 1% error.

Table 7.2 shows the best results since the early 2000s, presented as the error rates on the MNIST test set. It can be seen that the only models with an error rate below 0.5% are neural networks, mostly convolutional (CNN), with data augmentation by deforming the initial images (Section 7.13). In Table 7.2, 20C4 denotes a 20-map convolution layer with 4 x 4

Table 7.2 MNIST between 2003 and 2020.

Method	Error rate	Authors	Year
CNN (convolutional neural network)	0.40	Simard, Steinkraus and Platt	2003
CNN (convolutional neural network)	0.39	Ranzato, Poultney, Chopra and LeCun	2006
Committee (average) of 25 MLPs at a hidden layer 784-800-10 (top-2 error = 0.01%)	0.39	Meier, Cireşan, Gambardella and Schmidhuber	2011
5-hidden layer MLP 784-2500-2000-1500-1000-500-10	0.35	Cireşan, Meier, Gambardella and Schmidhuber	2010
CNN, 1-20-40-60-80-100-120-150FC-10	0.35	Cireşan, Meier, Masci, Gambardella and Schmidhuber	2011
Committee of 7 CNNs, 1-20C4-P2-40C5-P3-150FC-10 (57 committees formed)	0.27± 0.02	Cireşan, Meier, Gambardella and Schmidhuber	2011
Committee of 35 CNNs, 1-20C4-P2-40C5-P3-150FC-10	0.23	Cireşan, Meier and Schmidhuber	2012
Committee of 5 CNNs with DropConnect on the fully connected layer	0.21	Wan, Zeiler, Zhang, LeCun, and Fergus	2013
Random Multimodel Deep Learning (RMDL)	0.18	Kowsari, Heidarysafa, Brown, Meimandi, and Barnes	2018
Committee of 20 pre-trained ResNet networks with the "squeeze and excitation" architecture[1]	0.17	Hu, Shen, Albanie, Sun, and Wu	2020
Capsule network committee	0.13	Byerly, Kalganova, and Dear	2020

Note: [1] Jie Hu, Li Shen, Samuel Albanie, Gang Sun, and Enhua Wu Squeeze-and-Excitation Networks (2019). arXiv:1709.01507v4. This architecture won the ILSVRC2017 challenge, see below.

filters, P2 a max pooling layer with 2 x 2 filters, and 150FC a fully connected layer of 150 units.

In 2012, the lowest classification error rate obtained on MNIST came close to that of a human for the first time. It was obtained by a committee of 35 networks whose predictions were averaged. In 2013, the classification rate on MNIST was further improved, dropping to 0.21% on the test set. This result was achieved by using DropConnect (Section 7.11). The best result in 2020 was obtained with capsule networks (Section 7.17).

Image recognition was also applied more generally to Latin characters, with the NIST-SD19 database of more than 800,000 characters: upper case, lower case and numbers, written by 3600 people.[52] An error rate of 11.63% was obtained on this dataset, which is much higher than on the MNIST database. This is due to difficult distinctions such as {o,O,0}, {1,l,i,I}, {6,G}, {9,g}. There are also more specific databases of personal names (first names, family names).[53]

The recognition of Chinese characters has also been studied, on the CASIA-HWDB database[54] of more than 10^6 characters, as well as Japanese character recognition (Section 8.6.2).

airplane

automobile

bird

cat

deer

dog

frog

horse

ship

truck

Figure 7.20   CIFAR-10. *Source*: https://www.cs.toronto.edu/~kriz/cifar.html

One of the best-known image recognition databases is the CIFAR-10 dataset,[55] which is composed of 60,000 32 x 32 pixels color images, divided into ten classes (Figure 7.20) collected by Alex Krizhevsky, Vinod Nair, and Geoffrey Hinton. Its name comes from a laboratory that was among those at the forefront of deep learning research since 2006: the Canadian Institute For Advanced Research (CIFAR).

On this base (of which 10000 images are for test), achieving a test error rate as low as 3.47% (in 2015) was the result of significant effort, due to the variety of images (backgrounds, colors, size, centering) and the difficulty in distinguishing certain classes (cats/dogs, airplanes/birds). This was achieved[56] using data augmentation and fractional max-pooling (Section 7.9).

The CIFAR-100 base is a base of 60000 color images of 32 x 32 pixels like CIFAR-10, but divided into 100 classes of 600 photos each, so they are much more difficult to classify. In 2015, the best classification rate was 24.28%.

A list of the best results obtained on these different bases can be found on the Web.[57]

Another dataset, the ImageNet database has been collected since 2007 by Fei-Fei Li and his colleagues from Princeton University. It is very large, with 14,197,122 images from the Web, divided into 21,841 classes (divided into 27 major categories:[58] animals, devices, food, plants, individuals...), which was labeled by people on crowdsourcing: Amazon Mechanical Turk.[59] It can be downloaded on the Web.[60] Its important place in the training of computer vision algorithms comes from its richness, which means it is used as a support for an annual computer vision contest: the ImageNet Large-Scale Visual Recognition Challenge (ILSVRC). This contest took place between 2010 and 2017, and was based on an

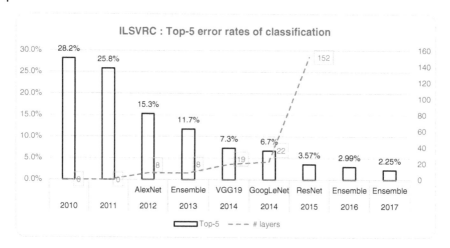

Figure 7.21 The ILSVRC Challenge.

extract of 1000 classes and a little more than 1000 images for each class, divided into 1.2 million images for training, 50,000 for validation and 100,000 for test, or about 27 gigabytes of data. This dataset is called ImageNet-1k. After object classification, object detection (Section 7.20.1) appeared in the ILSVRC2013 competition and object detection and scene classification in videos in the ILSVRC2015 competition.

The results of this challenge are often measured by the top-5 error: the proportion of test images whose class is not in the first five classes predicted by the model (Figure 7.21). The 1000-class classification is so complex that the usual error (top-1 error) would be too unfavorable a measure of model performance.

The ILSVRC2012 winner was Alex Krizhevsky, Ilya Sutskever, and Geoffrey Hinton's AlexNet network, which was more complex than LeNet, with 650,000 units and 60 million parameters on 5 convolution layers and 3 fully connected layers (Figure 7.22), using stochastic gradient descent with batches of 128 images, dropout (50%), ridge weight decay (0.0005), data augmentation, overlapping pooling, GPU training, and normalization and ReLU activation that were new at the time. Its top-5 error was equal to 16.4%. This edition of the challenge was a turning point, with the first victory of a convolutional network, a model of the neural networks that have since then always been winners of this competition.

The ILSVRC2013 competition was won by the start-up Clarifai and its neural network based on the principles of Matthew Zeiler and Rob Fergus' ZFNet,[61] which has the same structure and number of layers as AlexNet, but more maps in each layer. The top-5 error of ZFNet was 14.8% on the ILSVRC2012 data. It can be used online on the Web.[62] Clarifai achieved a top-5 error equal to 12.5% with a single network and 11.7% with an ensemble of ZFNet networks.[63]

The ILSVRC2014 winner was the GoogLeNet network[64] based on the Inception architecture (multiple convolutions performed in parallel with filters of different sizes), with 22 layers (plus 5 pooling layers) but "only" 5 million parameters, twelve times fewer parameters than AlexNet. Its top-5 error dropped to 6.67%. GoogLeNet is unique in that it replaced a fully connected layer with an average pooling layer, with filters of size 5 x 5 and

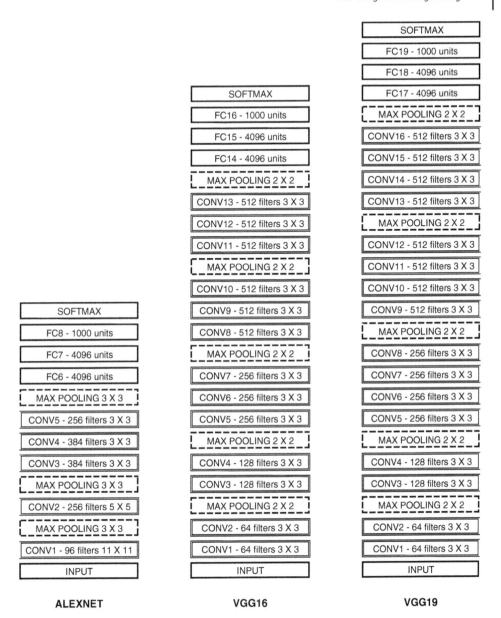

ALEXNET **VGG16** **VGG19**

Figure 7.22 AlexNet and VGG neural networks.

stride 3. It kept a fully connected layer on the output with 1024 units followed by a softmax activation. It has a fairly high dropout of 70% and unusually sized 1 x 1 convolution layers.

The runner-up in the ILSVRC2014 challenge was Karen Simonyan and Andrew Zisserman's VGG19 network (from the *Visual Geometry Group* at the University of Oxford),[65] implemented in the Caffe deep learning library, with 19 convolution and pooling layers (Figure 7.22), and ReLU activation. Its top-5 error was 7.3% on the test set.

Its layers consisted of small 3 x 3 filters for convolution and 2 x 2 filters (no overlap) for pooling (Figure 7.22). The reason for this choice of small filters was outlined in Section 7.7: in a convolution layer with a 7 x 7 filter, each unit is connected to 7 x 7 units of the previous layer, no more so than the stacking of three convolution layers with 3 x 3 filter, but with 49 parameters for the 7 x 7 filter versus 27 parameters for the stacking of three convolution layers with 3 x 3 filter. Small filters allow the same receptive field to be covered with less complexity. The same authors created a VGG16 network that is simpler but almost as accurate as the VGG19 network, with a top-5 error of 7.4%. Both VGG16 and VGG19 networks were made available to the community,[66] converted into Keras and MatConvNet models, and are now often used. It is important to point out their complexity, with the 138 million parameters of VGG16, and even more for VGG19. As has already been said, the fully connected layers represent a large part of these parameters, a little more than 100 million for the first fully connected layer of VGG16 alone.

The ILSVRC2015 winner was the 152-layer "ultra-deep" ResNet (ResNet152), and it achieved a top-5 classification error as low as 3.57%, lower for the first time than the human error of about 5%.[67] But human and algorithmic errors are not the same: the algorithm will be able to make fine distinctions between closely related categories (e.g. different breeds of cats) but may be more easily misled (e.g. by images taken out of context) and make serious classification errors. The training of the network used stochastic gradient descent with batches of 256 images, no dropout, a weight decay of 0.00001, and a single layer fully connected at the output with 1000 units. Most importantly, this network exploited the principle of residual neural networks (Section 7.4) which allows the vanishing gradient to be limited, and to build and train very deep networks.

As of 2016, the records seem to be able to be broken only by neural network ensembles.[68] The ILSVRC2016 winner was the Chinese team Trimps-Soushen with a top-5 classification error rate of 2.99%, obtained with ensembles of pre-trained Inception, ResNet, and Wide Residual Network (WRN) networks. A few months earlier, a top-5 error rate of 3.08% was obtained by a set of three Inception-ResNet-v2 networks and one Inception v4 network.[69] The ILSVRC2017 winner was the WMW team (researchers from Momenta and the University of Oxford) with a top-5 classification error rate of 2.25%, obtained with ensembles of pre-trained ResNet networks and a new "squeeze and excitation" architecture.[70]

Figure 7.23 is interesting because it shows the top-1 accuracy (i.e. the complement of the top-1 error) of the main convolutional networks as a function of the number of operations they require, with the area of the disks being proportional to the number of network parameters. It is clear that the greater complexity of VGG16 and VGG19 does not assure them an equivalent performance, and that in contrast GoogLeNet has a very good efficiency with about 5 million parameters that ensure a top-1 accuracy of about 70%, i.e. a "precision / mega-parameters" ratio of 14% that is the highest with that of ENet. Like the VGG networks, AlexNet also falls below the "regression line" of the scatterplot, due to its very large number of parameters. And it appears that the best performing networks, such as Inception v4, are beginning to stagnate in performance.

In 2018, one huge neural network achieved a top-1 error as low as 14.6% (and a top-5 error of 2.4%): the ResNeXt-101-32x48d network,[71] which has 829 million parameters.

Even approaching ten million units and one billion connections (but these numbers are growing fast), the largest deep neural networks are far from the human brain, which

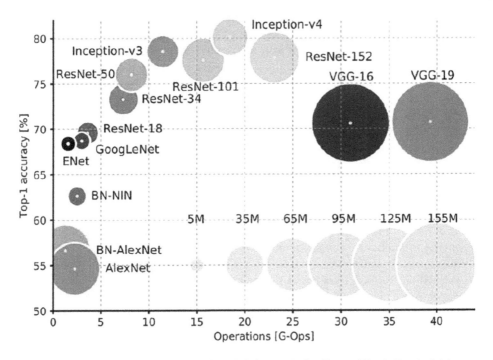

Figure 7.23 Accuracy of CNNs as a function of their complexity. *Source*: Alfredo Canziani, Adam Paszke, and Eugenio Culurciello. An Analysis of Deep Neural Network Models for Practical Applications (2017). arXiv:1605.07678.

has nearly 100 billion neurons and nearly 10,000 synapses per neuron, or on the order of 10^{15} synaptic connections.

As mentioned, convolutional network image recognition algorithms are also at work for real-time traffic sign and pedestrian recognition for driverless cars. The GTSRB (German Traffic Sign Benchmark) database of more than 50,000 images and 43 classes was used in a competition at the end of the IJCNN 2011 (International Joint Conference on Neural Networks),[72] with a lowest error rate of 0.54% achieved by Dan Cireşan, Ueli Meier, Jonathan Masci, and Jürgen Schmidhuber[73] with a committee of 25 convolutional neural networks. This result was the only one to exceed human performance (error of 1.16%), followed by another convolutional network model (error equal to 1.69%), and a random forest model (error equal to 3.86%).

House number recognition is implemented by Google on its Google Street View shots. A team of Google researchers achieved a lowest error rate of 2.16% in 2013[74] on the Street View House Numbers database,[75] which contains more than 200,000 street numbers with over 600,000 digits. Specifically, this 2.16% rate is calculated at the individual digit level, while the error rate in recognizing each street number is slightly higher and approaches 4%. This performance was achieved by an 11-layer network with 8 convolution layers and 3072 units, using data augmentation, max pooling, Maxout and ReLU activation functions (Section 7.3). The originality of their approach was that they did not attempt to slice the street numbers into their constituent digits and process them globally. Their network has been used to recognize 100 million street numbers in the world. It is fully operational since its recognition rate is of the order of magnitude of a human operator.

In 2019, Amazon announced a new feature of its mobile app, StyleSnap, which allows its user to take a photo of an item of clothing worn by a person in any situation and be offered by Amazon the clothes on its site that most resemble the ones photographed.

A very popular use of computer vision is face recognition. Some algorithms are well known. Facebook's DeepFace (2014) is a neural network with 9 layers and 120 million connections. It achieved 97.35% accuracy on the Labeled Faces in the Wild (LFW) database, which contains 13,000 face photos of 5,749 celebrities captured on the web. Here, the human achieved 98% accuracy. Google's FaceNet (2015) achieves even higher accuracy: 99.63% on the LFW database.

We can also mention the open source InsightFace library[76] for 2D&3D face analysis, which can use PyTorch or MXNet and is installed on Python 3.x ($x \geq 6$).

The difficulty of face recognition is that the face is constantly changing its appearance depending on emotions, hairstyle, smile …

Video image recognition can exploit the additional dimension of time, which makes the calculations very complex but can complement information that is missing or more difficult to detect in static images. This temporal dimension is best addressed by recurrent neural networks, which are described in Section 7.16. Video datasets are growing, the largest of which is YouTube-8M,[77] consisting of 6.1 million YouTube videos concerning 3862 categories (nature, animals, finance, fashion, sports, video games, fishing, car, music, piano, dance …) and representing more than 350,000 hours of video. The number of videos has decreased since the 8.2 million in September 2016 but their quality and the quality of their tagging have increased.

7.16   Recurrent Neural Networks

Recurrent neural networks (RNN) have proven to be among the best suited for natural language recognition, translation, speech recognition and generation, and even music generation.[78] These are neural networks that have recurrent connections in their hidden layers allowing at each moment a certain number of past states to be taken into account. Recurrent neural networks are adapted to situations in which the data are sequences, and where what we want to detect depends on the context and on a temporal evolution. In particular, for natural language processing, the "memory" of the network allows it to analyze each word, taking into account its context.

To do this, each unit of a hidden layer has two connections: the usual connection from the input layer, and a "recurrent" connection from the previous state of the hidden layer (Figure 7.24).

Each entry i_t corresponds to a word in a sequence of words, a sentence, for example, and more precisely to the coordinates corresponding to this word in a vector space in which it is embedded (Section 4.4). This vector space has one dimension per word of the vocabulary and the coordinates of a word in this vector space will be 1 for the dimension corresponding to this word, and 0 for the other dimensions. Such a representation, called "bag of words,"[79] is basic, and we will see that there are others that are much more elaborate.

Each hidden unit h_t receives a signal equal to:

$$h_t = activation(w_1 i_t + w_2 h_{t-1} + biais).$$

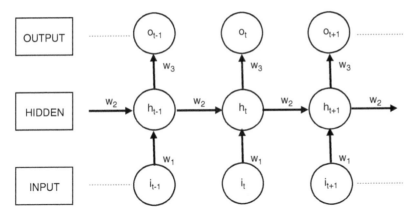

Figure 7.24 Recurrent neural network.

The activation function can be the hyperbolic tangent, the linear rectifier or another. Note that the weights w_1 and w_2 are constant (do not depend on t), hence the term "recurrent network." The last hidden unit h_t is followed by an output which can correspond to a set of words (for a translation), a category (sentiment analysis), etc.

But the use of recurrent networks soon ran into a difficulty: the memory of recurrent neural networks is often too short-term, limited to a few dozen iterations. This comes from the backpropagation mechanism, in which the unit weights are updated proportional to the gradient of the error with respect to these weights, starting with the layers of the network closest to the output layer. We have seen (Section 7.4) that the gradient often decreases exponentially as a function of the number of iterations and the number of layers, and this is what causes the rapid "forgetting of the past" by recurrent neural networks.

A solution was found in 1997 by Hochreiter and Schmidhuber[80] with the invention of recurrent neural networks with long short-term memory: LSTM networks.[81] A "memory unit" (cell state) is added to prevent the vanishing gradient problem and increase the memory depth of the network, which can reach thousands of iterations. This memory unit has a linear activation with a derivative equal to 1 that does not vanish.

More precisely, each hidden unit h_t is activated, not only by the previous unit h_{t-1} and the input i_t but also by a signal from the memory unit C_{t-1}. This memory unit has three "*gates*" (Figure 7.25, where i_t is noted x_t).

The *forget gate* reads h_{t-1} and i_t and determines how much of the information from C_{t-1} that is kept in C_t. This is done by applying the sigmoid activation function σ to $U_f h_{t-1} + W_f i_t + b_f$ (U_f and W_f being weight vectors, and b_f the bias), and multiplying the value of $f_t = \sigma(U_f h_{t-1} + W_f i_t + b_f)$ between 0 and 1 by C_{t-1}: a value of f_t close to 0 will forget a lot C_{t-1} while a value close to 1 will forget little C_{t-1}. This vector multiplication is done term by term, i.e. unit by unit.

The *input gate* reads h_{t-1} and i_t and determines the amount of new information coming from h_{t-1} and i_t which is taken into account in C_t. It is still a sigmoid activation σ applied to $U_i h_{t-1} + W_i i_t + b_i$ which determines the part of information that is integrated,

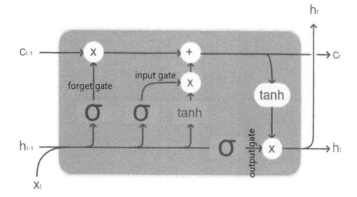

Figure 7.25 LSTM recurrent network. *Source*: Wikipedia: Guillaume Chevalier – LARNN: Linear Attention Recurrent Neural Network, CC BY-SA 4.0: https://commons.wikimedia.org/w/index.php?curid=99599411.

a part that is all the greater as $g_t = \sigma(U_i h_{t-1} + W_i i_t + b_i)$ is close to 1. This new information $\tilde{C}_t = tanh(U_c h_{t-1} + W_c i_t + b_c)$ is obtained by replacing the sigmoid activation by a hyperbolic tangent to update the memory unit with a value between -1 and +1 which can increase or decrease the content of the memory unit. With the sigmoid function, the content of the memory unit would always be updated with a positive value (between 0 and 1) and would increase indefinitely. The hyperbolic tangent also has a larger derivative than the sigmoid and thus a greater resistance to vanishing gradient. For the determination of the input gate two neural layers are therefore computed in parallel.

These two gates are combined to update the C_{t-1} in C_t: $C_t = (f_t * C_{t-1}) + (g_t * \tilde{C}_t)$. This vector addition is done unit by unit. The first term specifies to what extent a value remains in the memory unit, while the second term specifies to what extent new values flow into the memory unit.

Finally, the *output gate* sends part of the information from the memory unit C_t to the next unit h_t of the network: $h_t = o_t * tanh(C_t)$. This part of the information is again controlled by a sigmoid function σ which is multiplied by $tanh(C_t)$ to keep a proportion of C_t between 0 and 1, after its transformation by the hyperbolic tangent so that the information is added or subtracted to the next unit. This proportion is calculated as a function of h_{t-1} and i_t by the formula $o_t = \sigma(U_o h_{t-1} + W_o i_t + b_o)$.

The input gate therefore controls the influence of the signal on the state of the memory and may ignore it if it is not relevant. The forget gate can more or less clear the memory. As for the output gate, it allows the network to be immediately updated with new information or to keep it for a later state.

This makes it possible to process long sequences of words, but also sequences of images as in a video, whereas video recognition was a problem for recurrent neural networks with a short-term memory, because the duration of the video, at the end of which it can be classified, exceeded the duration of the network's memory. In a word sequence, the device

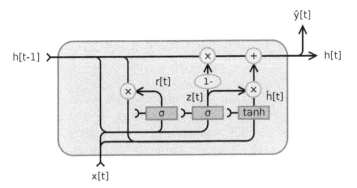

Figure 7.26 GRU recurrent network. *Source*: Wikipedia. Jeblad, Own work, CC BY-SA 4.0, https://commons.wikimedia.org/w/index.php?curid=66225938.

of forget, input, and output gates allows some less important words (e.g. stop words) to be forgotten, or the gender of a previous noun to be forgotten and replaced by the gender of the current subject. Words correspond to neural units, whose weights $U_f, W_f, U_i...$ are computed in the learning phase of the LSTM network.

The multiplication of the number of parameters to be trained in LSTM networks explains their main disadvantage, which is the very long training time, which is almost impossible in practice without a graphics processor (GPU). Faced with this drawback, a solution was discovered in 2014: gated recurrent networks, GRU (Gated Recurrent Units),[82] which differ from LSTM networks in that the forget and input gates are combined into a single *update gate*.

In the updating of the memory unit, the forgotten information is the one that is replaced by new information, and the updating of the memory unit is therefore done according to the formula:

$$C_t = (f_t * C_{t-1}) + ((1 - f_t) * \tilde{C}_t).$$

But in a GRU, the memory unit C_t and the hidden unit h_t are confused, so that the previous formula becomes:

$$h_t = (f_t * C_{t-1}) + ((1 - f_t) * \tilde{h}_t).$$

This can be seen in Figure 7.26 (where f_t is noted z_t). Furthermore, we have:

$$\tilde{h}_t = tanh(U_h r_t h_{t-1} + W_h i_t + b_c)$$

with

$$r_t = \sigma(U_r h_{t-1} + W_r i_t + b_r).$$

With fewer parameters, GRU networks may have a lower word representation capacity than LSTMs but they are faster. In some cases, they even manage to outperform LSTMs, for example, in speech recognition.[83] Examples of LSTM and GRU networks implementations will be given in Chapter 9.

We can also mention the Neural Turing Machines (NTM).[84] Their name comes from their memory mechanism which is similar to the Turing machine, with its ribbon on which one can read and write, but it is a Turing machine with a learning mechanism and which knows when to read and write. NTMs look promising, but their first stable implementation only dates back to 2018.

In the fight against over-fitting, one difficulty encountered in training recurrent networks is that batch normalization (Section 7.8) does not apply as is to recurrent networks, since this normalization applies "vertically" and not "horizontally." In other words, it applies between layers of a state t but not between states. Yet, normalization would be more efficient between states since a recurrent network is deeper in the time direction. However, solutions have been proposed for batch normalization of recurrent networks.[85]

In the same way, it was necessary to adapt the concept of dropout for recurrent networks with a "recurrent dropout"[86] which acts from one step to the next with always the same units of the network whose activation is canceled, without which the learning would not be improved but, on the contrary, degraded. The Keras library implements this recurrent dropout in its LSTM and GRU layers.

Convolutional networks are sometimes very efficient for language processing but they do not have the capacity of LSTM and GRU networks to take into account words in their sequences and not as isolated words. Note that there are bidirectional versions of the LSTM and GRU networks, which read the words of a sequence in both directions and can thus influence the state of a unit according to the preceding words but also the following words, and thus its entire context.

Recurrent networks are used for machine translation: one recurrent network is used to obtain the vector representation of words in a sentence written in language A, while another recurrent network uses this vector representation to generate a sentence in language B. Vector representations such as Word2Vec (Section 4.4.7) are used because they assign close positions to words with close meanings, which is well suited for translation where one wants to avoid misinterpretations. Vector representations of words provided by neural networks do not have the visual interpretation of images whose features are identified from the finest to the most global, but what corresponds to these visual features is the meaning of the words beyond their appearance and their expression in a particular language. This is why these vector representations of words and their construction by deep neural networks make it possible to move from one language to another, based on the meaning of words.

According to the same principle, another application that is developing is the automatic description of the content of an image. Annotating an image means associating a caption or keywords to it. A convolutional network converts the pixels of an image into vectors, and at the output of the convolution layers these vectors are understood by a recurrent network as representing words. One expected application among others is the description of an image for a blind person.

Researchers at Google have realized[87] such an automatic description by combining a convolutional network and a recurrent LSTM network. The convolutional network is used to recognize images, but its softmax classification layer (which assigns each image the probability of belonging to an image class) is replaced by an LSTM network that generates sentences. The combination of the two networks is trained on sets of annotated images to learn to describe images. The networks must capture the relationships of objects to each other and generate correct text.

Among the annotated image databases, we can mention Pascal VOC (Visual Object Classes), COCO (Common Objects in Context), Flickr8k, Flickr30k, SBU.

The Microsoft COCO database[88] consists of more than 330,000 images, of which more than 200,000 have been tagged as ImageNet by human volunteers on Amazon Mechanical Turk. They represent 1.5 million objects divided into 90 categories.[89] In addition to the fact that COCO images are segmented and annotated, they have the particularity of containing objects in their natural context, which implies the presence of several objects and even several classes of objects in each image, much more often than in the Pascal VOC database and especially in ImageNet database (Section 7.15) where 60% of the images contain only one category of object (but the ImageNet categories are much more numerous: 20,000).

LSTM networks are used in the Tesseract open source library for optical character recognition (OCR). This library was initially developed between 1985 and 1995 by Hewlett Packard engineers, then abandoned for ten years, before being revived in 2005 under the Apache open source license,[90] benefiting from numerous contributions including those from Google. Tesseract uses LSTM networks since version 4 and can be used in many languages. It can be used with Python (library `pytesseract`) and with R using its package `tesseract`.[91]

Finally, RNN recurrent networks and in particular LSTM are an alternative to ARIMA models for time series processing, interesting in principle but not necessarily more efficient in practice.

7.17 Capsule Networks

Convolutional neural networks can recognize shapes independently of their precise position (Section 7.1). A convolutional network can recognize eyes and mouths and detect them in an image, even without knowing their exact position, thanks to mechanisms like pooling (Section 7.9). But a convolutional network does not know how to take into account the context of a feature extracted from an image and in particular it does not know how to model the position of the components of an object in relation to each other. It will not be able to distinguish the *Portrait of Dora Maar* from a realistic face: this is called the "Picasso effect". Capsule neural networks (or CapsNet) were invented[92] to take into account the relative position of features in an image. Their training is based on a method called "dynamic routing between capsules."

In such a neural network, each layer is divided into groups of neurons called *capsules*. A capsule contains in its output vector information about the presence of an object in an image but also its "pose" (position, size, orientation). This output vector is the equivalent of the activation of classical neural networks. Unlike a classical convolutional network, a capsule network will be able to recognize an object in an image independently of its orientation and from viewpoints that may differ (and not only by translation as in convolutional networks). A capsule in one layer is only connected to capsules in the next layer that are sufficiently "matched," and in particular that correspond to objects (e.g. faces) containing objects in the capsule in the first layer (e.g. eyes). This selective connection is called "routing by agreement between capsules" and it replaces the pooling of classical convolutional networks, pooling which reduces the positional information. It is this agreement routing that allows parts to be associated with their whole provided that their poses are compatible. It can be represented by a "syntactic tree" (or "parse tree") where each level corresponds to a layer (the first ones at the bottom of the tree) and each node corresponds to a capsule. The construction of this tree is part of the training process of the neural network.

It seems that capsule networks achieve the same accuracy as convolutional networks with a smaller number of images (they have fewer parameters to calculate). They are even superior on a dataset such as the MNIST digits (Table 7.2 in section 7.15). On the other hand, they require more computing power and thus cannot be used on such large bases as convolutional networks.

Hinton noted the limitations of convolutional networks for understanding three-dimensional objects. The Stacked Capsule Autoencoder[93] (SCAE) is designed to overcome this problem. The model learns to represent objects independently of their orientation in space, so it can recognize objects despite variations in viewpoint, lighting, or the presence of noise.

7.18 Autoencoders

An autoencoder is a neural network whose output layer is equal to the input layer, with a central hidden layer (in the middle of possible other hidden layers) that contains a small number of units, often 2. Since the network must minimize the error between input and output that is equal to it, the idea with this 2-unit "bottleneck" is to force the network to find the two-dimensional representation of data that is as faithful as possible: the data has been "encoded" into a compressed form, with each observation summarized by its two values on the central units (Figure 7.27). Autoencoding is a dimension reduction method, like principal component analysis (which finds the directions over which the projected inertia

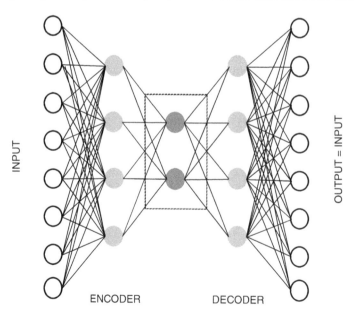

Figure 7.27 Autoencoder.

is maximum), but is non-linear, unlike principal component analysis. It is an unsupervised method.

Autoencoding can be used for the detection of abnormal observations. To do this, the data are passed through the autoencoder and the output data are compared with the input data: if one data has a large deviation for an observation, it is probably out of range.[94]

An autoencoder can also precede a supervised learning algorithm that will be applied to the compressed data and not to the initial data, which eliminates noise, and makes learning faster and perhaps easier if the data are few.

With the Keras library of neural networks, described in detail in Section 8.3, we can build an autoencoder. Here is an illustration on the MNIST dataset (Section 6.1). We build a fully connected seven-layer neural network whose activation function is the hyperbolic tangent. This network has nearly 830,000 weights.

```
> c(c(x_train, y_train), c(x_test, y_test)) %<-% dataset_mnist()
> x_train <- x_train / 255
> x_test <- x_test / 255

> model <- keras_model_sequential()
> model %>%
+    layer_dense(units = 400, activation = 'tanh', input_shape = ncol(x_train)) %>%
+    layer_dense(units = 200, activation = 'tanh') %>%
+    layer_dense(units = 100, activation = 'tanh') %>%
+    layer_dense(units = 2,   activation = 'tanh') %>%
+    layer_dense(units = 100, activation = 'tanh') %>%
+    layer_dense(units = 200, activation = 'tanh') %>%
+    layer_dense(units = 400, activation = 'tanh') %>%
+    layer_dense(units = ncol(x_train))
> model
Model
```

Layer (type)	Output Shape	Param #
dense_1 (Dense)	(None, 400)	314000
dense_2 (Dense)	(None, 200)	80200
dense_3 (Dense)	(None, 100)	20100
dense_4 (Dense)	(None, 2)	202
dense_5 (Dense)	(None, 100)	300
dense_6 (Dense)	(None, 200)	20200
dense_7 (Dense)	(None, 400)	80400
dense_8 (Dense)	(None, 784)	314384

```
Total params: 829,786
Trainable params: 829,786
Non-trainable params: 0
```

The model is compiled and trained in 100 epochs with the AdaMax optimization algorithm (Section 7.14). The repetition `x_train, x_train` in the parameters of the `fit()` function corresponds to the input and output data, and indicates that the model is trained on an output equal to the input:

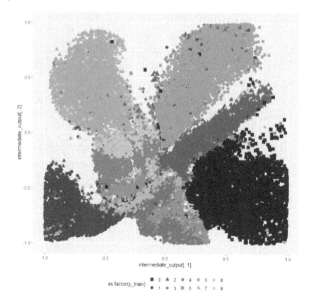

Figure 7.28 Keras autoencoder (400, 200, 100, 2, 100, 200, 400) and 100 epochs.

```
> model %>% compile(loss = "mean_squared_error", optimizer = "adamax")
> history <- fit(model, x_train, x_train, epochs = 100,
    batch_size = 64, validation_data = list(x_test, x_test),
    verbose=1)
```

We then extract the middle layer of the network using the get_layer() function of Keras, indicating the dense_4 name of this central layer which performs the autoencoding, and we apply the input data to it by the predict() function.

```
> layer_name <- 'dense_4'
> intermediate_layer_model <- keras_model(inputs = model$input,
    outputs = get_layer(model, layer_name)$output)
> intermediate_output <- predict(intermediate_layer_model,
    x_train)
```

We can then plot the data from this middle layer, where each image is represented by a dot in Figure 7.28, which shows that the digits are well separated:

```
> library(ggplot2)
> # in color
> qplot(intermediate_output[,1], intermediate_output[,2],
    colour = as.factor(y_train))
> # black and white
> p1 <- qplot(intermediate_output[,1], intermediate_output[,2])
> p2 <- p1 + geom_jitter(aes(shape = as.factor(y_train),
    color = as.factor(y_train)), size = 3) +
```

```
        scale_shape_manual(values = rep(15:19, len = 10),
        guide = guide_legend(nrow = 2)) + scale_color_grey() +
        theme(legend.position = "bottom")
> plot(p2)
```

We find that this unsupervised learning method does a very good job of identifying structures that have not been presented to it as labeled cases. In comparison, an unsupervised random forest does not separate the ten digits of the MNIST database as well. Figure 7.29 shows the proximity matrix of a 500-tree random forest, obtained by the following R code.

Recall that the proximity matrix is the n x n matrix (n being the number of individuals) in which each coefficient M_{ij} contains the number of trees constructed without i and without j, and of which one leaf contains both individuals i and j. To normalize the matrix, we divide M_{ij} by the number of trees constructed (trained) without i and j. This matrix is represented in two dimensions thanks to a multidimensional positioning method: each

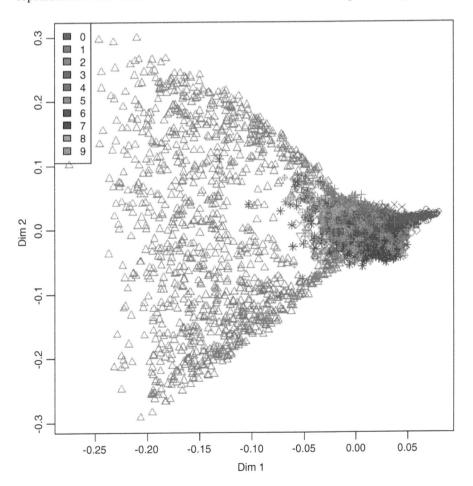

Figure 7.29 Representation of the proximity matrix of a random forest.

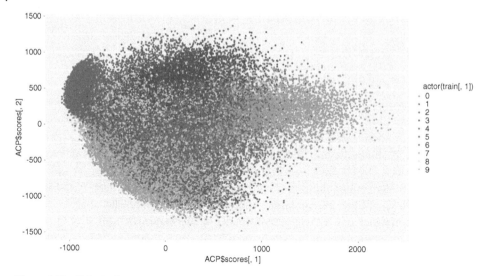

Figure 7.30 Principal component analysis on MNIST.

individual is positioned in a point (x_i, y_i) so that the distance between two individuals in this 2D representation is as close as possible to the dissimilarity matrix $1 - M_{ij}$.

```
> library(randomForest)
> rf <- randomForest(train[,-1], ntree=500, mtry=30, nodesize=5,
    proximity=TRUE, keep.forest=F)
> target <- as.factor(train[,1])
> MDSplot(rf, target, palette=rainbow(10), pch=as.numeric(target))
> legend("topleft", levels(target), col=rainbow(10), cex=0.8,
    fill=rainbow(10))
```

We can see that the `train[,-1]` matrix of the pixels is specified, but not the `train[,1]` digit to be predicted since the random forest is built here in an unsupervised way, which is allowed by the `randomForest` package. Each split of a tree is searched among a subset of 30 randomly selected pixels. It can be seen that the numbers 0 and 1 are very well distinguished, the others less so.

Of course, one can also perform a classical principal component analysis and represent the scatter plot in the first factorial plane (Figure 7.30) but the result is much less satisfactory than that of an autoencoding by deep neural network:

```
> ACP <- princomp(train[,-1])
> library(ggplot2)
> qplot(ACP$scores[,1], ACP$scores[,2], colour=as.factor(train[,1]))
```

7.19 Generative Models

Two techniques are mainly used for the generation of artificial data imitating existing data: generative adversarial networks and variational autoencoders. They are most often used for image generation but can also be used for sound or video generation.

7.19.1 Generative Adversarial Networks

In 2014, Generative Adversarial Networks[95] (or GAN) were invented, which are neural networks for unsupervised learning and in particular the generation of synthetic images that can be as realistic as a photograph.

A GAN model is composed of two models: a generative model G ("generator") which from a random distribution z (for example, Gaussian) in input generates in output data $G(z)$ according to a distribution p_g, and a discriminating model D ("discriminator"), which calculates the probability that an input sample comes from the training data x rather than from the generative model $G(z)$. We can see the value space z as a latent (underlying) representation, a coding, of the images to be generated. This is the idea of the autoencoders of the previous section, however, GANs only reproduce the "decoder" part because they do not know how to encode images. The goal of training the generative model is to maximize the probability that the discriminative model is wrong, a goal that is pursued because it has the effect of approximating the distribution p_{data} of the training data by the distribution p_g. The idea is to generate data, for example, images, indistinguishable from the original training data. It is a kind of visual Turing test, which would be passed by the machine (Section 10.1).

More precisely, the training of the model D will consist of maximizing the probability $D(x)$ (predict 1 for x from the training sample), minimize $D(G(z))$ (predict 1 for a data $G(z)$ generated by the model G), while the simultaneous training of the model G will consist of maximizing the probability $D(G(z))$, i.e. minimizing $1 - D(G(z))$. We see the adversarial system: we want to improve D and improve G so that it deceives D. This is shown in Figure 7.31 and in the following formula:

$$\min_G \max_D \{\mathbb{E}_x[log(D(x))] + \mathbb{E}_z[log(1 - D(G(z)))]\}.$$

The parameters of the model D are therefore adjusted during its training so that the output cost function of this model is low for the data of the training sample and high for the data generated by G. Simultaneously, the training of the model G will use the gradient of the previous cost function to adjust its parameters so that it generates data close to those of the training sample where the cost function is low. This is the gradient of the cost function of D with respect to its input, i.e. with respect to the output of G. The usual optimization algorithms, in particular ADAM (Section 7.14), apply in a satisfactory manner.[96] When they converge, it is towards a solution (called "Nash equilibrium" in game theory)[97] in

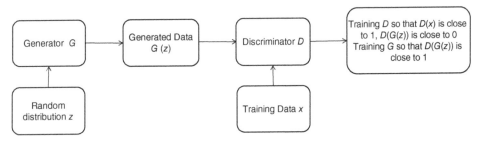

Figure 7.31 Principle of generative adversarial networks.

which the distribution p_g coincides with the distribution p_{data} and $D(x) = 0{,}5$ for all x: the discriminator is wrong one time out of two to recognize the real data.

In the first GANs, the models D and G were perceptrons, and then more efficient GANs appeared with convolutional networks: the Deep Convolutional Generative Adversarial Networks (DCGAN).[98] Conditional GANs have also appeared, in which the distribution z in input of the generator is a conditional distribution, the conditioning can be done, for example, on the class of an image or a text describing it.

Such a GAN model can also combine several images, for example photographs of two faces, to generate an image that blends features from both faces. One article shows how to generate photos of smiling men from photos of smiling women, non-smiling women and non-smiling men.[99] It also shows how to generate photos of women with glasses from photos of women without glasses and men with and without glasses. It also generates perfectly realistic bedroom photos from training examples in a way that is not limited to a combination of elements that might be inconsistent. The arithmetic "men with glasses – men without glasses + women without glasses = women with glasses" is reminiscent of another arithmetic (Word2Vec), at the word level (Section 4.4.7) the type "king" – "man" + "woman" = "queen." Whether it is a question of words or images, it is their immersion in an appropriate space that makes this type of operation possible.

GANs are thus used to manipulate images, to increase their resolution, to colorize them, to generate videos that are realistic and not simple averages of videos (therefore blurred) seen in training. GANs are also used to generate artificial images to enrich training samples for supervised models: it is a more sophisticated data augmentation (Section 7.13). GANs are also used in voice manipulation by lending the speech of an individual A to an individual B, of whom we have just a few minutes of recording. GANs are also used for text generation, in particular SeqGAN adapted to the generation of sequential data.[100]

Training GANs can be tricky due to some instability. A known drawback is "mode collapse" which occurs when the generator manages to trick the discriminator into generating only a portion of the possible data. If, for example, the data to be generated are the MNIST handwritten digits (Section 6.1), it is possible that the generator will succeed in fooling the discriminator very well by generating only one digit, in which case it will not generate the others. The unfortunate result is that the generator will only be able to produce one digit and the discriminator will only be able to recognize the generated images for one digit. Another situation is when, for each digit, only one type of handwriting is sufficient to perfectly fool the discriminator, in which case the other types of handwriting are not generated. Several solutions have been proposed to this problem,[101] such as making the discriminator detect if two generated samples are too close to each other.

7.19.2 Variational Autoencoders

Variational autoencoders (VAEs) created in 2013 by Kingma and Welling[102] and Rezende *et al.*[103] are a variant of autoencoders (Section 7.18), which are, let us recall, neural networks composed of an encoder (the first layers), a decoder (the last layers), and, in the middle, a constrained layer (the "code" or "latent variable space"), with the most common constraint being on the size of this central layer: often two units, or a latent space of dimension 2. The training of an autoencoder is done with an output layer equal to the input layer and its interest is to obtain in the central layer a compressed representation of the training data, having eliminated during the training what is not useful information in the data.

An autoencoder is used to generate images, obtained by applying the decoder to points in latent space. The difficulty of using a simple autoencoder to generate images becomes apparent if we look again at Figure 7.28, where we realize that some regions of the plane, between the classes, do not correspond to any digit image. An image generation from this autoencoder obtained by drawing points in the latent space can fall into discontinuities in the plane and produce outputs that do not correspond to any digits.

A variational autoencoder is a variant in which the latent space is continuous and not discontinuous. This latent space is obtained by having the encoder generate not one vector of dimension n ($n \geq 2$) for each input image, but two vectors of dimension n: a vector of means and a vector of standard deviations. Each input image of the autoencoder does not correspond to a point but to a probabilistic distribution, the one whose mean and standard deviation correspond to the image. The distribution can be a normal distribution. During the training of the autoencoder, each input image gives a probabilistic distribution, then a vector of dimension n is randomly drawn from this distribution, and the decoder reconstitutes from this vector an image which must be as close as possible to the input image. Training modifies the means and standard deviations with two objectives:

- the output images must be as close as possible to the input images;
- the distributions must cover the latent space as well as possible, without too much overlapping of the distributions corresponding to different image classes.

At the end of the training process, the decoder has learned to transform all the points of the latent space into images, without any indeterminate area, as happens with an ordinary autoencoder: if a point of the latent space corresponds to an image class, its neighboring points will generally correspond to the same class.

The variational autoencoder is ready to generate new images. For example, how can it add glasses to a face? We will take a face with and without glasses, obtain for each one an encoding in the latent space, calculate the difference of these two encodings, then add this difference to the encoding corresponding to the new face, the one to which we want to add a pair of glasses. The face with glasses will finally be generated by applying the decoder to this encoding. In the same way, we can transform a horse into a zebra by adding zebra stripes, or transform a zebra into a horse. We can transform a summer landscape into a winter landscape. This can be used in driving simulators. The generation of images becomes a manipulation of vectors.

The possibilities of generating animated images have been taking on alarming proportions in recent years, and especially since the work of researchers who showed in 2016 how to apply the expressions of another face to a face, in real time, using their algorithm Face2Face.[104] It is also possible to replace one face with another in a video, with increasing quality. In 2022, it is still possible to detect such tricks (called "deepfakes," a contraction of "deep learning" and "fake"), but for how long? The defects of these tricks are corrected one after another. For example, the blink of the eyes was once a way to detect a fake video, generated by an algorithm that was often trained on shots where people always had their eyes open: the blink of the eyes was not natural. But this defect was quickly corrected and the race is on between the creators and the deepfakes hunters.

7.20 Other Applications of Deep Learning

7.20.1 Object Detection

A more general problem than image recognition considered so far is that of detecting objects located in an image. It is both an object classification problem as before, combined with a regression problem to determine the coordinates of the edges of the boxes surrounding the objects and giving their position. This problem is of course crucial in applications such as autonomous vehicles and remote sensing. The difference between object detection and classification is that in the former problem (1) there may be several objects to be detected, the number of which may be unknown and (2) the position of these objects is unknown. The number of object classes and these classes are fixed.

There are two types of approaches to object detection: one-stage and two-stage detection. In one-stage detection, the classification of objects and the determination of their position by regression are done directly on the whole image. The main algorithms are YOLO (You Only Look Once) and its successors, SSD (Single Shot multibox Detector), MobileNet, CornerNet, and RetinaNet.

In two-stage detection, the first stage is to identify regions that may contain an object, and the second stage is to classify the objects in each candidate region and determine its precise position. Each of these stages requires optimization of its parameters, and these methods are therefore more time-consuming than methods consisting of a single training stage. The main algorithms are R-CNN (Regions with CNN features, or Region-based Convolutional Neural Networks), Fast R-CNN, Faster R-CNN, SPP-net, R-FCN and Mask R-CNN.

In all cases, the training of these models is done on databases that allow the training of object detection algorithms because they contain annotated images,[105] this annotation consists of: the class of the object, the outline of the rectangular box surrounding it, an indicator indicating that this box is not sufficient to contain the object, and an indicator signaling an object that is particularly difficult to recognize. The 2007 and 2012 Pascal VOC databases[106] (Section 7.16) are particularly used, and they allow comparison of the speed and predictive quality of the algorithms.

The speed of a detection algorithm is expressed in frames per second (FPS) and a real-time use in embedded systems requires a speed of at least 20 FPS. We mention FPS values for the following algorithms but they are of course only indicative as they depend on the machine on which the algorithm is executed. We use these indicative values only to rank the algorithms in terms of speed.

This algorithm produces models, and the quality of classification of objects by these models is evaluated in the following way. The prediction of a model is a probability of belonging to each class, and we choose a threshold of this probability, beyond which we assign the object to the class. Each threshold has two measures associated with it: recall and precision. *Recall* is the ratio TP / (TP + FN) of the number of true positives detected over the total number of positives. *Precision* is the ratio TP / (TP + FP) of the number of true positives over the number of predicted positives (true positives and false positives). For a given object class and probability threshold, the higher the recall, the more sensitive the model is, and the higher the precision, the less the model is wrong. For each class to be predicted, we define the precision recall curve which has one point for each probability threshold, the abscissa of the point being the recall and the ordinate being the precision. This curve is decreasing: the precision decreases when the recall increases, since the detection of a greater number of positives is done at the cost of some false positives. The area under this curve can be calculated, and it should be as high as possible. The predictive quality of the detection model is finally obtained by calculating the average mAP (mean average precision) of these areas for all classes. It is between 0 (the worst) and 1 (the best).

The objective of training an object detection model is of course to teach it to predict well the class of an object in a region, but also to teach it to localize it well. To evaluate the quality of the localization, we define a metric called "intersection over union," *IoU*. The ratio *IoU* of two regions is defined by the formula:

$$IoU(B_1, B_2) = \frac{area(B_1 \cap B_2)}{area(B_1 \cup B_2)}.$$

This ratio of the intersection area to the union area is between 0 and 1. In the training set, each region B_r actually surrounding an object is accurately known (it has been drawn by a human), and the prediction of the location of a region B_c will be all the better as the ratio $IoU(B_r, B_c)$ will be close to 1.

In general, two-stage methods are more accurate but slower, both in training and in application, which can be a problem in some uses such as autonomous vehicles.

But, on the other hand, two-stage methods allow a focus on rather small areas, while one-stage methods process a large area from the start, in which the objects to be detected (positive class) are therefore often much rarer than the background (negative class). Consequently, one-stage methods encounter the difficulty of classifying two very unbalanced frequency classes. Methods exist to deal with these cases of large imbalances: in particular, the use of modified loss functions, such as the balanced cross-entropy or the focal loss explained below.

A mixed approach was proposed[107] to get the best of each approach, with a first predictor distinguishing easy-to-classify images from hard-to-classify images: the former are sent to a one-stage algorithm, while the latter are sent to a two-stage algorithm. The difficulty predictor was trained on human annotator evaluations.

Let's start with the two-stage methods. An intuitively simple method is to arbitrarily split the image into smaller boxes, and apply a classification algorithm, such as a convolutional neural network, to each of these boxes. If for a box, the probability of one of the object classes is sufficiently high, the box is considered to contain an object of that class, and if not, no object has been detected in that box. The limit of this method is that the number of these boxes must be very large for the algorithm to be efficient.

R-CNN neural networks[108] follow a variant of this approach by partitioning the image into 2000 rectangular boxes of unequal size called *regions of interest*. They are trained in the following way.

We start with a pre-trained five-layer convolution CNN model based on AlexNet (Section 7.15) and retrain it on the 20 classes of the Pascal VOC 2007 database, to which we add the "no object" (or "background") class. This model is then applied to each of the 2000 boxes (all set to the same size 227 x 227 pixels) and the 4096 features extracted for each box by this model, the convolution filter activations, are used in linear kernel SVM models that classify the objects. The SVM models are binary and there is one model for each class to be predicted, with the "background" class added to the classes to be predicted. Each SVM model is fitted by considering as positive only the boxes containing the object under consideration and whose ratio *IoU* with the true region of the object exceeds a certain threshold set empirically at 0.3 by the authors. Then, for each box having a sufficient overlap with a region actually surrounding an object, a ridge regression model refines the position of the box by predicting the four coordinates of an optimal move of the box to bring it closer to the real region and thus to improve the classification of the object: the coordinates x and y of the center of the box, its height h and its width w.

If several boxes cover the same object, the so-called "non-maximum suppression" (or "non-max suppression") procedure is used to delete the redundant boxes. We select the box B_c whose ratio $IoU(B_r, B_c)$ with the real region B_r of the object is maximum, and we consider as redundant boxes to be deleted all the boxes B_d such that the ratio $IoU(B_d, B_c)$ exceeds a certain threshold (for example, 0.5). We then iterate the process by selecting, among all the non-deleted boxes, the box B_c whose ratio $IoU(B_r, B_c)$ with the true region of the object is maximum and by deleting all the boxes considered as redundant. We stop when no more boxes are deleted.

The detection speed of R-CNN is about 6 FPS and its accuracy mAP = 0.533 based on Pascal VOC 2007. This accuracy was the highest of all object detection methods when the R-CNN algorithm was published. But the slowness of this algorithm is prohibitive for real-time use: it comes from the fact that three models have to be successively trained: the convolutional model for feature extraction, the SVM model for object classification, and the regression model for the positioning of the boxes surrounding the objects.

The R-CNN network model has been improved by the Fast R-CNN model, and especially Faster R-CNN which is very accurate (mAP = 0.732) while reaching a speed of 17 FPS (based on Pascal VOC 2007) in some versions. But this is not enough for real-time use.

The Fast R-CNN model[109] saves time in two stages: on the one hand, the features extracted by the convolutional network are extracted at once for the whole image and not for each box, and on the other hand the SVM classifier is replaced by a softmax output (classification) of a network whose other output (regression) refines the box position. The learning of both position and classification is thus simultaneous.

The Faster R-CNN model[110] is even faster because the search phase of the regions of interest is integrated with the training of the objects detection and their location. This search is performed by a network called RPN (*Region Proposal Network*) which has convolutional layers shared with the Fast R-CNN network. These layers are used both to propose regions and to extract features sent to the classifier.

Finally, we mention the Mask R-CNN model,[111] which improves Faster R-CNN by allowing it to predict the object class of each pixel. It does not just enclose the object in a rectangle and predict the class of that rectangle, but the object is cut out from the rectangle and not all pixels in the rectangle, but only those of the identified object are associated with the class. This task is called instance segmentation.

Let's move on to one-stage detection methods.

In the YOLO algorithm,[112] one of the first and most widely used, the determination of the class of objects and the detection of their position are done simultaneously on the entire image, using a single neural network.

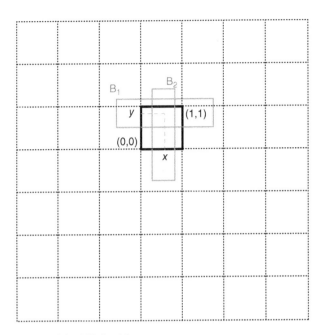

Figure 7.32 YOLO grid.

The image is divided into a grid of $S \times S$ cells with each of the S^2 cells itself divided into B finer boxes (Figure 7.32). A convolutional network is trained to simultaneously predict:

- for each of the S^2 cells of the grid and for each class of objects C_i ($1 \le i \le k$), the probability $P(C_i)$ that this cell contains an object of the class C_i;
- for each of the $S^2 B$ boxes, the set of coordinates (x, y, h, w) defined as above for the R-CNN networks, plus a fifth variable which is a confidence index that the box contains an object, estimated as shown below.

The coordinates (x, y) are related to the boundaries of the cell, while the coordinates (h, w) are related to the limits of the grid, so that they are all normalized between 0 and 1.

The boxes have sizes $h \times w$ determined by the training process, unlike the S^2 boxes of the grid which are all of the same size.

The neural network is inspired by GoogLeNet and has 24 convolution layers and 2 fully connected layers. The first 20 layers are pre-trained on ImageNet database (Section 7.15). It uses the leaky ReLU activation function (Section 7.3), dropout, data augmentation, and batches of 64 images. Its output is a tensor of dimension $S^2(5B + k)$ from the above.

In the training set, when a cell contains an object, we know the box B_r containing the object and we compute its overlap *IoU* with each of the candidate boxes B_c of the cell. The ratio $IoU(B_r, B_c)$ is an estimator of the confidence index of the box B_c mentioned above. The predicted candidate box is the one whose ratio $IoU(B_r, B_c)$ is maximal, just as the predicted object class is the one with maximal probability. When a cell does not contain an object, the confidence index of each of its boxes must be zero.

We can then calculate a quadratic loss function of the object localization at a cell level, calculating it only for the box B_c of the cell which has the largest ratio $IoU(B_r, B_c)$ and setting it to 0 for the other boxes (or the other box if $B = 2$). This loss function is the sum of the norm $\|(x_r, y_r) - ((x_c, y_c))\|^2$ and of the norm $\|\left(\sqrt{h_r}, \sqrt{w_r}\right) - \left((\sqrt{h_c}, \sqrt{w_c})\right)\|^2$. It is summed over all the cells containing an object. We take the square root of the width and height of the boxes so as not to give too much importance to large boxes, i.e. large objects.

The loss function of the object classification is calculated only for the cells containing an object, and is 0 for the others.

The loss function of the confidence index that the box contains an object is the sum of the values:

- $\|1 - IoU(B_r, B_c)\|^2$ for the cells containing an object and the boxes of maximum $IoU(B_r, B_c)$ ratio,
- $\|IoU(B_r, B_c)\|^2$ for the other cells and other boxes.

Finally, the loss function to be minimized during training is the weighted sum of these three loss functions, with a weighting of the location loss that is five times larger in the authors' paper.

It should be noted that, as with the two-stage methods, there may be a problem with the same object detected by several boxes because it covers all these boxes. The procedure of "non-maximum suppression" is used as before to remove the redundant boxes B_d, which are those whose ratio $IoU(B_d, B_c)$ with the best predicted B_c box exceeds a certain threshold.

The learning of YOLO is much faster than that of an R-CNN network because it is performed in a single pass on the image. Moreover, the values indicated in the authors' article are $S = 7$ and $B = 2$ and thus lead to a much smaller number of boxes than in an R-CNN network, which accentuates the speed of YOLO (but which prevents it from detecting many objects). However, its parameters and especially its learning rate must be well chosen to avoid the instability that comes from the fact that most of the boxes in the grid do not contain any object, which gives all the more weight to the other boxes.

The YOLO algorithm is implemented in the `image.darknet` package of R,[113] which produced Figure 7.33. It is currently on GitHub but not on CRAN.

Here is the code for installing and using this package. The file specified by the `weights` parameter (e.g. `yolov2.weights`) contains the pre-trained model used by the package. The parameters of the convolutional network are in the `cfg` parameter file and the names

Figure 7.33 Object detection with YOLO.

of the classes of objects identified by the model are in the `labels` file. A simple model (`tiny-yolo-voc`) is downloaded to the machine when the package is installed, but other models trained on the Microsoft COCO dataset (Section 7.16) can be downloaded from the Web.[114] The `image_darknet_model()` function can be used for image classification or detection depending on whether the `type` parameter is set to `classify` or `detect`. For classification, models are available on the web,[115] based on AlexNet, VGG16, ResNet50, ResNet152, and others.

```
> devtools::install_github("bnosac/image", subdir = "image.darknet",
    build_vignettes = TRUE)
> library(image.darknet)
> yolo_coco <- image_darknet_model(type = 'detect', model = "yolo2.cfg",
 weights = system.file(package = "image.darknet", "models",
 "yolo2.weights"), labels = system.file(package = "image.darknet",
 "include", "darknet", "data", "coco.names"))
> x <- image_darknet_detect(file = "C:/.../dot-cat.jpg", object = yolo_coco)
```

The result is a `predictions.png` file generated in the same directory on the machine as the one containing the initial image.

The performance of YOLO was compared to R-CNN and other methods on the 2007 and 2012 Pascal VOC bases (see above), for which we have $k = 20$ classes, resulting in a prediction tensor of size $7^2.30$. In its first version, YOLO has a speed of application of 45 FPS on Pascal VOC 2007. This allows it to be used on video images such as those from a webcam, to detect objects in real time. A demonstration is given on the authors' website.[116] Its mAP accuracy is 0.634.

A slightly less accurate but still faster (155 FPS) Fast YOLO variant uses only 9 convolutional layers instead of 24. The YOLO VGG16 variant is, on the contrary, more accurate but slower (21 FPS), and relies on VGG16 instead of GoogLeNet.

In all these variants, the YOLO algorithm is limited in its ability to detect numerous or closely spaced objects. This is due to the small number of boxes and the fact that only one object can be detected in each box. Therefore, no more than 49 objects can be detected, which must not be too different in size and which can only belong to 20 different classes, those of Pascal VOC.

Aside from these weaknesses, YOLO performs very well, due to the specificity that makes it so strong, in terms of its simplicity, speed, and detection capability. Because it sees the entire image when it classifies a box and determines its position, unlike two-stage algorithms that ignore the rest of the image when analyzing each box, YOLO can better account for the context surrounding each object. In addition, YOLO is superior to other algorithms in detecting objects in pictorial works, not just photographs.

Subsequent versions of YOLO have attempted to address its weaknesses and improve YOLO's accuracy, first by replacing GoogLeNet and VGG16 with models designed specifically for YOLO, trained on finer resolution images: DarkNet-19 (YOLOv2 and YOLO9000) and DarkNet-53 (YOLOv3) which have 19 and 53 convolutional layers, and average pooling layers. Other evolutions occurred from YOLOv2 onwards, with the use of batch normalization (Section 7.8), the ability to detect several objects per cell, a decoupling of the prediction of object classes and their position, and the consideration of images of different sizes. The boxes no longer contain only two boxes but a larger number t, determined by k-means, and an object can be associated to each of these boxes and not only to one box. The output of YOLOv2 is a tensor of dimension $S^2 t(5 + k)$ and no longer a tensor of dimension $S^2 (5.B + k)$ as in YOLO. In the article by its authors,[117] $t = 5$.

YOLO9000 and YOLOv3 can detect more than 9000 different object classes (again from ImageNet). YOLOv3 also introduced a ResNet residual network architecture with skip connections (Section 7.4). It uses logistic regression to predict the confidence index of the presence of an object in a box.[118]

These new algorithms are also very fast: 171 FPS for YOLOv2 and 78 FPS for YOLOv3 on Pascal VOC 2007.

The SSD algorithm[119] created shortly after the first version of YOLO offers another solution to the problem of detecting objects of various sizes. Its base is a pre-trained VGG16 model to which are added convolutional layers with filters of increasingly smaller size (pyramid structure) capable of detecting objects of increasingly larger size. These layers are all (not only the last one) connected to the output layer and avoid having to search for boxes of all different sizes as YOLO does. There is no separate prediction of whether an object exists in a box, and the "no object" class is simply added to the classes to be predicted. But the much higher frequency of this class is one of the difficulties of this type of object detection methods.

The loss function of SSD is the sum of a loss on the classification of objects and α times the loss on the regression of their position, the coefficient α being determined by cross-validation to optimize the detection.

SSD achieves both good speed (59 FPS) and accuracy (mAP $= 0.743$) measured on Pascal VOC 2007.

RetinaNet is another one-stage object detection algorithm. It is based on ResNet followed by a Feature Pyramid Network (FPN), a structure designed, as in the SSD algorithm, to detect objects of various sizes. RetinaNet is slower than YOLOv3 but it has a better object detection capability, and even one of the best of all the one-stage algorithms.

RetinaNet owes this ability to its original solution to the problem of class imbalance to be predicted: the introduction of the focal loss[120] that we define here. The loss function usually used in binary classification problems is the *cross-entropy* (Section 7.3) and gives the formula of the error function:

$$L(f, (xy)) = -\sum_i \left\{ y_i \log \left(f(x_i) \right) + (1 - y_i) \log \left(1 - f(x_i) \right) \right\}.$$

Here y_i is 1 if the box contains an object in the ith image and 0 otherwise, and $f(x_i)$ is the estimate of the probability that the box contains an object.

We note that this formula gives the same weight to each of the classification errors, which is a drawback when one of the classes to be predicted is much rarer than the other. Indeed, the small size of this class means that the errors concerning it are rarer and contribute less to the total error. The model therefore learns to predict the majority class and not the minority class, which is not always desired, as in object detection where the majority class is the background and the minority class the objects to be detected. This is why variants of cross-entropy have been devised.

The first is *balanced cross-entropy*. Since the background represents most of an image and a box rarely contains an object, we often have $y_i = 0$ and the main contributions to the error come from $- \log \left(1 - f(x_i) \right)$ especially when $f(x_i)$ is close to 1. The model will mostly learn not to predict the presence of an object when there is none, but we would like it to be able to detect an object when there is one and we would therefore like to give more weight to the error terms $-y_i \log (f(x_i))$. We multiply these terms by a factor α where $\alpha \in [0, 1]$, and we also multiply the error terms $-(1 - y_i) \log (1 - f(x_i))$ by a factor $(1 - \alpha)$. If, as here, it is the class $y_i = 1$ which is rarer, we choose a value $\alpha > 0,5$ which will give more importance to the prediction errors of this class. We thus define the balanced cross-entropy:

$$-\sum_i \left\{ \alpha y_i \log (f(x_i)) + (1 - \alpha)(1 - y_i) \log (1 - f(x_i)) \right\}.$$

This parameter restores the balance between majority and minority cases in the error calculation, by over-weighting the cases of the under-represented class.

However, it does not restore the balance between easy- and hard-to-classify cases. The easy-to-classify cases are those for which $y_i = 0$ and $f(x_i)$ is close to 0, or $y_i = 1$ and $f(x_i)$ is close to 1. According to the cross-entropy formula, the individual contribution to the error of these easy cases is small, but it can become globally predominant if they are numerous. We therefore want to modify the calculation of the error to give even less weight to these cases.

Therefore, when $y_i = 0$, we multiply the error terms $(1 - y_i) \log (1 - f(x_i))$ by a factor $f(x_i)^\gamma$, where $\gamma \geq 0$, which gives less weight to cases where $f(x_i)$ is close to 0. And when $y_i = 1$, we multiply the corresponding terms $-y_i \log (f(x_i))$ by a factor $(1 - f(x_i))^\gamma$, which gives less weight to the cases where $1 - f(x_i)$ is close to 0, i.e. where $f(x_i)$ is close to 1. This leads to the formula for the *focal loss*:

$$-\sum_i \left\{ (1 - f(x_i))^\gamma y_i \log (f(x_i)) + f(x_i)^\gamma (1 - y_i) \log (1 - f(x_i)) \right\}.$$

The optimal value of γ is generally between 0 and 5, with 0 giving the cross entropy, and the authors of the focal loss recommend the value $\gamma = 2$.

The interest of the focal loss is that it allows a specific weight to be given to each case, not based on its belonging to one or the other class, but based on the estimated probability of belonging to this class, by increasing the weight when the probability of belonging is lower, thus the case is more difficult to classify. Thus, the training process can be concentrated, over the course of the epochs, on the images that are difficult to classify.

We can combine the idea of focal loss and balanced entropy to simultaneously restore the balance between easy and hard to classify cases, and majority and minority cases, with balanced focal loss:

$$-\sum_i \left\{ \alpha (1 - f(x_i))^\gamma y_i \log (f(x_i)) + (1 - \alpha)f(x_i)^\gamma (1 - y_i) \log (1 - f(x_i)) \right\}.$$

The authors note that α should decrease when γ increases, and they recommend the values $\alpha = 0.25$ and $\gamma = 2$ for object detection.

The focal loss was tested on the YOLOv3 algorithm but did not improve its performance.[121]

7.20.2 Autonomous Vehicles

Tests of autonomous vehicles began in the 1980s and the first ones did not use deep learning. We can mention the ALVINN (*Autonomous Land Vehicle In a Neural Network*) project of Dean Pomerleau,[122] which used a classical, non-convolutional neural network. As in image recognition, these networks have been supplanted since the 2010s by deep neural networks.

The supervised learning of a deep network for car driving can consist in learning to detect road markings, safety rails, other vehicles in a first step, and to adapt its driving in a second step. Another approach is to directly learn to drive the vehicle and is described in a publication by NVIDIA researchers.[123]

In this approach, the vehicle is equipped with three cameras in the training phase, a central camera and two side cameras, while only the central camera is needed in the model application phase. The images from these cameras provide the training X data, and the driver's steering wheel angle, or rather the inverse Y of his turning radius, provides the labeled data. It is the inverse of the turning radius that is used to avoid an infinite value in a straight line and replace it with a zero value. The error to be minimized during training is the difference between the driver's Y value and the Y' value predicted by the neural network. The training data were collected during 72 hours of driving on various roads and in various weather and light conditions: driving on highways, on roads with or without markings, driveways, in tunnels. .., during day or night, in clear, cloudy, rainy, snowy, foggy weather. These data were augmented (Section 7.13) with slight deviations from the center of the lane, with the associated turning radius calculated as that required to return to the center of the lane in two seconds. The model is a convolutional network with three convolution layers of size 5 x 5, two convolution layers of size 3 x 3, and three fully connected layers. It has about 250,000 parameters.

After training, the model was tested in two ways. First, simulations were performed. Three hours of video footage from a vehicle driven by a human were provided as input to the network. The network calculated the turning radius at each instant, and a simulator then calculated the position of the vehicle resulting from the network's action: if it deviated more than one metre from the center of the road, manual intervention was considered necessary. Once the network was deemed sufficiently trained, it was used to drive a real vehicle on a route with a human driver: for 10 miles, the human driver had to intervene only 2% of the time.

The traditional approach to training an autonomous vehicle to drive is supervised learning, but reinforcement learning (Section 7.1) was used in 2018 by the start-up Wayve, which was able to train a vehicle to stay in its lane in a record time of 20 minutes.[124] During this learning, a human driver straightens the steering wheel every time the car moves out of its lane, and the reward function that is to be maximized is the amount of time the driver does not have to correct the vehicle's path.

The Berkeley DeepDrive Industrial Consortium[125] partners UC Berkeley with private companies to develop new technologies for autonomous vehicles, and is known for its large open source BDD100K database[126] of 100,000 driving videos, representing more than 1,000 hours of driving experience with more than 100 million images.

7.20.3 Analysis of Brain Activity

An extension of image recognition by convolutional neural networks came from the work of a team of researchers from the Computational Neuroscience Laboratories of Kyoto and Kyoto University,[127] who went from handwriting to thought.

They had individuals see or think about images and simultaneously analyzed their brain activity using functional magnetic resonance imaging (fMRI). Unlike previous work that aimed to directly predict the object seen or imagined from fMRI data, they trained their models not directly on the category of the object (airplane, truck, dolphin, leopard, etc.) but on the features built by convolutional neural networks (and other models) on these images.

A network was trained on 1000 categories from the ImageNet database and 1000 units were randomly extracted from each of the 7 convolution layers of the network, as well as the 1000 units from the output fully connected layer.

Sparse linear regressions were fitted on the fMRI signals to predict each of the values of these units, for 150 image categories. In these regressions, it was found that signals coming from low (respectively high) visual areas of the brain were more often selected by the regression to explain the units of the low (respectively high) layers of the network, which reinforces the analogy between the structure of convolutional neural networks (with its layers) and that of the human visual cortex (with its areas: V1, V2, V3, V4, LO ...)

In the application phase, when an individual imagines or sees an object, the regression models are applied to his brain imagery to predict the values of the units of each layer of the network. For each layer, we have a predicted vector of 1000 values, and we associate to it the category of objects whose average values of the units of the corresponding layer, values averaged for each category on the whole of the images of the category, are the most correlated to it.

The individuals have seen 150 categories of objects but the model can then predict 15,372 categories among those of the ImageNet database, thus categories never seen during the training. The originality of this method lies in the fact that it allows the prediction of object categories that were not seen during the training phase. Indeed, this training did not consist of learning an image category among a limited number of categories, but the value of units of a network able to recognize these image categories but others.

In short, we made humans and convolutional neural networks see the same images and we learned to predict the activity of a network (thus a certain object) from the activity of a brain.

In recent years, deep learning algorithms have been developed for brain-machine interfaces that can directly link a human brain and a computer, in order to control a computer, an exoskeleton, a prosthesis, a wheelchair or any other automated system by thought, without using the person's limbs. These interfaces can also be used to synthesize speech or write words solely by thought. They are composed of three elements: a system for acquiring brain signals (through electrodes implanted on or under the cranium), an algorithm that interprets and classifies these signals to send them to a system that transforms them into commands for a machine. In 2019, French researchers at the *Clinatec* biomedical research center created a brain-machine interface capable of piloting an exoskeleton by thought.[128] After two years of training, a young man who has been quadriplegic for four years was able to walk with this exoskeleton. The difficulty and the length of the training process are still an obstacle to the use of these brain-machine interfaces, another obstacle being of course the difficulty of implanting electrodes under the cranium.

In 2021, researchers at Stanford University created a brain-machine interface using a recurrent GRU neural network (Section 7.16) that could analyze the brain signals of a patient whose hand was paralyzed to type texts.[129] In the training phase of the neural network, the patient had to imagine that he was holding a pen and writing each letter of the alphabet. Sensors implanted under the cranium measured the activity of 200 neurons of the motor cortex during this training, which here took only about ten hours for a thousand sentences. It may seem complicated to ask the patient to imagine the movements he could make to draw letters, but these temporally complex movements are easier to decode. Once this was done, the recurrent network was able to decode the patient's brain activity and write at a speed of 90 letters per minute, with a raw accuracy of 94.1% online and an accuracy of over 99% offline with an automatic corrector. This is close to the normal writing speed of 120 letters per minute, and is twice as fast as eye-tracking systems in which you have to point a cursor at a screen.

7.20.4 Analysis of the Style of a Pictorial Work

Convolutional networks have been used to detect the style of a painter,[130] or more precisely, to exploit the hierarchical structure of such a network to distinguish the content of an image given by the upper layers of the network (low resolution), from its style restored by the hierarchy of convolution layers, the painter's touch in all its details corresponding to the lower layers of the network (high resolution). We can then synthesize an image by applying the style of one image to the content of another.

This idea of style transfer had been considered for years before finding an effective solution thanks to convolutional networks, and it was then quickly implemented in common applications for smartphones.

The basic idea of Gatys, Ecker, and Bethge is intuitive, consisting of minimizing the weighted sum of two loss functions:

1) between the content of the original image (in their article a photograph of the banks of the Neckar in Tübingen) and the generated image (Figure 7.34);
2) between the style of the reference image (a painting by Turner reproduced in Figure 7.34, Van Gogh, Munch, Picasso, or Kandinsky) and the generated image.

In reality, a third loss function is added to the first two: a regularization function that increases the spatial continuity and reduces the grain of the generated image.

The difficulty was to measure the distance between two images. The solution discovered by the authors is to use a convolutional neural network, and to consider the activations of the upper convolution filters of the network at the different positions of each of the images, original and generated, and to calculate the distance in L^2 norm of these activations: this gives the content loss function. Specifically, for a layer l of the network, the activation of the kth filter at the (i, j) position of the image is denoted $O^l_{i,j,k}$ for the original image and $G^l_{i,j,k}$ for the generated image, and the distance to be minimized is:

$$d^l_{content} = \frac{1}{2} \sum_{i,j,k} \left(G^l_{i,j,k} - O^l_{i,j,k} \right)^2.$$

The content loss function $L_{content}(G, O)$ is then obtained by a weighted sum of the distances $d^l_{content}$ over the different layers of the network.

The calculation of the style loss function is a bit more subtle, as it is not a measure of the distance of the lower filter activations but the correlations of the lower and upper

Andreas Praefcke

Joseph Mallord William Turner, *Shipwreck of the Minotaur*, about 1810, oil on canvas
Calouste-Gulbenkian Museum, Lisbon

Figure 7.34 Detecting the style of a painter. *Source*: L.A., Gatys, A S., Ecker, J., and M. Bethge, A Neural Algorithm of Artistic Style (2015). arXiv:1508.06576.

filter activations, with these correlations providing the texture and style. This correlation between the activations of two filters k and k' for a layer l of the generated image network is given by the Gram matrix:

$$G^l_{kk'} = \sum_i \sum_j G^l_{i,j,k} G^l_{i,j,k'}.$$

In this matrix, $G^l_{kk'}$ is increasingly larger as the activations of filters k and k' are simultaneous.

Similarly, we define the Gram matrix $R^l_{kk'}$ of the reference image, and the distance to be minimized for the style is:

$$d^l_{style} = \frac{1}{2} \sum_{k,k'} \left(G^l_{kk'} - R^l_{kk'} \right)^2.$$

The style loss function $L_{style}(G, R)$ is then obtained by a weighted sum of the distances d^l_{style} over the different layers of the network.

Finally, the overall loss function is a weighted average:

$$L(G) = \alpha L_{content}(G, O) + \beta L_{style}(G, R).$$

The weights α and β need to be fitted, but the style weight is always much higher (about a hundred times higher).

To obtain the activations of a convolutional network needed for these calculations, the authors did not specifically train a neural network but used the pre-trained VGG19 network (Section 7.15) with pooling by the mean. They used the quasi-Newton method L_BFGS (Section 3.2) to minimize the weighted sum of the loss functions. Their algorithm has been implemented in MXNet[131] and Keras.[132] The use of GPU is recommended to limit the time to generate an image.

Note that, since the low-resolution details of the original image are replaced by the characteristics of the reference image that give it its style, the style transfer works best if the original image is not identifiable by fine details.

7.20.5   Go and Chess Games

In Go, two players arrange stones on a board, each trying to expand territories and surround the opponent's stones to make prisoners. The territories and the prisoners earn points for the players and the winner is the player who has the most points at the end of the game. After a first victory in 1997 of a machine against a world chess champion[133] (IBM Deep Blue), the victory of a machine against a Go champion seemed much more inaccessible and distant, because of the immeasurable complexity of the game of Go: 10^{600} possible games for a 19 x 19 board against 10^{120} possible chess games. It follows that brute force[134] is much less efficient in Go than in chess, where Deep Blue estimated some two hundred million moves per second. This challenge stimulated research, notably from Google and Facebook, which developed its Darkforest program.

The victory in March 2016 of the AlphaGo program (from DeepMind) over the world champion Lee Sedol was therefore truly an event and a victory for artificial intelligence. It was won by two convolutional neural networks.[135] It was on this occasion that Google inaugurated the use of TPUs (Section 2.6.2), which are even faster than GPUs in deep learning calculations. Figure 7.35 suggests the analogy between image recognition and winning position recognition. The convolution mechanism can be applied to the game of Go as well as to an image, since we find translation invariance: the rules of the game are the same on the whole board (except for the limits imposed by the edges).

AlphaGo is based on a combination of deep learning and a Monte Carlo tree search (MTCS). The latter is used to simulate many, many games (a form of data augmentation), see if they win or lose, and deduce the value of the nodes in the tree that lead to those games. But not all possible games can be simulated, because there are so many of them. This is where deep learning comes in, to simulate only the most promising games. To do this, AlphaGo

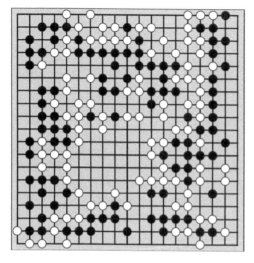

Figure 7.35   Go.

learns to find the best move from a position, by training a convolutional network based on tens of thousands of games and 30 million moves from expert players. It succeeded in improving the best move prediction rate far beyond previous approaches. It then improved this result by playing against itself, which is called reinforcement learning (Section 7.1). In this training, AlphaGo varies each parameter in a certain way, and if it wins more often this way, it knows to vary the parameter thus. The reinforcement-enhanced model wins 80% of the games against the original model. Finally, we go from predicting the next best move to predicting the best game, i.e., the best sequence of moves, through the Monte Carlo tree search, which relies on deep network predictions.

An even better performance was achieved the following year by AlphaGo Zero, also the work of DeepMind. Its feat was to train only by playing against itself, without seeing a single game by a human champion, and knowing only the rules of the game of Go at the outset. After three days of reinforcement learning and five million games, AlphaGo Zero defeated AlphaGo in October 2017 by 100 to 0! AlphaGo Zero exploits the invariance of the rules of Go through rotation and reflection, allowing it to use data augmentation by generating eight symmetries per position.

An even more generic algorithm, AlphaZero, was published two months later,[136] capable of playing Go, chess and shogi (Japanese chess). Because of the asymmetry of the chess and shogi rules, and the fact that some of the rules are position-dependent (e.g., moving pawns), it cannot rely on data augmentation. AlphaZero has other differences from AlphaGo Zero, such as the fact that in its game generation AlphaGo Zero only retains the games generated by the "best player" from previous iterations. AlphaZero's games are generated using the latest parameters without selection. What is remarkable is that an algorithm like AlphaZero, generic to the point of being able to play several games, has succeeded in defeating the best players each time: the strongest chess program (Stockfish),[137] the strongest shogi program (Elmo) and AlphaGo Zero in Go.

Unlike Stockfish and Elmo, and Deep Blue, which rely on grandmaster-calibrated position evaluation functions, optimized search functions (minimax algorithm with alpha-beta pruning) in possibility trees, and brute force, AlphaZero learned on its own, by reinforcement learning, without seeing a single grandmaster game, relying only on knowledge of the games' rules, like AlphaGo Zero in go. What's a little troubling is that in a sense, AlphaZero has an "intelligence" that is much closer to that of human players, examining only 80,000 positions in chess each second (compared to 70 million for Stockfish) and 40,000 positions in shogi (compared to 35 million for Elmo), but examining much deeper and more promising positions. After a few hours of learning, AlphaZero was able to obtain in a hundred games:

- in chess: 28 wins and 72 draws,
- in shogi: 90 wins, 2 draws and 8 losses,
- in Go: 60 wins and 40 losses.

Note in passing a particularity of chess and shogi compared to Go, which had to be taken into account in the learning process: the possibility of a draw.

A new milestone was reached in November 2019, when DeepMind presented its new algorithm, MuZero,[138] capable of playing chess and shogi as well as AlphaZero, Go better than AlphaZero, and 57 Atari games. Its novelty is that it is able to play without being taught the rules of these games. The only information it receives during its training process is the legality of each move made. To achieve this, DeepMind relied on an approach called lookahead tree search. Like AlphaZero, this algorithm relies on reinforcement learning, but by being able to quickly master a game without first knowing the rules, it takes another step towards unsupervised learning, adapted to complex situations where the rules are unknown. MuZero accomplishes this by trying to model (with the help of a deep network) only the three elements necessary for its anticipation:

- value function: how good is the current situation?
- action-selection policy: what is the best course of action?
- reward: how good is the last action?

7.20.6 Other Games

Researchers are now tackling games, such as bridge[139] or poker, which present a particular difficulty because some of the information is hidden since the other players' hands are not visible. Team games also add an extra level of complexity. Poker, on the other hand, presents an additional difficulty, with the misleading information of bluffing players. Nevertheless, in July 2019, researchers from Facebook and Carnegie-Mellon University announced [140] that they had succeeded in developing an artificial intelligence program that could defeat five top professional players in a single game. This artificial intelligence, named Pluribus, was trained by reinforcement and showed that it could use strategies unknown to professionals, and that it was also "bold" and capable of bluffing.

A perhaps more important challenge is the victory of an algorithm against a human player in a video game. Reinforcement learning is also used here, which allows a machine to play several games, for example, a range of games from the Atari 2600 console (Video Olympics, Breakout, Space Invaders, Seaquest, Beamrider, Enduro, etc.). The strategy game StarCraft is of particular interest to artificial intelligence researchers. It presents like card games the difficulty that some of the information is hidden since some parts of the territory are concealed. On January 24, 2019, DeepMind announced that its artificial intelligence AlphaStar had defeated two of the top players in the strategy game StarCraft II, in a series of five matches, each won with a score of 5 to 0, and it reached the title of "grandmaster" in October 2019.

The difficulty for the machine is planning strategies beyond the short term. This is what makes reinforcement learning so successful, as it maximizes a sum of long-term rewards, with a positive reward being given each time the player's score increases.

Deep learning models capable of playing with Atari can be built with common libraries such as TensorFlow or Keras,[141] but of course require enough computing power and in particular a GPU.

In another genre, Dr. Fill is an algorithm that won for the first time, in May 2021, a crossword competition with more than 1000 participants, the American Crossword Puzzle Tournament (ACPT).[142] Dr. Fill was created by Matt Ginsberg, a computer scientist and cruciverbalist, who enrolled him in ACPT since 2012, and partnered in 2021 with the Berkeley Natural Language Processing Group to bring Dr. Fill the benefits of deep neural learning methods. This learning is based on a dataset of six million pairs (definitions, solutions) published in various media, and allows Dr. Fill, when faced with a definition, to generate a large number of possible solutions, which are then ranked according to their probability and compatibility with other words in the grid. It can have difficulties when the definition is based on a set of words, and it sometimes makes mistakes, but these are now compensated in tournament by its greater speed than human cruciverbalists.

Notes

1 Mallat S. Understanding Deep Convolutional Networks, *Philosophical Royal Society*. A, 374 (2016), 20150203.

2 Hornik, K. Approximation Capabilities of Multilayer Feedforward Networks, *Neural Networks*, 4(2) (1991), 251–257.

3 Cybenko, G. Approximation by superpositions of a sigmoidal function, *Mathematics of Control, Signals and Systems*, 2(4) (1989), 303–314.

4 Park, S., Chulhee, Y., Lee, J., and Shin, J. Minimum Width for Universal Approximation (2020). arXiv:2006.08859.

5 Fukushima K. Neocognitron: A Self-Organizing Neural Network Model for a Mechanism of Pattern Recognition Unaffected by Shift in Position. *Biological Cybernetics*, 36(4) (1980),193–202.

6 LeCun, Y., Boser, B., Denker, J.S., Henderson, D., Howard, R.E., Hubbard, W., and Jackel, L.D. Backpropagation Applied to Handwritten Zip Code Recognition. *Neural Computation*, 1(4) (1989), 541–551.

7 LeCun, Y., Boser, B., Denker, J.S., Henderson, D., Howard, R.E., Hubbard, W., and Jackel, L.D. Handwritten Digit Recognition with a Back-Propagation Network. In D. Touretzky (Ed.), *Advances in Neural Information Processing Systems (NIPS 1989), Denver, CO* (Vol.. 2). (New York: Morgan Kaufmann, 1990).

8 LeCun, Y., Bottou, L., Bengio, Y., and Haffner, P. Gradient-Based Learning Applied to Document Recognition, *Proceedings of the IEEE*, 86(11) (1998), 2278–2323.

9 Zhang, X., Zhao, J., and LeCun, Y. Character-level Convolutional Networks for Text Classification (2016). arXiv:1509.01626v3.

10 Hochreiter, S. and Schmidhuber, J. Long Short-Term Memory, *Neural Computation*, 9(8) (1997), 1735–1780.

11 Hochreiter, S. Untersuchungen zu dynamischen neuronalen Netzen (Diploma thesis). (1991). Institut für Informatik, Technische Universität München.

12 Cho, K., van Merrienboer, B., Gulcehre, C., Bahdanau, D., Bougares, F., Schwenk, H., and Bengio, Y. Learning Phrase Representations using RNN Encoder-Decoder for Statistical Machine Translation (2014). arXiv:1406.1078.

13 https://www.fast.ai/.

14 https://course.fast.ai/.

15 This compilation can increase the computation time, which seems to be more the case on Theano than on TensorFlow where the functions corresponding to symbolic operations are precomputed.

16 Hinton, G.E. and Salakhutdinov, R.R. Reducing the Dimensionality of Data with Neural Networks. *Science*, 313(5786) (2006), 504–507.

17 Hahnloser, R., Sarpeshkar, R., Mahowald, M.A., Douglas, R.J., and Seung, H.S. Digital Selection and Analog Amplification Coexist in a Cortex-Inspired Silicon Circuit, *Nature*, 405 (2000), 947–951.

18 Glorot, X., Bordes, A., and Bengio, Y. Deep Sparse Rectifier Neural Networks, *Proceedings of the 14th International Conference on Artificial Intelligence and Statistics* (AISTATS). (2011).

19 Goodfellow *et al.* Maxout Networks (2013). arXiv:1302.4389v4.

20 Tufféry, S. *Data Mining and Statistics for Decision Making* (Hoboken, NJ: Wiley, 2011), § 11.8.6.

21 Nesterov, Y. A Method of Solving a Convex Programming Problem with Convergence Rate O($1/k^2$), *Soviet Mathematics Doklady*, 27 (1983), 372–376.

22 Aujol *et al.* *Optimal Convergence Rates for Nesterov Acceleration* (2018). arXiv:1805.05719.

23 Werbos, P.J. *Beyond Regression: New Tools for Prediction and Analysis in the Behavioral Sciences* (Cambridge, MA: Harvard University Press, 1974).

24 Rumelhart, D.E., Hinton, G.E., and Williams, R.J. (1986). Learning Internal Representations by Error Propagation. In Rumelhart, D.E., and McClelland, J.L. (Eds), *Parallel Distributed Processing: Explorations in the Microstructure of Cognition*. Vol. 1, *Foundations* (Cambridge, MA: MIT Press, 1986). See also the article: Rumelhart, D.E., Hinton, G.E., and Williams, R.J. Learning Representations by Back-Propagating Errors, *Nature*, 323 (1986), 533–536.

25 http://selbydavid.com/2018/01/09/neural-network/.

26 Hinton and Salakhutdinov, op. cit..

27 Kaiming *et al.* Deep Residual Learning for Image Recognition, *Conference on Computer Vision* and Pattern Recognition (2015). arXiv:1512.03385.

28 We will see later on other types of layers, for example, normalization.

29 http://cs.stanford.edu/people/karpathy/convnetjs/demo/cifar10.html.

30 http://playground.tensorflow.org/.

31 The so-called Hadamard product of two matrices.

32 Ioffe, S. and Szegedy, C. Batch Normalization: Accelerating Deep Network Training by Reducing Internal Covariate Shift (2015). arXiv:1502.03167.

33 Graham, B. Fractional Max-Pooling (2015). arXiv:1412.6071.

34 Yu, F. and Koltun, V. Multi-Scale Context Aggregation by Dilated Convolutions (2016). arXiv:1511.07122.

35 Hinton, G.E., Srivastava, N., Krizhevsky, A., Sutskever, I., and Salakhutdinov, R.R. Improving Neural Networks by Preventing Co-Adaptation of Feature Detectors (2012). arXiv:1207.0580.

36 Goodfellow, I., Bengio, Y., and Courville, A. *Deep Learning* (Cambridge, MA: MIT Press, 2016), § 7.12.

37 Wan, L., Zeiler, M., Zhang, S., LeCun, Y., and Fergus, R. Regularization of Neural Networks Using DropConnect, *Proceedings of the 30th International Conference on Machine Learning*, PMLR 28(3) (2013), 1058–1066.

38 http://proceedings.mlr.press/v28/wan13.pdf.

39 Cireşan, D.C., Meier, U., Masci, J., Gambardella, L.M., and Schmidhuber, J. High-Performance Neural Networks for Visual Object Classification (2011). arXiv:1102.0183, section 4.1.

40 Krizhevsky, A., Sutskever I., and Hinton G.E. ImageNet Classification with Deep Convolutional Neural Networks. *Proceedings of the 25th International Conference on Neural Information Processing Systems*, Vol. 1, (2012). 1097–1105.

41 Talebi, H. and Milanfar, P. Learning to Resize Images for Computer Vision Tasks (2021). arXiv:2103.09950v1.

42 Kornblith, S. and Shlens, J., and Le, Q.V. Do Better ImageNet Models Transfer Better? (2019). arXiv:1805.08974v3.

43 Duchi, J., Hazan, E., and Singer, Y. (2011). Adaptive Subgradient Methods for Online Learning and Stochastic Optimization, *Journal of Machine Learning Research*, 12 (2011), 2121–2159.

44 http://www.cs.toronto.edu/~tijmen/csc321/slides/lecture_slides_lec6.pdf

45 Tieleman, T. and Hinton, G. Lecture 6.5-rmsprop: Divide the Gradient by a Running Average f Its Recent Magnitude. *COURSERA: Neural Networks for Machine Learning*, 4(2). (2012).

46 Zeiler, M.D. ADADELTA: An Adaptive Learning Rate Method (2012). arXiv:1212.5701.

47 Kingma, D.P. and Ba, J.A.: A Method for Stochastic Optimization (2017). arXiv:1412.6980v9.

48 Ibid.

49 Dozat, T. (2016). Incorporating Nesterov Momentum into ADAM, *International Conference on Learning Representations* (ICLR).

50 See http://yann.lecun.com/exdb/mnist/.

51 LeCun, Y., Bottou, L., Bengio Y., and Haffner, P. Gradient-Based Learning Applied to Document Recognition. *Proceedings of the IEEE*, 86(11) (1998), 2278–2324, http://yann.lecun.com/exdb/publis/pdf/lecun-01a.pdf.

52 https://www.nist.gov/srd/nist-special-database-19. See also here for its import: https://github.com/Cerenaut/Preprocess-NIST-SD19.

53 https://www.kaggle.com/crowdflower/handwritten-names.

54 http://www.nlpr.ia.ac.cn/databases/handwriting/Home.html.

55 https://www.cs.toronto.edu/~kriz/cifar.html.

56 Graham, B.: Fractional Max-Pooling (2015). arXiv:1412.6071.

57 For results through 2016: http://rodrigob.github.io/are_we_there_yet/build/classification_datasets_results.html. The most recent results are here: https://paperswithcode.com/task/image-classification.

58 See http://www.image-net.org/about-stats.

59 http://www.mturk.com.

60 http://www.image-net.org/download-images.

61 Zeiler, M.D., Fergus, R.: Visualizing and Understanding Convolutional Networks (2013). arXiv:1311.2901.

62 horatio.cs.nyu.edu.

63 http://www.image-net.org/challenges/LSVRC/2013/results.php.

64 Szegedy, C., Liu, W.. Jia, Y., Sermanet, P., Reed, S., Anguelov, D., Erhan, D., Vanhoucke, V., Rabinovich, A. Going Deeper with Convolutions (2014). arXiv:1409.4842. Its name refers to Google and Yann LeCun's LeNet. It is also called Inception v1.

65 Simonyan, K. and Zisserman, A. Very Deep Convolutional Networks for Large-Scale Image Recognition (2017). arXiv:1409.1556.

66 http://www.robots.ox.ac.uk/~vgg/research/very_deep/.

67 See, for example, Dodge, S. and Karam, L. A Study and Comparison of Human and Deep Learning Recognition Performance Under Visual Distortions (2017). arXiv:1705.02498v1.

68 http://image-net.org/challenges/LSVRC/2016/results.

69 Szegedy *et al.* Inception-v4, Inception-ResNet and the Impact of Residual Connections on Learning (2016). arXiv:1602.07261v2.

70 http://image-net.org/challenges/LSVRC/2017/results.

71 Mahajan *et al.* Exploring the Limits of Weakly Supervised Pretraining (2018). arXiv:1805.00932.

72 http://benchmark.ini.rub.de/.

73 http://people.idsia.ch/~juergen/nn2012traffic.pdf.

74 Goodfellow, I.J., Bulatov, Y., Ibarz, J., Arnoud, S., and Shet, V. Multi-digit Number Recognition from Street View Imagery using Deep Convolutional Neural Networks (2013). arXiv:1312.6082.

75 Netzer, Y., Wang, T., Coates, A., Bissacco, A., Wu, B., and Ng, A.Y. Reading Digits in Natural Images with Unsupervised Feature Learning, *NIPS Workshop on Deep Learning and Unsupervised Feature Learning* (2011).

76 https://github.com/deepinsight/insightface.

77 https://research.google.com/youtube8m/.

78 See this example of Bach-style harmonization of musical notes chosen by the Internet user: https://www.google.com/doodles/celebrating-johann-sebastian-bach.

79 The "bag of words" representation of a document is obtained by adding the representations of the words that compose it. A document is thus represented by a vector whose i^{th} component is equal to the number of occurrences of the ith word in the document.

80 Hochreiter, S. and Schmidhuber, J. Long short-term memory, *Neural Computation* 9(8) (1997), 1735–1780.

81 This is sometimes also translated into short- and long-term memory networks.

82 Chung *et al.* Empirical Evaluation of Gated Recurrent Neural Networks on Sequence Modeling, *Conference on Neural Information Processing Systems* (2014). arXiv:1412.3555.

83 Khandelwal, S., Lecouteux, B., and Besacier, L. Comparing GRU and LSTM for Automatic Speech Recognition. (2016). [Research Report] LIG. 2016. hal-01633254.

84 Graves, A., Wayne, G., and Danihelka, I. Neural Turing Machines (2014). arXiv:1410.5401.

85 Cooijmans *et al.* Recurrent Batch Normalization (2017). arXiv:1603.09025.

86 Gal, Y. and Ghahramani, Z.A Theoretically Grounded Application of Dropout in Recurrent Neural Networks (2016). arXiv:1512.05287v5.

87 http://googleresearch.blogspot.fr/2014/11/a-picture-is-worth-thousand-coherent.html

88 Lin *et al.* Microsoft COCO: Common Objects in Context (2015). arXiv:1405.0312v3.

89 http://cocodataset.org/#home.

90 https://github.com/tesseract-ocr/tesseract/releases/tag/4.0.0.

91 https://cran.r-project.org/web/packages/tesseract/vignettes/intro.html.

92 Sabour, S., Froost, N., and Hinton, G.E. Dynamic Routing Between Capsules (2017). arXiv:1710.09829v2.

93 Kosiorek, A.R., Sabour, S., Whye Teh, Y., and Hinton, G.E. Stacked Capsule Autoencoders (2019). arXiv:1906.06818.

94 See https://h2o.gitbooks.io/h2o-training-day/content/hands-on_training/anomaly_detection.html.

95 Goodfellow, I., Pouget-Abadie, J., Mirza, M., Xu, B., Warde-Farley, D., Ozair, S., Courville, A., and Bengio, J. Generative Adversarial Networks, in *Advances in Neural Information Processing Systems* 27 (2014). arXiv:1406.2661 .

96 Goodfellow, I. *NIPS 2016* Tutorial: Generative Adversarial Networks (2016). arXiv:1701.00160.

97 Each player has an optimal strategy, given that of the other player. The generator has an optimal strategy given the discriminator's, and vice versa.

98 Radford, A., Metz, L., and Chintala S. Unsupervised Representation Learning with Deep Convolutional Generative Adversarial Networks (2015). arXiv:1511.06434.

99 Ibid.

100 Yu, L., Zhang, W., Wang, J., and Yu, Y. SeqGAN: Sequence Generative Adversarial Nets with Policy Gradient (2017). arXiv:1609.05473v6.

101 Huang, H., Yu, P.S., and Wang, C. An Introduction to Image Synthesis with Generative Adversarial Nets (2018). arXiv:1803.04469v2.

102 Kingma, D.P. and Welling, M. Auto-Encoding Variational Bayes (2013). arXiv:1312.6114.

103 Rezende, D.J., Mohamed, S., and Wierstra D. Stochastic Backpropagation and Approximate Inference in Deep Generative Models (2014). arXiv:1401.4082.

104 Thies, J., Zollhofer, M., Stamminger, M., Theobalt, C., and Nießner, M. Face2face: Real-Time Face Capture and Reenactment of RGB Videos. In: *Proceedings of the IEEE Conference on Computer Vision and Pattern Recognition*, (2016), 2387–2395.

105 http://host.robots.ox.ac.uk/pascal/VOC/voc2007/examples/index.html.

106 http://host.robots.ox.ac.uk/pascal/VOC/.

107 Soviany, P. and Ionescu, R.T. Optimizing the Trade-off between Single-Stage and Two-Stage Object Detectors Using Image Difficulty Prediction (2018). arXiv:1803.08707v3.

108 Girschick *et al.* Rich Feature Hierarchies for Accurate Object Detection and Semantic Segmentation, *Proceedings of the IEEE Conference on Computer Vision and Pattern Recognition* (2014). 580–587, arXiv:1311.2524.

109 Girschick, R. Fast R-CNN, *Proceedings of the IEEE International Conference on Computer Vision*: . (2015). 1440–1448, arXiv:1504.08083.

110 Ren *et al.* Faster R-CNN. Advances in Neural Information Processing Systems (2015). arXiv:1506.01497.

111 He *et al.* Mask R-CNN, *Proceedings of the IEEE International Conference on Computer Vision* (2017). 2980–2988, arXiv:1703.06870v3.

112 Redmon, J., Divvala, S., Girshick, R., and Farhadi, A. You Only Look Once: Unified, Real-Time Object Detection (2016). arXiv:1506.02640v5.

113 https://github.com/bnosac/image/tree/master/image.darknet/R.

114 https://pjreddie.com/darknet/yolo/.

115 https://pjreddie.com/darknet/imagenet/.

116 https://pjreddie.com/yolo/.

117 Redmon, J. and Farhadi, A. YOLO9000:Better, Faster, Stronger (2016). arXiv:1612.08242v1.

118 Redmon, J. and Farhadi, A. YOLOv3: An Incremental Improvement (2018). arXiv:1804.02767v1.

119 Liu, W., Anguelov, D., Erhan, D., Szegedy, C., Reed, S., Fu, C-Y. and Berg, A.C. SSD: Single Shot MultiBox Detector (2016). arXiv:1512.02325v5.

120 Lin, T.-Y., Goyal, P., Girshick, R., He, K., and Dollár, P. Focal Loss for Dense Object Detection (2017). arXiv:1708.02002.

121 Redmon, J. and Farhadi, A. YOLOv3: An Incremental Improvement (2018). arXiv:1804.02767v1.

122 Pomerleau, D.A. ALVINN, an Autonomous Land Vehicle in a Neural Network. Technical report, Carnegie Mellon University. (1989).

123 Bojarski *et al.* End to End Learning for Self-Driving Cars (2016). arXiv:1604.07316.

124 https://wayve.ai/blog/learning-to-drive-in-a-day-with-reinforcement-learning.

125 https://deepdrive.berkeley.edu/.

126 https://github.com/bdd100k/bdd100k.

127 Horikawa, T. and Kamitani, Y. Generic Decoding of Seen and Imagined Objects Using Hierarchical Visual Features, *Nature Communications*, 8 (2017). 15037.

128 Benabid, A.L., Costecalde, T., Eliseyev, A. *et al.* An Exoskeleton Controlled by an Epidural Wireless Brain-Machine Interface in a Tetraplegic Patient: A Proof-Of-Concept Demonstration, *The Lancet Neurology*, 18(12) (2019), 1112–1122.

129 Willett, F.R., Avansino, D.T., Hochberg, L.R., *et al.* High-Performance Brain-To-Text Communication Via Handwriting, *Nature*, 593 (2021). 249–254.

130 Gatys, L.A., Ecker, A.S., and Bethge, M.A Neural Algorithm of Artistic Style (2015). arXiv:1508.06576.

131 https://no2147483647.wordpress.com/2015/12/21/deep-learning-for-hackers-with-mxnet-2/.

132 Chollet, F. and Allaire, J.J. *Deep Learning with R* (Shelter Island, NY: Manning, 2018). See Section 8.3.3.

133 Read the interesting article by Pierre Nolot: https://interstices.info/jcms/int_65557/les-echecs-electroniques-histoire-d-une-confrontation-entre-l-humain-et-la-machine.

134 Not totally "brute," because the algorithms are sufficiently elaborate to know not to explore all the possibilities and to prune the configurations considered less interesting.

135 Silver *et al.* Mastering the Game of Go with Deep Neural Networks and Tree Search, *Nature*, 529(7587) (2016), 484–489.

136 Silver *et al.* Mastering Chess and Shogi by Self-Play with a General Reinforcement Learning Algorithm (2017). arXiv:1712.01815v1.

137 2016 Top Chess Engine Championship (TCEC) champion. But it seems that in the comparison with AlphaZero, Stockfish was not used to its best advantage: the version used wasn't the most recent, thinking time with a limit of one minute per move instead of a global limit, and a much less powerful machine than AlphaZero.

138 Schrittwieser, J., Antonoglou, I., Hubert, T., *et al.* Mastering Atari, Go, Chess and Shogi by Planning with a Learned Model, *Nature*, 588 (2020), 604–609. Also at: arXiv:1911.08265.

139 Ventos *et al.* Construction and Elicitation of a Black Box Model in the Game of Bridge (2022). arXiv:2005.01633v2.

140 Brown, N. and Sandholm, T. Superhuman AI for Multiplayer Poker, *Science* (2019). eaay2400. 10.1126/science.aay2400.

141 https://becominghuman.ai/lets-build-an-atari-ai-part-0-intro-to-rl-9b2c5336e0ec.

142 https://www.wired.com/story/crossword-ai-humans-way-with-words/.

8

Deep Learning for Computer Vision

Many libraries of deep learning algorithms have been written in C++ with a Python interface, but a growing number are also usable with R.[1] In this chapter, we see how to program deep neural network models in a few lines of code in order to solve computer vision problems, and we give some indications on the configurations and parameters allowing their optimization. In particular, we detail the configuration of a Windows machine for the use of a graphics processing unit (GPU) in deep learning. We also show how to do machine learning in a cloud, using the example of Kaggle, RStudio Cloud, and Google Colab and its Jupyter notebooks in Python. We implement the operations seen in Chapter 7: pooling, batch normalization, dropout, transfer learning, etc. We will see how effective they are for improving computer vision. Natural language processing with deep neural networks will be studied in Chapter 9.

8.1 Deep Learning Libraries

Before presenting the implementation of some of them in R (and in Python in Section 8.6.1), we start by comparing in Table 8.1 four of the main deep neural network libraries: MXNet, TensorFlow, Theano, and Torch. They can be used for computer vision, discussed in this chapter, but also for natural language processing, discussed in Chapter 9.

We mention Theano for its historical importance, even though it now seems destined to disappear, as mentioned in Section 7.2. The two libraries that are now in full expansion are TensorFlow and Torch, or rather PyTorch, which is the Python implementation of Torch and which absorbed the Caffe2 library in March 2018. Their competition is even more intense as TensorFlow is supported by Google and PyTorch by Meta. Their main difference was initially that TensorFlow models are described by static symbolic graphs that need to be "compiled" before the model is learned, while PyTorch models are described by NumPy-like Python code that is executed sequentially and for that reason is easier to debug since it can be executed step-by-step. Besides being more familiar to Python programmers, PyTorch code is also simpler, which favors its popularity, and allows more flexibility to create customized deep neural network architectures. It will probably be more appreciated by researchers. It is said to be faster than Keras but perhaps not faster than TensorFlow. For its part, TensorFlow has some additional features and probably a better deployment

Deep Learning: From Big Data to Artificial Intelligence with R, First Edition. Stéphane Tufféry.
© 2023 John Wiley & Sons Ltd. Published 2023 by John Wiley & Sons Ltd.
Companion website: www.wiley.com/go/Tuffery/DeepLearning

Table 8.1 Deep learning libraries.

Software	MXNet	TensorFlow	Theano	Torch
Creator (date)	DMLC (2015)	Google Brain Team (2015)	University of Montreal (2007–2017)	R. Collobert, K. Kavukcuoglu, C. Farabet (2002)
Open source	Yes	Yes	Yes	Yes
Platform	Linux, macOS, Windows, AWS, Android, iOS, JavaScript	Linux, macOS, Windows	Multiple	Linux, macOS, Android, iOS
Language	C++11	C++ (and Python)	Python	C, Lua
Interface	C++, Python, Julia, Matlab, JavaScript, R, Scala, Go	Python, C/C++, Java, R, Go	Python	LuaJT
Multi-GPU	Yes	Yes	Yes	Yes
Pre-trained models	Yes	Yes	*Model Zoo* of the *Lasagna* Library	Yes
Recurrent networks	Yes	Yes	Yes	Yes
Convolutional networks	Yes	Yes	Yes	Yes
Transformer models	Gluon API	Yes	No	Yes
Programming	Mixed ("mix-net")	Symbolic / Imperative	Symbolic	Imperative

capacity. Its handling is also facilitated by TensorBoard for the visualization of results and by the Keras interface, that we will present.

Recently, there has been a convergence of TensorFlow and PyTorch. On the one hand, PyTorch has become widely cited in the research world and has made a significant breakthrough into the business world, facilitated by the creation of the Captum library that makes it easier to read results, and the fastai interface that makes it easy to create advanced networks, as Keras does for TensorFlow. On the other hand, TensorFlow version 2.0 (September 2019) introduced *eager execution*, which is close to the imperative and dynamic programming of PyTorch and avoids the compilation of a static graph.

As for MXNet, which combines these two approaches (hence its name), it is currently, despite its qualities that we will see, rather an outsider. But everything we have just written about the different deep learning libraries can change quickly.

We will see that these libraries are not only usable with dedicated packages, including `torch` (or `PyTorch`), `mxnet`, `tensorflow` and `keras`, but also in the RStudio integrated development environment (IDE), and with the `h2o.deepwater()` function that gives H2O access to the TensorFlow, MXNet and Caffe libraries, or at least some of their functions.[2]

8.2 MXNet

MXNet[3] is a deep learning project written in C++11, portable (including on Android smartphones) and usable with Python, R, Julia, Go, JavaScript, in Linux, macOS, and Windows[4] environments. It has been developed as XGBoost in the framework of the open source project DMLC: Distributed (Deep) Machine Learning Common.

It benefits from optimized memory management, and can gain in speed thanks to GPU calculations on a machine that is equipped with one. But it is of course possible to perform all calculations in CPU. It is provided with a library of models.[5]

MXNet can be used in Python and in R with the mxnet package[6] which can be easily installed on Windows if you limit yourself to CPU calculations and if you use the compiled sources of mxnet rather than compiling them yourself:

```
> cran <- getOption("repos")
> cran["dmlc"] <- "https://apache-mxnet.s3-
  accelerate.dualstack.amazonaws.com/R/CRAN/"
> options(repos = cran)
> install.packages("mxnet")
```

Installing the GPU (and also CPU) capable version of mxnet is also straightforward, but it must be preceded by some preliminary configuration of the machine which is a bit complex, especially on Windows. These preliminaries are described in Section 8.4. Once they have been accomplished, the installation of the GPU version of the mxnet package is done with the following lines:

```
> cran <- getOption("repos")
> cran["dmlc"] <- "https://apache-mxnet.s3-
  accelerate.dualstack.amazonaws.com/R/CRAN/GPU/cu90"
> options(repos = cran)
> install.packages("mxnet")
```

We have the choice of the version of the CUDA toolkit: 10.0, 10.2 or 11.0 with the version 1.8.0 of the package in September 2021.

8.2.1 General Information about MXNet

MXNet allows the implementation of various and complex neural network structures. The input data must be matrices or tensors, which are the generalization of matrices to more than two dimensions.

Thus, MXNet allows a multilayer perceptron with its mx.mlp() function to be created. Its main parameters are the following:

- the number of units in each hidden layer (hidden_node parameter);
- the number of units in the output layer (out_node parameter);
- the activation function of hidden layers / output layer (parameters activation / out_activation, default value tanh / softmax);
- the dropout rate of the last hidden layer (equal to 0 by default);

- the learning rate;
- the momentum;
- the number of epochs for training (parameter `num.round`);
- the batch size (parameter `array.batch.size`);
- calculations in CPU (default) or GPU (`ctx` parameter).

Here is an example of MXNet code for a perceptron consisting of a ten-unit hidden layer and a ten-unit output layer for classification:

```
> model <- mx.mlp(train.x, train.y, hidden_node=10,
    out_node=10, out_activation="softmax", num.round=20,
    array.batch.size=128, learning.rate=0.07, momentum=0.9,
    eval.metric=mx.metric.accuracy)
```

Another way to build a perceptron is to define its elements one-by-one by functions `mx.symbol.xxx`.[6] In fact, the previous `mx.mlp()` function automatically generates the following elements:

```
# input data
> data <- mx.symbol.Variable("data")
# 10 units hidden layer
> fc1 <- mx.symbol.FullyConnected(data, name="fc1", num_hidden=100)
# hidden layer activation function
> act1 <- mx.symbol.Activation(fc1, name="relu1", act_type="relu")
# 10 units hidden layer
> fc2 <- mx.symbol.FullyConnected(act1, name="fc3", num_hidden=10)
> out <- mx.symbol.SoftmaxOutput(fc2, name="sm")
```

The training of the network to maximize the rate of good classification is done as follows:

```
> model <- mx.model.FeedForward.create(out, X=train.x,
    y=train.y, ctx=mx.cpu(), num.round=20, array.batch.size=128,
    learning.rate=0.07, momentum=0.9,
    eval.metric=mx.metric.accuracy)
```

Predictions are then made on a test sample:

```
> preds <- predict(model, test.x)
```

The `predict()` function produces a matrix with one row per class (digit) to be predicted and one column per case (image), which is transposed to obtain a matrix with one row per image, and the predicted digit corresponds to the column of maximum probability, subtracting 1 as the digits go from 0 to 9 and the column numbers from 1 to 10:

```
> pred.label <- max.col(t(preds)) - 1
```

8.2.2 Creating a Convolutional Network with MXNet

We then turn to the programming of a convolutional network, taking the example of a network such as LeNet[7] or one of its successors, applied to MNIST handwritten digit recognition (Section 6.1).

We start by reading the data, which are first transposed to have the 784 pixels in rows and one digit image per column. Then these data are transformed into the form expected by the MXNet convolution operator, namely tensors of order 4: width, height, channel, image number. Here, the channel is always "1" because the images are not in color but in grayscale, from 0 to 255, which we normalize between 0 and 1. There would be three channels (red, green, blue) for color images.

```
> train <- read.csv("/home/.../mnist_train.csv", header=TRUE)
> test <- read.csv("/home/.../mnist_test.csv", header=TRUE)
> train.x <- train[,-1]
> train.x <- t(train.x/255)
> train.y <- train[,1]
> test.x  <- test[,-1]
> test.x  <- t(test.x/255)
> train.array <- train.x
> dim(train.array) <- c(28, 28, 1, ncol(train.x))
> test.array <- test.x
> dim(test.array) <- c(28, 28, 1, ncol(test.x))
```

The images read in this way are rotated by 90° and the first two components of the tensor, i.e. the height and width, must be transposed by the aperm() function to straighten the images and obtain Figure 8.1. We will not do this here, as it is sufficient for our tests that the training and test sets are in the same format. It is the transformation of the train.x matrix into a train.array tensor that causes this rotation.

Figure 8.1 MNIST images.

Here is the code to display the first hundred digits of the base:

```
> train.array <- aperm(train.array,c(2,1,3,4))
> old <- par(no.readonly = TRUE)
> par(mfrow = c(10,10), mai = c(0,0,0,0))
> for(i in 1:100) {
+    plot(as.raster(train.array[,,,i]))
+    text(3, 0, train.y[i], cex = 2, col = gray(0.75),
        font=3, pos = c(3,4))
+ }
> par(old)
```

We will code with MXNet the neural network of the type LeNet (Section 7.15) whose formal definition is:

```
INPUT -> [CONV -> BN -> ACTI -> POOL]*2 -> FC -> BN ->
   ACTI -> FC -> SOFTMAX -> OUTPUT
```

Compared to a true LeNet network, however, we have added a batch normalization layer (Section 7.8) before each activation. We will see its effect later on.

```
> # input
> data <- mx.symbol.Variable('data')
> # first convolution layer
> conv1 <- mx.symbol.Convolution(data=data, kernel=c(5,5),
   num_filter=20)
> norm1 <- mx.symbol.BatchNorm(data=conv1)
> acti1 <- mx.symbol.Activation(data=norm1, act_type="relu")
> pool1 <- mx.symbol.Pooling(data=acti1, pool_type="max",
   kernel=c(3,3), stride=c(2,2))
> # second convolution layer
> conv2 <- mx.symbol.Convolution(data=pool1, kernel=c(5,5),
   num_filter=60)
> norm2 <- mx.symbol.BatchNorm(data=conv2)
> acti2 <- mx.symbol.Activation(data=norm2, act_type="relu")
> pool2 <- mx.symbol.Pooling(data=acti2, pool_type="max",
   kernel=c(3,3), stride=c(2,2))
> # first fully connected layer
> flatten <- mx.symbol.Flatten(data=pool2)
> drp    <- mx.symbol.Dropout(data=flatten, p=0.1)
> fc1    <- mx.symbol.FullyConnected(data=drp, num_hidden=600)
> norm3 <- mx.symbol.BatchNorm(data=fc1)
> acti3 <- mx.symbol.Activation(data=norm3, act_type="relu")
> # second fully connected layer
> fc2 <- mx.symbol.FullyConnected(data=acti3, num_hidden=10)
> # output
> lenet <- mx.symbol.SoftmaxOutput(data=fc2)
```

The network thus constructed consists of two convolution layers and two fully connected layers, separated by a dropout layer, and its structure can be noted: 20C5-BN-P-60C5-BN-P-DO-600FC-10.

Each convolution layer has:

- a 5 × 5 filter (and 20 cards for the first layer, 60 cards for the second)

```
mx.symbol.Convolution(data=, kernel=c(5,5), num_filter=20)
```

- batch normalization

```
mx.symbol.BatchNorm(data=)
```

- a ReLU activation function

```
mx.symbol.Activation(data=, act_type="relu")
```

- an overlapping max pooling of size (3,3) and stride (2,2)

```
mx.symbol.Pooling(data=, pool_type="max", kernel=c(3,3),
stride=c(2,2))
```

Convolution layers are followed by a 10% dropout:

```
mx.symbol.Dropout(data=, p=0.1)
```

The fully connected layers have 600 and 10 units:

```
mx.symbol.FullyConnected(data=, num_hidden=600)
mx.symbol.FullyConnected(data=, num_hidden=10)
```

There is batch normalization and ReLU activation between the two fully connected layers, and a softmax function between the last hidden layer and the output layer:

```
mx.symbol.BatchNorm(data=)
mx.symbol.Activation(data=, act_type="relu")
mx.symbol.SoftmaxOutput(data=)
```

The last convolution layer and the first fully connected layer are connected by a mandatory mx.symbol.Flatten step, as this is to connect a 2D or 3D convolution layer (height, width, channel) to a 1D fully connected layer, as illustrated in Figure 8.2. Note that each
unit of the flattening layer is connected to a single unit of the previous pooling layer, while each unit of a dense (fully connected) layer is connected to all the units of the previous layer, and in particular the flattening layer. This layer X of dimension 1 is connected to the output layer and the class to predict Y by a classical model $Y = f(X)$.

The essential function to create convolutional networks is the mxnet.symbol.Convolution() function which applies convolution to the input data and possibly adds a bias terme. Its main parameters are:

- data: input data;
- bias;
- kernel: size (y, x) of the convolution kernel;

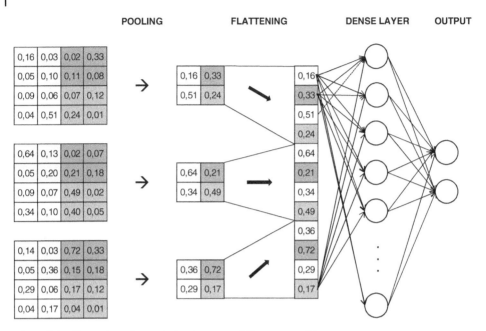

Figure 8.2 Flattening of convolution layers on fully connected layers.

- `stride`: stride (y, x) of convolution;
- `dilate`: coefficient (y, x) of dilation (see Section 7.10);
- `pad`: padding (y, x) of convolution;
- `num_filter`: number > 0 of convolution kernels;
- `workspace`: temporary space for convolution (default = 1024 MB), which can be reduced if memory is lacking, for example in a GPU calculation with a graphics card of limited capacity.

About padding (Section 7.6), we recall that a padding equal to $(n-1)/2$ on an $n \times n$ filter does not reduce the image size in the convolution, and that without padding (with a stride = 1), the image size is reduced from N to $(N - n + 1)$.

Therefore, the following values do not reduce the size of the images:

- `kernel = c(3,3), pad = c(1,1)`
- `kernel = c(5,5), pad = c(2,2).`

Once the convolutional network is defined, we move on to its training. First, we define the hardware configuration that will be used for the calculations. If, for example, we are doing CPU computations on 8 threads (execution sequences), we indicate it as follows:

```
> device <- lapply(0:7, function(i) { mx.cpu(i) })
```

If we want to perform GPU computations on 16 threads, we specify it as follows:

```
> device <- lapply(0:15, function(i) { mx.gpu(i) })
```

We can then define the training and specify the search for parameters that minimize the error. The following code creates a function that executes the mx.model.FeedForward.create() function dedicated to training a network that has as parameters the number of epochs nr, the learning rate lr and the momentum mm. The hardware configuration is the one just defined and the batches are composed of 128 images. With the parameter wd we specify a weight decay in L^2 norm. If the optimizer parameter is not specified, the learning algorithm will be the stochastic gradient (sgd). We ensure the reproducibility of the results with the mx.set.seed() function.

At the end of each epoch, the statement epoch.end.callback = mx.callback.log.train.metric(100) displays the rate of good classification in training and test, which allows us to track its evolution over the course of training. We could have the same information at the end of each iteration by replacing epoch.end.callback with batch.end.callback.

We could also save the model every epoch, using the statement epoch.end.callback = mx.callback.save.checkpoint("mnist"), which would create files mnist-0001.params, mnist-0002.params, mnist-0003.params...

These are predefined callback functions,[8] but you can create them yourself, to perform a treatment at the end of each period, if you want to program the interruption of the training or the update of the learning rate.

The following function also performs, after training the network, the prediction of the network on the test set, the calculation and display of the confusion matrix between real and predicted digits, and the calculation and display of the error rate:

```
> rnlenet <- function(nr = 10, lr = 0.05, mm = 0.9) {
+ mx.set.seed(235)
+ model   <- mx.model.FeedForward.create(lenet,
+   X = train.array, y = train.y,
+   ctx = device, num.round = nr, array.batch.size = 128,
+   learning.rate = lr, momentum = mm, wd = 0.00001,
+   eval.metric = mx.metric.accuracy,
+   epoch.end.callback=mx.callback.log.train.metric(100))
+ preds <- predict(model, test.array)
+ pred.label <- max.col(t(preds)) - 1
+ print(table(test$label,pred.label))
+ erreur <- (nrow(test)-sum(diag(table(test$label,pred.label))))/nrow(test)
+ preds <- predict(model, test.array)
+ print(erreur)
+ return(erreur)
+ }
```

The graph.viz() function of the mxnet package is used to represent the constructed network (Figure 8.3):

```
> graph.viz(model$symbol)
```

The search for parameters minimizing the error rate on the test set can be done by exploring a set of possible values of the learning rate and the momentum, using the previously defined function rnlenet(), whose parameters are the number of iterations, the learning rate (vector c1), and the momentum (vector c2).

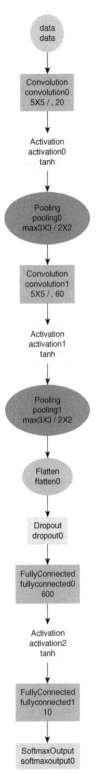

Figure 8.3 Convolutional neural network created with MXNet.

```
> c1 <- c(0.005,seq(0.01,0.04,0.01),seq(0.05,0.5,0.05))
> c2 <- seq(0.5,1,0.05)
> lenet.par   <- matrix(NA,length(c1),length(c2))
> lenet.res   <- matrix(NA,length(c1),length(c2))
> for (i in 1:length(c1)) {
+    for (j in 1:length(c2)) {
+      lenet.par[i,j] <- paste(c1[i],c2[j],collapse=" ")
+      lenet.res[i,j] <- rnlenet(30,c1[i],c2[j])
+ }
+ }
> lenet.par[which(lenet.res==min(lenet.res), arr.ind = T)]
```

Computing all possible combinations of parameters in this way may lead to a solution that will be satisfactory but probably not optimal, and will also involve long computations. It is better to implement one of the adaptive learning algorithms (Section 7.14) implemented in MXNet. The following example uses the RMSprop algorithm through the `optimizer="rmsprop"` specification. One could similarly use the ADAGRAD, ADADELTA, and ADAM algorithms.

The training of the neural network defined in the previous pages, with pooling and batch normalization, is then performed:

```
> logger <- mx.metric.logger$new()
> mx.set.seed(235)
> system.time(model <- mx.model.FeedForward.create(symbol=lenet,
    X=train.array, y=train.y, ctx=device, num.round=50,
    array.batch.size=128, optimizer="rmsprop",
    eval.data=list(data=test.array, label=test$label),
    wd=0.001, eval.metric = mx.metric.accuracy, epoch.end.
    callback = mx.callback.log.train.metric(100, logger)))
Auto-select kvstore type = local_update_cpu
Start training with 4 devices
[1]  Train-accuracy=0.964760283119658
[1]  Validation-accuracy=0.989319620253165
[2]  Train-accuracy=0.986640458422175
[2]  Validation-accuracy=0.99189082278481
[3]  Train-accuracy=0.991038113006397
[3]  Validation-accuracy=0.992088607594937
[4]  Train-accuracy=0.993003731343284
[4]  Validation-accuracy=0.993473101265823
...
[49] Train-accuracy=0.999966684434968
[49] Validation-accuracy=0.995945411392405
[50] Train-accuracy=0.999966684434968
[50] Validation-accuracy=0.995450949367089
utilisateur     système       écoulé
   10632.78     3398.26       3809.39
```

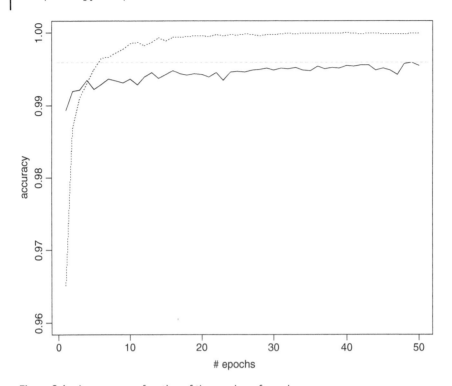

Figure 8.4 Accuracy as a function of the number of epochs.

At the end of each epoch, the instruction `epoch.end.callback = mx.callback.`
`log.train.metric(100, logger)` records the correct classification rate (accuracy)
in the previously declared `logger` file, which then allows us to display the evolution of
the accuracy in training (`logger$train`) and in test (`logger$eval`) as a function of
the number of epochs. Figure 8.4 shows the test accuracy as a solid line, and the training
accuracy as a dotted line.

```
> plot(logger$eval, type="l", ylim=c(0.96,1), ylab="accuracy",
    xlab="# epochs")
> abline(h=logger$eval[which.max(logger$eval)], lty=2)
> lines(logger$train, lty=3)
```

We apply the model from the training to the test set to calculate the confusion matrix:

```
> preds <- predict(model, test.array)
> pred.label <- max.col(t(preds)) - 1
> table(test$label,pred.label)
   pred.label
        0    1    2    3    4    5    6    7    8    9
   0  978    0    0    0    0    0    1    1    0    0
   1    0 1134    0    0    0    0    0    1    0    0
   2    1    0 1030    0    0    0    0    1    0    0
   3    0    0    1 1007    0    1    0    0    1    0
```

```
4     0     0     0     0   979     0     1     0     0     2
5     1     0     0     6     0   882     1     1     0     1
6     4     1     0     0     1     1   949     0     2     0
7     0     1     1     0     0     0     0  1024     0     2
8     1     1     0     0     0     0     0     0   971     1
9     1     0     0     0     3     1     0     2     1  1001
> sum(pred.label != test$label) / nrow(test)
[1] 0.0045
```

In just over an hour (on CPU) we obtained a model with an error rate on the test set as low as 0.45%.

We also tested variants of the previous neural network and other learning parameters, and plotted the corresponding correct classification rates on the test set in Figure 8.5, using the following code:

```
> library(RColorBrewer)
> CL <- brewer.pal(10, "Spectral")
> trait <- 1
> ggplot() +
+    geom_line(aes(seq(2,50), logger1$eval[2:50]), colour=CL[1],
         size=trait, linetype=1) +
+    geom_line(aes(seq(2,50), logger2$eval[2:50]), colour=CL[2],
         size=trait, linetype=2) +
...
+    xlab("# epochs") + ylab("accuracy") +
```

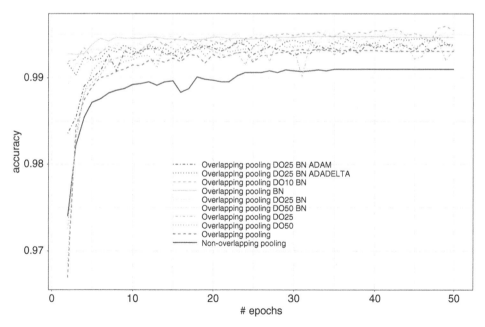

Figure 8.5 Comparison of the accuracy of several variants.

```
+    theme_bw() + theme(axis.text = element_text(size = 15)) +
        theme(axis.title = element_text(size = 18)) +
+    annotate("segment", x=15, xend=18, y=.971, yend=.971,
        colour=CL[1], size=trait, linetype=1) +
+    annotate("text", x=20, hjust="left", y=.971, label=
        "Non-overlapping pooling", colour="black", size=6) +
+    annotate("segment", x=15, xend=18, y=.972, yend=.972,
        colour=CL[2], size=trait, linetype=2) +
+    annotate("text", x=20, hjust="left", y=.972,
        label="Overlapping pooling", colour="black", size=6) +
...
```

The lowest curve, with a solid line, is obtained by the previous convolutional network from which the dropout and batch normalization layers have been removed, and in which the pooling is without overlap. This is the following basic network:

```
# input
data <- mx.symbol.Variable('data')
# first convolution layer
conv1 <- mx.symbol.Convolution(data=data, kernel=c(5,5),
    num_filter=20)
acti1 <- mx.symbol.Activation(data=conv1, act_type="relu")
pool1 <- mx.symbol.Pooling(data=acti1, pool_type="max",
    kernel=c(2,2), stride=c(2,2))
# second convolution layer
conv2 <- mx.symbol.Convolution(data=pool1, kernel=c(5,5),
    num_filter=60)
acti2 <- mx.symbol.Activation(data=conv2, act_type="relu")
pool2 <- mx.symbol.Pooling(data=acti2, pool_type="max",
    kernel=c(2,2), stride=c(2,2))
# first fully connected layer
flatten <- mx.symbol.Flatten(data=pool2)
#drp <- mx.symbol.Dropout(data=flatten, p=0.5)
#fc1 <- mx.symbol.FullyConnected(data=drp, num_hidden=500)
fc1 <- mx.symbol.FullyConnected(data=flatten, num_hidden=600)
acti3 <- mx.symbol.Activation(data=fc1, act_type="relu")
# second fully connected layer
fc2 <- mx.symbol.FullyConnected(data=acti3, num_hidden=10)
# output
lenet1 <- mx.symbol.SoftmaxOutput(data=fc2)
```

We then see that the overlapping pooling (`kernel=c(3,3)`, `stride=c(2,2)`) brings in a few epochs a very important gain compared to the non-overlapping pooling. The addition of the batch normalization layers, before each activation, brings a very important gain from the first epochs (which makes it the best model at the beginning) and the accuracy stabilizes from the 25th epoch, significantly above the accuracy of a neural network with pooling and without batch normalization.

Adding the dropout layer before the fully connected layer also improves the accuracy (correct classification rate) but less than batch normalization and not as consistently, due to the very principle of dropout which makes the correct classification rate fluctuate a bit over the epochs. The best models are those that combine dropout and batch normalization. It is therefore not always true that the regularization provided by batch normalization makes dropout unnecessary, as is sometimes thought. However, as indicated in the literature,[9] the use of batch normalization can decrease the dropout rate, which is observed here since the model with a batch normalization and a dropout rate of 10% has the best good classification rate, slightly higher than the models with rates of 25% and 50%. We have seen that this model reaches the excellent good classification rate of 99.59% on the 49th epoch. It is the one with the caption "Overlapping pooling DO10 BN." The adaptive algorithms ADADELTA and ADAM perform worse here than RMSprop. We have not reported the results of the ADAGRAD algorithm, but they are much worse.

8.2.3 Model Management with MXNet

It is possible to save a model created with `mxnet` and then apply it to other data.

The command `mx.model.save(model, xx, nnnn)` saves the model by creating two files: `xx-symbol.json` and `xx-nnn.params`:

```
> mx.model.save(model, 50, 1)
```

We can import these files with the command `mx.model.load(xx, iteration = nnnn)`:

```
> model.import <- mx.model.load("50", iteration = 1)
```

We can then apply the imported model to an image saved in JPEG format. Here is how. First, we load a package for image processing:

```
> library(imager)
```

Then we load an image that we created with Paint software (Figure 8.6). The four dimensions of the image's CImg class[10] are width, height, time, and channel. Here, the "time" dimension is "1" since the image is unique. The channel is "3" because the image is *a priori* in color:

```
> im <- load.image("digit4.jpg")
> dim(im)
[1] 1195  552    1    3
```

Figure 8.6 Handwritten number.

We invert the colors to have white on a black background, while we have drawn a black digit on a white background. We resize the image to 28 × 28 pixels, the same size as the MNIST database that was used to train the model. We then remove the colors using the `grayscale` command to keep only one channel. Then, we normalize the pixels so that they are between 0 and 1:

```
> im <- 1 - im
> resized <- resize(im, 28, 28)
> resized <- grayscale(resized)
> resized <- resized/max(resized)
```

We then transform the image into a tensor, which is the format expected by `mxnet`. Its dimension (28, 28, 1, 1) is the one treated by the model:

```
> test.array <- as.array(resized)
> dim(test.array)
[1] 28 28  1  1
```

But as mentioned in Section 8.2.2, the tensor transformation causes a 90° rotation of the image, as one could see by performing the following function:

```
> plot(as.raster(test.array[,,,1]))
```

This is not a problem, on the contrary, since the model was trained on MNIST data whose tensor loading for MXNet also has the same rotation. So we apply this model to the image and check that it has predicted the correct digit:

```
> preds <- predict(model.import, test.array)
> (pred.label <- max.col(t(preds)) - 1)
> 4
```

If one wanted to apply a model trained on images without rotation to this tensor (which is the case of the example with Keras in Section 8.3), one would have to transpose the height and width of the image into the tensor:

```
> pred <- predict_classes(model, aperm(test.array,c(1,3,2,4)))
```

It can be noted that the `image_to_array()` function of the `keras` package does not cause any rotation of the image during its transformation into a 3D tensor:

```
> img <- image_load("digit4.jpg", target_size = c(28,28),
    grayscale = TRUE)
> x <- image_to_array(img)
```

8.2.4 CIFAR-10 Image Recognition with MXNet

We have already mentioned (Section 7.15) the CIFAR-10 dataset, which is one of the best known and most used for testing image recognition algorithms. These images belong to ten classes that we need to predict well: airplane (class 0), car (1), bird (2), cat (3), deer (4), dog (5), frog (6), horse (7), boat (8) and truck (9).

The CIFAR-10 data can be retrieved in a format for Python on the CIFAR website,[11] but we extracted them from the dataset stored in the `keras` package to save them in CSV format, in six files: one file per color and per sample (training, test). Here is how we proceed for the training set.

The imported object `cifar10` is a list from which we extract the tensor `cifar10$train$x/255` of dimension (50000, 32, 32, 3). The division by 255 aims to set the pixels between 0 and 1. The instruction `adply(x_train[,,,1], c(2,3))` allows the first channel (red) `x_train[,,,1]`, which is a tensor (50000, 32, 32), to be transformed into a data frame of dimension (32 × 32, 50000), thanks to the function `adply()` of the package `plyr`. This data frame is then transposed into a matrix (50000, 32 × 32). We proceed in the same way for the green and blue channels:

```
> library(keras)
> cifar10 <- dataset_cifar10()
> x_train <- cifar10$train$x/255
> library(plyr)
> cifar <- t(adply(x_train[,,,1], c(2,3), .id=NULL))
> cifar <- data.frame("label"=cifar10$train$y, cifar)
> fwrite(cifar, "D:/Data/Images/CIFAR10/red_data_train.csv")
> cifar <- t(adply(x_train[,,,2], c(2,3), .id=NULL))
> cifar <- data.frame("label"=cifar10$train$y, cifar)
> fwrite(cifar, "D:/Data/Images/CIFAR10/green_data_train.csv")
> cifar <- t(adply(x_train[,,,3], c(2,3), .id=NULL))
> cifar <- data.frame("label"=cifar10$train$y, cifar)
> fwrite(cifar, "D:/Data/Images/CIFAR10/blue_data_train.csv")
```

A faster and less memory-intensive variant is obtained by replacing the `adply()` function of the `plyr` package with the `dcast()` function of the `data.table` package. We start by creating a data table that has 50000 × 32 × 32 rows and four columns. These four columns are V1 the image number (between 1 and 50000), V2 and V3 the pixel width and height indices (between 1 and 32), and `value` the pixel value. The function `dcast(DT, V1 ~ V3 + V2, value.var = "value")` then transforms this DT table into a data table that has 50000 rows (one per value of V1 on the left of the formula) and 32 × 32 columns (one per combination of V3 and V2 on the right of the formula), plus a first column (which we delete) containing the image number. The symbol `~ V3 + V2` in the `dcast()` function is equivalent to the symbol `c(2,3)` in the `adply()` function.

```
> DT <- as.data.table(x_train[,,,1])
> head(DT)
   V1 V2 V3       value
1:  1  1  1 0.2313725
2:  1  1  2 0.1686275
3:  1  1  3 0.1960784
4:  1  1  4 0.2666667
5:  1  1  5 0.3843137
6:  1  1  6 0.4666667
> cifar <- dcast(DT, V1 ~ V3 + V2, value.var = "value")[,-1]
> cifar <- data.table("label"=cifar10$train$y, cifar)
```

While this function dcast() allows a data table to be very quickly reorganized from a long format to a wide format, the function melt() allows a data table to be very quickly reorganized from a wide format to a long format.

We then read the six CSV files with the data.table package to reconstruct the CIFAR-10 database, and then transform the matrices into tensors, which is necessary for the convolution operator of mxnet. The channel variable here is set to "3" since the CIFAR-10 images are in color.

```
> cifar_red    <- fread("D:/Data/Images/CIFAR10/red_data_train.csv",
  header=TRUE)
> cifar_green  <- fread("D:/Data/Images/CIFAR10/green_data_train.csv",
  header=TRUE)
> cifar_blue   <- fread("D:/Data/Images/CIFAR10/blue_data_train.csv",
  header=TRUE)
> train.y      <- cifar_red[1:50000,1]
> train.array  <- array(data = NA, dim = c(32, 32, 3, 50000))
> train.array[,,1,] <- t(cifar_red[1:50000,-1])
> train.array[,,2,] <- t(cifar_green[1:50000,-1])
> train.array[,,3,] <- t(cifar_blue[1:50000,-1])
```

We do the same for the test set.

We then build a convolutional neural network, including batch normalization layers (Section 7.8) which also allow us to significantly reduce the error rate of the network. Note in the following code the use of the %>% (*pipe*) symbol of the dplyr package to chain the instructions:

```
> library(dplyr)
> cnn8 <- mx.symbol.Variable('data') %>%
+   # first convolution layer
+   mx.symbol.Convolution(kernel=c(3,3), pad=c(1,1), num_filter=64) %>%
+   mx.symbol.BatchNorm() %>%
+   mx.symbol.Activation(act_type="relu") %>%
+   # second convolution layer
+   mx.symbol.Convolution(kernel=c(3,3), pad=c(1,1), num_filter=64) %>%
+   mx.symbol.BatchNorm() %>%
+   mx.symbol.Activation(act_type="relu") %>%
+   mx.symbol.Pooling(pool_type="max", kernel=c(2,2), stride=c(2,2)) %>%
+   mx.symbol.Dropout(p=0.2) %>%
+   # third convolution layer
+   mx.symbol.Convolution(kernel=c(3,3), pad=c(1,1), num_filter=128) %>%
+   mx.symbol.BatchNorm() %>%
+   mx.symbol.Activation(act_type="relu") %>%
+   # fourth convolution layer
+   mx.symbol.Convolution(kernel=c(3,3), pad=c(1,1), num_filter=128) %>%
+   mx.symbol.BatchNorm() %>%
+   mx.symbol.Activation(act_type="relu") %>%
+   mx.symbol.Pooling(pool_type="max", kernel=c(2,2), stride=c(2,2)) %>%
+   mx.symbol.Dropout(p=0.2) %>%
+   # fifth convolution layer
```

```
+   mx.symbol.Convolution(kernel=c(3,3), pad=c(1,1), num_filter=256) %>%
+   mx.symbol.BatchNorm() %>%
+   mx.symbol.Activation(act_type="relu") %>%
+   # sixth convolution layer
+   mx.symbol.Convolution(kernel=c(3,3), pad=c(1,1), num_filter=256) %>%
+   mx.symbol.BatchNorm() %>%
+   mx.symbol.Activation(act_type="relu") %>%
+   mx.symbol.Pooling(pool_type="max", kernel=c(2,2), stride=c(2,2)) %>%
+   mx.symbol.Dropout(p=0.2) %>%
+   # first fully connected layer
+   mx.symbol.Flatten() %>%
+   mx.symbol.Dropout(p=0.5) %>%
+   mx.symbol.FullyConnected(num_hidden=512) %>%
+   mx.symbol.BatchNorm() %>%
+   mx.symbol.Activation(act_type="relu") %>%
+   # second fully connected layer
+   mx.symbol.Dropout(p=0.5) %>%
+   mx.symbol.FullyConnected(num_hidden=512) %>%
+   mx.symbol.BatchNorm() %>%
+   mx.symbol.Activation(act_type="relu") %>%
+   # output
+   mx.symbol.FullyConnected(num_hidden=10) %>%
+   mx.symbol.SoftmaxOutput()
```

We start the training of the network, recording as before the accuracy as a function of the number of epochs. We make 50 epochs:

```
> device <- lapply(0:3, function(i) { mx.cpu(i) })
> logger <- mx.metric.logger$new()
> mx.set.seed(235)
> model <- mx.model.FeedForward.create(symbol=cnn8,
    X=train.array, y=as.numeric(as.matrix(train.y)),
    ctx=device, num.round=50, array.batch.size=128,
    optimizer="rmsprop", eval.data=list(data=test.array,
    label=as.numeric(as.matrix(test.y))), wd=0.00001,
    eval.metric = mx.metric.accuracy, epoch.end.callback =
    optimizer="rmsprop", eval.data=list(data=test.array,
    mx.callback.log.train.metric(100, logger)))
Auto-select kvstore type = local_update_cpu
Start training with 4 devices
[1] Train-accuracy=0.38603766025641
[1] Validation-accuracy=0.538370253164557
[2] Train-accuracy=0.582920396419437
[2] Validation-accuracy=0.624505537974684
[3] Train-accuracy=0.668558184143223
[3] Validation-accuracy=0.685621044303797
[4] Train-accuracy=0.7106577685422
[4] Validation-accuracy=0.738825158227848
...
```

```
[47]  Train-accuracy=0.968829923273657
[47]  Validation-accuracy=0.87589003164557
[48]  Train-accuracy=0.970048753196931
[48]  Validation-accuracy=0.870747626582278
[49]  Train-accuracy=0.972526374680307
[49]  Validation-accuracy=0.876087816455696
[50]  Train-accuracy=0.972406489769821
[50]  Validation-accuracy=0.878757911392405
```

Applied to the test set, the resulting model shows an error rate of 12.12%. Although much higher than the error rate on the MNIST figures, this is a respectable rate, given the much greater complexity of the CIFAR images and the relative simplicity of the network trained here, which has only six convolution layers. The computation time, on an Intel Core i3 CPU, is, on the other hand, very long: about 20 hours.

```
> preds <- predict(model, test.array)
> pred.label <- max.col(t(preds)) - 1
> sum(pred.label != as.matrix(test.y)) / dim(test.y)[1]
[1]  0.1212
```

```
> table(as.matrix(test.y), pred.label)
   pred.label
       0    1    2    3    4    5    6    7    8    9
 0  897    4   15    9    6    1    8    7   40   13
 1    7  921    2    0    1    2    3    2    7   55
 2   33    1  821   17   37   29   37   16    5    4
 3   10    2   45  681   45  133   46   26    7    5
 4    2    0   35   11  886   20   15   27    3    1
 5    7    0   29   56   24  841   14   26    3    0
 6    3    1   20   10   10   14  934    5    2    1
 7    7    0    5    5   26   16    4  929    1    7
 8   28   11    4    4    0    0    4    0  930   19
 9    9   20    1    1    2    2    6    3    8  948
```

The most common errors are 133 cats mistaken for dogs, 56 dogs mistaken for cats, and 55 cars mistaken for trucks. Horses, frogs, boats, and trucks result in fewer mix-ups:

```
> plot(logger$eval, type="l", ylim=c(0.4,1), ylab="accuracy",
    xlab="epochs")
> abline(h=logger$eval[which.max(logger$eval)], lty=2,
    col="grey")
> lines(logger$train, lty=3)
```

Figure 8.7 shows the evolution of the training accuracy (dashed line) and the test accuracy (solid line).

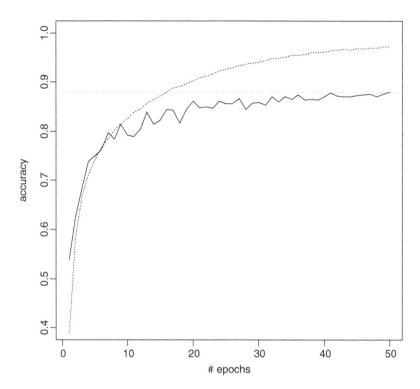

Figure 8.7   Accuracy as a function of the number of epochs.

8.3   Keras and TensorFlow

TensorFlow[12] is currently a reference library in deep learning, known among researchers and developers, for its deep neural network models. Its name comes from tensors, which are, as we have seen, the structures manipulated by convolutional networks, generalizing matrices in more than two dimensions. It is very complete but its language is not very simple and one often prefers to use a higher-level interface, Keras, to quickly create models with TensorFlow. However, there is a R tensorflow package which allows one to use this library directly. As for RStudio,[14, 15] it allows one to use either the "Core" interface giving access to all the TensorFlow functionalities, or the high-level Keras interface.

Here is an example of R code for tensorflow, which is not very user-friendly:[15]

```
cross_entropy <- tf$reduce_mean(-tf$reduce_sum(y_ * tf$log(y_conv),
  reduction_indices=1L))
train_step <- tf$train$AdamOptimizer(1e-4)$minimize
  (cross_entropy)
correct_prediction <- tf$equal(tf$argmax(y_conv, 1L),
  tf$argmax(y_, 1L))
accuracy <- tf$reduce_mean(tf$cast(correct_prediction,
  tf$float32))
```

```
sess$run(tf$global_variables_initializer())

for (i in 1:20000) {
  batch <- mnist$train$next_batch(50L)
  if (i %% 100 == 0) {
    train_accuracy <- accuracy$eval(feed_dict = dict(
        x = batch[[1]], y_ = batch[[2]], keep_prob = 1.0))
    cat(sprintf("step %d, training accuracy %g\n", i,
      train_accuracy))
  }
  train_step$run(feed_dict = dict(
    x = batch[[1]], y_ = batch[[2]], keep_prob = 0.5))
}

test_accuracy % fit(
        x = train_x, y = train_y,
        epochs=epochs, batch_size=batch_size,
        validation_data=valid)
```

Keras[16] is an open source library written in Python, usable in Linux, macOS, and Windows environments as an interface to TensorFlow, Theano, Microsoft Cognitive Toolkit, and PlaidML. It allows the simple implementation of complex structures of convolutional and recurrent neural networks. The same code can run on CPU or GPU.

Keras comes with pre-trained models on ImageNet: VGG16 and VGG19 (convolutional networks from the *Visual Geometry Group* of Oxford), ResNet50, InceptionV3.

Its installation on Windows for CPU calculations is very simple. However, it is necessary to have previously installed the Anaconda distribution of Python 3.x since Keras is written in Python. An alternative to installing Anaconda is Miniconda, which is a much lighter distribution than Anaconda. While Anaconda installs about 150 Python packages (Section 2.7), Miniconda only installs the Python package manager, conda, and the accompanying essential packages. This is an interesting solution if you do not plan to use Python for itself with its numerous packages. You start the installation by downloading Anaconda[17] or Miniconda,[18] You have to download and install the version corresponding to your operating system and the right version of Python, a version 3.x, for example, version 3.10 in November 2021. With Anaconda, all packages are automatically installed. With Miniconda, you yourself have to install the packages necessary for Keras: `numpy` (management of matrices and tensors), `scipy` (scientific calculation), `mkl-service` (optimization of mathematical functions), `libpython` (machine learning), and `m2w64-toolchain` (compiler). To do this, open a command window in Windows (type `cmd.exe` in the search window) and run the script:

```
c:\Users\<utilisateur>\Miniconda3\Scripts\activate.bat
```

This script launches the Anaconda command line on which you type:

```
conda install numpy scipy mkl-service m2w64-toolchain
```

The installation of the packages is then done quickly.

When installing TensorFlow using the R package, some Internet access problems can be solved by specifying proxies such as:

```
> Sys.setenv(https_proxy="http://<user>:<password>@proxy
   .server.com:port")
```

or simply:

```
> Sys.setenv(https_proxy="http://:@proxy.server.com:port")
```

When several installations of Python coexist on the same machine, an instruction can indicate to R the path of the version to use:

```
> Sys.setenv(RETICULATE_PYTHON = "D:/anaconda3")
```

We can check the installed and used versions:

```
> reticulate::py_config()
python:            D:/anaconda3/python.exe
libpython:         D:/anaconda3/python38.dll
pythonhome:        D:/anaconda3
version:           3.8.8 (default, Apr 13 2021, 15:08:03)
                      [MSC v.1916 64 bit (AMD64)]
Architecture:      64bit
numpy:             D:/anaconda3/Lib/site-packages/numpy
numpy_version:     1.20.1
tensorflow:        D:\ANACON~1\lib\site-
                      packages\tensorflow\__init__.p

python versions found:
 C:/Users/tuffery/Miniconda3/python.exe
 D:/anaconda3/python.exe
```

Keras can be used in R with the `keras` package of RStudio.[19] The `keras` package is available on GitHub but it can be installed from CRAN as well.

```
> install.packages("keras")
> library(keras)
> install_keras()
```

The `install_keras()` command is to be run the first time to install Keras and TensorFlow, as Keras uses TensorFlow by default.

We can also install Keras from a previously created Anaconda environment:

```
> install_keras(version="gpu", method = 'conda',
   conda = "D:/anaconda3/envs/tensorflow-gpu/",
   envname = 'tensorflow-gpu')
```

If you have a powerful enough NVIDIA graphics card, you can install the GPU version of TensorFlow by replacing the previous command with the following one. You can also install a specific version of TensorFlow. But, as for MXNet, you have to start by configuring your machine to use the GPU for deep learning, and in particular to install the appropriate CUDA and cuDNN (CUDA Deep Neural Network library) libraries. This configuration is not very simple and that is why it is the subject of a specific section (Section 8.4) at the end of the chapter.

```
> install_keras(tensorflow = "gpu")
> install_keras(tensorflow = "1.2.1")
> install_keras(tensorflow = "1.2.1-gpu")
```

For a user who does not have a machine with a GPU, Google offers its `cloudml` package which allows access with R to the Google Cloud Platform (where you will have opened an account)[20] and to its machine learning engine Google CloudML.[21]

```
> library(devtools)
> devtools::install_github("rstudio/cloudml")
> library(cloudml)
> gcloud_install()
```

We can use this package with RStudio as a terminal to launch and follow tasks on CloudML.[22] By default, this one works in CPU but you can simply work in GPU by executing, for example, one of the two following commands. The price is not the same as with CPU:

```
> cloudml_train("code.R", master_type = "standard_gpu")
> cloudml_train("code.R", master_type = "standard_p100")
```

The `keras` package is provided with pre-trained models (Section 8.3.3) and the MNIST, Fashion-MNIST (28×28 images of clothing), CIFAR10, CIFAR100, Reuters databases. On a Windows machine, they are stored in the `C:/Users/<user_name>/.keras` directory and downloaded automatically when first used.

There is another R package on the CRAN for using Keras, `kerasR`, but its installation is less simple, the function names are a bit different from those of Keras and it does not have the useful operator "%>%."

8.3.1 General Information about Keras

The central structure of Keras is the model, which defines the organization of the layers of the neural network. Each layer has an input and output tensor. The simplest and most common model is the *sequential model* which is a sequence of layers:

```
> model <- keras_model_sequential()
```

We can also define more complex architectures, with layer graphs, using the `keras_model()` function whose arguments are the input and output tensors:

```
> model <- keras_model(inputs = input_tensor, outputs =
    output_tensor)
```

We can eventually parallelize the computations on several GPU processors, by distributing the batches of data on each GPU. In the following example, each batch of *x* images will be divided into four sub-batches of $x/4$ images, each of which will be processed on a GPU. A new parallel_model is substituted for the initial model:

```
> parallel_model <- multi_gpu_model(model, pgus=4)
```

The defined model is then "compiled" for training and one can specify the loss function (see Table 7.1), the optimization algorithm (Stochastic Gradient Descent (SGD), ADAM, RMSprop, etc.) and its parameters if one does not use the default ones, and the metric to be monitored (e.g., the accuracy):

```
> model %>% compile(loss = 'categorical_crossentropy',
    optimizer = 'sgd', metrics = c('accuracy'))
```

The fit() function performs the training of the model on the training set:

```
> model %>% fit(x_train, y_train, epochs = 5, batch_size = 128)
```

The evaluate() function allows the evaluation of the model on the test set:

```
> model %>% evaluate(x_test, y_test, verbose = 0)
```

And the class is predicted thanks to the predict() function:

```
> pred <- predict_classes(model, x_test)
```

8.3.2 Application of Keras to the MNIST Database

Let's take the MNIST handwritten numbers example, the "Hello, World" of deep learning.

The data are loaded by the dataset_mnist() function and then transformed into fourth-order tensors whose values are normalized between 0 and 1. As with MXNet, these tensors are the form in which the data must necessarily be provided to the neural network convolution operator: image number, height, width, channel. The difference with MXNet is that the image number is the first element of the tensor instead of being the last element:[23]

```
> library(keras)
> c(c(x_train, y_train), c(x_test, y_test)) %<-% dataset_mnist()
> img_rows <- 28 # images width
> img_cols <- 28 # images height
> num_classes <- 10 # number of classes to predict
> x_train <- array(x_train,c(nrow(x_train),img_rows,img_cols,1))
> x_test  <- array(x_test,c(nrow(x_test),img_rows, img_cols,1))
> x_train <- x_train / 255
> x_test  <- x_test / 255
> input_shape <- c(img_rows, img_cols, 1)
```

The categorical variables to be explained y_train and y_test are transformed into binary matrices having one column per class of the variable, this column being 1 for the one corresponding to the class of the image and 0 otherwise:

```
> y_train <- to_categorical(y_train, num_classes)
> y_test  <- to_categorical(y_test, num_classes)
```

Here is how a model is coded in Keras with batch normalization, overlapping pooling, and dropout: 20C5-BN-P-60C5-BN-P-DO-600FC-10. The parameter names are very similar to those in `mxnet`. We did not specify the padding. In the `layer_conv_2d()` function, you can specify `padding="same"` or `padding="valid."` The second one is the default one, and means no padding, while `padding="same"` means that the padding is equal to $(n - 1)/2$, n being the size of the filter, to keep the size of the images, which otherwise decreases. This option is necessary if you want to follow the convolution layer with another convolution layer whose filters have the same size.

Another parameter that does not exist in MXNet but is mandatory here is `input_shape = c(height, width, channel)`.

```
> model <- keras_model_sequential()
> model %>%
+    layer_conv_2d(filter = 20, kernel_size = c(5,5),
+       input_shape = input_shape) %>%
+    layer_batch_normalization() %>%
+    layer_activation("relu") %>%
+    layer_max_pooling_2d(pool_size = c(3,3), strides
+       = c(2,2)) %>%
+
+    layer_conv_2d(filter = 60, kernel_size = c(5,5)) %>%
+    layer_batch_normalization() %>%
+    layer_activation("relu") %>%
+    layer_max_pooling_2d(pool_size = c(3,3), strides =
+       c(2,2)) %>%
+
+    layer_flatten() %>%
+    layer_dropout(0.5, seed=235) %>%
+    layer_dense(600) %>%
+    layer_batch_normalization() %>%
+    layer_activation("relu") %>%
+    layer_dense(num_classes) %>%
+    layer_activation("softmax")
```

The `summary()` function displays the characteristics of the defined model:

```
> summary(model)
```

Layer (type)	Output Shape	Param #
conv2d_1 (Conv2D)	(None, 24, 24, 20)	520
batch_normalization_1 (BatchNormal	(None, 24, 24, 20)	80
activation_1 (Activation)	(None, 24, 24, 20)	0
max_pooling2d_1 (MaxPooling2D)	(None, 11, 11, 20)	0
conv2d_2 (Conv2D)	(None, 7, 7, 60)	30060

batch_normalization_2 (BatchNormal	(None, 7, 7, 60)	240
activation_2 (Activation)	(None, 7, 7, 60)	0
max_pooling2d_2 (MaxPooling2D)	(None, 3, 3, 60)	0
flatten_1 (Flatten)	(None, 540)	0
dropout_1 (Dropout)	(None, 540)	0
dense_1 (Dense)	(None, 600)	324600
batch_normalization_3 (BatchNormal	(None, 600)	2400
activation_3 (Activation)	(None, 600)	0
dense_2 (Dense)	(None, 10)	6010
activation_4 (Activation)	(None, 10)	0

```
=================================================================
Total params: 363,910
Trainable params: 362,550
Non-trainable params: 1,360
```

We then compile the model by choosing cross-entropy as the loss function and the adaptive algorithm RMSprop as the optimization method:

```
> model %>% compile(loss = 'categorical_crossentropy',
    optimizer = 'rmsprop', metrics = c('accuracy'))
```

Then comes the training of the model, with the choice of 50 epochs, batches of 128 images, and a shuffling of observations triggered at each run by the shuffle=TRUE instruction, a shuffling which we recall is desirable for the training of a neural network (Section 7.13), so much so that this instruction is activated by default in the fit() function. The plot() function displays the training history, i.e., the evolution of loss and accuracy as a function of the number of epochs (Figure 8.8).

```
> system.time(history <- fit(model, x_train, y_train,
    epochs = 50, batch_size = 128, shuffle = TRUE,
    validation_data = list(x_test, y_test), verbose=0))
utilisateur      système        écoulé
    475.77        141.67        304.80
> plot(history)
```

Applying the model to the test set shows that the training resulted in an error rate as low as 0.58% in five minutes (on GPU):

```
> model %>% evaluate(x_test, y_test, verbose = 0)
      loss     accuracy
0.02249365 0.99420001
```

```
> pred <- model %>% predict(x_test) %>% k_argmax() %>%
    as.integer()
> test.label <- max.col(y_test) - 1
> table(test.label, pred)
```

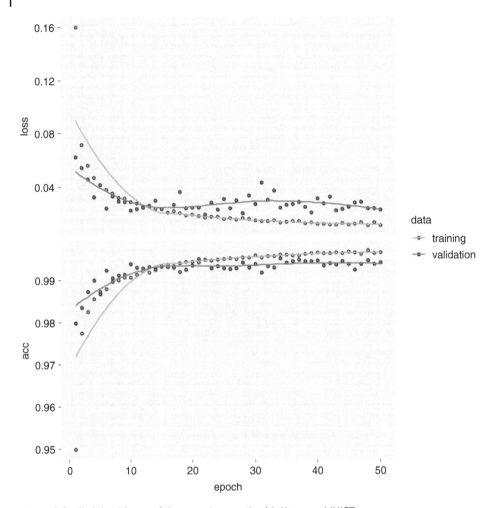

Figure 8.8 Training history of the neural network with Keras on MNIST.

```
            pred
test.label     0     1     2     3     4     5     6     7     8     9
         0   977     0     0     0     0     0     2     1     0     0
         1     1  1133     0     0     0     0     0     1     0     0
         2     1     1  1024     0     0     0     0     4     2     0
         3     0     0     0  1008     0     0     0     1     1     0
         4     0     0     0     0   975     0     1     1     0     5
         5     1     1     0     6     0   882     1     1     0     0
         6     3     6     0     0     0     1   946     0     2     0
         7     0     1     1     0     0     0     0  1024     1     1
         8     0     0     1     0     0     0     0     1   971     1
         9     0     0     0     1     3     1     0     2     0  1002
> mean(test.label != pred)
[1] 0.0058
```

8.3.3 Application of Pre-Trained Models

Like MXNet, Keras allows one to save a model, which can take a long time to train, in order to apply it to another dataset, or even to continue training it as in transfer learning (Section 7.13).

Keras allows you to save a model as a binary file:

```
> save_model_hdf5(model, "full_model.h5")
```

or save the model weights as a binary file:

```
> save_model_weights_hdf5(model, "weights_model.h5")
```

In the first case, the entire model is saved, with its architecture, weights, training parameters (loss function, optimization algorithm) and the training state that allows it to be resumed at the point where it was interrupted.

The model can then be read to apply the model or continue training:

```
> model <- load_model_hdf5("full_model.h5")
```

In the second case, only the weights of the model are saved, so that they can be loaded and applied to a new model that has the same layers as the initial model, or at least some layers in common:

```
> load_model_weights_hdf5(model, "weights_model.h5")
```

But Keras also allows us to use much more complex models than we could train with the computational power that is usually available to us. Indeed, it comes with very deep models that have been pre-trained on millions of images, such as VGG16 or VGG19 (Section 7.15), and that have then been made available to the community. They are therefore put to good use by Keras, which allows them to be loaded and used in two different ways.

The loading of these models is done with the functions `application_vgg16()`, `application_vgg19()`, `application_resnet50()`...

With the `include_top=TRUE` instruction of these functions, there is no transfer learning because the whole model is loaded and applied without modification of its weights up to its top, i.e. up to the fully connected layers that perform the classification. One can judge the complexity of this model, with its more than 138 million weights.

```
> vgg_model <- application_vgg16(weights = "imagenet", include_top = TRUE)
> summary(model_vgg)
```

Layer (type)	Output Shape	Param #
input_1 (InputLayer)	(None, 224, 224, 3)	0
block1_conv1 (Conv2D)	(None, 224, 224, 64)	1792
block1_conv2 (Conv2D)	(None, 224, 224, 64)	36928
block1_pool (MaxPooling2D)	(None, 112, 112, 64)	0
block2_conv1 (Conv2D)	(None, 112, 112, 128)	73856

block2_conv2 (Conv2D)	(None, 112, 112, 128)	147584
block2_pool (MaxPooling2D)	(None, 56, 56, 128)	0
block3_conv1 (Conv2D)	(None, 56, 56, 256)	295168
block3_conv2 (Conv2D)	(None, 56, 56, 256)	590080
block3_conv3 (Conv2D)	(None, 56, 56, 256)	590080
block3_pool (MaxPooling2D)	(None, 28, 28, 256)	0
block4_conv1 (Conv2D)	(None, 28, 28, 512)	1180160
block4_conv2 (Conv2D)	(None, 28, 28, 512)	2359808
block4_conv3 (Conv2D)	(None, 28, 28, 512)	2359808
block4_pool (MaxPooling2D)	(None, 14, 14, 512)	0
block5_conv1 (Conv2D)	(None, 14, 14, 512)	2359808
block5_conv2 (Conv2D)	(None, 14, 14, 512)	2359808
block5_conv3 (Conv2D)	(None, 14, 14, 512)	2359808
block5_pool (MaxPooling2D)	(None, 7, 7, 512)	0
flatten (Flatten)	(None, 25088)	0
fc1 (Dense)	(None, 4096)	102764544
fc2 (Dense)	(None, 4096)	16781312
predictions (Dense)	(None, 1000)	4097000

```
==============================================================================
Total params: 138,357,544
Trainable params: 138,357,544
Non-trainable params: 0
```

The previous VGG16 model can be applied to a new photograph in the following way. We load the example image in Figure 8.9 using the image_load() function in the keras package, sizing it to 224 × 224 pixels, and then transform it into a 3D tensor.

```
> img_path <- "C:/.../German_shepherd.jpg"
> img <- image_load(img_path, target_size = c(224,224))
> x <- image_to_array(img)
```

We then switch to a 4D tensor by adding a first component equal to 1 because we process a single image. We normalize the image by subtracting with the function imagenet_preprocess_input() the RGB average for each pixel. This is the only preprocessing done on the ImageNet database for the pre-trained model, and in particular the pixel values are not set between 0 and 1:

```
> x <- array_reshape(x, c(1, dim(x)))
> x <- imagenet_preprocess_input(x)
```

Figure 8.9 Image processed with Keras.

We can then apply the VGG16 model to the transformed image and the result is a vector containing the probabilities of each of the 1000 classes:

```
> preds <- vgg_model %>% predict(x)
> dim(preds)
[1]    1 1000
> imagenet_decode_predictions(preds, top = 3)[[1]]
  class_name class_description        score
1  n02106662    German_shepherd 9.983767e-01
2  n02105162           malinois 1.253263e-03
3  n02105412             kelpie 1.276684e-04
```

Having displayed the three most likely classes, we see that the German Shepherd is correctly predicted with a probability of 99.8%.

We can verify that animal breeds are well represented in the 1000 classes of the ImageNet database, with 90 dog breeds in particular.[24] The feline roots are also well represented, and we can distinguish between African and Asian elephants.

Now let's start with the same image, but replace the include_top=TRUE statement with the value FALSE and apply the VGG16 model:

```
> model_vgg <- application_vgg16(weights = "imagenet",
    include_top = FALSE)
> preds <- model_vgg %>% predict(x)
> dim(preds)
[1]    1    7    7  512
```

We see that instead of a vector of 1000 probabilities, i.e. the softmax output of the network, we have a tensor of dimension $7 \times 7 \times 512$. It corresponds in fact to the 512 maps of 7×7 pixels of which the previous summary(model_vgg) shows that they are the last maps, those of the layer noted block5_pool, before their flattening and the fully connected layers of the network.

This is because with the `include_top = FALSE` statement, only the convolution layers are retrieved, with their weights calculated on the ImageNet database. Using the `predict()` function, we can apply these pre-trained convolution layers to the images in our specific dataset, get the predicted tensor for each image and use it as input to a new predictive model, which can be a perceptron or another model, and which will be trained on our dataset.

But most often, we complete the convolution layers with fully connected layers, the whole forming a new neural model. As an input to this network, we need to specify the size of the images to be processed, which is done by adding the instruction `input_shape = c(224,224,3)` (the values 224 can be replaced by smaller values but at least equal to 32) in the function `application_vgg16()`.

However, in the training of this network, the weights of the fully connected layers are randomly initialized, as we have seen, which could have the effect of propagating important updates of these weights to the whole network, including the convolution layers whose weights had benefited from the computation on ImageNet and could unexpectedly be strongly deviated from their initial values. To avoid undoing the training of convolution layers, the practice is to "freeze" the weights of these layers before starting the training:

```
> freeze_weights(model_vgg)
```

The starting point for the specific training is then the set of 512 7 × 7 pixels maps output from the convolutional layers of VGG16. During training, the entire network is evaluated, but the weights of the convolutional layers are "frozen" at the values of the retrieved pre-trained model, and only the weights of the fully connected layers are updated by the training. In this way, we benefited from the image knowledge that a pre-trained model as large as VGG16 can have, while having adapted it to our specific dataset.

After this first training, we sometimes refine it ("fine tuning") by "unfreezing" some of the convolutional layers to retrain them on the new dataset. This is done by the following instruction, in which we specify the code of the convolution layer from which we must update the weights. This code is the one visible in the `summary(model_vgg)`:

```
> unfreeze_weights(model_vgg, from = "block3_conv1")
```

We then restart the training process.

In summary, what the `include_top = FALSE` statement of the `application_vgg16()` function allows is to perform transfer learning (Section 7.13). In such a learning process, a model learned on one dataset is used to help train another model on a different dataset.

How does this transfer learning proceed? We have seen that in a convolutional network, the first layers learn to recognize simple shapes, while the upper layers learn to recognize complex shapes, faces, objects. The first layers are therefore rather generic (detect general shapes) and can be used as a starting point for training another network: the first layers of the first network are kept, its last layers are removed and replaced by layers trained on the second dataset composed of different shapes to be recognized, which the first network may never have seen (e.g. satellite images). This training is (much) faster because it is not taken from the base, and it requires (much) less data. An example of such transfer learning is given in Section 8.3.6.

The layers that are removed are at least the fully connected layers because they are specific to the original problem. One cannot use a layer designed to predict 1000 classes and ask it to predict "cat" or "dog," or worse, to predict classes that would not be present in the classes of the original model.

Transfer learning can only be done between problems that are not too far apart. But if the two problems are still a bit far apart, a more subtle transfer learning can be done, in which not only the weights of the fully connected layers will be updated, but also the weights of the upper convolution layers, which are considered to have been learned on data too different to be kept. In this case, only the lower convolution layers are not retrained, because the very general shapes they correspond to are the same in both datasets. This is when we are led, as mentioned above, to "unfreeze" some of the convolutional layers to update their weights when learning on the new dataset.

This type of transfer is used for incremental deep learning, i.e., learning that can be performed on an evolving sample, without the need to retrain at each evolution at the starting point (see Section 1.1 for the notion of incremental learning). This is how a deep neural model can be trained on an image base that continues to grow over time, and transfer learning allows the model to be updated by integrating new images without having to recalculate all the weights of the network.[25]

8.3.4 Explain the Prediction of a Computer Vision Model

A predictive machine learning or deep learning model is explainable if its predictions can be justified by arguments that are understandable to a human. Several qualities are generally expected from a model explanation: it should be immediately understandable, reflect the actual influence of each feature of the observation, and provide similar explanations for similar cases.

The explanation often involves determining the influence (intensity and direction) of the characteristics of the observations in their prediction, and it is a question of knowing the importance of the characteristics in a model, either globally in the predictive power of the model, or locally in the explanation of the prediction of a given observation.

One can try to reconcile explainability and performance of a model by first fitting a complex model (neural network, ensemble) and then fitting a simple model (regression, decision tree) on the predictions of the complex model: the LIME method[26] (Local Interpretable Model-Agnostic Explanations) is this idea applied locally. It allows the interpretation of a model, whatever the modeling method used. Its calculations are faster than another popular method, the Shapley method. Its basic assumption is that a complex non-linear model can be approximated locally by a simpler linear model: a local regression at the point whose prediction we want to explain, the observations being weighted according to their proximity to the observation considered.

Here is the general algorithm of the LIME method.

For a given observation, we generate new observations in its neighborhood:

- this is done by sampling according to the empirical distribution of the explanatory variables, which has been calculated in a first step;
- the difficulty is to define the neighborhood: often by an exponential kernel whose window must be chosen (if it is narrow, only the closest observations will be taken into account for the explanation of the model).

Then we use the model to be explained to calculate the predicted values for these new observations. We calculate the distance between the chosen observation and each of those generated. We choose a number k of explanatory variables for the interpretation. We fit an explainable model with k variables on the generated observations, weighted by the distance of each observation from the original one. This model could be a decision tree but we often choose a GLM model, and particularly a Lasso or ridge regression with a penalty ensuring that we have exactly k explanatory variables.

The LIME method has been adapted to image processing, and in this case the new observations are generated by randomly permuting related sets of pixels, sets that are called "superpixels." These permutations allow us to know whether a superpixel is important or not in the prediction of the model. The superpixels must be large enough to cover recognizable portions of the image and have a significant impact when permuted, but they must be small enough to have well-defined prediction probabilities associated with them.

We will show how to explain the predictions of a deep image classification model using the `lime` package. This package is able to process various models from the packages `caret, mlr, MASS::lda, xgboost, ranger, h2o`... and `keras`. To process other models, we have to indicate the type of model (e.g. classification) with the `model_type()` function and the prediction function with the `predict_model()` function of `lime`:

```
> library(keras)
> library(lime)
```

Here we use the VGG16 pre-trained model for image class prediction:

```
> model <- application_vgg16(weights = "imagenet",
    include_top = TRUE)
```

We take the same example of image as in Section 8.3.3:

```
> img_path <- "C:/.../German_shepherd.jpg"
> preprocess_image <- function(x) {
+ arrays <- lapply(x, function(path) {
+ img <- image_load(path, target_size = c(224,224)) %>%
    image_to_array() %>% array_reshape(c(1, dim(.)))
+ imagenet_preprocess_input(img)
+ })
+ do.call(abind::abind, c(arrays, list(along = 1)))
+ }
```

The `lime()` function creates an "explainer" object that contains the model and information about the image whose prediction we want to explain. We tell `lime()` the path to the image as well as the name of the model and the name of the image preprocessing function. As in Section 8.3.3, this `preprocess_image()` function sizes the image to 224 × 224 pixels, then transforms it into a tensor, then normalizes it by subtracting the average RGB for each pixel with the `imagenet_preprocess_input()` function.

```
> explainer <- lime(img_path, model, preprocess_image)
```

Figure 8.10 Superpixels of LIME.

We can display the superpixels (Figure 8.10):

```
> plot_superpixels(img_path)
```

The `explain()` function then applies the LIME algorithm to the selected image and returns in a data frame the weights of the variables of the (`n_features`) most explanatory features of each image, as well as the R² of the local linear model, the prediction of the explained model and the explaining model.

We look for the features that explain the first of the values of the variable to be explained (`n_labels = 1`), the one with the highest probability. We can specify the number of images generated (1000 by default) and the number of superpixels (50 by default), two parameters that have an influence on the computation time, since the creation of new images is more cumbersome than the creation of new tabular or textual data cases. If we have enough memory, we can increase the size of the image batches, equal to 10 by default. We can also specify a seed to have a reproducible result:

```
> set.seed(235)
> explanation <- explain(img_path, explainer, n_labels = 1,
   n_features = 10, n_permutations = 500, n_superpixels = 50)
> explanation <- as.data.frame(explanation)
> explanation[1:5,c(3:5,7:8,10:11)]
  label label_prob   model_r2 model_prediction feature feature_weight       feature_desc
1 236   0.9983668 0.6731243         1.276119       8      0.4154103  [53-310], [208-428]
2 236   0.9983668 0.6731243         1.276119       3      0.2255576    [1-141], [268-451]
3 236   0.9983668 0.6731243         1.276119      22      0.1744751  [268-471], [568-728]
4 236   0.9983668 0.6731243         1.276119      28      0.1513520  [426-640], [584-813]
5 236   0.9983668 0.6731243         1.276119      21      0.1381075  [265-475], [281-494]
```

Figure 8.11 Explanation of LIME.

Each feature is a superpixel and the pixel range of the superpixel is used as a description. But this explanation is much less explicit than its display in the image itself, which the `lime` package can do with its `plot_image_explanation()` function:

```
> plot_image_explanation(explanation)
```

We can verify that the model, for the predicted class, focuses on the dog (Figure 8.11). We can also remove the context and display only the relevant superpixels, with the option `display = 'block'` (Figure 8.12).

8.3.5 Application of Keras to CIFAR-10 Images

We take the CIFAR-10 database (Section 7.15) already used to test MXNet (Section 8.2.3). The data are loaded and normalized (pixels divided by 255) to have values in the range [0,1]. The message "Down-loading data..." is displayed the first time the CIFAR-10 database is loaded because it is downloaded from the University of Toronto website. The download may take several minutes, depending on the speed of the Internet connection.

```
> cifar10 <- dataset_cifar10()
Using TensorFlow backend.
Downloading data from https://www.cs.toronto.edu/~kriz/cifar-
   10-python.tar.gz
> x_train <- cifar10$train$x/255
> x_test <- cifar10$test$x/255
> y_train <- to_categorical(cifar10$train$y, num_classes = 10)
> y_test <- to_categorical(cifar10$test$y, num_classes = 10)
```

Label: 236
Probability: 1
Explanation Fit: 0.67

Figure 8.12   Relevant superpixels in the explanation of LIME.

We then display the first 100 images (Figure 8.13):

```
> par(mfrow = c(10,10), mai = c(0,0,0,0))
> for(i in 1:100) {
+   plot(as.raster(x_train[i,,,]))
+   text(3, 0, cifar10$train$y[i], cex = 2,
     col = gray(0.75), font=3, pos = c(3,4))
+ }
```

Next, we define a Keras convolutional sequential model consisting of six convolution layers, each followed by a batch normalization and ReLU activation layer, with increasing numbers of filters, a dropout layer every two convolutional layers, then a flattening layer, a dropout, a fully connected layer, a normalization and activation layer, before the output layer to predict the ten classes:

```
> model <- keras_model_sequential() %>%
+
+   # first convolution layer
+   layer_conv_2d(filter = 64, kernel_size = c(3,3),
       padding = "same", input_shape = c(32, 32, 3)) %>%
+   layer_batch_normalization() %>%
+   layer_activation("relu") %>%
+   # second convolution layer
+   layer_conv_2d(filter = 64, kernel_size = c(3,3)) %>%
+   layer_batch_normalization() %>%
+   layer_activation("relu") %>%
```

Figure 8.13 First 100 images of CIFAR-10.

```
+   layer_max_pooling_2d(pool_size = c(2,2)) %>%
+   layer_dropout(0.2) %>%
+   # third convolution layer
+   layer_conv_2d(filter = 128, kernel_size = c(3,3),
+       padding = "same") %>%
+   layer_batch_normalization() %>%
+   layer_activation("relu") %>%
+   # fourth convolution layer
+   layer_conv_2d(filter = 128, kernel_size = c(3,3)) %>%
+   layer_batch_normalization() %>%
+   layer_activation("relu") %>%
+   layer_max_pooling_2d(pool_size = c(2,2)) %>%
+   layer_dropout(0.2) %>%
+   # fifth convolution layer
```

```
+    layer_conv_2d(filter = 256, kernel_size = c(3,3),
        padding = "same") %>%
+    layer_batch_normalization() %>%
+    layer_activation("relu") %>%
+    # sixth convolution layer
+    layer_conv_2d(filter = 256, kernel_size = c(3,3)) %>%
+    layer_batch_normalization() %>%
+    layer_activation("relu") %>%
+    layer_max_pooling_2d(pool_size = c(2,2)) %>%
+    layer_dropout(0.2) %>%
+ # first fully connected layer
+    layer_flatten() %>%
+    layer_dropout(0.5) %>%
+    layer_dense(512) %>%
+    layer_batch_normalization() %>%
+    layer_activation("relu") %>%
+ # second fully connected layer
+    layer_dropout(0.5) %>%
+    layer_dense(512) %>%
+    layer_batch_normalization() %>%
+    layer_activation("relu") %>%
+ # output layer
+    layer_dense(10) %>%
+ # output
+  layer_activation("softmax")
```

As before, we can display the characteristics of this model:

```
> summary(model)
```

Layer (type)	Output Shape	Param #
conv2d_7 (Conv2D)	(None, 32, 32, 64)	1792
batch_normalization_9 (BatchNormaliza	(None, 32, 32, 64)	256
activation_9 (Activation)	(None, 32, 32, 64)	0
conv2d_8 (Conv2D)	(None, 30, 30, 64)	36928
batch_normalization_10 (BatchNormaliz	(None, 30, 30, 64)	256
activation_10 (Activation)	(None, 30, 30, 64)	0
max_pooling2d_4 (MaxPooling2D)	(None, 15, 15, 64)	0
dropout_6 (Dropout)	(None, 15, 15, 64)	0
conv2d_9 (Conv2D)	(None, 15, 15, 128)	73856
batch_normalization_11 (BatchNormaliz	(None, 15, 15, 128)	512

activation_11 (Activation)	(None, 15, 15, 128)	0
conv2d_10 (Conv2D)	(None, 13, 13, 128)	147584
batch_normalization_12 (BatchNormaliz	(None, 13, 13, 128)	512
activation_12 (Activation)	(None, 13, 13, 128)	0
max_pooling2d_5 (MaxPooling2D)	(None, 6, 6, 128)	0
dropout_7 (Dropout)	(None, 6, 6, 128)	0
conv2d_11 (Conv2D)	(None, 6, 6, 256)	295168
batch_normalization_13 (BatchNormaliz	(None, 6, 6, 256)	1024
activation_13 (Activation)	(None, 6, 6, 256)	0
conv2d_12 (Conv2D)	(None, 4, 4, 256)	590080
batch_normalization_14 (BatchNormaliz	(None, 4, 4, 256)	1024
activation_14 (Activation)	(None, 4, 4, 256)	0
max_pooling2d_6 (MaxPooling2D)	(None, 2, 2, 256)	0
dropout_8 (Dropout)	(None, 2, 2, 256)	0
flatten_2 (Flatten)	(None, 1024)	0
dropout_9 (Dropout)	(None, 1024)	0
dense_3 (Dense)	(None, 512)	524800
batch_normalization_15 (BatchNormaliz	(None, 512)	2048
activation_15 (Activation)	(None, 512)	0
dropout_10 (Dropout)	(None, 512)	0
dense_4 (Dense)	(None, 512)	262656
batch_normalization_16 (BatchNormaliz	(None, 512)	2048
activation_16 (Activation)	(None, 512)	0
dense_5 (Dense)	(None, 10)	5130
activation_17 (Activation)	(None, 10)	0

```
=============================================================================
Total params: 1,945,674
Trainable params: 1,941,834
Non-trainable params: 3,840
```

Then comes the compilation and training of the model, which takes half an hour for 50 epochs on our machine. This time would be at least ten hours using only the CPU on the same machine. Note the very large number of parameters to be adjusted in this deep network: nearly two million! At compilation, we chose the RMSprop optimization algorithm (Section 7.14) with an initial learning rate equal to 10^{-3} and a decay parameter of the past gradients equal to 10^{-3}. This algorithm gives good results, but others are available for Keras: ADAGRAD, ADADELTA, ADAM.

```
> model %>% compile(loss = 'categorical_crossentropy', optimizer = optimizer_
    rmsprop(learning_rate = 1e-3, decay = 1e-3), metrics = 'accuracy')
> system.time(history <- fit(model, x_train, y_train, epochs = 50, batch_
    size = 128, shuffle = TRUE, validation_data = list(x_test, y_test),
    verbose=1))
Train on 50000 samples, validate on 10000 samples
Epoch 1/50
50000/50000 [==============================] - 44s 870us/step - loss: 1.4869 -
acc: 0.4585 - val_loss: 1.2687 - val_acc: 0.5921
Epoch 2/50
50000/50000 [==============================] - 35s 693us/step - loss: 0.9645 -
acc: 0.6569 - val_loss: 0.9923 - val_acc: 0.6636
Epoch 3/50
50000/50000 [==============================] - 36s 713us/step - loss: 0.7877 -
acc: 0.7228 - val_loss: 0.8681 - val_acc: 0.7013
Epoch 4/50
50000/50000 [==============================] - 35s 708us/step - loss: 0.6798 -
acc: 0.7655 - val_loss: 0.6857 - val_acc: 0.7526
...
Epoch 46/50
50000/50000 [==============================] - 37s 747us/step - loss: 0.1317 -
acc: 0.9532 - val_loss: 0.4633 - val_acc: 0.8735
Epoch 47/50
50000/50000 [==============================] - 37s 745us/step - loss: 0.1289 -
acc: 0.9543 - val_loss: 0.4546 - val_acc: 0.8752
Epoch 48/50
50000/50000 [==============================] - 37s 744us/step - loss: 0.1272 -
acc: 0.9550 - val_loss: 0.4587 - val_acc: 0.8728
Epoch 49/50
50000/50000 [==============================] - 37s 744us/step - loss: 0.1263 -
acc: 0.9551 - val_loss: 0.4718 - val_acc: 0.8722
Epoch 50/50
50000/50000 [==============================] - 37s 746us/step - loss: 0.1243 -
acc: 0.9560 - val_loss: 0.4594 - val_acc: 0.8769
utilisateur     système        écoulé
1102.95        1264.67        1841.53
```

We then display the training history (Figure 8.14) and evaluate the model on the test set:

```
> plot(history)
> model %>% evaluate(x_test, y_test, verbose = 0)
     loss     accuracy
0.4593773 0.87690001
```

We can verify the displayed correct classification rate by applying the model to the test set, and calculating the error rate which is found to be equal to 12.31%, comparable to that obtained with MXNet and a network of the same size discussed in Section 8.2.3.

When we compare this error rate to the 0.66% error rate obtained after a few minutes of training on the MNIST database, we see that the difficulty of classifying images representing objects is much greater than classifying handwritten digits:

```
> pred <- model %>% predict(x_test) %>% k_argmax() %>%
    as.integer()
> test.label <- max.col(y_test) - 1
> table(test.label, pred)
```

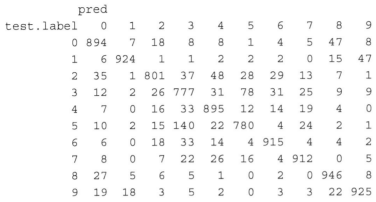

```
             pred
test.label   0    1    2    3    4    5    6    7    8    9
        0  894    7   18    8    8    1    4    5   47    8
        1    6  924    1    1    2    2    2    0   15   47
        2   35    1  801   37   48   28   29   13    7    1
        3   12    2   26  777   31   78   31   25    9    9
        4    7    0   16   33  895   12   14   19    4    0
        5   10    2   15  140   22  780    4   24    2    1
        6    6    0   18   33   14    4  915    4    4    2
        7    8    0    7   22   26   16    4  912    0    5
        8   27    5    6    5    1    0    2    0  946    8
        9   19   18    3    5    2    0    3    3   22  925
> mean(test.label != pred)
[1] 0.1231
```

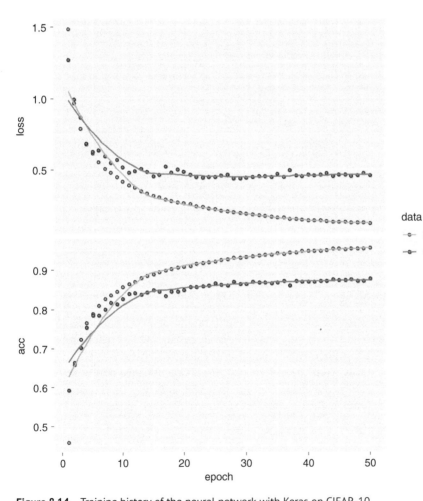

Figure 8.14 Training history of the neural network with Keras on CIFAR-10.

Figure 8.15 CIFAR-10 image classification errors.

We display the first 100 misclassified images (Figure 8.15).

```
> err100 <- head(which(test.label != pred), 100)
> par(mfrow = c(10,10), mai = c(0,0,0,0))
> for(i in err100) {
+   plot(as.raster(x_test[i,,,]))
+   text(3, 0, test.label[i], cex = 2, col = gray(0.75),
       font=3, pos = c(3,4))
+   text(3, 20, pred[i], cex = 2, col = gray(0.25), pos = c(3,4))
+ }
```

In Figure 8.15, the true classes are shown on the left and bottom of each image, and the predicted classes are shown on top. The first image is a dog (class 5) mistaken for a deer (class 4), the second a deer mistaken for a cat (class 3), etc.

We have already discussed data augmentation (Section 7.13), and the following code is an implementation of it with Keras. First, we specify the transformations that the images can randomly be transformed into. In the following example the images can be rotated between -15 and +15 degrees, horizontally or vertically translated up to 15% of their width or height, sheared (the mathematical term is "transvection") up to 15%, zoomed up to 15%. We did not retain horizontal flipping which would not make sense for these images.

```
> datagen <- image_data_generator(
+    rotation_range = 15,
+    width_shift_range = 0.15,
+    height_shift_range = 0.15,
+    shear_range = 0.15,
+    zoom_range = 0.15,
+    horizontal_flip = FALSE
+ )
```

Once this is done, we can perform the training of the neural network with the `fit_generator()` function which calls the previous parameters. Its difference with the previous `fit()` function is that it performs the training, not on a fixed specified dataset, but on a flow of generated data. Since the generation process is undefined, we need to specify its term, i.e. the number of images generated at each epoch. Since these images are generated in batches, a number of images equal to the batch size is generated each time. The `steps_per_epoch` parameter specifies the number of batches to be generated until the end of the epoch, and is therefore equal to the training set size divided by the size of each batch, at least if we want to generate a number of images equal to the training set size (but no more should be generated). The initial images of the training set with their labels, contained in `x_train` and `y_train`, are replaced by images generated by the `flow_images_from_data()` function using the generation `datagen` parameters.

We have specified in our code a callback function but without activating it here: the function `callback_early_stopping(monitor = 'val_loss', patience = 3)` which interrupts training when the error on the test set does not decrease for three consecutive epochs. This is another example of a callback function (Section 7.13) than the one we saw with MXNet (Section 8.2.2).

```
> history <- model %>% fit_generator(
+    flow_images_from_data(x_train, y_train, generator =
         datagen, batch_size = 128),
+    steps_per_epoch = as.integer(nrow(x_train)/128),
+    epochs = 50, validation_data = list(x_test, y_test)
+    # , callbacks = callback_early_stopping(monitor =
            'val_loss', patience = 3)
+ )
```

Another callback function would save the model weights at the end of each epoch, but only when its accuracy has improved over the test set.:

```
callbacks = callback_model_checkpoint(filepath =
    "best_model.h5", monitor = "val_loss", save_best_only = TRUE)
```

Other callback functions are provided in Keras (e.g. `callback_reduce_lr_on_plateau()` to reduce the learning rate when the error stops decreasing in validation) and the user can program their own callback functions.

At the end of the training process, we apply the model to the test set:

```
> pred <- predict_classes(model, x_test)
> test.label <- max.col(y_test) - 1
> table(test.label, pred)
            pred
test.label    0    1    2    3    4    5    6    7    8    9
         0  880   17   14    6    5    0    8    7   37   26
         1    3  949    0    0    0    0    4    1    1   42
         2   24    5  810   22   36   18   61   13    8    3
         3    9    6   24  722   33   96   70   19    6   15
         4    2    0   20   15  884    5   54   17    1    2
         5    0    4   13   89   23  796   29   36    1    9
         6    3    1    6    6    5    0  974    3    1    1
         7    3    2   10   16   19   17   12  914    0    7
         8   16    5    1    4    1    0    3    0  953   17
         9    3   30    2    1    1    1    1    1   10  950
> mean(test.label != pred)
[1] 0.1168
```

We note that the use of data augmentation allowed us, with the same number of epochs and the same computation time, to decrease the error in the test from 12.31% to 11.68%.

We end with an illustration of transfer learning, as described in Section 8.3.3, starting from the VGG16 pre-trained model. We will not start from the last convolutional layer of VGG16, as is often done and as will be shown in Section 8.3.6, but will start from an intermediate layer of VGG16, the third of five pooling layers (see Figure 7.23). We follow this layer with a dropout layer, a 512-unit dense layer (with ridge regularization), a batch normalization layer, and then a ReLU activation, and the output layer. This network has 3,840,330 weights, of which 3,839,306 are trainable, which is more than the 1,941,834 trainable weights of the original network, but much less than if we had started from all the convolution layers of VGG16: we would then have 14,983,498 trainable weights.

```
> base_model <- application_vgg16(include_top = FALSE, weights = "imagenet",
    input_shape = c(32, 32, 3))
> intermediate_layer_model <- keras_model(inputs = base_model$input,
    outputs = get_layer(base_model, 'block3_pool')$output)
> model <- keras_model_sequential() %>%
+ intermediate_layer_model %>%
+ layer_flatten() %>%
+   layer_dropout(0.5) %>%
+   layer_dense(units = 512, kernel_regularizer = regularizer_l2(0.0001)) %>%
+   layer_batch_normalization() %>%
+   layer_activation("relu") %>%
+ layer_dense(units = 10, activation = "softmax")
> model
Model
```

Layer (type)	Output Shape	Param #
model (Model)	(None, 4, 4, 256)	1735488
flatten (Flatten)	(None, 4096)	0
dropout (Dropout)	(None, 4096)	0
dense (Dense)	(None, 512)	2097664
batch_normalization (BatchNormalizat	(None, 512)	2048
activation (Activation)	(None, 512)	0
dense_1 (Dense)	(None, 10)	5130

```
Total params: 3,840,330
Trainable params: 3,839,306
Non-trainable params: 1,024
```

We freeze the set of convolution weights and recompile the model:

```
> for (layer in base_model$layers){ layer$trainable = FALSE }
> model %>% compile(loss = 'categorical_crossentropy', optimizer =
  optimizer_rmsprop(learning_rate = 1e-3, decay = 1e-3), metrics = 'accuracy')
> model
Model
```

Layer (type)	Output Shape	Param #
model (Model)	(None, 4, 4, 256)	1735488
flatten (Flatten)	(None, 4096)	0
dropout (Dropout)	(None, 4096)	0
dense (Dense)	(None, 512)	2097664
batch_normalization (BatchNormalizat	(None, 512)	2048
activation (Activation)	(None, 512)	0
dense_1 (Dense)	(None, 10)	5130

```
Total params: 3,840,330
Trainable params: 2,103,818
Non-trainable params: 1,736,512
```

We rerun the model training, with the same parameters as before but only ten epochs:

```
  > system.time(history <- fit(model, x_train, y_train, epochs = 10, batch_
size = 128, shuffle = TRUE, validation_data = list(x_test, y_test), verbose=1))
  Train on 50000 samples, validate on 10000 samples
  Epoch 1/10
  50000/50000 [==============================] - 16s 323us/step - loss: 0.1032 -
acc: 0.9832 - val_loss: 0.6969 - val_acc: 0.8667
  Epoch 2/10
  ...
  Epoch 9/10
  50000/50000 [==============================] - 15s 307us/step - loss: 0.0478 -
acc: 0.9936 - val_loss: 0.7369 - val_acc: 0.8724
```

```
Epoch 10/10
50000/50000 [==============================] - 15s 307us/step - loss: 0.0439 -
acc: 0.9944 - val_loss: 0.7352 - val_acc: 0.8714
   utilisateur       système        écoulé
        90.25        100.78        157.13
```

We find that after a training of less than three minutes, much shortened by the transfer of the VGG16 weights, we achieve a correct classification rate of 87.14%, at the same level as before. This shows the value of transfer learning.

8.3.6 Classifying Cats and Dogs

Cat and dog identification is a classic computer vision example. The database provided by Kaggle[27] in a 2013 competition is often used. This sample consists of 12500 cat images and 12500 dog images, representing nearly 600 megabytes of data. This dataset is the Asirra (Animal Species Image Recognition for Restricting Access) database, used as a CAPTCHA (Completely Automated Public Turing test to tell Computers and Humans Apart), that is to say, as a system to identify a human being who has to distinguish himself from a robot on a website. He does this by answering questions that are supposed to be easy for a human but difficult for a computer, such as spotting cars, bridges or cats and dogs in photographs. Asirra got these photographs through a partnership with Petfinder.com, the world's largest site dedicated to finding homes for abandoned pets. The interest of the photographs on this website is their great variety, and the fact that they are "tagged" with "cat," "dog," or other labels, and allow for supervised learning.

Once the database is downloaded, the dog pictures are stored in one directory and the cat pictures in another. For our illustration, we will extract from the Asirra database 5000 images of cats and dogs for the training set, and 2000 images for the test set. We start by creating a directory containing two subdirectories, one for training images and one for test images, each containing two subdirectories: one for dogs and one for cats. We have 2500 dog images and 2500 cat images in training, and 1000 dog images and 1000 cat images in test.

```
> library(keras)
> original_dataset_dir <- "D:/Data/DogsCats"
> base_dir <- "D:/Data/DogsCats/miniDogsCats"
> dir.create(base_dir)
> train_dir <- file.path(base_dir, "train")
> dir.create(train_dir)
> test_dir <- file.path(base_dir, "test")
> dir.create(test_dir)
> train_cats_dir <- file.path(train_dir, "cats")
> dir.create(train_cats_dir)
> train_dogs_dir <- file.path(train_dir, "dogs")
> dir.create(train_dogs_dir)
> test_cats_dir <- file.path(test_dir, "cats")
> dir.create(test_cats_dir)
> test_dogs_dir <- file.path(test_dir, "dogs")
> dir.create(test_dogs_dir)
```

We copy the images of dogs and cats in the specified directories:

```
> fnames <- paste0("cat.", 1:2500, ".jpg")
> file.copy(file.path(original_dataset_dir, "train", fnames),
    file.path(train_cats_dir))
> fnames <- paste0("cat.", 3001:4000, ".jpg")
> file.copy(file.path(original_dataset_dir, "train", fnames),
    file.path(test_cats_dir))
> fnames <- paste0("dog.", 1:2500, ".jpg")
> file.copy(file.path(original_dataset_dir, "train", fnames),
    file.path(train_dogs_dir))
> fnames <- paste0("dog.", 3001:4000, ".jpg")
> file.copy(file.path(original_dataset_dir, "train", fnames),
    file.path(test_dogs_dir))
```

We set the image size to 128×128 pixels:

```
> img_rows = 128
> img_cols = 128
> input_shape <- c(img_rows, img_cols, 3)
```

We define a neural model with three convolution layers, a 128-unit dense layer and a sigmoid output layer preceded by a 50% dropout. This model has 3,304,769 parameters.

```
> model <- keras_model_sequential() %>%
+   layer_conv_2d(filters = 32, kernel_size = c(3,3), activation = 'relu',
+     input_shape = input_shape) %>%
+   layer_max_pooling_2d(pool_size = c(2, 2)) %>%
+   layer_conv_2d(filters = 64, kernel_size = c(3,3), activation = 'relu') %>%
+   layer_max_pooling_2d(pool_size = c(2, 2)) %>%
+   layer_conv_2d(filters = 128, kernel_size = c(3,3), activation = 'relu') %>%
+   layer_max_pooling_2d(pool_size = c(2, 2)) %>%
+   layer_flatten() %>%
+   layer_dense(units = 128, activation = 'relu') %>%
+   layer_dropout(rate = 0.5) %>%
+   layer_dense(units = 1, activation = 'sigmoid')

> summary(model)
```

Layer (type)	Output Shape	Param #
conv2d_1 (Conv2D)	(None, 126, 126, 32)	896
max_pooling2d_1 (MaxPooling2D)	(None, 63, 63, 32)	0
conv2d_2 (Conv2D)	(None, 61, 61, 64)	18496
max_pooling2d_2 (MaxPooling2D)	(None, 30, 30, 64)	0
conv2d_3 (Conv2D)	(None, 28, 28, 128)	73856
max_pooling2d_3 (MaxPooling2D)	(None, 14, 14, 128)	0
flatten_1 (Flatten)	(None, 25088)	0

dense_1 (Dense)	(None, 128)	3211392
dropout_1 (Dropout)	(None, 128)	0
dense_2 (Dense)	(None, 1)	129

```
===============================================================================
Total params: 3,304,769
Trainable params: 3,304,769
Non-trainable params: 0
```

We compile the model by choosing the adaptive optimization algorithm RMSprop with an initial learning rate equal to 0.001, and the error function fitted to the binary sigmoid output:

```
> model %>% compile(
+    loss = 'binary_crossentropy',
+    optimizer = optimizer_rmsprop(lr=0.001),
+    metrics = c('accuracy')
+ )
```

We then specify to the convolutional network the data on which it should be trained. We have shown in Section 8.3.5 how the function `flow_images_from_data()` can generate batches of images according to certain parameters. We had previously created the tensors that this function called upon. Here, we use another function, `flow_images_from_directory()`, which allows us to provide batches of images to the network directly from images contained in a directory on the machine's hard disk. This function reads the JPEG images and automatically converts them into tensors of a fixed size `target_size`, to which it can apply transformations (here just a division by 255), and which it restores in batches of `batch_size` images. We tell it that the data labels are binary and must be formatted in 1D tensor. In this case, the function expects to find the images in two subdirectories, one per label, and this is how we have arranged the images. The same is done for the test images, the only difference being that the training images and not the test images are shuffled in the batches.

```
> train_datagen <- image_data_generator(rescale = 1/255)
> test_datagen  <- image_data_generator(rescale = 1/255)
> train_generator <- flow_images_from_directory(train_dir,
    train_datagen, target_size = c(img_rows,img_cols),
    shuffle = TRUE, seed = 235, batch_size = 64,
    class_mode = "binary")
Found 5000 images belonging to 2 classes.
> test_generator  <- flow_images_from_directory(test_dir,
    test_datagen, target_size = c(img_rows,img_cols),
    shuffle = FALSE, batch_size = 64, class_mode = "binary")
Found 2000 images belonging to 2 classes.
```

When starting the model training, we remember that the image batch generation process has no defined term, and that it must be specified, i.e., specify the number of images generated at each epoch. As these images are generated in batches, a number of images equal to the size of the batch is generated each time, i.e. 64 images. The parameter steps_per_epoch specifies the number of batches to be generated until the end of the epoch, and the value 79 means that at each epoch the network will have seen $79 \times 64 = 5056$ images, about the size of the training sample (the value 80 giving 5120 images would be too large). Similarly, a validation_steps parameter must specify the number of image batches to be generated for model validation, and it is set to 30 to have a number 30×64 very close to the number of images in the validation set. With the instruction shuffle = TRUE, we shuffle the images used for training. The images of the validation sample should not be shuffled in order to calculate the confusion matrix of the model.

```
> system.time(history <- model %>% fit_generator(train_generator, steps_per_
  epoch = 79, epochs = 30, validation_data = test_generator, validation_steps = 30))
Epoch 1/30
79/79 [==============================] - 76s 952ms/step - loss: 0.7699 -
acc: 0.5519 - val_loss: 0.6656 - val_acc: 0.6516
Epoch 2/30
79/79 [==============================] - 15s 185ms/step - loss: 0.6462 -
acc: 0.6449 - val_loss: 0.5850 - val_acc: 0.7000
Epoch 3/30
79/79 [==============================] - 17s 214ms/step - loss: 0.5910 -
acc: 0.7027 - val_loss: 0.5672 - val_acc: 0.7120
...
Epoch 28/30
79/79 [==============================] - 16s 196ms/step - loss: 0.0467 -
acc: 0.9855 - val_loss: 1.5777 -  val_acc: 0.7818
Epoch 29/30
79/79 [==============================] - 20s 249ms/step - loss: 0.0486 -
acc: 0.9846 - val_loss: 1.5532 - val_acc: 0.7828
Epoch 30/30
79/79 [==============================] - 15s 191ms/step - loss: 0.0446 -
acc: 0.9838 - val_loss: 1.5503 - val_acc: 0.7740
utilisateur     système      écoulé
     623.17      171.06      566.85
```

The fit_generator() function performs the training of the network on the data generated according to the previously defined parameters train_generator and test_generator. The number of epochs is set to 30.

As the training progresses, we see the accuracy evolve on the training and validation (test) sets, and we can determine the confusion matrix by applying the model to the validation set. The predict_generator() function returns the probabilities predicted by the model, based on steps = 30 batches of images provided by the test generator. This value of steps is identical to the value of validation_steps in the fit_ generator() function, but this is not mandatory. Indeed, we could specify a smaller value of validation_steps to compute the validation accuracy only on a smaller number of images, if we only want to have an estimate of the validation accuracy, and if we wait for the end of the training to apply the model to all the validation images.

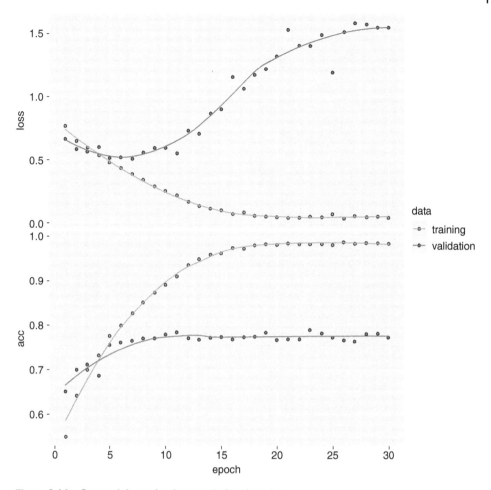

Figure 8.16 Cats and dogs: simple convolutional model.

```
> pred <- predict_generator(model, test_generator, steps = 30)
> table(head(test_generator$classes,length(pred)), (pred>0.5))

    FALSE TRUE
0    719   281
1    153   767
```

In less than ten minutes on the GPU, we obtained a model with an accuracy of up to
77% on the validation set, but with overfitting clearly visible in Figure 8.16, since the
accuracy curve in training is far above that in validation. We will try to correct it using
the already mentioned data augmentation procedure. We specify as in Section 8.3.5 the
transformations that the images can randomly be modified. The only addition is the
normalization of the pixels by division by 255.

```
> datagen <- image_data_generator(
+    rescale = 1/255,
+    rotation_range = 15,
+    width_shift_range = 0.15,
+    height_shift_range = 0.15,
+    shear_range = 0.15,
+    zoom_range = 0.15,
+    horizontal_flip = FALSE
+ )
> train_generator <- flow_images_from_directory(train_dir,
    datagen, target_size = c(img_rows,img_cols), shuffle = TRUE,
    batch_size = 64, class_mode = "binary")
Found 5000 images belonging to 2 classes.
```

Having modified the network image batch generator to include the data augmentation, we can perform the model training, as before in 30 epochs:

```
> system.time(history <- model %>% fit_generator(train_generator, steps_per_
  epoch = 79, steps_per_epoch = 79, epochs = 30, validation_data = test_generator,
  validation_steps = 40))
Epoch 1/30
79/79 [==============================] - 31s 385ms/step - loss: 8.0049 -
acc: 0.4979 - val_loss: 8.0220 - val_acc: 0.4968
Epoch 2/30
79/79 [==============================] - 25s 307ms/step - loss: 1.1434 -
acc: 0.5588 - val_loss: 0.6689 - val_acc: 0.5394
Epoch 3/30
79/79 [==============================] - 26s 330ms/step - loss: 0.6743 -
acc: 0.6025 - val_loss: 0.5753 - val_acc: 0.7436
...
Epoch 28/30
79/79 [==============================] - 27s 343ms/step - loss: 0.4206 -
acc: 0.8139 - val_loss: 0.4660 - val_acc: 0.8373
Epoch 29/30
79/79 [==============================] - 29s 360ms/step - loss: 0.4223 -
acc: 0.8059 - val_loss: 0.6663 - val_acc: 0.8145
Epoch 30/30
79/79 [==============================] - 27s 332ms/step - loss: 0.4256 -
acc: 0.8104 - val_loss: 0.4683 - val_acc: 0.8296
utilisateur     système     écoulé
    1062.63     210.75      854.47
```

Under the same conditions as before, we see that the data augmentation significantly increases the prediction accuracy from 78% to 83%. Figure 8.17 shows that the overfitting has disappeared.

Data augmentation is proving to be an effective way to train a neural network from a limited size dataset by generating new labeled images. A way that can be even more effective is to apply a pre-trained model to a much larger dataset using a much deeper neural network architecture, as explained in Section 7.13. It is this transfer learning that we now perform using the VGG16 model and its weights computed on the ImageNet dataset

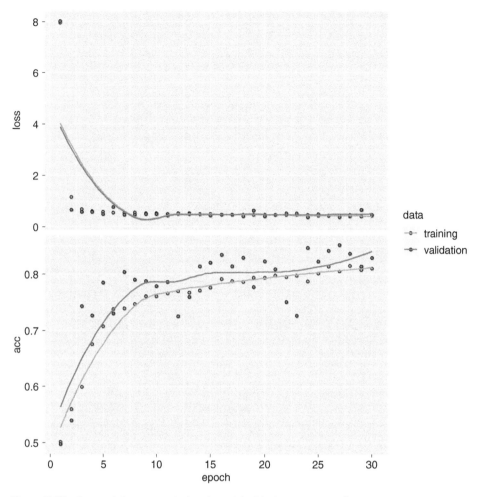

Figure 8.17 Cats and dogs: convolutional model with data augmentation.

(Section 7.15). We saw in Section 8.3.3 that the `include_top=FALSE` instruction retrieves the convolution layers of the VGG16 network and their 14,714,688 weights:

```
> base_model <- application_vgg16(include_top = FALSE, weights = "imagenet",
    input_shape = input_shape)
> base_model
Model
```

Layer (type)	Output Shape	Param #
input_1 (InputLayer)	(None, 128, 128, 3)	0
block1_conv1 (Conv2D)	(None, 128, 128, 64)	1792
block1_conv2 (Conv2D)	(None, 128, 128, 64)	36928
block1_pool (MaxPooling2D)	(None, 64, 64, 64)	0
block2_conv1 (Conv2D)	(None, 64, 64, 128)	73856

block2_conv2 (Conv2D)	(None, 64, 64, 128)	147584
block2_pool (MaxPooling2D)	(None, 32, 32, 128)	0
block3_conv1 (Conv2D)	(None, 32, 32, 256)	295168
block3_conv2 (Conv2D)	(None, 32, 32, 256)	590080
block3_conv3 (Conv2D)	(None, 32, 32, 256)	590080
block3_pool (MaxPooling2D)	(None, 16, 16, 256)	0
block4_conv1 (Conv2D)	(None, 16, 16, 512)	1180160
block4_conv2 (Conv2D)	(None, 16, 16, 512)	2359808
block4_conv3 (Conv2D)	(None, 16, 16, 512)	2359808
block4_pool (MaxPooling2D)	(None, 8, 8, 512)	0
block5_conv1 (Conv2D)	(None, 8, 8, 512)	2359808
block5_conv2 (Conv2D)	(None, 8, 8, 512)	2359808
block5_conv3 (Conv2D)	(None, 8, 8, 512)	2359808
block5_pool (MaxPooling2D)	(None, 4, 4, 512)	0

```
Total params: 14,714,688
Trainable params: 14,714,688
Non-trainable params: 0
```

We complete the model with a fully connected layer that is chosen to be identical to the previous models, so that we can compare the new model to the previous ones:

```
> model <- keras_model_sequential() %>%
+ base_model %>%
+ layer_flatten() %>%
+ layer_dense(units = 128, activation = "relu") %>%
+ layer_dropout(rate = 0.5) %>%
+ layer_dense(units = 1, activation = "sigmoid")
> model
Model
```

Layer (type)	Output Shape	Param #
vgg16 (Model)	(None, 4, 4, 512)	14714688
flatten_2 (Flatten)	(None, 8192)	0
dense_3 (Dense)	(None, 128)	1048704
dropout_2 (Dropout)	(None, 128)	0
dense_4 (Dense)	(None, 1)	129

```
Total params: 15,763,521
Trainable params: 15,763,521
Non-trainable params: 0
```

We can see that the new model created has 15,763,521 weights and of course we cannot train such a complex model on only 5000 images. This is why the training is done by "freezing" the weights of the convolutional layers to the values of the VGG16 model pre-trained on ImageNet, so that only the weights of the fully connected layer and the output layer added to the top of the VGG16 convolution layers are updated by the training. Since we start with 512 4×4 pixels maps from VGG16, flattening these convolutional layers gives $8192 = 512 \times 4 \times 4$ units, or $1{,}048{,}704 = 8193 \times 128$ weights between the flattening layer and the 128-unit fully connected layer ($8193 = 8192 +$ one bias unit). Finally, there are 129 weights between the fully connected layer and the binary output (counting one more bias unit). There are thus 1,048,833 weights to be updated during the training process (less than the 3,304,769 weights of the initial convolutional model).

```
> freeze_weights(base_model)
> model
Model
```

Layer (type)	Output Shape	Param #
vgg16 (Model)	(None, 4, 4, 512)	14714688
flatten_2 (Flatten)	(None, 8192)	0
dense_3 (Dense)	(None, 128)	1048704
dropout_2 (Dropout)	(None, 128)	0
dense_4 (Dense)	(None, 1)	129

```
Total params: 15,763,521
Trainable params: 1,048,833
Non-trainable params: 14,714,688
```

We need to compile the model to take into account the previous operations, and we do so by specifying the same optimization algorithm as before. For training purposes, we also keep the `train_generator` with the data augmentation and the batches of 64 images defined previously:

```
> model %>% compile(loss = 'binary_crossentropy', optimizer =
  optimizer_rmsprop(learning_rate = 0.001), metrics = 'accuracy')
> system.time(history <- model %>%
  fit_generator(train_generator, steps_per_epoch = 79,
  epochs = 30, validation_data = test_generator,
  validation_steps = 40))
Epoch 1/30
79/79 [==============================] - 42s 523ms/step - loss: 0.7007 -
acc: 0.6984 - val_loss: 0.3012 - val_acc: 0.8666
Epoch 2/30
79/79 [==============================] - 38s 479ms/step - loss: 0.4354 -
acc: 0.7961 - val_loss: 0.3035 - val_acc: 0.8649
```

```
Epoch 3/30
79/79 [==============================] - 42s 528ms/step - loss: 0.3971 -
acc: 0.8176 - val_loss: 0.2948 - val_acc: 0.8814
...
Epoch 28/30
79/79 [==============================] - 43s 540ms/step - loss: 0.2478 -
acc: 0.8912 - val_loss: 0.2591 - val_acc: 0.8941
Epoch 29/30
79/79 [==============================] - 43s 540ms/step - loss: 0.2375 -
acc: 0.9002 - val_loss: 0.2584 - val_acc: 0.8909
Epoch 30/30
79/79 [==============================] - 43s 541ms/step - loss: 0.2395 -
acc: 0.8967 - val_loss: 0.2459 - val_acc: 0.9022
utilisateur     système      écoulé
   1662.94       710.05      1348.17

> plot(history)
```

Figure 8.18 shows the very rapid convergence of the accuracy around 90% in validation, and a rapid convergence of the accuracy in training and in validation, which indicates an absence of overfitting. This is normal since we start with a pre-trained model on a very large base and only one million parameters remain to be estimated on the sample of 5000 cats and dogs. We can be surprised that during the first epochs, the training accuracy is much lower than the validation accuracy, contrary to what is often observed, but this can be attributed to the fact that the training is done on images voluntarily distorted by data increase, and therefore more difficult to recognize, even by a pre-trained model. On the contrary, the images of the validation sample are the original ones, probably closer to the ImageNet images than the distorted images.

Another reason is that the validation accuracy is calculated at the end of each epoch, when the model has started to converge, while the training accuracy is the average of the accuracies calculated on each batch of the epoch, this accuracy being naturally lower in the first batches.

Transfer learning based on the VGG16 model allowed us, by replacing the fully connected layers but keeping the same convolution layer configuration and training parameters (in particular the number of 30 epochs) to increase the accuracy of the model from 83% to about 90%. We can see from Table 8.2 that the VGG16 model is not the most sophisticated of those available in Keras, suggesting that we test other models. The number of weights shown in Table 8.2 includes both the weights of the convolution layers, the fully connected layers, and the output layer. The top-1 and top-5 accuracies were measured on the ImageNet database.

We tested the InceptionV3 model which, with its 21,802,784 convolution weights, allowed us to achieve 92.56% accuracy, again in 30 epochs. The huge Inception ResNetV2 model with 54,336,736 convolution weights allows us to achieve 93.75% accuracy. But it is the

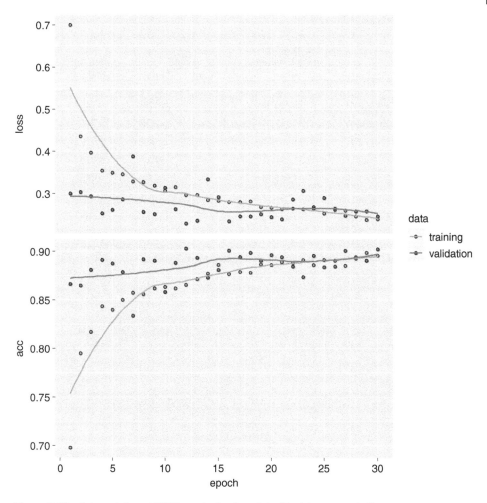

Figure 8.18 Cats and dogs: VGG16 pre-trained model with data augmentation.

Xception model, with "only" 20,861,480 convolution weights that allows us to reach the best accuracy in validation: 94.51%. So we detail it a bit:

```
> base_model <- application_xception(include_top = FALSE, weights =
'imagenet', input_shape = input_shape)
Downloading data from https://github.com/fchollet/deep-learning-models/
    releases/download/v0.4/xception_weights_tf_dim_ordering_tf_kernels_
    notop.h5
83689472/83683744 [==============================] - 717s 9us/step

> model <- keras_model_sequential() %>%
+ base_model %>%
+ layer_flatten() %>%
+ #layer_global_average_pooling_2d() %>%
+ layer_dense(units = 128, activation = "relu") %>%
+ layer_dropout(rate = 0.5) %>%
+ layer_dense(units = 1, activation = "sigmoid")
> model
```

Table 8.2 Keras pre-trained models.

Model	Image size	No. of weights of the complete model	Depth	File size	Top-1 accuracy	Top-5 accuracy
Xception	299 × 299	22,910,480	126	88 MB	0.790	0.945
VGG16	224 × 224	138,357,544	23	528 Mb	0.715	0.901
VGG19	224 × 224	143,667,240	26	549 Mb	0.727	0.,910
ResNet50	224 × 224	25,636,712	168	99 Mb	0.759	0.929
InceptionV3	299 × 299	23,851,784	159	92 MB	0.788	0.944
Inception ResNetV2	299 × 299	55,873,736	572	215 MB	0.804	0.953
MobileNet	224 × 224	4,253,864	88	17 Mb	0.665	0.871

Source: https://gogul09.github.io/software/flower-recognition-deep-learning.

```
Model

_____
Layer (type)                  Output Shape                  Param #
========================================================================
xception (Model)              (None, 4, 4, 2048)            20861480
_____
flatten_6 (Flatten)           (None, 32768)                 0
_____
dense_11 (Dense)              (None, 128)                   4194432
_____
dropout_6 (Dropout)           (None, 128)                   0
_____
dense_12 (Dense)              (None, 1)                     129
========================================================================
Total params: 25,056,041
Trainable params: 25,001,513
Non-trainable params: 54,528
```

As above, we freeze the weights of the convolutional layers at the values of the pre-trained Xception model, so that we only have to update the weights introduced by the fully connected layer and the output layer during the training. This represents 4,194,561 weights to be updated during the training process, which is performed after compilation with the same parameters as the previous ones:

```
> freeze_weights(base_model)
> model
Model
```

```
Layer (type)                    Output Shape                Param #
=====================================================================
xception (Model)                (None, 4, 4, 2048)          20861480

flatten_6 (Flatten)             (None, 32768)               0

dense_11 (Dense)                (None, 128)                 4194432

dropout_6 (Dropout)             (None, 128)                 0

dense_12 (Dense)                (None, 1)                   129
=====================================================================
Total params: 25,056,041
Trainable params: 4,194,561
Non-trainable params: 20,861,480
```

```
> model %>% compile(loss = 'binary_crossentropy', optimizer =
    optimizer_rmsprop(learning_rate = 0.001), metrics = 'accuracy')
> system.time(history <- model %>% fit_generator(train_generator,
    steps_per_epoch = 79, epochs = 30, validation_data = test_generator,
    validation_steps = 40))
Epoch 1/30
79/79 [==============================] - 50s 626ms/step - loss: 0.8351 -
acc: 0.7430 - val_loss: 0.2313 - val_acc: 0.9379
Epoch 2/30
79/79 [==============================] - 47s 584ms/step - loss: 0.4754 -
acc: 0.8024 - val_loss: 0.2416 - val_acc: 0.9399
Epoch 3/30
79/79 [==============================] - 46s 569ms/step - loss: 0.4142 -
acc: 0.8313 - val_loss: 0.3410 - val_acc: 0.9269
...
Epoch 28/30
79/79 [==============================] - 53s 666ms/step - loss: 0.2825 -
acc: 0.8889 - val_loss: 0.4622 - val_acc: 0.9375
Epoch 29/30
79/79 [==============================] - 53s 662ms/step - loss: 0.2938 -
acc: 0.8850 - val_loss: 0.4497 - val_acc: 0.9502
Epoch 30/30
79/79 [==============================] - 58s 719ms/step - loss: 0.2934 -
acc: 0.8912 - val_loss: 0.4977 - val_acc: 0.9451
utilisateur     système     écoulé
   1829.05      689.19     1469.28
```

Figure 8.19 shows the evolution of the error and accuracy in training and validation, which logically quickly is very high and approaches 95%. The gain is very important compared to the 78% accuracy obtained without a pre-trained model and without data augmentation, by a convolutional network which nevertheless has the same number of units in the fully connected layers and benefits from the same training parameters. We verify the interest of transfer learning.

Another possibility offered by the pre-trained models is to keep their convolutional layers to extract features from the images, and to complement them, not with a neural classifier (perceptron) with a dense layer as before, but with another model, which can be a regression model, gradient boosting model, etc.

Here we show how we combined the VGG16 pre-trained model with a LightGBM gradient boosting model (Section 3.4.5).

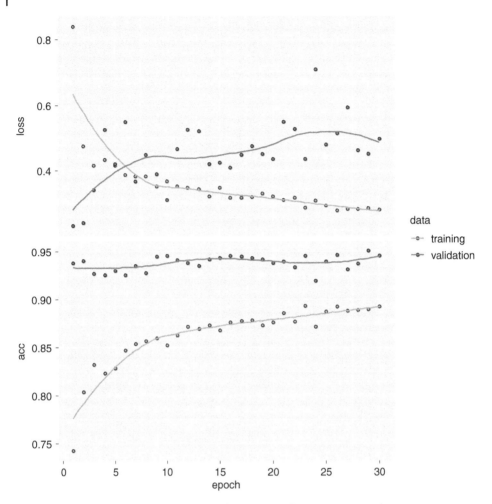

Figure 8.19 Cats and dogs: Xception pre-trained model with data augmentation.

```
> model_vgg <- application_vgg16(weights = "imagenet",
    include_top = FALSE, input_shape = c(128, 128, 3))
```

As before, we use the flow_images_from_directory() function to provide image batches in the form of tensors to the pre-trained model from JPEG images in the specified directory. Here we do not normalize the images by dividing the pixel values by 255 (no "rescaling" in image_data_generator()), as we can verify that this does not improve performance.

```
> train_generator <- flow_images_from_directory(train_dir,
    image_data_generator(), target_size = c(img_rows,img_cols),
    shuffle = FALSE, batch_size = 100, class_mode = "binary")
> test_generator   <- flow_images_from_directory(test_dir,
    image_data_generator(), target_size = c(img_rows,img_cols),
    shuffle = FALSE, batch_size = 100, class_mode = "binary")
```

The batches of images are processed by the pre-trained model and the image features are extracted into the 512 4 × 4 maps as output from VGG16. This is followed by a layer that "flattens" the 512 4 × 4 maps to 8192 units, and the values of these units are provided by the `predict_generator()` prediction function, which gives the predictions of a Keras model receiving data from an image generator. This function produces a matrix with 8192 columns. We create the variable to be explained `ytrain` which equals 0 for cats and 1 for dogs, and which comes from the `train_generator$classes` vector. Be careful, we must not mix the images in the generator and we must therefore specify `shuffle = FALSE`, otherwise the 0/1 labels of the cats and dogs will be mixed and a label will not correspond to its image.

```
> train <- keras_model_sequential() %>% base_model %>% layer_ flatten() %>%
    predict_generator(train_generator, steps=50)
> ytrain <- train_generator$classes[1:dim(train)[1]]
```

We do the same for the validation set:

```
> valid <- keras_model_sequential() %>% base_model %>%
    layer_ flatten() %>% predict_generator(test_generator, steps=20)
> yvalid <- test_generator$classes[1:dim(valid)[1]]
```

We then transform the previous data, features of the images extracted by VGG16, into LGB dataset:

```
> library(lightgbm)
> dtrain <- lgb.Dataset(data=train, label=ytrain)
> dvalid <- lgb.Dataset.create.valid(dtrain, valid,
    label=yvalid)
```

We train a LightGBM model on this data, with a ridge penalty, a training rate of 0.3, and an early stopping mechanism that activates at the 166th iteration. This computation takes 30 seconds on an ordinary machine without a GPU.

```
> lgb.grid = list(seed = 123, objective = "binary", metric =
    "auc", boosting = "gbdt", lambda_l2 = 0.0005, max_depth = 5,
    num_leaves = 32, eta = 0.3, num_threads = 4, feature_
    fraction = 0.5, n_iter = 1000, early_stopping_rounds = 10,
    num_threads = 4, verbosity=1)
> lgb.model <- lgb.train(params = lgb.grid, data = dtrain,
    valids = list(test = dvalid))
```

We compute on the validation set the confusion matrix and the accuracy of the LightGBM model applied to the cat and dog image features extracted by the VGG16 model:

```
> pred.lgb <- predict(lgb.model, valid)
> table(yvalid, (pred.lgb>0.5))

    FALSE TRUE
  0   939   61
  1    68  932

> sum(yvalid==(pred.lgb>0.5))/nrow(valid)
[1] 0.9355
```

We achieve an accuracy of 93.6% on the validation set, higher than that obtained with a perceptron over the VGG16 model, and with a much lower computation time.

An even smaller pre-trained model, MobileNet, with just over 4 million parameters (yet 16384 units on 1024 output maps, twice as many as VGG16), is used here to achieve the best accuracy by following it with a LightGBM gradient boosting model having the same parameters as before. Unlike the previous example with VGG16, we had to normalize the images with the `image_data_generator(rescale = 1/255)` option. Without normalization, the accuracy is only 76.9%, much lower than the one obtained with normalization:

```
> table(yvalid, (pred.lgb>0.5))

    FALSE  TRUE
  0   959    41
  1    25   975

> sum(yvalid==(pred.lgb>0.5))/nrow(valid)
[1] 0.967
```

In less than 3 minutes, on a simple machine without a GPU, an accuracy of 96.7% is achieved on the validation set. We can therefore profitably combine a deep pre-trained model for image feature extraction and a shallow model for image classification. The preliminary normalization of the images depends on the pre-trained model: it is necessary with MobileNet, Xception, InceptionV3 models, and even more so with Inception ResNetV2, but it degrades the results of VGG16, VGG19, and ResNet50 models.

8.4 Configuring a Machine's GPU for Deep Learning

The installation of the pure CPU versions of Torch, MXNet, and Keras is immediate, but the installation of their GPU versions requires a prior configuration of the machine, which is not very simple, especially on Windows. As the documentation for this configuration is disseminated on a number of websites,[28] we have gathered in this section all the details necessary for the reader to configure their Windows machine (using Windows 10 as an example). Of course, the software versions indicated are those valid at the date of writing these lines, in January 2022, and will change over time. It's the procedure itself that you need to remember.

8.4.1 Checking the Compatibility of the Graphics Card

The only graphics cards currently compatible with Keras, MXNet, and Torch when using CUDA are NVIDIA[29] cards. But not all NVIDIA cards are compatible. So you have to start by identifying the characteristics of your graphics card from the NVIDIA control panel, which you can access by right-clicking on the Windows desktop.[30] You obtain system information as in Figure 8.20.

It is necessary to consult the NVIDIA documentation[31] to know the computing capacity of the graphics card. This capacity must be greater than or equal to 3.5. This is the case with recent cards, for example, GeForce RTX 3060, 3070, 3080, 3090 with capacities equal to 8.6, TITAN RTX with capacity equal to 7.5, or TITAN X and GeForce GTX 1050, 1060, and 1080 with capacities equal to 6.1. If the graphics card is not GPU-compatible, there is unfortunately no way to go any further if you want to use CUDA.

8.4.2 NVIDIA Driver Installation

A computer can be equipped with an NVIDIA card without an appropriate driver being installed. This driver is a software program that allows the peripheral device, which is the graphics card, to function. The lack of a driver will probably be reported in the Windows Device Manager. It is possible to determine and download the correct driver from the NVIDIA website,[32] as in the example in Figure 8.21.

8.4.3 Installation of Microsoft Visual Studio

You may need Visual Studio, the integrated development environment of Microsoft. You can download the "community" version from the Microsoft website,[33] which is free and sufficient (but you have to register).

8.4.4 NVIDIA CUDA Toolkit Installation

Since CUDA (Compute Unified Device Architecture) is a programming language on graphics processing units (GPUs), developed by NVIDIA to provide GPUs with the equivalent of C for CPUs (Section 2.6.2), GPU computing, and especially deep learning, require
CUDA language development tools.

It is therefore necessary to install the NVIDIA CUDA Toolkit, which is a development kit for programming calculations on a graphics processor. We are interested here in

Figure 8.20 Graphics card information.

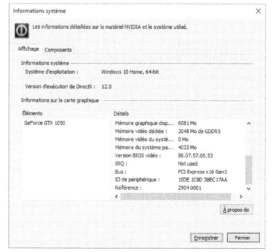

NVIDIA Driver Downloads

Select from the dropdown list below to identify the appropriate driver for your NVIDIA product.

Product Type:	GeForce ⌄
Product Series:	GeForce 10 Series ⌄
Product:	GeForce GTX 1050 ⌄
Operating System:	Windows 10 64-bit ⌄
Download Type:	Game Ready Driver (GRD) ⌄ ?
Language:	English (US) ⌄

SEARCH

GEFORCE GAME READY DRIVER

Version:	512.95 WHQL
Release Date:	2022.5.24
Operating System:	Windows 10 64-bit, Windows 11
Language:	English (US)
File Size:	786.42 MB

DOWNLOAD

Figure 8.21 Downloading the graphics card driver.

deep learning, but this kit is used for all applications using the GPU: video and audio encoding, digital imaging, scientific research, etc. It contains a compiler, a debugger, FFT (Fast Fourier Transform), and BLAS libraries, the CUDA runtime drive, and the CUDA programming manual.

Several versions of the NVIDIA CUDA Toolkit are available on the NVIDIA website. As of January 2022, Torch requires version 10.2 or 11.3, and TensorFlow 2.6 requires version 11.2. MXNet recommends version 9.2 or 9.0. In our example, we have chosen to install version 11.6. You can download[34] the executable file "cuda_11.6.0_511.23_windows.exe" and install it like any other program on Windows. The description of the installation can be found on the NVIDIA website,[35] but it is not normally difficult. You can still make sure that the "C:Program Files" directory contains the "cuDNN64_7.dll" file.

8.4.5 Installation of cuDNN

The final piece of the setup is the installation of NVIDIA's cuDNN, or CUDA Deep Neural Network library, which is a library of CUDA-programmed functions for deep neural network learning: convolution operators, pooling, normalization, and layer activation.

This library of powerful functions allows developers to focus on the advanced part of programming their neural networks, without having to program these already available functions. The cuDNN library is used by TensorFlow, Theano, Torch, PyTorch, MXNet, Microsoft
Cognitive Toolkit, and Caffe2.

Before you can download cuDNN,[36] you need to create an account on the NVIDIA website. As of January 2022, you had to use the most recent version of cuDNN for MXNet and a version at least equal to 8.1 for Keras. So we chose the 8.3.2 version and we downloaded the "cudnn-windows-x86_64-8.3.2.44_cuda10.2-archive.zip" file.

Once this file is downloaded, the installation is very simple. To summarize the guide of installation online,[37] after having decompressed the downloaded file (for example, in the folder \cuDNN), one obtains three folders and it is necessary to copy their contents in the folders of the same name in the directory of CUDA, which is for us "C:\Program Files\NVIDIA GPU Computing Toolkit\CUDA\v11.6." It is thus necessary to copy \cuDN\cuda\bin\cudn64_7.dll in the *bin* folder of CUDA, \cuDN\cuda\includecudnn.h in the *include* folder, and \cuDN\cuda\lib\x64\cudnn.lib in the *lib* folder of CUDA.

Finally, we need to create the environment variables with name PATH and values:

- C:\Program Files\NVIDIA GPU Computing Toolkit\CUDA\v11.6\bin
- C:\Program Files\NVIDIA GPU Computing Toolkit\CUDA\v11.6\extras\CUPTI\lib64
- C:\Program Files\NVIDIA GPU Computing Toolkit\CUDA\v11.6\include
- D:\cuDNN\cuda\v8.3\bin.

And you need to create the environment variable with the name CUDA_PATH and the value: C:Program FilesNVIDIA GPU Computing ToolkitCUDA\v11.6.

8.5 Computing in the Cloud

We detail in this section the free cloud offers for R and Python: the one from Kaggle which allows one to realize its challenges, Google Colab, which is of course less powerful and slower than the commercial offer from Google Cloud but still provided with GPU and TPU cards (Section 2.6.2), and RStudio Cloud.

The most complete and simple free cloud computing solution for R and Python is Kaggle.[38] As of March 2022, R is installed on Ubuntu Linux in its version 4.0.5.

You need to have a Kaggle account, which is very quick to create. When you log in, you have 16 GB of memory and 20 GB for data. This space allows you to upload your data, up to 1000 files or even more if they are in a compressed archive. You can also access all Kaggle datasets directly. You can use notebooks created by other users or your own notebooks, already created and automatically saved. To create a new one, you click on the "New Notebook" tab (Figure 8.22). You then create a new notebook or a new Python or R script (Figure 8.23).

A great advantage of Kaggle compared to other cloud offerings is that the R packages are all already installed and immediately usable after loading them with the `library()` command. Thus, one can use Keras without having to worry about installing Python, or use MXNet whose R package is not on the CRAN.

You can choose your "accelerator": none or GPU. Note that the number of hours of weekly use of a GPU is limited, a few dozen hours, the exact number of which varies according to the resources available.

With the "Notebook" choice, the code is executed in cells under which the results are displayed. You can see the metrics of the session and the resources used (Figure 8.24). The "Data" menu allows you to upload data.

With the "Script" choice, a console allows code to be executed.

Google has created its Google Cloud Platform program[39] to provide access to its cloud to academics and their students. This program also provides access to documentation. After signing up, one receives a free credit of a certain dollar amount to be used within 12 months.

Google Colab[40] (colaboratory) is a free offer for training and research, which just requires you to have a Google account. Colab is based on Python and on Jupyter notebooks that can be used with Python and saved in GitHub or Google Drive. It has an R kernel that can be accessed directly through a URL link[41] which allows you to create an R notebook, but you can also insert R code into a Python notebook by preceding it the first time with `%load_ext rpy2.ipython`, and then `%%R` at the beginning of each cell of R code. These commands for switching between Python and R environments are called R Magic

Figure 8.22 Creating a Kaggle notebook.

Figure 8.23 Creating an R notebook on Kaggle.

Figure 8.24   Configuring a notebook on Kaggle.

Figure 8.25   Number of cores allocated to a Google Colab session.

Figure 8.26   Google Colab notebook settings.

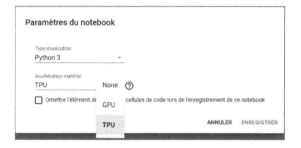

(and other commands allow you to switch between Python and Julia or Scala). Figure 8.25 shows you how to detect the number of allocated cores.

TensorFlow and Keras are of course available in Google Colab, as well as PyTorch and OpenCV (C/C++ toolkit for image and video processing), and `matplotlib` for visualization. The choice of a GPU or TPU is a parameter of each notebook created (Figure 8.26). The packages are not installed and you have to install them yourself.

Figure 8.27 shows an example Python 3 notebook for training a convolutional network on the MNIST database, as in Section 8.3.2.

Notice the similarity of the Python code with the R code already seen.

When using TPU cards, Google Colab computations can be as slow as with the CPU of a simple laptop, which is surprising for processors specifically designed for machine learning and deep learning. Using a GPU card, on the other hand, provides a computing speed that

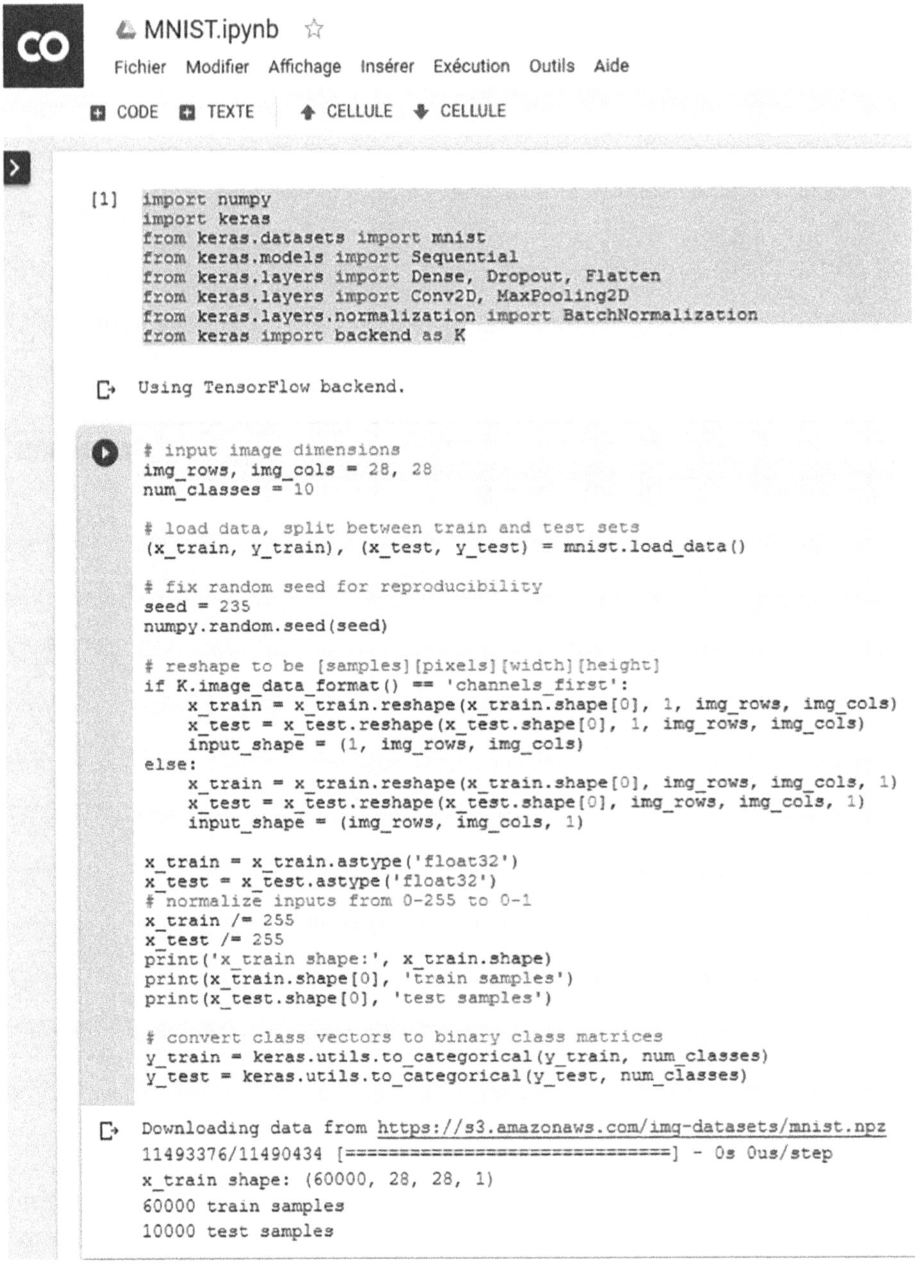

CO

△ MNIST.ipynb ☆

Fichier   Modifier   Affichage   Insérer   Exécution   Outils   Aide

⊞ CODE   ⊞ TEXTE   ⬆ CELLULE   ⬇ CELLULE

>

```python
[1]  import numpy
     import keras
     from keras.datasets import mnist
     from keras.models import Sequential
     from keras.layers import Dense, Dropout, Flatten
     from keras.layers import Conv2D, MaxPooling2D
     from keras.layers.normalization import BatchNormalization
     from keras import backend as K
```

⌐→ Using TensorFlow backend.

```python
     # input image dimensions
     img_rows, img_cols = 28, 28
     num_classes = 10

     # load data, split between train and test sets
     (x_train, y_train), (x_test, y_test) = mnist.load_data()

     # fix random seed for reproducibility
     seed = 235
     numpy.random.seed(seed)

     # reshape to be [samples][pixels][width][height]
     if K.image_data_format() == 'channels_first':
         x_train = x_train.reshape(x_train.shape[0], 1, img_rows, img_cols)
         x_test = x_test.reshape(x_test.shape[0], 1, img_rows, img_cols)
         input_shape = (1, img_rows, img_cols)
     else:
         x_train = x_train.reshape(x_train.shape[0], img_rows, img_cols, 1)
         x_test = x_test.reshape(x_test.shape[0], img_rows, img_cols, 1)
         input_shape = (img_rows, img_cols, 1)

     x_train = x_train.astype('float32')
     x_test = x_test.astype('float32')
     # normalize inputs from 0-255 to 0-1
     x_train /= 255
     x_test /= 255
     print('x_train shape:', x_train.shape)
     print(x_train.shape[0], 'train samples')
     print(x_test.shape[0], 'test samples')

     # convert class vectors to binary class matrices
     y_train = keras.utils.to_categorical(y_train, num_classes)
     y_test = keras.utils.to_categorical(y_test, num_classes)
```

⌐→ Downloading data from https://s3.amazonaws.com/img-datasets/mnist.npz
     11493376/11490434 [==============================] - 0s 0us/step
     x_train shape: (60000, 28, 28, 1)
     60000 train samples
     10000 test samples

Figure 8.27   Google Colab Jupyter notebook.

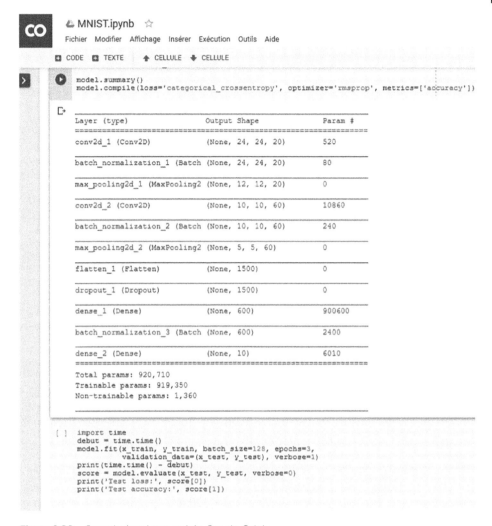

Figure 8.28 *Convolutional network in Google Colab.*

can be equivalent to that of a GPU such as a GTX 1050. In any case, one remains dependent on the variability of the resources made available in this type of cloud.

Here is the result of training the previous convolutional network (Figure 8.28), comparable to that in Section 8.3.2:

```
import time
start = time.time()
model.fit(x_train, y_train, batch_size=128, epochs=50, validation_
data=(x_test, y_test), verbose=1)
print(time.time() - debut)
score = model.evaluate(x_test, y_test, verbose=0)
print('Test loss:', score[0])
print('Test accuracy:', score[1])
```

```
Train on 60000 samples, validate on 10000 samples
Epoch 1/50
60000/60000 [==============================] - 9s 154us/step - loss: 0.0152 -
acc: 0.9952 - val_loss: 0.0244 - val_acc: 0.9935
Epoch 2/50
60000/60000 [==============================] - 9s 152us/step - loss: 0.0129 -
acc: 0.9957 - val_loss: 0.0209 - val_acc: 0.9942
Epoch 3/50
60000/60000 [==============================] - 9s 153us/step - loss: 0.0117 -
acc: 0.9961 - val_loss: 0.0207 - val_acc: 0.9937
...
Epoch 48/50
60000/60000 [==============================] - 9s 152us/step - loss: 0.0032 -
acc: 0.9991 - val_loss: 0.0336 - val_acc: 0.9945
Epoch 49/50
60000/60000 [==============================] - 9s 153us/step - loss: 0.0028 -
acc: 0.9991 - val_loss: 0.0385 -  val_acc: 0.9936
Epoch 50/50
60000/60000 [==============================] - 9s 153us/step - loss: 0.0034 -
acc: 0.9991 - val_loss: 0.0369 - val_acc: 0.9939
456.4405405521393
Test loss: 0.03687452462423585
Test accuracy: 0.9939
```

We should not expect exceptional performance from Google Colab, but we still achieve very satisfactory performance, comparable to that of a GPU, which all personal computers are far from being equipped with, and its use is very simple.

Accessing files on Google Drive may be possible with the R kernel but it is easier with the Python kernel, as in this example where we then switch back to R with R Magic (Figure 8.29). The instruction `drive.mount` requires a connection to Google.

A third free cloud offering for calculations with R is RStudio Cloud.[42] In March 2022, versions 4.1.2 of R and 3.8 of Python are installed there, in the Linux environment.

To use RStudio Cloud, you must first create an account. You can then create, save and share projects (Figure 8.30). The packages are not installed and you have to install them yourself (some are suggested if necessary) before loading them. The main limitation of RStudio is the low resources of its free version: 1 GB of allocated memory, only one CPU,

Figure 8.29 Reading a file with R in Google Colab.

Figure 8.30 RStudio Cloud.

50 projects, 25 hours of calculation per month and at most 1 hour of calculation per session. You have to upgrade to the premium version to get 8 GB of RAM, 4 CPUs, unlimited projects, 200 hours of computation per month and 48 hours of computation per session.[43] An interesting feature of RStudio Cloud is the presence of numerous tutorials in the form of notebooks and videos.[44]

8.6 PyTorch

The third deep neural network library described in this chapter is PyTorch, one of the most popular with TensorFlow. We outlined in Section 8.1 the main features that distinguish it from TensorFlow, including the fact that PyTorch code is executed as Python code, whereas TensorFlow models are represented by static graphs that must be compiled beforehand.

8.6.1 The Python `PyTorch` Package

We will show PyTorch in action in this section, using Python code that we will run on Google Colab (Section 8.5), which is therefore not limited to Keras and Google TensorFlow. Moreover, the Google Cloud Platform is open to fast.ai courses that are given on PyTorch.[45]

As a change from the MNIST database that we have extensively used, we will use the Fashion-MNIST dataset,[46] which is both very different from MNIST since it is composed of images of clothes (Figure 8.31), and which has many points in common with it (hence its name): Its 28×28 grayscale images (pixels are integers between 0 and 255), its training sample of 60,000 images and its test sample of 10,000 images, and its number of classes, ten, which in this case are T-shirts (class 0), trousers (1), pullovers (2), dresses (3), coats (4), sandals (5), shirts (6), sneakers (7), bags (8), and ankle boots (9).

This database was created using items from the Zalando online store to provide an interesting alternative to MNIST that is both less used, more representative of current image recognition tasks, and more difficult and therefore more challenging to process.[47]

Its format is identical to that of MNIST and allows the same programs to be applied to it, of course with parameters to be adapted to optimize image recognition. Fashion-MNIST

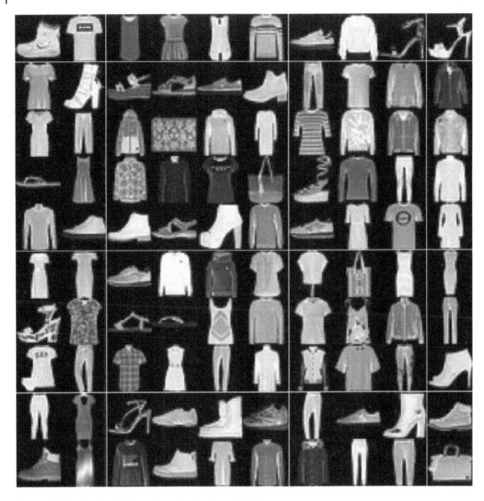

Figure 8.31 The first 100 articles in Fashion-MNIST.

images can be downloaded from the Web[48] but they are also provided in many libraries: PyTorch, TensorFlow, Keras, JuliaML, Kaggle, etc.

Loading these images into Keras in R is done as follows:

```
> mnist <- dataset_fashion_mnist()
```

These images are also in the PyTorch `torchvision` package, which contains many other datasets: MNIST, EMNIST, ImageNet, CIFAR, STL10, SVHN, Flickr, SBU, COCO, VOC, etc.

So we start by loading `torch` and `torchvision`:

```
import torch
from torchvision import datasets, transforms
```

Then we load the Fashion-MNIST data. The `transforms.Compose()` function of the `torchvision` package can perform transformations on the input data. It is necessary at least to transform them into tensors, as we do here, and eventually to normalize them by indicating their mean and standard deviation:

```
transfo = transforms.Compose([transforms.ToTensor()])
#transfo = transforms.Compose([transforms.ToTensor(),
    transforms.Normalize((0.1307,), (0.3081,))])
```

We then download the training data[49] by indicating the source and the transformations to be applied to them (here just the tensor transformation):

```
train_dataset = datasets.FashionMNIST('/files/', train=True,
    transform=transfo, download=True)
```

Then the data loader provides the data to the neural network, in batches of the indicated size, possibly shuffling them as here to improve learning:

```
batch_size = 64
train_loader =
torch.utils.data.DataLoader(dataset=train_dataset,
batch_size=batch_size, shuffle=True)
```

The test data are loaded in the same way:

```
test_dataset = datasets.FashionMNIST('/files/', train=False,
    transform=transfo, download=True)
    test_loader = torch.utils.data.DataLoader(dataset=test_
    dataset, batch_size=batch_size, shuffle=False)
```

```
Downloading http://fashion-mnist.s3-website.eu-central-
    1.amazonaws.com/train-images-idx3-ubyte.gz
Downloading http://fashion-mnist.s3-website.eu-central-
    1.amazonaws.com/train-labels-idx1-ubyte.gz
Downloading http://fashion-mnist.s3-website.eu-central-
    1.amazonaws.com/t10k-images-idx3-ubyte.gz
Downloading http://fashion-mnist.s3-website.eu-central-
    1.amazonaws.com/t10k-labels-idx1-ubyte.gz
Processing...
Done!
```

Before creating a neural network model, which here will be with three convolution layers, we need to import some submodules from PyTorch:

```
import torch.nn as nn
import torch.nn.functional as F
import torch.optim as optim
```

The optim module contains optimization algorithms for model learning. The nn.Module class is a PyTorch class that contains what is needed to create a deep neural network. The model will be created as an instance of a subclass of the nn.Module class, which is denoted ConvNet in our code. Recall that a Python class is an object type, and that we can create objects as instances of this class. Moreover, a class has attributes that define its state and methods that allow to modify it. As always in Python, to create a class, we need to define a __init__ function. It has here:

- attributes conv1, conv2... created from the Conv2d method of the nn.Module class for convolution;
- attributes conv1_bn, conv2_bn... created from the BatchNorm2d method for batch normalization;
- attributes fc1 and fc2 created from the Linear method for fully connected layers;
- a forward method which replaces the forward method of the nn.Module class, and indicates how the output of the network is calculated by passing from the input into its different layers.

We could have added a MaxPool2d attribute for pooling.

The Conv2d method has several arguments, in order:

- the number of input channels;
- the number of feature maps;
- the size of the convolution kernels (kernel_size);
- the convolution stride;
- padding.

Recall (Section 7.7) that the image produced by a kernel of size n, padding p and stride S has a size equal to $[N - n + (2p)]/S + 1$. In the following configuration, we have chosen $n = 5$, $p = 0$ and $S = 1$, and an image of volume size N is transformed into an image of size $N - 4$. At the input of the first layer, we have $N = 28$, which therefore gives an image of size 24 at the output, which is the input of the second layer, at the output of which we have an image of size 20. This second layer being followed by a 2×2 max pooling layer of stride 2, an image will be of size 10 at the output of this pooling, and of size 6 at the output of the third convolution layer, and finally of size 3 at the output of the last pooling layer and at the input of the fully connected layer. Furthermore, each layer is followed by a batch normalization layer.

There is only one channel at the input of the first convolution layer (Conv2d(1,...)) because the Fashion-MNIST images are grayscale; we would have three channels for color images. There are 32 maps output from this layer and input to the second, 32 maps output from the second layer and input to the third, and 64 maps output from the third convolution layer. The fully connected layer that follows it thus has $3 \times 3 \times 64$ units in input, since each of the 64 maps is, as we have seen, of dimension 3×3. This layer has 256 units in output and the last layer has 256 units in input and 10 in output, for the ten classes to be predicted. Unlike Keras, PyTorch forces one to specify the number of channels and not only the size of the filters, the padding and the stride.

After the layers are defined in the __init__ function, the forward function specifies the propagation of data in the network through these layers. The data stream passes through the convolution layer conv1, then the normalization layer conv1_bn, it is followed by an activation by the ReLU function, then a 10% dropout. This is repeated a second time with the addition of a max pooling layer, then a third time. The flatten(1) function then performs the flattening of the 64 3×3 maps onto the $3 \times 3 \times 64$ units of the fully connected layer that follows. The parameter 1 specifies the dimension in which the flattening is performed: for all the channels of an image, not on all the images of the batch. In an equivalent way, we can use the function view(-1, 3*3*64) which has the disadvantage of obliging one to specify the number of channels.

We end up with a batch normalization layer, a ReLU activation, a dropout, and a softmax layer of 10 classes.

Here is the code, in which you should note the indentations of four spaces typical of the Python language:

```python
class ConvNet(nn.Module):
    def __init__(self):
        super(ConvNet, self).__init__()
        self.conv1 = nn.Conv2d(1, 32, kernel_size=5, stride=1,
            padding=0)
        self.conv1_bn = nn.BatchNorm2d(32)
        self.conv2 = nn.Conv2d(32, 32, kernel_size=5, stride=1,
            padding=0)
        self.conv2_bn = nn.BatchNorm2d(32)
        self.conv3 = nn.Conv2d(32, 64, kernel_size=5, stride=1,
            padding=0)
        self.conv3_bn = nn.BatchNorm2d(64)
        self.fc1 = nn.Linear(3*3*64, 256)
        self.fc1_bn = nn.BatchNorm1d(256)
        self.fc2 = nn.Linear(256, 10)

    def forward(self, x):
        x = F.relu(self.conv1_bn(self.conv1(x)))
        x = F.dropout(x, p=0.1, training=self.training)
        x = F.relu(self.conv2_bn(self.conv2(x)))
        x = F.max_pool2d(x, kernel_size=2, stride=2)
        x = F.dropout(x, p=0.1, training=self.training)
        x = F.relu(self.conv3_bn(self.conv3(x)))
        x = F.max_pool2d(x, kernel_size=2, stride=2)
        x = F.dropout(x, p=0.1, training=self.training)
        #x = x.view(-1, 3*3*64)
        x = x.flatten(1)
        x = x.view(x.size(0), -1)
        x = F.relu(self.fc1_bn(self.fc1(x)))
        x = F.dropout(x, p=0.2, training=self.training)
        x = self.fc2(x)
        return F.log_softmax(x, dim=1)
```

The dim=1 option of the log_softmax() function indicates that the softmax function is applied line by line, and that it is the sum of the probabilities in line that is equal to 1 for each line, i.e. for all the classes of each image, whereas with the dim=0 option it would be necessary to add the probabilities in column to have a sum equal to 1.

We then create an instance of the `ConvNet` class, which will be our model, and we define an optimizer by specifying the optimization algorithm and its possible parameters if we do not use the default ones. We have chosen here the ADAM algorithm, but all the main algorithms are available in PyTorch:

```
model = ConvNet()
optimizer = torch.optim.Adam(model.parameters())
```

Then comes the training and test of the model, in ten epochs. This phase is more complex to write in PyTorch than in Keras. In each of the epochs, the training phase is followed by a test phase which allows us to compute the accuracy of the model trained so far on the test set. We specify that we are in the training or test phase of the model by the instructions `model.train()` and `model.eval()`, `model` being the name previously given to the instance of the `ConvNet` class. For the test, the function `model.eval()` disables the dropout and the batch normalization, which are not necessary in the model test phase.

In training, for each batch of images provided by the data loader, we compute the output of the model computed for this batch of `images`, using the instruction `model(images)` which calls the `forward` function previously defined. We also compute an error which is here the `cross_entropy`, other error functions being available in PyTorch. We record the error in a list (`loss_list`). Then we set the gradients of the error to zero (function `zero_grad()`), before recalculating them (function `backward()`) and backpropagating them according to the specified optimization algorithm to update the weights (function `optimizer.step()`). We compute the class of the predicted image using the `torch.max()` function, which returns the index of the maximum value of the specified tensor, in the specified direction: 0 in the first dimension, that of the batch images (from 0 to `batch_size` - 1), 1 in the second dimension, that of the classes (from 0 to 9). We then add the number of images in the batch (`total`), equal to `labels.size(0)`, and the number of these images whose class has been correctly predicted (`correct`), for each batch until the end of the epoch, when all the batches of images have been processed. We can then display the accuracy, which is the ratio `correct/total`.

In test, the `torch.no_grad()` instruction disables the `autograd` mechanism, which calculates the error gradient in the backpropagation by applying chain derivation. It is useless for model testing and slows down processing. We compute the accuracy as for the training set, to follow its evolution at each epoch.

```
n_epochs = 10
loss_list = []
for epoch in range(n_epochs):
    model.train()
    correct = 0
    total = 0
    for images, labels in train_loader:
        # forward propagation
        output = model(images)
        loss = F.cross_entropy(output, labels)
        loss_list.append(loss.item())
        # backpropagation
        optimizer.zero_grad() # setting the gradient to 0
        loss.backward()
        optimizer.step()
```

```
        # accuracy calculation
        _, predicted = torch.max(output.data, 1)
        total += labels.size(0)
        correct += (predicted == labels).sum().item()
        # item()allows to have the the tensor value
    print('Epoch [{}/{}], Train Loss: {:.4f}, Train Accuracy: {:.2f}%, '
        .format(epoch + 1, n_epochs, loss.item(), (correct /
        total) * 100), end='')
model.eval()
with torch.no_grad():
    correct = 0
    total = 0
    for images, labels in test_loader:
        output = model(images)
        _, predicted = torch.max(output.data, 1)
        total += labels.size(0)
        correct += (predicted == labels).sum().item()
    print('Test Accuracy: {:.2f}%'.format((correct /
        total) * 100))
```

During model training, the following outputs are displayed:

```
Epoch [1/10], Train Loss: 0.2800, Train Accuracy: 93.83%,
    Test Accuracy: 91.90%
Epoch [2/10], Train Loss: 0.0621, Train Accuracy: 94.21%,
    Test Accuracy: 91.87%
Epoch [3/10], Train Loss: 0.2202, Train Accuracy: 94.42%,
    Test Accuracy: 91.64%
Epoch [4/10], Train Loss: 0.2327, Train Accuracy: 94.61%,
    Test Accuracy: 92.14%
Epoch [5/10], Train Loss: 0.1209, Train Accuracy: 94.83%,
    Test Accuracy: 92.05%
Epoch [6/10], Train Loss: 0.3052, Train Accuracy: 95.16%,
    Test Accuracy: 92.15%
Epoch [7/10], Train Loss: 0.1464, Train Accuracy: 95.24%,
    Test Accuracy: 92.13%
Epoch [8/10], Train Loss: 0.1901, Train Accuracy: 95.45%,
    Test Accuracy: 92.27%
Epoch [9/10], Train Loss: 0.1479, Train Accuracy: 95.53%,
    Test Accuracy: 92.26%
Epoch [10/10], Train Loss: 0.0705, Train Accuracy: 95.73%,
    Test Accuracy: 92.53%
```

After ten epochs, we reach an accuracy of 92.5% on the Fashion-MNIST test sample, much lower than that obtained on the MNIST database, which is to be expected since clothes are much harder to recognize than handwritten digits. We obtained little better results with other optimization algorithms than ADAM: ADAMAX, RMSprop, and the Averaged Stochastic Gradient Descent (ASGD) algorithm.

8.6.2 The R `torch` Package

RStudio's "PyTorch for R" project started in 2020 to implement PyTorch in R. Unlike the Tensorflow and Keras packages, the `torch` package does not rely on Python and does not require its installation. It is based directly on C++. It is still recent and under development, but it is already rich and allows deep neural networks in image recognition applications, time series processing and written or spoken natural language processing to be implemented.[50]

It can be installed from CRAN or GitHub:

```
> install.packages("torch")
> remotes::install_github("mlverse/torch")
```

If a CUDA version at least 10.2 is detected during installation, a GPU version of `torch` will be installed. The `cuda_is_available()` function is used to check the availability of the GPU.

This installation can be completed by the `torchvision` package which is analogous to the Python package of the same name and contains some of its deep learning datasets (MNIST, Kuzushiji-MNIST, CIFAR10) and pre-trained models (VGG16, VGG16, AlexNet, ResNet-18). It also allows a number of transformations on the images to be performed.

We will see that the syntax of the `torch` package is close to that of the PyTorch package seen in the previous section. We will apply it to a new variant of the MNIST dataset: the Kuzushiji-MNIST[51] dataset, which is both very different from MNIST since it is composed of Japanese hiragana characters (Figure 8.32), and which has many points in common with it (hence its name): its 28 × 28 grayscale images (the pixels are integers between 0 and 255), its training set of 60,000 images and its test set of 10,000 images, and its number of classes, ten, which are here ten hiragana characters. One can also find on GitHub[52] a more complete dataset, Kuzushiji-49, which contains 49 hiragana characters in 270,912 images of size 28 × 28, and a dataset of 3832 kanji characters (sinograms) in 140,426 images of size 64 × 64.

We load the `torch` package as well as the `torchvision` package which contains the Kuzushiji-MNIST dataset:

```
> library(torch)
> library(torchvision)
```

We then load the dataset (downloaded the first time) and call the `dataloader()` function which will send the images as batches to the network.

```
dir <- "C:/temp/MNIST"
train_ds <- kmnist_dataset(dir, download = TRUE, transform =
    transform_to_tensor)
test_ds  <- kmnist_dataset(dir, download = TRUE, train = FALSE,
    transform = transform_to_tensor)
train_dl <- dataloader(train_ds, batch_size = 32,
    shuffle = TRUE)
test_dl  <- dataloader(test_ds, batch_size = 32)
```

Figure 8.32 The Kuzushiji-MNIST dataset.

We build a network with three convolution layers followed by batch normalization layers. We notice that the names of the functions are very close to the Python names and their arguments are identical. In particular, we find the arguments of the nn_conv2d() function: the number of input channels, the number of feature maps, the size of the convolution kernels and the convolution stride. Since the Kuzushiji-MNIST images are grayscale, we have a single channel as input to the first function nn_conv2d(). As with the Python package in Section 8.6.1, we have to specify the number of units in the input of the first dense layer, $3 \times 3 \times 64$, which comes from the fact that we have 64 maps of dimension 3×3 in the output of the last convolution layer. The calculation of this 3×3 dimension is explained in Section 8.6.1.

The initialize() function defines the layers of the network, and the forward() function describes the propagation of data in the network through these layers. These two functions make up the base class nn_module(), as in PyTorch:

```
ConvNet <- nn_module("Net",
  initialize = function() {
    self$conv1 <- nn_conv2d(1, 32, 5, 1)
    self$conv1_bn <- nn_batch_norm2d(32)
    self$conv2 <- nn_conv2d(32, 32, 5, 1)
    self$conv2_bn <- nn_batch_norm2d(32)
    self$conv3 <- nn_conv2d(32, 64, 5, 1)
    self$conv3_bn <- nn_batch_norm2d(64)
    self$dropout1 <- nn_dropout2d(0.1)
    self$dropout2 <- nn_dropout2d(0.1)
    self$fc1 <- nn_linear(3*3*64, 256)
    self$fc1_bn <- nn_batch_norm1d(256)
    self$fc2 <- nn_linear(256, 10)
  },
  forward = function(x) {
    x <- self$conv1(x)
    x <- self$conv1_bn(x)
    x <- nnf_relu(x)
    x <- self$conv2(x)
    x <- self$conv2_bn(x)
    x <- nnf_relu(x)
    x <- nnf_max_pool2d(x, 2)
    x <- self$conv3(x)
    x <- self$conv3_bn(x)
    x <- nnf_relu(x)
    x <- nnf_max_pool2d(x, 2)
    x <- self$dropout1(x)
    x <- torch_flatten(x, start_dim = 2)
    x <- self$fc1(x)
    x <- self$fc1_bn(x)
    x <- nnf_relu(x)
    x <- self$dropout2(x)
    output <- self$fc2(x)
    output
  }
)

model <- ConvNet()
```

We specify that the training of the model will be done on GPU if a suitable graphics card is available, and otherwise on CPU:

```
device <- if(cuda_is_available()) "cuda" else "cpu"
model$to(device = device)
```

We train the network in 30 epochs after specifying the loss function and choosing the optimization algorithm:

```
criterion <- nn_cross_entropy_loss()

#optimizer <- optim_sgd(model$parameters, lr = 0.01)
optimizer <- optim_rmsprop(model$parameters, lr = 0.001)
#optimizer <- optim_adam(model$parameters, lr = 0.001)

num_epochs <- 30
```

As with PyTorch, in training we loop over the image batches provided by the data loader, we set the error gradients to zero (`optimizer$zero_grad()`) at the beginning of the batch, we compute the output of the model for this batch `b` (`model(b[[1]]$to(device = device)))`), we compute the error (`loss`) and its gradient (`loss$backward()`), and we update the weights (`optimizer$step()`) by applying the chosen optimization algorithm.

We use in the test the instruction `with_no_grad()` which disables the computation of the gradient of the error useless for testing the model. We loop over the batches of images, apply the model to them, compute the loss, the predicted character and the accuracy.

At the end of each epoch, we display the loss in training and in test, and the accuracy in the test. A progress bar allows the training progress to be followed.

```
for (epoch in 1:num_epochs) {

  bar <- progress::progress_bar$new(
    total = length(train_dl),
    format = "[:bar] :eta Loss: :loss"
  )

  train_losses <- c()
  test_losses  <- c()
  correct <- 0
  total   <- 0

  coro::loop(for (b in train_dl) {
    optimizer$zero_grad()
    output <- model(b[[1]]$to(device = device))
    labels <- b[[2]]$to(device = device)
    loss <- criterion(output, labels)
    loss$backward()
    optimizer$step()
    train_losses <- c(train_losses, loss$item())
    bar$tick(tokens = list(loss = mean(train_losses)))
  })

  with_no_grad({
    coro::loop(for (b in test_dl) {
      model$eval()
      output <- model(b[[1]]$to(device = device))
      labels <- b[[2]]$to(device = device)
      loss <- criterion(output, labels)
      test_losses <- c(test_losses, loss$item())
      predicted <- torch_max(output$data(), dim = 2)[[2]]
      total <- total + labels$size(1)
      correct <- correct + (predicted == labels)$sum()$item()
      model$train()
    })
```

```
  })

  cat(sprintf("Epoch %d - Loss : [Train: %3f] [Test: %3f]
    Accuracy : [Test: %3f]\n", epoch, mean(train_losses),
    mean(test_losses), (correct/total))
}

Epoch 1 - Loss : [Train: 0.198370] [Test: 0.236853]  Accuracy : [Test: 0.930000]
Epoch 2 - Loss : [Train: 0.085183] [Test: 0.181194]  Accuracy : [Test: 0.950000]
Epoch 3 - Loss : [Train: 0.060101] [Test: 0.157434]  Accuracy : [Test: 0.959600]
Epoch 4 - Loss : [Train: 0.046951] [Test: 0.150087]  Accuracy : [Test: 0.962100]
Epoch 5 - Loss : [Train: 0.037176] [Test: 0.156986]  Accuracy : [Test: 0.961800]
Epoch 6 - Loss : [Train: 0.032142] [Test: 0.153699]  Accuracy : [Test: 0.964100]
Epoch 7 - Loss : [Train: 0.027509] [Test: 0.153295]  Accuracy : [Test: 0.965900]
Epoch 8 - Loss : [Train: 0.023577] [Test: 0.155254]  Accuracy : [Test: 0.965800]
Epoch 9 - Loss : [Train: 0.022410] [Test: 0.160301]  Accuracy : [Test: 0.965900]
Epoch 10 - Loss : [Train: 0.019610] [Test: 0.162534]  Accuracy : [Test: 0.966800]
Epoch 11 - Loss : [Train: 0.018561] [Test: 0.161956]  Accuracy : [Test: 0.969200]
Epoch 12 - Loss : [Train: 0.015712] [Test: 0.188385]  Accuracy : [Test: 0.964200]
Epoch 13 - Loss : [Train: 0.015341] [Test: 0.196262]  Accuracy : [Test: 0.964600]
Epoch 14 - Loss : [Train: 0.015846] [Test: 0.209294]  Accuracy : [Test: 0.965400]
Epoch 15 - Loss : [Train: 0.014924] [Test: 0.168412]  Accuracy : [Test: 0.970300]
Epoch 16 - Loss : [Train: 0.013735] [Test: 0.167678]  Accuracy : [Test: 0.971300]
Epoch 17 - Loss : [Train: 0.011623] [Test: 0.200627]  Accuracy : [Test: 0.967300]
Epoch 18 - Loss : [Train: 0.012190] [Test: 0.175519]  Accuracy : [Test: 0.970900]
Epoch 19 - Loss : [Train: 0.012045] [Test: 0.209019]  Accuracy : [Test: 0.967800]
Epoch 20 - Loss : [Train: 0.011552] [Test: 0.180781]  Accuracy : [Test: 0.968000]
Epoch 21 - Loss : [Train: 0.010010] [Test: 0.207223]  Accuracy : [Test: 0.968500]
Epoch 22 - Loss : [Train: 0.011681] [Test: 0.187927]  Accuracy : [Test: 0.967300]
Epoch 23 - Loss : [Train: 0.011208] [Test: 0.200534]  Accuracy : [Test: 0.970200]
Epoch 24 - Loss : [Train: 0.009762] [Test: 0.181169]  Accuracy : [Test: 0.972300]
Epoch 25 - Loss : [Train: 0.009288] [Test: 0.193658]  Accuracy : [Test: 0.969700]
Epoch 26 - Loss : [Train: 0.009520] [Test: 0.207335]  Accuracy : [Test: 0.969300]
Epoch 27 - Loss : [Train: 0.009439] [Test: 0.210408]  Accuracy : [Test: 0.968200]
Epoch 28 - Loss : [Train: 0.008613] [Test: 0.191292]  Accuracy : [Test: 0.971800]
Epoch 29 - Loss : [Train: 0.009056] [Test: 0.212872]  Accuracy : [Test: 0.969800]
Epoch 30 - Loss : [Train: 0.009359] [Test: 0.201459]  Accuracy : [Test: 0.971000]
```

In 30 epochs, we reach an accuracy of 97.1% on the Kuzushiji-MNIST test sample.

We could save the obtained model:

```
> torch_save(model, "torch.kmnist.30epochs")
```

We found that using the R `torch` package is a very close alternative to using the Python `PyTorch` package.

Notes

1 Incidentally, François Chollet, the creator of Keras, is the co-author of *Deep Learning with R*, published in 2018 by Manning, which follows his 2017 book *Deep Learning with Python* from the same publisher.

2 https://www.h2o.ai/wp-content/uploads/2018/01/DeepWater-BOOKLET.pdf.

3 https://www.cs.cmu.edu/~muli/file/mxnet-learning-sys.pdf.

4 https://github.com/apache/incubator-mxnet.

5 https://github.com/dmlc/mxnet-model-gallery.

6 https://mxnet.apache.org/versions/1.8.0/api/python/docs/api/symbol/symbol.html.

7 We take here LeNet as a generic name for a family of convolutional neural networks developed by Yann LeCun *et al.* that started with LeNet-1 and ended with LeNet-5, the most successful.

8 https://mxnet.apache.org/versions/1.7/api/r/docs/tutorials/callback_function.

9 Ioffe, S. and Szegedy, C. Batch Normalization: Accelerating Deep Network Training by Reducing Internal Covariate Shift (2015). arXiv:1502.03167.

10 http://cimg.eu/.

11 https://www.cs.toronto.edu/~kriz/cifar.html.

12 https://www.tensorflow.org/.

13 https://tensorflow.rstudio.com/.

14 https://blog.rstudio.com/2018/02/06/tensorflow-for-r/.

15 A book that introduces deep learning by illustrating it with examples using TensorFlow can be helpful: Buduma, N. *Fundamentals of Deep Learning* (Sebastopol, CA: O'Reilly, 2017).

16 https://keras.io/.

17 https://www.anaconda.com/download/#windows.

18 https://conda.io/miniconda.html.

19 https://tensorflow.rstudio.com/guide/keras/.

20 https://console.cloud.google.com/getting-started.

21 https://cloud.google.com/vertex-ai/.

22 https://tensorflow.rstudio.com/reference/cloudml/.

23 Theano adopts a third convention: image number, channel, height, width.

24 https://gist.github.com/yrevar/942d3a0ac09ec9e5eb3a.

25 Rebuffi *et al.* (2017). iCaRL: Incremental Classifier and Representation Learning. In *Conference on Computer Vision and Pattern Recognition*, CVPR 2017; Castro *et al.* End-to-End Incremental Learning. In *European Conference on Computer Vision*, ECCV 2018. (2018).

26 Ribeiro, M.T., Singh, S., and Guestrin, C. "Why Should I Trust You?": Explaining the Predictions of Any Classifier (2016). arXiv:1602.04938.

27 https://www.kaggle.com/c/dogs-vs-cats/data.

28 These include https://mxnet.apache.org/versions/1.0.0/install/windows_setup.html, https://www.tensorflow.org/install/gpu and https://keras.rstudio.com/reference/install_keras.html.

29 But Keras has a new backend, to the open source PlaidML deep learning library, which can use NVIDIA cards but also AMD and Intel (https://github.com/plaidml/plaidml), on Linux, macOS and Windows.

30 https://nvidia.custhelp.com/app/answers/detail/a_id/2040/~/identifying-the-graphics-card-model-and-device-id-in-a-pc.

31 https://developer.nvidia.com/cuda-gpus.

32 https://www.nvidia.com/Download/index.aspx?lang=en-us.

33 https://visualstudio.microsoft.com/

34 https://developer.nvidia.com/cuda-downloads.

35 https://docs.nvidia.com/cuda/cuda-installation-guide-microsoft-windows/index.html.

36 https://developer.nvidia.com/cudnn.

37 https://docs.nvidia.com/deeplearning/cudnn/install-guide/index.html.

38 https://www.kaggle.com/notebooks.

39 https://cloud.google.com/edu/.

40 https://colab.research.google.com/.

41 https://colab.research.google.com/notebook#create=true&language=r.

42 https://rstudio.cloud/.

43 https://rstudio.cloud/plans/compare.

44 https://rstudio.cloud/learn/guide.

45 https://course.fast.ai/.

46 Xiao, H., Rasul, K., and Vollgraf, R. Fashion-MNIST: A Novel Image Dataset for Benchmarking Machine Learning Algorithms (2017). arXiv:1708.07747.

47 https://github.com/zalandoresearch/fashion-mnist.

48 https://github.com/zalandoresearch/fashion-mnist#get-the-data.

49 http://fashion-mnist.s3-website.eu-central-1.amazonaws.com/.

50 https://torch.mlverse.org/.

51 Clanuwat *et al*. Deep Learning for Classical Japanese Literature (2018). arXiv:1812.01718.

52 https://github.com/rois-codh/kmnist.

9

Deep Learning for Natural Language Processing

After the application, in Chapter 8, of deep learning methods to computer vision, we now describe the application of deep learning methods to natural language processing, with examples of text classification and text generation. We focus on recurrent neural networks but also on transformer models, in particular, the BERT model, and we compare the classification of texts by a recurrent network LSTM and by a transformer model DistilBERT. This gives an overview of the use of such a model and its performance, but transformer models are capable of performing many other tasks, and this is what is remarkable about their operation: pre-trained on large-scale unlabeled corpora, they can then be fine-tuned on a wide variety of supervised tasks, or even on unsupervised tasks, such as text generation, and give very good results. Some generative models such as GPT-3 are even able to write texts that are difficult to distinguish from texts written by humans. As in computer vision, transfer learning is useful for natural language processing, especially when the corpora available for learning are small, for languages with few speakers or for vocabularies specific to a profession or a discipline.

9.1 Neural Network Methods for Text Analysis

We will now show some examples[1] of the implementation of deep neural networks, and, in particular, recurrent networks (Section 7.16). These recent tools are appropriate for natural language processing and show that, by learning, deep neural networks are capable of amazing performances, since they do not rely on a grammatical analysis of texts and are possible in any language, without even knowing its lexicon or *a fortiori* being able to perform part-of-speech tagging. However, these new methods require large enough datasets to be able to train complex neural networks. As for image recognition (Section 7.13), it is possible to "augment the data" by automatically generating new data from existing data. What is done by image deformations is done here by transforming texts by randomly adding or deleting words, or by replacing them by synonyms (using, for example, WordNet, Section 4.3.9) or by close words in a word embedding of the type of Word2Vec, GloVe, FastText, or BERT. It is also possible to add a synonym to the initial word instead of replacing it. One can randomly swap pairs of words in the text or within each sentence of the text. Another method is applied at the level of the sentence or part of the sentence, and consists of translating it into another language and then returning to the original language with a new translation. If the

Deep Learning: From Big Data to Artificial Intelligence with R, First Edition. Stéphane Tufféry.
© 2023 John Wiley & Sons Ltd. Published 2023 by John Wiley & Sons Ltd.
Companion website: www.wiley.com/go/Tuffery/DeepLearning

reverse translation differs from the original, it provides a text augmentation. Several intermediate languages can be used for translation, providing several possible different results. Whether using a thesaurus, word embedding, or back translation, it is possible to obtain several variants of the original text and thus vary the text augmentation.

One can also try to increase the robustness of models trained on textual data by injecting noise or even errors into them. Noise can be obtained by randomly deleting certain words or by replacing them, for example according to the empirical probability of the words in the text, a word being used more often for replacement the more frequent it is in the original text. Errors can be injected by referring to the most frequent errors, of which lists exist[2] and are used in some software, or by replacing certain letters by their neighbors on a QWERTY or AZERTY keyboard. It is also possible to randomly swap certain letters in words, certain words in sentences or certain sentences in the document. A more elaborate method consists of analyzing the sentence to transform it, for example, from an active form to the equivalent passive form. Finally, as for images (Section 7.19), it is possible to use GAN generative methods to generate new texts and enrich the original.

9.2 Text Generation Using a Recurrent Neural Network LSTM

We said in Section 7.16 that an LSTM recurrent network was able to generate sentences to automatically describe the content of an image. It is also able to generate a text imitating the vocabulary of a source text. The method implemented will depend on the length and richness of the source text.[3]

If the source text is very long or if its vocabulary is simple, the ratio "total number of words / number of different words" will be high and it will be possible to generate the new text word-by-word (Figure 9.1). Indeed, the network will be able to learn to predict each word because it will have seen it often enough in its training set. This solution generates texts that are more structured and faithful to the original, but the number of classes to predict is very large (one class per distinct word) and the training time of the LSTM network becomes enormous if one does not have a very large computing power.

If, on the other hand, the source text is short or its vocabulary is rich, the ratio "total number of words / number of different words" will be low and the network will have seen each distinct word too rarely to be able to predict it. In this case, the generation of the text must be done character-by-character, which has the major drawback that many assemblies of characters do not form words that exist in the language. This disadvantage decreases as the learning process progresses, but it takes many epochs for the generated text to start making sense, which still poses the problem of computing power. A small advantage of this method is that it increases the "creativity" of the network by allowing it to create words that are absent from the source text.

We can see that text generation will be easier for elementary texts than for literary texts. In this register, we can, however, imagine the possibilities of neural learning in literary productions such as those of the Oulipo, for example, to generate lipograms.

We will illustrate the second method with the construction of an LSTM network learning to predict the next character(s) following a given sequence of characters (Figure 9.1). It thus has a softmax output on all the characters of the source text. The model obtained is the probability of the next character given the previous characters. From this model, it is possible to generate a new text. We start from a string of n characters, we

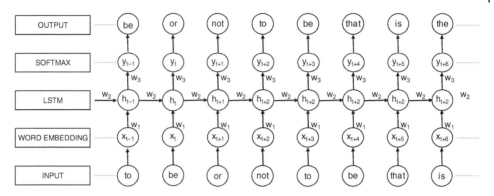

Figure 9.1 Word prediction with an LSTM network.

generate the $n+1^{th}$ character given the first n characters, then we generate the $n+2^{nd}$ character from the $n+1^{th}$ added to the first n characters, etc. To draw the $n+1^{th}$ character, we can always choose the most probable one but we will then obtain repetitive sequences that do not look like a real text at all. On the other hand, we can also draw the $n+1^{th}$ character at random according to a uniform distribution between the characters, but this will generate a high proportion of imaginary words. These two extremes correspond respectively to a minimal or maximal entropy, the entropy measuring as we have seen (Section 4.4.5) the homogeneity of the random sampling. We also talk about the "temperature" of the softmax output: a high temperature gives unpredictable and unstructured texts while a low temperature gives more deterministic and even repetitive texts.

We are going to apply the Keras LSTM network to text generation, based on Shakespeare's *Sonnets*,[4] and using the script provided by François Chollet on the Web[5] and in his book on deep learning with Keras.[6] We have taken this typical volume of Shakespeare's style, which contains a sufficient number of characters (nearly 100,000, including spaces), to train the network. François Chollet considers that we need at least 100,000 characters and that it is better to have a million characters. This would be the number of characters in several books of Shakespeare, but much more than 8 gigabytes of memory would be needed to train the network.

In general, training an LSTM network requires a large amount of data. Recurrent networks require a lot of computing power and it is strongly recommended to perform this type of computation on a GPU, which already takes several hours (and would take several days with a simple CPU), especially since in the first epochs, the generated words are mostly imaginary, and it is necessary to wait for several epochs to see understandable sentences appear. It also depends on the choice of the temperature and it takes several tries to find an adequate value.

The quality of the text generation depends on the size of the training set, its lexical simplicity, the depth of the network, its window size, the softmax temperature and the number of epochs.

We can start by checking whether the total number of words (function `ntoken()`) in the corpus is too small compared to the number of different words (function `ntype()`) to train a deep network to predict words, not characters. Here, this ratio is less than 7:

```
> path <- "../input/shakespeare/Shakespeare_Sonnets.txt"
> text <- read_lines(path) %>% str_to_lower() %>% str_c(collapse = "\n")
```

```
> library(quanteda)
> corpus <- corpus(text)
> ntoken(corpus)
text1
20516
> ntype(corpus)
text1
 3240
> ntoken(corpus) / ntype(corpus)
   text1
6.332099
```

Here is how to program the generation of a text by an LSTM network with Keras:

```
> library(keras)
> library(readr)
> library(stringr)
> library(tokenizers)
> maxlen <- 100
> step    <- 1
```

We start by reading the text, changing all the capitals to lower case, keeping the punctuation and spaces, and tokenize the text into characters. We display the total number of characters in the text, as well as the number of different characters, which will be the number of units in the softmax layer of the network output. There are 38 of them:

```
> text <- read_lines(path) %>% str_to_lower() %>% str_c(collapse = "\n") %>%
    tokenize_characters(strip_non_alphanum = FALSE,
    simplify = TRUE)
> print(sprintf("corpus length: %d", length(text)))
[1] "corpus length: 94051"
> chars <- text %>% unique() %>% sort()
> print(sprintf("total chars: %d", length(chars)))
[1] "total chars: 38"
```

The text is split into sequences of *maxlen* (here 100) characters, which overlap strongly because they follow each other at *step* (here 1) character(s) interval. An important overlap increases the size of the training set but also the quality of the result:

```
> library(purrr)
> dataset <- map(seq(1, length(text) - maxlen - 1, by = step),
    ~list(sentence = text[.x:(.x + maxlen - 1)], next_char =
    text[.x + maxlen]))
> dataset <- transpose(dataset)
```

The characters are coded in binary tensors which will be the input of the model. The tensor x is constructed from each sequence of characters, and for each of these 93,950 sequences, each of the 100 characters of the sequence is coded 0/1 for each of the 38 different possible characters, the tensor being 1 for the one of the 38 characters corresponding to the current character and 0 for the 37 other characters. The tensor y contains the next character of each sequence, also coded in 0/1 for each of the 38 possible characters. These tensors are very sparse:

```
> x <- array(0L, dim = c(length(dataset$sentence), maxlen, length(chars)))
```

```
> y <- array(0L, dim = c(length(dataset$sentence), length(chars)))
> for(i in 1:length(dataset$sentence)){
+    x[i,,] <- sapply(chars, function(x){as.integer(x == dataset$sentence[[i]])})
+    y[i,]  <- as.integer(chars == dataset$next_char[[i]])
+ }
> dim(x)
[1] 93950 100 38
> dim(y)
[1] 93950 38
```

We define the LSTM model predicting the next character. This is a three-layer model with 512 units, each followed by a 25% dropout. Increasing the number of layers and the number of units per layer greatly improves the ability of the model to generate meaningful and interesting text. When one LSTM layer is followed by another, the return_sequences=TRUE option must be specified to output a three-dimensional tensor, including time, and not a two-dimensional tensor containing only the last sequence of characters.

```
> model <- keras_model_sequential()
>
> model %>%
+    layer_lstm(units = 512, return_sequences=TRUE,
+        input_shape = c(maxlen, length(chars))) %>%
+    layer_dropout(0.25, seed=235) %>%
+    layer_lstm(units = 512, return_sequences=TRUE) %>%
+    layer_dropout(0.25, seed=235) %>%
+    layer_lstm(units = 512) %>%
+    layer_dropout(0.25, seed=235) %>%
+    layer_dense(length(chars)) %>%
+    layer_activation("softmax")
```

The model will be trained with the adaptive algorithm ADAM and the cross-entropy as a loss function:

```
> model %>% compile(loss = 'categorical_crossentropy',
+    optimizer = 'adam', metrics = c('accuracy'))
```

The following function draws the next character according to the predictions of the LSTM model:

```
> sample_next_char <- function(preds, temperature = 1){
+    preds <- log(preds)/temperature
+    exp_preds <- exp(preds)
+    preds <- exp_preds/sum(exp(preds))
+    which.max(t(rmultinom(1, 1, preds)))
+ }
```

We arrive at the function that generates texts of a prescribed number of characters (for example, here 600). At each epoch of the LSTM network and for several possible values of the temperature:

- we randomly draw a sample of text of length *maxlen*;
- we code this sample as before in the form of a matrix and then a 0/1 tensor of dimension 1 x *maxlen* (100) x number of different characters (38);

- we apply the LSTM model to it;
- we predict the next character (taking into account the temperature);
- we add this character to the generated text;
- the sample is shifted by one character and we return to the second coding step, until we have generated 600 characters.

This is done by a callback function, which, as we have seen (Section 7.13), allows some actions to be performed, depending on the intermediate results obtained during the training of the network, for example, at each new epoch.

```
> on_epoch_end <- function(epoch, logs) {
+   start_index <- sample(1:(length(text) - maxlen), size = 1)
+   cat(sprintf("epoch: %02d --------------------\n\n", epoch+1))
+   # test of several temperatures (entropies)
+   for(temperature in c(0.3, 0.5)){
+     cat(sprintf("temperature: %f --------------------\n",
+       temperature))
+     sentence  <- text[start_index:(start_index + maxlen - 1)]
+     generated <- ""
+     cat("text seed: ", sentence, "\n\n")
+     for(i in 1:600){
+       s <- sapply(chars, function(s){as.integer(s==sentence)})
+       s <- array_reshape(s, c(1, dim(s)))
+      # prediction of the next character according to the model
+       preds <- predict(model, s)
+       next_index <- sample_next_char(preds, temperature)
+       next_char  <- chars[next_index]
+       generated <- paste0(generated, next_char)
+      # update of the training sample
+       sentence <- c(sentence[-1], next_char)
+     }
+     cat(generated)
+     cat("\n\n")
+   }
+ }
```

The `generate_text` callback function executes the previous function at the end of each of the 30 training epochs:

```
> generate_text <- callback_lambda(on_epoch_end = on_epoch_end)
> set.seed(123)
> system.time(model %>% fit(x, y, batch_size = 128, epochs = 30,
    callbacks = generate_text))
```

Here are some samples of the poetry generated by our LSTM model, after more than five hours of computation on GPU:

```
epoch: 30   ---------------
```

```
temperature: 0.300000 ---------------
text seed:    i m a g e s   i   l o v ' d ,   i   v i e w   i n
    t h e e ,
  a n d   t h o u - - a l l   t h e y - - h a s t   a l l   t h e
    a l l   o f   m e .
i f   t h o u   s u r v i v e   m y   w e l
```

1-contented day,
when in dead night thy fair imperfect shade
thou art the fairest of thy shadow and thee back,
shall nightly thought i found, you did exceed
that thy unkindness lays upon my part:
and i what works in heaven in thy heart
to mourn for me since mourning doth thee grace,
and suit thy pity like in every part.
then will i swear against the thing they see;
for i have sworn deep oaths of thy deep kindness,
oaths of thy beauty though their did assure,
were it not sinful then, strength seem to decay,
and to the painter banquet bids my heart;
another time mine eye is my heart's guest,

```
temperature: 0.500000 ---------------
text seed:    i m a g e s   i   l o v ' d ,   i   v i e w   i n
    t h e e ,
  a n d   t h o u - - a l l   t h e y - - h a s t   a l l   t h e
    a l l   o f   m e .
i f   t h o u   s u r v i v e   m y   w e l
```

1-contented day,
when that shall vade, by verse distills your truth:
but when your pity is, shall be thy 'will,'
and you in every blessed shape which truth,
and summer's green all girded up in sheaves,
but is profan'd, if not thou gild'st the even.
but day doth daily draw my sorrows longer,
and in mine own love's strength seem to decay,
and to his paralle sail to be a devil,
wooing his parity with all compare.

can it be not to be receives reproving;
for when i should your great deserts repay,
for then despite of space i would be brought,
from limits far remote, where thou dost stay.

The result may seem light years away from a literary production, but one must remember that it was created by a neural network that has no knowledge of English literature, nor of the English language, nor any grammatical notion. And it only needed 5.3 million parameters where Shakespeare had a hundred billion neurons and thousands of synapses per neuron.

```
> summary(model)
```

Layer (type)	Output Shape	Param #

```
========================================================================
lstm_1 (LSTM)                  (None, 100, 512)              1128448
------------------------------------------------------------------------
dropout_1 (Dropout)            (None, 100, 512)              0
------------------------------------------------------------------------
lstm_2 (LSTM)                  (None, 100, 512)              2099200
------------------------------------------------------------------------
dropout_2 (Dropout)            (None, 100, 512)              0
------------------------------------------------------------------------
lstm_3 (LSTM)                  (None, 512)                   2099200
------------------------------------------------------------------------
dropout_3 (Dropout)            (None, 512)                   0
------------------------------------------------------------------------
dense_1 (Dense)                (None, 62)                    19494
------------------------------------------------------------------------
activation_1 (Activation)      (None, 62)                    0
========================================================================
Total params: 5,346,342
Trainable params: 5,346,342
Non-trainable params: 0
```

9.3 Text Classification Using a LSTM or GRU Recurrent Neural Network

LSTM recurrent networks are able to generate texts but can also be used in a more classical way to classify texts into several predefined categories, based on a training sample of texts whose category is known. Their strength lies in their ability to process sequential data by analyzing each element, for example, each word, by placing it in its context. We manipulate data sequences, which can be character sequences or word sequences. Character sequence analysis, as in the previous section, is more complex and less common, but it has advantages, such as being more resistant to unusual combinations of characters, such as those encountered in misspellings. Here we will analyze sequences of words.

We will use the *Consumer Complaint Database* produced by the Consumer Financial Protection Bureau, a U.S. government organization whose website[7] allows you to download a "Consumer_Complaints.csv" file of 1,282,355 consumer complaints (323,288 with a comment) about banking products.[8] This is a large file of over 600 megabytes. This file contains the date the complaint was received, the financial institution involved, the product concerned (credit card, consumer credit, mortgage credit), the subject of the complaint, its text, and the institution's response. We will try to predict the product concerned from the text of the complaint, contained in the "Consumer_complaint_narrative" variable.

We read the dataset using the `data.table` package and we only keep the product and the text of the complaint, and only when it is filled. The option `check.names = TRUE` avoids having spaces or special characters in the names of the variables.

```
> library(data.table)
> system.time(texts <- fread("D:/…/Consumer_Complaints.csv",
    check.names=TRUE))
> setnames(texts, old = "Consumer.complaint.narrative",
    new = "text")
> texts <- texts[, .(Product,text)]
> texts <- texts[text!=""]
```

We perform some transformations of the text:

```
> texts$text <- gsub("[^[:print:]]", "", texts$text) # remove
  non-printable characters
> texts$text <- gsub("\<\w{1,2}\\\>", "", texts$text) # remove
  words of 1 or 2 characters
> texts$text <- gsub("\\<[a-z]*[x]{2,}[a-z]*\\>", "", texts$text)
  # remove words containing a string of xx
> texts$text <- gsub("\<[a-z]*[X]{2,}[a-z]*\\>", "", texts$text)
  # remove words containing a string of XX
> texts$text <- gsub("[[:punct:]]", " ", texts$text) # remove
  punctuation (replace with a space)
> texts$text <- gsub("[[:space:]]{2,}", " ", texts$text) # remove
  multiple spaces
```

This dataset contains 18 products, two of which are rarer and will be excluded to simplify the prediction a bit:

```
> table(textes$Product)
```

```
                                     Bank account or service
                                                        14885
                                  Checking or savings account
                                                         9129
                                                Consumer Loan
                                                         9473
                                                  Credit card
                                                        18838
                                  Credit card or prepaid card
                                                        15212
                                             Credit reporting
                                                        31588
       Credit reporting, credit repair services, or other personal
       consumer reports
                                                        67018
                                              Debt collection
                                                        73938
             Money transfer, virtual currency, or money service
                                                         4202
                                              Money transfers
                                                         1497
                                                     Mortgage
                                                        48011
                                      Other financial service
                                                          292
                                                  Payday loan
                                                         1747
                      Payday loan, title loan, or personal loan
                                                         3074
```

```
                                            Prepaid card
                                                    1450
                                            Student loan
                                                   18852
                                    Vehicle loan or lease
                                                    4066
                                        Virtual currency
                                                      16
```

However, there are still 16 categories to predict, which is a much more difficult problem than predicting the two "spam/ham" categories (Section 4.4.7) or even the six job categories of the American site Craigslist (Section 4.4.2), for which we achieved a test accuracy of 81.3%.

```
> texts <- texts[!(texts$Product%in%c("Other financial
    service", "Virtual currency")),]
```

We will predict the Y vector containing the products from the X vector containing the text of the complaints. Before we begin modeling, we randomly permute the elements of the Y vector and will measure the proportion of those that remain in the same place. This will tell us the accuracy of a model with random predictions.

```
> X <- texts$text
> Y <- texts$Product
> Y <- as.numeric(factor(Y))
> y_test   <- Y
> pred <- sample(y_test)
> mean(y_test == pred)
[1] 0.1407311
```

The accuracy of a predictive model should be compared to the 14% accuracy of a random classification.

We then create training (226,086 complaints) and test (96,894 complaints) sets:

```
> set.seed(235)
> s <- sample(1:length(X),length(X)*0.7)
> x_train <- X[s]
> x_test   <- X[-s]
> y_train <- Y[s]
> y_test   <- Y[-s]
```

We then format the text into the form expected by the Keras LSTM network.

First, the categorical variables to be explained y_train and y_test must be transformed into binary matrices having one column per class of the variable, this column being 1 for the one corresponding to the class of the image and 0 otherwise:

```
> y_train <- to_categorical(y_train-1, num_classes)
> y_test   <- to_categorical(y_test-1, num_classes)
```

We tokenize the complaint texts into words, using the function tokenize_words() whose result is a list where each element is a document of the corpus, i.e. a complaint. The punctuation is removed but not the stop words:

```
> library(tokenizers)
```

```
> x_token <- tokenize_words(x_train, lowercase = TRUE,
    stopwords = NULL, strip_punct = TRUE, strip_numeric = FALSE,
    simplify = FALSE)
```

The function `text_one_hot(x, maxwords)` then allows us to transform each word into an integer which is the number of the word between 1 and `maxwords`. This parameter is equal to the number of words in the vocabulary and is set here to 5000, a value chosen small enough to limit the size of the objects created. Two different words can have the same number if `maxwords` is less than the total number of different words, but this encoding is based on an optimized hash function (it is not a one-hot encoding as the name of the function suggests).[9] Note that this function does not apply to each element x but to `paste(x, collapse=" ")`, because this function applies to strings of words "aaa bbb ccc…" and not to vectors ("aaa," "bbb," "ccc"…).

```
> maxwords <- 5000
> x_encode <- lapply(x_token, function(x) text_one_hot(paste(x,
    collapse=" "), maxwords, lower=FALSE))
```

We go from one form to another:

```
> head(x_token,1)
[[1]]
  [1] "when"        "loan"        "was"         "switched"    "over"
  [6] "navient"     "was"         "never"       "told"        "that"
 [11] "had"         "deliquint"   "balance"     "because"     "with"
 [16] "did"         "not"         "when"        "going"       "purchase"
 [21] "vehicle"     "discovered"  "credit"      "score"       "had"
 [26] "been"        "dropped"     "from"        "the"         "into"
 [31] "the"         "have"        "been"        "faithful"    "paying"
 [36] "student"     "loan"        "was"         "told"        "that"
 [41] "navient"     "was"         "the"         "company"     "had"
 [46] "delinquency" "with"        "contacted"   "navient"     "resolve"
 [51] "this"        "issue"       "you"         "and"         "kept"
 [56] "being"       "told"        "just"        "contact"     "the"
 [61] "credit"      "bureaus"     "and"         "expalin"     "the"
 [66] "situation"   "and"         "maybe"       "they"        "could"
 [71] "help"        "was"         "angry"       "that"        "just"
 [76] "hurried"     "and"         "paid"        "the"         "balance"
 [81] "off"         "and"         "then"        "after"       "tried"
 [86] "dispute"     "the"         "delinquency" "with"        "the"
 [91] "credit"      "bureaus"     "have"        "had"         "much"
 [96] "trouble"     "bringing"    "credit"      "score"       "back"
> head(x_encode,1)
[[1]]
  [1] 4799 4705 4161 1784 1178 4109 4161 3860 4204 1406 2110 2254  139 3973
 [15] 3846  222 2881 4799 2625 2139 1769 1451 1465 3455 2110 1642 2755 3465
 [29]  233 2145  233 1838 1642 2167 1148 4027 4705 4161 4204 1406 4109 4161
 [43]  233  963 2110   99 3846  682 4109 3314 2083 2171 2642 4118  129 3912
 [57] 4204 4877 4565  233 1465 2453 4118  953  233 3915 4118 1968 3916  609
 [71] 2319 4161   75 1406 4877 3309 4118 4899  233  139 1207 4118  926 1228
 [85]   40 2869  233   99 3846  233 1465 2453 1838 2110 2426 3061  100 1465
 [99] 3455 2229
```

We then apply the `pad_sequences()` function which transforms a list of n sequences of integers (here the word numbers) into a matrix of dimension (`n, maxlength`). Each sequence of integers corresponds to a complaint and there are thus 226,086 for the training set. The parameter `maxlength` is the common length set to all sequences. Sequences shorter than `maxlength` are filled with 0s at the beginning of the sequence, and sequences longer than that are truncated. Here, we set this `maxlength` parameter to 200, because 80% of the complaint texts have less than 200 words.

```
> quantile((sapply(1:length(x_token), function(x)
    length(x_token[[x]]))), 0.8)
80%
203
> maxlength <- 200
> x_train   <- pad_sequences(x_encode, maxlen = maxlength)
> dim(x_train)
[1] 226086    200
```

We do the same for the test sample, before building the neural network whose softmax output has a number of units equal to the number `num_classes` of products to predict:

```
> (num_classes <- length(table(y_train))
[1] 16
```

The first layer of the network is an embedding layer, whose input is a matrix that has one row per document in the corpus to be analyzed and one column per word in each sequence. It is here a 226086 x 200 matrix for the training sample. This layer will perform a word embedding, like the ones in Section 4.4. Its aim is to "embed" each word in a vector space of fixed but limited size, so that each word is associated with its coordinates in the vector space $\mathbb{R}^n$. We have seen (Section 4.4.7) the interest of such a vector representation, which is much more compact than a simple "bag of words" representation, since the dimension n is generally between 100 and 1000, much smaller than the number of different words.

This `layer_embedding` can be trained at the same time as the LSTM network as an integral part of a global model, it can be saved to be used later as an input for another neural network, or it can benefit from transfer learning by loading a pre-trained model of the Word2Vec, GloVe or fastText type, as seen above. It is the first possibility which is implemented here: the calculation of its weights is integrated in the global training of the deep model. Three parameters must be specified for the embedding layer: `input_dim` the size of the vocabulary of the texts (i.e. the number of different words), `output_dim` the dimension of the vector space in which the words are embedded, and `input_length` the length of the word sequences, which must be related to the number of words in each document.

The size of the vocabulary has been set above to `maxwords` = 5000, the dimension of the embedding to 100, and the length of the word sequences to `maxlength` = 200. The output of the `layer_embedding layer` is a 3D tensor whose first component corresponds to the document of the corpus, the second component corresponds to a word of the sequence, and the third component corresponds to a dimension of the embedding. The output is thus a tensor of dimension `nrow(x_train) x maxlength x output_dim` = `dim(x_train) x output_dim`. It can be the input of a fully connected layer (after flattening) or of an LSTM layer as here. Figure 9.2 shows the embedding of a document.

The first model tested consists of a single 128-unit LSTM layer, followed by a dense 64-unit layer, a 50% dropout and a softmax output layer:

```
> model <- keras_model_sequential()
```

mortgage	company	states	did	not	pay	months	mortgage
			↓ word indexing ↓				
1	2	3	4	5	6	7	1
			↓ word embedding ↓				
0.52	0.52	0.64	0.04	0.48	0.78	0.15	0.52
0.23	-0.08	0.88	0.11	0.24	0.55	0.32	0.23
...	...	...	...	...	...	...	...

Figure 9.2 Word embedding.

```
> model %>%
+    layer_embedding(input_dim = maxwords, output_dim = 100,
        input_length=maxlength) %>%
+    layer_lstm(units = 128) %>%
+    layer_dense(units = 64, activation = "relu") %>%
+    layer_dropout(0.5, seed=235) %>%
+    layer_dense(units = num_classes, activation = 'softmax')
> summary(model)
```

Layer (type)	Output Shape	Param #
embedding_5 (Embedding)	(None, 200, 100)	500000
lstm_2 (LSTM)	(None, 128)	117248
dense_9 (Dense)	(None, 64)	8256
dropout_6 (Dropout)	(None, 64)	0
dense_10 (Dense)	(None, 16)	1040

```
Total params: 626,544
Trainable params: 626,544
Non-trainable params: 0
```

We compile and train the network with the RMSprop algorithm for ten epochs:

```
> model %>% compile(loss = 'categorical_crossentropy',
    optimizer = 'rmsprop', metrics = c('accuracy'))

> system.time(history <- fit(model, x_train, y_train,
    batch_size = 128, epochs = 10, shuffle = TRUE,
    validation_data = list(x_test, y_test)))
Train on 226086 samples, validate on 96894 samples
Epoch 1/10
226086/226086 [==============================] - 663s 3ms/step -
    loss: 1.4566 - acc: 0.5370 - val_loss: 1.1673 - val_acc: 0.6188
Epoch 2/10
226086/226086 [==============================] - 669s 3ms/step -
    loss: 1.1159 - acc: 0.6265 - val_loss: 1.0409 - val_acc: 0.6399
Epoch 3/10
226086/226086 [==============================] - 663s 3ms/step -
    loss: 0.9806 - acc: 0.6585 - val_loss: 0.9040 - val_acc: 0.6764
Epoch 4/10
226086/226086 [==============================] - 710s 3ms/step -
    loss: 0.9047 - acc: 0.6835 - val_loss: 0.8709 - val_acc: 0.6894
Epoch 5/10
226086/226086 [==============================] - 670s 3ms/step -
    loss: 0.8594 - acc: 0.7022 - val_loss: 0.8627 - val_acc: 0.7005
Epoch 6/10
226086/226086 [==============================] - 727s 3ms/step -
    loss: 0.8280 - acc: 0.7149 - val_loss: 0.8386 - val_acc: 0.7086
Epoch 7/10
226086/226086 [==============================] - 729s 3ms/step -
    loss: 0.8031 - acc: 0.7243 - val_loss: 0.8467 - val_acc: 0.7102
Epoch 8/10
226086/226086 [==============================] - 730s 3ms/step -
    loss: 0.7824 - acc: 0.7320 - val_loss: 0.8266 - val_acc: 0.7180
Epoch 9/10
226086/226086 [==============================] - 730s 3ms/step -
    loss: 0.7637 - acc: 0.7369 - val_loss: 0.8933 - val_acc: 0.7197
Epoch 10/10
226086/226086 [==============================] - 729s 3ms/step -
    loss: 0.7474 - acc: 0.7424 - val_loss: 0.8491 - val_acc: 0.7175
utilisateur       système        écoulé
   13495.25       1611.78       7021.75
> plot(history)
> pred <- predict_classes(model, x_test)
> test.label <- max.col(y_test) - 1
> table(test.label, pred)
         pred
test.     0     1     2     3     4     5     6     7     8     9    10    11    12    13    14    15
label
  0    2836   341    48   411   166    17    80   129    47    67   185     4     8   107    17     2
  1    1228   918     7    77   221     8    52    85    73    23    56     2    11    30     2     0
  2      25     2  1255   126    12    30   347   476     2     4   147   108   146     2    69    78
  3     100    11    28  3916   584    79   257   465     4    17    63     4     8    36    23     0
  4     119    55    13  2075  1676    16   285   245    17    11    35     2    12   122    23     5
  5      13     3    19   144    23  5306  2964   773     0     4    94     1     2     1    18     2
  6      63    38   148   495   196  2607 14448  1514     4     3   396     7    21     1   250    12
  7      64    24   150   324   107   366  1187 19057    11    11   419    84    40     4   360    10
  8     120    93     2    35    51     2    11    25   711   133    19     1     2    20     7     0
  9      65     1     3    24    10     0     1    17   103   211     6     3     1    14     1     0
 10      65    15    67    87    39    33   245   262     0     2 13411    13    34     1    96     0
 11       7     0    28     4     5     1    15   173     0     4    10   182    74     0    13     0
 12      17    11   137    27    18     1    63   189     3     3    58   107   259     1    39     9
 13      29     6     0    32    61     1     3     9     2    12     2     0     0   256     0     0
 14       2     2    21    15    12     7   220   286     1     2    66    13    37     0  4965     0
 15       6     8   561    11    38     3   192   109     1     2    43     2    23     0    18   114
> mean(test.label != pred)
[1] 0.2825046
```

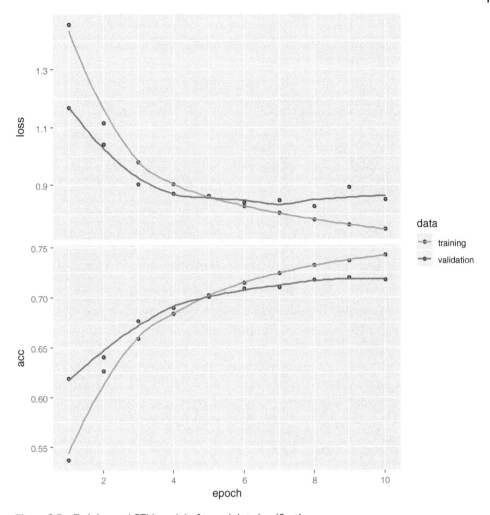

Figure 9.3   Training an LSTM model of complaint classification.

Figure 9.3 shows the evolution of the accuracy during training. The model reaches a test accuracy of 72%, compared to the 18% accuracy of a random model. This performance is all the more honorable since it was obtained by an elementary word embedding at the input of the LSTM network, not exploiting the power of a pre-trained Word2Vec and GloVe embedding like those seen previously. However, Keras allows us to use these pre-trained models in a neural model like the one we have built.[10]

We tested the addition of a second LSTM layer: the computation time increased significantly but not the accuracy.

We then tested a Gated Recurrent Units network (Section 7.16) with the same number of units as the previous network, and the same training parameters, to compare their accuracy. The only change in the following code is the replacement of the `layer_lstm` layer with the `layer_gru` layer. We check that the GRU layer has fewer parameters than the LSTM layer which is more complex.

```
> model <- keras_model_sequential()
> model %>%
+    layer_embedding(input_dim = maxwords, output_dim = 100,
        input_length=maxlength) %>%
+    layer_gru(units = 128) %>%
+    layer_dense(units = 64, activation = "relu") %>%
+    layer_dropout(0.5, seed=235) %>%
+    layer_dense(units = num_classes, activation = 'softmax')

> summary(model)
```

Layer (type)	Output Shape	Param #
embedding_2 (Embedding)	(None, 200, 100)	500000
gru_1 (GRU)	(None, 128)	87936
dense_3 (Dense)	(None, 64)	8256
dropout_2 (Dropout)	(None, 64)	0
dense_4 (Dense)	(None, 16)	1040

```
Total params: 597,232
Trainable params: 597,232
Non-trainable params: 0
```

The GRU layer has only 87,936 weights instead of the 117,248 weights of the LSTM layer. We compile and train the model with the same parameters as before:

```
> model %>% compile(loss = 'categorical_crossentropy',
    optimizer = 'rmsprop', metrics = c('accuracy'))
> system.time(history <- fit(model, x_train, y_train,
    batch_size = 128, epochs = 10, shuffle = TRUE,
    validation_data = list(x_test, y_test)))
Train on 226086 samples, validate on 96894 samples
Epoch 1/10
226086/226086 [==============================] - 656s 3ms/step -
    loss: 1.3750 - acc: 0.5483 - val_loss: 1.0299 - val_acc: 0.6342
Epoch 2/10
226086/226086 [==============================] - 634s 3ms/step -
    loss: 0.9936 - acc: 0.6506 - val_loss: 0.9147 - val_acc: 0.6670
Epoch 3/10
226086/226086 [==============================] - 642s 3ms/step -
    loss: 0.9083 - acc: 0.6804 - val_loss: 0.8635 - val_acc: 0.6906
Epoch 4/10
226086/226086 [==============================] - 682s 3ms/step -
    loss: 0.8607 - acc: 0.6997 - val_loss: 0.8516 - val_acc: 0.6962
Epoch 5/10
226086/226086 [==============================] - 673s 3ms/step -
    loss: 0.8269 - acc: 0.7138 - val_loss: 0.8287 - val_acc: 0.7108
Epoch 6/10
226086/226086 [==============================] - 599s 3ms/step -
    loss: 0.8010 - acc: 0.7227 - val_loss: 0.8220 - val_acc: 0.7156
Epoch 7/10
226086/226086 [==============================] - 601s 3ms/step -
    loss: 0.7809 - acc: 0.7308 - val_loss: 0.8249 - val_acc: 0.7171
Epoch 8/10
226086/226086 [==============================] - 611s 3ms/step -
    loss: 0.7631 - acc: 0.7371 - val_loss: 0.8502 - val_acc: 0.7175
```

```
Epoch 9/10
226086/226086 [==============================] - 707s 3ms/step -
    loss: 0.7456 - acc: 0.7430 - val_loss: 0.8249 - val_acc: 0.7182
Epoch 10/10
226086/226086 [==============================] - 628s 3ms/step -
    loss: 0.7270 - acc: 0.7493 - val_loss: 0.8479 - val_acc: 0.7179
utilisateur       système        écoulé
  11186.02        1699.48        6435.86
> plot(history)
> pred <- predict_classes(model, x_test)
> test.label <- max.col(y_test) - 1
> table(test.label, pred)
```

pred																
test. label	0	1	2	3	4	5	6	7	8	9	10	11	12	13	14	15
0	2638	680	34	325	178	11	77	94	132	54	153	5	3	69	11	1
1	988	1259	3	52	173	2	50	55	143	7	35	2	3	17	3	1
2	31	7	1241	149	68	18	280	440	10	8	165	72	129	1	63	147
3	130	27	9	3502	1093	46	242	419	19	15	46	1	4	32	10	0
4	134	111	6	1638	2201	7	236	193	36	11	31	2	3	88	12	2
5	14	5	30	165	73	5009	3063	866	6	0	106	2	1	2	22	3
6	75	68	197	398	400	2168	14672	1586	11	4	389	4	14	1	183	33
7	91	63	166	340	215	244	1051	19190	35	6	425	54	55	2	268	13
8	74	127	0	28	44	1	10	24	844	56	9	1	1	8	5	0
9	47	9	1	21	14	2	3	16	190	134	4	1	1	16	1	0
10	163	49	40	103	82	34	259	271	21	7	13248	4	21	2	62	4
11	8	2	24	7	6	1	10	162	4	2	25	182	70	0	13	0
12	18	19	115	38	39	1	63	180	6	0	83	90	233	0	36	21
13	34	17	0	29	87	1	1	8	16	5	1	0	0	213	1	0
14	4	4	12	25	34	6	237	367	6	0	115	8	27	0	4802	2
15	13	2	506	17	58	2	153	101	4	0	40	1	27	0	17	190

```
> mean(test.label != pred)
[1] 0.2821227
```

Figure 9.4 shows the evolution of the GRU network's accuracy over the course of the training, which ends with an accuracy of 72% in the test dataset, almost equal to the accuracy of the LSTM network, as one would expect in this type of analysis, but with a time saving of 8%.

Finally, we tested a bidirectional recurrent gate network with the same number of units as the previous network, and the same training parameters, to compare their accuracy. In the Keras code, the bidirectionality of the layer_gru layer was specified by bidirectional(layer_gru(units = 128)):

```
> model <- keras_model_sequential()
> model %>%
+   layer_embedding(input_dim = maxwords, output_dim = 100,
    input_length=maxlength) %>%
+   bidirectional(layer_gru(units = 128)) %>%
+   layer_dense(units = 64, activation = "relu") %>%
+   layer_dropout(0.5, seed=235) %>%
+   layer_dense(units = num_classes, activation = 'softmax')

> summary(model)
```

Layer (type)	Output Shape	Param #
embedding_3 (Embedding)	(None, 200, 100)	500000

```
bidirectional_1 (Bidirectional (None, 256)                175872

dense_5 (Dense)                  (None, 64)                 16448

dropout_3 (Dropout)              (None, 64)                 0

dense_6 (Dense)                  (None, 16)                 1040
================================================================
Total params: 693,360
Trainable params: 693,360
Non-trainable params: 0
```

```
...
> mean(test.label != pred)
[1] 0.2884802
```

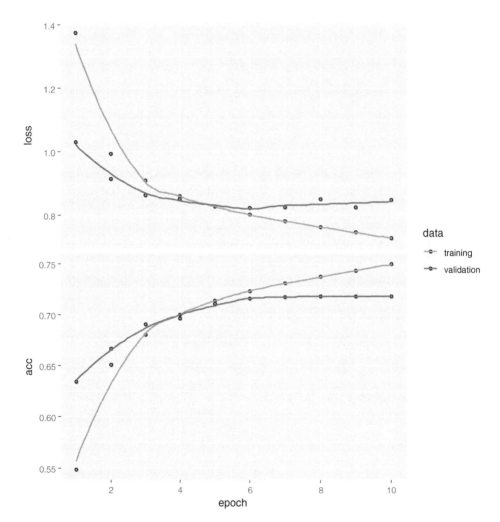

Figure 9.4   Training a GRU model of complaint classification.

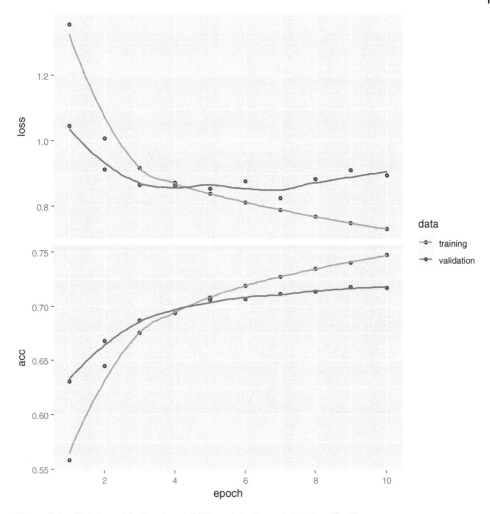

Figure 9.5 Training a bi-directional GRU model of complaint classification.

The number of parameters is naturally doubled in the GRU layer. Figure 9.5 shows the evolution of the accuracy of the bidirectional GRU network. Training turns out to be 1.6 times longer but the accuracy is almost unchanged. Here, bidirectionality did not improve the predictive power of the model. We also tested replacing the RMSprop algorithm with the ADAM adaptive optimization algorithm, but with no gain in accuracy.

Thus, the accuracy of the previous models is around 72% with no significant difference between the LSTM, GRU, and bidirectional GRU models. We rerun the first LSTM model by increasing the length of the word sequences (`maxlength` parameter) from 200 to 500, and by increasing the vocabulary from 5000 to 10000 words. The number of parameters of the embedding layer then increases from half a million to a million: 10000 words x 100 dimensions.

```
> summary(model)
```

Layer (type)	Output Shape	Param #
embedding_3 (Embedding)	(None, 500, 100)	1000000
lstm_2 (LSTM)	(None, 128)	117248
dense_5 (Dense)	(None, 64)	8256
dropout_3 (Dropout)	(None, 64)	0
dense_6 (Dense)	(None, 16)	1040

```
Total params: 1,126,544
Trainable params: 1,126,544
Non-trainable params: 0
```

```
> # predictions
> pred <- predict_classes(model, x_test)
> test.label <- max.col(y_test) - 1
> table(test.label, pred)
                pred
```

test. label	0	1	2	3	4	5	6	7	8	9	10	11	12	13	14	15
0	2896	675	37	236	117	10	93	84	19	57	159	1	9	54	11	7
1	972	1437	4	41	118	1	65	44	37	8	47	1	7	4	2	5
2	41	4	1356	78	28	22	288	353	1	2	159	35	210	0	36	216
3	178	24	15	3634	903	37	355	360	6	18	41	0	7	9	7	1
4	128	147	8	1527	2286	10	353	142	13	4	26	0	13	43	7	4
5	32	12	39	121	25	4826	3422	768	3	1	93	1	1	0	21	2
6	77	52	205	310	249	1994	15170	1428	4	2	356	0	32	0	267	57
7	125	42	193	327	152	197	1124	19158	6	14	438	36	61	1	306	38
8	119	187	2	26	42	2	14	17	658	133	14	1	7	4	5	1
9	88	13	3	21	6	0	1	12	64	238	6	0	5	3	0	0
10	92	23	22	36	38	22	370	180	2	2	13526	1	33	1	20	2
11	12	1	22	3	1	1	15	172	0	3	22	127	131	0	6	0
12	22	16	86	15	35	0	76	146	1	1	72	54	332	0	33	53
13	55	18	0	24	92	0	4	5	1	6	0	0	0	208	0	0
14	7	5	2	7	12	2	215	242	1	0	84	0	44	0	5026	2
15	4	8	398	7	25	1	214	56	0	3	40	0	27	0	8	340

```
> mean(test.label != pred)
[1] 0.2649906
```

We manage to improve the accuracy in the test dataset up to 73.5%, against 72% with sequences of length 200 and a vocabulary of 5000 words, but with 1.8 times more parameters to determine and at the end of a calculation three times longer. We also tested the use of a recurrent dropout `layer_lstm(units = 128, recurrent_dropout = 0.5)`, but with no significant gain in accuracy, neither with 50% nor with 20% dropout.

9.4   Text Classification Using a H2O Model

As a comparison, we will apply to the same Consumer Complaint Database two machine learning methods of the H2O software (Section 2.5.6): gradient boosting and a neural network, which H2O calls `deeplearning` but which is neither a convolutional network nor a recurrent network but an improved perceptron. This will be the opportunity to use the *grid search* function which allows H2O to compute in one a run large set of models of a given algorithm, differing according to some parameters.

We proceed as in Section 4.4.7. After loading the h2o package and starting the H2O cluster, we read the database excluding the two rarest products in the complaints. The 44,062,361 words in the database are extracted by the h2o.tokenize(x, "\\\\W+") function, which considers any character other than a letter or number as a word separator, and separates two complaints by a "NA." Next, we create Word2Vec vectors using the skip-gram model of the h2o.word2vec() function by retaining only words appearing in at least 50 complaints, with a 5-word sliding window around each word, a vector representation of dimension 100, and 10 epochs for training the Word2Vec model. The 100 Word2Vec vectors created for each word are then aggregated at the level of each complaint by the h2o.transform() function. These 100 vectors are assembled with the variable to be explained "Product" into a data frame that is then split into a training sample (70%) and a test sample (30%).

```
> library(h2o)
> h2o.init(max_mem_size = '6g', ice_root="C:/…/h2o", nthreads=2)
> textes <- h2o.importFile(path = "D:/…/Complaints.csv", header=TRUE, sep=",")
> textes <- textes[!(textes$Product%in%c("Other financial service",
  "Virtual currency")),]
> words <- h2o.tokenize(textes$text, "\\\\W+")
> dim(words)
[1] 44062361        1
> w2v.model <- h2o.word2vec(words, min_word_freq = 50, vec_size = 100,
  window_size = 5, epochs = 10)
> plot.vecs <- h2o.transform(w2v.model, words, aggregate = "average")
> dim(plot.vecs)
[1] 319529     100
> data <- h2o.cbind(textes["Product"], plot.vecs)
> data.split <- h2o.splitFrame(data, ratios = 0.7, seed = 235)
```

We can now start the modeling, i.e. the prediction of the product object of the complaint from the 100 Word2Vec vectors describing each complaint.

To start, we run the grid search on the deeplearning neural network. The name of this h2o function is therefore the first parameter of the h2o.grid() function. We decided to vary several of the parameters seen in Section 6.11: the activation function, the penalty of the ridge and Lasso weights, and the number of hidden units. We test the following configurations: two hidden layers of 25, 50 or 100 units each, and three hidden layers of 25 or 50 units each. The number of epochs will always be equal to 20.

```
> dl_params <- list(activation = c("Tanh","Rectifier"),
    l1 = c(1e-4,1e-5,1e-6,0), l2 = c(1e-4,1e-5,1e-6,0),
    hidden = c(c(25,25),c(50,50),c(100,100),c(25,25,25),c(50,50,50)))
> system.time(grid_dl <- h2o.grid(algorithm="deeplearning",
    grid_id="dl_grid", epochs=20, training_frame=data.split[[1]],
    validation_frame=data.split[[2]], x=names(plot.vecs),
    y="Product", seed=123, hyper_params=dl_params))
utilisateur     système      écoulé
     83.38       20.01    17429.06
```

After a long computation, we obtained 124 neural network models, which are ranked in the grid_dl result by increasing cross-entropy:

```
> grid_dl
```

```
H2O Grid Details
================

Grid ID: dl_grid
Used hyper parameters:
  -  activation
  -  hidden
  -  l1
  -  l2
Number of models: 124
Number of failed models: 0

Hyper-Parameter Search Summary: ordered by increasing logloss
    activation hidden     l1      l2          model_ids               logloss
1         Tanh   [100] 1.0E-6     0.0 dl_grid_model_408 0.9082633479585424
2         Tanh   [100]    0.0 1.0E-6 dl_grid_model_336 0.9099535196106062
3         Tanh   [100]    0.0     0.0 dl_grid_model_432 0.9100011837128597
4         Tanh   [100] 1.0E-5     0.0 dl_grid_model_384 0.9112289606259246
5         Tanh   [100]    0.0 1.0E-5 dl_grid_model_240 0.9113150465776803

—

    activation hidden     l1      l2          model_ids               logloss
119         Tanh    [50] 0.001 1.0E-5  dl_grid_model_68 0.9939510200586888
120         Tanh    [25] 0.001 1.0E-5  dl_grid_model_64 0.9972293262429055
121         Tanh    [25] 0.001 1.0E-4  dl_grid_model_32 0.9990807667878026
122         Tanh    [50] 0.001 1.0E-4  dl_grid_model_36 1.0019198348624039
123         Tanh    [25] 0.001   0.001  dl_grid_model_0 1.0167183555694421
124         Tanh    [50] 0.001   0.001  dl_grid_model_4 1.0197901193729948
```

We sort the models by increasing error in the test dataset, and display the grid parameters and their values for the best and worst models. The lowest error, 32.92%, or 67.08% accuracy, is obtained with a two-layer grid of 100 hidden units, the hyperbolic tangent as activation function, a Lasso penalty equal to 10^{-6} and no ridge penalty. This accuracy is therefore lower than the 72% accuracy obtained with a recurrent LSTM or GRU network (Section 9.3):

```
> models <- h2o.getGrid("dl_grid", sort_by="err", decreasing=FALSE)
> models
H2O Grid Details
================

Grid ID: dl_grid
Used hyper parameters:
  -  activation
  -  hidden
  -  l1
  -  l2
Number of models: 124
Number of failed models: 0

Hyper-Parameter Search Summary: ordered by increasing err
    activation hidden     l1      l2          model_ids                   err
1         Tanh   [100] 1.0E-6     0.0 dl_grid_model_408 0.32916997368311124
2         Tanh   [100] 1.0E-6 1.0E-5 dl_grid_model_216  0.3294937131876854
3    Rectifier   [100] 1.0E-4 1.0E-4  dl_grid_model_73  0.3306946823175571
4    Rectifier   [100] 1.0E-4 1.0E-4  dl_grid_model_73  0.3306946823175571
5         Tanh    [50] 1.0E-5 1.0E-5  dl_grid_model_84 0.33075734157650694
```

```
---
      activation hidden     l1      l2        model_ids                 err
119        Tanh    [50] 0.001 1.0E-5 dl_grid_model_68 0.34954467605163125
120        Tanh    [50] 0.001 1.0E-4 dl_grid_model_36  0.3496073353105811
121        Tanh    [25] 0.001 1.0E-5 dl_grid_model_64  0.3498579723463804
122        Tanh    [25] 0.001  0.001  dl_grid_model_0 0.35034880320815404
123        Tanh    [50] 0.001  0.001  dl_grid_model_4  0.3521450352980492
124        Tanh    [25] 0.001 1.0E-4 dl_grid_model_32 0.35256276369104805
```

We then run the grid search on the gradient boosting. We vary the learning rate, the number of trees and their maximum depth:

```
> gbm_params <- list(ntrees = c(100, 300), learn_rate = c(0.2,0.35,0.5),
    max_depth = c(5,10))
> system.time(grid_gbm <- h2o.grid(algorithm="gbm", grid_id="dl_grid",
    training_frame=data.split[[1]], validation_frame=data.split[[2]],
    x=names(plot.vecs), y="Product",
+   , seed=123, hyper_params=gbm_params))
utilisateur      système       écoulé
    3072.09       725.88    173184.00
```

The computation time of this grid is much longer, for only 12 models obtained, classified as before by increasing cross-entropy:

```
> grid_gbm
H2O Grid Details
================

Grid ID: dl_grid
Used hyper parameters:
  -  learn_rate
  -  max_depth
  -  ntrees
Number of models: 12
Number of failed models: 0

Hyper-Parameter Search Summary: ordered by increasing logloss
     learn_rate max_depth ntrees         model_ids              logloss
1           0.2         5    300   dl_grid_model_6 0.9539073628386971
2           0.2         5    100   dl_grid_model_0 0.9677672524489567
3          0.35         5    100   dl_grid_model_1 1.0852793596342336
4          0.35         5    300   dl_grid_model_7 1.0898507104886113
5           0.5         5    100   dl_grid_model_2 1.2096227997288944
6           0.5         5    300   dl_grid_model_8 1.2177563724456177
7           0.2        10    100   dl_grid_model_3 1.4567361586798697
8          0.35        10    100   dl_grid_model_4 1.4909849571066331
9          0.35        10    300  dl_grid_model_10  1.51167438196562
10          0.5        10    100   dl_grid_model_5 2.037270396992035
11          0.2        10    300   dl_grid_model_9 2.077143075972489
12          0.5        10    300  dl_grid_model_11 4.405635945458592
```

We sort the models by increasing error in test, and display the grid parameters for each model, along with its error. The lowest error, 32.03%, or 68% accuracy, is obtained with 300 trees of maximum depth equal to 5 and a learning rate equal to 0.2. This accuracy is slightly higher than that of the previous neural network but still lower than the accuracy of the recurrent LSTM and GRU networks.

```
> models <- h2o.getGrid("dl_grid", sort_by="err", decreasing=FALSE)
> models@summary_table
Hyper-Parameter Search Summary: ordered by increasing err
     learn_rate max_depth ntrees        model_ids                   err
1          0.2          5    300  dl_grid_model_6   0.3203350181711851
2          0.2         10    100  dl_grid_model_3   0.3241467897572998
3          0.2         10    300  dl_grid_model_9    0.334067839091023
4          0.2          5    100  dl_grid_model_0  0.33427670328752246
5         0.35          5    300  dl_grid_model_7   0.3491791637077572
6         0.35          5    100  dl_grid_model_1  0.34954467605163125
7         0.35         10    100  dl_grid_model_4   0.3597476920506287
8         0.35         10    300 dl_grid_model_10  0.35987301056852833
9          0.5          5    300  dl_grid_model_8  0.36416516980659175
10         0.5          5    100  dl_grid_model_2  0.36472910313714024
11         0.5         10    100  dl_grid_model_5   0.3895317264714483
12         0.5         10    300 dl_grid_model_11  0.40746271774092485
```

These results confirm the value of recurrent neural networks for the analysis of natural language in the form of word sequences.

9.5   Application of Convolutional Neural Networks

The words of a sentence can be represented in a way that allows convolutional neural networks to be naturally applied to them. Each sentence (or each email, each document) is a matrix that has one column per word of the vocabulary and one row per word of the sentence: the whole row is 0 except for the column corresponding to the word, which is 1. A word is thus the equivalent of a pixel, and a sentence or a segment of text corresponds to an image in its matrix form, as shown in Figure 9.6. We can also make the columns correspond to signs (letters, numbers, punctuation) and the rows to words, and have a non-zero value in the matrix when a character appears in a word.

Figure 9.7 illustrates the convolutional network mechanism applied to a text. The sentence "I like this movie very much!" has two filters of height 2, two filters of height 3 and two filters of height 4. If we consider the example of a filter of size 3, it could be centered on "I like this," "like this movie," "this movie very," "movie very much" or "very much!." So we have five units in the activation layer following the convolution layer. As with image convolution, the output of the convolution layer is larger, the narrower the convolution filter. A filter as wide as the input window would give an output reduced to one unit. We then have in the network a max pooling layer, and a flattening of the layers before the softmax output layer.

Another possible architecture is the word embedding architecture used previously with recurrent networks. The convolution layers are preceded by an embedding layer, whose output is a 3D tensor whose first component corresponds to the document or sentence, the second component corresponds to a word of the sequence and the third component corresponds to a dimension of the embedding. The difference with convolutional networks used for computer vision is that the convolution is here in one dimension, the temporal dimension, and not in two dimensions.

the	1	0	0	0	0	0	0	0	0	0
young	0	1	0	0	0	0	0	0	0	0
man	0	0	1	0	0	0	0	0	0	0
in	0	0	0	1	0	0	0	0	0	0
a	0	0	0	0	1	0	0	0	0	0
crowded	0	0	0	0	0	1	0	0	0	0
bus	0	0	0	0	0	0	1	0	0	0
in	0	0	0	1	0	0	0	0	0	0
the	1	0	0	0	0	0	0	0	0	0
middle	0	0	0	0	0	0	0	1	0	0
of	0	0	0	0	0	0	0	0	1	0
the	1	0	0	0	0	0	0	0	0	0
day	0	0	0	0	0	0	0	0	0	1

Figure 9.6 Matrix representation of a text.

We use the example of complaint message classification again, with a convolutional network instead of a recurrent network as in Section 9.3. The first convolution layer is followed by a max pooling layer and the second convolution layer is followed by a global pooling layer (which could be replaced by a flattening layer).

We keep the same parameters of vocabulary size (5000 words), embedding dimension (100), and word sequence length (200 words), the RMSprop optimization algorithm and the ten epochs for training the network:

```
> model <- keras_model_sequential()
> model %>%
+   layer_embedding(input_dim = maxwords, output_dim = 100,
      input_length=maxlength) %>%
+   layer_conv_1d(filters = 128, kernel_size = 7, activation = "relu") %>%
+   layer_max_pooling_1d(pool_size = 5) %>%
+   layer_conv_1d(filters = 128, kernel_size = 7, activation = "relu") %>%
+   layer_global_max_pooling_1d() %>%
+   layer_dense(units = 64, activation = "relu") %>%
+   layer_dropout(0.5, seed=235) %>%
+   layer_dense(units = num_classes, activation = 'softmax')

> summary(model)
```

Layer (type)	Output Shape	Param #
embedding_8 (Embedding)	(None, 200, 100)	500000
conv1d_15 (Conv1D)	(None, 194, 128)	89728
max_pooling1d_9 (MaxPooling1D)	(None, 38, 128)	0
conv1d_16 (Conv1D)	(None, 32, 128)	114816
global_max_pooling1d_5 (GlobalM	(None, 128)	0

dense_13 (Dense)	(None, 64)	8256
dropout_7 (Dropout)	(None, 64)	0
dense_14 (Dense)	(None, 16)	1040

```
====================================================================
Total params: 713,840
Trainable params: 713,840
Non-trainable params: 0
```

```
> model %>% compile(loss = 'categorical_crossentropy', optimizer = 'rm-
sprop', metrics = c('accuracy'))
> system.time(history <- fit(model, x_train, y_train, batch_size = 128,
    epochs = 10, shuffle = TRUE, validation_data = list(x_test, y_test)))
Train on 226086 samples, validate on 96894 samples
```

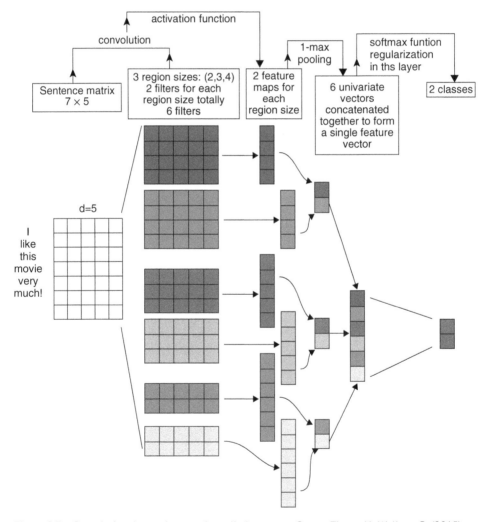

Figure 9.7 Convolutional neural network applied to a text. *Source*: Zhang, Y., Wallace, B. (2015). A Sensitivity Analysis of (and Practitioners' Guide to) Convolutional Neural Networks for Sentence Classification, arXiv:1510.03820.

```
Epoch 1/10
226086/226086 [==============================] - 45s 200us/step -
    loss: 1.2275 - acc: 0.5917 - val_loss: 1.0128 - val_acc: 0.6434
Epoch 2/10
226086/226086 [==============================] - 46s 201us/step -
    loss: 0.9833 - acc: 0.6555 - val_loss: 0.9044 - val_acc: 0.6706
Epoch 3/10
226086/226086 [==============================] - 46s 203us/step -
    loss: 0.9104 - acc: 0.6786 - val_loss: 0.9154 - val_acc: 0.6759
Epoch 4/10
226086/226086 [==============================] - 46s 205us/step -
    loss: 0.8617 - acc: 0.6976 - val_loss: 0.9980 - val_acc: 0.6599
Epoch 5/10
226086/226086 [==============================] - 49s 215us/step -
    loss: 0.8292 - acc: 0.7097 - val_loss: 0.9466 - val_acc: 0.6866
Epoch 6/10
226086/226086 [==============================] - 49s 216us/step -
    loss: 0.7999 - acc: 0.7199 - val_loss: 0.9660 - val_acc: 0.6926
Epoch 7/10
226086/226086 [==============================] - 49s 217us/step -
    loss: 0.7797 - acc: 0.7286 - val_loss: 1.0040 - val_acc: 0.6924
Epoch 8/10
226086/226086 [==============================] - 49s 217us/step -
    loss: 0.7661 - acc: 0.7349 - val_loss: 1.0750 - val_acc: 0.6757
Epoch 9/10
226086/226086 [==============================] - 47s 210us/step -
    loss: 0.7578 - acc: 0.7399 - val_loss: 1.1321 - val_acc: 0.6750
Epoch 10/10
226086/226086 [==============================] - 47s 207us/step -
    loss: 0.7518 - acc: 0.7440 - val_loss: 1.0682 - val_acc: 0.6867
utilisateur       système        écoulé
    400.11        336.50        473.97
```

We note the speed of training (on GPU). The model is then applied to the test sample:

```
> pred <- predict_classes(model, x_test)
> test.label <- max.col(y_test) - 1
> table(test.label, pred)
        pred
test.    0    1    2    3    4    5     6     7    8   9    10   11  12   13   14  15
label
    0 2562  570   50  304  138   27   108   156   78  54   332    3    3   59   20   1
    1 1174  930   12   75  162    9    79   102   61  16   137    1    2   13   18   2
    2   28    2 1186   87   30   22   486   400    3   1   233   24  116    0  137  74
    3  201   30   34 3003  933   69   579   519    9  13   140    0    2   24   37   2
    4  200   93   17 1644 1622   25   564   263   25   5   116    0    3   86   44   4
    5   23    4   31   72   22 4708  3485   872    1   0   110    1    2    0   35   1
    6   55   27  158  273  177 2612 14661  1579    4   0   377    2   12    1  246  19
    7   93   27  238  274  107  301  1611 18396    7   5   609   53   54    2  422  19
    8  153  106    8   35   35    1    31    39  660 106    41    0    0    9    8   0
    9   85   18    4   21   11    1    11    22  104 155    20    0    1    3    4   0
   10   63    7   58   51   45   45   474   262    3   1 13175    0   19    1  162   4
   11    8    2   46    3    4    1    20   182    0   1    36   95   76    0   42   0
   12   23    8  131   17   19    5    98   199    2   1   115   48  147    0  114  15
   13   45   10    1   47   65    1    16    11    7   7     3    0    0  198    1   1
   14    4    4   18    5   19    6   260   289    1   0   116    1   13    1 4911   1
   15    2    4  499    9   24    2   250    87    1   0    82    0    7    0   38 126
> mean(test.label != pred)
[1] 0.3133218
```

A two-layer convolutional neural network achieves 69% accuracy, which is lower than the 72% accuracy of an equivalent-sized LSTM network, but 15 times faster.

9.6 Spam Detection Using a Recurrent Neural Network LSTM

Finally, we take up the spam detection example we dealt with in Section 4.4.7 by applying a Word2Vec embedding to it using H2O software. We will now apply Keras embedding and an LSTM recurrent network to it.

The data preparation is done exactly as with the consumer complaint file, and we create a training set of 80% of the total base, and a test set of 20%. We set the size of the vocabulary (`maxwords`) to 10,000 and the length of the sequences (`maxlength`) to 25, which is much smaller than for the complaints because the SMS messages to be classified are much shorter.

The structure of the LSTM network is as follows:

```
> model <- keras_model_sequential()
> model %>%
+    layer_embedding(input_dim = maxwords, output_dim = 50,
+       input_length=maxlength) %>%
+    layer_lstm(units = 128, recurrent_dropout = 0.2) %>%
+    layer_dense(units = 64, activation = "relu") %>%
+    layer_dropout(0.5, seed=235) %>%
+    layer_dense(units = num_classes, activation = 'softmax')
> model
Model
```

Layer (type)	Output Shape	Param #
embedding_1 (Embedding)	(None, 25, 50)	500000
lstm_1 (LSTM)	(None, 128)	91648
dense_1 (Dense)	(None, 64)	8256
dropout_1 (Dropout)	(None, 64)	0
dense_2 (Dense)	(None, 2)	130

```
Total params: 600,034
Trainable params: 600,034
Non-trainable params: 0
```

The model is then trained with the ADAM optimization algorithm for ten epochs:

```
> model %>% compile(loss = 'categorical_crossentropy',
+    optimizer = 'adam', metrics = c('accuracy'))
> system.time(history <- fit(model, x_train, y_train,
+    batch_size = 128, epochs = 10, shuffle = TRUE,
+    validation_data = list(x_test, y_test)))
Train on 4451 samples, validate on 1113 samples
```

```
Epoch 1/10
4451/4451 [==============================] - 3s 611us/step -
    loss: 0.0022 - acc: 0.9991 - val_loss
...
Epoch 10/10
4451/4451 [==============================] - 2s 411us/step -
    loss: 5.1399e-05 - acc: 1.0000 - val_loss: 0.0337 - val_acc: 0.9964
utilisateur      système      écoulé
      37.88         4.54       19.93
```

The model predictions on the test set show an error of only 0.36%, much smaller than the 1.7% error previously obtained (Section 4.4.7) by gradient boosting on a Word2Vec embedding.

```
> pred <- predict_classes(model, x_test)
> test.label <- max.col(y_test) - 1
> table(test.label, pred)
          pred
test.label   0   1
         0 963   1
         1   3 146
> mean(test.label != pred)
[1] 0.00359389
```

This result shows the performance of LSTM neural networks in natural language processing.

9.7 Transformer Models, BERT, and Its Successors

We have studied word embedding methods such as Word2Vec (Section 4.4.7) and saw that they are NLP transfer learning models that can be applied to various problems after being trained on large corpora, just as image recognition models can be pre-trained on the ImageNet database. These methods have been improved by the ULMFiT (Universal Language Model Fine-Tuning),[11] ELMo (Embeddings from Language Models)[12] and BERT (Bidirectional Encoder Representations from Transformers)[13] algorithms which produce embeddings in which the same word has a different embedding if it is used in different contexts.[14] Tested on various benchmarks, GLU (General Language Understanding Evaluation), SQuAD (Stanford Question Answering Dataset), SNLI (Stanford Natural Language Inference) ..., these algorithms have shown a clear superiority. These three algorithms published in the same year have made the year 2018 referred to as the "ImageNet moment for natural language processing."

The last of these algorithms, BERT, is based on a new principle that is different from the other two: it is a transformer model.. These models appeared in 2017 and rely on the so-called self-attention mechanism.[15] When a word requires the knowledge of its context to be understood, for example, a pronoun that can refer to several people, the self-attention mechanism allows the model to incorporate, in the vector representation of the word, information that indicates its relevance to any other word in the sentence. Each word is encoded with its context: its importance depends on the presence and position of the other words in the sentence. It is this mechanism that allows the model to selectively focus on the segments of the input text that it has identified as the most relevant.

Transformer models are progressively replacing recurrent neural networks for complex natural language processing tasks, and in particular for translation or question answering. They are sometimes compared to LSTM recurrent networks for their ability to model long-term dependencies in sequential data. But transformer models are able to model longer-term dependencies than recurrent networks, especially since in an LSTM network, unlike a transformer model, the information between two non-adjacent words must pass through all intermediate words. We will see below that BERT is trained on tasks that by their very nature are designed to detect these long-range dependencies.

Their principle also means that they do not need to process sentences in order, from beginning to end, and can therefore be parallelized. This accelerates their training, which can be done on larger corpora. This is another advantage over LSTM recurrent networks.

A third advantage they have over both recurrent networks and previous word embedding methods is their universality: they are generically pre-trained on self-supervised tasks (see below) and can then be fine-tuned on a wide variety of supervised tasks, or even on unsupervised tasks such as text generation. Transformer models can thus be implemented in two ways:

- *for word embedding*: they are used to transform texts into numerical vectors representing the words of these texts, vectors often aggregated at the sentence or document level, and which are then used as input to another model, which can be a neural network, an ensemble model, a regression model ...
- *for transfer learning*: the initial transformer model (BERT or another one, most of them available in open source in deep learning libraries) is fine-tuned on the studied problem.

We will show later on the same dataset an example of each of these uses and we will compare the results obtained.

BERT (Bidirectional Encoder Representations from Transformers) is a transformer model pre-trained on an unlabeled dataset that can then be finely tuned by supervised learning for specific tasks. The value of this transfer learning is that the fine-tuning can be performed on a smaller corpus – and thus easier to obtain – than the training of the pre-trained model which requires a large corpus and long computations. Moreover, BERT pre-training is done for a wide variety of NLP tasks and does not have to be repeated to accomplish a specific task, only the fine-tuning of the training has to be done on the specific task.

Unlike the Word2Vec model and the other models seen in Section 4.4, BERT takes into account the different possible meanings of a word and the vector associated to this word will depend on its meaning in the sentence. The word "bank" will not have the same vector representation in "river bank" and "bank account." The word "cell" will not have the same vector representation in a judicial, phone, or biological context. The maximum length of BERT sequences is 512 words (or, rather, tokens), limiting the context taken into account for each to 511 words at most, which already requires complex calculations. Another feature of BERT is that it is bidirectional and takes into account the words that follow as well as the words that precede the analyzed word. This is a feature that ULMFiT does not have, nor even ELMo which is only superficially bidirectional with its two unidirectional recurrent networks.

BERT was trained on more than 16 gigabytes of data, 800 million words from the BookCorpus[16] and 2500 million words from the English Wikipedia, to perform two supervised tasks: (1) predict from their context a 15% proportion of randomly masked words (MLM: Masked Language Modeling); and (2) choose whether a sentence B follows a sentence A, for two given sentences in a sample composed of 50% consecutive pairs and 50% random pairs of sentences (NSP: Next Sentence Prediction). More precisely, we speak of self-supervised tasks because the texts have not been given any external information (labels), indicating, for example, the category of the text, but this information comes from the texts themselves: a part of a text is used to predict another part of this text. The interest of self-supervised learning is that it does not require human intervention and can therefore easily exploit very large text corpora (Wikipedia, Google News...) to train more and more complex models. Since Word2Vec (Section 4.4.7), word embedding methods have been based on self-supervised tasks, but we can see the evolution between Word2Vec and BERT: instead of looking for information in a small window around each word, information is looked for at a longer distance (in the whole text) in BERT and transformer models, hence this modeling of long-term dependencies.

It is remarkable that transfer learning is possible from a model pre-trained on self-supervised tasks, considering that transfer learning in the field of image recognition is often done from models trained on supervised tasks: labeled image recognition.

There are two versions of BERT: the $BERT_{BASE}$ model has 12 layers, 768 hidden units, 12 bidirectional attention heads, and 110 million parameters. Such an embedding model associates to each word a vector of dimension 768 and to each sentence a vector of the same dimension, which is a weighted average of the embedding of each word in the sentence. The $BERT_{LARGE}$ model is more complex (Table 9.1).

BERT has been followed by many variants, including RoBERTa[17] which is trained only on the MLM task. It was adapted to the French language in 2019 with the CamemBERT[18] model built on the architecture of RoBERTa and pre-trained on a 138 gigabyte corpus,

Table 9.1 Some transformer models.

Model	No. of layers	No. of hidden units	No. of attention heads	No. of parameters
$BERT_{BASE}$	12	768	12	110 million
$BERT_{LARGE}$	24	1024	16	340 million
$RoBERTa_{BASE}$	12	768	12	125 million
$RoBERTa_{LARGE}$	24	1024	16	355 million
$DeBERTa_{BASE}$	12	768	12	125 million
$DeBERTa_{LARGE}$	24	1024	16	390 million
DistilBERT	6	768	12	65 million
MobileBERT	24	512	4	25 million
CamemBERT	12	768	12	110 million
$FlauBERT_{BASE}$	12	768	12	138 million
$FlauBERT_{LARGE}$	24	1024	16	373 million

the OSCAR corpus which is a French section of the Common Crawl dataset (a dataset containing the texts of a large quantity of web pages). This French model was followed a few weeks later by the FlauBERT[19] model which was also pre-trained on the MLM task alone, on a corpus of 71 gigabytes of text, and which, despite its smaller training corpus, performed as well as CamemBERT on several tests, including the FLUE (French Language Understanding Evaluation) test adapted from GLUE by the creators of FlauBERT. In fact, these two models are complementary and give even better results when coupled. Like BERT, FlauBERT exists in two versions: the FlauBERT$_{BASE}$ model and the FlauBERT$_{LARGE}$ model. RoBERTa has also been improved by the DeBERTa model,[20] which achieves superior performance and even exceeds human performance on the SuperGLUE benchmark, albeit with a smaller training dataset.

There is a simplified and faster version of BERT, DistilBERT,[21] which has the same vocabulary, 97% of BERT's capabilities (measured on the GLUE benchmark), with a 40% smaller model size and 60% faster speed. DistilBERT is trained on the same corpus as BERT but with a "distillation" mechanism which consists in training a "student" model (here DistilBERT) to predict the predictions of a "teacher" model (here BERT). On the same principle, the MobileBERT[22] is an even more compressed variant of BERT, and it is 4.3 times smaller and, according to its authors, 5.5 times faster than BERT$_{BASE}$ while having comparable performances and universality. It must be said that when BERT was created in 2018, it was considered a big model, with its more than 100 million parameters, a number that was quickly far exceeded.

There are also specialized models, such as PubMedBERT,[23] pre-trained using abstracts from PubMed, the leading search engine for biological and medical bibliographic data. This model performs very well in several tests such as the BLURB: Biomedical Language Understanding and Reasoning Benchmark.

To show BERT at work, we will use the Python `transformers` library from the French start-up Hugging Face.[24] It contains more than 7000 models covering 140 languages, including French with CamemBERT and FlauBERT.[25] It contains the transformers GPT-2, BERT, and its variants, DistilBERT (created by Hugging Face), RoBERTa, DeBERTa, ALBERT, XLNet, T5 ... Its applications are translation, classification, text generation or summarization, named entity recognition, sentiment analysis, feature extraction (i.e. word embedding), etc. This library also contains transformer models for speech processing, image classification, object detection, image generation, video image prediction, visual question answering, etc. We will see at the end of this chapter that transformer models have also proved to be very effective in computer vision.

The `transformers` library can be used with PyTorch or TensorFlow. We can thus obtain the embedding of the words of a text in TensorFlow, using the DistilBERT library of Hugging Face:

```
from transformers import DistilBertTokenizer, TDdistilBertModel
tokenizer = DistilBertTokenizer.from_pretrained('distilbert-base-uncased')
model = TDdistilBertModel.from_pretrained("distilbert-base-uncased")
text = "Replace me by any text you'd like."
encoded_input = tokenizer(text, return_tensors='tf')
output = model(encoded_input)
```

And the same in PyTorch:

```
from transformers import DistilBertTokenizer, DistilBertModel
tokenizer = DistilBertTokenizer.from_pretrained('distilbert-base-uncased')
model = DistilBertModel.from_pretrained("distilbert-base-uncased")
text = "Replace me by any text you'd like."
encoded_input = tokenizer(text, return_tensors='pt')
output = model(**encoded_input)
```

For each transformer model of the library, the two basic elements are the tokenizer which prepares the data, and the model itself which processes them. These two elements are downloaded when they are first used. Even if the transformer models have the advantage over recurrent networks of being parallelizable, the use of GPUs quickly proves to be essential to avoid prohibitive computation times.

Here, we will use the `transformers` library with TensorFlow in an R program that uses Python thanks to the `reticulate` package. We can also mention the recent R package `text`[26] which also relies on `reticulate` to make the link with Python and which uses the `transformers` library provided that the Python libraries `torch`, `nltk` and `numpy` are also installed.

Remember that the `reticulate` package (Section 2.7) allows a Python session to be opened inside an R session, to install and import Python libraries (as here, possibly by specifying the version of the library, which sometimes permits errors to be solved), to access Python objects, and their content with the $ symbol, as we do below to access elements of the `transform` object:

```
> library(reticulate)
> reticulate::py_install('transformers', pip = TRUE)
> reticulate::py_install('transformers==4.6.0', pip = TRUE)
> transform = reticulate::import('transformers')
> tf = reticulate::import('tensorflow')
> builtins <- import_builtins()
```

To apply BERT to a classification problem, it is common to choose the $BERT_{BASE}$ model to obtain a word embedding of dimension 768 of the texts to be classified. There is a "cased" and an "uncased" version of this model, the latter not distinguishing upper and lower case.

This embedding must be preceded by the tokenization step (Section 4.3.3), which separates the different tokens: words, sub-words and punctuation marks. The beginning of each text sequence (sentence, document, SMS) is preceded by the token [CLS] and the sequences are separated by the token [SEP]. If a word is not part of BERT's vocabulary ("out of vocabulary"), BERT splits it into sub-words present in its vocabulary, such as "reading" broken down into "read" and "##ing." This algorithm is called "WordPiece."

This operation is required by BERT's limited vocabulary, about 30,000 tokens (with slight differences between variants), which cannot contain all the words but which contains sub-words allowing most of the words to be reconstituted. The words that are absent from the vocabulary and impossible to reconstitute are represented by the token [UNK]. The token [MASK] is not present during the application of the model but only during its pre-training on the MLM task. As BERT pre-training is also done on the NSP (Next Sentence Prediction) task, the token [SEP] is essential to BERT pre-training since it indicates the separation of the two sentences of the NSP task. While we will see that the token [CLS] plays an essential role when using BERT in classification, the tokens [SEP] and [MASK] play an essential role in its pre-training.

This tokenization step ends with the replacement of each token by a numerical identifier which is determined by the model. This identifier is by convention 101 for the token [CLS] and 102 for the token [SEP]. At the end of this step, each text sequence has been transformed into a sequence of numbers, one per token in the sequence.

The following command, using BERT tokenizer, here in its "uncased" version, downloads its vocabulary:

```
> tokenizer <- transform$BertTokenizer$from_pretrained('bert-base-uncased')
```

We display a few lines of this vocabulary, with the token identifiers:

```
> print(tokenizer$vocab[2000:2010])
$'in'
[1] 1999

$to
[1] 2000

$was
[1] 2001

$he
[1] 2002

$is
[1] 2003

$as
[1] 2004

$'for'
[1] 2005

$on
[1] 2006

$with
[1] 2007

$that
[1] 2008

$it
[1] 2009
```

We can check the size of the BERT$_{BASE}$ vocabulary and the maximum length (in number of tokens) of its sequences, as well as some options for pre-processing the sequences (see below) and the list of special tokens. We will limit this maximum length to a value lower than the one BERT$_{BASE}$ can reach (512), to avoid computations that would be too long and useless for the gain of accuracy which would be obtained. But it should be noted that the number of tokens in the sequences will always be greater than the initial number of words, due to the addition of special tokens and the splitting of complex words into several tokens. Compared to the example of the LSTM network (Section 9.3), we will therefore increase the length of the sequences, i.e. the number of tokens, from 200 to 250.

```
> str(tokenizer)
[1] PreTrainedTokenizer(name_or_path='bert-base-uncased',
    vocab_size=30522, model_max_len=512, is_fast=False,
    padding_side='right', special_tokens={'unk_token': '[UNK]',
    'sep_token': '[SEP]', 'pad_token': '[PAD]', 'cls_token':
    '[CLS]', 'mask_token': '[MASK]'})
> num_units <- 768    # embedding dimension
> maxlength <- 250L   # maximum length of sequences
```

Here is an example of tokenization, followed by the display of the encoded identifiers, the corresponding tokens, and their decoding. We notice that with an "uncased" model, the capital letters disappear during the encoding: "To" has the same identifier as "to" ("2000"):

```
> example <- tokenizer$encode('To be or not to be, that is the question.',
max_length=250, truncation=T, add_special_tokens=T, padding=T)
> print(example)
[1] 101 2000 2022 2030 2025 2000 2022 1010 2008 2003 1996 3160 1012 102
> print(tokenizer$convert_ids_to_tokens(example))
[1] "[CLS]" "to" "be" "or" "not" "to"
[7] "be" "," "that" "is" "the" "question"
[13] "." "[SEP]"
> print(tokenizer$decode(example))
[1] "[CLS] to be or not to be, that is the question. [SEP]"
```

Returning to our classification problem, we can apply the tokenizer to the training set, either sequence-by-sequence, or simultaneously to several sequences or to all the text sequences. For example, here is the result of tokenizing the first two sequences `x_train[1:2]`. We specify the maximum length of the text sequences, the fact that longer sequences are truncated and that shorter sequences are padded as shown below. The `return_tensors='tf'` statement is used to obtain TensorFlow tensors. If we had used PyTorch, we would have had to specify `return_tensors='pt'`.

```
> encode <- tokenizer(x_train[1:2], truncation=TRUE, padding=TRUE,
    max_length=maxlength, return_tensors='tf')
> encode
[1] {'input_ids': <tf.Tensor: shape=(2, 115), dtype=int32, numpy=
array([[  101,  1130,   161,  3190,  3190,  3190,   139, 23579,  2356,
        1143,  1126, 23692,  1223,  1103,  3341,   138,  3101,  6944,
        1895, 24387,  1665, 26073, 13069,  1116,  1788,  1115,   146,
        4452,  1111,   119,   146,  1108,  1280,  1194,   170,  1304,
        2846,  8126,  1105,  1125,   161,  3190,  3190,  3190,  1482,
```

```
          117,    170,   1554,   1159,   2261,   1105,   1185,   2027,   1619,
          119,   1188,   1788,   2356,   1143,  23692,   1948,   1105,   6695,
        19827,   1115,   1156,   1136,   1129,   3641,   1174,   1118,   1103,
          146,   8900,    119,   1438,    117,    139,  23579,   5770,    170,
          161,   3190,   3190,   3190,   1940,   1116,   1665,    119,   1939,
         1104,    170,    161,   3190,   3190,   3190,    117,   1105,   1208,
         1103,    146,   8900,   1110,   1170,   1143,   1111,   2212,    196,
          109,  21955,    119,   3135,    198,    119,    102],
      [   101,   1212,    170,   1374,   2767,   6070,    146,   1138,  11807,
         1114,   1155,    161,   3190,   3190,   3190,   4755,  18561,   1116,
          142,  18276,   8057,   1775,    117,    161,   3190,   3190,   3190,
          117,   1105,    161,   3190,   3190,   3190,  22383,   1106,    170,
         4755,   3621,   1114,    161,   3190,   3190,   3190,    170,  19515,
         1204,    108,    161,   3190,   3190,   3190,   1111,   1103,   2236,
         1104,   1314,   3246,    117,   7727,   1607,    117,   2781,    117,
         1344,   4755,   1105,   1103,   7287,   1108,   1608,  22480,    119,
          146,   1138,   1529,   1103,   4252,  14840,  12024,   1104,   1139,
         4755,   3756,   4000,   1293,   1292,   5756,   1132,   7516,    119,
          102,      0,      0,      0,      0,      0,      0,      0,      0,
            0,      0,      0,      0,      0,      0,      0,      0,      0,
            0,      0,      0,      0,      0,      0,      0]], dtype=int32)>,
  'token_type_ids': <tf.Tensor: shape=(2, 115), dtype=int32, numpy=
array([[0, 0, 0, 0, 0, 0, 0, 0, 0, 0, 0, 0, 0, 0, 0, 0, 0, 0, 0, 0, 0, 0,
        0, 0, 0, 0, 0, 0, 0, 0, 0, 0, 0, 0, 0, 0, 0, 0, 0, 0, 0, 0, 0, 0,
        0, 0, 0, 0, 0, 0, 0, 0, 0, 0, 0, 0, 0, 0, 0, 0, 0, 0, 0, 0, 0, 0,
        0, 0, 0, 0, 0, 0, 0, 0, 0, 0, 0, 0, 0, 0, 0, 0, 0, 0, 0, 0, 0, 0,
        0, 0, 0, 0, 0, 0, 0, 0, 0, 0, 0, 0, 0, 0, 0, 0, 0, 0, 0, 0, 0, 0,
        0, 0, 0, 0, 0],
       [0, 0, 0, 0, 0, 0, 0, 0, 0, 0, 0, 0, 0, 0, 0, 0, 0, 0, 0, 0, 0, 0,
        0, 0, 0, 0, 0, 0, 0, 0, 0, 0, 0, 0, 0, 0, 0, 0, 0, 0, 0, 0, 0, 0,
        0, 0, 0, 0, 0, 0, 0, 0, 0, 0, 0, 0, 0, 0, 0, 0, 0, 0, 0, 0, 0, 0,
        0, 0, 0, 0, 0, 0, 0, 0, 0, 0, 0, 0, 0, 0, 0, 0, 0, 0, 0, 0, 0, 0,
        0, 0, 0, 0, 0, 0, 0, 0, 0, 0, 0, 0, 0, 0, 0, 0, 0, 0, 0, 0, 0, 0,
        0, 0, 0, 0, 0]], dtype=int32)>, 'attention_mask': <tf.Tensor:
  shape=(2, 115), dtype=int32, numpy=
array([[1, 1, 1, 1, 1, 1, 1, 1, 1, 1, 1, 1, 1, 1, 1, 1, 1, 1, 1, 1, 1, 1,
        1, 1, 1, 1, 1, 1, 1, 1, 1, 1, 1, 1, 1, 1, 1, 1, 1, 1, 1, 1, 1, 1,
        1, 1, 1, 1, 1, 1, 1, 1, 1, 1, 1, 1, 1, 1, 1, 1, 1, 1, 1, 1, 1, 1,
        1, 1, 1, 1, 1, 1, 1, 1, 1, 1, 1, 1, 1, 1, 1, 1, 1, 1, 1, 1, 1, 1,
        1, 1, 1, 1, 1, 1, 1, 1, 1, 1, 1, 1, 1, 1, 1, 1, 1, 1, 1, 1, 1, 1,
        1, 1, 1, 1, 1],
       [1, 1, 1, 1, 1, 1, 1, 1, 1, 1, 1, 1, 1, 1, 1, 1, 1, 1, 1, 1, 1, 1,
        1, 1, 1, 1, 1, 1, 1, 1, 1, 1, 1, 1, 1, 1, 1, 1, 1, 1, 1, 1, 1, 1,
        1, 1, 1, 1, 1, 1, 1, 1, 1, 1, 1, 1, 1, 1, 1, 1, 1, 1, 1, 1, 1, 1,
        1, 1, 1, 1, 1, 1, 1, 1, 1, 1, 1, 1, 1, 1, 1, 1, 1, 1, 1, 1, 1, 1,
        1, 1, 1, 0, 0, 0, 0, 0, 0, 0, 0, 0, 0, 0, 0, 0, 0, 0, 0, 0, 0, 0,
        0, 0, 0, 0, 0]], dtype=int32)>}
```

We see that the tokenizer produces three components:

- `input_ids`: the token identifiers;
- `token_type_ids` (also called `segments_ids`): during BERT NSP pre-training, the value 0/1 of `token_type_ids` indicates whether the token belongs to the first or second sentence of each pair, and this is also the case in some tasks such as question/answering, but it is not the case in our example where this indicator is always 0; this component does not exist for transformer models trained on the MLM task only and not on the NSP task;
- `attention_mask`: a 1/0 flag indicating for each token if it should be taken into account or not in the attention mechanism.

Each of these components has as many elements as there are tokens in the sequences, starting with the token [CLS] (of identifier 101) and ending with the token [SEP] (of identifier 102). When the sequences do not have the same number of tokens because one is longer than the other, the parameter `padding=TRUE` has the effect of completing with tokens [PAD] (identifier = 0) the shorter sequence. These sequences do not end with identifiers 102 but 0, as can be seen here. As these null identifiers should not be taken into account in the further processing, they have 0 values in the 0/1 indicators of the "attention_mask" component.

As it is not a question here of pre-training BERT, when a sequence, which can correspond to an SMS, an email, a document, contains several sentences, they are then simply separated by periods and not by [SEP].

We can then apply the BERT$_{BASE}$ model to the tokenized sequences. Like any transformer model, BERT$_{BASE}$ associates a numerical vector, of dimension 768 for BERT$_{BASE}$, to each token (or, rather, each token identifier).

Transformer models, like all deep models, are composed of several layers. The number of these layers is indicated in Table 9.1 and BERT$_{BASE}$ has 12 of them. The output layer (`last_hidden_state`) is special because in this layer the token [CLS] output of each sequence is a vector that contains a summary of the information of all tokens in the sequence. However, the vector of the [CLS] token is not a simple average of the vectors of the other tokens: the i^e element (out of 768 for BERT$_{BASE}$) of the vector of [CLS] is not the average of this i^e element calculated on all the tokens of the sequence. Indeed, thanks to the self-attention mechanism, the [CLS] vector is calculated by recovering through the hidden layers the information of the greater or lesser importance of the different tokens, and it will give, for example, less importance to stop words, whereas in a simple average of the vectors, all the tokens would have had the same weight. This synthesis token [CLS] is used for classification but it is in fact always calculated, whatever the use of BERT. Some strategies mentioned by the authors of BERT[27] consist of using other layers and not only the last layer of the model: the average of all layers, the average of the last four layers, the concatenation of the last four layers ... These approaches consider that each attention head detects different and interesting information.

The following instruction calls the pre-trained transformer model, which we apply to the token identifiers:

```
> BERT = transform$TFBertModel$from_pretrained("bert-base-cased")
> bert <- BERT(encode)
> bert
[1] $last_hidden_state
tf.Tensor(
[[[ 4.5930078 6e-01  1.75250605e-01 -2.86377937e-01 ... -2.61458337e-01
    2.31851548e-01  7.93302134e-02]
  [ 6.56676054e-01 -4.76945341e-01  3.19912672e-01 ... -2.52701551e-01
    2.23027840e-01 -1.78228676e-01]
  [ 5.41331396e-02  1.43728673e-01  3.96955162e-01 ...  6.20874111e-03
    8.68899584e-01  1.24740101e-01]
  ...

  [ 1.10852465e-01  1.45019144e-01 -4.62199628e-01 ...  1.06219664e-01
   -1.78057969e-01  7.55754709e-01]
  [ 5.03614783e-01  3.48743945e-02 -3.35027516e-01 ... -2.84132928e-01
    4.35415879e-02 -9.51575786e-02]
  [ 6.91277564e-01  1.42955005e-01  3.86981875e-01 ...  2.89805830e-01
    2.87414193e-02 -3.62389684e-01]]]
```

```
[[ 4.11236435e-01 -1.96679346e-02 -2.71545611e-02 ... -1.58138886e-01
   4.07160163e-01  1.56565964e-01]
 [ 9.41895545e-01 -6.14444554e-01  5.59896588e-01 ... -4.07006592e-02
   4.08830583e-01  4.11947854e-02]
 [ 6.72990501e-01 -2.16137487e-02 -2.95354068e-01 ...  6.06363654e-01
   5.68442583e-01 -2.16522947e-01]
 ...
 [ 4.62135822e-02 -1.45172238e-01  1.85883731e-01 ... -4.60718125e-02
  -7.01415911e-03  1.66383147e-01]
 [-1.17880031e-02 -7.99364299e-02  1.98671445e-01 ...  2.25256234e-02
  -2.54098475e-02  1.33600906e-01]
 [ 6.56495616e-02  6.26237248e-04  2.21905023e-01 ...  8.03632364e-02
   4.67855409e-02  8.88305455e-02]]], shape=(2, 115, 768), dtype=float32)

$pooler_output
tf.Tensor(
[[-0.7291992   0.39572012  0.99981666 ...  0.9999496  -0.5903786
   0.9811175 ]
 [-0.74194086  0.31689128  0.99954736 ...  0.999874   -0.7845526
   0.97501856]], shape=(2, 768), dtype=float32)

> bert[[1]][[0]]
[1] tf.Tensor(
[[ 0.4593008   0.1752506  -0.28637794 ... -0.26145834  0.23185155
   0.07933021]
 [ 0.65667605 -0.47694534  0.31991267 ... -0.25270155  0.22302784
  -0.17822868]
 [ 0.05413314  0.14372867  0.39695516 ...  0.00620874  0.8688996
   0.1247401 ]
 ...
 [ 0.11085247  0.14501914 -0.46219963 ...  0.10621966 -0.17805797
   0.7557547 ]
 [ 0.5036148   0.03487439 -0.33502752 ... -0.28413293  0.04354159
  -0.09515758]
 [ 0.69127756  0.142955    0.38698187 ...  0.28980583  0.02874142
  -0.36238968]], shape=(115, 768), dtype=float32)
```

The BERT function applied to the sequences of token identifiers produces a list whose first element is the bert[[1]] tensor of the output layer, here of dimension 2 x 115 x 768. The second element bert[[2]] is the pooler output. The first dimension of bert[[1]] corresponds to the sequences of tokens, and as we have encoded two sequences here, we have two tensors bert[[1]][[0]] and bert[[1]][[1]], of dimensions (115,768), each corresponding to one of the sequences. We have highlighted above in gray the bert[[1]][[0]] tensor of the first sequence. The first dimension of this tensor is the number of tokens, and as we are interested in the token [CLS] which is the first token (in bold above), we extract the tensor bert[[1]][[0]][[0]] of dimension 768, the number of numerical elements associated with each token. Here is the vector representation of the token [CLS], which synthesizes the information extracted from the first sequence:

```
> bert[[1]][[0]][[0]]
[1] tf.Tensor(
[ 4.59300786e-01  1.75250605e-01 -2.86377937e-01 -3.22944641e-01
 -2.59090811e-01 -4.14340794e-02  4.22332168e-01 -1.09038934e-01
 -9.75909978e-02 -1.15462708e+00 -2.21406803e-01  1.54057488e-01
 -1.20750271e-01 -8.42202157e-02 -4.71113205e-01 -1.04463220e-01
```

```
 -4.85670418e-02   2.06990257e-01  -6.03705160e-02  -1.59272417e-01
...
  4.00695130e-02  -3.76803875e-01  -2.40698457e-01   1.56874284e-01
 -2.66413271e-01  -1.74781352e-01  -6.25788033e-01  -3.21883321e-01
  1.73246849e+00   1.07187301e-01   1.34559244e-01   1.50463209e-01
 -1.34077877e-01  -8.52571651e-02   2.19029009e-01   1.25317112e-01
  7.86448419e-02  -2.61458337e-01   2.31851548e-01   7.93302134e-02],
     shape=(768,), dtype=float32)
```

We can then transform this tensor into a Python matrix, and then into an R matrix thanks to the `py_to_r()` function of the `reticulate` package, which transforms a Python object into an R object:

```
> embed <- py_to_r(array_reshape(bert[[1]][[0]][[0]], c(1,num_units))
> str(embed)
[1] num [1, 1:768] 0.459 0.175 -0.286 -0.323 -0.259 ...
```

We can gather all these instructions in order to tokenize the set of documents in the `x_train` training set and then extract a R tensor of dimension 268279 x 250 x 768, equal to the number of documents x maximum length of the documents (number of tokens) x dimension of the vector representing each token:

```
> ntexts_train = length(x_train)
> bert_train <- py_to_r(array_reshape(BERT(tokenizer(x_train,
    truncation=TRUE, padding=TRUE, max_length=250L, return_tensors=
    'tf'))[[1]], c(1,ntexts_train,250,num_units))
> dim(bert_train)
[1] 1 268279 250 768
```

We then extract the vector of the first token of each document into a matrix of dimension 268279 x 768 with one row per document (text sequence) and 768 columns:

```
> bert_train <- bert_train[1,1:ntexts_train,1,1:num_units]
> bert_train[1:5,1:6]
A matrix: 5 × 6 of type dbl
0.4593005   0.17525052  -0.28637800  -0.32294428  -0.25909072  -0.04143417
0.4112364  -0.01966793  -0.02715456  -0.52252746  -0.14871584  -0.25878638
0.5917812   0.23830920   0.04439038  -0.18449011  -0.12478959  -0.05331802
0.6091980   0.25038838   0.06056030  -0.09247917  -0.16995628  -0.16487965
0.4797451   0.22863322  -0.07297292  -0.28891838  -0.08308525   0.15870406
```

We proceed in the same way for the validation dataset and we create a `bert_valid` matrix. Each coefficient (i, j) of the `bert_train` and `bert_valid` matrices contains the j^e ($1 \leq j \leq 768$) element of the BERT vector of the token [CLS] of the i^e document.

Instead of tokenizing and processing all the text sequences at once, we can also, using the code in the following example, process each sequence one by one in a loop. This avoids having to create a global tensor which can quickly become enormous if the number of sequences is large, especially since each sequence will have the same maximum length (with possible padding). With only 1000 sequences and a maximum length of 250 tokens, we produce a tensor of 192 million elements (1000 x 250 x 768) which may be impossible to store in memory. On the other hand, when processing sequences one-by-one, each sequence will be transformed into a sequence of tokens of length equal to that of the sequence, often less than the maximum length.

We will now put the above into practice and use a transformer model in the Consumer Complaint Database example already discussed in Section 9.3. Recall that the aim is to predict the bank product concerned from the text of the customer complaint. The DistilBERT model is used here, more precisely its "uncased" version which does not distinguish between upper and lower case letters. It is faster and as efficient as the BERT model. We set the maximum length of the sequences to 250 and we prepare the data in a simple way, removing non-printable characters and strings containing numbers or xx, lowercasing every word, but keeping punctuation and short words:

```
> model_type <- "distilbert-base-uncased"
> tokenizer <- transform$DistilBertTokenizer$from_pretrained(model_type)
> str(tokenizer)
[1] PreTrainedTokenizer(name_or_path='distilbert-base-uncased',
    vocab_size=30522, model_max_len=512, is_fast=False, padding_side=
    'right', truncation_side='right', special_tokens={'unk_token': '[UNK]',
    'sep_token': '[SEP]', 'pad_token': '[PAD]', 'cls_token': '[CLS]',
    'mask_token': '[MASK]'})

> num_units <- 768    # embedding dimension
> maxlength <- 250L   # maximum length of sequences
> BERT <- transform$TFDistilBertModel$from_pretrained(model_type)
> ntexts_train = length(x_train)
> ntexts_valid = length(x_valid)
> bert_train = matrix(NA, nrow=ntexts_train, ncol=num_units)
> bert_valid = matrix(NA, nrow=ntexts_valid, ncol=num_units)
```

We apply the DistilBERT model, first, to the training set, then to the validation dataset, processing each text one-by-one:

```
> bertha = function(i){
+ return(py_to_r(array_reshape(BERT(tokenizer(x_train[i],
    truncation=TRUE, padding=TRUE, max_length=maxlength,
    return_tensors='tf'))[[1]][[0]][[0]],c(1,num_units))))
+ }
> bert_train[1:ntexts_train,] <- t(vapply(1:ntexts_train, bertha,
    FUN.VALUE=numeric(num_units)))

> bertha = function(i){
+ return(py_to_r(array_reshape(BERT(tokenizer(x_valid[i],
    truncation=TRUE, padding=TRUE, max_length=maxlength,
    return_tensors='tf'))[[1]][[0]],c(1,num_units))))
+ }
> bert_valid[1:ntexts_valid,] <- t(vapply(1:ntexts_valid, bertha,
    FUN.VALUE=numeric(num_units)))
```

Finally, we apply a gradient boosting model (Section 3.4.5) to the DistilBERT embedding vectors:

```
> library(lightgbm)
> # transform matrix into LGB dataset
> dtrain <- lgb.Dataset(data=bert_train, label=y_train-1)
> dvalid <- lgb.Dataset.create.valid(dtrain, bert_valid,
    label=y_valid-1)
> # modeling
```

```
> lgb.grid = list(seed = 123, objective = "multiclass", num_class =
      num_classes, metric = "multi_error", boosting_type = "gbdt",
      max_depth = 6, num_leaves = 64, learning_rate = 0.2,
      feature_fraction = 0.25, bagging_fraction = 1, lambda_l1=0.0001,
      n_iter = 1000, early_stopping_rounds = 10, verbosity=1)
> lgb.model <- lgb.train(params = lgb.grid, data = dtrain, valids =
      list(test = dvalid))
[1]:     test's multi_error:0.65854
[2]:     test's multi_error:0.60379
[3]:     test's multi_error:0.575072
...
[499]:   test's multi_error:0.331701
[500]:   test's multi_error:0.331649
[501]:   test's multi_error:0.331527
```

Here are the predictions of the LightGBM model on the DistilBERT embedding:

```
> pred.lgb <- predict(lgb.model, bert_valid, reshape=TRUE)
> pred.lgb <- max.col(pred.lgb)
> sum(pred.lgb != y_valid) / nrow(bert_valid)
[1] 0.331422806300391
> table(pred.lgb, y_valid)
        y_valid
pred.     1     2    3    4     5     6     7     8     9   10    11   12   13   14   15   16
lgb
   1   1927  1066   47  300   235   24    61    99   159   77    91   15   31   33   15   15
   2    850  1445   12  101   227    5    55    50   176   33    34    3   18   26    9    8
   3     13     4  737   26    20   16    83   103     3    0    20   26   66    1   12  396
   4    280   118   80 2036  1265   77   205   170    52   48    57   12   29   68   18   14
   5    334   352   64 1378  2778   59   322   201   160   56    66    9   65  176   37   60
   6     21    13   30   82    59 3212  1152   266     4    1    66    4    6    4   33   11
   7    334   294  453  723   913 4699 23032  2528   117   14   551   23  185   21  409  324
   8    391   308  729  817   698 1107  2230 21510   178   90   903  274  454   72  641  308
   9     29    56    0    7    28    1     0     6   681   86     2    1    3   15    2    0
  10      3     3    0    0     3    0     0     2    23   20     0    0    0    0    0    1
  11    255   124  291  138   117  165   537   654    39   12 14049   75  247    2  346  156
  12      0     0    3    1     0    1     0     0     0    0     1   11    6    0    1    0
  13      0     1   32    2     3    0     2    10     0    0     6   50  120    1    9    2
  14      2     4    0    0    10    0     0     2     0    0     0    0    0   14    0    0
  15     21    10   83   28    30   56   224   306    11    2   173   40   86    4 4949   26
  16      3     2  233    5    12    2    68    43     1    1     2    0   15    1    4  350
```

The error rate of 33.1% is higher than that of the LSTM network in Section 9.3. We have not exploited the full capabilities of the DistilBERT model, since we have simply used the word embedding of the pre-trained model, without fine-tuning this model. However, the strength of transformer models is that they can be fine-tuned on a wide variety of natural language processing tasks.

We also did not explore the different possibilities of using the layers of the model, and we only used the last layer. This makes sense because we know that the layers take more into account the context of the words when we go from the first to the last layer, which is the interest of transformer models. But the last layer is also the most specific to BERT training tasks, which are distinct from our example application.

We will not explore these possibilities, and we will move on to the second mode of using a transformer model: fine-tuning its training on the NLP task at hand. We will therefore fine-tune DistilBERT on the complaint classification problem. Instead of using DistilBERT to extract the word embedding vectors in a first step, and using a supervised model (gradient boosting) on these vectors in a second step, it is DistilBERT that will perform the whole task, adjusting its parameters and thus its word embedding in order to improve the classification.

We keep the maximum sequence lengths equal to 250 and perform the same data pre-processing as before. Due to the very large volume of over 300,000 complaint texts to be loaded into memory, we limited ourselves to a sample of 100,000 complaints.

The Hugging Face library allows a large number of pre-tuned transformer models to be downloaded. Their fine-tuning can be performed on various types of tasks.[28] Since we have a classification task, we make use of the generic model `TFAutoModelForSequence Classification` (this is the same name without "TF" for PyTorch).

We download the classification model based on DistilBERT. For multiclass classification, we need to specify the option `problem_type = "multi_label_classification"` and the number of classes (calculated previously).

```
> model_type <- "distilbert-base-uncased"
> model_BERT <- with(training_args$strategy$scope(),
transform$TFAutoModelForSequenceClassification$from_pretrained (model_type,
num_labels=num_classes, problem_type="multi_label_classification"))
```

We then specify the training parameters, and in particular the learning rate, the weight decay and the "warmup" parameter which fixes the number of steps during which the learning rate increases linearly before reaching its specified value. To reduce the length of the computations, we limit the number of epochs to 3, but we will see that this number already allows us to obtain a good result. More epochs do not necessarily improve the accuracy, and this limited number of required epochs is understandable because we are fine-tuning an already pre-trained model. We do not modify the ADAM optimizer of this model.

```
> training_args = transform$TFTrainingArguments(
    output_dir='./results', # output directory
    num_train_epochs=3, # number of training epochs
    per_device_train_batch_size=32L, # batch size for training
    per_device_eval_batch_size=32L,  # batch size for
        validation
    learning_rate= 5e-5, # learning rate
    weight_decay=0.01,   # weight decay
    warmup_steps=100L
)
```

The model configuration can be displayed, including the number of layers, number of units, vocabulary size, etc.:

```
> model_BERT$config
```

```
DistilBertConfig {
  "_name_or_path": "distilbert-base-uncased",
  "activation": "gelu",
  "architectures": [
```

```
    "DistilBertForMaskedLM"
  ],
  "attention_dropout": 0.1,
  "dim": 768,
  "dropout": 0.1,
  "hidden_dim": 3072,
  "id2label": {
    "0": "LABEL_0",
    "1": "LABEL_1",
    "2": "LABEL_2",
    "3": "LABEL_3",
    "4": "LABEL_4",
    "5": "LABEL_5",
    "6": "LABEL_6",
    "7": "LABEL_7",
    "8": "LABEL_8",
    "9": "LABEL_9",
    "10": "LABEL_10",
    "11": "LABEL_11",
    "12": "LABEL_12",
    "13": "LABEL_13",
    "14": "LABEL_14",
    "15": "LABEL_15"
  },
  "initializer_range": 0.02,
  "label2id": {
    "LABEL_0": 0,
    "LABEL_1": 1,
    "LABEL_10": 10,
    "LABEL_11": 11,
    "LABEL_12": 12,
    "LABEL_13": 13,
    "LABEL_14": 14,
    "LABEL_15": 15,
    "LABEL_2": 2,
    "LABEL_3": 3,
    "LABEL_4": 4,
    "LABEL_5": 5,
    "LABEL_6": 6,
    "LABEL_7": 7,
    "LABEL_8": 8,
    "LABEL_9": 9
  },
  "max_position_embeddings": 512,
  "model_type": "distilbert",
```

```
  "n_heads": 12,
  "n_layers": 6,
  "pad_token_id": 0,
  "problem_type": "multi_label_classification",
  "qa_dropout": 0.1,
  "seq_classif_dropout": 0.2,
  "sinusoidal_pos_embds": false,
  "tie_weights_": true,
  "transformers_version": "4.6.0",
  "vocab_size": 30522
}
```

The number of parameters that will be adjusted by fine-tuning reaches almost 67 million. So we had to use a GPU processor to limit the computation time to about one hour:

```
> model_BERT$count_params()
[1] 66965776
```

As before, we must first tokenize the text sequences before applying the model, and here we use the tokenizer corresponding to the model, i.e. that of DistilBERT:

```
> tokenizer < - transform$AutoTokenizer$from_pretrained(model_type)
> train_encodings = tokenizer(x_train, truncation=TRUE, padding=TRUE,
    max_length=maxlength)
> test_encodings = tokenizer(x_valid, truncation=TRUE, padding=TRUE,
    max_length=maxlength)
```

We then create the training and validation datasets that will be used by TensorFlow for model fine-tuning. They contain the token identifiers and the attention masks indicators:

```
> train_dataset = tf$data$Dataset$from_tensor_slices(tuple
    (builtins$dict(train_encodings), y_train-1))
> valid_dataset = tf$data$Dataset$from_tensor_slices(tuple
    (builtins$dict(test_encodings), y_valid-1))
> str(train_dataset)
[1] < TensorSliceDataset shapes: ({input_ids: (250,),
attention_mask: (250,)}, ()), types: ({input_ids: tf.int32,
attention_mask: tf.int32}, tf.float32)>
```

For model fine-tuning we create a trainer object by specifying the pre-trained model, the set of training parameters, and the previously defined datasets:

```
> trainer = transform$TFTrainer(model=model_BERT, args=training_args,
    train_dataset=train_dataset, eval_dataset=valid_dataset)
```

The training of the model can be run, which will lead to the adjustment of the 67 million parameters of the pre-trained model:

```
> system.time(trainer$train())
    user    system   elapsed
2118.171   23.670 3027.185
```

The fine-tuned model can finally be applied to the validation dataset, and we obtain in the `predictions` object a list containing (1) the predicted logits for each class; (2) the actual values of the classes; and (3) the value of the loss function on the validation dataset:

```
> predictions <- trainer$predict(valid_dataset)
> predicted <- max.col(predictions['predictions'])
> actual <- predictions['label_ids']
```

The confusion matrix and error rate show a better prediction than those obtained previously: the 25% error rate is lower than the 33% error rate obtained by the LightGBM model applied to BERT word embedding, and lower than the 28% error rate obtained in Section 9.3 using a recurrent LSTM network:

```
> table(actual+1,predicted)
```

	1	2	3	4	5	6	7	8	9	10	11	12	13	14	15	16
1	699	253	9	61	29	4	26	26	20	8	45	0	2	7	1	1
2	224	598	3	6	46	3	32	17	31	0	18	0	6	4	2	1
3	7	4	340	25	10	4	70	96	0	1	20	14	34	0	12	102
4	33	5	10	917	297	15	119	98	3	3	15	1	3	2	3	1
5	33	47	6	364	972	7	114	59	8	1	7	0	6	23	1	4
6	5	1	11	11	13	1282	900	164	0	0	19	0	1	0	7	3
7	13	20	50	65	102	688	5521	464	4	0	89	0	16	0	60	49
8	26	17	54	99	44	89	396	5840	3	3	107	6	21	0	84	20
9	26	41	0	0	21	0	5	9	278	30	4	0	0	2	1	2
10	17	3	0	3	3	0	1	2	24	53	4	0	1	1	0	0
11	24	8	17	6	12	7	78	61	3	0	4003	0	8	0	15	2
12	1	1	10	1	1	1	1	49	0	0	0	36	28	0	2	0
13	4	6	37	5	10	0	25	55	1	0	16	15	139	0	9	5
14	10	3	0	6	26	0	1	2	4	1	0	0	0	58	0	0
15	3	2	9	0	7	1	82	98	0	0	17	1	5	0	1489	2
16	9	1	97	2	17	2	67	25	2	1	4	0	6	0	1	220

```
> mean((actual+1) != predicted)
[1] 0.251309249808199

> predictions['metrics']
[1] $eval_loss = 0.75050997250617
```

The DistilBERT model fine-tuned on our dataset proves to be superior to previous models and illustrates the predictive power of transformer models. This fine-tuned model could be saved and then applied to another dataset, and a model created with TensorFlow can even be reused with PyTorch, and *vice versa*.

We could use the RoBERTa$_{BASE}$ model, with a learning rate of 3e-5, a weight decay equal to 0.004, 100 warmup steps and 3 epochs for fine-tuning, and we will obtain an even lower error rate, equal to 24.47%, but at the cost of a doubled number of parameters and computation time.

Another transformer model is GPT-2 (Generative Pre-Training Transformer), created in February 2019 by OpenAI, a rival artificial intelligence company to DeepMind. Unlike BERT, the GPT model is not bidirectional. It can answer questions, translate text, summarize text, generate text from an example, and generally synthesize the next element of a word sequence. In its XL version, it has 1.5 billion parameters. It is available in the Hugging Face library. It is capable of very good performance on some tasks even without fine-tuning, which is called "zero-shot learning," a notion that also concerns the classification of classes never seen during training. The texts it generates, while far superior to those generated at the time by its competing models, eventually became repetitive or meaningless, and in May 2020 OpenAI introduced its much-improved successor: the GPT-3 language model.

With 175 billion parameters, GPT-3 was then the most powerful generative model ever developed for natural language processing[29]. It has been trained on 410 billion tokens from the Common Crawl corpus, 55 billion tokens from the Books2 corpus, 19 billion tokens from WebText2, and 3 billion tokens from Wikipedia. Its code is not open source but it is accessible through an API from OpenAI. Anyway, it requires 175 gigabytes of memory to run, which puts it out of reach of most computers. Early tests show it capable of writing text that is difficult to distinguish from human-written text, raising questions about the dangers of using it for disinformation. It is also capable of participating in a discussion, answering questions, making recommendations, summarizing a text or presenting it in tabular form, or translating a text into another language. Like GPT-2, although it is at a lower level, GPT-3 struggles to argue and its long texts can end up lacking meaning. In July 2020, it was still in beta version, while GPT-2 had been implemented in several websites,[30] but at the end of 2021 Microsoft made GPT-3 available to some customers of its Azure cloud, with security monitoring to detect possible abuse and misuse.

On October 11, 2021, an even more complex generative model was announced by Microsoft and NVIDIA[31]: the Megatron-Turing Natural Language Generation model (MT-NLG) has 530 billion parameters. It is also a transformer model. It has 105 layers and is claimed to be very accurate on many natural language processing tasks: automatic dialogue generation, translation, automatic summarization, semantic search ... It has been trained on 150 billion tokens from the Common Crawl corpus, 26 billion tokens from the Books3 corpus, 24 billion tokens from GitHub, 21 billion tokens from arXiv, 15 billion tokens from WebText2, 4 billion tokens from Wikipedia, 2.7 billion tokens from Project Gutenberg, etc. Its training required a supercomputer with 560 nodes of 8 GPUs each.

The record for the number of parameters in a transformer model was broken in 2021 by Google's Switch transformer model[32] (1600 billion parameters) and then by the Chinese model Wu Dao 2.0, which has 1750 billion parameters and has been trained on 4.9 terabytes of images and texts (including 1.2 terabytes of Chinese texts and as many English texts), and is capable of natural language processing or image recognition tasks, and of generating a text from an image or the reverse.

Since then, DeepMind has proposed transformer models (Gopher and RETRO)[33] that take different approaches to achieving such high performance with fewer parameters.

Since 2018, the diversification of uses for transformer models has gone along with the increase in their power.

Transfer learning is thus used in machine translation to translate rare languages. We start by training a deep network for the translation of two common languages, for example, English and French, and, as in image recognition (Section 8.3.3), we reuse the first layers of the network, which are more generic, and we replace the upper layers of the network by new layers trained this time on the rare languages considered. In natural language processing, the generic layers of a deep network would correspond to the structures common to all languages, following the idea of universal grammar of Noam Chomsky.[34]

Originally developed for natural language processing, transformer models have also proven to be very efficient in computer vision (the generative adversarial network TransGAN) and are competitors of convolutional neural networks.[35] They can generate images, recognize actions in videos, answer questions about their content, and classify proteins (AlphaFold 2: see Section 1.4.1). The self-attention mechanism, which considers how each element of a sequence is linked to all the other elements, allows a transformer model to analyze sequences of words, but also of pixels, video frames, or amino acids.

Recently, researchers have succeeded in training a transformer model to find the mathematical expression generating a given sequence of integers or real numbers.[36] This expression can be a function or a recurrence relation, such as an arithmetic or geometric progression. The training of the transformer model (8 hidden layers, 8 attention heads, and an embedding dimension of 512) has been done on five million expressions and on the sequences of numbers generated by these expressions. The obtained model has been tested on the OEIS: Online Encyclopedia of Integer Sequences.[37] But it can also handle real numbers, adding to the operations +, x, abs, modulo, division by an integer, the division by a real, the square root, the trigonometric functions, and the logarithm and exponential functions.

The field of application of transformer models is increasingly wide in deep learning, especially since they can be applied to a variety of problems, requiring little problem-specific knowledge and that can be pre-trained by self-supervised learning on large unlabeled datasets and then used by transfer learning with a simple fine-tuning.

Notes

1 See other examples at: https://keras.io/examples/.

2 In particular, https://github.com/makcedward/nlpaug/blob/5238e0be734841b69651d2043d f535d78a8cc594/nlpaug/res/word/spelling/spelling_en.txt.

3 Graves, A. Generating Sequences with Recurrent Neural Networks (2014). arXiv:1308.0850.

4 Available on the Project Gutenberg website: https://www.gutenberg.org/ebooks/1041.

5 https://keras.io/examples/generative/lstm_character_level_text_generation/.

6 Chollet, F. and Allaire, J.J. (*Deep Learning with R* (Sheltered Island: Manning, 2018). See section 8.1.4.

7 https://catalog.data.gov/dataset/consumer-complaint-database.

8 Also available on Kaggle: https://www.kaggle.com/selener/consumer-complaint-database.

9 We can also use another function of Keras: `text_hashing_trick()`.

10 https://blog.keras.io/using-pre-trained-word-embeddings-in-a-keras-model.html.

11 Howard, J. and Ruder S. Universal Language Model Fine-tuning for Text Classification (2018). arXiv:1801.06146.

12 Peters *et al.* Deep Contextualized Word Representations (2018). arXiv:1802.05365.

13 Devlin *et al. BERT*: Pre-training of Deep Bidirectional Transformers for Language Understanding (2018). arXiv:1810.04805v2.

14 We note the humor of their inventors who gave their algorithms the names of two Muppets: Bert and Elmo.

15 Vaswani *et al.* Attention Is All You Need (2017). arXiv:1706.03762.

16 Zhu *et al*. Aligning Books and Movies: Towards Story-like Visual Explanations by Watching Movies and Reading Books (2015). arXiv:1506.06724.

17 Liu *et al*. RoBERTa: A Robustly Optimized BERT Pretraining Approach (2019). arXiv:1907.11692.

18 Martin *et al*. CamemBERT: A Tasty French Language Model (2019). arXiv:1911.03894.

19 Le *et al* FlauBERT: Unsupervised Language Model Pre-training for French (2019). arXiv:1912.05372. See also Le *et al*. FlauBERT: Contextualized Pre-Trained Language Models for French. 6th joint conference Journées d'Études sur la Parole, 33rd edn (JEP, 2020), Traitement Automatique des Langues Naturelles (TALN), 27th edn, Rencontre des Étudiants Chercheurs en Informatique pour le Traitement Automatique des Langues (RÉCITAL), 22nd edn,. Volume 2: *Traitement Automatique des Langues Naturelles*, pp. 268–278, hal-02784776v3.

20 He *et al*. DeBERTa: Decoding-enhanced BERT with Disentangled Attention (2020). arXiv:2006.03654.

21 Sanh, V., Debut, L., Chaumond J., and Wolf T. DistilBERT, A Distilled Version of BERT: Smaller, Faster, Cheaper and Lighter (2019). arXiv:1910.01108.

22 Sun *et al*. MobileBERT: A Compact Task-Agnostic BERT for Resource-Limited Devices (2020). arXiv:2004.02984.

23 Gu *et al*. Domain-Specific Language Model Pretraining for Biomedical Natural Language Processing (2020). arXiv:2007.15779.

24 https://huggingface.co/docs/transformers/index.

25 https://huggingface.co/transformers/v3.4.0/pretrained_models.html.

26 Kjell, O.N.E., Giorgi, S., and Schwartz, H.A. Text: An R-package for Analyzing and Visualizing Human Language Using Natural Language Processing and Deep Learning. (2021). PsyArXiv. https://doi.org/10.31234/osf.io/293kt.

27 Devlin *et al*. note 13, op. cit., Section 5.3.

28 https://huggingface.co/docs/transformers/model_doc/auto.

29 Brown *et al*. Language Models Are Few-Shot Learners (2020). arXiv:2005.14165v4.

30 See, for example, "Write With Transformer" at https://transformer.huggingface.co/.

31 Smith *et al*. Using DeepSpeed and Megatron to Train Megatron-Turing NLG 530B, A Large-Scale Generative Language Model (2022). arXiv:2201.11990.

32 Fedus, W., Zoph, B., and Shazeer, N. Switch Transformers: Scaling to Trillion Parameter Models with Simple and Efficient Sparsity (2021). arXiv:2101.03961.

33 Borgeaud *et al*. Improving Language Models by Retrieving from Trillions of Tokens, (2021). arXiv:2112.04426.

34 Chomsky, N. *Syntactic Structures* (The Hague: Mouton, 1957).

35 Khan *et al*. Transformers in Vision: A Survey (2021). arXiv:2101.01169.

36 D'Ascoli *et al*. Deep Symbolic Regression for Recurrent Sequences (2022). arXiv:2201.04600.

37 https://oeis.org.

10

Artificial Intelligence

We conclude this book with an overview of recent developments in artificial intelligence, which rely heavily on deep learning methods to perform increasingly complex tasks of image, video, text or speech recognition, automatic text generation, translation, driving, and so on. These tasks are now even commonly combined in algorithms that, for example, can analyze images and automatically generate a textual description, or read the description of a scene and represent it; this is called multimodal artificial intelligence. These tasks that were previously inaccessible to automatic machine processing are now being performed by algorithms with a level of performance that sometimes approaches the human level. We examine what has allowed such an evolution of artificial intelligence, its progress, its limits and the questions it raises.

10.1 The Beginnings of Artificial Intelligence

Artificial intelligence, as a discipline, can be defined as the set of theories and techniques implemented in order to elaborate machines capable of performing cognitive tasks such as those performed by human intelligence: pattern recognition, face recognition, language understanding, dialogue, mathematical reasoning, games ... Another synthetic definition is: "Algorithms and systems leading to automated reasoning and actions, aimed at replacing and improving activities generally attributed to human intelligence and behavior."[1] Artificial intelligence also designates the achievements of this discipline, namely the capacity for machines to perform these tasks. It is this second meaning that can be compared to human intelligence (Section 10.2). We sometimes speak of a machine capable of performing some of these tasks as an artificial intelligence, with an indefinite article.

The realization of these first tasks is what we call "weak" artificial intelligence. The reasoning[2] and planning[3] tasks are much more complex, and we are not talking here about a machine being endowed with common sense,[4] nor even less with free will, the ability to set goals, consciousness and to feel (and not just simulate) feelings: this is "strong" artificial intelligence, which for a long time will probably remain an inaccessible fantasy. A very important and somewhat simpler task than reasoning and planning is to predict the next situation from a given situation. For example, it is to predict on the basis of certain signs that a pedestrian will cross the road without warning, which is obviously crucial for an autonomous vehicle.

Deep Learning: From Big Data to Artificial Intelligence with R, First Edition. Stéphane Tufféry.
© 2023 John Wiley & Sons Ltd. Published 2023 by John Wiley & Sons Ltd.
Companion website: www.wiley.com/go/Tuffery/DeepLearning

Even if this is still very far from strong artificial intelligence, some works are starting to allow an artificial intelligence to detect the emotions of a person, by observing their gestures, their facial movements, smiles, eyes, and the prosody of their voice (volume, flow, rhythm, accent, and intonation). This detection is difficult, because it is necessary to take into account the individual part and the cultural part which enter in the expression of the emotions, which can be expressed by the mouth, the glance, the eyebrows. The same perceptions do not necessarily correspond to the same interpretations. We can envisage interactions between the machine and the human being, which are beginning to be used in the treatment of autism. This is conversational artificial intelligence, whose objective is to interact with humans and not to solve problems. It can rely on the ability to detect imperceptible movements and associate them with an emotion, sometimes barely conscious in the person. In telephone calls to an emergency service, artificial intelligence can perceive the risk of cardiac arrest from the caller's answers but also from the tone of their voice and their breathing rhythm. Finally, emotional artificial intelligence can interact by detecting emotions but also by simulating them through the more or less anthropomorphic means of expression with which it has been equipped.

The first reflections on artificial intelligence can be found in the work of Alan Turing who, in the 1950s, wondered whether a machine could think, and translated this question into the more operational one of whether a machine could take the place of a human being in the "imitation game." Published in his article "Computing Machinery and Intelligence",[5] this question became the famous Turing test. It consists of making a person converse blindly with a machine and another human: if this person is not able to say which of their interlocutors is a machine, this one passes the test. Turing estimated that in the year 2000 machines with 128 megabytes of memory would be able to deceive about 30% of human judges during a five-minute test, and that we could then speak of artificial intelligence. This test has become a challenge for conversational agents and a challenge for natural language simulation. There are machines that now exceed a 50% success rate.

Another source of artificial intelligence can be found in a conference held in 1956 at Dartmouth College in the United States. It was attended by future greats of the new discipline, including John McCarthy and Marvin Minsky (MIT), Claude Shannon (Bell Labs), and Allen Newell and Herbert Simon (Carnegie-Mellon University). They wondered whether "every aspect of learning or any other characteristic of intelligence can be so precisely described that a machine can be designed to simulate it." McCarthy coined the term *artificial intelligence*.

In the years following the conference, the protagonists of the conference did a lot of work in this field,[6] especially in natural language processing, with machine translation being an important goal, and with the creation of ELIZA, the first conversational agent, in 1964–1966. It pretended to be a psychotherapist interviewing his patient, and its creator Joseph Weizenbaum (MIT) was surprised to see how much the people who took the patient's place felt that ELIZA really understood them. However, its performance was far from that of current conversational agents and it only asked questions that rephrased what the patient had just said. Since then, we call the "ELIZA effect" the fact of interacting with a machine as with a human being, and in particular to attribute empathy and other human feelings to it, and even to get emotionally involved, even though one knows that one is dealing with a machine, and despite the fact that it is not necessarily capable of passing the Turing test. It may be one believes in the gratitude of a machine displaying THANK YOU at the end of a transaction.

Problem-solving programs, such as the *General Problem Solver* (1959) by Herbert Simon, Cliff Shaw, and Allen Newell, were created, and it was envisaged that theorems could be proved, and even, in the following ten years, that new theorems could be discovered by artificial intelligence. The same decade would see a computer become the world chess champion.

These hopes were reinforced by the appearance of artificial neural networks: after the formal neuron of McCulloch and Pitts, the SNARC neural machine of Minsky and Edmonds, the perceptron of Rosenblatt (who had been a classmate of Marvin Minsky) and the ADALINE network of Widrow (who had participated in the Dartmouth conference) and his doctoral student Hoff.

The neuron of McCulloch and Pitts[7] was the first of the neural networks and was limited to a single neuron, admitting binary 0/1 values in input and output. The scalar product of the input values was calculated with weights equal to +1 (excitation) or −1 (inhibition), and when this scalar product exceeded a certain threshold, the output was +1, and if not, it was 0. Its 0/1 values reserved it for logical operations, and it had no learning mechanism: the weights of the neuron were fixed by their user.

In 1951, the SNARC (Stochastic Neural Analog Reinforcement Calculator) of Marvin Minsky and Dean Edmonds simulated with forty artificial neurons the behavior of a rat searching for food in a labyrinth, with synapses able to adjust their weighting in the presence of success or failure.

Rosenblatt's perceptron[8] brought three improvements to the neuron of McCulloch and Pitts: it can contain several neurons, its input values can be real numbers and not only 0/1, and it introduces for the first time a learning mechanism to update the weights of the neurons. This is called the *delta rule*. The output value +1/−1 of the perceptron is compared to the expected value: if the output value is lower, we increase the weights of the inputs that have a positive value and we decrease the other weights; and vice versa if the output value is higher.

Widrow and Hoff's ADALINE (ADAptive LInear NEuron) network[9] innovated by introducing a linear and therefore differentiable activation function: the output is simply the scalar product of the inputs by the weights. The error is the squared error and it is minimized by gradient descent. The interest of gradient descent on the delta rule is that all observations contribute to the learning, and not only the misclassified observations, i.e. with an expected value +1 and an output value −1 or the opposite.

However, it soon became apparent that most real problems required computing power far beyond the capabilities of computers of the time. The promising beginnings were followed by more modest achievements than expected.

As far as neural networks are concerned, one book had a devastating effect: *Perceptrons: An Introduction to Computational Geometry* (1969) by Marvin Minsky and Seymour Papert. They noticed that the neural networks of the time, with their single layer, were unable to represent non-linear functions, starting with the XOR, "or exclusive" true if only its two operands are both true or both false. Of course, they knew that it was possible to delimit non-linear domains by introducing hidden layers in the perceptrons: in the case of XOR, one has to introduce a hidden layer with two neurons, one for AND and the other for OR, and to combine these two neurons in the output layer. But at the time there was no mechanism for training a multi-layer network and Minsky and Papert considered efforts to find one to be fruitless. This work cooled the enthusiasm for the use of perceptrons for more than a decade and even caused the "first winter of artificial intelligence." In retrospect, given the current importance of neural networks in artificial intelligence, it is amusing to think that one of the "fathers" of artificial intelligence, Marvin Minsky, was the co-author of this book.

Artificial intelligence emerged from this winter in 1986 with the publication of a book by a group of researchers called the *Parallel Distributed Processing Research Group*. This book was a great success and especially the eighth chapter of its first volume,[10] written by Rumelhart, Hinton, and Williams and devoted to multilayer neural networks (Section 7.3). They generalized the Rosenblatt perceptron but with two novelties that make the multilayer perceptron more than a Rosenblatt perceptron with additional layers. First, its activation function is not a threshold, nor linear as in ADALINE, but any differentiable nonlinear function. In practice, sigmoidal functions are considered because they are the differentiable functions that most resemble the threshold function. On the other hand, the gradient descent algorithm used in ADALINE is extended to multi-layer networks thanks to the backpropagation mechanism (Section 7.3). This mechanism consists of computing the gradient of the error with respect to each of the weights of the network, from the last layer to the first, by considering the error as a function of the weights and applying the chain derivation. This is what makes it possible to adjust each weight by taking into account its contribution to the error, so as to minimize it. This idea, which is crucial for the development of multilayer neural networks, can be seen as a combination of the idea of gradient descent of Widrow and Hoff (applied by them to the single layer of ADALINE) and the idea of backpropagation introduced earlier, notably by Paul Werbos in his thesis in 1974. But it was not applicable to neural networks with binary output like Rosenblatt's perceptron and required networks with differentiable output like the linear function of ADALINE and the sigmoidal function of the multilayer perceptron of Rumelhart, Hinton, and Williams.

After a beautiful spring and first works on convolutional networks (Section 7.5), a second winter of neural networks and artificial intelligence occurred in the early 1990s, due to vanishing gradient problems making gradient backpropagation difficult on deep networks, until the new spring that around the year 2006 saw the appearance of several solutions to these problems (Section 7.4), coming from new ideas and increased computing power that led to the current supremacy of deep neural networks in artificial intelligence tasks, such as computer vision and natural language processing, especially since 2012 as we showed in Section 7.15.

Since the beginning of the twentieth century, artificial intelligence has been able to develop thanks to the availability of:

- very large labeled training datasets (the label being what the supervised system must predict) or not (for a self-supervised system);
- improved algorithms to solve optimization and gradient backpropagation problems posed by deep architectures (convolutional neural networks, recurrent networks, dropout, ReLU activation, batch normalization);
- more powerful machines, and in particular graphics processing units (GPU) for massively parallel calculations.

For computing power, we can also expect a lot from quantum computers but in the long term (Section 2.8).

Regarding large labeled training datasets, it should be noted that this labeling is expensive: for example, the ImageNet database (Section 7.15) required 49,000 "turkers" (Section 1.7) over a period of three years to annotate the 14 million images into nearly 22,000 categories. Moreover, if one wants to transfer a computer vision model trained on such a labeled dataset to apply it to another dataset containing different images, transfer learning is possible but still requires retraining part of the model (at least its dense layers) on the new dataset. Self-supervised training (see below) is the most common solution to this problem, finding supervision in the data itself and not in external labeling.

In some cases, a solution has been provided by multimodal artificial intelligence (see below) and the CLIP[11] (Contrastive Language-Image Pre-training) system from OpenAI.[12] This multimodal system learns from text-image pairs which have the advantage of being abundantly available on the Internet. In other words, CLIP learns to associate each image not with a label but with its corresponding caption. CLIP does not require specific tagging, performed on a dataset, and transfers to a wide variety of visual classification tasks without the need for additional training examples. To apply CLIP to a new task, one simply tells CLIP's text encoder the names of the visual representations in the task, e.g., "this is a picture of an animal called xxx," and it will produce a classifier of the visual representations. CLIP is trained by encoding the images and associated texts, then learning to associate the encoding of a text with the encoding of its corresponding image. Then, for prediction, a new image will be encoded, each possible caption will be encoded and the predicted caption will be the one whose encoding is predicted by the image encoding. The accuracy of CLIP is often comparable to that of models obtained in a fully supervised way, but it sometimes performs less well, especially in the finest classification tasks, for example, between close species or different marks of the same object.

Another self-supervised multimodal system, MERLOT[13] (Multimodal Event Representation Learning Over Time), is trained not on static text-image pairs like CLIP, but on videos accompanied by their text transcripts. MERLOT learns to associate image and text representations, but also to guess masked words in the text and to reorder scrambled images. It can retrieve the temporal sequence of images in a video and answer questions about individual images.

Over the course of this history, several artificial intelligence researchers have been awarded the ACM Turing Award created to honor Turing's memory and given annually for major contributions to computer science: Marvin Minsky (1969), John McCarthy (1971), Allen Newell and Herbert Simon (1975), Judea Pearl (2011), Yoshua Bengio, Geoffrey Hinton, and Yann Le Cun (2018).

The applications of artificial intelligence are numerous and varied today: biometrics with facial and fingerprint recognition, voice recognition and synthesis allowing dialogue with a machine, driverless vehicles ... The fields concerned are of course robotics, but also medicine, transport, games, finance, marketing, journalism, law, etc.

But an artificial intelligence is unable to have "ideas" and therefore cannot solve a problem by a new method. It can sometimes help verify a mathematical proof but cannot have the idea of an original proof like a mathematician who discovers a new approach to solve a difficult problem. At least that's the situation now, as DeepMind founder Demis Hassabis aims to solve Nobel Prize-level scientific problems by 2030. In addition to analyzing the 3D structure of proteins (Section 10.3), DeepMind has launched work in quantum chemistry, which could lead, among other things, to the manufacture of new materials.

Today, artificial intelligence can reproduce what it has been shown without having been given the rules, by only providing it with examples, and this is already remarkable. In terms of creation, it is capable of pastiche but not of originality. It is capable of painting "in the manner of" Van Gogh, Picasso or Turner (Section 7.20.4) but so can an excellent amateur. It will not become the Picasso of tomorrow, until proven otherwise, even though on October 25, 2018 was sold at auction at Christie's in New York, for $432,500 (!), *The Portrait of Edmond de Belamy*,[14] the first painting entirely created by an artificial intelligence, more precisely a generative adversarial network (Section 7.19.1) developed by the *Obvious* collective composed of Hugo Caselles-Dupré, Pierre Fautrel, and Gauthier Vernier. The signature of this painting has all the characteristics of a GAN:

$$\min_{G} \max_{D} \mathbb{E}_x[log(D(x))] + \mathbb{E}_z[log(1 - D(G(z)))].$$

Its training was based on a selection of 15,000 portraits painted between the fifteenth and twentieth centuries, hence the very academic aspect of *The Portrait of Edmond de Belamy* and the fact that it is not the painting itself but its author who made it sell. The trick would be to sell a painting painted by an artificial intelligence without revealing that it was painted by an artificial intelligence.

Similarly, artificial intelligence can produce texts resembling those of an existing author (Section 9.2) but cannot itself become a new author, with an original style and a new sensitivity. This is true for everything that concerns deep learning, which relies on examples and cannot detach itself from them as much as Proust detaches himself from Flaubert. And even then, the imitation is only local, with sentences that could have been written by the princeps author but which, put together, do not make much sense. We see this in a book that is quite difficult to read, *1 The Road*[15] written by an artificial intelligence in a Cadillac on a Kerouac-like road trip, and connected to a GPS, a clock, cameras and microphones that provide it with its "sensations." However, this situation can change quite quickly, as shown by the performance of the GPT-3 language model (Section 9.7), presented in May 2020 by the company OpenAI, which is capable of writing texts that are difficult to distinguish from texts written by humans.

However, artificial intelligence today is not capable of a truly literary translation, translating the letter but also the spirit of an author, and transforming a text of high literary quality in one language into a text of equal literary quality in another language.

10.2 Human Intelligence and Artificial Intelligence

It must be said here that talking about artificial intelligence is a misuse of language as the differences between artificial intelligence and human intelligence are so great. Indeed, human intelligence:

- finds tasks very simple that are quite complex for artificial intelligence (recognizing a face, walking, driving a car...);
- finds tasks very difficult that are simple for artificial intelligence (doing calculations on large numbers...);
- in the supervised domain: can learn with a (very) small number of cases;

- excels in the unsupervised domain, when a task is not defined, a goal not known, so much so that most of human learning is unsupervised, with humans learning a lot by observing the world without having to be told the name or function of everything they observe;
- proceeds by transferring knowledge and skills (obtained by unsupervised learning or supervised learning with labels from other tasks) from one domain to another (whereas transfer learning must be explicitly specified to an artificial intelligence algorithm);
- can generalize reasoning;
- is plastic and universal (AlphaGo can only play Go, WaveNet can talk like a human but do nothing else, an image recognition system does only that, and a joke says that a medical algorithm could diagnose measles in a rusted car);
- will understand a situation and predict the next situation (reasoning and planning) when artificial intelligence will only be able to recognize objects in a photograph;
- is autonomous, can define its own goals and motivations;
- can have new ideas, create without having a model.

Some of the previous oppositions should be put into perspective: it is likely that a human being is better at avoiding a sudden swerve by another driver and that the algorithm is better at performing parallel parking. An algorithm will be able to distinguish finely between animal species, but will make serious classification errors more often than a human being. Human and machine errors are not the same.

For its part, artificial intelligence:

- sees in an image only a set of objects and individuals;
- has no concept of causality;
- does not understand a text that it reads or translates, can introduce an absurd sentence in the middle of a perfect translation, and cannot discern what is plausible and what is absurd;
- is not self-learning (see below).

Thus, for the moment, even the deep learning algorithms used in artificial intelligence only see in an image a set of objects and individuals, and not underlying concepts, historical-socio-cultural references to a fund of knowledge shared by humanity, concrete situations where we know why such objects and such beings are brought together, for what purpose, how they are going to interact, what is going to happen and, on the contrary, what cannot happen, taking into account the constraints of the real world and in particular the laws of physics, etc. This limits enormously the autonomy of robots intended, for example, to help people, but which will be unable to detect a dangerous situation for the people they accompany, and which may themselves cause a dangerous situation. Robots are far from being able to respect Isaac Asimov's first law of robotics (*Runaround*, 1942): "a robot may not harm a human being, nor, by remaining passive, allow a human being to be exposed to danger."

The lack of common sense also limits the ability of virtual assistants to answer unexpected questions, react in unexpected situations, or accomplish a new task.

Artificial intelligence today has no notion of causality. In the same way, a deep learning algorithm processing natural language does not understand what it reads or translates, and cannot discern what is plausible and what is absurd (it even struggles to process handwritten notes in which the text is interspersed with sketches, erasures, and references). It should be able to learn more about semantic understanding, human reasoning, common sense, psychology, and even humor. Even an algorithm as powerful as GPT-3 (Section 9.7) does not understand anything of the elaborate texts it writes.

This distinction between the real understanding of language and the formal manipulation of symbols was illustrated by John Searle's thought experiment known as the "Chinese room." In this chamber, a prisoner receives questions in Chinese from the outside world and has to answer in the same language, using ideograms whose meaning he does not know, but a book tells him which ones to use when he is shown a particular ideogram.

In fact, artificial intelligence has mainly developed in the supervised domain, when it is a question of reaching a fixed objective, of making a choice between several identified solutions. Currently, it relies heavily on machine learning and deep learning, in which the machine learns itself from examples instead of having to formalize knowledge in the form of well-structured rules, as in the expert systems we discuss in the next section. But we have seen that this has not always been the case.

Even for this trained form of artificial intelligence, it is wrong to speak of self-learning algorithms. Supervised or reinforcement learning algorithms do not give artificial intelligence the status of autonomy, since humans must determine the classes to predict or the quantities to evaluate (supervised algorithms), the pretext tasks (self-supervised training) or the reward function (reinforcement algorithms). It is therefore an exaggeration to speak of self-learning algorithms as we often hear. They are self-learning only in the sense that they do not need to be told in detail what to do to achieve a certain result, but this result must be specified to them and examples must be provided for them to learn. The machine does not set its own goals and does not find the means to achieve them. It is not given the rules but the goal and the means to find the rules to reach the goal. Moreover, these means still require a good deal of annotation and labeling of data by human workers, "digital labor workers" (Section 1.5).

10.3 The Different Forms of Artificial Intelligence

The two forms of artificial intelligence are rule-based artificial intelligence, or symbolic artificial intelligence, and learning-based artificial intelligence, which could be called "empirical" insofar as it is based on data, and which is sometimes called "connectionist" by reference to artificial neural networks. In the early days of artificial intelligence, it was thought that machines had to be told how to perform the desired tasks: this is symbolic artificial intelligence. Experts were asked to formalize the knowledge of their domain in the form of facts and rules, and an inference engine was developed that was able to link facts and rules to deduce new facts that answered the questions asked.

One of the most successful expert systems was MYCIN, developed in the 1970s to prescribe antibiotics for bacterial infections. Programmed in Lisp and based on a database of about 600 rules, MYCIN listed the bacteria most likely to be involved and proposed the appropriate treatment for each one. Since 1987, the MedVir expert system,[16] designed by French emergency physicians, has been developed to consider 750 diagnoses based on the symptoms described by patients during a standardized and complete interview. It covers all medical specialties, can assess the severity of the patient's condition, and suggest medication.

The symbolic approach was also implemented by the American researcher Douglas Lenat, whose thesis in 1976 at Stanford described a program (Automated Mathematician) in the Lisp language that was to discover and prove new mathematical theorems. It was followed by the Eurisko program, but Lenat considered in 1984 that an artificial intelligence could not go very far without having a vast knowledge base of "common sense." He then started an ambitious project of universal artificial intelligence ("Cyc") based on a gigantic knowledge base of twenty-four million assertions and rules covering all basic human knowledge, assimilated by millennia of evolution, experience, and culture, and translated into a formal language, CycL. This language, whose users call themselves "cyclists", is based on predicate calculus and its syntax is similar to that of the Lisp language. However, the Cyc project has been criticized for its excessiveness (more than 2000 person-years of work) and the resulting necessary incompleteness. A limited open source version of its knowledge base has been released under the name OpenCyc, and it already contains several million assertions.

Another illustration of this approach is the principle of classical chess programs, such as Deep Blue, which rely on rules for evaluating positions on the board that have not been discovered by the algorithm but have been taught to it, unlike an algorithm such as AlphaZero (Section 7.20.5), which discovered the best moves and openings on its own.

IBM's Watson program[17] may represent a middle ground between machine learning and symbolic artificial intelligence, since Watson, which won the Jeopardy! quiz game against human champions in 2011, relied on classical machine learning and natural language processing tools that required the usual data preparation and knowledge compilation work, coupled with a fast information retrieval system. However, this compilation was not made from a closed database such as Lenat's, but from all the sources of information that Watson can consult: Wikipedia, encyclopedias, dictionaries, literary works, articles, news agency dispatches, etc. Let's add that the success of Watson owes a lot to the hardware and the enormous computing power that a company like IBM is able to implement: 2880 POWER7 processors and 16 terabytes of memory to store Watson's documentation. If this had been stored on hard drives, Watson would have been too slow to beat human players. More elaborately, IBM's *Debater* project used GRU recurrent networks (Section 7.16) to develop a model capable of debating by finding arguments, expressing them logically, and refuting the opposing side's arguments.[18]

Despite the successes of symbolic artificial intelligence, it is gradually disappearing, especially since data, algorithms, and computational capabilities have allowed the development of trained artificial intelligence. Much of our knowledge of the world around us is not formalized in written rules that can be taught to a computer. Moreover, symbolic artificial intelligence has serious drawbacks, such as the necessary availability of experts, the difficulty of synthesizing their opinions, the exponential growth of the number of inferences according to the number of rules, and the cumbersome nature of updating an expert system.

In deep learning, no rules are taught to the machine, as could be done by writing a program, but the machine detects these rules itself from a large number of examples that are provided to it. These rules are represented in a complex way in very elaborate models, most often neural networks.

This path of artificial intelligence is more general than the one that originally prevailed: the machine is not told how to recognize a cat from a dog according to very precise criteria;

it is shown cats and dogs by telling it who is who, and the machine elaborates its own knowledge. Its limit is that it is helpless in a new situation, which it finds problematic. It is even helpless in a situation rarely encountered in the training dataset, and there are examples of animals not being recognized by an artificial intelligence (whereas a child would know them without hesitation), simply because these animals are placed in an unusual context, for example, outside their habitat.[19]

Training autonomous vehicles is thus very difficult, because it requires data covering all possible situations, all the behaviors of other vehicles (whose human drivers are sometimes unpredictable), all types of roads, all weather conditions, and so on. If it has never seen a baby on the side of the road, an algorithm may not be able to identify it. It takes thousands of hours of training for an autonomous driving algorithm, whereas a human driver only needs about 20 hours (but this algorithm can be implemented in millions of vehicles).

Similarly, to approach (but not reach) the literary translation quality of a professional human translator, today's algorithms should read more translated texts than a human can read in a lifetime. Unlike human translators, these algorithms cannot answer a question about what they have just translated. And today's image recognition algorithms still need to see more images than a human can see in a lifetime to identify the most complex images. Again, images are universal and generally unambiguous, unlike texts which belong to a language, or even a dialect, and which can be subject to numerous interpretation difficulties because of the polysemy of many words, and the ambiguity of certain expressions. Learning a language requires a corpus in the same language, but this is not enough: learning on the basis of articles from *The Times* is not very effective for analyzing tweets. And a corpus of texts cannot be automatically augmented like a set of images by transforming them through simple operations of rotation, translation, zoom, etc.[20] This is perhaps one of the reasons why artificial intelligence currently seems to be more successful in the field of medical imaging, when it comes to analyzing photographs or X-rays, than when it comes to analyzing medical literature on the symptoms of a pathology, as the experiments of Deep Mind and IBM Watson have shown.

Despite an intense marketing campaign around the prowess of its Watson product in the field of oncology, IBM has indeed achieved only limited results[21] and its Watson Health division created in 2015 was sold in 2022 to the investment fund Francisco Partners. IBM claims that Watson is capable of searching large medical databases, and helping oncologists find the best available treatment for each patient. In fact, IBM partnered in 2012 with Memorial Sloan Kettering Cancer Center in New York, where a dozen doctors entered their own recommendations into Watson's database, and it is these recommendations that are then returned. Watson does not create any new knowledge, but only restores the knowledge that doctors have ingested over several years. The concordance rate of its recommendations with those of medical specialists is sometimes high but sometimes lower. This can be explained by the fact that Watson's recommendations are biased by the training and practices of the Memorial Sloan Kettering Cancer Center, which are not those of the entire profession, and which are linked to a certain geographically and sociologically circumscribed patient base. This is in line with the general question often asked in artificial intelligence about the bias imposed on an algorithm by the data used to train it (Section 10.4).

Other difficulties were encountered in the project that was to lead the University of Texas M.D. Anderson Cancer Center to fight cancers by enabling physicians "to find personalized treatments for each cancer patient by comparing disease and treatment histories, genetic data, scans, and symptoms with the vast universe of medical knowledge."[22] Unfortunately, the medical literature is vast, but of uneven interest, and useful medical information is harder to find and label than learning data in other fields. Nearly 80% of medical information is textual, and these data are more difficult to compare than sensor-based measurements. In addition, medical data are recorded in a certain population, in a certain context, which is important to know so as not to bias the analyses. It is also necessary that these data can be shared on the basis of standards, hence the creation in recent years of ontologies to describe genes, phenotypes, and diseases.

The road to true medical artificial intelligence is still long, but specialized companies such as DeepMind have also taken up the challenge.

DeepMind has partnered with the United Kingdom's health system (NHS) and London's Moorfields Eye Hospital, the world's oldest eye hospital, to learn how to detect two serious ophthalmic diseases which are age-related macular degeneration (AMD) and diabetic retinopathy, a serious complication of type 2 diabetes that causes retinal vessels to burst, on medical imaging (optical coherence tomography). This work resulted in a paper published in late 2016 in the *Journal of the American Medical Association*[23] describing the application of a deep learning algorithm to detect diabetic retinopathy. After learning to recognize pathologic fundus on a base of 128,000 images, the algorithm produced a correct diagnosis with results comparable to those obtained by well-trained ophthalmologists.

In April 2018, the U.S. Food and Drug Administration (FDA) announced the first marketing approval for a medical device using artificial intelligence to detect diabetic retinopathy in certain adults.[24] The device, IDx-DR, developed by IDx LLC, achieves 90% accuracy, exceeding the minimum 85% threshold required by the FDA for approval.

However, a general study by Harvard Medical School[25] has shown that doctors are currently twice as capable as an algorithm of making the right diagnosis. Artificial intelligence excels in detecting certain pathologies, such as melanoma from photographs, but radiologists are still much better at identifying multiple sclerosis. Moreover, artificial intelligence can only be applied to pathologies that are sufficiently frequent for the images to be numerous enough for the models to train. That said, the contribution of artificial intelligence in medical imaging is not limited to training classification models, but can also provide tools for searching for similar images in large masses of already diagnosed images (e.g. recent work of the University of Paris, Philips Healthcare).

These examples raise the question of the primacy of data or algorithms. For some, data are primary because artificial intelligence algorithms are trained on very large samples, and algorithms are secondary, at least from an economic point of view, because many algorithms are available in open source. This is especially true for translation and computer vision, where algorithms today have an insatiable need for data. As an example, the classification of objects into several categories (of images for example) requires about 5000 training cases per category for correct performances and ten million cases per category to reach human performances. The need for this very large number of examples comes from the fact that each object must be present in all possible contexts, otherwise it may not be correctly identified. It is particularly difficult to recognize an object that is not in its usual context, when it is, for example, surrounded by objects that do not usually surround it. For example, water helps to identify fish and savannah helps to identify giraffes. The importance of data has recently given rise to a new type of data challenge: "data-centric" competitions[26] in which the usual process is reversed since it is the model that is provided and the training dataset that must be improved (by recoding the data, correcting labels, applying data augmentation, etc.) in order to improve the performance of the model by training it on the improved dataset.

For others, on the contrary, it is indeed the algorithms, and in particular those of deep learning, that have allowed lightning progress in image or speech recognition. Moreover, it is undoubtedly the refinements of these algorithms that will one day allow them to learn with less data: a recent example is given by AlphaGo Zero (Section 7.20.5) which became the best player in the world without any data, without having seen any game played before, just by knowing the rules of the game of Go and by using reinforcement learning. However, while reinforcement learning is unsupervised and does not require labeled data, it is limited to problems with a pass/fail criterion and today requires huge amounts of computation. It is therefore not a panacea for artificial intelligence.

Another way is self-supervised learning, which trains a model from unlabeled data, replacing the labels with information available within the data. It is widely used in natural language processing (Section 4.4.7) where some words are hidden and the model is asked to guess them. It has more recently come into use in image recognition, where the problem of rare languages does not arise and where labeled databases such as ImageNet have been very successful in training models. But even in the image domain, labeling can be painful (when violent content must be viewed to identify it) or difficult (when radiologists must analyze many medical images to make diagnoses), and in any case unlabeled images are much more numerous and less expensive to obtain than labeled ones. In computer vision, self-supervised learning involves several tasks performed on modified images:

- we cut an image into several pieces and mix them like a puzzle to ask the model to find their initial positions;
- a hole is made in an image and the model must find the missing part;
- we rotate an image and the model has to find the initial orientation;
- we swap sequences of a video and the model has to find the right order;
- we ask the model to find the color of some parts of an image.

Like the autoencoders, these self-supervised tasks do not directly teach the model which images represent, for example, cats and which represent dogs, but they teach it indirectly, by forcing it to reconstruct images of cats and dogs and consequently to acquire knowledge of these animals which will be useful for classifying them. But the great interest of self-supervised learning is not only that it does not need labels: it is also that this relatively generic learning, not linked to a precise task, allows a transfer of learning to various downstream tasks (classification is only one of them) which only require "fine tuning" on a dataset that can be smaller.

But however great its successes may be today, deep learning may not be the last word in artificial intelligence, and we can imagine that other paths will emerge in the future, which could, for example, combine deep learning and the symbolic approach, so as to involve representations of the world and *a priori* knowledge in the manipulation of concepts, and not just a representation of the training data provided. It is known in machine learning that the introduction of *a priori* knowledge can reduce the need for training data: this idea is the basis of Bayesian statistics. This reduction is quantitative (a smaller volume of data is sufficient to fit the model) and qualitative (the model fit is less sensitive to imperfections and variations in the data). Today, a deep learning algorithm can recognize an image very well, and not recognize it at all after a slight transformation of this image. It would also be a matter of artificial intelligence achieving a better understanding of causality and a better anticipation of behaviors and situations.

In the shorter term, another new direction in artificial intelligence is multimodal learning, which combines several tasks such as natural language processing and computer vision. We give an example of this in the next section.

10.4   Ethical and Societal Issues of Artificial Intelligence

The design of data-driven learning may lead one to believe that artificial intelligence algorithms are completely neutral. This is not the case, as learning remains dependent on the choice of datasets on which it relies. We know the anecdote of Microsoft's conversational agent Tay, tested in 2016 to exchange words on Twitter, and which had to be stopped by Microsoft after only 16 hours of operation because of the misogynistic and racist words it was starting to utter. It did so because it had received numerous tweets from malicious interlocutors containing such remarks, and it responded in kind.

The representativeness of the training samples, whether they are classical databases, genome-wide databases (Section 1.4.1), image banks or text corpora, raises the crucial question of the possibility of biases in the models, which can lead to systematic errors and even discrimination toward certain individuals or groups of individuals, unacceptable discriminations when they induce decisions in the fields of justice or police (monitoring certain people), banking and insurance (granting a loan and insuring a risk) and health (deciding on a medical treatment).

Note that this notion of bias is becoming multifaceted in current debates. On the one hand, this notion no longer applies only to estimators as in classical statistics, but to everything that can be produced by machine learning and artificial intelligence: predictions, models, algorithms and samples, whereas for the latter we should rather talk about lack of representativeness. On the other hand, there is a tendency to consider a sample (and the resulting models) as "biased" not because it does not represent a reality in a representative way, but because it represents a reality that we consider (often rightly) unfair and that we want to change. Thus, an algorithm will be considered biased if it has been trained on a dataset containing male and female professional situations that have historically been to the disadvantage of the latter. Algorithms are asked to make ethical situations that are not ethical situations. We can see that we are moving away from the technical notion of bias, even if it is clear that in this case the algorithm should not reflect the historical situation. On the contrary, let us say that it should be "biased" so that it does not reflect the known situation but the one we wish to see happen. But we understand that this correction is far from simple and that it can in turn involve prejudices specific to their designers. The fact that these prejudices are generous does not change the fact that one must be aware of their existence and of their non-immanent character to the phenomena that one wants to model.

The situation can become more complex when the result of a model can itself lead to decisions influencing the modeled phenomenon. If a credit risk score leads to a decision not to lend money to certain risky client profiles, these clients will no longer have to repay and will then appear to be less risky. When an epidemiological model leads to certain prophylactic measures being taken, individuals will ultimately be less affected than the model predicted. This does not mean that the model is faulty, as we sometimes hear in times of pandemic, but it does mean that the model is more interesting for the risk factors that it highlights and quantifies, than for the predictions that it allows. This brings us back to the classical conception of statistics, which is not only interested in the accuracy of the predictions of the models but also in their parameters and the information they provide on the phenomena studied.

In the preceding examples, the use of models tends to minimize the phenomenon that is predicted. These are self-defeating predictions, in contrast to the criticism often made of models for producing self-fulfilling predictions. An example is given of the use of models in the legal field to decide on releases: a prediction of a high risk of recidivism can delay a release and could increase the desocialization of the person concerned and ultimately increase their risk of recidivism.[27] It is also said that a prediction of a high credit risk could result in a higher interest rate, and therefore higher repayments, which increase the risk of default. But in reality, with consumer credits of short duration, the impact of the rate on the amount of the monthly credit payments is limited,[28] and the use of the model can, on the contrary, lead to a refusal of the credit and a decrease of the risk.

In other cases, the algorithm is directly influenced by the point of view of its designers, such as driverless cars, where, in a fatal event, the designers would have to choose between the lives of the car's occupants and the lives of people outside. It is therefore crucial to know why a driverless car would fail to detect a pedestrian in such a situation.

This raises the increasingly debated question of the explainability (or interpretability) of the results of artificial intelligence and machine learning algorithms. It is part of the ethical and societal questions raised by artificial intelligence, and it has recently become a legal question with the entry into force of the GDPR, the General Data Protection Regulation protecting the personal data of Europeans (Section 1.6). The European citizen can ask for an explanation of a decision taken on the basis of an algorithm, and the person responsible for this algorithm must be able to show them that this decision is fair. The explanation of the results provided by increasingly complex and "black box" algorithms is a subject of growing research[29] and conferences.[30] It is not required with the same exigency in all sectors, because it is much less important to know on what basis such an image was identified or such an item was offered to a customer than to know why such a medical treatment was proposed for a patient or why such an answer was given to a bank customer credit application. But, in general, algorithmic transparency is a growing issue in artificial intelligence.

Initiatives have multiplied in favor of ethical artificial intelligence. Google, Facebook, Microsoft, IBM, and Amazon are leading reflections on ethical rules to be put in place around artificial intelligence and announced on September 28, 2016 the launch of their initiative *Partnership on Artificial Intelligence to Benefit People and Society*,[31] since joined by other companies. Concerns about ethical artificial intelligence have since led several major IT players to limit the capabilities of several of their tools, particularly in facial recognition. One understands the interest of these digital companies whose business model is built on the acceptance of individuals to let them collect and use their personal data, acceptance that is based on the interest they find in the services rendered by these companies, but which will also increasingly rely on the trust they place in them.

In early December 2018, the University of Montreal released the "Montreal Declaration for a Responsible Development of Artificial Intelligence,"[32] developed after a year of work and consultations with citizens, experts, public officials, industry stakeholders, civil society organizations, and professional orders. This declaration sets out ten principles to ensure that artificial intelligence serves the common good: well-being, respect for autonomy, protection of privacy, solidarity, democratic participation, equity, diversity, prudence, human responsibility, and sustainability of development.

Another challenge posed by artificial intelligence algorithms is their great need for electrical energy. A study cited by ADEME[33] estimates the number of connected objects in the world in 2020 to be between 50 billion and 80 billion, and the share of global electricity consumption linked to digital technology is estimated at between 5% and 10%. Data centers are huge consumers of energy and producers of heat, which is why they have been the focus of research into solutions such as locating them under the sea or in cold regions of the world.

But the deep learning algorithms themselves are huge energy consumers: while a human brain consumes about 20 watts, training an artificial intelligence like AlphaGo (Section 7.20.5) requires 20,000 watts. The training of the basic model of BERT by NVIDIA takes 79 hours on 64 Tesla V100 GPUs, which represents a CO_2 emission of about 650 kg,[34] more than the 500 kg of an air flight from Paris to New York.[35] And the CO_2 emission of the GPT-3 model training would be 85,000 kg.

Calculations represent only a very small part of this consumption, and it is mainly the data exchanges between the memory and the processors that consume a lot of energy: 100 times more than the calculations themselves. However miniaturized they may be, integrated circuits are much less so than the brain, since an electronic card capable of competing with the 20 billion neurons of the cerebral cortex (one hundred billion neurons in the entire human brain) would measure 300 meters on one side.

We can measure the efficiency of the human cerebral cortex: one watt is enough to run a billion neurons that will perform about 10^{17} operations per second, when the best GPUs and TPUs in 2018 consume one watt for 10^{11} operations per second. Figure 7.23 shows that these 100 billion operations allow processing of the order of a dozen images: less than the rate of a movie.

A GPU card today consumes about 100 watts to perform 10^{13} operations per second, and the most powerful artificial intelligence systems run more than a hundred GPUs, which makes them capable of performing 10^{15} (soon 10^{16}) operations per second, a thousand times less than the human brain for a consumption a thousand times higher. The brain consumes a million times less energy! And of course, even if a machine managed to perform as many (10^{18}) operations per second as the human brain, the operations it would perform would most probably not allow it to reach the performance of the human brain. To take the example of image processing, the brain probably does not need to perform 10 billion operations to recognize an image.

This energy saving and speed of the brain come from the fact that the tasks of calculation and memorization are combined, in the neurons for calculation and in their synapses for memory.

The search for power in artificial intelligence is coming up against the physical limits of current electronic architectures. Several research laboratories have therefore embarked on the design of neuromorphic chips that will bring memory and calculations closer together. These chips imagined by Carver Mead[36] gather up to several million low-power neurons in very large-scale integrated circuits (VLSI). These chips will themselves implement the code for deep neural networks, which today is written not in computer chips, but in lines of programs. Current work on neuromorphic engineering is developing in several directions. One of its most spectacular applications is the *Human Brain Project*,[37] which aims to successfully simulate the functioning of the human brain, which would allow the development of new and more effective therapies for neurological diseases.

In 2016, the first phase-change neuron appeared, and in July 2017 the first nano-neuron, designed by a CNRS/Thales research team, capable of recognizing spoken digits as efficiently as much larger neurons.[38] A next step is to combine these nano-neurons with artificial nanoscale electronic synapses. Reaching 10,000 synapses per neuron in the brain is a formidable challenge.

These synapses are present in spiking neural networks (SNN),[39] which do not learn by gradient descent but by the exchange of impulses across their synapses. A neuron receives activations that increase its activation potential, and it is only when its activation potential exceeds a given threshold that the neuron is activated in turn. The activation potential decreases in the absence of new activations, and for it to exceed the threshold, and for the neuron to be activated, a sufficient quantity of activations must arrive within a certain time window. These networks are therefore not activated at each propagation cycle, which leads to a lower energy consumption. This operation is similar to that of biological neurons. In these neural networks, the encoding of information is binary and temporal. Learning can be supervised or not. They can be implemented in neuromorphic chips.

Another way to reduce the energy consumption of machine learning and deep learning algorithms is optical chips (OPU: Optical Processing Unit), in which photons replace electrons. This research has not yet led to very efficient solutions for supervised learning, but it is very active, notably with the NeuRAM project of neuromorphic chips led by the CEA since 2016.

Another approach to quickly train deep neural networks is the SLIDE (Sub-LInear Deep learning Engine) algorithm proposed by researchers at Rice University.[40] It consists of not activating all the neurons of the network each time the gradient is updated during training, the neurons to be activated being found thanks to a hash function. According to its authors, SLIDE would be much faster than TensorFlow and would make CPUs competitive with GPUs in terms of computing time.

It is also worth mentioning that graphics processors specifically designed for transformer models are starting to emerge in 2022.

Work is also under way to limit the share of electricity consumption of autonomous cars that is linked to artificial intelligence and which today represents 20% of the car's consumption.

10.5 Fears and Hopes of Artificial Intelligence

There are concerns about the development of artificial intelligence, as expressed by Stephen Hawking, Nick Bostrom, and others, stating that artificial intelligence could dominate human intelligence, the so-called "(technological) singularity," or even lead to machines wanting to destroy humans. It is perhaps not irrelevant to note that one of these personalities, Elon Musk, warns against artificial intelligence while participating in 2015 in the creation of the company OpenAI (for a "friendly artificial intelligence")[41] and while announcing that he wants to create a company that will promote transhumanism, that is, the improvement of human beings by external bionic elements.[42]

But even if an artificial intelligence could have feelings, there is no reason why its feelings towards human beings should be negative. It is not clear why an artificial intelligence should be aggressive or have to harm humans, unlike humans themselves who have had to fight against competing species to survive during their evolution.

But positive feelings could still lead the artificial intelligence to want to do good to humans in spite of themselves, and thus to deprive them of freedom to prevent them from harming each other. And its power of planning could enable it to carry out its plans to control humans.

However, for years to come, it seems that artificial intelligence is less to be feared than the human intelligence behind artificial intelligence. We have already recalled its role in the manipulation of opinion and mass surveillance in some countries (Section 1.4.3). We are also seeing the development of military drones, some for the detection of explosive devices or the tracking of opposing forces, others armed and equipped with facial recognition systems that allow them to autonomously aim at human targets. This can be frightening when one considers that it only takes a few pixels change in an image for a computer vision model to be fooled into confusing the image with a completely different image (Section 1.5.6).

On the issues of artificial intelligence applied to medicine, one can read a comprehensive White Paper published in France in 2018 by the National Council of the Order of Physicians, under the coordination of Dr. Jacques Lucas and Professor Serge Uzan, entitled "Doctors and Patients in the World of Data, Algorithms and Artificial Intelligence."[43] Faced with a growing shortage of doctors in certain regions, there is a fear of a two-tier medicine, in which doctors would only be able to treat a more privileged part of the population, while the other sector would be offered a remote diagnosis with the sending of elements such as photographs by smartphone and the automatic receipt of a prescription by email.

The development of artificial intelligence not only raises fears, but also hopes for useful developments for our societies and economies in various fields: transport, security, health, education (personalized follow-up), robotics (deliveries, cleaning...). On this subject, we can consult the interesting report, *Artificial Intelligence and Life in 2030* by Stanford University in 2016,[44] followed by its update, *Gathering Strength, Gathering Storms* in 2021.[45]

Another aspect to be taken into account, highlighted by many reports, is the transformation of the labor market that the development of artificial intelligence will bring about, and the danger that the development of artificial intelligence represents for employment in certain professions, including professions such as white-collar workers that have been relatively spared by previous industrial revolutions. This is understandable, as machines are replacing not only humans in simple tasks, but also in well-paid ones. A trading algorithm is cheaper than a trader. We can also imagine that telephone and telemarketing agents will be replaced by algorithms, as well as cab and truck drivers, and even accountants. For all these categories of workers, it is necessary to think quickly about the evolution of their job and their possible retraining. For some economists, technological innovations generally create more work than they destroy, but the work created may be difficult for those who have lost theirs. There is also a risk that those who use artificial intelligence tools in their work will have such an unbalanced relationship with these tools, which are so powerful and omniscient, that they will abandon a large part of their initiative and decision-making to them.

In its 2019 report on *Work in Change*,[46] the World Bank considers that the development of robots, even those with artificial intelligence, does not threaten employment and can even help to develop it, increasing productivity, income, and consumption. Moreover, it notes, "In 2018, the Republic of Korea, Singapore and Germany have the highest number of robots per worker. For all that, in all these countries, the employment rate remains high despite this high robotization."

More than previous technological revolutions, the development of artificial intelligence raises the question of replacing or "augmenting" humans in certain tasks that are currently assigned to them, either because they are complex or because they require human interaction, as in personal assistance.

We can think that there will not always be a replacement of human intelligence by artificial intelligence, but rather a collaboration of the two, or more precisely the use of the latter by the former. One example is medical robotics. With the help of imaging, calculations, and artificial intelligence, surgical robots can help human surgeons to understand the surgical scene, to plan their movements and to have safer, more precise, less invasive procedures and sometimes even some that would be impossible for a human hand. However, these surgical robots are not autonomous and we cannot imagine them completely replacing humans, at least not for a long time. That said, it is very optimistic to imagine that it is always the machine that serves humans and relieves them of tedious tasks: a counter-example is provided by click workers (Section 1.7) who have to watch tedious videos or read boring texts for hours in order to provide labeled training data to algorithms.

We can also take the example of journalism, in which we are beginning to consider robot-journalists: it is easy to see how artificial intelligence could detect fake news,[47] but it is more difficult to see how it could understand a political strategy and make elaborate analyses. Artificial intelligence can, however, be used on simpler datasets, such as sports results or company results. They are published in a sufficiently standardized form to allow for automated extraction of information and automatic writing of a summary. This makes it possible to produce an initial article a few seconds after the publication of a company's results, a precious speed when important decisions can be derived from this information. For example, since 2017, the *Associated Press* has been using artificial intelligence to write some of its dispatches, which has allowed it to increase the number of companies it covers tenfold. On September 8, 2018, *The Guardian* published the article "Are you scared yet, human?" in which the author wanted to convince his readers that they had nothing to fear from artificial intelligence. The author beginning the article with "I am not a human. I am a robot" was none other than the transformer model GPT-3.

Even when artificial intelligence is not writing the stories itself, it can help, through its analysis of social networks and all the sources of information on the Web, to alert journalists to the topics they should be interested in and write about. Moreover, artificial intelligence can relieve journalists of time-consuming tasks, such as transcribing interviews. Hours of work per week can be saved by a machine that can transcribe an interview, translate it into several languages and automatically highlight the most interesting passages.

Artificial intelligence can also perform illustrative work, such as the DALL-E model,[48] announced in January 2021 by OpenAI, which is a transformer model derived from GPT-3, which with only 12 billion parameters is able to create images that it has heard described in natural language.[49] These can be realistic images or as crazy as a baby radish in a tutu walking a dog on a leash. This means that it is able to create images from scratch, not just copy them. It has been trained with text-picture pairs as the CLIP model (Section 10.1). It is often able to draw very faithfully what is asked of it, but sometimes it can also make very strange drawings. It could compete, however, not only with illustrators, but also with fashion and furniture designers. This is an example of multi-modal artificial intelligence that will develop. Another OpenAI model, GLIDE,[50] with "only" 3.5 billion parameters, is able to generate images judged by human evaluators to be often more realistic than those from DALL-E. DALL-E was also improved in April 2022 by DALL-E 2 and in May 2022 by Google Brain's Imagen model. Imagen uses a transformative model to obtain a vector embedding of the input text, and these vectors are converted to images by a new type of models, called diffusion models. Other algorithms are able to generate an image from a text accompanied by a sketch to better control the generated image. We are far from the psychedelic images generated by Google's DeepDream. Another example of multi-modal artificial intelligence is the GPV-I model, which is trained simultaneously to perform several tasks and is capable of describing an image, answering questions about its content, captioning it, and locating and classifying objects.[51]

In any case, it will be necessary to make the public and the government aware of the development and use of artificial intelligence, and not to neglect the importance of training in the face of the evolution of professions. Losing one's job because one has been replaced by an artificial intelligence is a greater short-term risk than being exterminated by an artificial intelligence. And, of course, those who will losetheir jobs will rarely be the ones who will fill the new jobs in data science.

Beyond the professional sphere, the citizens surrounded by artificial intelligence applications will have to have basic knowledge of the data that is collected about them, by whom it is collected and used, for how long, for which purpose, with which algorithms, with which repercussions and which risks for them. The extreme personalization made possible by artificial intelligence and the exploitation of big data raises other questions. We will arrive at personalized recommendations, personalized content, completely personalized media: will everyone have their own newspaper, television or radio program, or music program? What about the social link if two people never see the same content, never share the same experiences, never talk about the same things? What about the pleasure of discovery, and even simply the possibility of discovery, if the choices are no longer made by individuals, or at least are strongly oriented by algorithms that presuppose their centers of interest and that, moreover, may not always be neutral either, as mentioned above, and may have an interest in promoting this or that choice. Do we evaluate all the consequences of the "algorithmic containment" of individuals to whom the recommendation systems only propose articles and videos that correspond to their tastes and opinions, and thus only show contents in favor of the flatness of the Earth to those who are convinced of it? As some authors write, "a robotized humanity is more to be feared than the multiplication of humanized robots."[52]

What will happen to democratic life, not to mention the risks of manipulation of public opinions, created by the possibilities of deepfakes (photo and video faking by deep learning) and amplified by social networks? Personalities could soon not only be victims of deepfakes but also users of them, using them in videos shot in their place, possibly showing them in a more advantageous light than the reality. And what will happen to life in society, if everyday gestures such as making an appointment no longer allow us to speak with a person but only with a vocal robot? The advent of artificial intelligence in our lives raises many questions.

10.6 Some Dates of Artificial Intelligence

Finally, we give some chronological references in Table 10.1, obviously far from being exhaustive.

Table 10.1 Timeline of artificial intelligence.

Date	Event
1642	Blaise Pascal's calculating machine
1654	Blaise Pascal's "Problem of points," the first theorization of the probability calculus
1843	Charles Babbage's analytical machine and Ada Lovelace's first calculation program
1943	Formal neuron of the neurophysiologist Warren Mc Culloch and the logician Walter Pitts
1950	Turing test
1956	Dartmouth conference and creation of the term "artificial intelligence"
1958	Frank Rosenblatt's perceptron (with threshold activation)
1959	General Problem Solver (GPS) by Herbert Simon, Cliff Shaw, and Allen Newell
1960	ADALINE (Adaptive Linear Neuron) network of Widrow and Hoff (with linear activation)
1964	ELIZA, the first conversational agent
1969	Minsky and Papert's XOR problem
~ 1970	Beginning of the first winter of artificial intelligence
1974	Paul Werbos's gradient descent backpropagation algorithm
1980	Fukushima's Neocognitron, ancestor of convolutional neural networks
1985	Bayesian networks of Judea Pearl
1986	Application of the backpropagation mechanism by Rumelhart, Hinton, and Williams to multilayer neural networks (with any activation)
1986	End of the first winter of artificial intelligence
1989	Application of the backpropagation mechanism by Le Cun *et al.* to convolutional neural networks
1991	Vanishing gradient problem (Hochreiter's thesis)
~ 1990	Start of the second winter of artificial intelligence
1995	Vapnik and Cortes's support vector machines
1997	LSTM (Long Short-Term Memory) neural networks by Hochreiter and Schmidhuber

(Continued)

Table 10.1 (Continued)

Date	Event
1997	Spiking neural networks
2004	Training traditional neural networks on GPUs (graphics processors)
2006	Training convolutional neural networks on GPUs (graphics processors)
2006	Deep neural networks: end of the second winter of artificial intelligence
2007	CUDA language for GPU programming
2011	Rectified linear function (ReLU) for neural networks
2012	First victory for convolutional neural networks at the annual ILSVRC ImageNet competition
2012	Dropout for reducing the overfitting of neural networks
2013	Word2Vec embedding model of Mikolov *et al.*
2014	Generative adversarial networks (GAN) of Goodfellow *et al.*
2016	First victory of an artificial intelligence algorithm against the Go world champion
2017	First nano-neuron
2017	Hinton's capsule networks
2017	Transformer models for natural language processing
2018	BERT (Bidirectional Encoder Representations from Transformers) model by Devlin *et al.*
2018	Turing Award given to Yoshua Bengio, Geoffrey Hinton, and Yann Le Cun
2019	AlphaStar artificial intelligence becomes grandmaster at StarCraft II strategy game
2019	Pluribus artificial intelligence defeats professional poker players
2020	The MuZero artificial intelligence is able to play chess, shogi, Go, and 57 Atari games
2020	GPT-3 (Generative Pre-trained Transformer) model for natural language
2021	DALL-E multimodal model for generating images from a textual description

Notes

1 Aimetti, J-P., Coppet, O., and Saporta, G. *Manifeste pour une intelligence artificielle comprise et responsable* (Cent Mille Milliards, 2022), p. 16.

2 According to CNRTL Centre National de Ressources Textuelles et Lexicales, "reasoning" is defined as "the faculty of analyzing reality, of perceiving the relationships between beings, the relationships between objects, present or not, of understanding facts," http://www.cnrtl.fr/definition/raisonnement.

3 According to CNRTL, "planning" is defined as " a method of choosing objectives and proposing means to achieve them," http://www.cnrtl.fr/definition/planification.

4 According to CNRTL, " common sense" is defined as "central sense, faculty bringing together and coordinating the data of all the senses by relating them to a single object and thus allowing perception of it." https://www.cnrtl.fr/definition/sens.

5 *Mind*, 59 (236) (October 1950).

6 Read, for example, https://web.media.mit.edu/~minsky/papers/steps.html.

7 McCulloch, S.W. and Pitts, W. Logical Calculus of Ideas Immanent In Neural Activity. *Bulletin of Mathematical Biophysics*, 5 (1943), 115–133.

8 Rosenblatt, F. The Perceptron: A Probabilistic Model for Visual Perception. In: *Proceedings of the 15th International Congress of Psychology* (North Holland, 1957), pp. 290–297.

9 Widrow, B. and Hoff, M.E. *Adaptive Switching Circuits* (No. TR-1553-1). (Stanford, CA: Stanford Electronics Labs, Stanford University, 1960).

10 Rumelhart, D.E., Hinton, G.E., and Williams, R.J. Learning Internal Representations by Error Propagation. In: Rumelhart, D.E. and McClelland, J.L. (eds) *Parallel Distributed Processing: Explorations in the Microstructure of Cognition*. Vol. 1: *Foundations* (Cambridge, MA: MIT Press, 1986).

11 Radford *et al.* Learning Transferable Visual Models from Natural Language Supervision (2021). arXiv:2103.00020v1.

12 https://openai.com/blog/clip/.

13 Zellers *et al.* MERLOT: Multimodal Neural Script Knowledge Models (2021). arXiv:2106.02636.

14 The name is a tribute to Goodfellow, one of the inventors of the GAN.

15 Ross Goodwin (Jean Boîte Éditions, 2018).

16 https://medvir.fr/.

17 In a funny twist, an Indian company launched a new computer in 2016 called HOLMES: Heuristics and Ontology-based Learning Machines and Experiential Systems.

18 Slonim, N., Bilu, Y., Alzate, C., *et al.* An Autonomous Debating System. *Nature*, 591 (2021): 379–384.

19 To be complete, we must add that this possibility of deception is not totally specific to artificial intelligence vision systems: human vision is also sensitive to certain optical illusions. We sometimes see in convolutional neural networks a structure similar to that of the cortex cells in charge of human vision, but the act of seeing is not only a matter of the mechanism of vision but also of a more complex mechanism of perception and comprehension of reality, which contextualizes what is seen and makes it possible that two people facing the same scene do not always see the same thing.

20 Conversely, it is true that the learning of a language can be based on the existence of a structure, the grammar, which is absent from the images.

21 Read the STAT article: https://www.statnews.com/2017/09/05/watson-ibm-cancer/.

22 https://www.healthnewsreview.org/2017/02/md-anderson-cancer-centers-ibm-watson-project-fails-journalism-related/.

23 Gulshan, *et al.* Development and Validation of a Deep Learning Algorithm for Detection of Diabetic Retinopathy in Retinal Fundus Photographs. *JAMA*, 316(22) (2016), 2402–2410. doi:10.1001/jama.2016.17216.

24 https://www.fda.gov/newsevents/newsroom/pressannouncements/ucm604357.htm.

25 Semigran, H.L., Levine, D.M., Nundy, S., and Mehrotra, A. Comparison of Physician and Computer Diagnostic Accuracy. *JAMA Internal Medicine*, 176(12) (2016), 1860–1861. doi:10.1001/jamainternmed.2016.6001.

26 https://https-deeplearning-ai.github.io/data-centric-comp/.

27 Chouldechova, A. Fair Prediction with Disparate Impact: A Study of Bias in Recidivism Prediction Instruments (2017). arXiv:1703.00056.

28 For a loan of €5000 repaid over 3 years, when the rate increases from 4% to 8%, the monthly payment increases from €147.62 to €156.68.

29 Friedler, S.A., Scheidegger, C., and Venkatasubramanian, S. On the (Im)possibility of Fairness (2016). arXiv:1609.07236; Kleinberg, J., Mullainathan, S., and Raghavan, M. Inherent Trade-Offs in the Fair Determination of Risk Scores (2016). arXiv:1609.05807.

30 AIMLAI: Advances in Interpretable Machine Learning and Artificial Intelligence.

31 https://www.partnershiponai.org/.

32 https://www.declarationmontreal-iaresponsable.com/.

33 https://librairie.ademe.fr/cadic/1893/developpement_objects_connectes_rapport_doc.pdf.

34 Strubell, E., Ganesh, A., and McCallum, A. Energy and Policy Considerations for Deep Learning in NLP (2019). arXiv:1906.02243v1.

35 https://eco-calculateur.dta.aviation-civile.gouv.fr/

36 Mead, C. Neuromorphic Electronic Systems, *Proceedings of the IEEE*, 78(10) (1990), 1629–1636.

37 https://www.humanbrainproject.eu/en/.

38 Grollier, J. *et al.* Neuromorphic Computing with Nanoscale Spintronic Oscillators, *Nature*, 547, (2017). 428–431.

39 Maass, W. Networks of Spiking Neurons: The Third Generation of Neural Network Models. *Neural Networks*, 10(9) (1997), 1659–1671.

40 Chen *et al. SLIDE:* In Defense of Smart Algorithms over Hardware Acceleration for Large-Scale Deep Learning Systems (2019). arXiv:1903.03129v2.

41 First a nonprofit, then, as of 2019, a capped for profit company, with a partnership with Microsoft that brought it for $1 billion and privileged access to its cloud.

42 Some transhumanists believe (or dream) that nanotechnology will allow artificial intelligence devices to be connected to the brain and transform man into a cybernetic organism. In an extreme scenario, machines and artificial intelligence would eventually replace the entire brain and only man's consciousness would remain, which could be transferred ("uploaded") to a machine, allowing him to approach immortality. The mind totally dissociated from the body! In a less futuristic way, chatbots capable of conversing like a deceased person are beginning to develop, thanks to training based on the person's sound and written archives. There is also talk of video bots created from films of the person. For example, the start-up StoryFile is working in 2021 on a videobot of the interpreter of Captain Kirk from the *Star Trek* series.

43 https://www.conseil-national.medecin.fr/sites/default/files/external-package/edition/od6gnt/cnomdata_algorithmes_ia_0.pdf.

44 https://ai100.stanford.edu/sites/g/files/sbiybj18871/files/media/file/ai100report10032016 fnl_singles.pdf.

45 https://ai100.stanford.edu/sites/g/files/sbiybj18871/files/media/file/AI100Report_MT_10 .pdf

46 http://www.banquemondiale.org/fr/publication/wdr2019.

47 In June 2018, Facebook launched a system for authenticating photographs and videos to detect those that have been manipulated or presented in a context other than their own, with images that do not match the text or other images. This is an application of artificial intelligence to "fact checking."

48 DALL-E is the contraction of the name of the surrealist painter Salvador Dali and the name of the robot WALL-E from an animated film of anticipation of Pixar.

49 https://openai.com/blog/dall-e/.

50 Nichol *et al.* GLIDE: Towards Photorealistic Image Generation and Editing with Text-Guided Diffusion Models (2022). arXiv:2112.10741v3.

51 Gupta, T., Kamath, A., Kembhavi, A., and Hoiem, D. Towards General Purpose Vision Systems (2021). arXiv:2104.00743.

52 Aimetti, *et al.*, op. cit., p. 49.

Conclusion

Even if artificial intelligence worries us as much as it makes us dream, even if data science is nourished by decades of work and discoveries in statistics and machine learning (which we have briefly recalled), even if deep learning is a logical extension of it, even if big data is not the announced revolution, we hope to have shown what they can bring to our lives in the form of help and new services (from the chatbots to autonomous vehicles), what they can bring to us when we are sick (for example, the detection of cancers on medical images), what they can bring to companies for their customers and their processes, what they can bring to administrations for their users, and all the interest they present for the data scientist in terms of theoretical methods, machine learning techniques, and computer architectures. We have also shown that deep neural networks are finally succeeding, after decades of hopes based on a superficial analogy between artificial and natural neural networks, in mimicking the simplest productions of human intelligence, starting with image recognition. But, even if they do not create intelligence and even if they do not have an original idea, deep neural networks are increasingly capable of copying human inspiration and imitating its productions with a disconcerting quality, whether it is the generation of better and better written texts, pictorial works or chess and go games in which the machine offers, in a better manner, a real strategy to replace brute force. Of course, the time of the technological singularity has not yet arrived, and the machine will probably soon be able to write a novel, but not to have the idea or the desire to write a novel. It will not invent new artistic forms, and in the scientific field its first Nobel Prize is far off. Just as a deep neural network has to see thousands of images of cats and dogs before it can correctly classify them, an artificial intelligence would have to see thousands of apples fall before it has a small chance of being able to formulate Newton's theory of gravitation.

But perhaps in a few decades, after advances in quantum computing, neuroscience, neuromorphic chips, and new ideas in data science and deep learning that we cannot yet imagine, we will look at current artificial intelligence methods as we look at the first vacuum tube computer today.

We have also seen that algorithms raise questions about the protection of personal data and privacy, since they massively exploit all the traces of our behaviour, our movements, our purchases, and our searches, and can even recognize our faces. They are having an increasingly important impact on the life of our democracies, confronted with the omnipresence of algorithms on the Web and in social networks, and with the increasingly

Deep Learning: From Big Data to Artificial Intelligence with R, First Edition. Stéphane Tufféry.
© 2023 John Wiley & Sons Ltd. Published 2023 by John Wiley & Sons Ltd.
Companion website: www.wiley.com/go/Tuffery/DeepLearning

rapid, and not always controlled, dissemination of true or false information. They make decisions   or intervene in decisions that have consequences in our lives, in loans or work contracts that are granted or refused, which raises the crucial question of possible biases in their use, and puts forward the "responsible AI." Artificial intelligence also raises the essential question of the replacement or augmentation of humans by machines. It also raises energetic and environmental questions because of the enormous computing power on which it relies.

According to a report, conducted by the European Investment Bank, the European Union accounts for only 7% of annual equity investments in AI and blockchain, while the US and China together account for 80%.[1] However, the EU excels in research and has the largest pool of digital talents. It would be a pity for Europe to remain on the sidelines of this groundswell, whereas the deep learning pioneers Bengio, Hinton, and Le Cun were born in France and the United Kingdom. The EU must develop its training of data scientists, and create major players in data storage and processing, digital services, search engines, social networks, cloud computing, and artificial intelligence, who can hold significant market shares. The information economy can be expected to contribute to the global economy. Above all, big data, data science, and deep learning are the gateway to artificial intelligence.

Beyond big data, which has largely developed already known data processing methods, such as incremental learning and ridge and Lasso penalized regression, deep learning is beginning to rapidly develop certain fundamental concepts. It too relies on some tools that it did not invent, first of all, artificial neural networks, but it has introduced profound evolutions in them and solved some old problems, such as the vanishing gradient in gradient descent backpropagation. Strongly helped by new computer architectures (distributed computing, parallelism of graphics processors), deep learning has revolutionized computer vision, written and spoken language processing and strategy games, and is about to revolutionize other fields, notably in scientific research, medicine, and transport. It does so by moving from approaches based on complex rules taught to the machine, to rules discovered by the machine itself, based on sufficient examples provided to it. An even more innovative approach could even eliminate the need to provide a large number of examples for model training: reinforcement learning, provided that there is a success or failure criterion to provide feedback and guide model training.

Of course, all these problems will not disappear, and we have seen how delicate the tuning of deep learning algorithms is. It is interesting to note that these adjustments call upon some age-old concepts in statistical learning, such as control of the model complexity, dimension reduction, the use of penalization, etc. Under the shimmering exterior of the multiple methods described and implemented in this book, the deep unity of data science shines through.

Note

1 https://www.eib.org/fr/products/advising/innovfin-advisory/ai-blockchain-and-future-of-europe-report.

Annotated Bibliography

The books and articles cited are classified by topic.

On Big Data and High Dimensional Statistics

Mokrane Bouzeghoub and Rémy Mosseri (ed.) (2017). *Les Big Data à découvert*, CNRS Éditions.

A comprehensive overview of the big data, with many quick and enjoyable two-page articles by top experts on data collection, storage, and processing; information retrieval from the Web and social networks; scientific, medical, and societal/life applications.

Peter Bühlmann and Sara van de Geer (2011). *Statistics for High-Dimensional Data*, Springer.

Big data from the theoretical point of view of statistics, with long developments on the methods of penalization and particularly the Lasso.

Arthur Charpentier (ed.) (2014). *Computational Actuarial Science with R*, Chapman and Hall/CRC.

The edited work directed by Arthur Charpentier is devoted to statistical methods used in actuarial science and combines theoretical reminders and examples treated with R. Its 16 chapters are divided into four parts: (1) presentation of R and basic statistical methods, (2) statistical methods in life insurance, (3) methods in financial analysis, and (4) methods used in non-life insurance.

Fabrice Demarthon, Denis Delbecq, and Grégory Fléchet (2012). La déferlante des octets, *Journal du CNRS*, November–December 2012, n° 269, pp. 20–27. http://www.cnrs.fr/fr/pdf/jdc/JDC269.pdf.

A file of three articles presenting simply some issues and some applications of big data.

Mireille Gettler Summa, Léon Bottou, Bernard Goldfarb, Fionn Murtagh, Catherine Pardoux, and Myriam Touati (eds) (2012). *Statistical Learning and Data Science*, Chapman & Hall/CRC.

A collection of articles on various topics ranging from stochastic gradient descent to learning theory, correspondence analysis, SVM, semi-supervised analysis, social network analysis, structural equations, functional data, and other topics, covered by specialists such as Vladimir Vapnik, Alexey Chervonenkis, Françoise Fogelman Soulié, Léon Bottou, Jean-Paul Benzécri, David Hand, Avner Bar-Hen, Gilbert Saporta, and others.

Trevor Hastie, Robert Tibshirani, and Jerome H. Friedman (2009). *The Elements of Statistical Learning: Data Mining, Inference and Prediction*, Springer, 2nd edition. It can be downloaded here: https://web.stanford.edu/~hastie/ElemStatLearn/index.html.

One of the best references on the statistical aspects of machine learning, written by renowned researchers, inventors of several important methods in data science.

Trevor Hastie, Robert Tibshirani and M. Wainwright (2015). *Statistical Learning with Sparsity: The Lasso and Generalizations*, Chapman and Hall/CRC. It can be downloaded here (in a corrected version in 2016): http://web.stanford.edu/~hastie/StatLearnSparsity/index.html.

A book on the statistical analysis of sparse data, that is to say, when one observes fewer individuals than characteristics of these individuals, that is to say, when one analyzes tables that have more columns than rows, or tables with many zero elements. The methods discussed are the Lasso and its generalizations (Group Lasso, Fused Lasso), LAR regression, SVD decomposition of matrices, k-means, principal component analysis, and sparse linear discriminant analysis, etc.

Dawn E. Holmes (2017). *Big Data: A Very Short Introduction*, Oxford University Press.

A book of simple and non-theoretical presentation.

Myriam Maumy-Bertrand, Gilbert Saporta, and Christine Thomas-Agnan (eds.) (2018). *Apprentissage statistique et données massives*, Éditions Technip.

The contributions of many specialists to the Journées d'étude en statistique organized by the Société Française de Statistique in 2016, on machine learning, classical and deep neural networks, massive data processing, social network analysis, and recommender systems.

Éric Moulines (2015). Les mathématiques des Big Data, *Gazette des mathématiciens de la Société Française de Mathématique*, n° 144, pp. 5–12.

This very interesting article manages to review in a few pages the principles, achievements, and challenges of big data, while describing precisely the mathematical tools at work to study them.

Eric Siegel (2016). *Predictive Analytics: The Power to Predict Who Will Click, Buy, Lie, or Die*, Wiley.

In seven non-technical chapters, the book contains seven case studies, on IBM Watson, Netflix, Chase Bank, etc.

Chun Wang, Ming-Hui Chen, Elizabeth Schifano, Jing Wu, and Jun Yan (2015). A Survey of Statistical Methods and Computing for Big Data, arXiv:1502.07989.

An article on statistical methods, R packages and other software.

http://wikistat.fr/.

Very informative and comprehensive course vignettes as they cover the field of classical statistics, machine learning, and big data.

https://github.com/wikistat/.

Tutorials that are also very interesting and educational, with an introduction to Python and PySpark.

On Deep Learning

Charu C. Aggarwal (2018). *Neural Networks and Deep Learning: A Textbook*, Springer.

All issues related to neural networks are covered in this book. It starts with the basics, backpropagation learning, vanishing or exploding gradient or explosion problems, overfitting, the multilayer perceptron, and then moves on to other types of neural networks, the radial basis function (RBF) network, the restricted Boltzmann machine, Kohonen's self-organizing maps, convolutional and recurrent networks, generative adversarial networks, autoencoders, and reinforcement learning. Optimization methods are explained in detail, including adaptive gradient descent algorithms and second derivative-based algorithms (quasi-Newton, conjugate gradient). Everything that is useful for learning neural networks is discussed: regularization methods, early stopping, dropout, etc. Applications are indicated for recommender systems, automatic translation, image annotation, image classification, games and even natural language processing with the Word2Vec word embedding method. Exercises and software guidelines are given.

Vincent Barra, Antoine Cornuéjols, and Laurent Miclet (2021). *Apprentissage artificiel. Concepts et algorithmes, de Bayes et Hume au Deep Learning*, Eyrolles, 4th edition.

A comprehensive book, which covers not only deep neural networks, but also reinforcement learning and semi-supervised learning, Bayesian networks, Markov models, and inductive logic programming.

Yoshua Bengio (2012). Practical Recommendations for Gradient-Based Training of Deep Architectures, arXiv:1206.5533.

A practical guide to tuning the learning parameters of a deep neural network.

François Chollet (2022). *Deep Learning with Python*, Manning, 2nd edition.

A book that simply recalls the principles of deep learning and illustrates them with many examples with Keras, which go in a pedagogical way from the simplest to the most elaborate to generative models, giving many explanations. The first version of the book was written for Python and then rewritten with R code without changing the rest of the book.

François Chollet and J.J. Allaire (2018). *Deep Learning with R*, Manning.

The codes of the examples are on GitHub.
https://github.com/fchollet/deep-learning-with-python-notebooks;
https://github.com/jjallaire/deep-learning-with-r-notebooks.

Nikhil Duduma, Nicholas Locascio (2022). *Fundamentals of Deep Learning*, O'Reilly Media, 2nd edition.

A book that clearly recalls the principles of deep learning and illustrates them with numerous examples using TensorFlow. It discusses convolutional neural networks, recurrent neural networks, LSTM, word embedding and concludes with reinforcement learning.

Ian Goodfellow, Yoshua Bengio, and Aaron Courville (2016). *Deep Learning*, MIT Press. http://www.deeplearningbook.org

A very complete reference book, written by recognized specialists, which covers everything from deep learning to generative models.

Andrey Kurenkov (2015). *A 'Brief' History of Neural Nets and Deep Learning.* https://www.skynettoday.com/overviews/neural-net-history

An enjoyable and informative history of neural networks and deep learning. https://www.college-de-france.fr/site/yann-lecun/course-2015-2016.htm. *Yann LeCun's lecture at the Coll de France, downloadable in video and audio format.*

Yann LeCun, Yoshua Bengio, and G. Hinton (2015). Deep Learning, *Nature*, 521, 436–444.

A review article on deep learning and its applications.

https://www.college-de-france.fr/site/stephane-mallat/course-2017-2018.htm
https://www.college-de-france.fr/site/stephane-mallat/course-2018-2019.htm
https://www.college-de-france.fr/site/stephane-mallat/course-2019-2020.htm
https://www.college-de-france.fr/site/stephane-mallat/course-2020-2021.htm
https://www.college-de-france.fr/site/stephane-mallat/course-2021-2022.htm

Stéphane Mallat's lectures at the Collège de France. Downloadable in video and audio format, on learning with the curse of high dimension (January to March 2018), on deep neural network learning (January to March 2019), on multiscale models and convolutional neural networks (January to March 2020), on parsimonious representations (January to March 2021), and on information and complexity (January to March 2022):

Grégoire Montavon, Geneviève Orr, and Klaus-Robert Müller (eds) (2012). *Neural Networks: Tricks of the Trade*, Lecture Notes in Computer Science (Book 7700), Springer, 2nd edition.

A collection of numerous articles by the best specialists advising the best methods and practices to optimize the learning of neural networks, especially deep networks, by covering all aspects, from backpropagation to reinforcement, including early stopping, weight decay, regularization, gradient descent, Boltzmann machines, recurrent networks, the use of unsupervised methods, etc.

Jürgen Schmidhuber (2015). Deep Learning in Neural Networks: An Overview. *Neural Networks* 61, 85–117, arXiv:1404.7828.

A very complete historical study.

Jürgen Schmidhuber (2015). *Critique of Paper by "Deep Learning Conspiracy."* http://people.idsia.ch/~juergen/deep-learning-conspiracy.html.

Historical additions to the aforementioned article by LeCun, Bengio, and Hinton.

Eli Stevens, Luca Antiga, and Thomas Viehmann (2020). *Deep Learning with PyTorch*, Manning.

A book about PyTorch in three parts: the first one is a general presentation, the second is a complete implementation in a project on lung cancer detection on medical images, and the third on the deployment of a PyTorch model, in a web service, a C++ program or a cell phone Natural language processing is very quickly mentioned, as well as LSTM neural networks.

Richard S. Sutton and Andrew G. Barto (2018). *Reinforcement Learning: An Introduction*, MIT Press, 2nd edition.

A reference book on reinforcement learning.

Aston Zhang, Zachary C. Lipton, Mu Li, and Alexander J. Smola, (2021). Dive into Deep Learning, arXiv:2106.11342.

A very comprehensive course published on arXiv with an online interactive version (https://www.d2l.ai/) fully provided with MXNet, PyTorch and TensorFlow notebooks, which can be run while reading the course, either on a personal computer or on a cloud.

IPOL Journal - Image Processing On Line.http://www.ipol.im/

An online scientific journal on image processing, where each article is reviewed and accompanied by controlled source code.

http://cs231n.github.io/convolutional-networks/ and http://cs231n.stanford.edu/

Simple and enlightening Stanford University Course (CS231b) on Convolutional Neural Networks for Visual Recognition.

https://github.com/afshinea/stanford-cs-230-deep-learning/tree/master/en and https://stanford.edu/~shervine/teaching/cs-230

Afshine Amidi and Shervine Amidi's nice cheat sheets on deep learning.

https://course.fast.ai/

The famous MOOC "Practical Deep Learning for Coders" from the fast.ai group created in 2016 by Jeremy Howard and Rachel Thomas.

On Artificial Intelligence

Jean-Paul Aimetti, Olivier Coppet, and Gilbert Saporta (2022). *Manifeste pour une intelligence artificielle comprise et responsable*, Cent Mille Milliards.

A small book to be put in all hands as it is enlightening and full of remarks both deep and common sense far from the commonplaces on this subject.

Margaret A. Boden (2018). *Artificial Intelligence: A Very Short Introduction*, Oxford University Press.

A recent synthesis on artificial intelligence.

Yann Le Cun (2019). *Quand la machine apprend*, Éditions Odile Jacob.

A history of and thoughts on deep learning and artificial intelligence by one of its creators, accessible and very interesting.

Stuart Russel and Peter Norvig (2022). *Artificial Intelligence: A Modern Approach*, Pearson Education Limited, 4th edition, global edition; http://aima.cs.berkeley.edu/global-index.html

This classic book covers the entire discipline from the history of artificial intelligence to robotics, intelligent agents, logical inference, planning, machine learning, deep learning, reinforcement learning, and the philosophical foundations of artificial intelligence.

On the Use of R and Python in Data Science and on Big Data

Monica Bécue-Bertaut (2018). *Analyse textuelle avec R*, Presses Universitaires de Rennes.

Factor analysis applied to textual data processing, with the help of the Xplortext *package.*

Aurélien Géron (2019). *Hands-On Machine Learning with Scikit-Learn, Keras, and Tensorflow: Concepts, Tools, and Techniques to Build Intelligent Systems*, O'Reilly Media.

A very detailed practical book that illustrates with Python (Scikit-Learn, TensorFlow and Keras) the main machine learning methods, from linear regression to deep learning.

Gareth James, Daniela Witten, Trevor Hastie, and Robert Tibshirani (2021). *An Introduction to Statistical Learning, with Applications in R*, Springer, 2nd edition; https://www.statlearning.com/

The book covers more or less the same topics as the classic "Elements of Statistical Learning", with two authors in common. But it is simpler and, moreover, it contains in each chapter a "Lab" section with examples treated with R. The second edition includes new material and in particular new chapters on survival analysis and deep learning.

Hobson Lane, Cole Howard Hannes, and Max Hapke (2023). *Natural Language Processing in Action: Understanding, Analyzing, and Generating Text with Python*, Manning.

A book on deep learning methods applied to NLP.

Ludovic Lebart, Bénédicte Pincemin, and Céline Poudat (2019). *Analyse des données textuelles*, Presses de l'Université du Québec.

The Python codes of the book can be downloaded here: http://www.dtmvic.com/07_Python_Text_F.html. The R codes of the book can be downloaded here: http://www.dtmvic.com/07_R_F.html.

This book is a continuation of the famous "Statistique textuelle" by L. Lebart and A. Salem, which it updates with recent methods and software (many examples with Python). Still very much rooted in data analysis, it is a "Text Mining for Text Lovers, which respects the text and places it at the heart of the analysis."

Aloysius Lim and William Tjhi (2015). *R High Performance Programming*, Packt Publishing Limited.

This book provides ways to optimize computations with R, ranging from memory management to the use of graphics processing units (GPUs) to parallelization, code compilation, the use of external databases and Hadoop.

https://cran.r-project.org/web/views/HighPerformanceComputing.html

The CRAN page dedicated to R packages for parallelization and big data processing.

https://cs231n.github.io/python-numpy-tutorial

Python Tutorial by Stanford University associated with a notebook available in Google Colab.

Index

a

Activation function   275
Activation map   289
Ad exchange   211
ADADELTA algorithm   302
ADAGRAD algorithm   302
ADAM algorithm   302
Adaptive optimization
        algorithms   301
AlphaGo   338
AlphaGo Zero   339
AlphaZero   339
Amdahl's law   52
Anaphora   124
Annotation (image)   316
Anonymization   38
Artificial intelligence   479
Attributed graph   188
Autoencoder   318
Automated readability index   126

b

Backpropagation algorithm   281
Bag of words   312
Bagging   89
Balanced cross entropy   332
Batch gradient   279
Batch normalization   292
BERT model   460
Betweenness centrality   190
Bidirectional neural network   316
Big Data   3
Boosting   92

Brain-machine interfaces   335
Brown corpus   118

c

Callback function   301
CamemBERT model   461
Capsule neural networks   317
Cassandra   56
CatBoost algorithm   99
CBOW model   164
CIFAR   307
CIFAR-10   307
CIFAR-100   307
Clique   189
Closeness centrality   190
Cloud   62
Cloud Act   43
Cloud computing   411
Clustering coefficient   189
COCO database   317
Coleman–Liau readability index   127
Collaborative filtering   106
Column-oriented DBMS   56
Conjugate gradient   83
Connected graph   189
Content-based filtering   107
Convolution   288
Convolutional neural networks   272
Coordinate descent   83
Coordinate relaxation method   83
Coreference resolution   124
CoreNLP library   120
CouchDB   57

Deep Learning: From Big Data to Artificial Intelligence with R, First Edition. Stéphane Tufféry.
© 2023 John Wiley & Sons Ltd. Published 2023 by John Wiley & Sons Ltd.
Companion website: www.wiley.com/go/Tuffery/DeepLearning

CPU (central processing unit)   52
Cross-entropy   278
CUDA   61
Curse of dimensionality   32

d

DALL-E model   497
Damped Newton algorithm   84
Data augmentation   300
Data lake   56
Davidson-Harel simulated annealing   192
DeBERTa model   462
Deep Convolutional Generative Adversarial
      Networks (DCGAN)   324
Deepfakes   325
Degree centrality   190
Degree prestige   190
Dense graph   189
Differential privacy   40
Dilated convolution   295
Directed graph   188
Discrete AdaBoost   92
DistilBERT model   462
Distributed computing   52
Distributed Recursive Layout   192
DropConnect   297
Dropout   295

e

Elastic net   88
ELIZA effect   480
ELMo model   459
ELU (Exponential Linear Unit)   277
Energy consumption of algorithms   494
Ensemble methods   89
Epoch   279
Exploding gradient   284
Extra-Trees   91

f

Fast R-CNN model   328
Faster R-CNN model   328
FastText representation   176
Feature map   289
Federated learning   40

FlauBERT model   462
Flesch-Kincaid readability index   127
Focal loss   333
FOG readability index   127
Fractional Max-Pooling   294
Fruchterman-Reingold algorithm   192

g

GDPR   41
Generative Adversarial Networks
      (GAN)   323
Genome-wide association studies   26
Gentle AdaBoost   94
Girvan-Newman method   202
GloVe representation   174
GLUE benchmark   462
Google Flu Trends   23
Google Trends   10
GPT-2 model   475
GPT-3 model   476
GPU (graphics processing unit)   61
Gradient boosting   95
Gradient descent   76
Graph   188
Grid architecture   52
Grover's algorithm   68
GRU (Gated Recurrent Units) networks   315
Guiraud lexical diversity index   128

h

H2O   58
Hadoop   54
HBase   57
HDFS   54
Hellinger distance   157
Herdan lexical diversity index   128
Hierarchical Dirichlet process   160
Hoeffding bound   73
Huber function   95
Hugging Face transformer models   462
Hughes effect   32

i

ILSVRC challenge   307
ImageNet database   307

Incremental learning   5
Instance segmentation   328
Intersection over union (IoU)   327
Iteratively reweighted least squares   85

k

Kamada-Kawai algorithm   192
k-anonymization   39
Keras   368
keras package   369

l

Large Graph Layout   192
Lasso regression   87
Latent Dirichlet allocation   152
Latent semantic analysis   144
Layout (graph)   192
l-diversity   39
Leading eigenvector method   202
Leaky ReLU   277
Learning rate   279
Lemmatization   124
Levenberg-Marquardt algorithm   84
Lexical diversity indices   128
LightGBM algorithm   100
LIME method   379
Link mining   208
LogitBoost   95
Louvain method   203
LSTM (Long Short-Term Memory)
       networks   313

m

Markov Cluster algorithm   204
Max pooling   293
Mechanical Turk   44
MedVir expert system   486
Megatron-Turing Natural Language
       Generation model   476
Milgram experiment   190
MLlib (Spark)   58
MobileBERT model   462
Mode collapse   324
Modularity   201
Modularity matrix   201

Momentum   280
MongoDB   57
Monte Carlo search tree   338
MTLD lexical diversity index   128
Multimodal AI   491
MuZero   339
MXNet   349
mxnet package   349
MYCIN expert system   486

n

Named entity recognition   119
Nash equilibrium   323
Nesterov Accelerated Gradient   280
Netflix prize   107
Network   187
Neuromorphic chips   494
Newman-Girvan modularity   201
Newman's greedy algorithm   203
Newton algorithm   74
n-gram   115
NoSQL   55

o

Object detection   326
Oblivious trees   99
Ockham's razor   50
Online gradient   279
On-line random forests   73
Ontology   130
Opinion mining   180
Ordered boosting   99
Overlapping pooling   294

p

PageRank   191
Parallel computing   51
Part-of-speech tagging   117
Penn Treebank corpus   119
Perceptron   275
Perplexity   159
Pluribus   340
Pooling   293
POS tagging   117
Predictive maintenance   18

Programmatic advertising   211
Proust (Marcel)   147
Pseudonymization   39
PubMedBERT model   147
Python   63

q

Quantum computing   67
Quantum entanglement   67
Quasi-clique   200
Quasi-Newton methods   75
Qubits   67

r

R   63
Random forests   89
R-CNN neural networks   327
Readability indices   126
Real AdaBoost   92
Real-time bidding   211
Receptive field   291
Recommendation systems   105
Recurrent neural networks   312
Reinforcement learning   271
ReLU (Rectified Linear Unit)   276
Residual neural network   284
Retargeting (behavioral)   212
RetinaNet algorithm   332
Ridge regression   87
RMSprop algorithm   302
RoBERTa model   461

s

SCAD penalty   50
Scalability   54
Scale-free graph   188
Self-attention   459
Self-supervised learning   461, 477
Sentiment analysis   180
Simplex algorithm   84
Singular value decomposition   145
Skip connection   284
Skip-gram model   164
Small-world graph   188
SMOG readability index   127

Social network   187
Softmax   277
SpaCy   120
Spark   58
Sparse graph   189
Spiking neural networks   494
Spurious correlations   35
SSD algorithm   332
Stemming   129
Stochastic gradient   279
Stump   94
Style transfer   336
Stylometry   112
Subsampling   293
Sugiyama algorithm   192
Support vector machines (SVM)   100
Symbolic artificial intelligence   486

t

Tensor   349
TensorFlow   367
Text mining   112
TF-IDF weighting   142
Theano   348
3 V of Big Data   3
Thesaurus   130
Tokenization   116
Topic modeling   155
Torch   348
torch package   424
t-proximity   40
TPU (tensor processing unit)   61
Transfer learning   300
Transformer model   459
TreeBoost algorithm   98
TTR lexical diversity index   128
Turing Award   483
Turing test   481

u

Udpipe   121
ULMFiT model   459
Unipartite graph   188
Universal grammar   476

V

Vanishing gradient   284
Variational autoencoder   324

W

Walktrap algorithm   204
Weight decay   300
Word cloud   220
Word n-gram   116
Word2Vec
        representation   163

X

XGBoost algorithm   249

Y

Yield management   6
YOLO algorithm   328
YOLOv2 algorithm   331
YouTube-8M dataset   312

Z

Zipf law   111